Next Generation Assessment Teacher Edition

4

STRATEGIES FOR
write.rs

D1317086

Senior Author
Rebecca Bowers Sipe, Ed.D.
Eastern Michigan University

Consulting Authors
Julie Coiro, Ph.D.
University of Rhode Island

Amy Humphreys, Ed.M., NBCT
Educational Consultant

Sara B. Kajder, Ph.D.
Shady Side Academy,
Pittsburgh, Pennsylvania

James Scott Miller, M.Ed.
National Writing Consultant

Mark Overmeyer, M.A.
Cherry Creek School District, Colorado

ZB **Zaner-Bloser**

Program Reviewers

Zaner-Bloser wishes to thank these educators who reviewed portions
of this program and provided comments prior to publication.

ISBN 978-1-4531-1229-8

Credits

Photo credits: Cover and title page: © Shiroh Yabe/SEBUN PHOTO/amanaimages/Corbis; Z4: © Rubberball/Nicole Hill/Getty Images; Z5: © Ocean/Corbis; Z7(t), Z15(b): © Courtesy of Logitech; Z7(b), Z11(t), Z16(t): © Zaner-Bloser, Inc.; Z17: © Jose Luis Pelaez Inc/Getty Images; Z18: © John Lund/Drew Kelly/Getty Images

Zaner-Bloser, Inc.
1-800-421-3018
www.zaner-bloser.com

Printed in the United States of America

2 3 4 5 6 13880 18 17 16 15 14

ZB Code 15

Body stock is FutureMark® 90+% Recycled Paper
WWW.FUTUREMARKPAPER.COM

SUSTAINABLE FORESTRY INITIATIVE
Certified Chain of Custody
Promoting Sustainable Forestry
www.sfiprogram.org
SFI-01171

This SFI label applies to the text paper.

Table of Contents

Introduction to Strategies for Writers

Narrative Writing

Informative/Explanatory Writing

Opinion Writing

More Writing Practice:

Appendices

Scope and Sequence

Index

STRATEGIES FOR
writers

The Next Generation of Writing Instruction!

Are your students ready to succeed on Next Generation Assessments?

Today's standards put a new emphasis on writing to ensure that students are ready for the rigors of college and the expectations of today's workplace. *Strategies for Writers* is a flexible writing and grammar resource for the next generation of students.

CCSS
Meets 100% of the writing and writing related Common Core State Standards

Be CCSS Ready

- Provide ample writing practice for a range of **tasks, purposes, and audiences** within **Narrative, Informative/Explanatory, and Opinion or Argument** text types.

- Help students master the **mechanics and conventions** of the English language with flexible digital and print practice materials.

- **Analyze writing models and practice close reading** to build comprehension and writing proficiency.

- **Diagnose students' writing proficiency** with integrated pretests for each of the CCSS text types.

Prepare for Next Generation Assessments

- Prepare for high-stakes success with instructional **Next Generation Assessment chapters** tailored to the new assessments.

- Build confidence with **explicit instruction, modeling, and practice** for each of the writing text types.

- Address common testing problem areas with **comprehension mini-lessons** that provide explicit instruction in comprehension strategies.

- Get ready for testing with **interactive practice assessments** modeled on **Partnership for Assessment of Readiness for College and Careers** (PARCC) and **Smarter Balanced Assessment Consortium** (SBA) sample tests.

Write Across the Curriculum

- Prepare students for success in academic coursework with **writing practice across all subject areas.**

- **Build proficiency in Informative/Explanatory and Opinion or Argument** text types critical for academic success.

Build 21st Century Skills

- Build digital media literacy by **producing and publishing in a variety of media:**
  - Podcasts
  - Blogs
  - Videos and more

- **Encourage collaboration** with peer learning opportunities, class discussions, and shared digital workspaces.

Plan and Teach With Confidence

- Simplify writing instruction with **clear, concise lessons that follow a consistent lesson plan.**

- Tailor instruction to your classroom with a **flexible mix of digital and print materials.**

- Meet individual needs with **differentiated skill instruction and practice and ELL support.**

- Deepen your professional knowledge of the most relevant writing topics and instructional strategies with **integrated professional development podcasts and screencasts.**

Strategies for Writers Online Writing Center is Perfect for 1:1 Computing

Supercharge your writing instruction with the *Strategies for Writers* Online Writing Center, a flexible learning environment built for collaboration, engagement, and ease of use.

Students can:

- Compose essays, submit assignments, and receive teacher feedback with **My Writing Pad.**

- Collaborate in the writing process with **Peer Groups and Teacher-Led Conferencing.**

- Collect projects and monitor growth in writing proficiency with **My Writing Portfolio.**

- Access all of the student interactive resources including **grammar games, proofreading activites, eBooks, and more**!

Teachers can:

- Manage assignments and differentiate instruction with the **Classroom Management System.**

- Give students **feedback at each step of the writing process** and **assess** students' completed assignments.

- Model and instruct the writing process using the collaborative writing tool, **Class Writing Pad.**

- Access all of the **student and teacher interactive resources, including anchor papers, videos, the interactive lesson library, eBooks, assessments, and more**!

- Access all teaching masters, including **rubrics, graphic organizers, mini-lessons,** and more, in the **Virtual File Cabinet.**

Flexible materials for fully digital, print-based, or blended classroom environments

For students:

- **Student Edition** (iPad-compatible eBook edition or print): Maximize success with clear, consistent lessons.

- **Grammar, Usage & Mechanics Practice Book**: Reinforce writing mechanics with a comprehensive 5-step lesson for each skill.

- **Online Grammar Games and Proofreading Activities**: Make practice fun and effective.

For teachers:

- **Teacher Edition** (iPad-compatible eBook edition or print): Plan with confidence with easy-to-follow lesson plans and tips for differentiation.

- **Grammar Practice Masters:** Provide additional practice to support the Grammar, Usage & Mechanics Practice Book.

- **Grammar, Usage & Mechanics Teacher Edition:** Build basic skills with lessons to support the Grammar, Usage & Mechanics Practice Book.

- **Digital Resources:** Easily access anchor papers, rubrics, grammar games, writing process videos, graphic organizers, and more for interactive whiteboards.

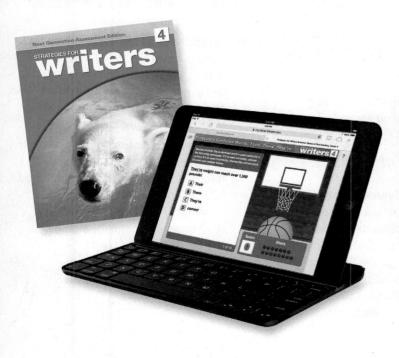

Free Online Resources at www.sfw.z-b.com

- Customizable presentations
- Rubrics
- Graphic organizers
- Next Generation Assessment Practice
- Differentiated Instruction Activities and more!

Learner Verification Research

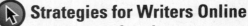
Strategies for Writers Online
Go to **www.sfw.z-b.com** for
• Podcasts/Screencasts
• Professional Development Articles
• Hundreds of Printable Resources

In the fall of 2012, the University of Cincinnati Evaluation Services Center and Saperstein Associates undertook a one-year longitudinal study to assess the efficacy of *Strategies for Writers*. The study continued through the spring of 2013.

Based on a quasi-experimental design, the study involved:

- 22 schools in 8 states, split evenly into treatment and control groups;
- 25 teachers (13 treatment and 12 control);
- 704 students
  - 342 students in Grade 4 (186 treatment and 156 control)
  - 362 students in Grade 7 (252 treatment and 110 control).

Teachers and students in the treatment group used *Strategies for Writers,* while teachers in the control group used

(1) teacher- or school-made materials;

(2) a standalone writing program or framework, including *Write Source*™ (Houghton Mifflin Harcourt) and *Units of Study*™ from Lucy Calkins (Heinemann); or

(3) a basal or comprehensive reading program, including *Journeys*™ (Houghton Mifflin Harcourt) and *Treasures*™ (McGraw-Hill).

During the first weeks of school, every participating student completed a pretest consisting of grade-appropriate prompts for informative/explanatory and opinion or argument writing. The pretest utilized an Educational Testing Service (ETS) measure. During the final weeks of school, the participating students completed a corresponding posttest. Responses to these prompts were scored using a six-point rubric by *Criterion*™, an online product from ETS.

An analysis of the scores produced by Criterion revealed that, overall, students using *Strategies for Writers* demonstrated growth compared to students using a variety of other materials. These gains were noteworthy in informative/explanatory and opinion writing at grade 4 and in argument writing at grade 7.

At **Grade 4,** the greatest gains (on a 6-point scale) were in informative/explanatory writing.

- For the **informative/explanatory text type,** students using *Strategies for Writers* demonstrated more growth than did students using other instructional materials. Specifically, the average gain for students in the treatment condition is 1.02 (on a 6-point scale) compared with .60 for

students in the control condition. This difference is statistically significant.

- For the **opinion text type,** students using *Strategies for Writers* once again demonstrated more growth than did students using other instructional materials. Here, the average gain for students in the treatment condition is .94 compared with .77 for students in the control condition.

At **Grade 7,** students using *Strategies for Writers* demonstrated more growth (on a 6-point scale) than did students using other instructional materials.

- For the **informative/explanatory text type,** the average gain for students in the treatment condition is 1.00 compared with .51 for students in the control condition. This difference is statistically significant.

- For the **argument text type,** the average gain for students in the treatment condition is 1.17 compared with .46 for students in the control condition. Again, the observed difference is statistically significant.

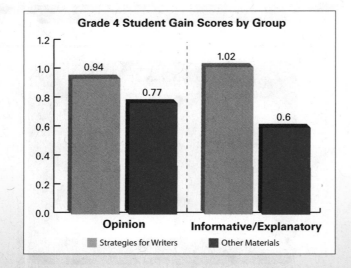

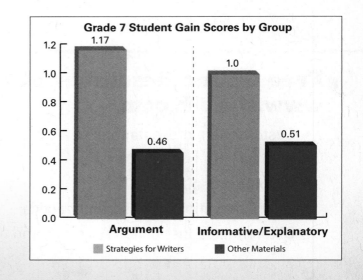

Writing in the Content Areas

Professional Development Podcasts and Screencasts

Go to **www.sfw.z-b.com** for a podcast on **writing in the content areas.**

According to the Common Core State Standards, writing in the content areas is essential. Why? Writing is one of the very best ways for students to comprehend and retain content area knowledge. Writing in the content area is far more cognitively demanding than worksheets and other activities that require only the recognition of the correct answers.

Content-Area Connections Each grade level includes a content-area writing experience for each Common Core text type. Look for one of these four content area tags in the Student Edition Table of Contents.

LITERATURE CONNECTION

MATH CONNECTION

SCIENCE CONNECTION

SOCIAL STUDIES CONNECTION

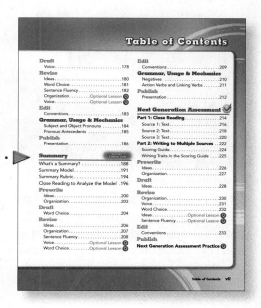

Content-Area Information The topics of the writing models throughout the lesson are tied to science, math, social studies, or literature.

What Is Photosynthesis?
Summary MODEL

by Leah Flora
Summary by Mitchell Martino

main ideas

All living things need food to live and grow. People do this by eating food. Plants do this by making their own food in a process called photosynthesis.

Plants need three things to make food—energy, carbon dioxide, and water. Plants get energy from the sunlight, carbon dioxide from the air, and water from the soil. With these three ingredients, plants can perform photosynthesis, which means "putting together with light." *Photo* means "light" and *synthesis* means "putting together."

organization

All the action happens in the leaves of green plants. Plants are green because of chlorophyll. The green chlorophyll is inside structures called chloroplasts. The chloroplasts collect energy from sunlight. (That's the "light" part of *photosynthesis*.) Carbon dioxide enters the underside of leaves through tiny holes called stomata, and water from the roots moves up the plant through tubes called xylem. With energy from sunlight, the chloroplasts combine the carbon dioxide and water. (That's the "putting together" part.) As a result, plants create sugars, or food, as well as give off oxygen during the process of photosynthesis.

supporting details

We need plants to survive. Plants store some of the food they make, and that's how fruits, such as apples, and vegetables, such as carrots, give our own bodies energy. Because plants also give off oxygen, we have fresh air to breathe. Life on this planet would not be possible without plants.

one-page length

Summary 191

Process-Based, Trait-Driven Instruction All of the content-area lessons follow a consistent and proven instructional framework. The lessons are process-based and support a fully developed composition. Trait-specific mini-lessons are provided within each lesson.

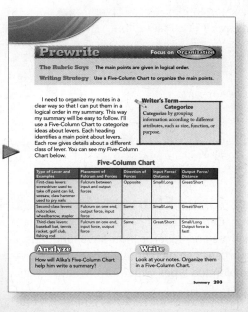

Prewrite Focus on **Organization**

The Rubric Says The main points are given in logical order.

Writing Strategy Use a Five-Column Chart to organize the main points.

I need to organize my notes in a clear way so that I can put them in a logical order in my summary. This way my summary will be easy to follow. I'll use a Five-Column Chart to categorize ideas about levers. Each heading identifies a main point about levers. Each row gives details about a different class of lever. You can see my Five-Column Chart below.

Writer's Term
Categorize
Categorize by grouping information according to different attributes, such as size, function, or purpose.

Five-Column Chart

Type of Lever and Examples	Placement of Fulcrum and Forces	Direction of Forces	Input Force/Distance	Output Force/Distance
First-class levers: screwdriver used to take off paint can lid, seesaw, claw hammer used to pry nails	Fulcrum between input and output forces	Opposite	Small/Long	Great/Short
Second-class levers: nutcracker, wheelbarrow, stapler	Fulcrum on one end, output force, input force	Same	Small/Long	Great/Short
Third-class levers: baseball bat, tennis racket, golf club, fishing rod	Fulcrum on one end, input force, output force	Same	Great/Short	Small/Long Output force is fast!

Analyze
How will Alika's Five-Column Chart help him write a summary?

Write
Look at your notes. Organize them in a Five-Column Chart.

Summary 203

Exploring the Text Types

Professional Development Podcasts and Screencasts
Go to **www.sfw.z-b.com** for a screencast on **CCSS and the text types.**

The **Common Core State Standards** (CCSS) identify three types of writing in which students must be proficient. These three **"text types"** represent broad categories that can be used to organize specific writing genres. To support teachers and students in meeting these standards, the lessons in *Strategies for Writers* are organized by text type.

Narrative Writing focuses on telling a story or sharing an experience and may be factual and informative or creative fiction. Description enhances the narrative by developing elements such as characters, settings, events, plots, and movements. Many language structures are used in narrative writing, including dialogue, vocabulary choices to evoke emotions and sensory experiences, and literary devices such as similes and personification to develop mood, tone, and audience considerations.

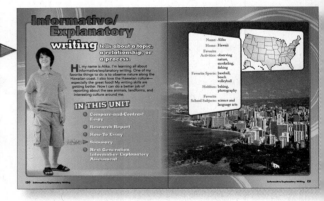

Informative/Explanatory Writing provides accurate information that is clearly organized to suit the topic. This text type may be organized around sequential/chronological order, cause-effect, topic with main idea(s) and supporting details, or compare-contrast. Citing sources and examples, adding descriptive detail, and including anecdotes add to the goal of helping the reader understand the information.

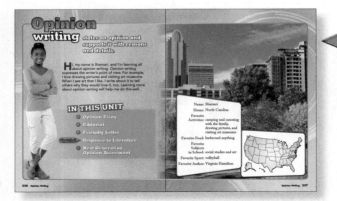

Opinion or Argument Writing requires students to state a position and defend it with appropriate information. Students write opinions and arguments and support their thinking with facts, evidence from sources, and data. Whether responding to a literary question using text evidence, a scientific position using data from sources or experiments, or the benefit or detriment of a historical action taken, multiple sources may be used to make a claim and defend the reasoning behind it.

Descriptive Elements in the Text Types Strong description enhances every type of writing. Careful use of precise, rich vocabulary adds accuracy, deeper understanding, and interest. Adjectives and adverbs, figurative language, and the use of references such as dictionaries and thesauruses can be taught via descriptive elements. *Strategies for Writers* includes instruction in these blended types with More Writing Practice (pp. T352–T443).

Grammar, Usage, and Mechanics

Professional Development Podcasts and Screencasts
Go to **www.sfw.z-b.com** for a podcast on **CCSS** standards for grammar, usage, and mechanics.

Proper use of English conventions demonstrates proficiency in the mechanics of grammar, usage, and punctuation. As students draft, revise, and edit their compositions, correct use of conventions makes the composition more interesting, readable, and considerate of the reader.

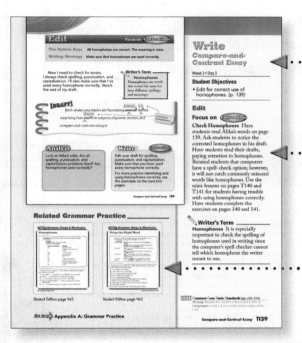

Explicit instruction for grammar, usage, and mechanics is integrated into the writing process at the editing step.

Students **analyze** how the skill is reflected in the model writing and then apply that knowledge to their own writing.

Related Grammar Practice provides additional opportunities for students to practice important grammar, usage, and mechanics skills.

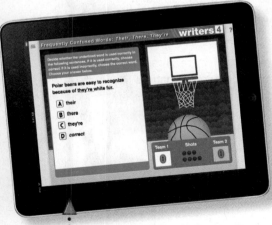

iPad-compatible interactive Grammar Games for all skills help students demonstrate their understanding in a **fun, engaging** way.

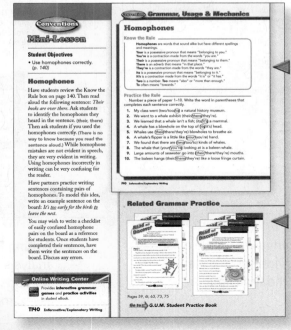

Conventions **Mini-Lessons** extend the targeted skill. Two mini-lessons follow every **Edit** lesson.

Grammar, Usage, and Mechanics Practice Book reinforces skills and provides additional practice through a comprehensive 5-step lesson.

Preparing Students for Close Reading on Next Generation Assessments

Today's writing assessments require both strong reading and writing skills. Each **Next Generation Assessment** chapter in *Strategies for Writers* walks students step-by-step through the process of taking a two-part assessment for each of the three text types.

Part 1: Close Reading teaches students to **analyze authentic text or video sources,** take notes, and answer comprehension questions. Students practice close reading to go beyond simple recall and engage in **deep critical thinking.**

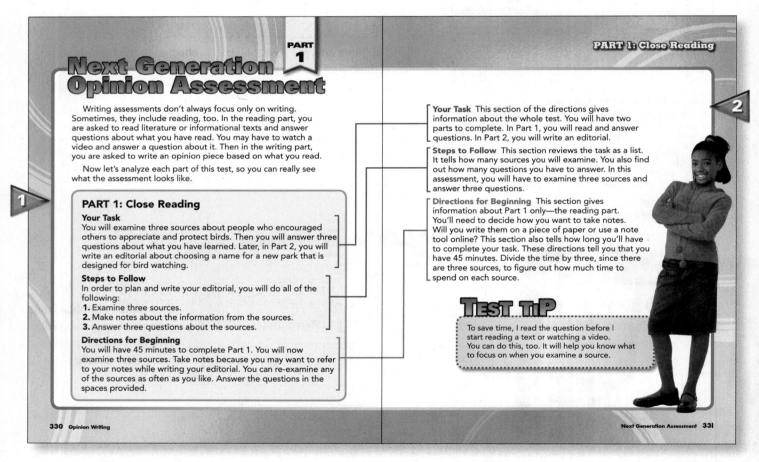

Next Generation Opinion Assessment

PART 1

Writing assessments don't always focus only on writing. Sometimes, they include reading, too. In the reading part, you are asked to read literature or informational texts and answer questions about what you have read. You may have to watch a video and answer a question about it. Then in the writing part, you are asked to write an opinion piece based on what you read.

Now let's analyze each part of this test, so you can really see what the assessment looks like.

PART 1: Close Reading

Your Task
You will examine three sources about people who encouraged others to appreciate and protect birds. Then you will answer three questions about what you have learned. Later, in Part 2, you will write an editorial about choosing a name for a new park that is designed for bird watching.

Steps to Follow
In order to plan and write your editorial, you will do all of the following:
1. Examine three sources.
2. Make notes about the information from the sources.
3. Answer three questions about the sources.

Directions for Beginning
You will have 45 minutes to complete Part 1. You will now examine three sources. Take notes because you may want to refer to your notes while writing your editorial. You can re-examine any of the sources as often as you like. Answer the questions in the spaces provided.

PART 1: Close Reading

Your Task This section of the directions gives information about the whole test. You will have two parts to complete. In Part 1, you will read and answer questions. In Part 2, you will write an editorial.

Steps to Follow This section reviews the task as a list. It tells how many sources you will examine. You also find out how many questions you have to answer. In this assessment, you will have to examine three sources and answer three questions.

Directions for Beginning This section gives information about Part 1 only—the reading part. You'll need to decide how you want to take notes. Will you write them on a piece of paper or use a note tool online? This section also tells how long you'll have to complete your task. These directions tell you that you have 45 minutes. Divide the time by three, since there are three sources, to figure out how much time to spend on each source.

TEST TIP

To save time, I read the question before I start reading a text or watching a video. You can do this, too. It will help you know what to focus on when you examine a source.

1. **Part 1 Directions** clearly explain the close reading task and provide specific steps to follow, as well as the time limit for completing Part 1.

2. **Writing Partner** guides students in an analysis of the Part 1 directions and supports students throughout the assessment writing process.

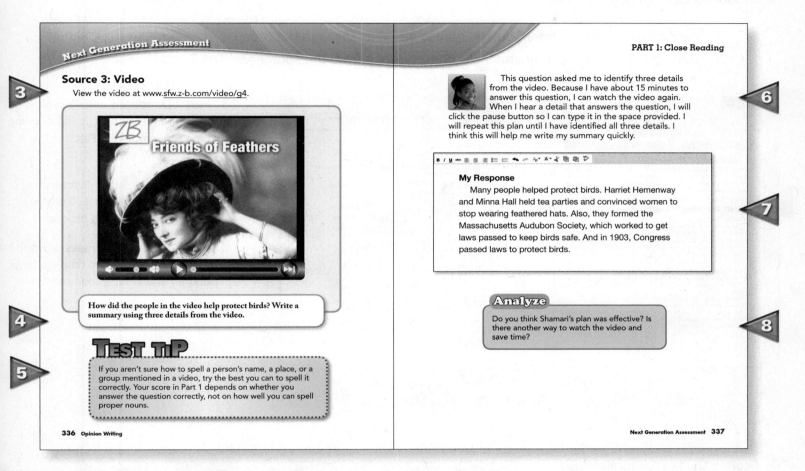

Next Generation Assessment

PART 1: Close Reading

Source 3: Video
View the video at www.sfw.z-b.com/video/g4.

Friends of Feathers

How did the people in the video help protect birds? Write a summary using three details from the video.

TEST TIP
If you aren't sure how to spell a person's name, a place, or a group mentioned in a video, try the best you can to spell it correctly. Your score in Part 1 depends on whether you answer the question correctly, not on how well you can spell proper nouns.

This question asked me to identify three details from the video. Because I have about 15 minutes to answer this question, I can watch the video again. When I hear a detail that answers the question, I will click the pause button so I can type it in the space provided. I will repeat this plan until I have identified all three details. I think this will help me write my summary quickly.

My Response
    Many people helped protect birds. Harriet Hemenway and Minna Hall held tea parties and convinced women to stop wearing feathered hats. Also, they formed the Massachusetts Audubon Society, which worked to get laws passed to keep birds safe. And in 1903, Congress passed laws to protect birds.

Analyze
Do you think Shamari's plan was effective? Is there another way to watch the video and save time?

336 Opinion Writing

Next Generation Assessment 337

3. **Source Texts or Videos** provide authentic, contemporary source content that relates to the writing task in Part 2 of the assessment.

4. **Comprehension Questions** require students to use comprehension skills and close reading strategies to find evidence in each source.

5. **Test Tips** provide strategies for successful testing experiences. The tips include time management, planning, and rechecking strategies.

6. **Think Aloud** shows how the writing partner "thinks aloud" as he or she demonstrates how to answer each comprehension question.

7. **My Response** provides the writing partner's response to the comprehension question, which is shown in a word-processing pane to simulate the test-taking experience.

8. **Analyze features** ask students to evaluate what the writing partner has done. In the process, students learn strategies to apply during an assessment.

Preparing Students for Writing to Multiple Sources on Next Generation Assessments

Part 2: Writing to Multiple Sources guides students through the process of writing for an assessment and including evidence from the sources in Part 1.

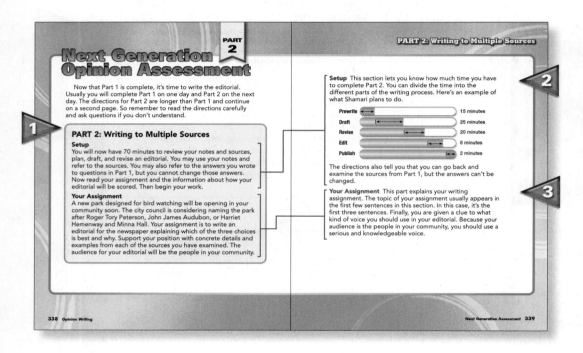

1. **Part 2 Directions** clearly explain the writing assignment and the time limit for completing Part 2 of the assessment.

2. **Setup** shows students how to manage their time based on the phases of the writing process.

3. **Your Assignment** breaks down the writing assignment to help students understand what is required.

4. **Scoring Guide** explains the criteria on which the writing will be scored and aligns to the writing traits.

5. **Writing Traits in the Scoring Guide** links questions in the scoring guide to the writing traits.

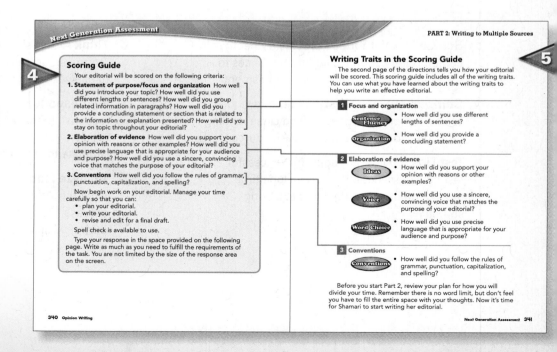

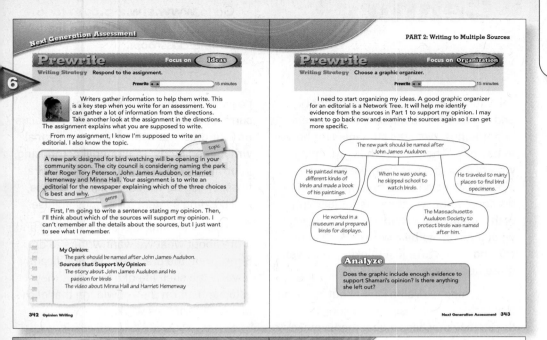

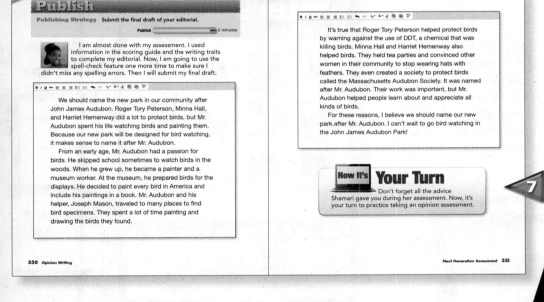

Professional Development Podcasts and Screencasts

Go to **www.sfw.z-b.com** for a screencast on **Next Generation Assessments** and **writing to multiple sources.**

6. Writing Process Instruction Students learn how to apply writing strategies during all phases of the writing process when taking an assessment.

7. Now It's Your Turn After students learn how to take a Next Generation Assessment, they will be ready to practice taking the assessment with **Zaner-Bloser Next Generation Assessment Practice**.

The **Zaner-Bloser Next Generation Assessment Practice** is designed to simulate an online test experience. Like the Next Generation Assessment chapters, the practice tests include authentic, engaging text and video sources tied to a two-part performance task for each text type.

Zaner-Bloser Next Generation Assessment Practice – Student Edition

Extending 21ˢᵗ Century Literacies

Professional Development Podcasts and Screencasts
Go to **www.sfw.z-b.com** for a screencast on **technology in the writing classroom.**

Skilled writers now work with more than putting pen to paper. We now write across modes and media, leveraging digital tools wherever purposeful. As a result, teaching writers today requires us to know both how to write an effective thesis statement *and* which social media tool helps us tap an engaged audience.

Learning and writing with digital media allows teachers and students to learn together. As much as we still inhabit our roles as lead-writers in our classrooms, teachers must also model thinking,

selection processes, and uses of print and digital tools that help us do new and better things. We need strategies for how to navigate what's new while equipping writers to be flexible, purposeful, and effective. We also need to remember that we come to these moments for learning with a great deal of expertise in knowing what it means to be a writer. We aren't starting over. We're just thinking in newer, more open ways.

The teaching we value isn't about knowing the flashiest tool. Instead, we consider the literacy practices digital media make

possible and how those sit within our current practices. In these pages, we focus on four practices with roots in traditional writing pedagogy: multimodal composing, information literacy practices with digital texts, engaging with an online audience, and creating content for purposeful use.

The goal is to think less about the tool and more about what we want writers to do. Simply put, the practices live significantly beyond the shelf life of a tool, and they value and affirm the knowledge that each of us brings to this work.

Every unit includes a **21ˢᵗ Century Literacies** page for teachers. Each page outlines suggested websites and how to incorporate them into the lessons.

Additional online resources are referenced at point of use and available at **www.sfw.z-b.com.**

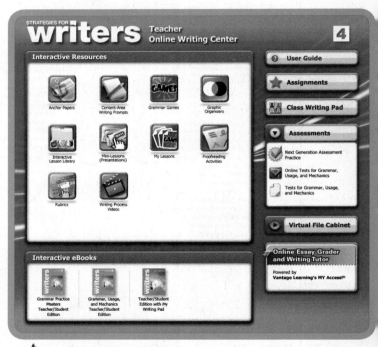

Access additional digital content in the **Online Writing Center.** Reminders for the variety of interactive resources are included throughout the Teacher Edition.

Tech Tips This feature recommends websites, apps, and other resources that are age-appropriate and engaging to help teachers incorporate technology in meaningful ways.

Formative and Summative Assessments

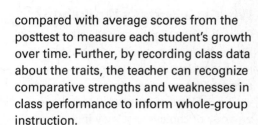
Professional Development Podcasts and Screencasts
Go to **www.sfw.z-b.com** for a screencast on **formative and summative assessments.**

The act of writing is a complex task requiring the management of myriad skills. For this reason, measuring students' writing proficiency (and their growth over time) requires a carefully crafted assessment regimen including a pretest and a posttest for each Common Core text type.

Pretests
for Formative Assessment

There are many things to consider when creating or selecting a pretest. A clear writing prompt with comprehensible instructions is a necessity. An effective pretest should also yield diagnostic information to identify areas of deficiency to be addressed with targeted mini-lessons. A Common Core State Standards-based, trait-specific rubric is ideal for this purpose. Trait-based assessment reveals specific strengths and weakness in student writing and can track improvement in specific measurable characteristics over time.

Posttests
for Summative Assessment

In some situations, teachers may choose to use the same prompt for both the pretest and the posttest to ascribe qualitative differences between the two samples to direct instruction. In other situations, teachers may choose to use different prompts for the pretest and posttest. In such cases, the posttest should approximate the pretest in format, readability, and rigor.

Analyzing Data

A critical part of this process is the collection and analysis of data. The combined use of a trait-based rubric and a simple spreadsheet can capture individual performance and whole-group trends.

By recording students' strengths in the different traits, teachers can differentiate instruction based upon each student's identified needs. This data may later be compared with average scores from the posttest to measure each student's growth over time. Further, by recording class data about the traits, the teacher can recognize comparative strengths and weaknesses in class performance to inform whole-group instruction.

Once pretest scores (individual and class average) are recorded in the spreadsheet, instructional needs become observable. Teachers should praise and reinforce specific areas of proficiency and address areas of weakness with specific targeted mini-lessons.

Strategies for Writers Pretests and Posttests

Strategies for Writers provides pretests and posttests for each Common Core text type.

- For flexibility, two prompts per text type are provided.
- Student responses (both pretest and posttest) can be scored with a Common Core-based, trait-specific rubric.
- Scores can be recorded on a provided spreadsheet with trait-specific scores for each student and for the class.

Strategies for Writers suggests and provides specific mini-lessons based upon students' trait-specific scores. These mini-lessons may be used to reteach specific skills in a whole-group setting, or to differentiate based upon the needs of individuals or small groups.

Strategies for Writers employs diagnostic pretests, specific instructional remedies, and congruent posttests to foster and demonstrate students' growth in writing proficiency.

Writer's Workshop

Professional Development Podcasts and Screencasts
Go to **www.sfw.z-b.com** for a screencast on the **writer's workshop model.**

What Is a Writer's Workshop?

Writer's Workshop is a highly effective format for process writing instruction that incorporates authentic practices within a consistent structure. As students write within the Workshop model, they have an array of choices that may include (but are not limited to) topic, genre, ideas, organization, and tone. Students then move freely and at a comfortable pace through the writing process. Some students might move through the steps sequentially. Others might forge their own path, skipping or repeating steps in a unique progression. In the Writer's Workshop classroom, this is normal, natural, and encouraged.

In such an environment, it is common for one student to be prewriting while another is drafting (and yet another may be revising). The Writer's Workshop helps teachers oversee and support each student's writing process while also facilitating sharing and feedback in a variety of groups, such as peer-to-peer, peer-groups, and teacher-led conferences.

How is this extraordinary combination of authenticity, flexibility, and oversight possible? The secret to Writer's Workshop lies in its unique structure and routines. That structure revolves around **time, space, mini-lessons and focus lessons, models, choice, conferences, and whole-group sharing.**

Strategies for Writers Supports Writer's Workshop

Time

Students can work at their own pace in *Strategies for Writers.* Student Writing Partners are introduced at the beginning of each unit and speak directly to your students in a friendly, first-person voice, guiding them through the steps of the writing process.

Space

Strategies for Writers **digital resources and posters** include useful reference material to display in your Writer's Workshop classroom.

Mini-Lessons and Focus Lessons

Each lesson features:

- **Explicit instruction** for all steps of the writing process and for each of the six traits

- **A clear, trait-specific writing goal** supported by a clearly explained writing strategy

- Trait-specific revising and editing strategies for **targeted mini-lessons**, including multiple mini-lessons for conventions

Models

Accessible student writing models are provided and annotated for genre-specific composition strategies. Each lesson rubric helps students identify the trait-specific strengths in the writing models. **Mentor text exemplars** for each text type and genre are listed in the Teacher Edition.

Choice

Flexible lesson prompts allow students to choose their own topics. Authentic purposes for writing are established to increase student engagement with the writing task. "Write" sections encourage students to use what they've learned as they continue to work on their own compositions.

Conferences

Students develop a common writing language for conferences as they work with the student-friendly rubrics before they start writing. "Analyze" sections provide questions that students can ask and answer during peer-to-peer and peer-group conferences. Suggestions for peer-to-peer, peer-group, and teacher-led conferences are included in the Teacher Edition.

Whole-Group Sharing

A variety of **publishing and presentation suggestions** promote creative options for students to share their work with the class or other audiences.

Writing Traits & Common Core State Standards

Professional Development Podcasts and Screencasts
Go to **www.sfw.z-b.com** for a screencast on **writing traits**.

***Strategies for Writers* leverages the power of trait-based instruction to exceed the rigorous expectations of the CCSS.**

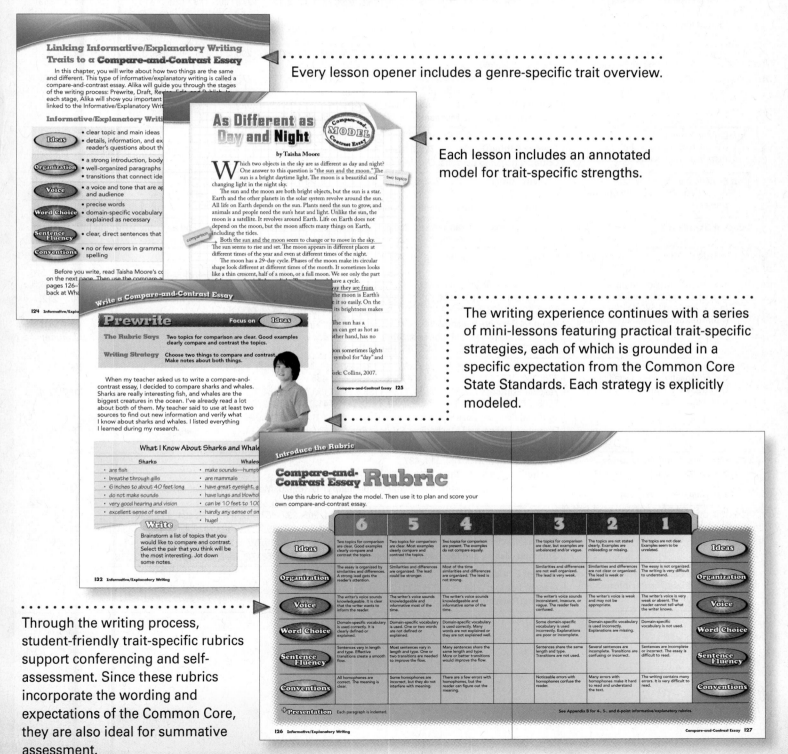

Every lesson opener includes a genre-specific trait overview.

Each lesson includes an annotated model for trait-specific strengths.

The writing experience continues with a series of mini-lessons featuring practical trait-specific strategies, each of which is grounded in a specific expectation from the Common Core State Standards. Each strategy is explicitly modeled.

Through the writing process, student-friendly trait-specific rubrics support conferencing and self-assessment. Since these rubrics incorporate the wording and expectations of the Common Core, they are also ideal for summative assessment.

STANDARD	CORRELATION

WRITING   Text Types and Purposes

Anchor Standard 1: Write arguments to support claims in an analysis of substantive topics or texts, using valid reasoning and relevant and sufficient evidence.

Standard 1: Write opinion pieces on topics or texts, supporting a point of view with reasons and information.

1a: Introduce a topic or text clearly, state an opinion, and create an organizational structure in which related ideas are grouped to support the writer's purpose.	**Student Edition:** 248, 249, 250, 251, 252, 253, 274, 275, 276, 277, 296, 297, 298, 315, 318, 319, 342, 343 **Teacher Edition:** T248, T249, T250, T251, T252, T253, T274, T275, T276, T277, T296, T297, T298, T315, T318, T319, T342, T343 **Optional Revising Lessons:** Opinion: 24 **Grammar, Usage, and Mechanics:** *Student Practice Book:* 10; *Teacher Edition:* T17
1b: Provide reasons that are supported by facts and details.	**Student Edition:** 248, 249, 250, 251, 252, 253, 274, 275, 276, 277, 279, 296, 297, 298, 300, 318, 319, 320, 321, 322, 323, 342, 343, 344, 345 **Teacher Edition:** T248, T249, T250, T251, T252, T253, T274, T275, T276, T277, T279, T296, T297, T298, T300, T318, T319, T320, T321, T322, T323, T342, T343, T344, T345 **Optional Revising Lessons:** Opinion: 21, 23, 29 **Grammar, Usage, and Mechanics:** *Student Practice Book:* 10; *Teacher Edition:* T17
1c: Link opinion and reasons using words and phrases (e.g., *for instance, in order to, in addition*).	**Student Edition:** 248, 254, 293, 323, 487 **Teacher Edition:** T248, T254, T293, T323, T487 **Optional Revising Lessons:** Opinion: 25, 30
1d: Provide a concluding statement or section related to the opinion presented.	**Student Edition:** 250, 251, 252, 253, 275, 276, 277, 279, 297, 319, 346, 347 **Teacher Edition:** T250, T251, T252, T253, T275, T276, T277, T279, T297, T319, T346, T347 **Grammar, Usage, and Mechanics:** *Student Practice Book:* 10; *Teacher Edition:* T17

Anchor Standard 2: Write informative/explanatory texts to examine and convey complex ideas and information clearly and accurately through the effective selection, organization, and analysis of content.

Standard 2: Write informative/explanatory texts to examine a topic and convey ideas and information clearly.

2a: Introduce a topic clearly and group related information in paragraphs and sections; include formatting (e.g., headings), illustrations, and multimedia when useful to aiding comprehension.	**Student Edition:** 133, 134, 135, 136, 155, 156, 157, 164, 177, 178, 179, 186, 187, 203, 204, 205, 207, 212, 213, 222, 223, 226, 227, 228, 229, 408, 409, 410, 411, 432, 433, 437 **Teacher Edition:** T133, T134, T135, T136, T155, T156, T157, T164, T177, T178, T179, T186, T187, T203, T204, T205, T207, T212, T213, T222, T223, T226, T227, T228, T229, T408, T409, T410, T411, T432, T433, T437 **Optional Revising Lessons:** Informative/Explanatory: 11 **Grammar, Usage, and Mechanics:** *Student Practice Book:* 32, 36, 57, 64, 66, 68, 72, 96, 109, 118, 135; *Teacher Edition:* T22, T25, T30, T33, T34, T35, T43, T46, T50, T54
2b: Develop the topic with facts, definitions, concrete details, quotations, or other information and examples related to the topic.	**Student Edition:** 132, 133, 134, 135, 136, 138, 150, 151, 154, 155, 158, 159, 176, 177, 180, 181, 186, 203, 206, 207, 224, 228, 232, 408, 409, 410, 411, 412, 413, 432, 434, 435, 436 **Teacher Edition:** T132, T133, T134, T135, T136, T138, T150, T151, T154, T155, T158, T159, T176, T177, T180, T181, T186, T203, T206, T207, T224, T228, T232, T408, T409, T410, T411, T412, T413, T432, T434, T435, T436 **Optional Revising Lessons:** Informative/Explanatory: 11, 13, 18, 19; More Writing Practice: 31, 33, 38 **Grammar, Usage, and Mechanics:** *Student Practice Book:* 32, 36, 57, 64, 66, 68, 72, 96, 109, 118, 135; *Teacher Edition:* T22, T25, T30, T33, T34, T35, T43, T46, T50, T54
2c: Link ideas within categories of information using words and phrases (e.g., *another, for example, also, because*).	**Student Edition:** 173, 182, 413, 487 **Teacher Edition:** T173, T182, T413, T487 **Optional Revising Lessons:** Informative/Explanatory: 12, 15, 20; More Writing Practice: 34, 36
2d: Use precise language and domain-specific vocabulary to inform about or explain the topic.	**Student Edition:** 116, 117, 138, 159, 180, 181, 201, 204, 205, 232, 407, 412, 413, 432, 434, 435, 436 **Teacher Edition:** T116, T117, T138, T159, T180, T181, T201, T204, T205, T232, T407, T412, T413, T432, T434, T435, T436 **Optional Revising Lessons:** Informative/Explanatory: 11, 13, 18, 19; More Writing Practice: 38 **Grammar, Usage, and Mechanics:** *Student Practice Book:* 57, 66, 68, 72; *Teacher Edition:* T30, T34, T35
2e: Provide a concluding statement or section related to the information or explanation presented.	**Student Edition:** 156, 157, 176, 177, 230, 231 **Teacher Edition:** T156, T157, T176, T177, T230, T231 **Optional Revising Lessons:** Informative/Explanatory: 14

STANDARD	CORRELATION
Anchor Standard 3: Write narratives to develop real or imagined experiences or events using effective technique, well-chosen details, and well-structured event sequences.	

Standard 3: Write narratives to develop real or imagined experiences or events using effective technique, descriptive details, and clear event sequences.

3a: Orient the reader by establishing a situation and introducing a narrator and/or characters; organize an event sequence that unfolds naturally.	**Student Edition:** 15, 18, 19, 36, 37, 38, 40, 58, 59, 60, 61, 62, 84, 85, 89, 98, 99, 110, 111, 112, 113, 114, 115, 366, 367, 370, 374, 386, 387, 388, 389 **Teacher Edition:** T15, T18, T19, T36, T37, T38, T40, T58, T59, T60, T61, T62, T84, T85, T89, T98, T99, T110, T111, T112, T113, T114, T115, T366, T367, T370, T374, T386, T387, T388, T389 **Optional Revising Lessons:** Narrative: 5 **Grammar, Usage, and Mechanics:** *Student Practice Book:* 32, 36, 136; *Teacher Edition:* T22, T54
3b: Use dialogue and description to develop experiences and events or show the responses of characters to situations.	**Student Edition:** 16, 17, 18, 20, 32, 33, 36, 38, 58, 59, 60, 61, 62, 63, 86, 87, 88, 89, 116, 117, 364, 365, 366, 367, 368, 370, 386, 387, 388, 389, 390, 391 **Teacher Edition:** T16, T17, T18, T20, T32, T33, T36, T38, T58, T59, T60, T61, T62, T63, T86, T87, T88, T89, T116, T117, T364, T365, T366, T367, T368, T370, T386, T387, T388, T389, T390, T391 **Optional Revising Lessons:** Narrative: 1, 3, 6, 7, 8, 9 **Grammar, Usage, and Mechanics:** *Student Practice Book:* 32, 36, 136; *Teacher Edition:* T22, T54
3c: Use a variety of transitional words and phrases to manage the sequence of events.	**Student Edition:** 10, 38, 39, 64, 114, 115, 368, 369, 385, 386, 388, 389, 487 **Teacher Edition:** T10, T38, T39, T64, T114, T115, T368, T369, T385, T386, T388, T389, T487 **Optional Revising Lessons:** Narrative: 4; More Writing Practice: 36
3d: Use concrete words and phrases and sensory details to convey experiences and events precisely.	**Student Edition:** 13, 16, 17, 18, 20, 32, 33, 41, 62, 63, 86, 87, 88, 89, 116, 360, 361, 364, 366, 367, 368, 370, 390, 391 **Teacher Edition:** T13, T16, T17, T18, T20, T32, T33, T41, T62, T63, T86, T87, T88, T89, T116, T360, T361, T364, T366, T367, T368, T370, T390, T391 **Optional Revising Lessons:** Narrative: 1, 8, 9; More Writing Practice: 38
3e: Provide a conclusion that follows from the narrated experiences or events.	**Student Edition:** 15, 18, 59, 60, 85, 89, 388, 389 **Teacher Edition:** T15, T18, T59, T60, T85, T89, T388, T389

WRITING Production and Distribution of Writing

Anchor Standard 4: Produce clear and coherent writing in which the development, organization, and style are appropriate to task, purpose, and audience.	

Standard 4: Produce clear and coherent writing in which the development and organization are appropriate to task, purpose, and audience. (Grade-specific expectations for writing types are defined in standards 1–3 above.)

	Student Edition: 114, 15, 16, 17, 18, 19, 20, 21, 24, 25, 36, 37, 38, 39, 40, 41, 42, 43, 46, 47, 58, 59, 60, 61, 62, 63, 64, 65, 68, 69, 70, 71, 84, 85, 86, 87, 88, 89, 90, 91, 94, 95, 96, 97, 118, 119, 132, 133, 134, 135, 136, 137, 138, 139, 142, 143, 154, 155, 156, 157, 158, 159, 160, 161, 164, 165, 176, 177, 178, 179, 180, 181, 182, 183, 186, 187, 200, 201, 202, 203, 204, 205, 206, 207, 208, 209, 212, 213, 234, 235, 248, 249, 250, 251, 252, 253, 254, 255, 256, 257, 260, 261, 262, 263, 274, 275, 276, 277, 278, 279, 280, 281, 284, 285, 296, 297, 298, 299, 300, 301, 302, 303, 306, 307, 318, 319, 320, 321, 322, 323, 324, 325, 328, 329, 348, 349, 350, 351, 364, 365, 366, 367, 368, 369, 370, 371, 374, 375, 386, 387, 388, 389, 390, 391, 392, 393, 396, 397, 408, 409, 410, 411, 412, 413, 414, 415, 418, 419, 420, 421, 432, 433, 434, 435, 436, 437, 438, 439, 442, 443 **Teacher Edition:** T14, T15, T16, T17, T18, T19, T20, T21, T24, T25, T36, T37, T38, T39, T40, T41, T42, T43, T46, T47, T58, T59, T60, T61, T62, T63, T64, T65, T68, T69, T70, T71, T84, T85, T86, T87, T88, T89, T90, T91, T94, T95, T96, T97, T118, T119, T132, T133, T134, T135, T136, T137, T138, T139, T142, T143, T154, T155, T156, T157, T158, T159, T160, T161, T164, T165, T176, T177, T178, T179, T180, T181, T182, T183, T186, T187, T200, T201, T202, T203, T204, T205, T206, T207, T208, T209, T212, T213, T234, T235, T248, T249, T250, T251, T252, T253, T254, T255, T256, T257, T260, T261, T262, T263, T274, T275, T276, T277, T278, T279, T280, T281, T284, T285, T296, T297, T298, T299, T300, T301, T302, T303, T306, T307, T318, T319, T320, T321, T322, T323, T324, T325, T328, T329, T348, T349, T350, T351, T364, T365, T366, T367, T368, T369, T370, T371, T374, T375, T386, T387, T388, T389, T390, T391, T392, T393, T396, T397, T408, T409, T410, T411, T412, T413, T414, T415, T418, T419, T420, T421, T432, T433, T434, T435, T436, T437, T438, T439, T442, T443 **Optional Revising Lessons:** Narrative: 1–10; Informative/Explanatory: 11–20; Opinion: 21–30; More Writing Practice: 31–38 **Grammar, Usage, and Mechanics:** *Student Practice Book:* 10, 32, 36, 57, 64, 66, 68, 72, 96, 109, 118, 135, 136; *Teacher Edition:* T17, T22, T25, T30, T33, T34, T35, T43, T46, T50, T54

STANDARD	CORRELATION
Anchor Standard 5: Develop and strengthen writing as needed by planning, revising, editing, rewriting, or trying a new approach.	
Standard 5: With guidance and support from peers and adults, develop and strengthen writing as needed by planning, revising, and editing. (Editing for conventions should demonstrate command of Language standards 1–3 up to and including grade 4.)	

	Student Edition: 14, 15, 16, 17, 18, 19, 20, 21, 36, 37, 38, 39, 40, 41, 42, 43, 58, 59, 60, 61, 62, 63, 64, 65, 84, 85, 86, 87, 88, 89, 90, 91, 114, 115, 118, 119, 132, 133, 134, 135, 136, 137, 138, 139, 154, 155, 156, 157, 158, 159, 160, 161, 176, 177, 178, 179, 180, 181, 182, 183, 200, 201, 202, 203, 204, 205, 206, 207, 208, 209, 234, 235, 248, 249, 250, 251, 252, 253, 254, 255, 256, 257, 274, 275, 276, 277, 278, 279, 280, 281, 296, 297, 298, 299, 300, 301, 302, 303, 318, 319, 320, 321, 322, 323, 324, 325, 348, 349, 350, 351, 364, 365, 366, 367, 368, 369, 370, 371, 386, 387, 388, 389, 390, 391, 392, 393, 408, 409, 410, 411, 412, 413, 414, 415, 418, 419, 432, 433, 434, 435, 436, 437, 438, 439
	Teacher Edition: T14, T15, T16, T17, T18, T19, T20, T21, T36, T37, T38, T39, T40, T41, T42, T43, T58, T59, T60, T61, T62, T63, T64, T65, T84, T85, T86, T87, T88, T89, T90, T91, T114, T115, T118, T119, T132, T133, T134, T135, T136, T137, T138, T139, T154, T155, T156, T157, T158, T159, T160, T161, T176, T177, T178, T179, T180, T181, T182, T183, T200, T201, T202, T203, T204, T205, T206, T207, T208, T209, T234, T235, T248, T249, T250, T251, T252, T253, T254, T255, T256, T257, T274, T275, T276, T277, T278, T279, T280, T281, T296, T297, T298, T299, T300, T301, T302, T303, T318, T319, T320, T321, T322, T323, T324, T325, T348, T349, T350, T351, T364, T365, T366, T367, T368, T369, T370, T371, T386, T387, T388, T389, T390, T391, T392, T393, T408, T409, T410, T411, T412, T413, T414, T415, T418, T419, T432, T433, T434, T435, T436, T437, T438, T439
	Optional Revising Lessons: Narrative: 1–10; Informative/Explanatory: 11–20; Opinion: 21–30; More Writing Practice: 31–38
	Grammar, Usage, and Mechanics: *Student Practice Book:* 27, 28, 31, 32, 53, 54, 56, 57, 79, 80, 83, 84, 105, 106, 109, 110, 131, 132, 135, 136; *Teacher Edition:* T21, T22, T29, T30, T37, T38, T45, T46, T53, T54

Anchor Standard 6: Use technology, including the Internet, to produce and publish writing and to interact and collaborate with others.	
Standard 6: With some guidance and support from adults, use technology, including the Internet, to produce and publish writing as well as to interact and collaborate with others; demonstrate sufficient command of keyboarding skills to type a minimum of one page in a single sitting.	

	Student Edition: 4, 6, 8, 12, 14, 15, 16, 20, 22, 24, 25, 28, 30, 34, 36, 38, 42, 44, 46, 47, 50, 52, 56, 58, 59, 60, 64, 66, 68, 69, 74, 78, 82, 84, 85, 86, 90, 92, 94, 95, 110, 111, 116, 117, 118, 119, 124, 125, 126, 127, 130, 132, 134, 138, 140, 143, 146, 148, 152, 154, 156, 160, 162, 165, 168, 170, 174, 175, 176, 178, 182, 184, 187, 190, 194, 198, 202, 203, 204, 208, 210, 232, 240, 242, 246, 248, 250, 256, 258, 260, 261, 266, 268, 272, 273, 274, 275, 276, 280, 282, 284, 285, 288, 290, 294, 295, 296, 298, 300, 301, 302, 303, 304, 306, 307, 310, 312, 316, 317, 318, 319, 320, 324, 326, 328, 329, 340, 342, 343, 348, 349, 356, 358, 362, 364, 366, 370, 372, 374, 375, 378, 380, 384, 386, 388, 392, 394, 396, 397, 400, 402, 408, 410, 414, 416, 418, 419, 424, 426, 430, 432, 434, 438, 440, 442, 443
	Teacher Edition: T4, T6, T8, T12, T14, T15, T16, T20, T22, T24, T25, T28, T30, T34, T36, T38, T42, T44, T46, T47, T50, T52, T56, T58, T59, T60, T64, T66, T68, T69, T74, T78, T82, T84, T85, T86, T90, T92, T94, T95, T110, T111, T116, T117, T118, T119, T124, T125, T126, T127, T130, T132, T134, T138, T140, T143, T146, T148, T152, T154, T156, T160, T162, T165, T168, T170, T174, T175, T176, T178, T182, T184, T187, T190, T194, T198, T202, T203, T204, T208, T210, T232, T240, T242, T246, T248, T250, T256, T258, T260, T261, T266, T268, T272, T273, T274, T275, T276, T280, T282, T284, T285, T288, T290, T294, T295, T296, T298, T300, T301, T302, T303, T304, T306, T307, T310, T312, T316, T317, T318, T319, T320, T324, T326, T328, T329, T340, T342, T343, T348, T349, T356, T358, T362, T364, T366, T370, T372, T374, T375, T378, T380, T384, T386, T388, T392, T394, T396, T397, T400, T402, T408, T410, T414, T416, T418, T419, T424, T426, T430, T432, T434, T438, T440, T442, T443
	Optional Revising Lessons: Informative/Explanatory: 18
	Grammar, Usage, and Mechanics: *Student Practice Book:* 10, 22, 86; *Teacher Edition:* T17, T20, T29, T40
	Online Writing Center: Anchor Papers, Class Writing Pad, Content-Area Prompts, Grammar Games, Graphic Organizers, Mini-Lessons, My Writing Pad, Proofreading Activities, Rubrics, Writing Process Videos
	Digital Resources: Anchor Papers, Content-Area Prompts, Grammar Games, Graphic Organizers, Mini-Lessons, Proofreading Activities, Rubrics, Writing Process Videos
	Online Grammar Games and Proofreading Activities

WRITING Research to Build and Present Knowledge	
Anchor Standard 7: Conduct short as well as more sustained research projects based on focused questions, demonstrating understanding of the subject under investigation.	
Standard 7: Conduct short research projects that build knowledge through investigation of different aspects of a topic.	

	Student Edition: 132, 134, 154, 155, 156, 157, 158, 159, 160, 161, 164, 165, 214, 215, 222, 223
	Teacher Edition: T132, T134, T154, T155, T156, T157, T158, T159, T160, T161, T164, T165, T214, T215, T222, T223
	Optional Revising Lessons: Informative/Explanatory: 13

STANDARD	CORRELATION
Anchor Standard 8: Gather relevant information from multiple print and digital sources, assess the credibility and accuracy of each source, and integrate the information while avoiding plagiarism.	
Standard 8: Recall relevant information from experiences or gather relevant information from print and digital sources; take notes and categorize information, and provide a list of sources.	
	Student Edition: 14, 15, 16, 17, 35, 36, 37, 38, 84, 106, 107, 110, 111, 132, 133, 134, 142, 143, 151, 152, 154, 155, 156, 164, 165, 176, 177, 200, 201, 202, 203, 226, 227, 248, 249, 274, 275, 296, 297, 300, 314, 315, 318, 319, 332, 333, 334, 335, 336, 337, 338, 339, 364, 365, 386, 387, 408, 409, 432, 433 **Teacher Edition:** T14, T15, T16, T17, T35, T36, T37, T38, T84, T106, T107, T110, T111, T132, T133, T134, T142, T143, T151, T152, T154, T155, T156, T164, T165, T176, T177, T200, T201, T202, T203, T226, T227, T248, T249, T274, T275, T296, T297, T300, T314, T315, T318, T319, T332, T333, T334, T335, T336, T337, T338, T339, T364, T365, T386, T387, T408, T409, T432, T433 **Grammar, Usage, and Mechanics:** *Student Practice Book:* 10, 32, 57, 64, 66, 118, 135, 136; *Teacher Edition:* T17, T22, T30, T33, T34, T50, T54
Anchor Standard 9: Draw evidence from literary or informational texts to support analysis, reflection, and research.	
Standard 9: Draw evidence from literary or informational texts to support analysis, reflection, and research.	
9a: Apply *grade 4 Reading standards* to literature (e.g., "Describe in depth a character, setting, or event in a story or drama, drawing on specific details in the text [e.g., a character's thoughts, words or actions].").	**Student Edition:** 83, 318, 319, 320, 321, 322, 323, 324, 325, 328, 329, 386, 387, 388, 389, 390, 391, 392, 393, 396, 397, 408, 409, 410, 411, 412, 413, 414, 415, 418, 419, 420, 421 **Teacher Edition:** T83, T318, T319, T320, T321, T322, T323, T324, T325, T328, T329, T386, T387, T388, T389, T390, T391, T392, T393, T396, T397, T408, T409, T410, T411, T412, T413, T414, T415, T418, T419, T420, T421 **Optional Revising Lessons:** Narrative: 1, 3, 5, 6, 7, 8, 9 **Zaner-Bloser Next Generation Assessment Practice:** Narrative: www.sfw.z-b.com
9b: Apply *grade 4 Reading standards* to informational texts (e.g., "Explain how an author uses reasons and evidence to support particular points in a text").	**Student Edition:** 200, 201, 202, 203, 204, 205, 206, 207, 208, 209, 212, 213, 216, 217, 218, 219, 220, 221, 226, 227, 228, 229, 230, 231, 232, 233, 234, 235, 344, 345, 348, 349 **Teacher Edition:** T200, T201, T202, T203, T204, T205, T206, T207, T208, T209, T212, T213, T216, T217, T218, T219, T220, T221, T226, T227, T228, T229, T230, T231, T232, T233, T234, T235, T344, T345, T348, T349 **Optional Revising Lessons:** Informative/Explanatory: 11, 13, 14, 19; Opinion: 21, 23, 24 **Zaner-Bloser Next Generation Assessment Practice:** Informative/Explanatory, Opinion: www.sfw.z-b.com
WRITING Range of Writing	
Anchor Standard 10: Draw evidence from literary or informational texts to support analysis, reflection, and research.	
Standard 10: Write routinely over extended time frames (time for research, reflection, and revision) and shorter time frames (a single sitting or a day or two) for a range of discipline-specific tasks, purposes, and audiences.	
	Student Edition: 114, 15, 16, 17, 18, 19, 20, 21, 24, 25, 36, 37, 38, 39, 40, 41, 42, 43, 46, 47, 58, 59, 60, 61, 62, 63, 64, 65, 68, 69, 70, 71, 84, 85, 86, 87, 88, 89, 90, 91, 94, 95, 96, 97, 98, 99, 100, 101, 102, 103, 104, 105, 110, 111, 114, 115, 116, 117, 118, 119, 132, 133, 134, 135, 136, 137, 138, 139, 142, 143, 154, 155, 156, 157, 158, 159, 160, 161, 164, 165, 176, 177, 178, 179, 180, 181, 182, 183, 186, 187, 200, 201, 202, 203, 204, 205, 206, 207, 208, 209, 212, 213, 214, 215, 216, 217, 218, 219, 220, 221, 222, 223, 226, 227, 228, 229, 230, 231, 232, 233, 234, 235, 248, 249, 250, 251, 252, 253, 254, 255, 256, 257, 260, 261, 262, 263, 274, 275, 276, 277, 278, 279, 280, 281, 284, 285, 296, 297, 298, 299, 300, 301, 302, 303, 306, 307, 318, 319, 320, 321, 322, 323, 324, 325, 328, 329, 330, 331, 332, 333, 334, 335, 336, 337, 342, 343, 344, 345, 346, 347, 348, 349, 350, 351, 364, 365, 366, 367, 368, 369, 370, 371, 374, 375, 386, 387, 388, 389, 390, 391, 392, 393, 396, 397, 408, 409, 410, 411, 412, 413, 414, 415, 418, 419, 420, 421, 432, 433, 434, 435, 436, 437, 438, 439, 442, 443 **Teacher Edition:** T14, T15, T16, T17, T18, T19, T20, T21, T24, T25, T36, T37, T38, T39, T40, T41, T42, T43, T46, T47, T58, T59, T60, T61, T62, T63, T64, T65, T68, T69, T70, T71, T84, T85, T86, T87, T88, T89, T90, T91, T94, T95, T96, T97, T98, T99, T100, T101, T102, T103, T104, T105, T110, T111, T114, T115, T116, T117, T118, T119, T132, T133, T134, T135, T136, T137, T138, T139, T142, T143, T154, T155, T156, T157, T158, T159, T160, T161, T164, T165, T176, T177, T178, T179, T180, T181, T182, T183, T186, T187, T200, T201, T202, T203, T204, T205, T206, T207, T208, T209, T212, T213, T214, T215, T216, T217, T218, T219, T220, T221, T222, T223, T226, T227, T228, T229, T230, T231, T232, T233, T234, T235, T248, T249, T250, T251, T252, T253, T254, T255, T256, T257, T260, T261, T262, T263, T274, T275, T276, T277, T278, T279, T280, T281, T284, T285, T296, T297, T298, T299, T300, T301, T302, T303, T306, T307, T318, T319, T320, T321, T322, T323, T324, T325, T328, T329, T330, T331, T332, T333, T334, T335, T336, T337, T342, T343, T344, T345, T346, T347, T348, T349, T350, T351, T364, T365, T366, T367, T368, T369, T370, T371, T374, T375, T386, T387, T388, T389, T390, T391, T392, T393, T396, T397, T408, T409, T410, T411, T412, T413, T414, T415, T418, T419, T420, T421, T432, T433, T434, T435, T436, T437, T438, T439, T442, T443 **Optional Revising Lessons:** Narrative: 1–10; Informative/Explanatory: 11–20; Opinion: 21–30; More Writing Practice: 31–38 **Grammar, Usage, and Mechanics:** *Student Practice Book:* 10, 32, 36, 57, 64, 66, 68, 72, 96, 109, 118, 135, 136; *Teacher Edition:* T17, T22, T25, T30, T33, T34, T35, T43, T46, T50, T54

STANDARD	CORRELATION
LANGUAGE **Conventions of Standard English**	
Anchor Standard 1: Demonstrate command of the conventions of standard English grammar and usage when writing or speaking.	
Standard 1: Demonstrate command of the conventions of standard English grammar and usage when writing or speaking.	
1a: Use relative pronouns (*who, whose, whom, which, that*) and relative adverbs (*where, when, why*).	**Student Edition:** 325, 327, 328 **Teacher Edition:** T325, T327, T328
1b: Form and use the progressive (e.g., *I was walking; I am walking; I will be walking*) verb tenses.	**Student Edition:** 461, 481 **Teacher Edition:** T461, T481
1c: Use modal auxiliaries (e.g., *can, may, must*) to convey various conditions	**Student Edition:** 454, 455, 479, 487 **Teacher Edition:** T454, T455, T479, T487 **Grammar, Usage, and Mechanics:** *Student Practice Book:* 45, 46, 167; *Teacher Edition:* T27 **Grammar Practice Masters:** 39, 40
1d: Order adjectives within sentences according to conventional patterns (e.g., *a small red bag* rather than *a red small bag*).	**Student Edition:** 416, 418 **Teacher Edition:** T416, T418
1e: Form and use prepositional phrases.	**Student Edition:** 436, 439, 440, 441, 442, 448, 458, 477, 480, 488 **Teacher Edition:** TT436, T439, T440, T441, T442, T448, T458, T477, T480, T488 **Grammar, Usage, and Mechanics:** *Student Practice Book:* 17, 18, 49, 50, 161, 168, 206; *Teacher Edition:* T19, T28 **Grammar Practice Masters:** 17, 18, 43, 44
1f: Produce complete sentences, recognizing and correcting inappropriate fragments and run-ons.	**Student Edition:** 21, 22, 23, 24, 42, 43, 44, 46, 62, 64, 90, 160, 208, 280, 322, 324, 392, 393, 394, 395, 396, 412, 414, 431, 438, 445, 446, 474, 476, 485 **Teacher Edition:** T21, T22, T23, T24, T42, T43, T44, T46, T62, T64, T90, T160, T208, T280, T322, T324, T392, T393, T394, T395, T396, T412, T414, T431, T438, T445, T446, T474, T476, T485 **Optional Revising Lessons:** Narrative: 2, 10; Informative/Explanatory: 12, 13, 20; Opinion: 22, 30; More Writing Practice: 32 **Grammar, Usage, and Mechanics:** *Student Practice Book:* 7, 8, 9, 10, 14, 16, 18, 19, 20, 22, 23, 24, 25, 26, 27, 28, 30, 31, 32, 36, 38, 42, 44, 46, 52, 56, 57, 58, 64, 66, 68, 70, 72, 74, 78, 86, 88, 90, 92, 94, 96, 100, 102, 104, 109, 110, 112, 114, 116, 118, 120, 121, 124, 126, 128, 130, 135, 136, 201, 202; *Teacher Edition:* T16, T17, T18, T19, T20, T21, T22, T25, T26, T27, T29, T30, T33, T34, T35, T36, T37, T40, T41, T42, T43, T44, T45, T46, T48, T49, T50, T51, T52, T53, T54 **Grammar Practice Masters:** 7, 8, 9, 10, 11, 12, 13, 14, 19, 20, 21, 22, 23, 24, 25, 26, 30, 36, 38, 40, 42, 45, 46, 48, 52, 56, 58, 60, 64, 66, 68, 70, 72, 74, 76, 78, 80, 82, 84, 86, 87, 88, 90, 98, 100, 101, 102, 104, 106
1g: Correctly use frequently confused words (e.g., *to, too, two; there, their*).	**Student Edition:** 136, 139, 140, 141, 142, 257, 258, 259, 327, 462, 463, 481, 482 **Teacher Edition:** T136, T139, T140, T141, T142, T257, T258, T259, T327, T462, T463, T481, T482 **Grammar, Usage, and Mechanics:** *Student Practice Book:* 59, 60, 61, 62, 63, 64, 67, 68, 69, 70, 73, 74, 75, 76, 79, 80, 81, 82, 83, 84, 169, 170, 171, 172, 173, 209, 210; *Teacher Edition:* T32, T33, T34, T35, T36, T37, T38 **Grammar Practice Masters:** 47, 48, 49, 50, 51, 52, 55, 56, 57, 58, 61, 62, 63, 64, 73, 74, 75, 76
Anchor Standard 2: Demonstrate command of the conventions of standard English capitalization, punctuation, and spelling when writing.	
Standard 2: Demonstrate command of the conventions of standard English capitalization, punctuation, and spelling when writing.	
2a: Use correct capitalization.	**Student Edition:** 21, 43, 65, 66, 91, 117, 139, 158, 161, 162, 163, 164, 183, 186, 209, 212, 233, 257, 281, 303, 304, 305, 325, 348, 349, 371, 393, 394, 415, 439, 446, 447, 469, 470, 484 **Teacher Edition:** T21, T43, T65, T66, T91, T117, T139, T158, T161, T162, T163, T164, T183, T186, T209, T212, T233, T257, T281, T303, T304, T305, T325, T348, T349, T371, T393, T394, T415, T439, T446, T447, T469, T470, T484 **Grammar, Usage, and Mechanics:** *Student Practice Book:* 27, 28, 35, 36, 53, 54, 60, 62, 64, 70, 74, 76, 79, 80, 82, 90, 105, 106, 107, 111, 112, 113, 114, 115, 116, 117, 118, 128, 131, 132, 133, 134, 135, 136, 164, 179, 180, 196, 197, 198, 203; *Teacher Edition:* T21, T25, T29, T37, T45, T48, T49, T50, T52 **Grammar Practice Masters:** 29, 30, 34, 50, 52, 58, 60, 62, 72, 87, 88, 89, 90, 91, 92, 93, 94, 100, 106
2b: Use commas and quotation marks to mark direct speech and quotations from a text.	**Student Edition:** 60, 61, 65, 66, 68, 322, 390 **Teacher Edition:** T60, T61, T65, T66, T68, T322, T390 **Grammar, Usage, and Mechanics:** *Student Practice Book:* 127, 128, 129, 130, 131, 132, 133, 134, 136, 183, 198, 200; *Teacher Edition:* T52, T53, T54 **Grammar Practice Masters:** 103, 104, 105, 106

STANDARD	CORRELATION
Language Standard 2 continued	
2c: Use a comma before a coordinating conjunction in a compound sentence.	**Student Edition:** 160, 393, 394, 395, 396, 446, 459, 476, 480, 487 **Teacher Edition:** T160, T393, T394, T395, T396, T446, T459, T476, T480, T487 **Optional Revising Lessons:** Narrative: 2; Opinion: 30 **Grammar, Usage, and Mechanics:** *Student Practice Book:* 23, 24, 25, 26, 27, 28, 30, 32, 51, 52, 56, 125, 126, 182, 200, 202; *Teacher Edition:* T20, T21, T29, T52 **Grammar Practice Masters:** 23, 24, 25, 26, 45, 46, 101, 102
2d: Spell grade-appropriate words correctly, consulting references as needed.	**Student Edition:** 21, 65, 67, 91, 117, 136, 139, 140, 141, 142, 161, 183, 209, 212, 233, 257, 260, 281, 282, 283, 284, 303, 304, 305, 325, 348, 349, 363, 371, 372, 393, 412, 415, 417, 439, 452, 461, 462, 463, 465, 466, 468, 478, 481, 482, 483 **Teacher Edition:** T21, T65, T67, T91, T117, T136, T139, T140, T141, T142, T161, T183, T209, T212, T233, T257, T260, T281, T282, T283, T284, T303, T304, T305, T325, T348, T349, T363, T371, T372, T393, T412, T415, T417, T439, T452, T461, T462, T463, T465, T466, T468, T478, T481, T482, T483 **Grammar, Usage, and Mechanics:** *Student Practice Book:* 27, 28, 37, 38, 47, 48, 53, 54, 59, 60, 61, 62, 63, 64, 69, 70, 73, 74, 75, 76, 79, 80, 95, 96, 99, 100, 103, 104, 105, 106, 115, 116, 119, 120, 131, 132, 165, 167, 169, 170, 171, 172, 173, 177, 178, 180, 181, 197, 198, 199, 205, 206, 207, 208, 209, 210; *Teacher Edition:* T21, T25, T28, T29, T32, T33, T35, T36, T37, T43, T44, T45, T49, T50, T53 **Grammar Practice Masters:** 31, 32, 41, 42, 47, 48, 49, 50, 51, 52, 61, 62, 63, 64, 77, 78, 81, 82, 85, 86, 95, 96
LANGUAGE Knowledge of Language	
Anchor Standard 3: Apply knowledge of language to understand how language functions in different contexts, to make effective choices for meaning or style, and to comprehend more fully when reading or listening.	
Standard 3: Use knowledge of language and its conventions when writing, speaking, reading, or listening.	
3a: Choose words and phrases to convey ideas precisely.	**Student Edition:** 113, 16, 17, 18, 20, 32, 33, 40, 41, 57, 62, 63, 86, 87, 116, 138, 152, 158, 159, 180, 181, 204, 205, 229, 232, 254, 256, 279, 300, 301, 318, 320, 321, 348, 360, 361, 364, 365, 366, 367, 368, 370, 390, 391, 407, 412, 413, 432, 434, 435, 436 **Teacher Edition:** T13, T16, T17, T18, T20, T32, T33, T40, T41, T57, T62, T63, T86, T87, T116, T138, T152, T158, T159, T180, T181, T204, T205, T229, T232, T254, T256, T279, T300, T301, T318, T320, T321, T348, T360, T361, T364, T365, T366, T367, T368, T370, T390, T391, T407, T412, T413, T432, T434, T435, T436 **Optional Revising Lessons:** Narrative: 1, 8, 9; Informative/Explanatory: 18; Opinion: 24, 28; More Writing Practice: 31, 33, 38 **Grammar, Usage, and Mechanics:** *Student Practice Book:* 17, 18, 21, 22, 28, 30, 31, 32, 47, 48, 49, 50, 54, 56, 57, 67, 68, 79, 80, 82, 83, 93, 94, 103, 104, 109, 113, 114, 115, 116, 119, 120, 161, 162, 167, 168, 171, 176, 178, 179, 180, 181, 197, 199, 203, 206, 207, 208, 212, 213; *Teacher Edition:* T19, T20, T21, T22, T28, T29, T30, T34, T37, T38, T42, T45, T46, T49, T50 **Grammar Practice Masters:** 21, 22, 41, 42, 43, 44
3b: Choose punctuation for effect.	**Student Edition:** 62, 90, 445, 449, 460, 476, 481 **Teacher Edition:** T62, T90, T445, T449, T460, T476, T481 **Grammar, Usage, and Mechanics:** *Student Practice Book:* 7, 8, 28, 29, 32, 111, 112, 123, 124, 131, 132, 133, 134, 136, 159, 179, 182, 199, 200, 201; *Teacher Edition:* T16, T21, T22, T48, T51, T53, T54 **Grammar Practice Masters:** 7, 8, 87, 88

STANDARD	CORRELATION
Language Standard 3 continued	
3c: Differentiate between contexts that call for formal English (e.g., presenting ideas) and situations where informal discourse is appropriate (e.g., small-group discussion).	**Student Edition:** 4, 5, 6, 7, 8, 9, 10, 11, 12, 13, 15, 17, 19, 25, 26, 27, 28, 29, 30, 31, 32, 33, 34, 35, 37, 39, 41, 47, 48, 49, 50, 51, 52, 53, 54, 55, 56, 57, 59, 61, 63, 70, 71, 72, 73, 74, 75, 76, 77, 78, 79, 80, 81, 82, 83, 85, 87, 89, 96, 97, 122, 123, 124, 125, 126, 127, 128, 129, 130, 131, 132, 133, 135, 137, 142, 143, 144, 145, 146, 147, 148, 149, 150, 151, 152, 153, 155, 157, 159, 165, 166, 167, 168, 169, 170, 171, 172, 173, 174, 175, 187, 188, 189, 190, 191, 192, 193, 194, 195, 196, 197, 198, 199, 202, 205, 207, 213, 216, 217, 218, 219, 220, 221, 238, 239, 240, 241, 242, 243, 244, 245, 246, 247, 249, 251, 255, 262, 264, 265, 266, 267, 268, 269, 270, 271, 272, 273, 275, 277, 279, 285, 286, 287, 288, 289, 290, 291, 292, 293, 294, 295, 297, 299, 301, 307, 308, 309, 310, 311, 312, 313, 314, 315, 316, 317, 319, 321, 323, 329, 354, 355, 356, 357, 358, 359, 360, 361, 362, 363, 365, 367, 369, 375, 376, 377, 378, 379, 380, 381, 382, 383, 384, 385, 387, 389, 391, 397, 398, 399, 400, 401, 402, 403, 404, 405, 406, 407, 409, 411, 413, 420, 422, 423, 424, 425, 426, 427, 428, 429, 430, 431, 433, 435, 437, 487 **Teacher Edition:** T4, T5, T6, T7, T8, T9, T10, T11, T12, T13, T15, T17, T19, T25, T26, T27, T28, T29, T30, T31, T32, T33, T34, T35, T37, T39, T41, T47, T48, T49, T50, T51, T52, T53, T54, T55, T56, T57, T59, T61, T63, T70, T71, T72,, T73, T74, T75, T76, T77, T78, T79, T80, T81, T82, T83, T85, T87, T89, T96, T97, T122, T123, T124, T125, T126, T127, T128, T129, T130, T131, T132, T133, T135, T137, T142, T143, T144, T145, T146, T147, T148, T149, T150, T151, T152, T153, T155, T157, T159, T165, T166, T167, T168, T169, T170, T171, T172, T173, T174, T175, T187, T188, T189, T190, T191, T192, T193, T194, T195, T196, T197, T198, T199, T202, T205, T207, T213, T216, T217, T218, T219, T220, T221, T238, T239, T240, T241, T242, T243, T244, T245, T246, T247, T249, T251, T255, T262, T264, T265, T266, T267, T268, T269, T270, T271, T272, T273, T275, T277, T279, T285, T286, T287, T288, T289, T290, T291, T292, T293, T294, T295, T297, T299, T301, T307, T308, T309, T310, T311, T312, T313, T314, T315, T316, T317, T319, T321, T323, T329, T354, T355, T356, T357, T358, T359, T360, T361, T362, T363, T365, T367, T369, T375, T376, T377, T378, T379, T380, T381, T382, T383, T384, T385, T387, T389, T391, T397, T398, T399, T400, T401, T402, T403, T404, T405, T406, T407, T409, T411, T413, T420, T422, T423, T424, T425, T426, T427, T428, T429, T430, T431, T433, T435, T437, T487 **Optional Revising Lessons:** Narrative: 7; Informative/Explanatory: 16, 17; Opinion: 26, 27; More Writing Practice: 33, 35, 37 **Grammar, Usage, and Mechanics:** *Student Practice Book:* 214; *Teacher Edition:* T16, T17, T18, T19, T20, T21, T24, T25, T26, T27, T28, T29, T32, T33, T34, T35, T36, T37, T40, T41, T42, T43, T44, T45, T48, T49, T50, T51, T52, T53

LANGUAGE   Vocabulary Acquisition and Use

Anchor Standard 4: Determine or clarify the meaning of unknown and multiple-meaning words and phrases by using context clues, analyzing meaningful word parts, and consulting general and specialized reference materials, as appropriate.

Standard 4: Determine or clarify the meaning of unknown and multiple-meaning words and phrases based on *grade 4 reading and content,* choosing flexibly from a range of strategies.

4a: Use context (e.g., definitions, examples, or restatements in text) as a clue to the meaning of a word or phrase.	**Student Edition:** 44, 45, 136, 139, 140, 141, 142, 158, 159, 160, 184, 185, 210, 258, 259, 326, 327, 373, 416, 417, 462, 463, 464, 465, 468, 481, 482 **Teacher Edition:** T44, T45, T136, T139, T140, T141, T142, T158, T159, T160, T184, T185, T210, T258, T259, T326, T327, T373, T416, T417, T462, T463, T464, T465, T468, T481, T482 **Grammar, Usage, and Mechanics:** *Student Practice Book:* 8, 16, 18, 34, 40, 46, 48, 50, 58, 59, 60, 61, 62, 63, 64, 67, 68, 73, 74, 75, 76, 78, 81, 82, 83, 84, 126, 169, 170, 171, 172, 173, 209, 210; *Teacher Edition:* T32, T33, T34, T36, T37, T38
4c: Consult reference materials (e.g., dictionaries, glossaries, thesauruses), both print and digital, to find the pronunciation and determine or clarify the precise meaning of key words and phrases.	**Student Edition:** 62, 139, 256, 284, 301, 320, 325 **Teacher Edition:** T62, T139, T256, T284, T301, T320, T325 **Optional Revising Lessons:** Informative/Explanatory: 18; Opinion: 28 **Grammar, Usage, and Mechanics:** *Student Practice Book:* 212, 213

Anchor Standard 5:   Demonstrate understanding of figurative language, word relationships, and nuances in word meanings.

Standard 5: Demonstrate understanding of figurative language, word relationships, and nuances in word meanings.

5a: Explain the meaning of simple similes and metaphors (e.g., *as pretty as a picture*) in context.	**Student Edition:** 420, 422, 434, 435, 436 **Teacher Edition:** T420, T422, T434, T435, T436 **Optional Revising Lessons:** More Writing Practice: 38
5b: Recognize and explain the meaning of common idioms, adages, and proverbs.	**Student Edition:** 391 **Teacher Edition:** T391

STANDARD	CORRELATION
Anchor Standard 6:	Acquire and use accurately a range of general academic and domain-specific words and phrases sufficient for reading, writing, speaking, and listening and the college and career readiness level; demonstrate independence in gathering vocabulary knowledge when encountering an unknown term important to comprehension or expression.

Standard 6: Acquire and use accurately grade-appropriate general academic and domain-specific words and phrases, including those that signal precise actions, emotions, or states of being (e.g., *quizzed, whined, stammered*) and that are basic to a particular topic (e.g., *wildlife, conservation,* and *endangered* when discussing animal preservation).

Student Edition: 10, 13, 14, 15, 16, 17, 18, 19, 20, 22, 23, 32, 33, 36, 37, 38, 39, 40, 41, 43, 59, 60, 61, 62, 63, 64, 65, 66, 67, 80, 85, 86, 87, 88, 89, 90, 91, 92, 93, 128, 129, 132, 133, 136, 138, 139, 140, 141, 150, 153, 155, 156, 158, 159, 162, 163, 172, 173, 177, 180, 181, 182, 183, 184, 185, 196, 200, 201, 203, 204, 205, 206, 209, 210, 211, 228, 229, 232, 244, 246, 248, 249, 250, 254, 256, 257, 258, 259, 270, 271, 274, 275, 276, 278, 281, 282, 283, 292, 293, 296, 297, 300, 303, 304, 305, 315, 318, 319, 320, 323, 325, 326, 327, 360, 361, 364, 365, 366, 367, 368, 369, 370, 371, 372, 373, 385, 386, 387, 388, 389, 390, 391, 393, 394, 395, 407, 409, 412, 413, 415, 416, 417, 428, 432, 433, 434, 435, 436, 439, 440, 441, 450, 451, 452, 453, 454, 455, 456, 457, 464, 465, 466, 467, 468, 471, 472, 473, 475, 477, 478, 479, 480, 482, 482, 483, 484, 485, 486

Teacher Edition: T10, T13, T14, T15, T16, T17, T18, T19, T20, T22, T23, T32, T33, T36, T37, T38, T39, T40, T41, T43, T59, T60, T61, T62, T63, T64, T65, T66, T67, T80, T85, T86, T87, T88, T89, T90, T91, T92, T93, T128, T129, T132, T133, T136, T138, T139, T140, T141, T150, T153, T155, T156, T158, T159, T162, T163, T172, T173, T177, T180, T181, T182, T183, T184, T185, T196, T200, T201, T203, T204, T205, T206, T209, T210, T211, T228, T229, T232, T244, T246, T248, T249, T250, T254, T256, T257, T258, T259, T270, T271, T274, T275, T276, T278, T281, T282, T283, T292, T293, T296, T297, T300, T303, T304, T305, T315, T318, T319, T320, T323, T325, T326, T327, T360, T361, T364, T365, T366, T367, T368, T369, T370, T371, T372, T373, T385, T386, T387, T388, T389, T390, T391, T393, T394, T395, T407, T409, T412, T413, T415, T416, T417, T428, T432, T433, T434, T435, T436, T439, T440, T441, T450, T451, T452, T453, T454, T455, T456, T457, T464, T465, T466, T467, T468, T471, T472, T473, T475, T477, T478, T479, T480, T482, T483, T484, T485, T486

Optional Revising Lessons: Narrative: 1, 2, 4, 5, 7, 8; Informative/Explanatory: 11, 13, 15, 18; Opinion: 25, 28; More Writing Practice: 31, 33, 34, 37

Grammar Practice Masters: 7, 8, 9, 10, 11, 12, 13, 14, 15, 16, 17, 18, 19, 20, 21, 22, 23, 24, 25, 26, 27, 28, 29, 30, 31, 32, 33, 34, 35, 36, 37, 38, 39, 40, 41, 42, 43, 44, 45, 46, 47, 48, 49, 50, 51, 52, 53, 54, 55, 56, 57, 58, 59, 60, 61, 62, 63, 64, 65, 66, 67, 68, 69, 70, 71, 72, 73, 74, 75, 76, 77, 78, 79, 80, 81, 82, 83, 84, 85, 86, 87, 88, 89, 90, 91, 92, 93, 94, 95, 96, 97, 98, 99, 100, 101, 102, 103, 104, 105

Grammar, Usage, and Mechanics: *Student Practice Book:* 7, 8, 9, 10, 11, 12, 13, 14, 15, 16, 17, 18, 19, 20, 21, 22, 23, 24, 25, 26, 27, 28, 29, 30, 31, 32, 33, 34, 35, 36, 37, 38, 39, 40, 41, 42, 43, 44, 45, 46, 47, 48, 49, 50, 51, 52, 53, 54, 55, 56, 57, 58, 59, 60, 61, 62, 63, 64, 65, 66, 67, 68, 69, 70, 71, 72, 73, 74, 75, 76, 77, 78, 79, 80, 81, 82, 83, 84, 85, 86, 87, 88, 89, 90, 91, 92, 93, 94, 95, 96, 97, 98, 99, 100, 101, 102, 103, 104, 105, 106, 107, 108, 109, 110, 111, 112, 113, 114, 115, 116, 117, 118, 119, 120, 121, 122, 123, 124, 125, 126, 127, 128, 129, 130, 131, 132, 133, 134, 135, 136, 159, 160, 161, 162, 163, 164, 165, 166, 167, 168, 169, 170, 171, 172, 173, 174, 175, 176, 177, 178, 179, 180, 181, 182, 183, 197, 198, 199, 200, 201, 202, 203, 204, 205, 206, 207, 208, 209, 210, 211, 212, 213; *Teacher Edition:* T16, T17, T18, T19, T20, T21, T22, T24, T25, T26, T27, T28, T29, T30, T32, T33, T34, T35, T36, T37, T38, T40, T41, T42, T43, T44, T45, T46, T48, T49, T50, T51, T52, T53, T54

SPEAKING AND LISTENING   Comprehension and Collaboration

Anchor Standard 1: Prepare for and participate effectively in a range of conversations and collaborations with diverse partners.

Standard 1: Engage effectively in a range of collaborative discussions (one-on-one, in groups, and teacher-led) with diverse partners on *grade 4 topics and texts,* building on others' ideas and expressing their own clearly.

1a: Come to discussions prepared, having read or studied required material; explicitly draw on that preparation and other information known about the topic to explore ideas under discussion.	**Student Edition:** 4, 5, 6, 7, 8, 9, 10, 11, 12, 13, 15, 17, 19, 25, 26, 27, 28, 29, 30, 31, 32, 33, 34, 35, 37, 39, 41, 47, 48, 49, 50, 51, 52, 53, 54, 55, 56, 57, 59, 61, 63, 70, 71, 72, 73, 74, 75, 76, 77, 78, 79, 80, 81, 82, 83, 85, 87, 89, 96, 97, 98, 99, 100, 101, 102, 103, 104, 105, 108, 109, 110, 111, 112, 113, 114, 115, 116, 117, 122, 123, 124, 125, 126, 127, 128, 129, 130, 131, 132, 133, 134, 135, 136, 137, 142, 143, 144, 145, 146, 147, 148, 149, 150, 151, 152, 153, 155, 157, 159, 165, 166, 167, 168, 169, 170, 171, 172, 173, 174, 175, 187, 188, 189, 190, 191, 192, 193, 194, 195, 196, 197, 198, 199, 202, 207, 213, 214, 215, 216, 217, 218, 219, 220, 221, 222, 223, 224, 225, 226, 227, 228, 229, 230, 231, 232, 233, 234, 235, 238, 239, 240, 241, 242, 243, 244, 245, 246, 247, 249, 251, 255, 262, 264, 265, 266, 267, 268, 269, 270, 271, 272, 273, 275, 277, 279, 285, 286, 287, 288, 289, 290, 291, 292, 293, 294, 295, 297, 299, 301, 307, 308, 309, 310, 311, 312, 313, 314, 315, 316, 317, 319, 321, 323, 329, 330, 331, 332, 333, 334, 335, 336, 337, 338, 339, 340, 341, 342, 343, 344, 345, 346, 347, 348, 349, 350, 351, 354, 355, 356, 357, 358, 359, 360, 361, 362, 363, 365, 367, 369, 375, 376, 377, 378, 379, 380, 381, 382, 383, 384, 385, 387, 389, 391, 397, 398, 399, 400, 401, 402, 403, 404, 405, 406, 407, 409, 411, 413, 420, 422, 423, 424, 425, 426, 427, 428, 429, 430, 431, 433, 435, 437, 443 **Teacher Edition:** T4, T5, T6, T7, T8, T9, T10, T11, T12, T13, T15, T17, T19, T25, T26, T27, T28, T29, T30, T31, T32, T33, T34, T35, T37, T39, T41, T47, T48, T49, T50, T51, T52, T53, T54, T55, T56, T57, T59, T61, T63, T70, T71, T72, T73, T74, T75, T76, T77, T78, T79, T80, T81, T82, T83, T85, T87, T89, T96, T97, T98, T99, T100, T101, T102, T103, T104, T105, T108, T109, T110, T111, T112, T113, T114, T115, T116, T117, T122, T123, T124, T125, T126, T127, T128, T129, T130, T131, T132, T133, T134, T135, T136, T137, T142, T143, T144, T145, T146, T147, T148, T149, T150, T151, T152, T153, T155, T157, T159, T165, T166, T167, T168, T169, T170, T171, T172, T173, T174, T175, T187, T188, T189, T190, T191, T192, T193, T194, T195, T196, T197, T198, T199, T202, T207, T213, T214, T215, T216, T217, T218, T219, T220, T221, T222, T223, T224, T225, T226, T227, T228, T229, T230, T231, T232, T233, T234, T235, T238, T239, T240, T241, T242, T243, T244, T245, T246, T247, T249, T251, T255, T262, T264, T265, T266, T267, T268, T269, T270, T271, T272, T273, T275, T277, T279, T285, T286, T287, T288, T289, T290, T291, T292, T293, T294, T295, T297, T299, T301, T307, T308, T309, T310, T311, T312, T313, T314, T315, T316, T317, T319, T321, T323, T329, T330, T331, T332, T333, T334, T335, T336, T337, T338, T339, T340, T341, T342, T343, T344, T345, T346, T347, T348, T349, T350, T351, T354, T355, T356, T357, T358, T359, T360, T361, T362, T363, T365, T367, T369, T375, T376, T377, T378, T379, T380, T381, T382, T383, T384, T385, T387, T389, T391, T397, T398, T399, T400, T401, T402, T403, T404, T405, T406, T407, T409, T411, T413, T420, T422, T423, T424, T425, T426, T427, T428, T429, T430, T431, T433, T435, T437, T443 **Grammar, Usage, and Mechanics:** *Student Practice Book:* 214; *Teacher Edition:* T16, T17, T18, T19, T20, T21, T24, T25, T26, T27, T28, T29, T32, T33, T34, T35, T36, T37, T40, T41, T42, T43, T44, T45, T48, T49, T50, T51, T52, T53

STANDARD	CORRELATION
Speaking and Listening Standard 1 continued	

1b: Follow agreed-upon rules for discussions and carry out assigned roles.

Student Edition: 4, 5, 6, 7, 8, 9, 10, 11, 12, 13, 15, 17, 19, 25, 26, 27, 28, 29, 30, 31, 32, 33, 34, 35, 37, 39, 41, 47, 48, 49, 50, 51, 52, 53, 54, 55, 56, 57, 59, 61, 63, 70, 71, 72, 73, 74, 75, 76, 77, 78, 79, 80, 81, 82, 83, 85, 87, 89, 96, 97, 122, 123, 124, 125, 126, 127, 128, 129, 130, 131, 132, 133, 134, 135, 136, 137, 142, 143, 144, 145, 146, 147, 148, 149, 150, 151, 152, 153, 155, 157, 159, 165, 166, 167, 168, 169, 170, 171, 172, 173, 174, 175, 187, 188, 189, 190, 191, 192, 193, 194, 195, 196, 197, 198, 199, 202, 205, 207, 213, 230, 231, 232, 233, 238, 239, 240, 241, 242, 243, 244, 245, 246, 247, 249, 251, 255, 262, 264, 265, 266, 267, 268, 269, 270, 271, 272, 273, 275, 277, 279, 285, 286, 287, 288, 289, 290, 291, 292, 293, 294, 295, 297, 299, 301, 307, 308, 309, 310, 311, 312, 313, 314, 315, 316, 317, 319, 321, 323, 329, 330, 331, 332, 333, 334, 335, 336, 337, 354, 355, 356, 357, 358, 359, 360, 361, 362, 363, 365, 367, 369, 375, 376, 377, 378, 379, 380, 381, 382, 383, 384, 385, 387, 389, 391, 397, 398, 399, 400, 401, 402, 403, 404, 405, 406, 407, 409, 411, 413, 420, 422, 423, 424, 425, 426, 427, 428, 429, 430, 431, 433, 435, 437, 443

Teacher Edition: T4, T5, T6, T7, T8, T9, T10, T11, T12, T13, T15, T17, T19, T25, T26, T27, T28, T29, T30, T31, T32, T33, T34, T35, T37, T39, T41, T47, T48, T49, T50, T51, T52, T53, T54, T55, T56, T57, T59, T61, T63, T70, T71, T72, T73, T74, T75, T76, T77, T78, T79, T80, T81, T82, T83, T85, T87, T89, T96, T97, T122, T123, T124, T125, T126, T127, T128, T129, T130, T131, T132, T133, T134, T135, T136, T137, T142, T143, T144, T145, T146, T147, T148, T149, T150, T151, T152, T153, T155, T157, T159, T165, T166, T167, T168, T169, T170, T171, T172, T173, T174, T175, T187, T188, T189, T190, T191, T192, T193, T194, T195, T196, T197, T198, T199, T202, T205, T207, T213, T230, T231, T232, T233, T238, T239, T240, T241, T242, T243, T244, T245, T246, T247, T249, T251, T255, T262, T264, T265, T266, T267, T268, T269, T270, T271, T272, T273, T275, T277, T279, T285, T286, T287, T288, T289, T290, T291, T292, T293, T294, T295, T297, T299, T301, T307, T308, T309, T310, T311, T312, T313, T314, T315, T316, T317, T319, T321, T323, T329, T330, T331, T332, T333, T334, T335, T336, T337, T354, T355, T356, T357, T358, T359, T360, T361, T362, T363, T365, T367, T369, T375, T376, T377, T378, T379, T380, T381, T382, T383, T384, T385, T387, T389, T391, T397, T398, T399, T400, T401, T402, T403, T404, T405, T406, T407, T409, T411, T413, T420, T422, T423, T424, T425, T426, T427, T428, T429, T430, T431, T433, T435, T437, T443

Grammar, Usage, and Mechanics: *Student Practice Book:* 214; *Teacher Edition:* T16, T17, T18, T19, T20, T21, T24, T25, T26, T27, T28, T29, T32, T33, T34, T35, T36, T37, T40, T41, T42, T43, T44, T45, T48, T49, T50, T51, T52, T53

1c: Pose and respond to specific questions to clarify or follow up on information, and make comments that contribute to the discussion and link to the remarks of others.

Student Edition: 4, 5, 6, 7, 8, 9, 10, 11, 12, 13, 15, 17, 19, 25, 26, 27, 28, 29, 30, 31, 32, 33, 34, 35, 37, 39, 41, 47, 48, 49, 50, 51, 52, 53, 54, 55, 56, 57, 59, 61, 63, 70, 71, 72, 73, 74, 75, 76, 77, 78, 79, 80, 81, 82, 83, 85, 87, 89, 96, 97, 98, 99, 100, 101, 102, 103, 104, 105, 108, 109, 110, 111, 112, 113, 114, 115, 116, 117, 118, 119, 122, 123, 124, 125, 126, 127, 128, 129, 130, 131, 132, 133, 134, 135, 136, 137, 142, 143, 144, 145, 146, 147, 148, 149, 150, 151, 152, 153, 155, 157, 159, 165, 166, 167, 168, 169, 170, 171, 172, 173, 174, 175, 187, 188, 189, 190, 191, 192, 193, 194, 195, 196, 197, 198, 199, 202, 205, 207, 213, 214, 215, 216, 217, 218, 219, 220, 221, 222, 223, 224, 225, 226, 227, 228, 229, 230, 231, 232, 233, 234, 235, 238, 239, 240, 241, 242, 243, 244, 245, 246, 247, 249, 251, 255, 262, 264, 265, 266, 267, 268, 269, 270, 271, 272, 273, 275, 277, 279, 285, 286, 287, 288, 289, 290, 291, 292, 293, 294, 295, 297, 299, 301, 307, 308, 309, 310, 311, 312, 313, 314, 315, 316, 317, 319, 321, 323, 329, 330, 331, 332, 333, 334, 335, 336, 337, 340, 341, 342, 343, 344, 345, 346, 347, 348, 349, 350, 351, 354, 355, 356, 357, 358, 359, 360, 361, 362, 363, 365, 367, 369, 375, 376, 377, 378, 379, 380, 381, 382, 383, 384, 385, 387, 389, 391, 397, 398, 399, 400, 401, 402, 403, 404, 405, 406, 407, 409, 411, 413, 420, 422, 423, 424, 425, 426, 427, 428, 429, 430, 431, 433, 435, 437, 443

Teacher Edition: T4, T5, T6, T7, T8, T9, T10, T11, T12, T13, T15, T17, T19, T25, T26, T27, T28, T29, T30, T31, T32, T33, T34, T35, T37, T39, T41, T47, T48, T49, T50, T51, T52, T53, T54, T55, T56, T57, T59, T61, T63, T70, T71, T72, T73, T74, T75, T76, T77, T78, T79, T80, T81, T82, T83, T85, T87, T89, T96, T97, T98, T99, T100, T101, T102, T103, T104, T105, T108, T109, T110, T111, T112, T113, T114, T115, T116, T117, T118, T119, T122, T123, T124, T125, T126, T127, T128, T129, T130, T131, T132, T133, T134, T135, T136, T137, T142, T143, T144, T145, T146, T147, T148, T149, T150, T151, T152, T153, T155, T157, T159, T165, T166, T167, T168, T169, T170, T171, T172, T173, T174, T175, T187, T188, T189, T190, T191, T192, T193, T194, T195, T196, T197, T198, T199, T202, T205, T207, T213, T214, T215, T216, T217, T218, T219, T220, T221, T222, T223, T224, T225, T226, T227, T228, T229, T230, T231, T232, T233, T234, T235, T238, T239, T240, T241, T242, T243, T244, T245, T246, T247, T249, T251, T255, T262, T264, T265, T266, T267, T268, T269, T270, T271, T272, T273, T275, T277, T279, T285, T286, T287, T288, T289, T290, T291, T292, T293, T294, T295, T297, T299, T301, T307, T308, T309, T310, T311, T312, T313, T314, T315, T316, T317, T319, T321, T323, T329, T330, T331, T332, T333, T334, T335, T336, T337, T340, T341, T342, T343, T344, T345, T346, T347, T348, T349, T350, T351, T354, T355, T356, T357, T358, T359, T360, T361, T362, T363, T365, T367, T369, T375, T376, T377, T378, T379, T380, T381, T382, T383, T384, T385, T387, T389, T391, T397, T398, T399, T400, T401, T402, T403, T404, T405, T406, T407, T409, T411, T413, T420, T422, T423, T424, T425, T426, T427, T428, T429, T430, T431, T433, T435, T437, T443

Grammar, Usage, and Mechanics: *Student Practice Book:* 214; *Teacher Edition:* T16, T17, T18, T19, T20, T21, T24, T25, T26, T27, T28, T29, T32, T33, T34, T35, T36, T37, T40, T41, T42, T43, T44, T45, T48, T49, T50, T51, T52, T53

STANDARD	CORRELATION

Speaking and Listening Standard 1 continued

1d: Review the key ideas expressed and explain their own ideas and understanding in light of the discussion.

Student Edition: 4, 5, 6, 7, 8, 9, 10, 11, 12, 13, 15, 17, 19, 25, 26, 27, 28, 29, 30, 31, 32, 33, 34, 35, 37, 39, 41, 47, 48, 49, 50, 51, 52, 53, 54, 55, 56, 57, 59, 61, 70, 71, 72, 73, 74, 75, 76, 77, 78, 79, 80, 81, 82, 83, 85, 87, 89, 96, 97, 98, 99, 100, 101, 102, 103, 104, 105, 108, 109, 110, 111, 112, 113, 114, 115, 116, 117, 118, 119, 122, 123, 124, 125, 126, 127, 128, 129, 130, 131, 132, 133, 134, 135, 136, 137, 142, 143, 144, 145, 146, 147, 148, 149, 150, 151, 152, 153, 155, 157, 159, 165, 166, 167, 168, 169, 170, 171, 172, 173, 174, 175, 187, 188, 189, 190, 191, 192, 193, 194, 195, 196, 197, 198, 199, 202, 205, 207, 213, 214, 215, 216, 217, 218, 219, 220, 221, 222, 223, 224, 225, 226, 227, 228, 229, 230, 231, 232, 233, 234, 235, 238, 239, 240, 241, 242, 243, 244, 245, 246, 247, 249, 251, 255, 262, 264, 265, 266, 267, 268, 269, 270, 271, 272, 273, 275, 277, 279, 285, 286, 287, 288, 289, 290, 291, 292, 293, 294, 295, 297, 299, 301, 307, 308, 309, 310, 311, 312, 313, 314, 315, 316, 317, 319, 321, 323, 329, 330, 331, 332, 333, 334, 335, 336, 337, 340, 341, 342, 343, 344, 345, 346, 347, 348, 349, 350, 351, 354, 355, 356, 357, 358, 359, 360, 361, 362, 363, 365, 367, 369, 375, 376, 377, 378, 379, 380, 381, 382, 383, 384, 385, 387, 389, 391, 397, 398, 399, 400, 401, 402, 403, 404, 405, 406, 407, 409, 411, 413, 420, 422, 423, 424, 425, 426, 427, 428, 429, 430, 431, 433, 435, 437, 443

Teacher Edition: T4, T5, T6, T7, T8, T9, T10, T11, T12, T13, T15, T17, T19, T25, T26, T27, T28, T29, T30, T31, T32, T33, T34, T35, T37, T39, T41, T47, T48, T49, T50, T51, T52, T53, T54, T55, T56, T57, T59, T61, T70, T71, T72, T73, T74, T75, T76, T77, T78, T79, T80, T81, T82, T83, T85, T87, T89, T96, T97, T98, T99, T100, T101, T102, T103, T104, T105, T108, T109, T110, T111, T112, T113, T114, T115, T116, T117, T118, T119, T122, T123, T124, T125, T126, T127, T128, T129, T130, T131, T132, T133, T134, T135, T136, T137, T142, T143, T144, T145, T146, T147, T148, T149, T150, T151, T152, T153, T155, T157, T159, T165, T166, T167, T168, T169, T170, T171, T172, T173, T174, T175, T187, T188, T189, T190, T191, T192, T193, T194, T195, T196, T197, T198, T199, T202, T205, T207, T213, T214, T215, T216, T217, T218, T219, T220, T221, T222, T223, T224, T225, T226, T227, T228, T229, T230, T231, T232, T233, T234, T235, T238, T239, T240, T241, T242, T243, T244, T245, T246, T247, T249, T251, T255, T262, T264, T265, T266, T267, T268, T269, T270, T271, T272, T273, T275, T277, T279, T285, T286, T287, T288, T289, T290, T291, T292, T293, T294, T295, T297, T299, T301, T307, T308, T309, T310, T311, T312, T313, T314, T315, T316, T317, T319, T321, T323, T329, T330, T331, T332, T333, T334, T335, T336, T337, T340, T341, T342, T343, T344, T345, T346, T347, T348, T349, T350, T351, T354, T355, T356, T357, T358, T359, T360, T361, T362, T363, T365, T367, T369, T375, T376, T377, T378, T379, T380, T381, T382, T383, T384, T385, T387, T389, T391, T397, T398, T399, T400, T401, T402, T403, T404, T405, T406, T407, T409, T411, T413, T420, T422, T423, T424, T425, T426, T427, T428, T429, T430, T431, T433, T435, T437, T443

Grammar, Usage, and Mechanics: *Student Practice Book*: 214; *Teacher Edition*: T16, T17, T18, T19, T20, T21, T24, T25, T26, T27, T28, T29, T32, T33, T34, T35, T36, T37, T40, T41, T42, T43, T44, T45, T48, T49, T50, T51, T52, T53

Anchor Standard 2: Integrate and evaluate information presented in diverse media and formats, including visually, quantitatively, and orally.

Standard 2: Paraphrase portions of a text read aloud or information presented in diverse media and formats, including visually, quantitatively, and orally.

Student Edition: 6, 7, 8, 9, 11, 14, 28, 29, 30, 31, 50, 51, 52, 53, 54, 55, 74, 75, 76, 77, 78, 79, 124, 125, 126, 127, 146, 147, 148, 149, 168, 169, 170, 171, 190, 191, 192, 193, 194, 195, 240, 241, 242, 243, 266, 267, 268, 269, 288, 289, 290, 291, 310, 311, 312, 313, 332, 333, 334, 335, 336, 337, 356, 357, 358, 359, 378, 379, 380, 381, 400, 401, 402, 403, 424, 425, 426, 427

Teacher Edition: T6, T7, T8, T9, T11, T14, T28, T29, T30, T31, T50, T51, T52, T53, T54, T55, T74, T75, T76, T77, T78, T79, T124, T125, T126, T127, T146, T147, T148, T149, T168, T169, T170, T171, T190, T191, T192, T193, T194, T195, T240, T241, T242, T243, T266, T267, T268, T269, T288, T289, T290, T291, T310, T311, T312, T313, T332, T333, T334, T335, T336, T337, T356, T357, T358, T359, T378, T379, T380, T381, T400, T401, T402, T403, T424, T425, T426, T427

Anchor Standard 3: Evaluate a speaker's point of view, reasoning, and use of evidence and rhetoric.

Standard 3: Identify the reasons and evidence a speaker provides to support particular points.

Student Edition: 4, 5, 6, 7, 8, 9, 10, 11, 12, 13, 15, 17, 19, 25, 26, 27, 28, 29, 30, 31, 32, 33, 34, 35, 37, 39, 41, 47, 48, 49, 50, 51, 52, 53, 54, 55, 56, 57, 59, 61, 63, 70, 71, 72, 73, 74, 75, 76, 77, 78, 79, 80, 81, 82, 83, 85, 87, 89, 96, 97, 100, 101, 102, 103, 104, 105, 122, 123, 124, 125, 126, 127, 128, 129, 130, 131, 132, 133, 135, 137, 142, 143, 144, 145, 146, 147, 148, 149, 150, 151, 152, 153, 155, 157, 159, 165, 166, 167, 168, 169, 170, 171, 172, 173, 174, 175, 187, 188, 189, 190, 191, 192, 193, 194, 195, 196, 197, 198, 199, 202, 205, 207, 213, 214, 215, 216, 217, 218, 219, 220, 221, 238, 239, 240, 241, 242, 243, 244, 245, 246, 247, 249, 251, 255, 262, 264, 265, 266, 267, 268, 269, 270, 271, 272, 273, 275, 277, 279, 285, 286, 287, 288, 289, 290, 291, 292, 293, 294, 295, 297, 299, 301, 307, 308, 309, 310, 311, 312, 313, 314, 315, 316, 317, 319, 321, 323, 329, 354, 355, 356, 357, 358, 359, 360, 361, 362, 363, 365, 367, 369, 375, 376, 377, 378, 379, 380, 381, 382, 383, 384, 385, 387, 389, 391, 397, 398, 399, 400, 401, 402, 403, 404, 405, 406, 407, 409, 411, 413, 420, 422, 423, 424, 425, 426, 427, 428, 429, 430, 431, 433, 435, 437

Teacher Edition: T4, T5, T6, T7, T8, T9, T10, T11, T12, T13, T15, T17, T19, T25, T26, T27, T28, T29, T30, T31, T32, T33, T34, T35, T37, T39, T41, T47, T48, T49, T50, T51, T52, T53, T54, T55, T56, T57, T59, T61, T63, T70, T71, T72, T73, T74, T75, T76, T77, T78, T79, T80, T81, T82, T83, T85, T87, T89, T96, T97, T100, T101, T102, T103, T104, T105, T122, T123, T124, T125, T126, T127, T128, T129, T130, T131, T132, T133, T135, T137, T142, T143, T144, T145, T146, T147, T148, T149, T150, T151, T152, T153, T155, T157, T159, T165, T166, T167, T168, T169, T170, T171, T172, T173, T174, T175, T187, T188, T189, T190, T191, T192, T193, T194, T195, T196, T197, T198, T199, T202, T205, T207, T213, T214, T215, T216, T217, T218, T219, T220, T221, T238, T239, T240, T241, T242, T243, T244, T245, T246, T247, T249, T251, T255, T262, T264, T265, T266, T267, T268, T269, T270, T271, T272, T273, T275, T277, T279, T285, T286, T287, T288, T289, T290, T291, T292, T293, T294, T295, T297, T299, T301, T307, T308, T309, T310, T311, T312, T313, T314, T315, T316, T317, T319, T321, T323, T329, T354, T355, T356, T357, T358, T359, T360, T361, T362, T363, T365, T367, T369, T375, T376, T377, T378, T379, T380, T381, T382, T383, T384, T385, T387, T389, T391, T397, T398, T399, T400, T401, T402, T403, T404, T405, T406, T407, T409, T411, T413, T420, T422, T423, T424, T425, T426, T427, T428, T429, T430, T431, T433, T435, T437

Grammar, Usage, and Mechanics: *Student Practice Book*: 214; *Teacher Edition*: T16, T17, T18, T19, T20, T21, T24, T25, T26, T27, T28, T29, T32, T33, T34, T35, T36, T37, T40, T41, T42, T43, T44, T45, T48, T49, T50, T51, T52, T53

STANDARD	CORRELATION

SPEAKING AND LISTENING   Presentation of Knowledge and Ideas

Anchor Standard 4:   Present information, findings, and supporting evidence such that listeners can follow the line of reasoning and the organization, development, and style are appropriate to task, purpose, and audience.

Standard 4: Report on a topic or text, tell a story, or recount an experience in an organized manner, using appropriate facts and relevant, descriptive details to support main ideas or themes; speak clearly at an understandable pace.

Student Edition: 14, 36, 46, 68, 69, 84, 85, 94, 173, 197, 204, 213, 245, 250, 260, 261, 276, 298, 314, 315, 418, 443
Teacher Edition: T14, T36, T46, T68, T69, T84, T85, T94, T173, T197, T204, T213, T245, T250, T260, T261, T276, T298, T314, T315, T418, T443
Grammar, Usage, and Mechanics: *Teacher Edition:* T16, T24, T32, T34, T36, T40, T41, T42, T45, T48, T50, T51

Anchor Standard 5:   Make strategic use of digital media and visual displays of data to express information and enhance understanding of presentations.

Standard 5: Add audio recordings and visual displays to presentations when appropriate to enhance the development of main ideas or themes.

Student Edition: 46, 68, 69, 94, 260, 328, 418, 443
Teacher Edition: T46, T68, T69, T94, T260, T328, T418, T443

Anchor Standard 6:   Adapt speech to a variety of contexts and communicative tasks, demonstrating command of formal English when indicated or appropriate.

Standard 6: Differentiate between contexts that call for formal English (e.g., presenting ideas) and situations where informal discourse is appropriate (e.g., small-group discussions); use formal English when appropriate to task and situation. (See grade 4 Language standards 1 for specific expectations.)

Student Edition: 4, 5, 6, 7, 8, 9, 10, 11, 12, 13, 15, 17, 19, 25, 26, 27, 28, 29, 30, 31, 32, 33, 34, 35, 37, 39, 41, 47, 48, 49, 50, 51, 52, 53, 54, 55, 56, 57, 59, 61, 63, 70, 71, 72, 73, 74, 75, 76, 77, 78, 79, 80, 81, 82, 83, 85, 87, 89, 96, 97, 122, 123, 124, 125, 126, 127, 128, 129, 130, 131, 135, 137, 143, 144, 145, 146, 147, 148, 149, 150, 151, 152, 153, 155, 157, 159, 165, 166, 167, 168, 169, 170, 171, 172, 173, 174, 175, 187, 188, 189, 190, 191, 192, 193, 194, 195, 196, 197, 198, 199, 202, 205, 207, 213, 214, 215, 216, 217, 218, 219, 220, 221, 238, 239, 240, 241, 242, 243, 244, 245, 246, 247, 249, 251, 255, 262, 264, 265, 266, 267, 268, 269, 270, 271, 272, 273, 275, 277, 279, 285, 286, 287, 288, 289, 290, 291, 292, 293, 294, 295, 297, 299, 301, 307, 308, 309, 310, 311, 312, 313, 314, 315, 316, 317, 319, 321, 323, 329, 354, 355, 356, 357, 358, 359, 360, 361, 362, 363, 365, 367, 369, 375, 376, 377, 378, 379, 380, 381, 382, 383, 384, 385, 387, 389, 391, 397, 398, 399, 400, 401, 402, 403, 404, 405, 406, 407, 409, 411, 413, 420, 422, 423, 424, 425, 426, 427, 428, 429, 430, 431, 433, 435, 437
Teacher Edition: T4, T5, T6, T7, T8, T9, T10, T11, T12, T13, T15, T17, T19, T25, T26, T27, T28, T29, T30, T31, T32, T33, T34, T35, T37, T39, T41, T47, T48, T49, T50, T51, T52, T53, T54, T55, T56, T57, T59, T61, T63, T70, T71, T72, T73, T74, T75, T76, T77, T78, T79, T80, T81, T82, T83, T85, T87, T89, T96, T97, T122, T123, T124, T125, T126, T127, T128, T129, T130, T131, T135, T137, T143, T144, T145, T146, T147, T148, T149, T150, T151, T152, T153, T155, T157, T159, T165, T166, T167, T168, T169, T170, T171, T172, T173, T174, T175, T187, T188, T189, T190, T191, T192, T193, T194, T195, T196, T197, T198, T199, T202, T205, T207, T213, T214, T215, T216, T217, T218, T219, T220, T221, T238, T239, T240, T241, T242, T243, T244, T245, T246, T247, T249, T251, T255, T262, T264, T265, T266, T267, T268, T269, T270, T271, T272, T273, T275, T277, T279, T285, T286, T287, T288, T289, T290, T291, T292, T293, T294, T295, T297, T299, T301, T307, T308, T309, T310, T311, T312, T313, T314, T315, T316, T317, T319, T321, T323, T329, T354, T355, T356, T357, T358, T359, T360, T361, T362, T363, T365, T367, T369, T375, T376, T377, T378, T379, T380, T381, T382, T383, T384, T385, T387, T389, T391, T397, T398, T399, T400, T401, T402, T403, T404, T405, T406, T407, T409, T411, T413, T420, T422, T423, T424, T425, T426, T427, T428, T429, T430, T431, T433, T435, T437
Grammar, Usage, and Mechanics: *Student Practice Book:* 214; *Teacher Edition:* T16, T17, T18, T19, T20, T21, T24, T25, T26, T27, T28, T29, T32, T33, T34, T35, T36, T37, T40, T41, T42, T43, T44, T45, T48, T49, T50, T51, T52, T53

4

STRATEGIES FOR
writers

Senior Author
Rebecca Bowers Sipe, Ed.D.
Eastern Michigan University

Consulting Authors
Julie Coiro, Ph.D.
University of Rhode Island

Amy Humphreys, Ed.M., NBCT
Educational Consultant

Sara B. Kajder, Ph.D.
Shady Side Academy, Pittsburgh, Pennsylvania

James Scott Miller, M.Ed.
National Writing Consultant

Mark Overmeyer, M.A.
Cherry Creek School District, Colorado

ZB **Zaner-Bloser**

Program Reviewers

Zaner-Bloser wishes to thank these educators who reviewed portions of this program and provided comments prior to publication.

Joe Anspaugh
Shelbyville Middle School
Shelbyville, IN

Michele Barto, Ed.D.
Fairleigh Dickinson University
Madison, NJ

Jackie Blosser
Lima City Schools
Lima, OH

Kim Bondy
South Arbor Academy
Ypsilanti, MI

Kelly Caravelli
Meadowbrook Middle School
Poway, CA

Cathy Cassy
St. Louis Public Schools
St. Louis, MO

Penny Clare
Educational Consultant
Lee, NH

Mary Dunton
Literacy Consultant
Sparks, NV

Emily Gleason
Beaverton School District
Beaverton, OR

Denise Gray, Ed.D.
Whiteriver Elementary School
Whiteriver, AZ

Laura Hall
Walton Charter Academy
Pontiac, MI

Donna Jett
Rockwood South Middle School
Fenton, MO

Christine Johnson, Ed.D.
Boonton Public Schools
Boonton, NJ

Dr. Roma Morris
Columbia School District
Columbia, MS

Rosanne Richards
Southern Nevada Regional
Professional Development Program
North Las Vegas, NV

Sharlene E. Ricks
Alpine School District
American Fork, UT

Debbie Rutherford
Independent National Consultant
Omaha, NE

Melinda Springli
Lawton Public Schools
Lawton, OK

Kerry Stephenson
Pendleton County School District
Butler, KY

Photography: Cover © PHOTO/ananimages/Corbis; Interior models, George C. Anderson; Stopwatch image © Royalty-Free/Corbis; p. 3 © Tim McGuire/Corbis; p. 12 © Tom Walker/Getty Images; p. 106 © Comstock; p. 121 © Toyohiro Yamada/Getty Images; p. 237 © iStockphoto.com/Jill Lang; p. 384 © Panoramic Images/Getty Images

Art Credits: pp. 4, 26, 48, 122, 144, 166, 238, 264, 286, 354, 376, 398 Paul Montgomery; pp. 72, 188, 193, 201, 308, 422 Chris Vallo; pp. 69, 70, 71 Heidi Chang

Literature Credits: pp. 100-101 *The American Adventure: The Gold Rush*, by Sally Senzell Isaacs © 2004 by Heinemann Library, an imprint by Capstone Global Library, LLC Chicago, Illinois. All rights reserved; pp. 218-219 From "Seeing Through Dorothea's Eyes" by Sudipta Bardhan. Copyright © 2005 Highlights for Children, Inc., Columbus, Ohio. All rights reserved. Used by permission; pp. 220-221 From *Hour of Freedom: American History in Poetry* compiled by Milton Meltzer. Copyright © 2003 by Milton Meltzer. Published by WordSong, an imprint of Boyds Mills Press, Inc. Used by permission; pp. 332-333 From *For the Birds: The Life of Roger Tory Peterson* by Peggy Thomas. Copyright © 2008 by Peggy Thomas. Published by Calkins Creek, an imprint of Boyds Mills Press, Inc. Used by permission; pp. 334-335 From *On the Frontier with Mr. Audubon* by Barbara Brenner. Copyright ©1977 by Barbara Brenner. Published by Boyds Mills Press, Inc. Used by permission.

ISBN 978-1-4531-1222-9

Zaner-Bloser, Inc.
1-800-421-3018
www.zaner-bloser.com
Printed in the United States of America

ZB Code 15

Body stock is FutureMark® 90+% Recycled Paper
WWW.FUTUREMARKPAPER.COM

SUSTAINABLE FORESTRY INITIATIVE
Certified Chain of Custody
Promoting Sustainable Forestry
www.sfiprogram.org
SFICOC-01042

2 3 4 5 6 25170 18 17 16 15 14

Hi, there!

We're your *Strategies for Writers Writing Partners!*

We're here to guide you step-by-step through the stages of the writing process: Prewrite, Draft, Revise, Edit, and Publish.

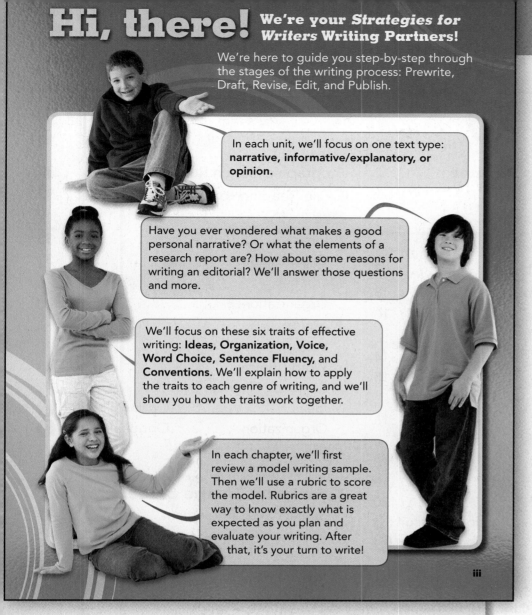

In each unit, we'll focus on one text type: **narrative, informative/explanatory, or opinion.**

Have you ever wondered what makes a good personal narrative? Or what the elements of a research report are? How about some reasons for writing an editorial? We'll answer those questions and more.

We'll focus on these six traits of effective writing: **Ideas, Organization, Voice, Word Choice, Sentence Fluency,** and **Conventions.** We'll explain how to apply the traits to each genre of writing, and we'll show you how the traits work together.

In each chapter, we'll first review a model writing sample. Then we'll use a rubric to score the model. Rubrics are a great way to know exactly what is expected as you plan and evaluate your writing. After that, it's your turn to write!

iii

Introduce the Writing Partners

An important element of becoming a writer is viewing oneself as a writer. In order to help students "see themselves as writers," *Strategies for Writers* introduces all instruction through a **Writing Partner.** Each of the four students pictured on this page will guide your students through one *Strategies for Writers* unit. The **Writing Partners** will

- introduce the genre of writing in each chapter.
- help students deconstruct the writing model.
- develop their own piece of writing based on the model.

Through the **Writing Partner,** your students will see a new piece of writing evolve. As the **Writing Partner** explains his/her writing strategy and "thinks aloud" about what he/she is writing, your students will have a window into the mind of a young writer like themselves.

To ensure students understand the **Writing Partner's** role,

- invite students to take turns reading the **Writing Partners'** comments on this page.
- use the first two pages in each unit to introduce the unit **Writing Partner.**
- encourage students to discuss the **Writing Partner's** comments and explanations throughout the unit.

Narrative writing

🖱 Optional Revising Lessons available at **www.sfw.z-b.com/NGAE/G4**

Table of Contents

Table of Contents

Informative/Explanatory writing

🔲 Optional Revising Lessons available at **www.sfw.z-b.com/NGAE/G4**

Table of Contents

Opinion writing

🖱 Optional Revising Lessons available at **www.sfw.z-b.com/NGAE/G4**

Table of Contents

Tviii

Table of Contents

More Writing Practice

Descriptive Elements in the Text Types

🖱Optional Revising Lessons available at **www.sfw.z-b.com/NGAE/G4**

Table of Contents

Table of Contents

Appendices

Table of Contents

Table of Contents

Narrative writing

Personal Narrative
Pages T4A–T25

This genre opens the door to narrative writing by encouraging students to relate writing to their own lives by drawing on personal experiences.

Prewrite   Make notes about an interesting personal experience.
Make a Sequence Chain to organize the notes.

Draft   Include details about the characters so the reader can form a clear picture.

Revise   Check to see that the events are in order.
Use first-person point of view.
Use clear and specific words to tell the story.

Edit   Make sure there are no sentence fragments.

Publish   Post the narrative on the class bulletin board.

Biographic Sketch
Pages T26A–T47

This genre gives students an opportunity to explore the life, work, and accomplishments of an interesting person.

Prewrite   Make a list of interesting questions for an interview.
Make a Timeline to organize the important events.

Draft   Organize information using transition words.

Revise   Use third-person point of view.
Take out any words that are not needed.
Combine short sentences to improve flow.

Edit   Make sure all verbs are correct.

Publish   Share the final paper in an author's circle.

Adventure Story
Pages T48A–T71

This genre gives students a chance to use their imaginations as they write about exciting events and heroic deeds.

Prewrite   Choose a lead character and a problem.
Make a Story Map to organize the events.

Draft   Write dialogue that sounds like real people.

Revise   Use details to help the reader imagine characters, setting, and plot.
Change common verbs to exciting action verbs.
Use transition words to begin sentences.

Edit   Check the punctuation.

Publish   Publish the story as a big book to read to younger students.

Professional Development Podcasts and Screencasts

Go to **www.sfw.z-b.com** to access the variety of professional development **podcasts** and **screencasts**.

Unit Overview

Play ◄ SOCIAL STUDIES CONNECTION

Pages T72A–T97

Students will express their understanding of a social studies concept or event in the creative form of a play.

Prewrite   Choose a topic for the play. Then collect details that fit the story.
Use a Story Map to plan a play.

Draft   Choose words and phrases to convey ideas precisely.

Revise   Put details in the dialogue and stage directions.
Let the readers know what's happening right away.
Choose punctuation for effect.

Edit   Check to make sure commas are used correctly.

Publish   Publish copies of the play for classmates to perform.

Next Generation Narrative Assessment

Pages T98A–T119

Students will learn and practice how to take a next generation narrative assessment. They will learn to read and analyze the directions for each part of the assessment, plan their time effectively, and follow the steps of the writing process to write a narrative piece that includes evidence from sources they have examined.

Prewrite   Respond to the assignment.
Choose a graphic organizer.

Draft   Remember your purpose as you write.

Revise   Use transitions to guide the reader.
Use first-person point of view.
Add concrete words and sensory details.

Edit   Check the grammar, spelling, capitalization, and punctuation.

Online Writing Center

iPad® and IWB Ready

Complete Digital Writing Instruction!

- My Writing Pad
- Interactive Rubrics
- Anchor Papers
- Graphic Organizers

- Content-Area Writing Prompts
- Grammar Games
- Proofreading Activities
- Instructional Videos

- Virtual File Cabinet
- eBooks
- Assessments

For information, go to www.sfw.z-b.com

21st Century Literacies
Technology, Digital Media & Writing

by **Julie Coiro, Ph.D.,** University of Rhode Island & **Sara B. Kajder, Ph.D.,** Shady Side Academy

 INSPIRE Websites to Spark Ideas

Publishing Personal Narratives

The Internet provides a number of safe online environments for children to share their writing with the world. Many websites feature easy-to-use forms and organize student work in an attractive format that motivates even the most struggling writers to want to publish their work. Four websites where students can publish their personal narratives include:

- **Kids on the Net (www.kidsonthenet.com),** one of the foremost sites on the Internet for children's writing, was founded to give children an international voice. The website encourages submissions from children at home or at school from all over the world.

- **Pinky Dinky Doo Story Podcasts (www. pinkydinkydoo.com/podcasts.html)** is a fun and easy-to-use tool to help younger students create their own video story podcasts. Simply select a type of story (e.g., scary story, silly story, fairy tale); use picture cues to fill in the sentence template for the beginning, middle, and end of the story; and then have it read aloud and added to the database. A powerful motivator for reluctant writers.

- **Cyberkids (www.cyberkids.com/he/html/submit. html)** publishes original stories, poems, articles, multimedia, and product reviews by children aged 7–12, with preference given to humor and submissions with a visual component.

Writing Biographic Sketches

Many websites can spark ideas for students who are not quite sure whom to write about for a biographic sketch or for those who want to know more about a particular person. These websites offer students opportunities to link their writing to topics such as science, math, social studies, and art. Here are a few online biography collections your students can visit:

- **Biographies for Kids: Famous Leaders for Young Readers (http://gardenofpraise.com/leaders)** includes stories of presidents, inventors, athletes, educators, scientists, and business men and women to inspire students to follow their examples of courage, determination, and honesty.

- **Achiever Gallery (www.achievement.org/ galleryachieve.html),** from the Academy of Achievement website, is an interactive resource with multimedia information on a variety of notable people. The site includes biographies, career profiles, video interviews, and photo galleries.

- **The HistoryMakers African American History Archive (www.thehistorymakers.com)** includes biographical information and audio and video clips about African Americans who have influenced history.

- **Women of the Century (http://school. discoveryeducation.com/schooladventures/ womenofthecentury),** sponsored by Discovery Education, features a collection of biographies about inspirational females in space, science, arts, government, sports, and exploration.

- **Meet Amazing Americans (www.americaslibrary. gov/aa/index.php),** from the Library of Congress America's Story website, connects younger students with information about famous Americans who made this country what it is today.

Narrative writing tells a story about real or imaginary events.

Hi, my name is Jack. I'm learning all about narrative writing. I love telling stories to my friends! I also like listening to my grandfather tell me stories about when he was growing up. In school, I can write his stories as biographic sketches. I can also write stories in science and social studies. Now, I'm going to learn strategies for turning stories into good pieces of writing.

IN THIS UNIT

- Personal Narrative
- Biographic Sketch
- Adventure Story

SOCIAL STUDIES CONNECTION ▶ Play

- Next Generation Narrative Assessment

Name: Jack
Home: Washington
Favorite Sports: soccer and hockey
Favorite Book: *S.O.R. Losers* by Avi

To differentiate instruction and maximize student achievement, use the Differentiated Instruction Activities available at **www.sfw.z-b.com.**

Created by Amy Humphreys, Ed.M., these engaging activities can be used to meet a wide range of learner needs. Each activity uses a combination of visual, written, oral, and kinesthetic elements, and deliberately leverages the power of collaboration and conversation so students learn to think like writers in fun and engaging ways.

Meet Your Writing Partner, Jack

The writing partner for this chapter is Jack, a boy from the state of Washington. You may wish to explore with students how Jack's background, hobbies, interests, and personality connect with his choices of writing topics. Explain to students that Jack will use what he knows to make decisions about his topics and that this helps to make his writing special and real. Encourage students to use their own background knowledge, interests, and personalities as they write, as well. Narrative writing tells stories, and your students will have many interesting, unique, and authentic stories to tell.

Personal Narrative Planner

WEEK 1

Day 1
Introduce
Personal Narrative

Student Objectives
- Review the elements of a personal narrative.
- Consider purpose and audience.
- Learn the traits of narrative writing.

Student Activities
- Read and discuss **What's in a Personal Narrative?** (p. 4)
- Read and discuss **Why Write a Personal Narrative?** (p. 5)
- Read **Linking Narrative Writing Traits to a Personal Narrative.** (p. 6)

Day 2
Analyze
Close Reading of the Model

Student Objectives
- Read a model personal narrative.

Student Activities
- Read **"My Leap for Loons."** (p. 7)

Day 3
Analyze
Introduce the Rubric

Student Objectives
- Learn to read a rubric.

Student Activities
- Review **"My Leap for Loons."** (p. 7)
- Read and discuss the **Personal Narrative Rubric.** (pp. 8–9)

WEEK 2

Day 1
Write
Prewrite: Ideas

Student Objectives
- Read and understand a prewriting strategy.

Student Activities
- Read and discuss **Prewrite: Focus on Ideas.** (p. 14)
- Apply the prewriting strategy.

Day 2
Write
Prewrite: Organization

Student Objectives
- Create a Sequence Chain to organize notes.

Student Activities
- Read and discuss **Prewrite: Focus on Organization.** (p. 15)
- Reflect on the model Sequence Chain.
- Apply the prewriting strategy to create a Sequence Chain.
- Participate in a peer conference.

Day 3
Write
Draft: Ideas

Student Objectives
- Use a Sequence Chain to begin writing.

Student Activities
- Read and discuss **Draft: Focus on Ideas.** (p. 16)
- Reflect on the model draft. (p. 17)
- Apply the drafting strategy by using a Sequence Chain to write a draft.

WEEK 3

Day 1
Write
Revise: Voice

Student Objectives
- Revise to use first-person point of view.

Student Activities
- Read and discuss **Revise: Focus on Voice.** (p. 19)
- Reflect on the model draft.
- Apply the revising strategy.
- Participate in a peer conference.

Day 2
Write
Revise: Word Choice

Student Objectives
- Revise to use clear and specific words.

Student Activities
- Read and discuss **Revise: Focus on Word Choice.** (p. 20)
- Reflect on the model draft.
- Apply the revising strategy.

Note: Optional Revising Lessons are located at **www.sfw.z-b.com.**

Day 3
Write
Edit: Conventions

Student Objectives
- Edit for sentence fragments.

Student Activities
- Read and discuss **Edit: Focus on Conventions.** (p. 21)
- Reflect on the model draft.
- Apply the editing strategy.

Note: Teach the Conventions mini-lessons (pp. 22–23) if needed.

Day 4

Analyze
Close Reading for the Traits

Student Objectives
- Read a model personal narrative.
- Use the personal narrative rubric.
- Use the model personal narrative to study Ideas, Organization, and Voice.

Student Activities
- Review **"My Leap for Loons."** (p. 7)
- Review the rubric. (pp. 8–9)
- Read and discuss **Using the Rubric to Analyze the Model.** (pp. 10–11)

Day 5

Analyze
Close Reading for the Traits

Student Objectives
- Read a model personal narrative.
- Use the personal narrative rubric.
- Use the model personal narrative to study Word Choice, Sentence Fluency, and Conventions.

Student Activities
- Review **"My Leap for Loons."** (p. 7)
- Read and discuss **Using the Rubric to Analyze the Model.** (pp. 12–13)

Day 4

Write
Draft

Student Objectives
- Complete a draft.

Student Activities
- Finish the draft.
- Participate in a peer conference.

Day 5

Write
Revise: Organization

Student Objectives
- Revise to ensure the events are in order.

Student Activities
- Read and discuss **Revise: Focus on Organization.** (p. 18)
- Reflect on a model draft.
- Apply the revising strategy.

Day 4

Write
Publish: +Presentation

Student Objectives
- Discuss preparation for publishing and presentation.
- Use a final editing checklist to publish their work.

Student Activities
- Read and discuss **Publish: +Presentation.** (p. 24)
- Apply the publishing strategy.

Day 5

Write
Publish: +Presentation

Student Objectives
- Use a personal narrative rubric.
- Share a published personal narrative.

Student Activities
- Share their work.
- Use the rubric to reflect upon and evaluate the model and their own writing. (pp. 8–9, 25)

To complete the chapter in fewer days, combine the learning objectives and activities in a way that supports students as they write.

Resources at-a-Glance

Grammar, Usage & Mechanics

Differentiating Instruction
For additional Differentiating Instruction activities, see Strategies for Writers *Differentiated Instruction Activities at www.sfw.z-b.com.*

English Language Learners

Collaborative Conferencing

Tech Tips

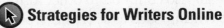 **Strategies for Writers Online**

Go to **www.sfw.z-b.com** for additional online resources for students, teachers, and parents.

Online Writing Center

Provides IWB resources, assessments, interactive games and practice activities, videos, eBooks, and a virtual file cabinet.

Introduce
Personal Narrative

Student Objectives

- Review the elements of a personal narrative. *(p. 4)*
- Consider purpose and audience. *(p. 5)*
- Learn the traits of narrative writing. *(p. 6)*

What's a Personal Narrative?

Discuss the definition of a personal narrative with students. Explain that when someone tells or writes about an experience that he or she has had, that story is called a personal narrative. Ask students whether any of them keep a journal or diary or have a blog. Point out that anytime they retell the events of their day or recall an experience from their lives, they are using the personal narrative genre.

What's in a Personal Narrative?

Direct students to page 4. Read and discuss each of the featured elements of a personal narrative with students. Explain that many of these elements are also common to other forms of writing, such as short story, biography, and play. Discuss the important role each element plays when a writer is creating a unique story.

 Strategies for Writers Online
Go to **www.sfw.z-b.com** for additional online resources for students, teachers, and parents.

What's a Personal Narrative?

It's a story I write about myself!

What's in a Personal Narrative?

Narrator
That's me! The narrator is the person who tells the story.

Setting
This is where and when the story happens. It could be yesterday at my school or last year in Arizona when we took a family camping trip.

Characters
These are the people in my story. I might be the only character, or I might include other people.

Plot
It's the action! This is what happens in the story.

Tone
This is the mood I want to express to my readers. It could be funny, serious, suspenseful, or sad.

Narrative Text Exemplars (Personal Narrative)

Perez, Amada Irma. *My Diary from Here to There/ Mi diario de aqui hasta alla*. Children's Book Press, 2009. Amada expresses uncertainty and apprehension as she prepares to move to Los Angeles from her home in Mexico. While at first she records her doubts in her diary, Amada is eventually reassured by family and friends that this new experience will be a positive one.

Uhlberg, Myron. *Dad, Jackie, and Me*. Peachtree Publishers, 2010. When Jackie Robinson is added to the Brooklyn Dodgers lineup, a little boy and his deaf father who is hearing impaired begin attending the baseball games. Through their time spent together, the boy's embarrassment of his father's disability fades and the two develop an everlasting bond.

Why write a Personal Narrative?

There are plenty of reasons to write a personal narrative. Here are a few.

To Entertain
Sometimes something happens that is so exciting that I just have to share it with someone else. It's such a good story that my reader will be really entertained.

To Reflect
Sometimes, writing a personal narrative can help me think about things in my life from a different perspective.

To Inform
Some events can be really informative. I can write a personal narrative about something that happened to me. I can share the information about what I've learned.

Why write a Personal Narrative?

Read and discuss with students the reasons for writing a personal narrative. Point out that all writing has a purpose. Writers write for many reasons and for a variety of audiences, and these authentic purposes help to shape the writing. Someone writing to entertain may use a tone that conveys excitement, humor, or suspense. A writer who is writing for personal reflection may focus on feelings and thoughts. A person writing to inform may include many facts and explanations to help the audience understand. Encourage students to think about their reasons for writing a personal narrative and how these reasons will affect the tone and focus of their writing.

Steptoe, John. *Creativity.* **Sandpiper, 2003.** A boy named Charles helps Hector, a student who just moved from Puerto Rico, adjust to his new life. However, Charles is confused because although they look different, they share the same language and heritage.

Quattlebaum, Mary. *Jackson Jones and the Mission Greentop.* **Yearling, 2005.** Jackson Jones learns that big city developers want to tear down the community garden. He must work with his friends to save the community garden and avoid a bully in the process.

CCSS **C**ommon **C**ore **S**tate **S**tandards (pp. Z20–Z30)
Writing: W.4.6
Language: L.4.3c
Speaking and Listening: SL.4.1a, SL.4.1b, SL.4.1c, SL.4.1d, SL.4.3, SL.4.6

Introduce
Personal Narrative

Linking Narrative Writing Traits to a Personal Narrative

Tell students you are going to share something that happened to you. Choose something interesting or exciting, such as finding an object that you thought was lost forever, celebrating a family occasion, helping with a community project, or getting a new pet. Ask students to listen to how you refer to yourself. Then share the experience, using many personal pronouns (*I, me, mine, we, our*). Ask students which words you used to refer to yourself. Tell or remind the class that *I, me, mine, we,* and *our* are personal pronouns. When you use these pronouns to tell about an experience, you are sharing a personal story. A narrative is a story. A personal narrative is a story that you share about yourself.

Read page 6 aloud to help students understand that they will follow Jack as he models using the writing process and the narrative writing traits together.

Linking Narrative Writing Traits to a Personal Narrative

In this chapter, you will write a story about an experience you want to share. This type of narrative writing is called a personal narrative. Jack will guide you through the stages of the writing process: Prewrite, Draft, Revise, Edit, and Publish. In each stage, Jack will show you important writing strategies that are linked to the Narrative Writing Traits below.

Narrative Writing Traits

Trait	Description
Ideas	• a topic that is just the right size, not too big or too small • details and facts that develop the narrative
Organization	• a natural and logical sequence • a strong beginning and a satisfying ending • transitions that signal the sequence of events
Voice	• a voice and tone that are perfect for the writing • dialogue that, when used, sounds just right for the characters
 Word Choice	• concrete words and phrases that describe the characters and events
 Sentence Fluency	• a variety of sentence lengths to make the story flow smoothly
 Conventions	• no or few errors in spelling, grammar, punctuation, and capitalization

Before you write, read Stephen Jensen's personal narrative on the next page. Then use the personal narrative rubric on pages 8–9 to decide how well he did. (You might want to look back at What's in a Personal Narrative? on page 4, too!)

Narrative Writing Traits in a Personal Narrative

 **Ideas** The writer focuses on one event that is neither too large nor too small for a piece of writing this size. Memorable and vivid details are included to help the reader imagine the events being described.

 **Organization** Chronological order is effective in a personal narrative. The reader can then easily follow the story's events and better connect with the narrative. The beginning pulls readers in, and the ending satisfies.

 **Voice** A good writer uses a voice or tone that is appropriate for both the purpose and the audience. First-person point of view and an energetic voice are best for a personal narrative.

MY LEAP FOR LOONS

Personal MODEL Narrative

by Stephen Jensen

first-person narrator

I'm not the outdoors type. Every time my sister Jennifer invited me to go on a canoe trip, I tried my best to get out of it. "I'm busy that weekend," I would say. Jennifer didn't give up, though. One day, I just gave in.

tone in beginning

A few weeks later, Jennifer and I were floating on a lake in northern Minnesota. As our paddles cut through clean waters, we pushed past green, wooded land. We never saw other people. Jennifer went wild every time she saw deer or moose drinking at the shore. One day, we heard a *whoosh* and saw an eagle swoop down to grab a fish. My sister got so excited, I thought she was going to fall out of the boat.

characters

setting

"Wow," I'd say, but I didn't really care. I was counting the hours until we'd pack up the car and drive home. While Jennifer went on and on about moose, I thought about a hot shower followed by a movie.

tone in middle

plot

On our last day, however, even I got excited. We heard a high-pitched wailing sound. Jennifer said "ah" softly, smiled at me, and pointed across the lake. I saw the shadow of a bird gliding slowly over the water. Then we heard a reply. It was coming from right next to our campsite.

In the fading light of day, I spotted my first loon. I couldn't take my eyes off this beautiful creature, whose wail and laugh I would hear in my mind ever after. Before nightfall, we saw many loons. Their backs were delicately etched with a checkered pattern, but their bills were shaped like daggers. Their eyes glowed a spooky red.

These amazing birds dive deep, and they can swim long distances underwater. Just when I thought one had disappeared forever, it popped up halfway across the lake!

tone in end

I can't say I went totally loony for loons. However, when we were driving home, I found myself thinking more about those loons than about a shower or a movie.

Personal Narrative 7

Word Choice A good writer uses concrete, descriptive words and phrases to bring a story to life. Clear, specific words help make the characters and events "real" for the reader.

Sentence Fluency A variety of sentence types and structures are used to give the writing energy and flow. The writing is a pleasure to listen to or read aloud.

Conventions A good writer carefully edits his or her work prior to publishing. Mistakes in spelling, punctuation, capitalization, and grammar will confuse the reader and obscure the author's purpose.

Analyze
Close Reading of the Model

Week 1 • Day 2

Student Objectives

- Read a model personal narrative. (*p. 7*)

Read the Model

Read "My Leap for Loons" on page 7 aloud. Before you read, remind students to listen for the writing traits outlined on page 6.

Elements of a Personal Narrative

Use the notes on the model to discuss the various elements of a personal narrative. Discuss Stephen Jensen's use of personal pronouns to establish that he is the narrator. How does he help the reader envision the setting? Is the sequence of events easy to follow? What tone does Stephen use throughout the story? You may wish to have students refer back to What's in a Personal Narrative? on page 4 for review.

CCSS **C**ommon **C**ore **S**tate **S**tandards (pp. Z20–Z30)
Writing: W.4.6
Language: L.4.3c
Speaking and Listening: SL.4.1a, SL.4.1b, SL.4.1c, SL.4.1d, SL.4.2, SL.4.3, SL.4.6

Analyze
Introduce the Rubric

Week 1 • Day 3

Student Objectives

- Learn to read a rubric. *(pp. 8–9)*

Introduce the Rubric

Explain the Rubric Explain that a rubric is a tool that helps you plan, improve, and evaluate a piece of writing. Tell students that a rubric helps a writer focus on key elements, or traits, in writing (**Ideas, Organization, Voice, Word Choice, Sentence Fluency, Conventions,** and **Presentation**). Draw students' attention to the six columns to explain how the scoring system works. Explain that column 6 describes a very good personal narrative, one that has received the highest score in all categories. This is what students should strive for in their own writing.

Discuss the Rubric Guide students in a discussion of the rubric. Read the descriptors that go with each trait. Note how the descriptors vary as you move from column to column. Remind students to keep the rubric in mind when they write their own personal narrative and again when they revise it.

Online Writing Center

Provides a variety of **interactive rubrics,** including 4-, 5-, and 6-point models.

Personal Narrative Rubric

Use this rubric to analyze the model. Then use it to plan and score your own personal narrative.

	6	**5**	**4**	
Ideas	The writing focuses on one experience. Interesting, descriptive details bring the experience to life for the reader.	The writing focuses on one experience. Most details bring the experience to life for the reader.	The writing focuses on one experience. More details are needed to bring the experience to life for the reader.	
Organization	The events are organized into a clear beginning, middle, and end. The sequence of events is easy to follow.	One or two events may be out of order. Most of the story is easy to follow.	Several events appear to be out of order. Part of the story is hard to follow.	
Voice	The writer uses a first-person voice to engage the reader. The tone sets the right mood.	The writer uses a first-person voice to engage the reader. The tone may not maintain the right mood.	The writer uses a first-person voice at first. The tone sets the right mood at first.	
Word Choice	Concrete, vivid language describes a clear picture for the reader.	Most language is concrete and vivid. The description is clear most of the time.	Many words are vague or too general. They do not form a clear picture.	
Sentence Fluency	Sentences vary in length and structure, making the story enjoyable to read.	Many sentences vary in length and structure. Most of the story flows.	Many sentences are different lengths and sentence structures, but they do not always flow well.	
Conventions	All sentences are complete. There are no sentence fragments.	A few errors are present, but they do not confuse the reader. All sentences are complete.	Some minor errors are noticeable, but the message is clear. A few sentences are incomplete.	

✛ Presentation   The narrative is legible and neat. The title and writer's name are at the top of the page.

CCSS Common Core State Standards
Personal Narrative

Each of the rubrics and strategies for the personal narrative is solidly based on the Narrative Writing standards; however, several strategies and exercises echo Speaking & Listening, Reading/Literature, and Language standards as well.

The Ideas and Organization rubrics are reflected in standard **W.4.3a,** which addresses focusing on one event and presenting events in a clear, logical order. The Organization rubric also reflects standard **W.4.3,** which emphasizes including a conclusion that follows from the narrated experience. Standard **W.4.3b** lists several narrative techniques, including dialogue and description to develop both plot and characters.

3	2	1	
The writing introduces one experience. Details may be too general to bring the experience to life for the reader.	The experience is not clear. Details may be weak or unrelated.	The writing is not focused. Details may be unrelated or not provided.	**Ideas**
Events may be out of order. The middle part of the story may be hard to follow.	Events are out of order. The end may be incomplete or missing.	The writing is not organized. It is impossible to follow.	**Organization**
The voice may shift to third-person in several places. The tone may be hard to determine.	The voice and/or tone may not be appropriate. Frequent shifts in voice confuse the reader.	The voice and tone are very weak or absent. The writer does not engage the reader.	**Voice**
Some words are overused or too ordinary to form a clear picture.	The words are ordinary or dull. Some are used incorrectly.	Many words are used incorrectly. The reader cannot form a picture.	**Word Choice**
Several sentences in a row have the same length or structure, making the writing less interesting.	Many sentences are the same length or structure, making the writing choppy in places.	Sentences are incomplete or unclear.	**Sentence Fluency**
Distracting errors make the text difficult to read and understand in some places. Some sentences are incomplete.	Noticeable errors confuse the reader. Some sentences are incomplete.	The writing contains many errors. Sentences are incorrect. Many sentence fragments are present.	**Conventions**

See Appendix B for 4-, 5-, and 6-point narrative rubrics.

Find Evidence in the Model

Small-Group Collaboration Organize students into six groups. Assign each group a trait. Have students search the model on page 7 for strong examples of their assigned trait as described by the rubric.

Teacher-Led Discussion Bring the class back together and ask one person from each group to report their findings to the class. Remind students that the point of this exercise is not to score the model, but to further their understanding of each trait and to practice identifying the traits within a piece of writing.

Additional Rubrics

Appendix B includes 4-, 5-, and 6-point rubrics that can be used with any piece of narrative writing. The rubrics are also available as blackline masters in the back of this Teacher Edition.

Both the Voice and Word Choice rubrics encompass standards **W.4.3c** and **W.4.3d**, which focus on the careful use of words to both guide the reader through the story and clearly and vividly describe characters, setting, and events.

The editing pages in this chapter, as in all of the chapters throughout the Narrative unit, reflect standards **L.4.1** and **L.4.2**. As this chapter focuses on recognizing and fixing sentence fragments, standard **L.4.1f** is included as well.

CCSS **C**ommon **C**ore **S**tate **S**tandards (pp. Z20–Z30)
Writing: W.4.6
Language: L.4.3c
Speaking and Listening: SL.4.1a, SL.4.1b, SL.4.1c, SL.4.1d, SL.4.2, SL.4.3, SL.4.6

Analyze
Close Reading for the Traits

Week 1 • Day 4

Student Objectives

- Read a model personal narrative. (*p. 7*)
- Use the personal narrative rubric. (*pp. 8–9*)
- Use the model personal narrative to study **Ideas, Organization,** and **Voice**. (*pp. 10–11*)

Find Evidence in the Model

Evaluate the Model Have students turn to pages 10–11. Explain that these pages show how the model on page 7 uses the writing traits described in the rubric.

Read each section with students. Use these questions to initiate the discussion. Be sure students can back up their answers with specific examples from the model.

Discuss Audience, Task, Purpose Ask students one or more of the following questions as they analyze the model:

- **Audience** Who is the audience? (Possible response: all readers)

- **Task** How does Stephen Jensen share his personal experience in his story? (Possible response: He uses interesting details to bring his experience to life for the reader.)

- **Purpose** What was Stephen's purpose for writing this story? (Possible response: to tell about an event in his life)

Using the Personal Narrative Rubric to Analyze the Model

Did you notice that the model on page 7 points out some key elements of a personal narrative? As he wrote "My Leap for Loons," Stephen Jensen used these elements to help him write about a personal experience. He also used the 6-point rubric on pages 8–9 to plan, draft, revise, and edit the writing. A rubric is a great tool to evaluate writing during the writing process.

Now let's use the same rubric to score the model. To do this, we'll focus on each trait separately, starting with Ideas. We'll use the top descriptor for each trait (column 6), along with examples from the model, to help us understand how the traits work together. How would you score Stephen on each trait?

 **Ideas**
- The writing focuses on one interesting experience.
- Interesting, descriptive details bring the experience to life for the reader.

I didn't know anything about loons before I read this story, so I found his story really interesting! All of the details help me imagine Stephen's canoe trip. He paints a vivid picture of his experience by describing how he *cut through clean waters* and *pushed past green, wooded land.*

A few weeks later, Jennifer and I were floating on a lake in northern Minnesota. As our paddles cut through clean waters, we pushed past green, wooded land.

English Language Learners

BEGINNING

Sequencing Using pictures, tell a short story to students. Post the pictures on the board in random order. Hold up one finger and ask, *Which happened first?* Have a student write *First* or *1* next to the first picture. Model the sentence *This happened first.* Continue for the remaining pictures using words such as *second, then, next, last,* and *finally.*

INTERMEDIATE

The 5 W's Tell students, *Let's plan a party!* Draw a blank party invitation on the board with *Party!* at the top. Ask students, *What kind of party will we have?* If students say, for example, *a birthday party*, write *What: birthday* on the invitation. Repeat for the remaining 5 W's.

Organization
- The events are organized into a clear beginning, middle, and end.
- The sequence of events is easy to follow.

The writer tells everything in order. He starts with his sister's invitation and ends with the last day of their trip. There is a clear beginning, middle, and end. He also uses transition words and phrases like *on our last day* that help me follow the story.

On our last day, however, even I got excited. We heard a high-pitched wailing sound.

Voice
- The writer uses a first-person voice to engage the reader.
- The tone sets the right mood.

Right from the beginning, the writer draws me into the story by using first-person point of view. It seems like he is speaking directly to me. The feelings that Stephen shares set the tone for the rest of the story.

I'm not the outdoors type. Every time my sister Jennifer invited me to go on a canoe trip, I tried my best to get out of it.

Discuss the Traits Ask students one or more of the following questions to discuss the traits in the model.

Ideas Choose another descriptive detail and tell why it helps the story come alive for you. (Possible response: *One day we heard a* woosh *and saw an eagle swoop down to grab a fish.* I feel like I can hear and see the eagle.)

Organization Why does Stephen choose to tell the events in order? (The order makes it easy to understand what happened.)

Voice What voice or tone does Stephen use? What does this tell you about his purpose? (Possible response: His voice is humorous. Stephen wants to entertain us with a funny story.)

ADVANCED
Sequencing Read a short story to students. The story should clearly answer the 5 W's and follow a logical order. After you read the story the first time, give students 3 minutes to work quietly with a partner to fill out a Sequence Chain graphic organizer. After 3 minutes, read the story again. Have partners revise their Sequence Chains as necessary. Have students review as a group.

ADVANCED HIGH
Identifying the 5 W's Give each student a language-level-appropriate narrative to read, such as a newspaper article, decodable book, or leveled reader. Then have them fill in a 5 W's chart. Tell them that they may have to use other clues, such as pictures, to gather the information. Have students trade selections and charts with a partner. The partner should read the selection and review the chart for mistakes.

CCSS **Common Core State Standards** (pp. Z20–Z30)
Writing: 4.3c
Language: L.4.3c, L.4.6
Speaking and Listening: SL.4.1a, SL.4.1b, SL.4.1c, SL.4.1d, SL.4.2, SL.4.3, SL.4.6

Analyze
Close Reading for the Traits

Week 1 • Day 5

Student Objectives

- Read a model personal narrative. (p. 7)
- Use the personal narrative rubric. (pp. 8–9)
- Use the model personal narrative to study **Word Choice, Sentence Fluency,** and **Conventions.** (pp. 12–13)

Discuss the Traits Ask students one or more of the following questions to discuss the traits in the model.

Word Choice Point out some of the concrete, vivid language Stephen uses to help his readers "see" the setting and events. (Possible responses: *green, wooded land; swoop; high-pitched wailing sound; delicately etched with a checkered pattern*)

Sentence Fluency How does Stephen vary sentence length in the first paragraph?
(He starts and ends with short sentences and has long sentences in between.)

Conventions How does Stephen's careful editing show in this narrative?
(Possible responses: He makes sure that all the sentences are complete. He corrected any fragments that he found in his narrative.)

Strategies for Writers Online
Go to **www.sfw.z-b.com** for additional online resources for students, teachers, and parents.

Using the Rubric to Analyze the Model
Personal Narrative

Word Choice • Concrete, vivid language describes a clear picture for the reader.

When Stephen describes the loons, he uses very clear and vivid words. Even though I have never seen a loon before, I am able to picture one. Phrases such as *checkered pattern* and *shaped like daggers* give me a clear picture.

Their backs were delicately etched with a checkered pattern, but their bills were shaped like daggers.

Sentence Fluency • Sentences vary in length and structure, making the story enjoyable to read.

Stephen uses a lot of different kinds of sentences in his personal narrative. For example, some sentences are longer and some are shorter. This helps the story flow smoothly.

In the fading light of day, I spotted my first loon. I couldn't take my eyes off this beautiful creature, whose wail and laugh I would hear in my mind ever after. Before nightfall, we saw many loons.

12 Narrative Writing

Tech Tips
Online Images

Use Pictures Online Opening up modes of communication to students as they prepare to write their personal narratives means creating storyboards, prewriting by sequencing images, or even recording a spoken-word narration that is then transcribed into a draft. Some students are quick to pick up a pencil and write; others will discover the stories they have to tell by tapping into image or sound. Model this process for them as the skilled writer in the classroom. Unpack a series of images to create a text they can work from (see Pics4Learning for image ideas) and pay attention to the steps you take in moving from image to print text.

See **www.sfw.z-b.com** for further information about and links to these websites and tools.

Conventions
- All sentences are complete.
- There are no sentence fragments.

I looked through the whole story, and every word is spelled correctly. All the sentences are capitalized and punctuated correctly. Every sentence is complete, and there are no sentence fragments.

These amazing birds dive deep, and they can swim long distances under water. Just when I thought one had disappeared forever, it popped up halfway across the lake!

⁺Presentation
The narrative is legible and neat. The title and writer's name are at the top of the page.

My Turn!
Now it's my turn to write a personal narrative! I'll use the 6-point rubric on pages 8–9 and good writing strategies to help me. Follow along to see how I do it.

⁺Presentation Point out that the trait of Presentation is just as important as any other trait. Explain that the greatest of stories cannot be enjoyed if the writing is so messy that it can't be read. Students must keep in mind that legible, neat writing is essential in their final copies. Also remind students to be sure they include the title of their personal narrative and their name at the top of the page. Explain that the title is the first thing a reader will see, and just like any other first impression, it should be engaging and neatly presented.

Using a computer is an excellent way to create clean, legible text. Encourage students to use a word processing program and to choose one legible font for the text of their personal narrative.

Think About the Traits

Once students have thoroughly discussed the model, ask them which traits they think are most important in a personal narrative and have them explain why. (Possible response: Ideas are very important, as this trait is at the heart of a good story. Voice is very important because it helps the reader get to know the writer or narrator.)

Differentiating Instruction

ENRICHMENT
Exploring Creativity Ask students to choose a setting to describe. Give them the categories Sight, Sound, Smell, Taste, and Feeling/Texture. Instruct students to brainstorm concrete, vivid words that fall under each category to describe their chosen settings. Have each student read his or her list of words to the group.

REINFORCEMENT
Working With Vivid Language To help students better understand the importance of vivid, concrete language, create four columns on the board using the following words: *house, noise, bread,* and *odor.* Explain that these words are vague and overused. Ask students for creative, vivid words to replace each vague word. Discuss how the new words will help a reader better envision the story.

CCSS **Common Core State Standards** (pp. Z20–Z30)
Writing: W.4.3d, W.4.6
Language: L.4.3a, L.4.3c, L.4.6
Speaking and Listening: SL.4.1a, SL.4.1b, SL.4.1c, SL.4.1d, SL.4.3, SL.4.6

Write
Personal Narrative

Week 2 • Day 1

Student Objectives

- Read and understand a prewriting strategy. *(p. 14)*

Prewrite

Focus on ⟨Ideas⟩

Narrow Topic Read page 14 aloud. Point out that Jack chose a story that was just the right size for this writing assignment. It's important that students do not select a story that is too long or detailed, or they may easily become overwhelmed. Instruct students to think about something interesting that has happened to them. You may want to use the following questions to get your students thinking:

- Have any new people moved into your neighborhood in the past year? Who are they? What are they like?

- Has anyone had any experiences volunteering or doing something helpful for other people? How did you feel while helping them?

- Can you remember a day that you thought was going to be like any other day yet ended up being surprisingly exciting? What happened?

Take Notes Once students have decided on a topic, have them take some notes about the event just as Jack has done.

Online Writing Center

 Provides **interactive graphic organizers** as well as a variety of graphic organizers in PDF format.

Write a Personal Narrative

Prewrite   Focus on ⟨Ideas⟩

The Rubric Says	The writing focuses on one experience.
Writing Strategy	Make notes about an interesting personal experience.

My teacher said we could write about any experience that we think the rest of the class will find interesting.

I think I'll write about the day the Saddok family moved in next door to us. Many of my classmates live in big apartment buildings like mine. I'm sure they have neighbors from other countries, too. They'll probably be interested in my experience. First I'll jot down some notes on what I remember about that day.

My Notes

- ✔ Mrs. Saddok did not want to shake Dad's hand.
- ✔ Mr. Saddok put his right hand over his heart.
- ✔ No one said anything.
- ✔ We helped pick up everything.
- ✔ It all started with a big noise.

Write

Think about interesting events in your life. Brainstorm some ideas and pick one event you think will be the most interesting. Jot down some notes about the event.

14 Narrative Writing

English Language Learners

BEGINNING/INTERMEDIATE

What Is a Personal Narrative? Tell a very brief story using simple words that students know. Try to include all of the 5 W's. Have volunteers retell the story, one event at a time. Tell students, *A story is a narrative.* Have students repeat that sentence. Write it on the board. Have students say the sentence again, first as a group and then individually. Repeat the process for the sentence, *A story about you is a personal narrative.* Review usage of the pronouns *I* and *me.*

ADVANCED/ADVANCED HIGH

Making Notes Ask students to think of a story about themselves that they would like to tell. As they tell the story to a partner, the partner should make notes on a piece of paper. After the story is completed, have students review their partner's notes, then switch roles and repeat the activity. Finally, using the notes as a starting point, students should add other details to their personal narratives.

Prewrite

Focus on Organization

The Rubric Says	The events are organized into a clear beginning, middle, and end.
Writing Strategy	Make a Sequence Chain to organize my notes.

The rubric says the events in my story need to follow each other in order. I'll use a graphic organizer to put my notes in order. I think a Sequence Chain would be the best one for ordering my notes this time. A Sequence Chain helps me to place the events first, second, third, and so on.

Writer's Term

Sequence Chain A Sequence Chain organizes events in the order in which they happen.

Sequence Chain

	The Day We Met Our New Neighbors
First Event	There was a loud noise outside our door.
Second Event	We said hello and offered to help. Nobody said a word to us.
Third Event	Dad told his name and wanted to shake hands with the new neighbors.
Fourth Event	We started picking up all the things. We helped a lot.

Analyze

Look at Jack's notes and the Sequence Chain. How will they help him organize the events in his personal narrative?

Write

Use your notes to make a Sequence Chain. Be sure to put the events in order.

Personal Narrative **15**

Collaborative Conferencing

PEER TO PEER Have pairs exchange and read each other's Sequence Chains. Each student should then write on sticky notes two questions or comments regarding the organization of events in the chain.

PEER GROUPS Divide students up into groups of five or six. Students should then take turns reading their Sequence Chains aloud. The other group members then get to offer one comment or question each to help strengthen or clarify the organization of events.

TEACHER-LED Work with one or two students at a time. Instruct students to close their eyes and envision the events as you read their Sequence Chains aloud. Guide them to notice where events could be better sequenced for clarity.

Write
Personal Narrative

Week 2 • Day 2

Student Objectives

- Create a Sequence Chain to organize notes. (p. 15)

Prewrite

Focus on Organization

Make a Sequence Chain Read page 15 aloud to students. Explain that all good writers first gather their information and then organize it. Explain that a Sequence Chain is a great tool to use when writing a personal narrative or any story. (Go to **www.sfw.z-b.com** for the downloadable graphic organizers.) The chain helps the writer put each event in the story in the proper, logical order. Allow time for students to create Sequence Chains for their personal narratives.

Writer's Term

Sequence Chain A Sequence Chain helps writers organize all the events in their story prior to writing. This organization ensures the story is logical and readers will not feel confused. Using a short and familiar story such as "Goldilocks and the Three Bears," diagram a Sequence Chain on the board for students to see. Verbally walk them through the process, being sure to use the labels *First Event, Second Event,* and so on.

CCSS Common Core State Standards (pp. Z20–Z30)
Writing: W.4.3a, W.4.3e, W.4.4, W.4.5, W.4.6, W.4.8, W.4.10
Language: L.4.3c, L.4.6
Speaking and Listening: SL.4.1a, SL.4.1b, SL.4.1c, SL.4.1d, SL.4.2, SL.4.3, SL.4.4, SL.4.6

Write
Personal Narrative

Week 2 • Day 3

Student Objectives

• Use a Sequence Chain to begin writing. *(pp. 16–17)*

Draft

Focus on Ideas

Begin a Draft Explain to students that the main goal of writing a draft is to get their ideas down on paper without having to worry about making mistakes. Assure them that there will be time set aside later when they can fix any errors they might have made.

Then read page 16, including the Writer's Term box, aloud. Take a moment to discuss how including plenty of vivid details enhances and enlivens writing.

Have students use their Sequence Chains to write drafts of their personal narratives. Remind them to include plenty of details to paint the clearest picture possible. Point out that Jack repeatedly refers to the rubric as he writes.

Writer's Term

Details The writer should try to include details that are surprising or intriguing to the audience, rather than details that the audience already knows or expects.

Online Writing Center

Provides an **interactive writing pad** for drafting, revising, editing, and publishing.

Draft   Focus on Ideas

The Rubric Says   Interesting, descriptive details bring the experience to life for the reader.

Writing Strategy   Include details about the characters so the reader can form a clear picture.

Writer's Term

Details

Details are words or phrases that give more information about a person or event. Details make writing more interesting.

Now it's time to start writing. I'll use my notes and Sequence Chain to write my draft. I'll make sure that I focus on sharing my experience.

According to the rubric, I also need to use interesting details so my reader will understand what's happening. I'll include descriptive details about my characters that show what they're saying and doing. I want the reader to understand what we experienced.

As usual, I won't worry too much about my grammar, punctuation, and spelling. I know that I can fix errors when I edit my writing.

16 Narrative Writing

Differentiating Instruction

ENRICHMENT

Practice Adding Details Have students write a "bare-bones" sentence about something they can see in the classroom. Then challenge them to add as many specific and vivid details to their sentences as they can. You may wish to have a contest to see who can include the most details in a sentence.

REINFORCEMENT

List Details Before Drafting Work with individual students before they begin drafting. Look at each student's Sequence Chain and discuss which details he or she can include for each step in the Sequence Chain. Students should write down the details so they can refer to them in the Sequence Chain when drafting.

Proofreading Marks

⏋ Indent	ℓ Take out something
≡ Make uppercase	⊙ Add a period
/ Make lowercase	¶ New paragraph
∧ Add something	SP Spelling error

[DRAFT]

The Day We Met Our New Neighbors

Noise outside the door. Jack's dad ran out, and Jack followed him.

Dad said, "Hi, do you need help?" Not a word! They just looked at us. — *details*

In the hallway were for strangers. The woman wore cloths I'd never seen before. The rest of the family wore unusual cloths too.

Dad held out his hand to the man Dad said, "Hi, I'm Ken Washington, and I live here." The man took Dad's hand. He shook it a little. Didn't say a word. My dad held out his hand to the woman. Turned away.

We could see that a big wooden box had split open. We helped pick up everything. — *details*

Analyze

Read Jack's draft. Which details help you picture what is happening?

Write

Use your notes and Sequence Chain to write a draft. Be sure to include details that show the characters and the action in your story.

Personal Narrative **17**

Collaborative Conferencing

PEER TO PEER Have pairs of students exchange their Sequence Chains and drafts. Pairs discuss if any events are missing or out of order.

PEER GROUPS Give sticky notes to each student in the group. Students read each draft and write on a sticky note where a detail is needed. This process is repeated until each draft has been read by each student.

TEACHER-LED Meet with pairs of students. Have students read their drafts aloud. Encourage the listening student to explain what he or she could easily envision from the story, as well as what events are confusing or vague and need more details.

Write
Personal Narrative

Week 2 • Day 4

Student Objectives

• Complete a draft. *(p. 17)*

Continue Drafting Read Jack's draft on page 17 aloud. Have students turn back to page 15 to review Jack's Sequence Chain. Ask if Jack followed his Sequence Chain. Encourage students to point out examples to show how the events in the draft follow the order in the Sequence Chain. Then ask if Jack included any descriptive details to help his readers envision his story. Guide a discussion about how these details help enrich and enliven the narrative. Ask students to discuss where they feel Jack could have included more details to help readers visualize his story.

Review the proofreading marks at the top of page 17. Explain to students that they will be using these marks when they revise and edit their writing.

CCSS **Common Core State Standards** (pp. Z20–Z30)
Writing: W.4.3b, W.4.3d, W.4.4, W.4.5, W.4.6, W.4.8, W.4.10
Language: L.4.3a, L.4.3c, L.4.6
Speaking and Listening: SL.4.1a, SL.4.1b, SL.4.1c, SL.4.1d, SL.4.3, SL.4.6

Write
Personal Narrative

Week 2 • Day 5

Student Objectives

- Revise to ensure the events are in order. *(p. 18)*

Revise

Focus on

Keep Events in Order Explain how every good, complete story has a beginning, middle, and end. Each section serves a different role, but each is equally important. The beginning of a story should pull the reader in. It provides important information, such as who is in the story and where the action takes place. The middle is where most of the action takes place. The end is where the events are wrapped up: challenges are overcome, problems are solved, and the reader is left with a sense of satisfaction.

Read Jack's words at the top of page 18. Explain that it is important for a writer to keep events in a logical order when writing a story, or the reader will become confused. A confusing story is difficult to read. Then read Jack's draft excerpt both before and after his revision. Discuss how his reordering events helped clarify the story. Have students revise their drafts to ensure their story events are in order. Remind students to refer to their Sequence Chains if needed.

 Strategies for Writers Online
Go to **www.sfw.z-b.com** for additional online resources for students, teachers, and parents.

Revise

Focus on **Organization**

The Rubric Says	The events are organized into a clear beginning, middle, and end.
Writing Strategy	Check to see that the events are in order.

After writing my draft, I looked back at the rubric. It says that the events are organized into a clear beginning, middle, and end. I read my draft again. I'll follow my Sequence Chain to put the events in the correct order.

[DRAFT]

> Dad said, "Hi, do you need help?" Not a word! They just looked at us.
>
> In the hallway were for strangers. The woman wore cloths I'd never seen before. The rest of the family wore unusual cloths too.

changed order of events

Write
Read your draft. Put events in the correct order so your story is easy to follow.

English Language Learners

BEGINNING/INTERMEDIATE
Personal Pronouns Review usage of the first-person pronouns *I, me,* and *my.* Give several simple examples, such as *I live in Texas. Mom loves me. My name is Ana.* Write other examples on the board, but do not include the pronouns. Have Beginning ELLs fill in the appropriate pronouns, and ask Intermediate ELLs to check for mistakes.

ADVANCED/ADVANCED HIGH
Using Vivid Words Write a generic word, such as *pretty,* on the board. Use a Web or Continuum Scale graphic organizer to brainstorm other words that have the same meaning as *pretty* or have stronger meanings. For example, on a Continuum Scale, you could write *pretty, lovely, handsome, beautiful, stunning,* and so on. Tell students to use this idea when choosing words for their personal narratives.

Revise

Focus on **Voice**

The Rubric Says The writer uses a first-person voice to engage the reader.

Writing Strategy Use a first-person point of view.

Writer's Term

First-Person Point of View
Point of view tells the reader who is telling the story. In a personal narrative, the point of view is **first person** because the writer is telling his or her own story. Writers using the **first-person point of view** use words such as **I, me, my, mine, we, us, our,** and **ours** to tell their story.

I have to remember that a personal narrative is my own story. My audience needs to know that I'm actually in the story. This means I need to use personal pronouns such as *I, me,* and *my* to tell my story.

[DRAFT]

used first-person point of view

My

Noise outside the door. ~~Jack's~~ dad ran out, and

I
~~Jack~~ followed him.

Analyze
Look at Jack's revision. Why is it important to use first-person point of view in a personal narrative?

Write
Use personal pronouns (*I, me, my, mine, we, us, our,* and *ours*) to tell your story.

Personal Narrative **19**

Collaborative Conferencing

PEER TO PEER Have partners read each other's drafts aloud. Instruct students to listen for places where first-person point of view should be used, then make revisions as needed.

PEER GROUPS Have students tell the group whether they want feedback on event order or first person. Each student reads his or her draft aloud, and the others make one comment each relating to either Organization or Voice.

TEACHER-LED Meet with students who are struggling with the idea of first-person point of view. Have students listen as you read their drafts aloud. Guide them to notice any pronouns that are not first person but should be.

Write
Personal Narrative

Week 3 • Day 1

Student Objectives

• Revise to use first-person point of view. (*p. 19*)

Revise

Focus on **Voice**

Use First Person Remind students that when they write a personal narrative, they are telling a story that happened to them. Read Jack's words and the Writer's Term box at the top of page 19. Then read Jack's draft excerpt both before and after his revisions. Guide students in a discussion about how the revisions helped clarify that Jack himself is involved in the story. Then direct students to revise for first person in their own drafts.

Writer's Term

First-Person Point of View First-person point of view allows a writer to be a part of the action, as well as share personal thoughts and feelings about the events. When a writer uses first person, the reader feels a stronger connection to the story. Using first person also brings the story to life as the readers feel they are hearing the story firsthand.

CCSS Common Core State Standards (pp. Z20–Z30)
Writing: W.4.3a, W.4.3b, W.4.3e, W.4.4, W.4.5, W.4.10
Language: L.4.3a, L.4.3c, L.4.3d, L.4.6
Speaking and Listening: SL.4.1a, SL.4.1b, SL.4.1c, SL.4.1d, SL.4.3, SL.4.6

Write
Personal Narrative

Week 3 • Day 2

Student Objectives

• Revise to use clear and specific words. *(p. 20)*

Revise

Focus on Word Choice

Paint a Picture Explain to students that writers are like artists—they create pictures for their readers, only they use words instead of paint or pencil. Good writers use plenty of vivid, descriptive words to help create the clearest and most accurate image possible. The easier it is for the reader to "see" and "hear" the action, the more he or she will enjoy the story.

Write the following sentence on the board: *I carried my stuff to school.* Invite students to suggest specific words that describe concrete items you could use to replace *stuff* in the sentence (*all my books, my folders and lunchbox, my science project*). Discuss how using clear, specific words would help them explain to someone exactly what and how much they lugged to school.

Read page 20 aloud. Discuss how Jack's revisions helped students "see" and "hear" the books spilling out of the trunk. Then instruct students to check their drafts to see if they can make any of their word choices clearer and more specific for their readers.

Online Writing Center

Provides **interactive proofreading activities** for each genre.

Revise — Focus on Word Choice

The Rubric Says Concrete, vivid language describes a clear picture for the reader.

Writing Strategy Use clear and specific words to tell the story.

The rubric says to use vivid language to tell my story. That means that I should use words that help the reader "see" and "hear" what is happening. I'll read through my draft again. Then I'll add clear, specific words to describe the scene. For example, the word *trunk* gives the reader a better picture than *box*.

[DRAFT]

used specific words

trunk

We could see that a big wooden box had split

That was the loud crashing noise we heard. the books that had spilled out open. We helped pick up everything.

clear words

Write

Read your draft again. Look for parts that aren't clear. Use clear and specific words to make your writing clearer.

Optional Revising Lessons

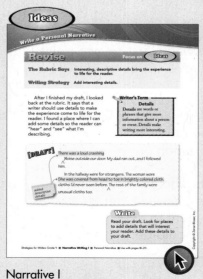

Narrative I

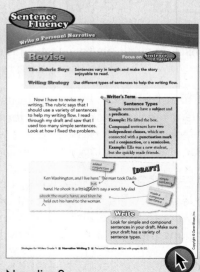

Narrative 2

Go to *Strategies for Writers* at www.sfw.z-b.com

Edit — Focus on Conventions

The Rubric Says   All sentences are complete.

Writing Strategy   Make sure there are no sentence fragments.

Next I'll check my spelling, punctuation, and capitalization. I will also check for sentence fragments. A sentence fragment is an incomplete thought. It needs either a subject or a predicate. I'll fix any sentence fragments I find.

[DRAFT]

At the end of the day, Mr. Saddok put his right hand over
his heart, and then he ~~nodded~~ nodded. Later, we learned that the
Saddoks were from algeria. ✗ That was their Algerian way to say
a sincere thank you.

corrected sentence fragment

Analyze
Look at the words that Jack changed. Do they change the picture you have in your mind? Look at the edits. How did Jack fix a sentence fragment?

Write — Conventions
Edit your draft for spelling, punctuation, and capitalization errors. Fix any sentence fragments.

For more practice writing complete sentences and fixing sentence fragments, use the exercises on the next two pages.

Personal Narrative 21

Related Grammar Practice

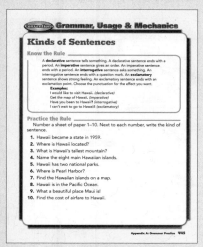

Student Edition page 445

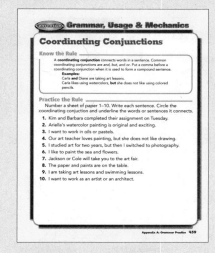

Student Edition page 459

Go to ➡ Appendix A: Grammar Practice

Write
Personal Narrative

Student Objectives
- Edit for sentence fragments. (p. 21)

Edit

Focus on Conventions

Check for Sentence Fragments

Explain to students that every sentence must contain a subject and a predicate and express a complete thought. Write this phrase on the board: *Headed for the library.* Ask if it is a complete sentence. **(No.)** If not, what is missing? **(The subject is missing.)** Encourage volunteers to add the missing subject. **(Possible responses: We/The new librarian/ A new shipment of books headed for the library.)**

Read page 21 aloud. Review each of the edits Jack made to his draft excerpt. Instruct students to check their own narratives to correct any sentence fragments.

If some or many of your students are having trouble identifying sentence fragments, teach the mini-lessons on pages T22 and T23. Then have students complete the exercises on pages 22 and 23.

CCSS Common Core State Standards (pp. Z20–Z30)
Writing: W.4.3b, W.4.3d, W.4.4, W.4.5, W.4.6, W.4.10
Language: L.4.1f, L.4.2a, L.4.2d, L.4.3a, L.4.6

Conventions

Mini-Lesson

Student Objectives

- Learn to identify the complete subject and predicate within a sentence. *(p. 22)*

Complete Subject and Predicate

The simple subject tells who or what the sentence is about; a complete subject is who or what the sentence is about, as well as any related words or phrases. The simple predicate tells what the subject is doing; a complete predicate contains the verb and any words or phrases relating to it.

Write the following sentences on the board:

The hungry squirrel scavenged for acorns for the winter.

Dozens of kittens played with balls of yarn and wind-up mice for hours.

Help students identify the complete subjects (**The hungry squirrel, Dozens of kittens**) and the complete predicates (**the remainder of each sentence**).

Online Writing Center

Provides **interactive grammar games** and **practice activities** in student eBook.

Complete Subject and Predicate

Know the Rule

The **complete subject** of a sentence tells who or what the sentence is about. It includes the subject and all the words that modify the subject.

Example: My best friend Olivia lives in California.

A **compound subject** (two or more subjects) can share the same predicate.

Example: My best friend Olivia and my cousin met in California.

The **complete predicate** of the sentence tells what happens in the sentence. It includes the verb and all the words that modify the verb.

Example: We <u>drove to the beach with her family</u>.

A **compound predicate** (two or more predicates) can share the same subject(s).

Example: My cousin and I <u>drove to the beach with her family and dug for clams</u>.

Practice the Rule

Number a sheet of paper 1–10. Then write each sentence below. Circle the complete subject. Underline the complete predicate.

1. My family offered to help our neighbors with their packing.
2. They and their golden retriever were moving to California.
3. Shipping boxes were sorted by size and stacked to the ceiling.
4. My brother and I chose the room with the fewest boxes.
5. We went to the small study at the back of the house.
6. Neither of us had ever seen that many books in one bookshelf.
7. Mysteries, adventure stories, and old comic books lined three shelves.
8. My brother forgot all about packing and read a book about California.
9. I kept packing and filled six boxes.
10. I liked hearing the story and dreamed of heading west someday.

Related Grammar Practice

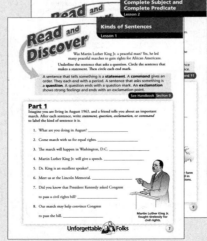

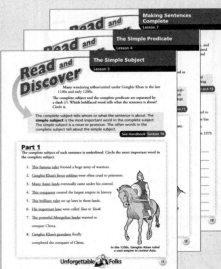

Pages 7, 9, 11, 13, 19

Go to ➡ **G.U.M. Student Practice Book**

Sentence Fragments

Know the Rule

A **sentence** tells a complete thought. A sentence needs a subject (what the sentence is about) and a predicate (what the subject does).
Example:
I love living in the new apartment.

A **sentence fragment** is a group of words that is missing a subject, a predicate, or both.
Example:
Living in the new apartment.

Practice the Rule

Number a sheet of paper 1–12. Write **F** for each sentence fragment. Write **C** for complete sentence. If the sentence is a fragment, write **S** if the subject is missing. Write **P** if the predicate is missing.

1. My new neighbors in the next apartment.   F, P
2. A huge truck began to unload boxes.   C
3. Looked out the window at the people outside.   F, S
4. Several men carried tables and chairs up the stairs.   C
5. Rested and ate their lunch under a tree.   F, S
6. Everyone came out and welcomed them to the neighborhood.   C
7. Cookies and lemonade.   F, P
8. Moving day turned into a celebration.   C
9. Played music from other countries.   F, S
10. Soon our new neighbors seemed like old friends.   C
11. Felt very tired.   F, S
12. Moving days can be very busy for the people moving in.   C

Personal Narrative 23

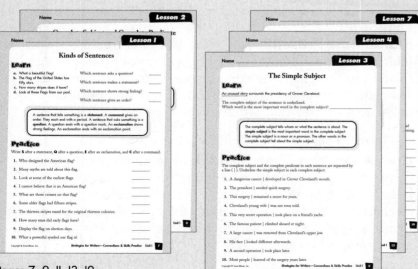

Pages 7, 9, 11, 13, 19

Go to ➡ Grammar Practice Masters

Mini-Lesson

Student Objectives

- Learn to identify and correct sentence fragments. (p. 23)

Sentence Fragments

Explain to students that a complete sentence contains a subject and a predicate and expresses a complete thought. Write the following phrase on the board: *The three girls.* Ask students if this is a complete sentence or a sentence fragment. (a sentence fragment) What is the fragment missing? (a predicate) Ask volunteers how to make the fragment a complete sentence. (Possible response: The three girls heard a loud noise in the hall.) Write *was very exciting* on the board and ask students what is missing. (a subject) Ask volunteers to supply a subject to complete the sentence. (Possible response: Moving day was very exciting.)

Write several more sentence fragments on the board and call on volunteers to add a subject or predicate to complete the sentences. Ask students to specify whether they are adding a subject or a predicate.

CCSS Common Core State Standards (pp. Z20–Z30)
Writing: W.4.6
Language: L.4.1f, L.4.6

Write
Personal Narrative

Week 3 • Day 4

Student Objectives

- Discuss preparation for publishing and presentation. *(p. 24)*
- Use a final editing checklist to publish their work. *(p. 24)*

Publish ⁺Presentation

Publishing Strategy Remind students that they have worked hard on their personal narratives, and choosing the right publishing method is important.

Read page 24 aloud. Ask students if they like Jack's choice for sharing his personal narrative. Remind them that he might also include this narrative in a journal or send it to a friend or relative. Ask students to suggest different ways to publish their personal narratives. The class can all agree to one method, such as creating a personal narrative compilation or journal, or each student can choose a method individually.

Review Jack's final checklist with students. Then have students make a checklist of their own to check their narratives. Along with their chosen mode of publishing, encourage them to give or send copies to friends and relatives who would enjoy reading about the experience they described.

▶ Strategies for Writers Online
Go to **www.sfw.z-b.com** for additional online resources for students, teachers, and parents.

Publish ⁺Presentation

Publishing Strategy	Post narrative on the class bulletin board.
Presentation Strategy	Use neat handwriting or word processing.

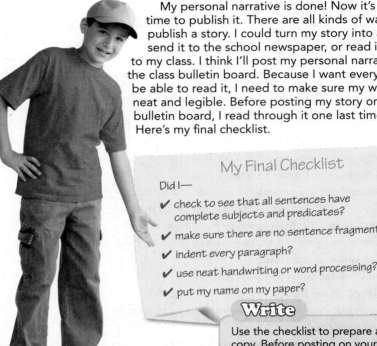

My personal narrative is done! Now it's time to publish it. There are all kinds of ways to publish a story. I could turn my story into a book, send it to the school newspaper, or read it aloud to my class. I think I'll post my personal narrative on the class bulletin board. Because I want everyone to be able to read it, I need to make sure my writing is neat and legible. Before posting my story on the bulletin board, I read through it one last time. Here's my final checklist.

My Final Checklist

Did I—

✔ check to see that all sentences have complete subjects and predicates?

✔ make sure there are no sentence fragments?

✔ indent every paragraph?

✔ use neat handwriting or word processing?

✔ put my name on my paper?

Write
Use the checklist to prepare a final copy. Before posting on your class bulletin board or website, add illustrations or drawings that enhance your personal narrative.

24 Narrative Writing

Differentiating Instruction

ENRICHMENT
Multimedia Presentation Have students create a multimedia presentation with short videos or photographs relating to their experience to display along with the text. The video or photographs can come from their personal collection, or they can gather images online.

REINFORCEMENT
Create Practice Time Set aside time for students with less computer experience to experiment on the class computer before they type their final copy. Make a list of features for students to explore, such as using the tab key, setting side margins, selecting font and font size, selecting line spacing, and saving and printing text.

The Day We Met Our New Neighbors
by Jack

There was a loud crashing noise outside our door. My dad ran out, and I followed him.

In the hallway were four strangers. The woman wore clothes I'd never seen before. She was covered from head to toe in brightly colored cloth. The rest of the family wore unusual clothes, too.

Dad said, "Hi, do you need help?" Nobody said a word! They just looked at us as if we were from another planet! Dad held out his hand to the man. Dad said, "Hi, I'm Ken Washington, and I live here." The man took Dad's hand. He shook it a little, but didn't say a word. My dad shook the man's hand, and then he held out his hand to the woman. She turned away.

We could see that a big wooden trunk had split open. That was the loud crashing noise we had heard. We helped pick up the books that had spilled out. Then Dad and I helped the family with the rest of the suitcases and trunks. Soon we knew they didn't speak English.

At the end of the day, Mr. Saddok put his right hand over his heart, and then he nodded to us all. Later, we learned that the Saddoks were from Algeria. That was their Algerian way to say a sincere thank you.

Analyze

Use the rubric to evaluate Jack's story. Are all the traits of a good personal narrative there? Don't forget to evaluate your own story against the rubric on pages 8–9.

Personal Narrative **25**

Student Objectives

- Use a personal narrative rubric. (pp. 8–9)
- Share a published personal narrative. (p. 25)

Presentation Strategy Explain to students that all their hard work will go to waste if their work is messy and hard to read. If students are using a computer, they should choose a simple, easy-to-read font. Mention that their name and the title of the narrative should appear at the top of each page of their narrative, which can be set up with the header function in a word-processing program.

Reflecting on a Personal Narrative

Ask students to reflect on the experience of writing a personal narrative. Ask:

- What did you enjoy the most about writing your personal narrative?
- Which part was the most difficult for you?
- What did you learn about improving your writing from this experience?

Tech Tips
Digital Images and Audio

Reflect on Using Images and Sound Consider leading students to examine how working from an image or a sound early in their writing impacted the emotion within their personal narrative. Did they dig deeper into a memory or use stronger language? How does an image work differently from audio in expressing and evoking meaning? As important as it is for students to think with images and other multimodal texts as they prewrite and draft, reflecting on what that meant to their work helps them carry the practice into other writing tasks.

CCSS **Common Core State Standards** (pp. Z20–Z30)
Writing: W.4.4, W.4.6, W.4.10
Language: L.4.1f, L.4.3c
Speaking and Listening: SL.4.1a, SL.4.1b, SL.4.1c, SL.4.1d, SL.4.3, SL.4.6

Personal Narrative **T25**

Biographic Sketch Planner

WEEK 1

Day 1
Introduce
Biographic Sketch

Student Objectives
- Review the elements of a biographic sketch.
- Consider purpose and audience.
- Learn the traits of narrative writing.

Student Activities
- Read and discuss **What's in a Biographic Sketch?** *(p. 26)*
- Read and discuss **Why Write a Biographic Sketch?** *(p. 27)*
- Read **Linking Narrative Writing Traits to a Biographic Sketch.** *(p. 28)*

Day 2
Analyze
Close Reading of the Model

Student Objectives
- Read a model biographic sketch.

Student Activities
- Read **"Listening for a Living."** *(p. 29)*

Day 3
Analyze
Introduce the Rubric

Student Objectives
- Learn to read a rubric.

Student Activities
- Review **"Listening for a Living."** *(p. 29)*
- Read and discuss the **Biographic Sketch Rubric.** *(pp. 30–31)*

WEEK 2

Day 1
Write
Prewrite: Ideas

Student Objectives
- Read and understand a prewriting strategy.

Student Activities
- Read and discuss **Prewrite: Focus on Ideas.** *(p. 36)*
- Apply the prewriting strategy.

Day 2
Write
Prewrite: Organization

Student Objectives
- Create a Timeline to organize information.

Student Activities
- Read and discuss **Prewrite: Focus on Organization.** *(p. 37)*
- Reflect on the model Timeline.
- Apply the prewriting strategy to create a Timeline.
- Participate in a peer conference.

Day 3
Write
Draft: Organization

Student Objectives
- Use a Timeline to begin writing.

Student Activities
- Read and discuss **Draft: Focus on Organization.** *(p. 38)*
- Reflect on the model draft. *(p. 39)*
- Apply the drafting strategy by using a Timeline to write a draft.

WEEK 3

Day 1
Write
Revise: Word Choice

Student Objectives
- Revise to take out unnecessary words.

Student Activities
- Read and discuss **Revise: Focus on Word Choice.** *(p. 41)*
- Reflect on the model draft.
- Apply the revising strategy.
- Participate in a peer conference.

Day 2
Write
Revise: Sentence Fluency

Student Objectives
- Revise to combine short sentences.

Student Activities
- Read and discuss **Revise: Focus on Sentence Fluency.** *(p. 42)*
- Reflect on the model draft.
- Apply the revising strategy.

Note: Optional Revising Lessons are located at **www.sfw.z-b.com**

Day 3
Write
Edit: Conventions

Student Objectives
- Edit to make sure all verbs are correct.

Student Activities
- Read and discuss **Edit: Focus on Conventions.** *(p. 43)*
- Apply the editing strategy.

Note: Teach the Conventions mini-lessons *(pp. 44–45)* if needed.

Day 4 — Analyze: Close Reading for the Traits

Student Objectives
- Read a model biographic sketch.
- Use the biographic sketch rubric.
- Use the model biographic sketch to study Ideas, Organization, and Voice.

Student Activities
- Review **"Listening for a Living."** (p. 29)
- Review the rubric. (pp. 30–31)
- Read and discuss **Using the Rubric to Analyze the Model.** (pp. 32–33)

Day 5 — Analyze: Close Reading for the Traits

Student Objectives
- Read a model biographic sketch.
- Use the biographic sketch rubric.
- Use the model biographic sketch to study Word Choice, Sentence Fluency, and Conventions.

Student Activities
- Review **"Listening for a Living."** (p. 29)
- Read and discuss **Using the Rubric to Analyze the Model.** (pp. 34–35)

Day 4 — Write: Draft

Student Objectives
- Complete a draft.

Student Activities
- Finish the draft.
- Participate in a peer conference.

Day 5 — Write: Revise: Voice

Student Objectives
- Revise to use third-person point of view.

Student Activities
- Read and discuss **Revise: Focus on Voice.** (p. 40)
- Reflect on the model draft.
- Apply the revising strategy.

Day 4 — Write: Publish: +Presentation

Student Objectives
- Discuss preparation for publishing and presentation.
- Use a final editing checklist to publish their work.

Student Activities
- Read and discuss **Publish: +Presentation.** (p. 46)
- Apply the publishing strategy.

Day 5 — Write: Publish: +Presentation

Student Objectives
- Use a biographic sketch rubric.
- Share a published biographic sketch.

Student Activities
- Share their work.
- Use the rubric to reflect upon and evaluate the model and their own writing. (pp. 30–31, 47)

To complete the chapter in fewer days, combine the learning objectives and activities in a way that supports students as they write.

 Strategies for Writers Online

Go to **www.sfw.z-b.com** for additional online resources for students, teachers, and parents..

Online Writing Center

Provides IWB resources, assessments, interactive games and practice activities, videos, eBooks, and a virtual file cabinet.

Introduce
Biographic Sketch

Week 1 • Day 1

Student Objectives

- Review the elements of a biographic sketch. (p. 26)
- Consider purpose and audience. (p. 27)
- Learn the traits of narrative writing. (p. 28)

What's a Biographic Sketch?

Ask students to name magazines or television shows that introduce them to real people. Discuss reasons they enjoy learning about the lives of others. Point out that when a writer tells the story of some aspect of another person's life, this kind of narrative is called a biographic sketch.

What's in a Biographic Sketch?

Read and discuss the elements of a biographic sketch with students. Ask students why each of the elements is essential in a biographic sketch. (Basic Facts tell the person's background; Characteristics tell what the person is like; Accomplishments tell why the reader should be interested in the person; Interesting Details make the person come alive for the reader.)

Strategies for Writers Online
Go to **www.sfw.z-b.com** for additional online resources for students, teachers, and parents.

What's a Biographic Sketch?
It's a story written in third person that tells something important about someone else.

What's in a Biographic Sketch?

Basic Facts
Facts are important pieces of information, such as the person's first and last name, where he or she lives, and specific events that helped the person become who he or she is.

Characteristics
These are the special qualities that the person has, such as courage, determination, concern for others, or talents.

Accomplishments
This is what the person has achieved. It could be winning at sports, finding success as an artist, helping others, or discovering something new.

Interesting Details
These are interesting facts about the person, such as favorite activities, how the person feels about what he or she does, and any challenges the person has faced.

Narrative Text Exemplars (Biographic Sketch)

Davies, Jacqueline. *The Boy Who Drew Birds: A Story of John James Audubon.* Houghton Mifflin, 2004. John James Audubon loved the outdoors, especially birds. To pursue his passion, he roamed the woods around his home to observe and study wildlife. His interest in birds led him to become one of America's greatest painters of birds and wildlife.

Yoo, Paula. *Sixteen Years in Sixteen Seconds: The Sammy Lee Story.* Lee and Low, 2010. Yoo tells the story of Sammy Lee, an Asian American boy who was determined to overcome adversity. Not only did Sammy become the first Asian to win an Olympic gold medal for the United States, but the talented diver also fulfilled his father's dream by earning a medical degree from the University of Southern California.

Why write a Biographic Sketch?

People write biographic sketches for a lot of different reasons. Here are a few of them.

To Inspire
Some people do amazing things that I might like to do, too. It's interesting to learn how they got started, who helped them, and how they became successful.

To Admire
I may not want to do what other people have done, but I can look up to them. I might want to do a biographic sketch of a person who I think is special in some way.

To Inform
I can learn all kinds of things by finding out about another person. I might find out what it feels like to come here from another country or how someone makes music with a computer. Finding out about other people can lead to fascinating discoveries.

Biographic Sketch **27**

Why write a Biographic Sketch?

Direct students to read and discuss the reasons for writing a biographic sketch listed on page 27. Remind students that all writing has a purpose. Writers have many reasons to write, and they write for a variety of audiences. These authentic purposes influence how the writing develops. Someone writing to inspire will use words and a tone that connect with the reader's feelings to motivate the reader. A writer who is writing out of admiration will focus on showing the reader why someone is special. A person writing to inform will include many facts and details that help the reader learn about the subject, find out something new, or discover interesting connections to other people and events. Encourage students to choose their own reasons for writing a biographic sketch and think about how these reasons will affect the tone and focus of their writing.

Ryan, Pam Muñoz. *Riding Freedom*. Scholastic Paperbacks, 1999. *Riding Freedom* is a fictionalized biography of Charlotte Parkhurt, a girl who knew that the world of the 1860s held more opportunities for boys than girls. So she cut off her hair, acted as a boy, and became the first woman to vote in the United States.

Ryan, Pam Muñoz and Brian Selznick. *When Marian Sang: The True Recital of Marian Anderson*. Scholastic Press, 2002. The talented singer Marian Anderson was often overlooked because of her race. This story chronicles her life, from her days as a struggling artist to her performance at the Metropolitan Opera.

CCSS **Common Core State Standards** (pp. Z20–Z30)
Language: L.4.3c
Speaking and Listening: SL.4.1a, SL.4.1b, SL.4.1c, SL.4.1d, SL.4.3, SL.4.6

Introduce
Biographic Sketch

Linking Narrative Writing Traits to a Biographic Sketch

Share a true story about another person with students. Ask students to listen to how you refer to the person you are talking about. Tell your story using as many third-person pronouns as possible.

Then ask students:

- Was I talking about myself? (No.)

- Was I talking about you? (No.)

- Was I talking about a third person who isn't here? (Yes.)

Explain to students that this is called the *third-person point of view.* Then ask students which words you used to refer to this third person. (Possible responses: the person's name, *he* or *she,* and *him* or *her*) Explain that when you share a true story or information about another person, you are sharing a biographic sketch. A biographic sketch is told from the third-person point of view.

Read page 28 aloud to help students understand that they will follow Jack as he models using the writing process and the narrative writing traits together.

Linking Narrative Writing Traits to a Biographic Sketch

In this chapter, you will write a story about something that happened to someone else. This type of narrative writing is called a biographic sketch. Jack will guide you through the stages of the writing process: Prewrite, Draft, Revise, Edit, and Publish. In each stage, Jack will show you important writing strategies that are linked to the Narrative Writing Traits below.

Narrative Writing Traits

 Ideas
- a topic that is just the right size, not too big or too small
- details and facts that develop the narrative

 Organization
- a natural and logical sequence
- a strong beginning and a satisfying ending
- transitions that signal the sequence of events

 Voice
- a voice and tone that are perfect for the writing
- dialogue that, when used, sounds just right for the characters

 Word Choice
- concrete words and phrases that describe the characters and events

 **Sentence Fluency**
- a variety of sentence lengths to make the story flow smoothly

 **Conventions**
- no or few errors in spelling, grammar, punctuation, and capitalization

Before you write, read Jacob Gadski's biographic sketch on the next page. Then use the biographic sketch rubric on pages 30–31 to decide how well he did. (You might want to look back at What's in a Biographic Sketch? on page 26, too!)

Narrative Writing Traits in a Biographic Sketch

 **Ideas** The writer focuses on one person. Interesting and accurate details help make the subject come to life for the reader.

 **Organization** The writer presents the events of the subject's life in chronological order. Time-order transition words help guide the reader.

 **Voice** Using just the right voice shows respect for the subject and helps the writer better connect with the audience. Realistic dialogue, if used, conveys the subject's personality.

Listening for a Living

by Jacob Gadski

characteristic

Tim Farley should be called "Ears" Farley. That's because <u>he listens</u> all day long. In fact, he listens for a living.

basic facts

Mr. Farley works in a city called Sprintfield. Like many cities, Sprintfield has a lot of noise. Several years ago, in 2003, Mr. Farley saw an ad for a job as a "noise detective." Right away, he decided it was the job for him.

First he went for an interview. He learned the purpose of the job. It was to measure and record exactly how much noise was coming from different places in the city. He would go all around Sprintfield with a sound meter, a little machine that measured decibel levels. Decibels are units that measure sound.

interesting details

Mr. Farley got the job. During the spring of 2004, he worked along the freeway and on other roads. First, he gathered information. Later, he focused on sounds above 80 decibels. These sounds are really loud! In fact, they are louder than in most places in the United States.

accomplishments

After Mr. Farley had been working for a few months, he had a lot of information. By fall of 2004, he knew the city's major sources of noise. The worst source was the sound of car and truck traffic. The second major source was the sound of trains. The third major source was the sound of commercial and industrial activities. Soon, Mr. Farley's job included finding out how to solve the noise problems.

Mr. Farley loved to solve problems. But he learned that some were not easy to fix. In 2005 he recommended that the city put up walls to help block noise. The high walls were ugly. In 2006 he recommended that the city also plant trees and shrubs. These were attractive, but they did not block noise very well.

interesting detail

accomplishments

Mr. Farley keeps listening and looking for the answers to the city's noise problems. When it comes to his job, he is definitely "all ears"!

Word Choice The writer carefully chooses precise, concrete words and phrases to describe the subject. The language is never vague or confusing.

Sentence Fluency The writing is a pleasure to both read and hear read aloud. A variety of long and short sentences gives the writing energy and makes it engaging.

Conventions The writing has been carefully edited for spelling, grammar, punctuation, and capitalization errors. The reader finds the biographic sketch easy to read and understand, as all subjects and verbs agree and all forms of the verb *be* are used correctly.

Analyze
Close Reading of the Model

Student Objectives

- Read a model biographic sketch. *(p. 29)*

Read the Model

Read "Listening for a Living" on page 29 aloud. Before you read, remind students to listen for the writing traits outlined on page 28.

Elements of a Biographic Sketch

Use the notes on the model to discuss the various elements of a biographic sketch. Ask students if Jacob's introduction clearly states the subject of the sketch. Is the introduction engaging? How does Jacob organize the events in the biographic sketch? Does his organization help students follow along? Do students feel Jacob included enough interesting details and accomplishments to help them get a good sense of who Tim Farley is and what he does? You may wish to have students refer back to What's in a Biographic Sketch? on page 26 for review.

CCSS **C**ommon **C**ore **S**tate **S**tandards (pp. Z20–Z30)
Writing: W.4.6
Language: L.4.3c
Speaking and Listening: SL.4.1a, SL.4.1b, SL.4.1c, SL.4.1d, SL.4.2, SL.4.3, SL.4.6

Analyze
Introduce the Rubric

Week 1 • Day 3

Student Objectives

• Learn to read a rubric. *(pp. 30–31)*

Introduce the Rubric

Explain the Rubric Explain that a rubric is a tool that helps you plan, improve, and evaluate a piece of writing. Tell students that a rubric helps a writer focus on key elements, or traits, in writing (**Ideas, Organization, Voice, Word Choice, Sentence Fluency, Conventions,** and **Presentation**).

The 6-point rubric on pages 30–31 can be used to evaluate a biographic sketch. Draw students' attention to the six columns to explain how the scoring system works. Explain that column 6 describes a very good biographic sketch, one that has received the highest score in all categories. This is what students should strive for in their own writing.

Discuss the Rubric Guide students in a discussion of the rubric. Note how the descriptors vary as you move from column to column.

Remind students to keep the rubric in mind when they write their own biographic sketch and again when they revise it.

Online Writing Center

Provides a variety of **interactive rubrics,** including 4-, 5-, and 6-point models.

Biographic Sketch Rubric

Use this rubric to analyze the model. Then use it to plan and score your own biographic sketch.

	6	**5**	**4**	
Ideas	The sketch tells important events in the person's life. Interesting details make the subject come alive.	Most of the details are interesting. Most make the subject real for the reader.	More memorable details would make the subject real for the reader.	
Organization	Events are arranged in a sequence that unfolds naturally. Transition words make the sequence of events clear.	Events are arranged in a sequence that unfolds naturally. Transition words could be added in one or two places.	A few events are not in a natural sequence. Transition words are too few or are overused.	
Voice	It is clear that the writer respects the subject. The voice connects with the audience.	The voice shows that the writer respects the subject. The voice connects with the audience most of the time.	The voice sounds sincere most of the time. It fails to connect with the audience in places.	
Word Choice	Each word has a job to do, so no unnecessary words are used.	One or two unnecessary words distract the reader.	Some sentences are too wordy, distracting the reader.	
Sentence Fluency	There is a balance of short and long sentences, which makes writing clear and easy to read.	Most sentences vary in length. One or two longer sentences could be shortened.	The sentences are clear, but several sentences in a row are too long or too short.	
Conventions	Subjects and verbs agree. Forms of the verb *be* are used correctly.	There are a few minor errors in agreement and forms of *be*, but they do not confuse the reader.	Some errors in verb agreement and forms of *be* confuse the reader.	

✛Presentation The sketch is neat and legible.

CCSS Common Core State Standards
Biographic Sketch

Writing in the Narrative text type engages the Common Core State Standards for Narrative writing. Each of the rubrics and strategies for the biographic sketch is solidly based on the Narrative Writing standards, and several strategies and exercises echo Speaking & Listening, Reading/Literature, and Language standards as well. The Ideas and Organization rubrics are reflected in standard **W.4.3a,** which addresses focusing on the important events in one person's life, and presenting interesting details and events in a natural and logical order. Standard **W.4.3b** lists several narrative techniques, including dialogue and description, which resonate throughout the Ideas, Organization, Voice, and Word Choice traits. The

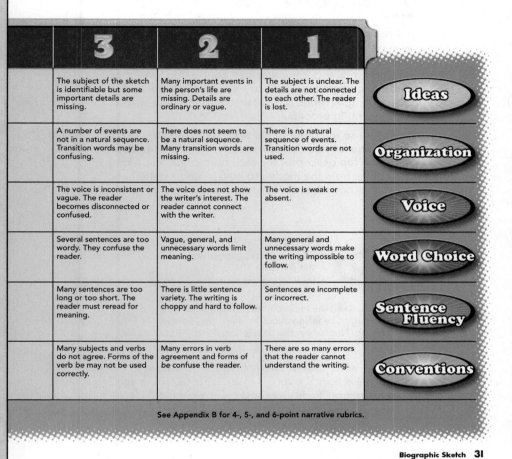

	3	2	1	
	The subject of the sketch is identifiable but some important details are missing.	Many important events in the person's life are missing. Details are ordinary or vague.	The subject is unclear. The details are not connected to each other. The reader is lost.	**Ideas**
	A number of events are not in a natural sequence. Transition words may be confusing.	There does not seem to be a natural sequence. Many transition words are missing.	There is no natural sequence of events. Transition words are not used.	**Organization**
	The voice is inconsistent or vague. The reader becomes disconnected or confused.	The voice does not show the writer's interest. The reader cannot connect with the writer.	The voice is weak or absent.	**Voice**
	Several sentences are too wordy. They confuse the reader.	Vague, general, and unnecessary words limit meaning.	Many general and unnecessary words make the writing impossible to follow.	**Word Choice**
	Many sentences are too long or too short. The reader must reread for meaning.	There is little sentence variety. The writing is choppy and hard to follow.	Sentences are incomplete or incorrect.	**Sentence Fluency**
	Many subjects and verbs do not agree. Forms of the verb *be* may not be used correctly.	Many errors in verb agreement and forms of *be* confuse the reader.	There are so many errors that the reader cannot understand the writing.	**Conventions**

See Appendix B for 4-, 5-, and 6-point narrative rubrics.

Find Evidence in the Model

Small-Group Collaboration Assign students to small groups and tell them to evaluate the model using the rubric. Assign one person in each group to record the group's findings and one person to report the findings to the class. Instruct students to score the model for each trait based on evidence in the text. Remind students to read closely to identify examples to support their high or low scores. Note: Although the models were written to score high in each trait, students should not assume each trait would receive a 6, the top score.

Teacher-Led Discussion Bring the class back together, and have the reporters present their findings and scores. Prompt groups to provide evidence and examples for their scores from the model as needed.

Additional Rubrics

Appendix B includes 4-, 5-, and 6-point rubrics that can be used with any piece of narrative writing. The rubrics are also available as blackline masters in the back of this Teacher Edition.

Organization rubric also reflects standard **W.4.3c,** which emphasizes the use of transition words to guide the reader from one event to the next. Standard **W.4.3d** is reflected in the Word Choice rubric, which focuses on the careful choice of words to clearly and vividly describe the subject and his or her life and accomplishments.

Standards **L.4.1** and **L.4.2** are clearly reflected throughout the editing pages of the chapter, while standard **W.4.6** echoes through the Narrative unit, as students are encouraged to take full advantage of the word processing programs available to them.

CCSS **Common Core State Standards** (pp. Z20–Z30)
Writing: W.4.6
Language: L.4.3c
Speaking and Listening: SL.4.1a, SL.4.1b, SL.4.1c, SL.4.1d, SL.4.2, SL.4.3, SL.4.6

Analyze
Close Reading for the Traits

Week 1 • Day 4

Student Objectives

- Read a model biographic sketch. *(p. 29)*
- Use the biographic sketch rubric. *(pp. 30–31)*
- Use the model biographic sketch to study **Ideas, Organization,** and **Voice.** *(pp. 32–33)*

Find Evidence in the Model

Evaluate the Model Have students turn to pages 32–33. Explain that these pages show how the model on page 29 uses the writing traits described in the rubric.

Read each section with students. Use questions such as the following to discuss each section. Be sure students can back up their answers with examples from the model.

Discuss Audience, Task, Purpose Ask students one or more of the following questions as they analyze the model:

- **Audience** Who is the audience? (Possible response: all readers)

- **Task** How does Jacob Gadski make the person in the sketch seem real? (Possible response: He includes interesting details that make the person come alive.)

- **Purpose** What was Jacob Gadski's purpose for writing this story? (Possible response: to tell about the life of an interesting person)

Using the Rubric to Analyze the Model
Biographic Sketch

Did you notice that the model on page 29 points out some key elements of a biographic sketch? As he wrote "Listening for a Living," Jacob Gadski used these elements to help him write about another person. He also used the 6-point rubric on pages 30–31 to plan, draft, revise, and edit the writing. A rubric is a great tool to evaluate writing during the writing process.

Now let's use the same rubric to score the model. To do this, we'll focus on each trait separately, starting with Ideas. We'll use the top descriptor for each trait (column 6), along with examples from the model, to help us understand how the traits work together. How would you score Jacob on each trait?

 Ideas
- The sketch tells important events in the person's life.
- Interesting details make the subject come alive.

Jacob tells all about the important events and when they happened. He begins by telling about an interesting person, Mr. Tim Farley, and his job. Notice how the details help bring the story to life.

> Mr. Farley works in a city called Sprintfield. Like many cities, Sprintfield has a lot of noise. Several years ago, in 2003, Mr. Farley saw an ad for a job as a "noise detective." Right away, he decided it was the job for him.

32 Narrative Writing

English Language Learners

BEGINNING

Identifying Characteristics Show a photo of a person who students know. Say, *Describe the person. What does he or she do?* If students supply one-word answers, model a few descriptive sentences using their answers. For example, *She is Mrs. Stewart. She is the lunch lady. She is friendly. She helps us clean our tables.* Write the sentences on the board and have students repeat them. Then ask students to write the sentences on paper. Have students repeat the activity with a photo of a family member.

INTERMEDIATE

Describing a Famous Person Have students choose a famous person. Ask each student to write answers to the following questions. *Who is the famous person? Why is the person famous? What are some of his or her accomplishments?* Have students discuss their answers with a partner.

Organization
- Events are arranged in a sequence that unfolds naturally.
- Transition words make the sequence of events clear.

The writer uses transition words to signal when things happen. The transition words *during, first,* and *later* in this example make the sequence of events easy to follow.

> Mr. Farley got the job. During the spring of 2004, he worked along the freeway and on other roads. First, he gathered information. Later, he focused on sounds above 80 decibels.

Voice
- It is clear that the writer respects the subject.
- The voice connects with the audience.

Right away the reader can see that Jacob respects his subject. He explains why he suggests a different name for the subject.

> Tim Farley should be called "Ears" Farley. That's because he listens all day long. In fact, he listens for a living.

Biographic Sketch 33

Discuss the Traits Ask students one or more of the following questions to discuss the traits in the model.

Ideas Which detail do you think does the best job of making Tim Farley come alive for the reader? Why? (Possible response: *Mr. Farley loved to solve problems.* This detail explains why he works hard at his job.)

Organization What other transitions or temporal words does Jacob use to show the passage of time? (Possible responses: *Several years ago, During the spring of 2004, After Mr. Farley had been working for a few months*)

Voice Why is Jacob's voice appropriate for his subject and audience? (Possible response: Showing respect for the subject helps the reader understand why he or she could care about Tim Farley.)

ADVANCED
Personality Descriptions As a class, brainstorm different personality traits, such as *determined, grumpy, inquisitive, shy,* and so on. Have partners think of a person who exemplifies each personality trait and tell why they think so.

ADVANCED HIGH
Role-Play Assign partners a personality trait and have them write a role-play in which they can demonstrate the meaning of the word. For example, if the trait is *determined,* the students might act out a situation in which one student has a problem (such as being locked inside a room or working on a difficult math assignment) and tries several different solutions before succeeding. You might ask the class to use the clues in each role-play to guess the trait that was assigned to each pair.

CCSS **Common Core State Standards** (pp. Z20–Z30)
Writing: W.4.3b, W.4.3d
Language: L.4.3a, L.4.3c, L.4.6
Speaking and Listening: SL.4.1a, SL.4.1b, SL.4.1c, SL.4.1d, SL.4.3, SL.4.6

Analyze
Close Reading for the Traits

Week 1 • Day 5

Student Objectives

- Read a model biographic sketch. (p. 29)
- Use the biographic sketch rubric. (pp. 30–31)
- Use the model biographic sketch to study **Word Choice, Sentence Fluency,** and **Conventions**. (pp. 34–35)

Discuss the Traits Ask students one or more of the following questions to discuss the traits in the model.

 Why is it important in good writing to avoid using unnecessary words? (**Possible response: Too many words can bore or confuse the reader.**)

 Find another passage with an interesting mix of sentence lengths. (**Possible response:** *Mr. Farley got the job. During the spring of 2004, he worked along the freeway and other roads. First he gathered information.*)

Conventions Can you find any errors in Jacob's biographic sketch? Do all his subjects and verbs agree? (**Possible response: There are no errors in the sketch.**)

Strategies for Writers Online
Go to **www.sfw.z-b.com** for additional online resources for students, teachers, and parents.

Using the Rubric to Analyze the Model
Biographic Sketch

Word Choice
- Each word has a job to do, so no unnecessary words are used.

The writer does a good job of telling about Mr. Farley without using a lot of unnecessary words. Jacob has chosen his words carefully, and they work well.

> Mr. Farley loved to solve problems. But he learned that some were not easy to fix. In 2005 he recommended that the city put up walls to help block noise. The high walls were ugly. In 2006 he recommended that the city also plant trees and shrubs.

Sentence Fluency
- There is a balance of short and long sentences, which makes the writing clear and easy to read.

Jacob uses lots of different kinds of sentences in his biographic sketch. For example, some sentences are longer and some are shorter. Usually, long and short sentences follow each other. This helps the story flow smoothly. It makes the biographic sketch easy to read, too.

> First he went for an interview. He learned the purpose of the job. It was to measure and record exactly how much noise was coming from different places in the city.

Tech Tips — Slide Shows

Create Slide Shows Perspective and point of view are important elements of multimodal writing. Sequences of slides in VoiceThread or other slide shows often pair spoken word with image and motion. This "layering" works to communicate more than what we'd have with just one "mode" of writing. As students prepare to write their biographic sketch, use these elements, perhaps when building content on a PowerPoint slide, to discuss how the meaning of a composition changes as we "layer" the writing.

See **www.sfw.z-b.com** for further information about and links to these websites and tools.

Conventions

- Subjects and verbs agree.
- Forms of the verb *be* are used correctly.

All the subjects and verbs agree in number. Singular subjects have singular verbs, and plural subjects have plural verbs. In these sentences, the subject, *source*, is singular, so the verb, *was*, is also singular.

The worst source was the sound of car and truck traffic. The second major source was the sound of trains. The third major source was the sound of the commercial and industrial activities.

⊹Presentation The sketch is neat and legible.

My Turn!

Now it's my turn to write a biographic sketch! I'll use the 6-point rubric on pages 30–31 and good writing strategies to help me. Read along to see how I do it.

Differentiating Instruction

ENRICHMENT

Preparing for an Interview Challenge students to write a series of interview questions for the model story, "Listening for a Living." What questions do they think Jacob asked Tim Farley? What other aspects of Mr. Farley's job or career could the author have investigated? What additional questions could he have asked to get that information?

REINFORCEMENT

Using Questions to Gather Information Help students understand how to ask personal interview questions. Review *who, what, when, where, why,* and *how* questions. Model using each type of question in a personal interview. Then have students practice asking each other *who, what, when, where, why,* and *how* questions.

⊹Presentation Point out that excellent writing cannot be enjoyed or understood if it is messy to the point of being illegible. Explain to students that neat handwriting, even margins, and indented paragraphs are some of the features they must consider when writing their final copies. Also remind students that their biographic sketches will need a title, and their name must be at the top of each page.

One way to ensure neat and legible writing is to use a computer. Encourage students to type their sketches using a word processing program if possible.

Think About the Traits

Once students have thoroughly discussed the model, ask them which traits they think are most important in a biographic sketch and have them explain why. (Possible response: Ideas are very important, as details about the subject are what pull the reader in. Organization is very important because events in a person's life must be presented in a logical order.)

CCSS Common Core State Standards (pp. Z20–Z30)
Writing: W.4.6, W.4.8
Language: L.4.3c
Speaking and Listening: SL.4.1a, SL.4.1b, SL.4.1c, SL.4.1d, SL.4.3, SL.4.6

Write
Biographic Sketch

Week 2 • Day 1

Student Objectives

• Read and understand a prewriting strategy. *(p. 36)*

Prewrite

Focus on (Ideas)

Prepare for an Interview Explain that Jack first selected something in his life that he was interested in—the hand-carved stone bear. This led him to write about the artist who created the bear. Remind students that when they write about something they are interested in, it is easier for them to get their readers interested, too.

Asking Questions Review the six kinds of questions students should ask to gather information: *who, what, where, when, why,* and *how.* Discuss the questions Jack created to send to the Inuit artist. Can students think of any other questions that would be helpful to ask? Review the Writer's Term box. Then instruct students to write interview questions of their own.

✎ Writer's Term _____

Interview An interview does not have to occur face-to-face. Many interviews occur over the phone or via e-mail.

Online Writing Center

Provides **interactive graphic organizers** as well as a variety of graphic organizers in PDF format.

Prewrite

Focus on (Ideas)

The Rubric Says   Interesting details make the subject come alive.

Writing Strategy   Make a list of interesting questions for an interview.

My mom has a little stone bear carved by an Inuit artist. I have always wondered about the person who made it.

When my teacher asked us to write a biographic sketch, I decided to write about the Inuit artist who made that stone bear. I knew I had to gather information, so I sent the artist an e-mail with interview questions. This will help me get information about the object and give me more than just simple details like the artist's name.

✎ Writer's Term _____

Interview
An **interview** is the process of asking questions of another person and listening to and recording that person's answers.

Questions for My Interview

✔ What kinds of objects do you make?

✔ Why do you like to carve?

✔ When did you first start to carve in stone?

✔ How did you learn to carve?

✔ What skills do you need to be a stone carver?

Write

Think about a person you would like to write about. List interesting questions you could ask. Then interview the person.

36   Narrative Writing

English Language Learners

BEGINNING/INTERMEDIATE

Timeline Ask students to tell about a common routine, such as preparing for bed or a morning routine at school. Draw a timeline on the board. Label the timeline using actual times or numbers to indicate order. Then ask, *What happens first, next,* and so on. Then have volunteers use the timeline to tell about the routine again.

ADVANCED/ADVANCED HIGH

Timeline Have students think of an event that happened recently that they would like to share with a friend. Introduce the Timeline graphic organizer. Ask them to write the events in order on the timeline, including labels to indicate time. Then have them trade timelines with a partner. The partner should follow along on the timeline as the first student tells the story.

Prewrite

The Rubric Says   Events are arranged in a sequence that unfolds naturally.

Writing Strategy   Make a Timeline to organize the important events.

I know from the rubric that organization is important. I want to find a natural order for my biographic sketch. During the interview, Mr. Aniksak, the artist, told me when the main events of his life happened and why they are important. If I put the events in the order in which he experienced them, my paper will make sense to the reader. I can put these events on a Timeline to help me stay organized.

Writer's Term

Timeline
A **Timeline** is a graph that shows events in the order in which they happened. A Timeline also shows dates.

Timeline

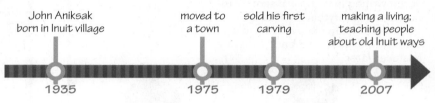

John Aniksak born in Inuit village	moved to a town	sold his first carving	making a living; teaching people about old Inuit ways
1935	1975	1979	2007

Analyze

Look at Jack's questions and Timeline. Is there enough information? Think of a few more interview questions to ask.

Write

Look at your interview notes. Use a Timeline to arrange events in a sequence that unfolds naturally.

Biographic Sketch   **37**

Collaborative Conferencing

PEER TO PEER   Have partners exchange Timelines. Tell students to write three comments on a separate sheet of paper regarding the organization or completeness of their partner's Timeline.

PEER GROUPS   Have students give a brief summary of their interviews and share their Timelines with the group. Each group member comments on whether all the information from the interview seems to be represented in the Timeline.

TEACHER-LED   Meet with individual students and discuss how well their Timelines represent their notes from the interview.

Write
Biographic Sketch

Week 2 • Day 2

Student Objectives

- Create a Timeline to organize information. *(p. 37)*

Prewrite

Focus on  **Organization**

Create a Timeline Read page 37 aloud. Explain that a Timeline is a graphic organizer that helps writers organize events chronologically. (Go to **www.sfw.z-b.com** for the downloadable graphic organizer.) Then when the writer begins writing, the information is already in an accurate and logical order.

Review Jack's Timeline with students. Help them understand how he arranged his gathered information along the line in chronological order according to year. Tell students that they will create a Timeline of their own using the information they gathered from their interviews.

Writer's Term

Timeline A Timeline is a great visual tool that helps a writer organize and "see" how much time has passed between events in the subject's life. Students should figure out how to space the segments of time. The more time has passed between events, the greater the distance between the plotted points on the Timeline.

CCSS Common Core State Standards (pp. Z20–Z30)
Writing: W.4.3a, W.4.3b, W.4.4, W.4.5, W.4.6, W.4.8, W.4.10
Language: L.4.3c, L.4.6
Speaking and Listening: SL.4.1a, SL.4.1b, SL.4.1c, SL.4.1d, SL.4.3, SL.4.4, SL.4.6

Write
Biographic Sketch

Week 2 • Day 3

Student Objectives

• Use a Timeline to begin writing. *(pp. 38–39)*

Draft

Focus on  Organization

Begin a Draft Ask students what a draft is. How does it differ from a finished piece of writing? Be sure they understand that a draft is a temporary or "rough" form of a written piece. It will be changed and corrected several times before it is finished.

Read page 38 and the Writer's Term box aloud. Ask volunteers for additional time-order transition words, which you write on the board. Tell students to keep time-order words in mind as they review their Timelines prior to drafting. (See page 487 for a list of transitions.)

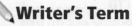
Writer's Term

Transition Words Transition words such as *first, then, soon after,* and *during* are like helpful signs along the road—they help guide the reader from the beginning of the reading "road trip" to the end.

Online Writing Center

 Provides an **interactive writing pad** for drafting, revising, editing, and publishing.

Draft

Focus on **Organization**

The Rubric Says Events are arranged in a sequence that unfolds naturally. Transition words make the sequence of events clear.

Writing Strategy Organize information using transition words.

Now it's time to tell the whole story. I will use the answers that Mr. Aniksak e-mailed back and my Timeline to write a draft. I am going to use my Timeline to make sure I include all the important events and when they happened. The rubric says I need to arrange the events in a sequence that unfolds naturally. I will use transition words and dates to organize the events.

Right now I'm not going to worry about writing in complete sentences or whether everything I write is spelled perfectly. I know I'll have a chance to fix grammar and spelling mistakes later.

Writer's Term

Transition Words

Transition words make a sequence of events clear. They help the writing move naturally from one event to the next.

Here are some transition words:

**after   during   finally   first   later
now   soon   then   until**

38 Narrative Writing

Differentiating Instruction

ENRICHMENT

In-Depth Interview Have students review their notes from their interviews and think of at least three follow-up questions to elicit additional information. Students should set up a follow-up interview with their subject and then incorporate the new information into their notes and Timelines.

REINFORCEMENT

Practice Using Transitions Write the following sentences on the board: *I awoke. I dressed and made my bed. I felt very full, so I knew a walk would do me good. I was ready to go. My legs were so tired that I sat on a park bench and watched some pigeons.* Have students add these transitions to the sentences: *Within ten minutes; Two hours later; At dawn; After a few moments; After a huge breakfast.*

[DRAFT]

Carving Art from Stone

John Aniksak carves stone bears, dear, seals, and other animals. He was not always a stone carver, though. Mr. Aniksak was born in an Inuit village in 1935. He and his family are from Canada. The Inuit people have lived in Canada for a very long time. It was a very different kind of life. You would be surprised. He lived very far from roads, stores, and factorys. In 1975, Mr. Aniksak moved to a town. He had to get use to a new way of life. He need a new way to earn a living. He took up carving. He found and chose stone. He learn about carving tools. He is also able to use many skills from his days in the wilderness. His knowledge of artic animals were especially importent. Mr. Aniksak learned his new skill well. In 1979, he sold his first carving, a seal. Everyone who sees his animals really like them. Many of his pieces have be sold. People from all over the country buy his carvings now.

transition words

Analyze

Are the events in Jack's draft organized in a sequence that unfolds naturally? Which transition words help make the sequence of events clear?

Write

Use your interview notes and Timeline to write your own draft. Remember to use transition words.

Biographic Sketch 39

Collaborative Conferencing

PEER TO PEER Have partners exchange drafts. Each student suggests two transitions that could be added to his or her partner's draft.

PEER GROUPS Have students read their drafts aloud to the group. Each student in the group suggests a transition word that could replace one of the transition words in the reader's draft. The reader may decide whether to take the suggestions or keep the original transitions.

TEACHER-LED Meet with individuals who are having trouble adding transitions to their drafts. Point out passages that could use transitions and give students options to choose from.

Write
Biographic Sketch

Week 2 • Day 4

Student Objectives

• Complete a draft. (p. 39)

Continue Drafting Read Jack's draft on page 39 aloud. Then instruct students to refer to Jack's Timeline on page 37. Ask them if Jack followed his Timeline. Did he leave out any important or interesting information?

Besides the transitions highlighted on page 39, can students find any places where Jack indicated time passing? Discuss other ways Jack might have indicated the order of events in his biographic sketch. For example, he might have written *four years later* instead of giving a specific date. Remind students to use a variety of transitions in their writing to show the order of events.

Use Your Own Words Tell students to always use their own words when drafting. Explain that using someone else's words *as their own* is called plagiarism, and it is not acceptable. Make sure students understand that if they use their subject's exact words in a biographic sketch, the words should have quotation marks around them.

CCSS **C**ommon **C**ore **S**tate **S**tandards (pp. Z20–Z30)
Writing: W.4.3a, W.4.3b, W.4.3c, W.4.4, W.4.5, W.4.6, W.4.8, W.4.10
Language: L.4.3c, L.4.6
Speaking and Listening: SL.4.1a, SL.4.1b, SL.4.1c, SL.4.1d, SL.4.3, SL.4.6

Write
Biographic Sketch

Week 2 • Day 5

Student Objectives

• Revise to use third-person point of view. (p. 40)

Revise

Focus on Voice

Third-Person Point of View Read Jack's words at the top of page 40 aloud. Remind students that the purpose of a biographic sketch is to inform the reader about a person's life. Keeping oneself out of a biographic sketch keeps the subject clear and shows respect for the person.

Have a volunteer read Jack's draft excerpt. Guide students in a discussion about how using third person helps Jack connect with his readers and show proper respect for Mr. Aniksak.

Writer's Term
Third-Person Point of View
When writers use only third-person pronouns in their writing, they show respect by staying out of the story. It is equally important that writers avoid using the second-person pronouns *you* and *yours*. Although the goal is to connect with the reader, a biographic sketch is truly only about the chosen subject.

 Strategies for Writers Online
Go to **www.sfw.z-b.com** for additional online resources for students, teachers, and parents.

Revise   Focus on Voice

The Rubric Says   It is clear that the writer respects the subject. The voice connects with the audience.

Writing Strategy   Use the third-person point of view.

Writer's Term
Third-Person Point of View
Writers use **third-person point of view** to tell about the experiences of others and to show that they are not part of the story. For third person, we use the person's name and words such as **he, she, him, her, his, hers, they, them,** and **theirs**.

My biographic sketch is about Mr. Aniksak. That means I need to take myself out of the writing and use third-person point of view. The rubric says that my sketch should show respect for the subject, Mr. Aniksak, and should connect to the audience. So I will use events from Mr. Aniksak's life to show why he is a special artist.

[DRAFT]

used third-person point of view

John Aniksak carves stone bears, dear, seals, and other animals. He was not always a stone carver, though.

Write
Read your draft. Change any words if needed to make sure you have used third-person point of view throughout your draft.

40 Narrative Writing

English Language Learners

BEGINNING/INTERMEDIATE
Third-Person Point of View Review usage of the third-person pronouns *she, he, they, her, him,* and *them*. Give several simple examples, such as *He is from Japan. She was a scientist. No one believed them.* Write other examples on the board, but do not include the pronouns. Have Beginning ELLs fill in the appropriate pronouns, and ask Intermediate ELLs to check for mistakes.

ADVANCED/ADVANCED HIGH
Avoid Unnecessary Words Review third-person personal pronouns. Give each student a short newspaper article. Have them underline compound or complex sentences. Discuss the varied sentence lengths within the article. Finally, have students rewrite it using pronouns in place of people's names.

Revise
Focus on Word Choice

The Rubric Says	Each word has a job to do, so no unnecessary words are used.
Writing Strategy	Take out any words that are not needed.

I reread my story and noticed that some parts were unclear. I remembered the rubric said that each word has a job to do. I should choose each word carefully. Wordy writing can be confusing to readers. I looked for unnecessary words to take out of my sketch.

[DRAFT]

took out unnecessary words

Today he still loves his work ~~as a carver.~~ He ~~still~~ makes his living by carving animals and ~~he also~~ uses ~~his carved animals~~ them to teach people about the old Inuit way of life.

Analyze
Look at Jack's revisions. How does removing unnecessary words improve his writing?

Write
Read your draft again. Take out any words that are not needed.

Biographic Sketch 41

Collaborative Conferencing

PEER TO PEER Have partners exchange drafts. Students circle, in pencil, up to three words they think are unnecessary or phrases that could be replaced with something shorter.

PEER GROUPS Have students pass their drafts around the group. Each student circles, in pencil, a word or phrase that he or she feels is unnecessary. When students get their drafts back, they may make edits to remove one or more of the words and discuss their edits with the group.

TEACHER-LED Meet with pairs of students. Have each student read his or her draft aloud. Prompt students with suggestions if they are having trouble pointing out unnecessary words in their partner's draft.

Write
Biographic Sketch

Week 3 • Day 1

Student Objectives
- Revise to take out unnecessary words. *(p. 41)*

Revise

Focus on  Word Choice

Avoid Unnecessary Words Explain that repeated or unnecessary words are like carrying around a large number of pennies. Just as the pennies weigh a person down, excess words weigh the writing down. A person could have the same amount of money simply by holding two quarters rather than fifty pennies that keep falling and rolling away. In the same way, one or two precise and descriptive words are much more effective than a number of vague or unnecessary words.

Read Jack's words at the top of page 41. Then have one volunteer read Jack's draft excerpt prior to his revisions. Have a second volunteer read it with the revisions made. Guide students in a discussion about how much clearer and smoother Jack's writing is after his changes. Tell students that they are now to remove any unnecessary or repeated words from their drafts and replace them with clearer, more precise words.

CCSS **Common Core State Standards** (pp. Z20–Z30)
Writing: W.4.3a, W.4.3d, W.4.4, W.4.5, W.4.10
Language: L.4.3a, L.4.3c, L.4.6
Speaking and Listening: SL.4.1a, SL.4.1b, SL.4.1c, SL.4.1d, SL.4.3, SL.4.6

Write
Biographic Sketch

Week 3 • Day 2

Student Objectives

• Revise to combine short sentences. (p. 42)

Revise

Focus on  Sentence Fluency

Improve Flow Explain to students that good writing should flow smoothly, have an energy that keeps the reader interested, and easily move the reader along from the beginning to the end. When many short sentences are used in a row, the rhythm of the writing becomes choppy and inconsistent. Readers find choppy reading difficult to enjoy and connect with. Explain that good writers use a variety of sentence lengths to give their writing energy and flow.

Read Jack's words at the top of page 42. Then have two volunteers read the draft excerpt before and after Jack's revisions. Ask:

• What has Jack's revision done to the flow of his writing? (Possible response: The flow feels more natural and less choppy.)

Point out that this revision did not change the information—it simply created smoother writing that is easier and more enjoyable to read.

Online Writing Center

Provides **interactive proofreading activities** for each genre.

Revise

Focus on Sentence Fluency

The Rubric Says There is a balance of short and long sentences, which makes the writing clear and easy to read.

Writing Strategy Combine short sentences to improve flow.

The next thing I need to do is check my sentences. The rubric says I shouldn't use all short or all long sentences. So I need to go back to be sure there is variety in my sentences. I'll look for short sentences in a row to see if I can combine them, too.

[DRAFT]

combined set of short sentences

Everyone who sees his animals really like them. Many of his pieces have be ~~sold. People~~ , and people from all over the country buy his carvings now.

Write

Check your draft to be sure you have variety in your sentences. Revise sentences for balance and flow.

Optional Revising Lessons

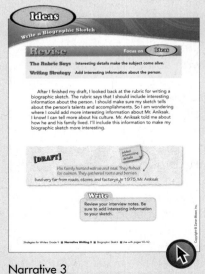

Ideas

Write a Biographic Sketch

Revise
Focus on **Ideas**

The Rubric Says Interesting details make the subject come alive.

Writing Strategy Add interesting information about the person.

After I finished my draft, I looked back at the rubric for writing a biographic sketch. The rubric says that I should include interesting information about the person. I should make sure my sketch tells about the person's talents and accomplishments. So I am wondering where I could add more interesting information about Mr. Aniksak. I know! I can tell more about his culture. Mr. Aniksak told me about how he and his family lived. I'll include this information to make my biographic sketch more interesting.

[DRAFT]

added interesting details

His family hunted walrus and seal. They fished for salmon. They gathered roots and berries.

lived very far from roads, stores, and factorys. In 1975, Mr. Aniksak

Write
Review your interview notes. Be sure to add interesting information to your sketch.

Strategies for Writers Grade 4 • Narrative Writing 3 • Biographic Sketch • Use with pages 40–42

Narrative 3

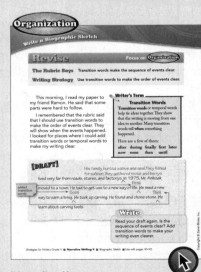

Organization

Write a Biographic Sketch

Revise
Focus on **Organization**

The Rubric Says Transition words make the sequence of events clear.

Writing Strategy Use transition words to make the order of events clear.

This morning, I read my paper to my friend Ramon. He said that some parts were hard to follow. I remembered that the rubric said that I should use transition words to make the order of events clear. They will show when the events happened. I looked for places where I could add transition words or temporal words to make my writing clear.

Writer's Term
_____
Transition Words
Transition words or temporal words help tie ideas together. They show that the writing is moving from one idea to another. Many transition words tell **when** something happened.
Here are a few of them:
after during finally first later now soon then until

[DRAFT]

His family hunted walrus and seal. They fished for salmon. They gathered roots and berries.

lived very far from roads, stores, and factorys. In 1975, Mr. Aniksak

added transition words

First moved to a town. He had to get use to a new way of life. He need a new Soon Then way to earn a living. He took up carving. He found and chose stone. He learn about carving tools.

Write
Read your draft again. Is the sequence of events clear? Add transition words to make your writing even clearer.

Strategies for Writers Grade 4 • Narrative Writing 4 • Biographic Sketch • Use with pages 40–42

Narrative 4

Go to → **Strategies for Writers** at **www.sfw.z-b.com**

Edit

Focus on Conventions

The Rubric Says	Subjects and verbs agree. Forms of the verb *be* are used correctly.
Writing Strategy	Make sure all verbs are correct.

Now I need to check for errors. I know from the rubric that I always need to check spelling, capitalization, and punctuation. I'll also make sure that all my subjects and verbs agree and that I use the correct forms of the verb *be*.

Writer's Term

Subject-Verb Agreement
Subject-Verb Agreement means that subjects and verbs must agree in number. Singular nouns or pronouns take singular verbs, and plural nouns or pronouns take plural verbs. In the present tense, singular verbs often end in **-s** or **-es**.

corrected subject-verb agreement errors

corrected form of the verb "be"

[DRAFT]

likes
Everyone who sees his animals really ~~like~~ them. Many of his pieces have been
~~be~~ sold, and people from all over the country buy his carvings now.

Analyze

Look at how Jack combined two short sentences. What do you think of the result? Look at the edits. Why did Jack make the changes?

Write
Conventions

Reread your work to make sure that subjects and verbs agree.

For more practice with subject-verb agreement and *be*, use the exercises on the next two pages.

Biographic Sketch 43

Related Grammar Practice

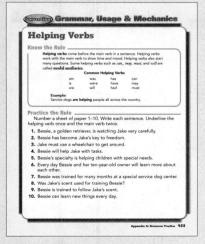

Convention **Grammar, Usage & Mechanics**

Helping Verbs

Know the Rule

Helping verbs come before the main verb in a sentence. Helping verbs work with the main verb to show time and mood. Helping verbs also start many questions. Some helping verbs such as *can, may, must,* and *will* are called **modal auxiliaries.**

Common Helping Verbs

am	was	has	can
is	were	have	may
are	will	had	must

Example:
Service dogs **are helping** people all across the country.

Practice the Rule
Number a sheet of paper 1–10. Write each sentence. Underline the helping verb once and the main verb twice.

1. Bessie, a golden retriever, is watching Jake very carefully.
2. Bessie has become Jake's key to freedom.
3. Jake must use a wheelchair to get around.
4. Bessie will help Jake with tasks.
5. Bessie's specialty is helping children with special needs.
6. Every day Bessie and her ten-year-old owner will learn more about each other.
7. Bessie was trained for many months at a special service dog center.
8. Was Jake's scent used for training Bessie?
9. Bessie is trained to follow Jake's scent.
10. Bessie can learn new things every day.

Appendix A: Grammar Practice 455

Student Edition page 455

Go to ⟹ **Appendix A: Grammar Practice**

Student Objectives

• Edit to make sure all verbs are correct. *(p. 43)*

Edit

Focus on Conventions

Check for Errors Instruct students to check their own biographic sketches to ensure all subjects and verbs agree and that the proper forms of *be* have been used. Remind them that they should always check their spelling, grammar, punctuation, and capitalization as well.

If any of your students are having trouble with subject-verb agreement or with using the verb *be*, you may wish to teach the mini-lessons on T44 and T45. Then have students complete the exercises on pages 44 and 45. Review the answers with them.

Writer's Term

Subject-Verb Agreement Errors that are made in writing are not typically made while speaking. That is why it can be very helpful for a student to read the sentence out loud—because errors in subject-verb agreement are more easily caught when spoken or heard.

CCSS **C**ommon **C**ore **S**tate **S**tandards (pp. Z20–Z30)
Writing: W.4.4, W.4.5, W.4.6, W.4.10
Language: L.4.1f, L.4.2a, L.4.6

Mini-Lesson

Student Objectives

- Use correct subject-verb agreement. *(p. 44)*

Subject-Verb Agreement

Remind students that subjects and verbs must agree in number.

Write the following sentence on the board: *My friend plays baseball after school.*

Ask students to identify the subject and verb. **(The subject is *friend*; the verb is *plays*.)** Ask if the subject is singular or plural. **(singular)** Then ask if the subject and verb agree. **(yes)** Now add an *-s* to the word *friend*. Ask if the subject now is singular or plural. **(plural)** Ask if the verb now agrees with the subject. **(no)** Ask what change needs to be made to the verb. **(remove the *s*)**

Write the following on the board: *The books is on the floor.*

Ask students to identify the subject and verb. **(*books, is*)** Then ask if the subject and verb agree. **(no)** Ask students for suggestions on how to write the sentence so that the subject and verb agree. **(Possible responses: The books are on the floor. The book is on the floor.)**

Online Writing Center

Provides **interactive grammar games** and **practice activities** in student eBook.

Subject-Verb Agreement

Know the Rule

Add **-s** or **-es** to a regular verb in the present tense when the subject is a singular noun or **he, she,** or **it.**

Examples:
John throws the ball. She catches the ball.

Do not add **-s** or **-es** to a regular verb in the present tense when the subject is a plural noun or **I, you, we,** or **they.**

Examples:
We watch the game. They take pictures.

Practice the Rule

Number a separate sheet of paper 1–12. Decide which verb in parentheses agrees with the subject. Then write the correct verb.

1. Historians (feel/feels) that art is an important part of history.
2. Civilizations (use/uses) art in many ways.
3. Early art forms (tell/tells) us much about the people who created them.
4. Art (remain/remains) an important part of any culture.
5. Artists sometimes (carve/carves) on cave walls and rocks.
6. They (learn/learns) to use certain tools.
7. Carvers must (know/knows) the final form they wish to create.
8. Carvers cannot (correct/corrects) a mistake.
9. Therefore, they usually (make/makes) a small clay model first.
10. Some artists (do/does) all the stone cutting themselves.
11. Many carvers (give/gives) the simple cutting jobs to an assistant.
12. The style of carving (change/changes) over time.

Related Grammar Practice

Pages 69, 95, 97

Go to G.U.M. Student Practice Book

Forms of *Be*

Know the Rule

The linking verb *be* connects the subject to a noun or an adjective in the predicate. The verb *be* does not show action. It has different forms for different tenses. Use *is* or *was* after a singular subject or with the pronouns *he, she,* and *it.* Remember to use *am* after the pronoun *I.* Use *are* or *were* after a plural subject or with the pronouns *we, you,* or *they.* Remember to use *has* or *have* with *been.*

Examples:
Andy **is** tall. Andy **was** taller than I. Now I **am** taller.
They **are** in Europe. **Were** you there last year?
It **has been** rainy for days. I **have been** in the house.

Practice the Rule

Number a separate sheet of paper 1–10. Decide which form of *be* agrees with the underlined subject. Then write the correct verb.

1. My <u>grandfather</u> (is/are) the only furniture maker in our town.
2. His furniture <u>designs</u> (is/are) beautiful.
3. Last month, my <u>grandfather and brother</u> (was/were) in England.
4. Many English <u>artisans</u> (is/are) talented wood carvers.
5. A four-poster <u>bed</u> from England (is/are) now for sale at my grandfather's store.
6. Detailed <u>carvings</u> (is/are) on the headboard, footboard, and four posts.
7. <u>Wood carving</u> (is/are) an art.
8. My <u>brother</u> (has been/have been) an apprentice wood carver for a year.
9. At first, <u>he</u> (was/were) interested in cabinet making.
10. <u>Men</u> in my family (has been/have been) furniture makers for six generations.

Biographic Sketch **45**

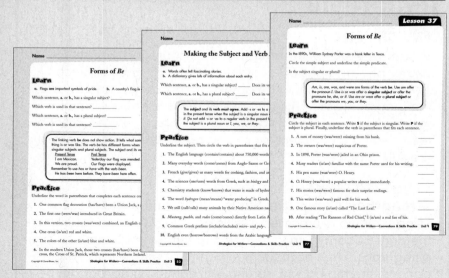

Pages 53, 77, 79

Go to ⇨ Grammar Practice Masters

Student Objectives

• Learn to use the correct form of the linking verb *be.* (p. 45)

Forms of *Be*

Write the following chart on the board:

Present

Singular	Plural
I am	we are
you are	you are
he/she/it is	they are

Past

Singular	Plural
I was/have been	we were/have been
you were/have been	you were/have been
he/she/it was/has been	they were/have been

Review the chart with students. Explain that the plural form of *you* is used when the speaker is speaking to several people. Call upon volunteers to create sentences using each form of the verb *be* on the board. Encourage students to replace pronouns with specific names.

CCSS Common Core State Standards (pp. Z20–Z30)
Writing: W.4.6
Language: L.4.1f, L.4.4a

Biographic Sketch **T45**

Write
Biographic Sketch

Week 3 • Day 4

Student Objectives

- Discuss preparation for publishing and presentation. (p. 46)
- Use a final editing checklist to publish their work. (p. 46)

Publish ⁺Presentation

Publishing Strategy Remind students that choosing the right publishing method for their work is an important detail. They have worked hard to write engaging and informative biographic sketches, and it's important that a large audience gets to enjoy their work.

Read page 46 aloud. Discuss Jack's choice of publishing strategies. If you do not already have a set publishing plan established, ask students how they wish to publish their work. Encourage them to send a copy not only to the subject of their writing (if possible) but also to friends and family members.

Review Jack's final checklist with students. Have a volunteer read page 47. Review how Jack's checklist helped him produce a well-written and accurate final copy. Then have students create their own checklists to use when checking over their biographic sketches.

 Strategies for Writers Online
Go to **www.sfw.z-b.com** for additional online resources for students, teachers, and parents.

Publish ⁺Presentation

Publishing Strategy   Share your final paper in an author's circle.

Presentation Strategy   Use neat handwriting or word processing.

I have finished my biographic sketch. Now I will publish it by sharing it with my class. My classmates will be interested in hearing the story of the artist. The author's circle will be a good way to publish this piece. I need to use neat handwriting or word processing for my final copy so it is legible. I also plan to e-mail a copy to the artist. I'll use a final checklist to make sure it's ready to publish.

My Final Checklist

Did I—

✔ check to see that all subjects and verbs agree?

✔ check to see that I used the correct form of *be*?

✔ indent every paragraph?

✔ use neat handwriting or word processing?

✔ put my name on my paper?

Write
Use this checklist for your biographic sketch. Then make a neat final copy to share.

46 Narrative Writing

Differentiating Instruction

ENRICHMENT

Visual or Audio Enhancement Encourage students to gather photographs or recordings related to their subject. The photographs could be of the person interviewed for the biographic sketch or images of the person's accomplishments. Audio recordings could be the interview itself, a song recorded by the subject, or a song related to some aspect of the subject's life.

REINFORCEMENT

Strengthen Computer Skills Allow students to practice using their word-processing skills on a computer, including the print option. Instruct students to type a few short paragraphs. Then have them experiment with line spacing options, the tab button, setting left/right and top/bottom margins, and selecting a font and font size.

Carving Art from Stone
by Jack

John Aniksak carves stone bears, deer, seals, and other animals. He was not always a stone carver, though.

Mr. Aniksak was born in an Inuit village in 1935. He and his family are from Canada. The Inuit people have lived in Canada for a very long time. It was a very different kind of life. You would be surprised. He lived very far from roads, stores, and factories. His family hunted walrus and seals. They fished for salmon. They gathered roots and berries.

In 1975, Mr. Aniksak moved to a town. He had to get used to a new way of life. First, he needed a new way to earn a living. Soon, he took up carving. He found and chose stone. Then, he learned about carving tools. Now he was also able to use many skills from his days in the wilderness. His knowledge of Arctic animals was especially important.

Mr. Aniksak learned his new skill well. In 1979, he sold his first carving, a seal. Everyone who sees his carvings really likes them. Many of his pieces have been sold, and people from all over the country buy his carvings now.

Today he still loves his work. He makes his living by carving animals and uses them to teach people about the old Inuit way of life.

Analyze
Use the rubric to evaluate Jack's biographic sketch. Then use the rubric to score your own biographic sketch.

Tech Tips
Online Tools

Use Word Clouds Multimodal texts don't have to have bells, whistles, and lots of glitz. Writing across modes is about ratcheting up what we can communicate or about providing a different lens into our work. Ask students to use the written draft of their biographic sketch to create a word cloud using an online tool such as Wordle. By transforming their print text into a visual image (in which repeated words are larger and the writer can adjust color, layout, and font), students can examine what they said and how they said it and set goals for later work.

See **www.sfw.z-b.com** for further information about and links to these websites and tools.

Write
Biographic Sketch

Week 3 • Day 5

Student Objectives
- Use a biographic sketch rubric. (pp. 30–31)
- Share a published biographic sketch. (p. 47)

Presentation Strategy Remind students of the importance of the trait of Presentation. If students are using computers, remind them of the word-processing functions that can help them easily prepare a neat final copy. Selecting the double-space setting prior to printing also helps to create a neat copy.

Ask students what score they would assign Jack for each trait. Be sure students can support their answers. Remind students to refer to the rubric to assess their own stories.

Reflecting on a Biographic Sketch

Ask students to reflect on the experience of writing a biographic sketch. Ask:

- With which part of your biographic sketch are you the most pleased? Why?

CCSS **C**ommon **C**ore **S**tate **S**tandards (pp. Z20–Z30)
Writing: W.4.4, W.4.6, W.4.10
Language: L.4.1f, L.4.3c
Speaking and Listening: SL.4.1a, SL.4.1b, SL.4.1c, SL.4.1d, SL.4.3, SL.4.4, SL.4.5, SL.4.6

Adventure Story Planner

WEEK 1

Day 1
Introduce
Adventure Story

Student Objectives
- Review the elements of an adventure story.
- Consider purpose and audience.
- Learn the traits of narrative writing.

Student Activities
- Read and discuss **What's in an Adventure Story?** (p. 48)
- Read and discuss **Why Write an Adventure Story?** (p. 49)
- Read **Linking Narrative Writing Traits to an Adventure Story**. (p. 50)

Day 2
Analyze
Close Reading of the Model

Student Objectives
- Read a model adventure story.

Student Activities
- Read **"The Unexpected Voyage."** (p. 51)

Day 3
Analyze
Introduce the Rubric

Student Objectives
- Learn to read a rubric.

Student Activities
- Review **"The Unexpected Voyage."** (p. 51)
- Read and discuss the **Adventure Story Rubric.** (pp. 52–53)

WEEK 2

Day 1
Write
Prewrite: Ideas

Student Objectives
- Read and understand a prewriting strategy.

Student Activities
- Read and discuss **Prewrite: Focus on Ideas.** (p. 58)
- Apply the prewriting strategy.

Day 2
Write
Prewrite: Organization

Student Objectives
- Create a Story Map to organize information.

Student Activities
- Read and discuss **Prewrite: Focus on Organization.** (p. 59)
- Reflect on the model Story Map.
- Apply the prewriting strategy to create a Story Map.
- Participate in a peer conference.

Day 3
Write
Draft: Voice

Student Objectives
- Use a Story Map to begin writing.

Student Activities
- Read and discuss **Draft: Focus on Voice.** (p. 60)
- Reflect on the model draft. (p. 61)
- Apply the drafting strategy by using a Story Map to write a draft.

WEEK 3

Day 1
Write
Revise: Word Choice

Student Objectives
- Revise to add action verbs.

Student Activities
- Read and discuss **Revise: Focus on Word Choice.** (p. 63)
- Reflect on the model draft.
- Apply the revising strategy.
- Participate in a peer conference.

Day 2
Write
Revise: Sentence Fluency

Student Objectives
- Revise to use transitions to begin sentences.

Student Activities
- Read and discuss **Revise: Focus on Sentence Fluency.** (p. 64)
- Apply the revising strategy.

Note: Optional Revising Lessons are located at **www.sfw.z-b.com.**

Day 3
Write
Edit: Conventions

Student Objectives
- Edit to correct all punctuation.

Student Activities
- Read and discuss **Edit: Focus on Conventions.** (p. 65)
- Reflect on the model draft.
- Apply the editing strategy.

Note: Teach the Conventions mini-lessons (pp. 66–67) if needed.

Day 4

Analyze
Close Reading for the Traits

Student Objectives
- Read a model adventure story.
- Use the adventure story rubric.
- Use the model adventure story to study Ideas, Organization, and Voice.

Student Activities
- Review **"The Unexpected Voyage."** (p. 51)
- Review the rubric. (pp. 52–53)
- Read and discuss **Using the Rubric to Analyze the Model.** (pp. 54–55)

Day 5

Analyze
Close Reading for the Traits

Student Objectives
- Read a model adventure story.
- Use the adventure story rubric.
- Use the model adventure story to study Word Choice, Sentence Fluency, and Conventions.

Student Activities
- Review **"The Unexpected Voyage."** (p. 51)
- Read and discuss **Using the Rubric to Analyze the Model.** (pp. 56–57)

Day 4

Write
Draft

Student Objectives
- Complete a draft.

Student Activities
- Finish the draft.
- Participate in a peer conference.

Day 5

Write
Revise: Ideas

Student Objectives
- Revise to include character, setting, and plot details.

Student Activities
- Read and discuss **Revise: Focus on Ideas.** (p. 62)
- Reflect on a model draft.
- Apply the revising strategy.

Day 4

Write
Publish: +Presentation

Student Objectives
- Discuss preparation for publishing and presentation.
- Use a final editing checklist to publish their work.

Student Activities
- Read and discuss **Publish: +Presentation.** (p. 68)
- Apply the publishing strategy.

Day 5

Write
Publish: +Presentation

Student Objectives
- Use an adventure story rubric.
- Share a published adventure story.

Student Activities
- Share their work.
- Use the rubric to reflect upon and evaluate the model and their own writing. (pp. 52–53, 69–71)

To complete the chapter in fewer days, combine the learning objectives and activities in a way that supports students as they write.

Resources at-a-Glance

Grammar, Usage & Mechanics

Differentiating Instruction

For additional Differentiating Instruction activities, see Strategies for Writers *Differentiated Instruction Activities at* **www.sfw.z-b.com.**

English Language Learners

Collaborative Conferencing

Tech Tips

▶ Strategies for Writers Online

Go to **www.sfw.z-b.com** for additional online resources for students, teachers, and parents.

Online Writing Center

Provides IWB resources, assessments, interactive games and practice activities, videos, eBooks, and a virtual file cabinet.

Introduce
Adventure Story

Student Objectives

- Review the elements of an adventure story. *(p. 48)*
- Consider purpose and audience. *(p. 49)*
- Learn the traits of narrative writing. *(p. 50)*

What's an Adventure Story?

Ask students what words come to mind when they hear the word *adventure*. **(Possible responses: excitement, fun, danger, heroes)** Read aloud and discuss the definition of an adventure story on page 48. Invite students to name or identify examples of adventure stories that they have seen or read. If necessary, remind them of stories they have read in school or seen on television or at the movies.

What's in an Adventure Story?

Read and discuss the elements of an adventure story with students. Choose an adventure story the students are familiar with and have students name the problem, setting, and lead character in the story. Ask students if they can quote some dialogue from the story.

 Strategies for Writers Online
Go to **www.sfw.z-b.com** for additional online resources for students, teachers, and parents.

What's an Adventure Story?

It's a tale about a character who does something exciting. It can be something that really happened to someone, or it can be made up. Most adventure stories are fiction—invented by the author.

What's in an Adventure Story?

A Problem
The story is built around a problem or challenge that has to be faced. What happens around the problem is called the **plot**.

Setting
This is when and where the story happens. It could be last week at the soccer field or in 2150 on Saturn.

I'LL SAVE YOU!

A Lead Character
This is the main person in the story. She or he must face dangers or take risks in order to solve the problem. The lead character may not look like a hero at first.

Dialogue
These are the conversations that characters in the story have. Dialogue should sound like how people talk in real life.

Narrative Text Exemplars (Adventure Story)

Farley, Walter. *The Black Stallion.* **Random House Books for Young Readers, 2008.** Young Alec Ramsey is shipwrecked on a deserted island with a wild black stallion. The stallion becomes an important part of Alec's life as he depends on the horse for survival. Together, the pair form a wonderful and lifelong friendship.

Lin, Grace. *Where the Mountain Meets the Moon.* **Little, Brown, 2009.** *Where the Mountain Meets the Moon* is an adventure about Minli, a young girl from a poor village, who embarks on an epic journey with a dragon that cannot fly. The pair set out to find the Old Man of the Moon and change their family's fortune.

Why write an Adventure Story?

People write adventure stories for different reasons. Here are two good reasons to write them.

To Entertain

Adventure stories get you excited and involved. You can imagine yourself as the brave and daring hero. Both the author and the reader can enjoy solving difficult problems in an invented world. Sometimes heroes do things we would never do. This can make it fun and exciting to write about.

To Understand

Stories about heroes can help us understand others. We can learn how different people solve problems and how they find the courage to face danger.

O'Dell, Scott. *Island of the Blue Dolphins.* **Sandpiper, 2010.** A young girl leaps from a rescue ship and spends eighteen years living alone on a deserted island. The girl must find food, fight off predators, and find courage and self-reliance in order to survive.

Burnford, Sheila. *The Incredible Journey.* **Yearling, 1997.** A captivating story of a Labrador retriever, bull terrier, and Siamese cat who set out through the Canadian wilderness to find their way home. The three pets face death and danger as they try to make it home to the family they love.

Why write an Adventure Story?

Write the words *Entertainment* and *Understanding* on the board. Then read the reasons for writing an adventure story on page 49. Discuss ways in which both writing and reading adventure stories are used for the purposes of entertainment and understanding. Next, remind students that the setting for an adventure story can be anywhere, real or imagined. Ask students to suggest places in the world—near to home or far away—that would make an interesting setting for an adventure story. Where would they like to take their readers? Stress that good writers keep their audience in mind as they write, providing all the details necessary to capture the imagination and curiosity of the readers and bring them along on the adventure. Urge students to consider their purpose for writing and their audience carefully as they develop their adventure story.

CCSS Common Core State Standards (pp. Z20–Z30)
Language: L.4.3c
Speaking and Listening: SL.4.1a, SL.4.1b, SL.4.1c, SL.4.1d, SL.4.3, SL.4.6

Introduce
Adventure Story

Linking Narrative Writing Traits to an Adventure Story

Prepare a brief adventure story to read aloud, or share an adventure that happened to you. Ask students to listen closely to the story. Stop the story at its climax, before the resolution. Ask students the following:

- Who is the lead character?

- What is the problem that needs to be solved?

- Does the story have a setting and action?

- What do you think is going to happen?

Finish the story, and then direct students' attention to the narrative writing traits listed on page 50. Call on individuals to read each trait aloud. Discuss each trait as it is read and, when suitable, use your story as an example to clarify the trait descriptions.

Tell students that they will follow Jack as he models using the writing process and the narrative writing traits together to write an adventure story.

Linking Narrative Writing Traits to an Adventure Story

In this chapter, you will write a story about something exciting! This type of narrative writing is called an adventure story. Jack will guide you through the stages of the writing process: Prewrite, Draft, Revise, Edit, and Publish. In each stage, Jack will show you important writing strategies that are linked to the Narrative Writing Traits below.

Narrative Writing Traits

 Ideas
- a topic that is just the right size, not too big or too small
- details and facts that develop the narrative

 Organization
- a natural and logical sequence
- a strong beginning and a satisfying ending
- transitions that signal the sequence of events

 Voice
- a voice and tone that are perfect for the writing
- dialogue that, when used, sounds just right for the characters

 Word Choice
- concrete words and phrases that describe the characters and events

 **Sentence Fluency**
- a variety of sentence lengths to make the story flow smoothly

 Conventions
- no or few errors in spelling, grammar, punctuation, and capitalization

Before you write, read Becky Silver's adventure story on the next page. Then use the adventure story rubric on pages 52–53 to decide how well she did. (You might want to look back at What's in an Adventure Story? on page 48, too!)

50 Narrative Writing

Narrative Writing Traits in an Adventure Story

 **Ideas** The writer chooses a plot that is not too large and not too small. The writer uses plenty of vivid, descriptive details to help the audience envision the plot, characters, and setting.

 **Organization** Each of the events unfolds in a natural and logical order. The beginning grabs the reader's attention, the climax is clearly identifiable, and the ending shows how the problem is resolved in a satisfying way.

 **Voice** The writer uses a voice that is energetic and engaging. Realistic-sounding dialogue is used to develop the characters and move the plot along.

The Unexpected Voyage

by Becky Silver

setting

"We never should have gone by ourselves," said Jeremy. "I'll bet we're lost."

"Don't worry," answered Samantha. "Our stop is probably next." The subway train stopped again. The doors opened. Passengers got off. New people came on. The train started up again.

lead characters

dialogue

problem

"But it shouldn't take so long to get to the nature museum," said Jeremy. "When we go with Mom and Dad, it doesn't take long at all. If we don't get there soon, we're going to miss Dr. Forrest and his amazing change-of-seasons machine."

Jeremy looked out the window. By twisting a little, he could see where the train was headed. It seemed about to leave the dark underground. In a split second, the train broke into bright daylight. Two things happened at once. Samantha and Jeremy couldn't see for a few seconds because of the blinding sunlight, and the train conductor announced, "We will arrive in Brighton at 11 o'clock. No stops between here and Brighton."

Brighton! Samantha and Jeremy looked at each other in disbelief. Brighton was miles and miles from where they lived. The nature museum was just a few city subway stops from home.

dialogue

"I know!" yelled Jeremy. "We must have gotten on the train in the wrong direction! We should have been traveling south, and instead we've been going north!"

Jeremy thought he should be upset, but instead he felt like laughing. The train was speeding toward Brighton. He and Samantha looked out the window. The train raced along so fast that the sunny world seemed to change color as they moved. Trees that had been green now flamed red and gold. Acorns fell from branches and thudded against the train. Fluffy white clouds danced in an endless, brilliant blue sky.

problem solved

"We can take the train back once we get to Brighton," said Jeremy.

"Meanwhile, we can watch the real change-of-seasons show from right here!" exclaimed Samantha.

Adventure Story **51**

Word Choice Strong, exciting verbs are used to depict the action. Precise, descriptive words bring the story and characters to life. The reader feels excited to keep reading and see how the story ends.

Sentence Fluency The writer uses a variety of sentence beginnings, which keeps the reading interesting and energetic.

Conventions The writer takes great care to use all punctuation, including quotation marks and apostrophes, accurately. The reader is able to focus on the story and characters, as there are no errors to slow the reading.

Analyze
Close Reading of the Model

Week 1 • Day 2

Student Objectives

- Read a model adventure story. *(p. 51)*

Read the Model

Read "The Unexpected Voyage" on page 51 aloud. Before you read, remind students to listen for the writing traits outlined on page 50.

Elements of an Adventure Story

Use the notes on the model to discuss the various elements of an adventure story. Ask students if it was easy to visualize the main characters and setting based on the details Becky used. Did they feel the dialogue was realistic sounding? Was the problem clearly identifiable? How did students feel about the ending? Was the problem solved in a satisfying way? You may wish to have students refer back to What's in an Adventure Story? on page 48 for review.

CCSS **Common Core State Standards** (pp. Z20–Z30)
Writing: W.4.6
Language: L.4.3c
Speaking and Listening: SL.4.1a, SL.4.1b, SL.4.1c, SL.4.1d, SL.4.2, SL.4.3, SL.4.6

Analyze
Introduce the Rubric

Week 1 • Day 3

Student Objectives

• Learn to read a rubric.
  (pp. 52–53)

Introduce the Rubric

Explain the Rubric Explain that a rubric is a tool that helps you plan, improve, and evaluate a piece of writing. Tell students that a rubric helps a writer focus on key elements, or traits, in writing (**Ideas, Organization, Voice, Word Choice, Sentence Fluency, Conventions,** and **Presentation**).

The 6-point rubric on pages 52–53 can be used to evaluate an adventure story. Explain that it is based on the same traits for an adventure story that students read on page 50. Draw students' attention to the six columns to explain how the scoring system works. Explain that column 6 describes a very good adventure story, one that has received the highest score in all categories. This is what students should strive for in their own writing.

Discuss the Rubric Guide the students in a discussion of the rubric. Remind students to keep the rubric in mind when they write and revise their own adventure story.

Online Writing Center

Provides a variety of **interactive rubrics,** including 4-, 5-, and 6-point models.

Adventure Story Rubric

Use this rubric to analyze the model. Then use it to plan and score your own adventure story.

	6	5	4
Ideas	Story elements work together successfully. Details develop the characters, setting, and plot.	Story elements work together most of the time. Most details develop the characters, setting, and plot.	Story elements work together some of the time. Some details do not develop the characters, setting, and plot.
Organization	The sequence unfolds naturally. The story builds to a high point, and the problem is solved at the end.	Most of the details build to a high point and problem solution.	Some more details are needed to develop the problem and solution for the reader.
Voice	The voice is strong and natural. The dialogue makes the characters sound real.	The voice is strong. The dialogue sounds real most of the time.	The voice is clear much of the time. Some dialogue does not sound real.
Word Choice	The writer uses strong verbs that make the story come to life and convey events precisely.	The writer uses strong verbs most of the time. One or two are weak.	The writer uses weak verbs most of the time. Some events are not conveyed well.
Sentence Fluency	Sentence beginnings are varied. Transition words connect ideas.	Most of the sentence beginnings are varied and use transition words to connect ideas.	Many sentences are varied. The writer uses a few transition words.
Conventions	Quotation marks, apostrophes, and other punctuation marks are used correctly.	A few minor errors in punctuation are present, but they do not distract the reader.	Some punctuation errors are noticeable but do not confuse the reader.

+Presentation The story is legible and neat. Illustrations, if used, are complete.

52 Narrative Writing

CCSS Common Core State Standards
Adventure Story

Writing in the Narrative text type engages the Common Core State Standards for Narrative writing. Each of the rubrics and strategies for the adventure story chapter is solidly based on the Narrative Writing standards, and several strategies and exercises echo Speaking & Listening, Reading/Literature, and Language standards as well. Standards **W.4.3a** and **W.4.3e** are reflected in the Organization rubric, which focuses on presenting the sequence of events in a natural order and writing an ending in which the problem is solved in a satisfying way. Standard **W.4.3b** resonates throughout both the Ideas and Voice rubrics, which emphasize the use of story elements, such as details and dialogue, to develop characters, setting, and plot. The Sentence Fluency rubric

3	2	1	
Story elements don't work together in the middle. Details may not be related in this part of the story.	Story elements don't work together. Details are unrelated or incomplete.	The writing is not a story. Details are not provided.	Ideas
Some details do not build to the high point and they cause confusion. The solution is not clear.	The story does not build to a high point. The solution does not follow the problem.	The writing is not organized. It is difficult or impossible to follow.	Organization
The voice is inconsistent. The dialogue sounds flat or forced at times.	The voice is insincere and/ or vague. Dialogue is awkward or missing.	The voice is absent. There is no dialogue.	Voice
The writer's verbs are weak or repeated. Events are not conveyed well.	The verbs are weak or confusing. They make the story dull.	Overused, poorly chosen, or repetitive verbs cause confusion.	Word Choice
Several sentences sound the same and slow the flow. Few transitions are used.	Some sentences are short and choppy. Some are too long. There are no transitions.	Sentences are incomplete or incorrect. The writing is impossible to follow.	Sentence Fluency
Noticeable punctuation errors confuse the reader. Some quotation marks are used incorrectly.	The writing contains many errors. Quotation marks are missing. Apostrophes may be missing or used incorrectly.	Many major errors in punctuation make the text difficult to read and understand. The writer is not in control of conventions.	Conventions

See Appendix B for 4-, 5-, and 6-point narrative rubrics.

Find Evidence in the Model

Small-Group Collaboration
Assign a small group of students to check the model for each trait. One student in each group should be responsible for recording one or two strong examples of the trait as described by the rubric.

Teacher-Led Discussion Bring the class back together and ask one person from each group to report their findings to the class. Ensure that students understand that the point of this exercise is not to score the model, but rather to practice identifying the traits within a piece of writing.

Additional Rubrics

Appendix B includes 4-, 5-, and 6-point rubrics that can be used with any piece of narrative writing. The rubrics are also available as blackline masters in the back of this Teacher Edition.

clearly reflects standard **W.4.3c,** which stresses the use of transitional words and phrases to show the sequence of events and connect ideas. Standard **W.4.3d** is reflected in both the Ideas and Word Choice rubrics, which focus on the use of descriptive, precise language and details to bring the story and characters to life.

Standards **L.4.1** and **L.4.2** are clearly reflected throughout the editing pages of the chapter, while standard **W.4.6** resonates throughout the Narrative unit, particularly in the Publishing +Presentation pages, as students are encouraged to take full advantage of the word processing programs available to them.

CCSS **Common Core State Standards** (pp. Z20–Z30)
Writing: W.4.6
Language: L.4.3c
Speaking and Listening: SL.4.1a, SL.4.1b, SL.4.1c, SL.4.1d, SL.4.2, SL.4.3, SL.4.6

Analyze
Close Reading for the Traits

Week 1 • Day 4

Student Objectives

- Read a model adventure story. (*p. 51*)
- Use the adventure story rubric. (*pp. 52–53*)
- Use the model adventure story to study **Ideas, Organization,** and **Voice**. (*pp. 54–55*)

Find Evidence in the Model

Evaluate the Model Have students turn to pages 54 and 55. Explain that these pages show how the model on page 51 uses the writing traits described in the rubric.

Read each section with students. Use questions such as the following to discuss each section. Be sure students can back up their answers with examples from the model.

Discuss Audience, Task, Purpose Ask students one or more of the following questions as they analyze the model:

- **Audience** Who is the audience? (Possible response: all readers)
- **Task** How does Becky Silver make her adventure story exciting? (Possible response: She includes descriptive details and builds the story to a high point.)
- **Purpose** What is the writer's purpose for writing this story? (Possible response: to entertain the readers)

Using the Rubric to Analyze the Model
Adventure Story

Did you notice that the model on page 51 points out some key elements of an adventure story? As she wrote "The Unexpected Voyage," Becky Silver used these elements to help her write an exciting story. She also used the 6-point rubric on pages 52–53 to plan, draft, revise, and edit the writing. A rubric is a great tool to evaluate writing during the writing process.

Now let's use the same rubric to score the model. To do this, we'll focus on each trait separately, starting with Ideas. We'll use the top descriptor for each trait (column 6), along with examples from the model, to help us understand how the traits work together. How would you score Becky on each trait?

- Story elements work together successfully.
- Details develop the characters, setting, and plot.

The beginning of the story sets up everything. I find out that the story has two main characters, Jeremy and Samantha, and that the setting is a subway train. Later on, I find out the problem. The subway train is not taking Jeremy and Samantha to the nature museum. The action of the story shows the train taking Jeremy and Samantha farther and farther away.

The subway train stopped again. The doors opened. Passengers got off. New people came on. The train started up again.

English Language Learners

BEGINNING

Parts of a Story Draw a stick person on one side of the board and a house on the other. Read a simple story to students. Make sure the story has characters and an obvious setting. After you finish reading, say the name of the character(s) (for example, *Little Red Riding Hood*) in the story you read. Ask, *Is Red Riding Hood a person or a place? Is Grandmother's house a person or a place?* Introduce the terms *character* and *setting*. Write them on the board and have students repeat.

INTERMEDIATE

Parts of a Story Have a volunteer tell his or her favorite story, either from childhood or from a book he or she has recently read. Ask other students to listen carefully and identify the characters, setting, and basic plot of the story. Discuss as a class.

Organization
- The sequence unfolds naturally.
- The story builds to a high point, and the problem is solved at the end.

I know right away that Jeremy and Samantha are worried that something is wrong. They will have to solve the problem by themselves. Their worry builds until they find out just how far from the museum they are. I wonder what I would do if I were alone on a train going the wrong way.

Brighton! Samantha and Jeremy looked at each other in disbelief. Brighton was miles and miles from where they lived. The nature museum was just a few city subway stops from home.

Voice
- The voice is strong and natural.
- The dialogue makes the characters sound real.

I could tell right away that Jeremy and Samantha are about my age. They are trying to get to the museum by themselves. Jeremy reacts the way that I might react if I were lost. The opening dialogue shows that Jeremy is upset. Samantha's words show that she is trying to stay calm.

"We never should have gone by ourselves," said Jeremy. "I'll bet we're lost."
"Don't worry," answered Samantha. "Our stop is probably next."

Adventure Story **55**

Discuss the Traits Ask students one or more of the following questions to discuss the traits in the model.

Ideas What details does Becky include to help the reader understand the setting?
(Possible responses: the subway's doors and window, the dark tunnel and blinding sunlight, flame-red trees, fluffy white clouds, brilliant blue sky)

Organization How is the problem solved?
(Possible response: Samantha and Jeremy realize they are headed in the wrong direction and that they can get off the train and go back the other way.)

Voice How does Becky write realistic-sounding dialogue?
(Possible response: She uses words and phrases that kids our age use every day, such as "I'll bet we're lost." and "I know!")

ADVANCED
Characters and Plot Ask students to think about some of the (real or fictional) heroes they know about. List them on the board. Discuss the problem each hero faced and the dangers or risks he or she had to take in order to solve the problem. Did the hero have any enemies? Weaknesses? Have students use this information to develop their characters and plot.

ADVANCED HIGH
Story Map Review the elements of a story. Ask, *What can you find in a story?* Students should be able to answer questions such as *What is a character/setting/plot?* Students should know that the *conflict* in the story is the problem, and the *resolution* is the solution. Have partners brainstorm ideas for an adventure story and complete a Story Map as a prewriting activity.

CCSS **C**ommon **C**ore **S**tate **S**tandards (pp. Z20–Z30)
Language: L.4.3c
Speaking and Listening: SL.4.1a, SL.4.1b, SL.4.1c, SL.4.1d, SL.4.2, SL.4.3, SL.4.6

Analyze
Close Reading for the Traits

Week 1 • Day 5

Student Objectives

- Read a model adventure story. (p. 51)
- Use the adventure story rubric. (pp. 52–53)
- Use the model adventure story to study **Word Choice, Sentence Fluency,** and **Conventions.** (pp. 56–57)

Discuss the Traits Ask students one or more of the following questions to discuss the traits in the model.

Word Choice Aside from the example given on page 56, point out some strong verbs that Becky used to bring her story to life. (Possible responses: *twisting, broke, announced, exclaimed*)

Sentence Fluency Find another example of varied sentence beginnings. (Possible response: *Jeremy thought he should be upset, but instead he felt like laughing. The train was speeding toward Brighton.*)

Conventions How has Becky's careful attention to punctuation affected your reading experience? (Possible response: If there were lots of punctuation mistakes, especially in the dialogue, I would have felt confused and maybe even frustrated.)

Strategies for Writers Online
Go to **www.sfw.z-b.com** for additional online resources for students, teachers, and parents.

Using the Rubric to Analyze the Model
Adventure Story

- The writer uses strong verbs that make the story come to life and convey events precisely.

The writer uses some strong verbs that really pull me into the story. Don't you think that the sentences below are much stronger than *the trees were green and gold* and *acorns fell on the train?*

The train raced along so fast that the sunny world seemed to change color as they moved. Trees that had been green now flamed red and gold. Acorns fell from branches and thudded against the train. Fluffy white clouds danced in an endless, brilliant blue sky.

- Sentence beginnings are varied.
- Transition words connect ideas.

Becky's story moves along at a good pace. The dialogue helps, but she also varies sentences in the narrative part to hold the reader's interest. Look at the way she uses a short sentence to highlight the sudden events. She also uses the transition words *In a split second* to connect her ideas.

By twisting a little, he could see where the train was headed. It seemed about to leave the dark underground. In a split second, the train broke into bright daylight. Two things happened at once.

56 Narrative Writing

Tech Tips
Online Resources

Find a Place Online Place is an integral part of any adventure story. Try using the Street View tools in Google Earth to research the buildings, imagery, and terrain in an unfamiliar place. Then set a familiar story in that place. You'll want to tinker with the tool ahead of time to ensure that the imagery is deep enough to stimulate curiosity (and writers) more than a conventional map would. Ask students to write both before and after exploring the new setting. How does their writing change based on what they see?

See **www.sfw.z-b.com** for further information about and links to these websites and tools.

Conventions • Quotation marks, apostrophes, and other punctuation marks are used correctly.

I've checked the whole story and can't find any spelling or punctuation errors. All the direct quotations are punctuated correctly. They begin and end with quotation marks. A new paragraph shows when another person is speaking.

"We can take the train back once we get to Brighton," said Jeremy.

"Meanwhile, we can watch the real change-of-seasons show from right here!" exclaimed Samantha.

+Presentation The story is neat and legible. Illustrations, if used, are complete.

My Turn!

Now it's my turn to write an adventure story! I will use the 6-point rubric on pages 52–53 and good writing strategies to help me. Read along to see how I do it.

Adventure Story **57**

Differentiating Instruction

ENRICHMENT
Write a Sequel Challenge students to write a sequel to the model story on page 51 involving a problem on the return trip. For example, the train might have a mechanical problem, or Jeremy and Samantha might fall asleep on the train and miss their stop.

REINFORCEMENT
Practice With Action Verbs On the board, write the following sentences that contain common verbs: *The old house <u>was</u> dark and empty. I <u>said</u>, "Open the door." The door <u>opened</u>.* Ask students to suggest action verbs to replace the common verbs. (**Possible responses: The old house stood dark and empty. I hissed, "Open the door." The door creaked open.**) Discuss how these change what the sentences communicate.

+Presentation Explain to students that many writers choose to illustrate some of the key events in their stories. These visuals strengthen the readers' experience with the characters and plot. Tell students that they will be adding a few illustrations to their own adventure stories. Explain that thoughtfully inserted drawings will add a visual dimension to the story and help readers better connect with the excitement and suspense. Remind students also that their stories must be legible and neatly presented.

Think About the Traits

Once students have thoroughly discussed the model, ask them which traits they think are most important in an adventure story and have them explain why.

(Possible response: Ideas is very important, as readers will rely on vivid, descriptive details to help them envision the characters, setting, and plot. Organization is very important because if the story does not have a clearly defined climax and satisfying resolution, the reader may feel frustrated or confused.)

CCSS **Common Core State Standards** (pp. Z20–Z30)
Writing: W.4.6
Language: L.4.3a, L.4.3c
Speaking and Listening: SL.4.1a, SL.4.1b, SL.4.1c, SL.4.1d, SL.4.3, SL.4.6

Write
Adventure Story

Week 2 • Day 1

Student Objectives

- Read and understand a prewriting strategy. (p. 58)

Prewrite

Focus on ⟨Ideas⟩

Record Ideas Read page 58 aloud to students. Explain that every good adventure story starts as an idea. The writer needs to first determine the lead character and what problem or challenge he or she will overcome. Call attention to the way Jack clearly defines the problem that he will need to solve. Once the main character and problem have been figured out, then the other details can be determined. Have students brainstorm how Jack might solve his problem.

Ask students if they have ever solved a problem that would make a good adventure story. Start the conversation by sharing an interesting problem you have faced, such as being stuck in heavy traffic while running late for an appointment or dropping your keys in a lake while fishing with friends. Write students' suggestions on the board.

Now tell students it is time for them to decide on a main character and a problem for their own adventure story. Instruct them to jot down their ideas.

Online Writing Center

Provides **interactive graphic organizers** as well as a variety of graphic organizers in PDF format.

Prewrite
Focus on ⟨Ideas⟩

The Rubric Says	Story elements work together successfully.
Writing Strategy	Choose a lead character and a problem.

I know that all the parts of an adventure story need to work together. First I need to choose my lead character and a problem to solve. Then I'll think about the setting, other characters, and the plot.

I'd like to make myself the lead character. I know! My problem can be when a little girl in our neighborhood is surrounded by bees. I can make myself the hero of a story about rescuing her! I'll start by writing down the problem I plan to solve in my story.

The Problem

A little girl is surrounded by bees. She is so scared she cannot move.

Write

Have you ever solved a problem that would make a good adventure story? Write out the problem. Then write out how you solved it.

58 Narrative Writing

English Language Learners

BEGINNING/INTERMEDIATE

Create a Story Map Give students a story idea, such as *hike to the treasure of Eagle Island.* Have partners use a story map to plan an adventure story. Make sure they include characters' names, a description of the setting, a problem (conflict), plot events, and a resolution. They may use just a few words to describe each.

ADVANCED/ADVANCED HIGH

Developing Ideas Ask groups of three to work together to finalize the story map and plot ideas they started during prewriting. Ask a volunteer from each group to describe the story characters, setting, and plot to the rest of the class. The plot should include several events leading up to the climax of the story.

Prewrite

The Rubric Says   The sequence unfolds naturally. The story builds to a high point, and the problem is solved at the end.

Writing Strategy   Make a Story Map to organize the events.

I have written down a problem for my adventure story. A Story Map can help me organize my story. By focusing on the problem, I can think about using a natural sequence to build my story to a high point, or climax. That's what keeps the reader interested.

Story Map

Setting	**Where**	a road near my house
	When	an August day
Characters		Amy Sisson, Mom, Michael, and me
Problem		Amy Sisson is scared by bees.
Plot Events		Michael and I hear Amy screaming.
		We run to help her.
		I am scared, but I act like Superkid.
		I help Amy get away from the bees.
Ending		Amy gets home safely.

Writer's Term ——

Story Map
A Story Map organizes the setting, characters, problem, events, and ending of a story.

Analyze

Look at Jack's Story Map. How did it help him organize his ideas?

Write

Make a Story Map to organize your story. List ideas that show the setting, character(s), problem, events, and ending.

Adventure Story   **59**

Collaborative Conferencing

PEER TO PEER   Have partners exchange Story Maps. Each student gives a brief summary of the story he or she wants to tell. The partner points out any details from the story that are missing from the Story Map.

PEER GROUPS   Divide students into groups of five and have students pass their Story Maps around the group. Give each student sticky notes, and have students write one comment or question on a note to attach to each Story Map they read.

TEACHER-LED   Meet with individual students who are having difficulty completing the Story Map. Determine which element is presenting the biggest challenge and provide additional information or discussion. Guide students as they fill in the missing information on the Story Map.

Write
Adventure Story

Student Objectives

- Create a Story Map to organize information. (p. 59)

Prewrite

Focus on **Organization**

Create a Story Map Explain that every good story has a climax, or high point, where the tension is at its highest. This is where a reader will feel the most excited and want to read on to see how the problem is resolved. All the elements of a story build up to the climax. Creating a Story Map is an effective way for a writer to map out these elements. (Go to **www.sfw.z-b. com** for the downloadable graphic organizers.) Review Jack's Story Map with students, and then have them create their own Story Maps.

Writer's Term _____

Story Map Explain to students that a Story Map is just what it sounds like—a map that will guide them when they write their stories. Taking the time to fill in this organizer pays off when it comes time to draft. A well-written Story Map helps keep the writer focused on the plot and reminds him or her to include each of the important elements, such as setting and characters.

CCSS **C**ommon **C**ore **S**tate **S**tandards (pp. Z20–Z30)
Writing: W.4.3a, W.4.3b, W.4.3e, W.4.4, W.4.5, W.4.6, W.4.10
Language: L.4.3c, L.4.6
Speaking and Listening: SL.4.1a, SL.4.1b, SL.4.1c, SL.4.1d, SL.4.3, SL.4.6

Write
Adventure Story

Week 2 • Day 3

Student Objectives

- Use a Story Map to begin writing. *(pp. 60–61)*

Draft

Focus on Voice

Realistic-Sounding Dialogue Ask students if they understand that *draft* refers to a temporary or early form of a written document. A draft is often changed and corrected several times before it is ready to be published. Then read Jack's words on page 60 aloud.

Remind students that using a strong story-telling voice will help the reader connect with the story. Writing realistic-sounding dialogue is another important technique writers use to engage the reader. If dialogue sounds stiff or unnatural, the characters will seem boring, and the reader will lose interest. Review the Writer's Term box with students.

Instruct students to use their Story Maps to draft their adventure stories. Encourage them to write dialogue that sounds realistic for the characters and setting. Remind them that they will have time later to correct any mistakes they might make. Review the proofreading marks found on page 61.

Online Writing Center

 Provides an **interactive writing pad** for drafting, revising, editing, and publishing.

Draft

Focus on (Voice)

The Rubric Says	The voice is strong and natural. The dialogue makes the characters sound real.
Writing Strategy	Write dialogue that sounds like real people.

I'm ready to start writing my adventure story. I'll use my Story Map to make sure my story has a clear setting, characters, problem, events, and ending.

I will use my story-telling voice to connect with the reader. To make my story come to life, I need to remember to use dialogue. My teacher says, "Your characters should sound like real people talking." I want my readers to understand my characters and hear their voices, too.

I'll do my best with grammar and spelling as I write, but I won't worry about mistakes right now. I know I'll have a chance to fix them later.

> **Writer's Term**
> **Dialogue**
> In a story, **dialogue** refers to the conversation between characters.

60 Narrative Writing

Differentiating Instruction

ENRICHMENT
Internal Challenges Explain that not all problems faced by main characters are external. Many stories students may be familiar with include internal challenges such as fear and self-doubt. Challenge students to create a list of internal problems and then draft an adventure story in which the main character must overcome one.

REINFORCEMENT
Identifying Elements To help students better understand the elements of an adventure story, write the following questions on the board: *Who is the main character? What is the setting? What is the problem that needs to be solved? What is the climax? How is the problem resolved?* Then read aloud a familiar fairy tale. Discuss the answers to the questions with students to ensure they can identify each element.

[DRAFT]

Just Call Me Superkid

setting → It was a hot day. I was playing superhero with my little brother. I

was pretending to take on the bad guy when Michael herd something.

He yelled, "What's that noise?"

dialogue →

"I dont hear anything," I said.

I listened, too. Sure enough, I herd someone. Then I saw little Amy

Sisson standing in the road.

event →

I saw what was making Amy scream. A beehive had fallen about

five feet from her. Bees were everywhere. Amy was frozen with fear.

I knew she wouldn't be able to move by herself. I had to help her.

clear problem   high point

I was plenty scared of those bees, too, but I was five years older

than Amy. More importantly, I felt like Superkid.

Analyze
Read Jack's draft. In what ways does it hold your interest?

Write
Use your Story Map to write your own draft. Don't forget to include dialogue.

Adventure Story **61**

Collaborative Conferencing

PEER TO PEER Have students read their draft aloud to a partner. The partner listens carefully to the dialogue and offers one or two comments either on making the dialogue more realistic or adding dialogue in places.

PEER GROUPS Have each student read his or her draft aloud to the group. Each student points out one element of the story that he or she liked and makes one suggestion for adding dialogue or making it more realistic.

TEACHER-LED Meet with individual students. Read the student's draft aloud to him or her. Together, discuss how the dialogue sounded to the student and how he or she might add or change dialogue.

Write
Adventure Story

Student Objectives
• Complete a draft. *(p. 61)*

Continue Drafting Read Jack's draft on page 61. Have volunteers identify the setting, the characters, the problem, the events leading up to the climax, and the climax itself. Ask:

• Does Jack's dialogue sound realistic? Did he include enough dialogue to keep you engaged? **(Possible response: The dialogue sounds realistic, but I wish there was more so I could better "hear" the characters.)**

✏ Writer's Term
Dialogue To help the reader follow dialogue, the writer must follow the rules for punctuating it. Dialogue should always be enclosed by quotation marks, and the writer must start a new line when a new speaker is introduced. End punctuation for sentences spoken in dialogue goes inside the quotation marks.

CCSS **Common Core State Standards** (pp. Z20–Z30)
Writing: W.4.3a, W.4.3b, W.4.3e, W.4.4, W.4.5, W.4.6, W.4.10
Language: L.4.2b, L.4.3c, L.4.6
Speaking and Listening: SL.4.1a, SL.4.1b, SL.4.1c, SL.4.1d, SL.4.3, SL.4.6

Write
Adventure Story

Week 2 • Day 5

Student Objectives

- Revise to include character, setting, and plot details. *(p. 62)*

Revise

Focus on Ideas

Add Details Explain to students that now that they have drafted their adventure stories, it is time to revise and strengthen their writing.

Illustrate vivid details for students. Write on the board: *It was a good day.* Explain that you are going to add descriptive details to the sentence. Then write *It was a glorious, sunny day* and *It was a good day for skiing.* Discuss how adding details allowed you to convey two different, clear images. Have volunteers suggest other ways to revise the sentence by adding details.

Have a volunteer read Jack's draft excerpt before and then after his revisions. Ask:

- How do the new details help you visualize this event in the story? (Possible response: The new details really helped me "see" Jack as a Superkid.)

Now have students add descriptive details to their own stories.

 Strategies for Writers Online
Go to **www.sfw.z-b.com** for additional online resources for students, teachers, and parents.

Revise

Focus on ⟨ **Ideas** ⟩

The Rubric Says	Details develop the characters, setting, and plot.
Writing Strategy	Use details to help the reader imagine the characters, setting, and plot.

The rubric reminds me to use details to develop the setting, characters, and plot. I'll add a few details in the beginning to help my reader picture me better. In this story, I'm a character playing a character!

I also want to make sure that all the details—including the dialogue—build interest and suspense. Then the reader will want to keep reading to find out what happens next.

[DRAFT]

long,   August

It was a hot day. I was playing superhero with my little brother.
I was dressed up as Superkid.
I was pretending to take on the bad guy when Michael herd something. He
yelled, "What's that noise?"
                    I went on chasing the make-believe theif.
"I dont hear anything," I said.

added details

Write

Read your draft. Add details to help develop the characters, setting, and plot.

English Language Learners

BEGINNING/INTERMEDIATE

Word Choice Write the following words on the board or on index cards: *gripe, whisper, stumble, parade, mumble, say, reply, gab, tramp, trudge, march, skip, gossip, stroll, trip, chat.* Then have students work in pairs to sort the words into *walk* words and *talk* words. They may use a dictionary. Encourage them to try to use more interesting words in their writing.

ADVANCED/ADVANCED HIGH

Using Different Kinds of Sentences Write the following sentence on the board: *That is a treasure map.* Ask students to supply a sentence that gives the same information but sounds more dramatic; for example, *Could that tattered and yellowing paper actually be the legendary map to the treasure of Eagle Island?* Write other plain sentences on the board, and have students suggest ways to make them more dramatic by using questions, exclamations, or commands.

Revise

Focus on Word Choice

The Rubric Says	The writer uses strong verbs that make the story come to life and convey events precisely.
Writing Strategy	Change common verbs to exciting action verbs.

When I read the rubric again, I saw that strong verbs build suspense. I'll go through my draft and replace dull verbs with exciting verbs. For example, I can write *ordered* instead of *tells*. See how much more interesting my story becomes when I use exciting action verbs? Now I just have to make sure that my verbs agree with their subjects.

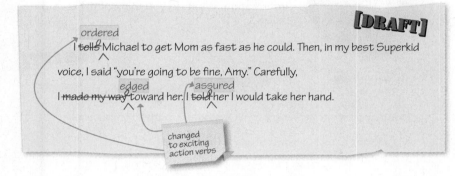

[DRAFT]

ordered

I ~~tells~~ Michael to get Mom as fast as he could. Then, in my best Superkid voice, I said "you're going to be fine, Amy." Carefully,

edged   assured

I ~~made my way~~ toward her. I ~~told~~ her I would take her hand.

changed to exciting action verbs

Analyze

Look at Jack's revisions. How do the verbs help to build suspense in this part of the story?

Write

Look at your draft again. Replace dull or overused verbs with exciting ones. Make sure these verbs agree with their subjects.

Adventure Story **63**

Collaborative Conferencing

PEER TO PEER Have pairs of students exchange drafts and look for common verbs that could be replaced with exciting action verbs. Students note common verbs and suggestions for replacements on a separate sheet of paper and give the paper to their partner.

PEER GROUPS Have students list the verbs they have already written in their drafts. Then divide the class into small groups. Each student takes a turn reading his or her list of verbs aloud. Other group members suggest possible action-verb alternatives.

TEACHER-LED Meet with pairs of students. Have partners read their drafts aloud, using as much expression as they can. Choose one or two verbs that sounded ordinary from each student's draft and help students discuss more exciting verbs that could be used in their place.

Write
Adventure Story

Week 3 • Day 1

Student Objectives

- Revise to add action verbs. (p. 63)

Revise

Focus on  Word Choice

Use Strong Verbs Read Jack's words on page 63 aloud. Explain that common verbs are boring and do not help the reader picture the events in a story vividly. In fact, boring, overused verbs can actually deplete a story of excitement for the reader. Using creative and exciting action verbs helps the reader feel the excitement and suspense the writer wants to convey.

Write the following words on the board: *run, walk, said, sat, think.* Ask volunteers to offer some creative verbs to replace each. Write students' suggestions next to the "boring" verb. (**Possible responses:** *sprint, stride, mumbled, lounged, wonder*)

Direct students to study the draft paragraph on page 63. Discuss how these new verbs add action and excitement to the scene. Have students read their own drafts and change common verbs to exciting action verbs.

CCSS **C**ommon **C**ore **S**tate **S**tandards (pp. Z20–Z30)
Writing: W.4.3a, W.4.3b, W.4.3d, W.4.4, W.4.5, W.4.10
Language: L.4.1f, L.4.3a, L.4.3b, L.4.3c, L.4.4c, L.4.6
Speaking and Listening: SL.4.1a, SL.4.1b, SL.4.1c, SL.4.3, SL.4.6

Write
Adventure Story

Week 3 • Day 2

Student Objectives

• Revise to use transitions to begin sentences. *(p. 64)*

Revise

Focus on Sentence Fluency

Use Transitions Explain to students that using a variety of sentence structures and types is a great way to give their writing flow and energy. An easy way to vary sentence structure is to begin some sentences with transitions. Remind students that transitions are words that signal to the reader that time has passed, guide the reader through a series of steps, or connect ideas.

Read Jack's words on page 64. Have a volunteer read the draft once without Jack's revisions and once with them. Discuss as a class how the revisions strengthened Jack's writing. Tell students to read over their drafts to see where they can use transitions to begin sentences. Allow them time to make the revisions. (See page 487 for a list of transitions.)

Revise

Focus on **Sentence Fluency**

The Rubric Says Sentence beginnings are varied. Transition words connect ideas.

Writing Strategy Use transition words to begin sentences.

Now it's time to check all my sentences. The rubric says I need to vary my sentence beginnings. By putting transition words at the beginning of a sentence, I do two things. One is that I vary the way my sentences begin, which helps to make them flow smoothly. The other thing is that I give the reader a little bit more information. What do you think of my revision below?

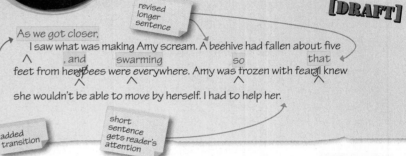

[DRAFT]

revised longer sentence

As we got closer,
I saw what was making Amy scream. A beehive had fallen about five
, and   swarming   so   that
feet from her. Bees were everywhere. Amy was frozen with fear. I knew

she wouldn't be able to move by herself. I had to help her.

added transition

short sentence gets reader's attention

Write

Check your draft again. Revise sentences to vary the rhythm and get your reader's attention.

64 Narrative Writing

Optional Revising Lessons

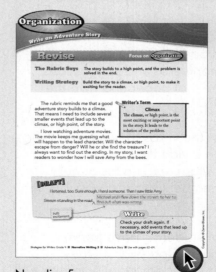

Narrative 5

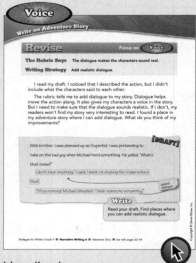

Narrative 6

Go to **Strategies for Writers** at www.sfw.z-b.com

Edit

Focus on Conventions

The Rubric Says   Quotation marks, apostrophes, and other punctuation marks are used correctly.

Writing Strategy   Check the punctuation.

I'm ready to check my spelling, punctuation, and capitalization. I also need to check all the dialogue in my story. Each direct quotation should begin and end with quotation marks. A new paragraph shows that a new speaker is talking. I'll also check to make sure I've punctuated contractions correctly.

Writer's Term

Direct Quotations

Direct quotations give the exact words of someone speaking. Put quotation marks around a direct quotation. Also, indent the first line of each new speaker.

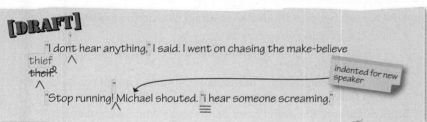

[DRAFT]

"I dont hear anything," I said. I went on chasing the make-believe
thief ∧
theif.

indented for new speaker

"Stop running! Michael shouted. "i hear someone screaming."

Analyze

Look at the way Jack revised his sentences. What do you think of his revisions? Look at Jack's edits. Are they correct? How do quotation marks help you read the dialogue?

Write

Conventions

Edit your draft carefully. Check that you have used quotation marks and apostrophes correctly.

For more practice using quotation marks and apostrophes, use the exercises on the next two pages.

Adventure Story **65**

Related Grammar Practice

Student Edition page 449

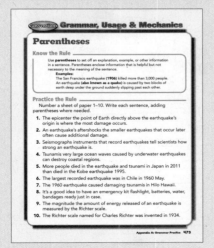

Student Edition page 473

Go to ▷ **Appendix A: Grammar Practice**

Student Objectives

• Edit to correct all punctuation. *(pp. 65–67)*

Edit

Focus on Conventions

Check Punctuation   Ask, *How do Jack's edits help how you enjoy this part of his adventure story?* (Possible response: If Jack hadn't inserted quotation marks, I wouldn't have understood when characters started or stopped speaking.)

If students have difficulty with quotations and apostrophes, teach the mini-lessons on pages T66 and T67 and then have students complete pages 66 and 67.

Writer's Term

Direct Quotations   Direct quotations are words spoken by a character. The reader understands these are the speaker's actual words because there are quotation marks at both the beginning and ending of the quote. In indirect quotations, the writer tells what someone said without quoting the person directly (*Marie said that we had to leave soon.*). Indirect quotations do not use quotation marks.

CCSS **Common Core State Standards** (pp. Z20–Z30)
Writing: W.4.3c, W.4.4, W.4.5, W.4.6, W.4.10
Language: L.4.1f, L.4.2a, L.4.2b, L.4.2d, L.4.6

Conventions

Mini-Lesson

Student Objectives

- Understand how to correctly punctuate direct quotations. (p. 66)

Direct Quotations

Explain to students that quotation marks are used to enclose direct quotations. Note that commas, periods, question marks, and exclamation points are placed inside the closing quotation mark. Write the following sentence on the board: *Hello, he said.*

Ask students to point out where the quotation marks should be placed. (before *Hello* and after the comma)

Remind students that every time a speaker changes, the new line of dialogue should be indented. Have student volunteers tell you where to add the appropriate quotation marks and where to indent new lines: *Mother asked, Where are you going? Outside to play, I said. Oh no, you're not! she exclaimed. You have homework.*

(Correct response:

   Mother asked, "Where are you going?"

   "Outside to play," I said.

   "Oh no, you're not!" she exclaimed. "You have homework.")

Online Writing Center

Provides **interactive grammar games** and **practice activities** in student eBook.

Direct Quotations

Know the Rule

A **direct quotation** is a speaker's exact words. Use quotation marks at the beginning and end of the speaker's exact words. Use a comma to separate the speaker's exact words from the rest of the sentence. Begin a direct quotation with a capital letter and add end punctuation before the last quotation mark.

Examples:
The child shouted, **"Wow!"**
"I'm not surprised," the man replied.

Practice the Rule

Number a sheet of paper 1–10. Read each sentence. If the sentence has errors in punctuation, rewrite the sentence correctly. If the sentence uses punctuation correctly, write **Correct**.

1. Our teacher said, "Kids, we're going to visit an apiary." Correct
2. "What's an apiary?" asked Gina.
3. "An apiary is a place where a beekeeper keeps hives of bees," explained Mr. Frantz.
4. Mr. Frantz continued, "The beekeeper takes care of the bees and then harvests honey from each hive." Correct
5. Ryan asked, "But aren't bees dangerous? Won't we get stung?"
6. Mr. Frantz said, "No, we won't be touching any hives, and the bees are peaceful if we leave them alone."
7. "Beekeepers wear protective clothes when it's time to harvest the honey," Mr. Frantz said. Correct
8. "Oh, I see" exclaimed Gina.
9. "That way the beekeeper can't get stung," she added. Correct
10. "A beekeeper's work is very interesting," said Mr. Frantz.

Related Grammar Practice

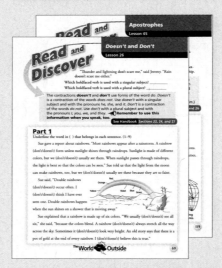

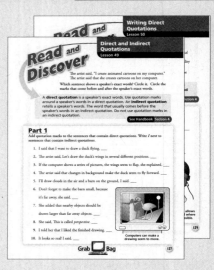

Pages 69, 119, 127, 129

 Go to G.U.M. Student Practice Book

Apostrophes

Know the Rule

A **possessive noun** shows ownership. Add an **apostrophe (')** and an -s to a singular noun to show ownership.
> **Example:**
> I hurried to **Ms. Garcia's** classroom.

Add an apostrophe after the -s of a plural noun to show ownership.
> **Example:**
> I found the **students'** books in her room.

Use an apostrophe and an -s if the plural noun doesn't end in an -s.
> **Example:**
> The **children's** room was a mess!

A **contraction** is made of two words put together, like *doesn't* (does not). An apostrophe takes the place of one or more letters.
> **Example:**
> The children **hadn't** (had not) cleaned up their art project.

Practice the Rule

Rewrite each sentence on a separate sheet of paper, adding apostrophes as needed. Sometimes two apostrophes are needed in one sentence.

1. There's a nest of bees in Tony's backyard.
2. Tony's father saw it, but he hasn't disturbed it.
3. We aren't allowed to go anywhere near it.
4. They've seen many bees swarming around.
5. Tony's mom is worried that we'll get stung.
6. I haven't been stung by a bee, yet!
7. I'm pretty sure that it's painful, though.
8. For now, we'll just have to play in our backyard.
9. As far as we know, there isn't a bees' nest at my house.
10. We've looked all around, but we can't find one.

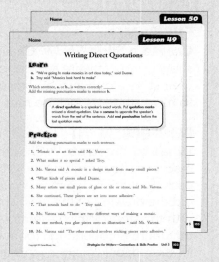

Pages 57, 95, 103, 105

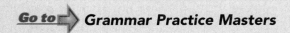 **Grammar Practice Masters**

Mini-Lesson

Student Objectives

- Learn how to use apostrophes correctly. *(p. 67)*

Apostrophes

Explain that apostrophes serve two purposes in writing: They show possession, and they are used in contractions.

Write the following examples on the board: *the department of the men; the barn of the three horses; the room of the girl.*

Ask for volunteers to change these phrases into possessive nouns using -s and an apostrophe. (**the men's department; the horses' barn; the girl's room**)

Write the following phrases on the board: *will not, should not, it is, I am, you are, we have, you will.* Ask for volunteers to change these phrases into contractions. (**won't, shouldn't, it's, I'm, you're, we've, you'll**) Point out that *will not* does not become *willn't* and that this change in spelling is an exception to the rule.

Have students complete page 67 for more practice with apostrophes.

CCSS **C**ommon **C**ore **S**tate **S**tandards (pp. Z20–Z30)
Writing: W.4.6
Language: L.4.2a, L.4.2b, L.4.2d, L.4.6

Write
Adventure Story

Week 3 • Day 4

Student Objectives

- Discuss preparation for publishing and presentation. *(p. 68)*
- Use a final editing checklist to publish their work. *(p. 68)*

Publish ⁺Presentation

Add Illustrations Remind students that the method of publishing should be appropriate for the writing. As this is an adventure story, Jack's choice makes sense. Discuss how adding drawings that illustrate specific events will help readers enjoy the story more.

Discuss other publishing choices Jack could have made, such as making an audio recording of his story. Challenge students to consider several ways they could publish their own adventure stories.

Read through Jack's publishing checklist. Be sure students understand that the checklist relates to the writing traits and strategies they have been using. Allow time in class for students to illustrate and check over their stories. Then help students arrange to read their stories to groups of younger students. Encourage them to share their published work with a parent or other family members.

 Strategies for Writers Online
Go to **www.sfw.z-b.com** for additional online resources for students, teachers, and parents.

Publish ⁺Presentation

Publishing Strategy	Publish my story as a big book to read to younger students.
Presentation Strategy	Add illustrations that support and clarify the story elements.

My adventure story is done! Now it's time to publish it. There are many ways to publish a story. I think that younger students would really enjoy my adventure, so I think I'll publish it in a big book. A big book has the story's words printed very large. Each page has a picture that shows what is happening in the story. I need to be sure my writing is neat and my illustrations are clear. Before I draw the pictures and make the big book, I want to check my story one last time. Here's the checklist I will use.

My Final Checklist

Did I—

✔ use quotation marks for direct quotes?

✔ use apostrophes correctly?

✔ use illustrations to support my story?

✔ use neat handwriting or word processing?

✔ put my name on my story?

Write

Use the checklist to prepare your final copy for publication.

68 Narrative Writing

Differentiating Instruction

ENRICHMENT

Create a Slide Show Challenge students to create a slide show using software such as paint.net. Have students read their story aloud as they present the slide show. You may wish to have students include music in their presentation as well.

REINFORCEMENT

What to Illustrate? Choose an illustrated short story to read and show to students. When the story is over, discuss what each illustration depicted. Were all the characters shown? How did the drawing of the main character help students connect with the story? Which events were *not* illustrated? Explain that there is not enough room for every single event to be illustrated; only major events and characters are shown to help enhance the reader's experience of the story.

Just Call Me Superkid
by Jack

It was a long, hot August day. I was playing superhero with my little brother. I was dressed up as Superkid, and I was pretending to take on the bad guy when Michael heard something. He yelled, "What's that noise?"

"I don't hear anything," I said. I went on chasing the make-believe thief.

Week 3 • Day 5

Student Objectives

• Use an adventure story rubric. *(pp. 52–53)*
• Share a published adventure story. *(pp. 69–71)*

Presentation Strategy Remind students of the importance of presentation. Even the most exciting adventure stories will not be read or enjoyed by readers if the handwriting or type is messy or illegible. When students put effort into presentation, they are showing the proper respect for all of the hard work they have put into their writing.

Remind students that they can still illustrate their stories if they choose to type their work. Many computers have illustrating programs that allow students to draw their illustrations and then copy and paste the drawing into the text. Or students can simply leave blank spaces in the text where they will later hand-draw their illustrations.

Have students refer to the rubric on pages 52–53 as you read "Just Call Me Superkid" on pages 69–71. Ask students what score they would assign Jack for each trait. Be sure students can support their answers. Take a vote to see how well Jack did overall in the eyes of your class. Remind students to refer to the rubric to assess their own stories.

Tech Tips

Online Tools

Use Audio Feedback Student writers are hungry for feedback from peers, teachers, and other writers. Provide an opportunity for students to compose in a different mode by offering audio feedback to students' work. You could do this by using the comment feature in VoiceThread, recording audio and movement using a screencast tool like Jing, or using an audio editor like Audacity or GarageBand. Encourage students to return to the recording as they work on subsequent texts, as it is meant to be a tool and an artifact.

See **www.sfw.z-b.com** for further information about and links to these websites and tools.

CCSS **C**ommon **C**ore **S**tate **S**tandards (pp. Z20–Z30)
Writing: W.4.4, W.4.6, W.4.10
Language: L.4.2b
Speaking and Listening: SL.4.4, SL.4.5

Reflecting on an Adventure Story

Have students think back on this assignment as a whole. Encourage students to share how they feel about the experience. You might ask:

- Were you surprised by any of the steps or methods for writing an adventure story?

- How difficult was it to think of a main character and a problem?

- How was writing an adventure story different from other types of writing you have done?

- What part of the writing process did you enjoy the most?

- Will you ever write another adventure story? If so, what will you do differently?

Have students write their answers to these questions in their journals, or have them discuss their reflections as a class or in small groups.

"Stop running!" Michael shouted. "I hear someone screaming."

I listened, too. Sure enough, I heard someone. Then I saw little Amy Sisson standing in the road. Michael and I flew down the street to her to find out what was wrong.

As we got closer, I saw what was making Amy scream. A beehive had fallen about five feet from her, and bees were swarming everywhere. Amy was so frozen with fear that I knew she wouldn't be able to move by herself. I had to help her.

70 Narrative Writing

Strategies for Writers Online

Go to **www.sfw.z-b.com** for additional online resources for students, teachers, and parents.

I was plenty scared of those bees, too, but I was five years older than Amy. More importantly, I felt like Superkid. I didn't get any closer to the bees, but I did tell Amy quietly in my most soothing voice that I could help her. I told her not to be afraid. Superkid was there.

I ordered Michael to get Mom as fast as he could. Then, in my best Superkid voice, I said, "You're going to be fine, Amy." Carefully I edged toward her. I assured her that I would take her hand. I said that we would walk slowly backward from the hive. I don't know how I made myself go to Amy, but I did. The first step was the hardest. Soon Mom was there, taking steps backward with us. Only five minutes later, we were far away from the buzzing bees, walking Amy to her front door.

As soon as Amy got inside, she cried, "Daddy! Daddy! Superkid saved me!" Well, I guess Amy was right.

Analyze

Use the rubric to evaluate Jack's story. Which trait is strongest? Weakest? Be sure to use the rubric to score your own adventure story.

Adventure Story 71

CCSS **Common Core State Standards** (pp. Z20–Z30)
Writing: W.4.4, W.4.10
Language: L.4.3c
Speaking and Listening: SL.4.1a, SL.4.1b, SL.4.1c, SL.4.1d, SL.4.3, SL.4.6

Play Planner

WEEK 1

Day 1
Introduce
Play

Student Objectives
- Review the elements of a play.
- Consider purpose and audience.
- Learn the traits of narrative writing.

Student Activities
- Read and discuss **What's in a Play?** (p.72)
- Read and discuss **Why Write a Play?** (p. 73)
- Read **Linking Narrative Writing Traits to a Play.** (p. 74)

Day 2
Analyze
Close Reading of the Model

Student Objectives
- Read a model play.

Student Activities
- Read **"A Short Trip to Tomorrow."** (pp. 75–77)

Day 3
Analyze
Introduce the Rubric

Student Objectives
- Learn to read a rubric.

Student Activities
- Review **"A Short Trip to Tomorrow."** (pp. 75–77)
- Read and discuss the **Play Rubric.** (pp. 78–79)

WEEK 2

Day 1
Write
Prewrite: Ideas

Student Objectives
- Read and understand a prewriting strategy.

Student Activities
- Read and discuss **Prewrite: Focus on Ideas.** (p. 84)
- Apply the prewriting strategy.

Day 2
Write
Prewrite: Organization

Student Objectives
- Create a Story Map to organize ideas.

Student Activities
- Read and discuss **Prewrite: Focus on Organization.** (p. 85)
- Reflect on the model Story Map.
- Apply the prewriting strategy to create a Story Map.
- Participate in a peer conference.

Day 3
Write
Draft: Word Choice

Student Objectives
- Use a Story Map to begin writing.

Student Activities
- Read and discuss **Draft: Focus on Word Choice.** (p. 86)
- Apply the drafting strategy by using a Story Map to write a draft.

WEEK 3

Day 1
Write
Revise: Organization

Student Objectives
- Revise the beginning.

Student Activities
- Read and discuss **Revise: Focus on Organization.** (p. 89)
- Reflect on the model draft.
- Apply the revising strategy.
- Participate in a peer conference.

Day 2
Write
Revise: Sentence Fluency

Student Objectives
- Revise to use punctuation for effect.

Student Activities
- Read and discuss **Revise: Focus on Sentence Fluency.** (p. 90)
- Reflect on the model draft.
- Apply the revising strategy.

Note: Optional Revising Lessons are located at **www.sfw.z-b.com.**

Day 3
Write
Edit: Conventions

Student Objectives
- Edit for correct comma usage.

Student Activities
- Read and discuss **Edit: Focus on Conventions.** (p. 91)
- Reflect on the model draft.
- Apply the editing strategy.

Note: Teach the Conventions mini-lessons (pp. 92–93) if needed.

Analyze
Close Reading for the Traits

Student Objectives
- Read a model play.
- Use the play rubric.
- Use the model play to study Ideas, Organization, and Voice.

Student Activities
- Review **"A Short Trip to Tomorrow."** (pp. 75–77)
- Review the rubric. (pp. 78–79)
- Read and discuss **Using the Rubric to Analyze the Model.** (pp. 80–81)

Analyze
Close Reading for the Traits

Student Objectives
- Read a model play.
- Use the play rubric.
- Use the model play to study Word Choice, Sentence Fluency, and Conventions.

Student Activities
- Review **"A Short Trip to Tomorrow."** (pp. 75–77)
- Read and discuss **Using the Rubric to Analyze the Model.** (pp. 82–83)

Write
Draft

Student Objectives
- Complete a draft.

Student Activities
- Finish the draft.
- Reflect on the model draft. (p. 87)
- Participate in a peer conference.

Write
Revise: Ideas

Student Objectives
- Revise to provide details in the dialogue and stage directions.

Student Activities
- Read and discuss **Revise: Focus on Ideas.** (p. 88)
- Reflect on a model draft.
- Apply the revising strategy.

Write
Publish: +Presentation

Student Objectives
- Discuss preparation for publishing and presentation.
- Use a final editing checklist to publish their work.

Student Activities
- Read and discuss **Publish: +Presentation.** (p. 94)
- Apply the publishing strategy.

Write
Publish: +Presentation

Student Objectives
- Use a play rubric.
- Share a published play.

Student Activities
- Share their work.
- Use the rubric to reflect upon and evaluate the model and their own writing. (pp. 78–79, 95–97)

To complete the chapter in fewer days, combine the learning objectives and activities in a way that supports students as they write.

Resources at-a-Glance

Grammar, Usage & Mechanics

Differentiating Instruction

For additional Differentiating Instruction activities, see Strategies for Writers Differentiated Instruction Activities *at www.sfw.z-b.com.*

English Language Learners

Collaborative Conferencing

Tech Tips

 Strategies for Writers Online

Go to **www.sfw.z-b.com** for additional online resources for students, teachers, and parents.

Online Writing Center

Provides IWB resources, assessments, interactive games and practice activities, videos, eBooks, and a virtual file cabinet.

Introduce
Play

Student Objectives

- Review the elements of a play. *(p. 72)*
- Consider purpose and audience. *(p. 73)*
- Learn the traits of narrative writing. *(p. 74)*

What's a Play?

Read page 72 aloud and discuss the definition of a play with students. Explain that a play is a story that is performed live on a stage for an audience. Ask if anyone has seen a play or performed in one. Ask what was different about seeing a play versus watching a movie in a theater. As a play is made up mostly of dialogue, all other details must be revealed through stage directions and setting.

What's in a Play?

Discuss a school play students have seen or performed in. (If only a few students have seen a play, choose a movie or television show students have seen.) Have students identify the story elements and problem in the play. Ask them to quote lines of dialogue they found memorable. Prompt students to imagine what the stage directions might have been.

Strategies for Writers Online
Go to **www.sfw.z-b.com** for additional online resources for students, teachers, and parents.

What's a Play?
It's a piece of writing that tells a story that can be acted out.

What's in a Play?

Stage Directions
Stage directions are written instructions that tell the characters and stage crew what to do. Stage directions also help explain the characters, setting, and plot.

Story Elements
A play has characters, a setting, and a plot, just like a story. Most plays have at least two characters. The setting tells where and when the play takes place. The plot is the action of the play.

Dialogue
The story is told through dialogue. Dialogue is the conversation, or spoken lines, among characters. Spoken lines come after the name of the character that is speaking.

Problem
Like all good stories, a good play has a problem the characters must overcome or solve.

Narrative Text Exemplars (Play)

Ransom, Candice F. *George Washington and the Story of the U.S. Constitution.* **Lerner Classroom, 2011.** Filled with details regarding the writing of the US constitution, this book provides students with a great history lesson. A readers' theater script about the Constitutional Convention accompanies the text.

Peterson, Carol. *Around the World through Holidays: Cross Curricular Readers Theatre.* **Libraries Unlimited, 2005.** This compilation of readers' theater scripts touches on holidays celebrated by different cultures around the world. This informative and entertaining book includes 12 plays, one for each month of the year.

Why write a Play?

There are many reasons to write a play. Here are two important ones.

> **To Explore**
> Writing a play helps me explore and experience a specific time period. For example, I can write a play about the life of an important historical character or an exciting event I learned about in my social studies class.

> **To Entertain**
> When you put on a play, you get to work with other people. It's fun to write and act out a play with friends.

Evan-Moor Educational Publishers. *Leveled Readers' Theater, Grade 4.* Evan-Moor Educational Publishers, 2008. The scripts provided in this readers theater book address multiple fourth-grade content areas while keeping students interested and engaged. A few of the 15 titles include "Louis Pasteur: A Scientist Serving Humanity," "The Sager Children," and "How Animals Got Their Beautiful Coats."

Fredericks, Anthony D. *Frantic Frogs and Other Frankly Fractured Folktales for Readers Theatre.* Teacher Ideas Press, 1993. Fredericks brings comedy to the classroom in this unique collection of readers theater stories. With over 20 scripts that put a humorous spin on well-known folktales, these plays are sure to entertain even the most uninterested student.

Why write a Play?

Perhaps the most common reason for writing a play is to entertain an audience. However, explain that writers can also use the play form to explore a subject, event, or time period that interests them. By writing, the playwright can gain a deeper understanding of the subject and share it with others. Whatever the purpose of writing, it is very rewarding for a writer to watch his or her characters come to life on a stage.

Ask students to suggest ideas for plays they would enjoy watching. Write their suggestions on the board. Now ask them what would be the purpose for writing each play. For example, a play about World War I might aim to help the audience understand the soldier's experience, whereas a play about a roaming band of mischievous farm animals would be for entertainment.

No matter what the reason, a good writer will keep both purpose and audience in mind as the play is being written. That way, the writer is sure to write in a way that effectively connects with the audience and clearly depicts the characters and plot.

CCSS **Common Core State Standards** (pp. Z20–Z30)
Language: L.4.3c
Speaking and Listening: SL.4.1a, SL.4.1b, SL.4.1c, SL.4.1d, SL.4.3, SL.4.6

Introduce
Play

Linking Narrative Writing Traits to a Play

Find a short play to read aloud to the class. Before you begin reading, write each of the characters' names on the board, as well as the location and time period. Then write an example of dialogue and stage directions on the board. Explain that dialogue is spoken aloud by the character whose name appears right before the line. Stage directions appear inside parentheses and are not spoken; rather, they tell the actors how to say their lines or how to move around the stage while speaking.

Finish the play, and then direct students' attention to the narrative writing traits listed on page 74. Call on individuals to read each trait aloud. Discuss each trait as it is read and, when suitable, use the play you just finished as an example to clarify the trait descriptions.

Tell students that they will follow Jack as he models using the writing process and the narrative writing traits together to write a play.

Online Writing Center

Provides six **interactive anchor papers** for each text type.

Linking Narrative Writing Traits to a

In this chapter, you will write a story that can be acted out. This type of narrative writing is called a play. Jack will guide you through the stages of the writing process: Prewrite, Draft, Revise, Edit, and Publish. In each stage, Jack will show you important writing strategies that are linked to the Narrative Writing Traits below.

Narrative Writing Traits

 Ideas
- a topic that is just the right size, not too big or too small
- details and facts that develop the narrative

 Organization
- a natural and logical sequence
- a strong beginning and a satisfying ending
- transitions that signal the sequence of events

 Voice
- a voice and tone that are perfect for the writing
- dialogue that, when used, sounds just right for the characters

 **Word Choice**
- concrete words and phrases that describe the characters and events

 Sentence Fluency
- a variety of sentence lengths to make the story flow smoothly

Conventions
- no or few errors in spelling, grammar, punctuation, and capitalization

Before you write, read Lanie Song's play on the next three pages. Then use the play rubric on pages 78–79 to decide how well she did. (You might want to look back at What's in a Play? on page 72, too!)

Narrative Writing Traits in a Play

 **Ideas** The writer chooses a topic that can be depicted in no more than four scenes. Details are engaging and accurate and help move the plot forward.

 **Organization** A play is a story, so the most effective way to present the play's events is in a natural, chronological order. The beginning pulls the audience in, the middle presents the events that lead to the climax, and the ending reveals how the problem is solved.

 **Voice** The dialogue sounds natural and reveals all the information the audience needs to easily understand each character and follow the events of the plot.

A Short Trip to Tomorrow
by Lanie Song

CHARACTERS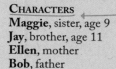
Maggie, sister, age 9
Jay, brother, age 11
Ellen, mother
Bob, father

SETTING: Seattle, Washington, April 1962 — *setting*

SCENE 1: *Family sitting around the kitchen table, just finishing dinner*

Ellen: Did you hear the news? The World's Fair just started! Maggie and I heard the announcement over the radio. President Kennedy opened it.

Bob: Is he in town?

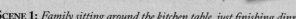 **Maggie:** (*excitedly*) No, he announced it over the telephone. And guess what? This is the coolest! They used a sound from a faraway star to open the fair. The star is light years away!

dialogue

Jay: (*rolling his eyes, not impressed*) There you go again, Maggs, dreaming about outer space. Get real. ← *stage direction*

Ellen: It's true, Jay. Your sister has it right. Scientists intercepted sound waves that came from a distant star. The sound began over 10,000 years ago!

Bob: I'd say that goes along with the space age theme of the fair.

Maggie: I'll say! There are all kinds of really neat things to do, like you can take a rocket trip through outer space, and…

Jay: (*interrupts Maggie*) Yeah, and you can wait in long lines with gazillions of other people. Sheesh! That's not for me.

Bob: (*rubs his chin, thinking*) Jay's probably right, there. Many people from all over the world will be coming to Seattle for the World's Fair. Still, it isn't every day it's in your own hometown. What do you think, Ellen? Should we take the kids and go?

Ellen and Maggie: Yes!!

Bob: What about it, Jay?

Jay: (*sighs and mumbles*) I guess so. But I don't have to like it!

Word Choice Concrete, descriptive words depict the play's characters and events. Each word serves a purpose and needs to be strong and accurate.

Sentence Fluency As a play consists of mostly dialogue, it is important that the dialogue sounds natural and realistic. We speak using a wide variety of sentence types and structures; thus a well-written play will do the same.

Conventions Errors in spelling, grammar, punctuation, or capitalization may confuse the reader as well as the actor attempting to learn or speak his or her lines. Commas are used correctly to ensure proper flow and clarify meaning.

Analyze
Close Reading of the Model

Student Objectives
• Read a model play. *(pp. 75–77)*

Read the Model

Read aloud "A Short Trip to Tomorrow" by Lanie Song on pages 75–77. Use a slightly different voice for stage directions and each of the characters to help students experience the different elements of a play. Before you read, remind students to listen for the writing traits outlined on page 74.

Elements of a Play

Use the notes on the model to discuss the various elements of a play. Ask students if they found it awkward or difficult to understand how the play is set up. Explain that although the format is different from the other forms of narrative writing they have studied, once they have a little practice reading a play, the format is easier to follow and understand.

Point out that the character list consists of only four characters. Explain that there is not enough time in a play to develop many characters, yet having only one or two characters may not be enough to fully develop a plot. Remind students to keep this point in mind as they think about topics for their own plays.

CCSS **Common Core State Standards** (pp. Z20–Z30)
Writing: W.4.6
Language: L.4.3c
Speaking and Listening: SL.4.1a, SL.4.1b, SL.4.1c, SL.4.1d, SL.4.2, SL.4.3, SL.4.6

Take a moment to focus on stage directions. Ask a volunteer to point out several examples of stage directions in the model. To help students understand this element better, ask:

- What purpose do these stage directions serve? (Possible response: They help show a character's personality, and they explain the setting.)

- How do these stage directions help you visualize the play? (Possible response: If it wasn't for the stage directions, I might have imagined a character saying his or her lines in a completely different way. For example, if the stage directions didn't tell me that Jay rolled his eyes before saying, "There you go again, Maggs, dreaming about outer space," I might not have understood he was teasing her.)

Explain that just as a book has chapters, a play consists of scenes. Each scene takes place in one setting and depicts a specific development of the plot. Ask a volunteer to tell you how many scenes there are in the model play. (four) Ask:

- In which scene does the climax occur? (scene 3)

Strategies for Writers Online

Go to **www.sfw.z-b.com** for additional online resources for students, teachers, and parents.

Play MODEL

SCENE 2: *Family boards a monorail train car that rides high above the city's streets*

Maggie: This is so cool!

Ellen: It sure is! They built this train for the fair, you know, to transport people from the city's center.

Bob: I heard that the engineers designed it to carry 10,000 people to their destinations in an hour!

Jay: (*grumpily*) What did I tell you about the crowds and long lines?

Maggie: (*excitedly, with face pressed against window*) Hey! I can see Puget Sound! And the Cascade Mountains! I love being high in the sky!   *stage direction*

Ellen: We're here! Let's see the fair!

Bob: (*as family exits the monorail*) Now listen, kids. Stick together and keep track of each other. We don't want to spend any time in line at the lost children's booth! C'mon! Let's head for the Science Pavilion first.

Maggie: Sounds good to me! C'mon, Jay!

Jay: (*reluctantly follows*) Sheesh! I've never seen so many people in one place. Get a look at those lines!

SCENE 3: *After tour, family gathers outside pavilion*

Bob: Well, what did you make of that tour, kids?

Maggie: Oh, Dad, that was the coolest—an imaginary rocket ride! I saw Jupiter, Saturn, Neptune, and Pluto! We must have traveled millions of miles!

Ellen: And all we had to do was look up at the world's largest movie screen to take that journey.

Maggie: Whaddya think, Jay? Worth the wait in line?

Jay: (*staring up at a tall structure in the distance*) Maggs, quit buggin' me! It was just a dumb movie, not a real ride.   *stage direction*

Bob: Just imagine, Son. Ordinary people like us will travel in spaceships someday, much in the same way we travel by car today.

Maggie: You tell him, Dad! John Glenn just orbited Earth three times a couple of months ago! That's a first, but I don't think it will be the last!

76 Narrative Writing

Ellen: And don't forget President Kennedy said that we'd have a real "man on the moon" by the end of this decade.

Jay: (*still staring up in amazement*) Man, look at that Space Needle!

Maggie: (*follows Jay's gaze*) Wow! Doesn't the top look like a flying saucer?

Jay: (*still looking up, in awe*) It sure does!

Maggie: The Space Needle is the tallest building west of the Mississippi. It's as high as a 60-story building! And, did you know that it's the symbol of this fair?

Ellen: (*turns to speak to Bob*) Honey, at the top of the Needle is a restaurant. What do you say we take the kids there for lunch?

Bob: My thoughts, exactly, but there's probably a very long line. Do you think Jay will mind?

Jay: (*responds loudly as he overhears his parents*) Who cares? We have to go up there!

Bob: (*looks up at the Needle as he thinks out loud*) …heard that the restaurant spins slowly…makes a complete circle every hour or so…should get some great views from up there. (*then says loudly*) All right, Team Mercury, let's go!

SCENE 4: *Family sitting at a lunch table in the Space Needle's restaurant, far above the fairgrounds*

Jay: (*looking out the window at the action far below*) This really is cool, isn't it, Dad?

Bob: Sure is, Jay. This really does feel like the future, doesn't it?

Maggie: It's exciting to think about what could happen in the future and what the world will be like then.

Jay: Well, I saw an exhibit sign for The World of Tomorrow. Let's go there next.

Ellen: (*smiling*) Jay, that's a great idea, but are you sure you won't mind the long line?

Jay: (*smiling back*) Mom, it's not every day the World's Fair comes to my hometown!

Play **77**

Explain that in this particular play, scenes one, two, and three depict events that lead to the climax, or highest point in excitement in the play. The last scene, scene 4, is where the excitement subsides and the main goal is achieved. The last scene is where all loose ends are wrapped up and all questions are answered. Remind students to keep this in mind as they draft their own plays.

CCSS **Common Core State Standards** (pp. Z20–Z30)
Language: L.4.3c
Speaking and Listening: SL.4.1a, SL.4.1b, SL.4.1c, SL.4.1d, SL.4.2, SL.4.3, SL.4.6

Analyze
Introduce the Rubric

Week 1 • Day 3

Student Objectives

• Learn to read a rubric. (pp. 78–79)

Introduce the Rubric

Explain the Rubric Explain that a rubric is a tool that helps you plan, improve, and evaluate a piece of writing. Tell students that a rubric helps a writer focus on key elements, or traits, in writing (**Ideas, Organization, Voice, Word Choice, Sentence Fluency, Conventions,** and **Presentation**).

The 6-point rubric on pages 78–79 can be used to evaluate a play. Draw students' attention to the six columns and explain how the scoring system works. Explain that column 6 describes a very good play, one that has received the highest score in all categories. This is what students should strive for in their own writing.

Discuss the Rubric Guide the students in a discussion of the rubric. Read the descriptors that go with each trait. Note how the descriptors vary as you move from column to column.

Remind students to keep the rubric in mind when they write their own play and again when they revise it.

Online Writing Center

Provides a variety of **interactive rubrics,** including 4-, 5-, and 6-point models.

Play Rubric

Use this rubric to analyze the model. Then use it to plan and score your own play.

	6	5	4
Ideas	Details are accurate and appropriate for the situation in the play. Dialogue and stage directions develop the characters, setting, and plot.	Details are accurate and appropriate. Most of the dialogue and stage directions develop the play.	Details are mostly accurate and appropriate. Some of the dialogue and stage directions develop the play.
Organization	Events happen in logical sequence. The script has a clear beginning, middle, and end.	Most events happen in logical sequence. The script has a clear beginning, middle, and end.	Some events are out of sequence. The script does not have a clear beginning, middle, and end.
Voice	The dialogue sounds natural and fits the characters.	Most of the dialogue sounds natural and fits the characters.	Dialogue sounds unrealistic or awkward in a few places.
Word Choice	Concrete words and phrases describe the events precisely.	Concrete words and phrases describe most events precisely.	Concrete words and phrases describe most events.
Sentence Fluency	A variety of sentence types helps the dialogue flow smoothly.	Most sentences help the dialogue flow smoothly.	Several sentences in a row share the same structure.
Conventions	The writing contains no errors. All commas are used correctly.	A few errors are present but do not confuse the reader. Commas are used correctly.	Several errors confuse the reader. Some commas are used incorrectly.

✛ **Presentation**   Play format is easy to follow.

78   Narrative Writing

CCSS Common Core State Standards

Play

Writing in the Narrative text type engages the Common Core State Standards for Narrative writing. Each of the rubrics and strategies for the play chapter are solidly based on the Narrative Writing standards, and several strategies and exercises echo Speaking & Listening, Reading/Literature, and Language standards as well.

Standards **W.4.3b** and **W.4.3d,** which emphasize the use of descriptive and sensory details to establish and develop characters, plot, and setting, are reflected in the Ideas and Word Choice rubrics. Standard **W.4.3b** resonates throughout the Ideas and Voice rubrics, which encourage the use

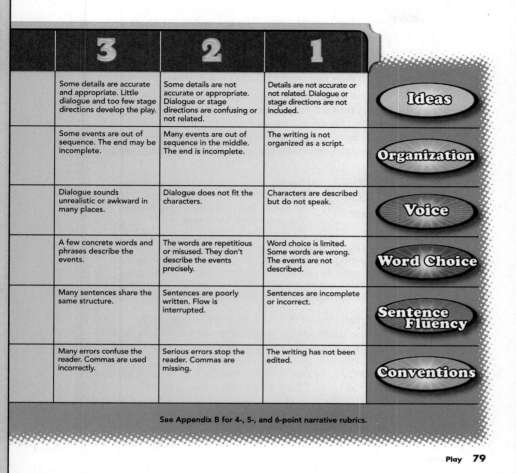

3	2	1	
Some details are accurate and appropriate. Little dialogue and too few stage directions develop the play.	Some details are not accurate or appropriate. Dialogue or stage directions are confusing or not related.	Details are not accurate or not related. Dialogue or stage directions are not included.	**Ideas**
Some events are out of sequence. The end may be incomplete.	Many events are out of sequence in the middle. The end is incomplete.	The writing is not organized as a script.	**Organization**
Dialogue sounds unrealistic or awkward in many places.	Dialogue does not fit the characters.	Characters are described but do not speak.	**Voice**
A few concrete words and phrases describe the events.	The words are repetitious or misused. They don't describe the events precisely.	Word choice is limited. Some words are wrong. The events are not described.	**Word Choice**
Many sentences share the same structure.	Sentences are poorly written. Flow is interrupted.	Sentences are incomplete or incorrect.	**Sentence Fluency**
Many errors confuse the reader. Commas are used incorrectly.	Serious errors stop the reader. Commas are missing.	The writing has not been edited.	**Conventions**

See Appendix B for 4-, 5-, and 6-point narrative rubrics.

of realistic-sounding dialogue to enhance the narrative and develop characters and plot. Standard **W.4.3a** is also clearly reflected in the Organization rubric, which stresses the importance of logically ordered events. Standard **W.4.3e** is also reflected in the Organization rubric, which outlines the need for the play to have a clear beginning, middle, and end.

Standards **L.4.1** and **L.4.2** are clearly reflected throughout the editing pages of the chapter, while standard **W.4.6** resonates throughout the Narrative unit, particularly in the Presentation +Publishing pages, as students are encouraged to take full advantage of the word processing programs available to them.

Find Evidence in the Model

Small-Group Collaboration
Assign students to small groups and tell them to evaluate the model using the rubric. Assign one person in each group to record the group's findings and one person to report the findings to the class. Instruct students to score the model for each trait based on evidence in the text. Remind students to read closely to identify examples to support their high or low scores. Note: Although the models were written to score high in each trait, students should not assume each trait would receive a 6, the top score.

Teacher-Led Discussion Bring the class back together, and have the reporters present their findings and scores. Prompt groups to provide evidence and examples for their scores from the model as needed.

Additional Rubrics

Appendix B includes 4-, 5-, and 6-point rubrics that can be used with any piece of narrative writing. The rubrics are also available as blackline masters in the back of this Teacher Edition.

CCSS **Common Core State Standards** (pp. Z20–Z30)
Writing: W.4.6
Language: L.4.3c
Speaking and Listening: SL.4.1a, SL.4.1b, SL.4.1c, SL.4.1d, SL.4.2, SL.4.3, SL.4.6

Analyze
Close Reading for the Traits

Week 1 • Day 4

Student Objectives

- Read a model play. *(pp. 75–77)*
- Use the play rubric. *(pp.78–79)*
- Use the model play to study **Ideas, Organization,** and **Voice**. *(pp. 80–81)*

Find Evidence in the Model

Evaluate the Model Have students turn to pages 80–81. Explain that these pages show how the model on pages 75–77 uses the writing traits described in the rubric.

Read each section with students. Use questions such as the following to discuss each section. Be sure students can back up their answers with examples from the model.

Discuss Audience, Task, Purpose Ask students one or more of the following questions as they analyze the model:

- **Audience** Who is the audience? (Possible response: people who are interested in going to a play)

- **Task** How does Lanie Song show what each character is supposed to do and say? (Possible response: She starts each speaker on a new line that starts with the character's name.)

- **Purpose** What is Lanie Song's purpose for writing this play? (Possible response: to entertain an audience)

Using the Play Rubric to Analyze the Model

Did you notice that the model on pages 75–77 points out some key elements of a play? As she wrote "A Short Trip to Tomorrow," Lanie Song used these elements to help her write her play. She also used the 6-point rubric on pages 78–79 to plan, draft, revise, and edit the writing. A rubric is a great tool to evaluate writing during the writing process.

Now let's use the same rubric to score the model. To do this, we'll focus on each trait separately, starting with Ideas. We'll use the top descriptor for each trait (column 6), along with examples from the model, to help us understand how the traits work together. How would you score Lanie on each trait?

 **Ideas**
- Details are accurate and appropriate for the situation in the play.
- Dialogue and stage directions develop the characters, setting, and plot.

Most of the action in Lanie Song's play takes place at the 1962 World's Fair in Seattle, Washington. She includes many factual, interesting details that help bring this time period to life. You also learn about the time period through the dialogue, the conversations among the characters in the play. The scene changes and stage directions help explain the events, too.

SCENE 1: *Family sitting around the kitchen table, just finishing dinner*
Ellen: Did you hear the news? The World's Fair just started! Maggie and I heard the announcement over the radio. President Kennedy opened it.
Bob: Is he in town?
Maggie: (*excitedly*) No, he announced it over the telephone. And guess what? This is the coolest! They used a sound from a faraway star to open the fair. The star is light years away!
Jay: (*rolling his eyes, not impressed*) There you go again, Maggs, dreaming about outer space. Get real.

80 Narrative Writing

English Language Learners

BEGINNING

Types of Performances If available via the Internet or on video, show students a bit of a play. Say, *This is a play.* Have students repeat. Write *play* on the board. Repeat for *movie, television program,* and *musical.*

INTERMEDIATE

Parts of a Story Introduce a play by showing students a short video or a photograph of a stage production. Teach the terms *play, actors, scene,* and *stage.* Review the elements of a story with students: *characters, setting, plot, conflict,* and *resolution.* Tell students that a play has all the same elements as a story, and it also includes *stage directions,* which tell the actors where to stand and how to interact with each other.

Organization
- Events happen in logical sequence.
- The script has a clear beginning, middle, and end.

The play opens as the family talks about the World's Fair coming to their hometown. In Scene 2, the family rides the monorail to the fair and decides to visit the Science Pavilion. In Scene 3, they decide to have lunch at the new Space Needle. I could really follow the action in each scene, and the order of events makes sense. I like the way the writer ties the ending to the beginning, too. In the end, Jay decides long lines aren't so bad after all.

Ellen: (*smiling*) Jay, that's a great idea, but are you sure you won't mind the long line?

Jay: (*smiling back*) Mom, it's not every day the World's Fair comes to my hometown!

Voice
- The dialogue sounds natural and fits the characters.

Maggie shows excitement about going to the fair, but Jay complains at first. I think their dialogue really shows their personalities by what they say and how they say it. All of their conversations sound like real people talking.

I also like the way the writer includes casual expressions, such as *yeah*, *gazillions*, and *sheesh*. She even has the characters interrupt one another, just like real people sometimes interrupt each other. This makes the dialogue sound very realistic.

Maggie: I'll say! There are all kinds of really neat things to do, like you can take a rocket trip through outer space, and...

Jay: (*interrupts Maggie*) Yeah, and you can wait in long lines with gazillions of other people. Sheesh! That's not for me.

Play **81**

Discuss the Traits Ask students one or more of the following questions to discuss the traits in the model.

Ideas How does the information in italics help you better understand the opening scene? (Possible response: It tells who is in the scene and where they are.)

Organization How does Lanie organize the events in the play? (Possible response: The events are given in chronological order, which makes the action easy to follow.)

Voice How does Lanie adjust the dialogue to accurately portray each character? (Possible response: The parents sound just like adults, while Maggie and Jay sound like two normal siblings who like to tease each other.)

ADVANCED
Reasons for Writing a Play Introduce the concept of a stage play, if students are unfamiliar. Ask students the reasons for writing a play and what types of stories might be a good plot for a play. Have a class discussion about the topic. Introduce sentence frames for students to practice, such as, *One reason to write a play would be to _____. I think/I don't think a good plot for a play would be _____.*

ADVANCED HIGH
Story Map Review the elements of a story. Ask, *What can you find in a story?* Students should be able to answer questions such as *What is a character/setting/plot?* Students should know that the *conflict* in the story is the problem, and the *resolution* is the solution. Have partners brainstorm ideas for a play and complete a Story Map as a prewriting activity.

CCSS **Common Core State Standards** (pp. Z20–Z30)
Language: L.4.3c, L.4.6
Speaking and Listening: SL.4.1a, SL.4.1b, SL.4.1c, SL.4.1d, SL.4.3, SL.4.6

Analyze
Close Reading for the Traits

Week 1 • Day 5

Student Objectives

- Read a model play. *(pp. 75–77)*
- Use the play rubric. *(pp. 78–79)*
- Use the model play to study **Word Choice, Sentence Fluency,** and **Conventions.** *(pp. 82–83)*

Discuss the Traits Ask students one or more of the following questions to discuss the traits in the model.

 Choose one word or phrase in the play that gave you a very clear image of the action. (Possible response: *I've never seen so many people in one place.* This line gives a clear idea of how crowded it is.)

Sentence Fluency Do you think the dialogue in the play sounds realistic? Why? (Possible responses: Yes, because there's a mix of exclamations, questions, and statements. Yes, because Maggie and Jay use words that kids often use in real life.)

Conventions How does Lanie's careful editing affect your experience with the play? (Possible response: The play is easy to read because there are no mistakes.)

Strategies for Writers Online

Go to **www.sfw.z-b.com** for additional online resources for students, teachers, and parents.

Using the Play Rubric to Analyze the Model

Word Choice • Concrete words and phrases describe the events precisely.

> Maggie and Jay are about my age and use words that I use. I noticed that their parents use more precise words. For example, Ellen uses the words *transport* and *city's center*, and Bob uses *engineers, designed,* and *destinations.* Their words give clear, accurate information about the fair.

Maggie: This is so cool!
Ellen: It sure is! They built this train for the fair, you know, to transport people from the city's center.
Bob: I heard that the engineers designed it to carry 10,000 people to their destinations in an hour!
Jay: (*grumpily*) What did I tell you about the crowds and long lines?
Maggie: (*excitedly, with face pressed against window*) Hey! I can see Puget Sound! And the Cascade Mountains! I love being high in the sky!

Sentence Fluency • A variety of sentence types helps the dialogue flow smoothly.

> In the dialogue, some sentences make statements, others ask questions, and some show excitement, just like real conversations. I noticed that the sentences vary in length, too. They kept my interest and moved the play along at a good pace.

Bob: Well, what did you make of that tour, kids?
Maggie: Oh, Dad, that was the coolest—an imaginary rocket ride! I saw Jupiter, Saturn, Neptune, and Pluto! We must have traveled millions of miles!
Ellen: And all we had to do was look up at the world's largest movie screen to take that journey.

82 Narrative Writing

Tech Tips

Online Resources

Use Apps Writers often speak of how they envision their texts as plays or movies that they see in their minds and transfer to writing. To facilitate that work as students compose, consider using storytelling apps like Toontastic to create two different "castings" and "stagings" of one scene in their work. Bringing their imagined story to life (and motion) puts interesting pressure on their writing, challenging students to be specific, to revise, and to consider how their script comes alive. As an alternative, students could exchange papers and have a peer create the staging based on the directions supplied in the script.

See **www.sfw.z-b.com** for further information about and links to these websites and tools.

- The writing contains no errors.
- All commas are used correctly.

It's clear to me that the writer edited her play carefully. Her spelling, punctuation, and capitalization are correct. I noticed that she placed commas where they are needed, too. I also noticed that Lanie used a word processor to prepare her final copy.

Bob: Just imagine, Son. Ordinary people like us will travel in spaceships someday, much in the same way we travel by car today.
Maggie: You tell him, Dad! John Glenn just orbited Earth three times a couple of months ago! That's a first, but I don't think it will be the last!
Ellen: And don't forget President Kennedy said that we'd have a real "man on the moon" by the end of this decade.

✛Presentation Play format is easy to follow.

My Turn!
Now it's my turn to write a play. I'll use the 6-point rubric on pages 78–79 and good writing strategies to help me. Follow along to see how I do it.

Play **83**

ENRICHMENT
Play vs. Movie Encourage students to speculate on how a play script and a movie script are the same or different. In what ways does the playwright get across what the characters and action are like? How does a screenwriter do the same?

REINFORCEMENT
Review a Play Choose an age-appropriate play or scene and provide each student with a copy. Write the following words on the board: *characters, personalities, setting, problem/challenge.* Read the play or scene aloud. Then ask students to provide as much information as possible about each of the terms on the board, based on the dialogue and stage directions.

✛Presentation Explain to students that a play is written in a specific format. The list of characters is given before the play begins. The setting is provided before each scene and, if typed, is set in italics to alert the reader that it is not to be spoken. Characters' names are given before the lines they are to speak, but the character names themselves are not spoken. Stage directions appear inside parentheses and in italics so the reader or actor does not confuse them with dialogue.

Think About the Traits

Once students have thoroughly discussed the model, ask them which traits they think are most important in a play and have them explain why. **(Possible responses: Voice is very important, as the play is made up almost entirely of dialogue. If the dialogue does not sound natural and appropriate for the characters, the play will be weak and unenjoyable. Word Choice is very important because accurate and descriptive words convey vital information to the reader or audience.)**

CCSS Common Core State Standards (pp. Z20–Z30)
Writing: W.4.6, W.4.9a
Language: L.4.3c
Speaking and Listening: SL.4.1a, SL.4.1b, SL.4.1c, SL.4.1d, SL.4.3, SL.4.6

Write
Play

Week 2 • Day 1

Student Objectives

- Read and understand a prewriting strategy. (p. 84)

Prewrite

Focus on Ideas

Gather Information Read page 84 aloud to students. Explain that the first step to any writing assignment is choosing a topic you find interesting and appropriate for the genre. Jack was asked by his teacher to write a play about moving to Washington. Once his topic was selected, he then knew where to search for relevant information.

Instruct students to begin brainstorming about the subject of their plays. Remind them that it will be easier to write a play based on a topic that they themselves find interesting; when a writer is excited about a topic, the reader or audience feels it and becomes interested and excited about the subject as well.

Once they have selected a topic, instruct students to gather information from several places—the Internet, the school library, and perhaps even a travel agency, as Jack has considered. Remind students to use only reliable websites and to keep track of their sources.

Online Writing Center

Provides **interactive graphic organizers** as well as a variety of graphic organizers in PDF format.

T84 Narrative Writing

Prewrite

Focus on Ideas

The Rubric Says	Details are accurate and appropriate for the situation in the play.
Writing Strategy	Choose a topic for the play. Then collect details that fit the story.

We are studying state history in social studies. So my teacher has asked us each to write a play about moving to Washington. I will need to do some research to find accurate details in order to make my play realistic. I can go to the library to find books and articles. I can also go to reliable websites on the Internet for pictures about my topic. I might even visit a travel agency for brochures that show places to visit. I'll remember to take good notes and keep track of my sources as I collect my ideas.

My Topic—
Moving to Tacoma, Washington

✔ Tacoma is the third-largest city in Washington.

✔ It's a port city that exports and imports goods.

✔ Native Americans call Mt. Rainier *Tacobet,* meaning "mother of the waters."

✔ The first steam train reached Tacoma in 1873.

✔ Tacoma became known as City of Destiny.

Write

Get ready to write your play. Choose a topic you want to explore. Then list the details you know about it. Collect more details from books, the Internet, and other good sources. Be sure to take good notes and keep track of your sources.

84 Narrative Writing

English Language Learners

BEGINNING/INTERMEDIATE

Fill in a Story Map Read a brief story to students, such as *The Three Little Pigs.* Have partners complete a story map using information from the story. Make sure they include characters' names, a description of the setting, a problem (conflict), plot events, and a resolution. They may use just a few words to describe each.

ADVANCED/ADVANCED HIGH

Create a Story Map Give students a story idea, such as *lost in the woods.* Have partners use a Story Map to plan a play. Make sure they include characters' names, a description of the setting, a problem (conflict), plot events, and a resolution. They may use just a few words to describe each. Ask a volunteer from each group to describe the play's characters, setting, and plot to the rest of the class. The plot should include several events leading up to the climax of the story.

The Rubric Says   Events happen in logical sequence.

Writing Strategy   Use a Story Map to plan a play.

A play is a special form of a story. It has the same parts—a setting, interesting characters, and a good plot. My teacher suggested using a Story Map. A Story Map will help me plan the events of the play in order.

Writer's Term

Story Map
A Story Map organizes the setting, characters, problem, action, and end of a story.

Story Map

Setting   **Where** Tucson, Arizona   **When** Present time

Characters   Marissa, Ethan, Ms. Crane

Problem   Marissa tells Ethan that she is moving away. She doesn't want to go and lose her friends.

Action   Ethan wants to cheer up Marissa. He heads to the library to find out about Tacoma, Washington.

End   Ethan tells Marissa what he learns and helps change her mind about moving.

Analyze

Look at Jack's notes and Story Map. How will it help him write a play?

Write

Plan your play. Use a Story Map to organize your ideas for the setting, characters, problem, action, and end.

Play   85

Collaborative Conferencing

PEER TO PEER Have partners exchange Story Maps. Each partner points out something he or she finds interesting in the other student's Story Map and asks one question to clarify a detail or the organization.

PEER GROUPS Students take turns giving a brief oral summary of the story they want to tell in their play and showing their Story Maps to the others. Group members comment on any items in the Story Maps that are missing or different from the oral summary.

TEACHER-LED Meet with individual students to review their Story Maps. Point out the aspects of each student's Story Map that are well executed. Discuss the aspects each student found more difficult.

Write
Play

Week 2 • Day 2

Student Objectives

• Create a Story Map to organize ideas. (p. 85)

Prewrite

Focus on **Organization**

Create a Story Map Review Jack's Story Map with students and explain that it will serve as a model for students to create their own Story Maps. (Go to **www.sfw.z-b. com** for the downloadable graphic organizer.) Once they organize their notes, the Story Map will guide their writing.

Writer's Term

Story Map A Story Map serves as a "supplies list" and a "map" when writing a story or play. The list of characters and setting description—or supplies list—is placed at the beginning of the Story Map. The second part of the Story Map outlines the problem, action, and ending, or how the problem is solved. This is the "map" section of the organizer, which guides the writer from the beginning of the story to the end.

CCSS **Common Core State Standards** (pp. Z20–Z30)

Writing: W.4.3a, W.4.3e, W.4.4, W.4.5, W.4.6, W.4.8, W.4.10
Language: L.4.3c, L.4.6
Speaking and Listening: SL.4.1a, SL.4.1b, SL.4.1c, SL.4.1d, SL.4.3, SL.4.4, SL.4.6

Write
Play

Student Objectives

- Use a Story Map to begin writing. *(pp. 86–87)*

Draft

Focus on **Word Choice**

Choose Precise Language Remind students that a draft is not expected to be error free. There will be time later to edit for any mistakes. Point out the proofreading marks on page 87 for future reference.

Remind students that a play consists almost entirely of dialogue, so using precise language to express character and plot development or setting is very important. Common or vague words will leave the audience with an incomplete image. Write the following words on the board: *bird, beverage, said.* Ask volunteers to come up with precise and creative words to replace each. **(Possible responses: colorful parrot, steaming hot chocolate topped with whipped cream, mumbled)** Write students' suggestions on the board. Discuss how the precise words help create a more vivid and accurate image for the reader.

Instruct students to use their Story Maps to begin drafting their plays.

Online Writing Center

Provides an **interactive writing pad** for drafting, revising, editing, and publishing.

Draft

Focus on **Word Choice**

The Rubric Says	Concrete words and phrases describe the events precisely.
Writing Strategy	Choose words and phrases to convey ideas precisely.

I think I'm ready to draft my play now. I can use my notes and Story Map to help me get started.

Choosing the right words is always important, but it's especially important when writing a play. Everything the characters say has to give precise information to the audience about the characters, the setting, and the plot.

> **Writer's Term**
>
> **Play Format**
> Write the speaker's name and a colon before each spoken line or set of lines. Place stage directions in parentheses. Notice that dialogue in a play is not enclosed in quotation marks. Lines that carry over to the next line are indented so that the speakers' names stand out.

Since I'm writing about the state of Washington, there may be some precise words I can use in my play, like *port* (a harbor where ships load and unload goods) or *salmon canneries* (processing plants for fish). These words tell about specific things that are found there, and they add factual information to my play.

As I write my draft, I'll use a word processor so that I can format the play. I'll also try to avoid making mistakes, but I know I can fix them later when I edit. Here's my draft.

86 Narrative Writing

Differentiating Instruction

ENRICHMENT
Revealing Stage Directions Write the following sentence on the board: *Oh, how I love macaroni and cheese.* Then list the following emotions: *sarcastic, sincere, overjoyed, disgusted.* Instruct students to write stage directions to reflect how a character would say the line and use his or her body or face to show the emotions on the list.

REINFORCEMENT
Support for Precise Words Help students practice thinking of more precise words to replace *person* and *stuff.* Prompt students with examples such as *toddler, newscaster, soccer equipment,* or *school supplies.*

[DRAFT]

Destiny, Here I Come!

SCENE 1: *Marissa's house*

Marissa: My life is ruined!

Ethan: Why? What happened?

Marissa: My mom just told me that we're moving. Oh, Ethan, I don't… I won't…

Ethan: What? Moving? Where?

Marissa: Washington! We have to start packing. But I don't want to go!

Ethan: Which city are you moving to?

Marissa: Tacoma. I guess it's pretty big, but not as big as Tucson, my mom said.

Ethan: Well it's no desert. Tucson's far from an ocean gets almost no rain and hardly changes with the seasons. I hear it rains a lot in Washington, and everything's green in the summer. I bet Tacoma's air smells like the sea.

Marissa: But Ethan I like it here!

SCENE 2: *School library*

Ethan: Hi, Ms. Crane.

Ms. Crane: Hi, Ethan.

Ethan: I'd like to find out everything I can about Tacoma, Washington. My friend Marissa is moving there.

Ms. Crane: Yes, she did mention moving when she returned her books. She seemed pretty upset, and she didn't stay to visit like she usually does. Let's see if we can find some facts about Tacoma that might make her feel better.

Ethan: Wow! There are several books and articles right here.

precise words describe the topic

Analyze
Read the beginning of Jack's draft. How does it follow the format of a play?

Write
Use your notes and Story Map to write your draft. Be sure to use precise words and phrases.

Play 87

Collaborative Conferencing

PEER TO PEER Have partners exchange drafts. Students lightly circle in pencil any places where their partner has not used proper play format.

PEER GROUPS Have students read the drafts aloud as a group, with students taking the roles in the play and one student reading the setting and stage directions aloud. After each reading, have group members make suggestions for precise words that could be added to the lines they read.

TEACHER-LED Meet with pairs of students. Read students' drafts aloud with expression so that they can hear their plays read in a new voice. Together, discuss whether more precise words can be added to the drafts.

Write
Play

Student Objectives
• Complete a draft. *(p. 87)*

Continue Drafting Read Jack's draft on page 87. Be sure to point out specific features of a play format, as well as story features such as the characters, problem, and setting. Discuss the precise words highlighted on the page. Emphasize how this precise language helps the reader better understand the story. Encourage students to refer to this page to help them format their own plays.

✎ Writer's Term
Play Format The function of play format is to make the play easy to read for actors and directors. Character names are made to stand out so that actors can quickly find their lines. Scene divisions are always clear. Text that is not meant to be spoken is in italics and/or parentheses. Even though we read plays as text in class, students should never forget that a play is intended to be read aloud and performed.

CCSS Common Core State Standards (pp. Z20–Z30)
Writing: W.4.3b, W.4.3d, W.4.4, W.4.5, W.4.6, W.4.10
Language: L.4.3a, L.4.3c, L.4.6
Speaking and Listening: SL.4.1a, SL.4.1b, SL.4.1c, SL.4.1d, SL.4.3, SL.4.6

Write
Play

Student Objectives

- Revise to provide details in the dialogue and stage directions. (p. 88)

Revise

Focus on Ideas

Include Details Remind students that all details must be relayed through dialogue and stage directions. Then direct students to review Jack's draft excerpt at the bottom of the page. Point out how the added stage directions provide important details necessary for the audience to fully understand the action. Ask students what key bit of information the added detail gives.
(the reason for the move)

✏ Writer's Term

Dialogue and Stage Directions
Stage directions inform actors how and where to move, how to say their lines, and even what props they might be holding. Without this information, the action is incomplete, and dialogue can easily be misinterpreted. For example, the line *You're the best cook we've ever had!* could be said sorrowfully or sarcastically. Stage directions ensure action is meaningful and dialogue is expressive.

▶ Strategies for Writers Online
Go to **www.sfw.z-b.com** for additional online resources for students, teachers, and parents.

Write a Play

Revise
Focus on **Ideas**

The Rubric Says	Dialogue and stage directions develop the characters, setting, and plot.
Writing Strategy	Put details in the dialogue and stage directions.

The rubric reminds me how important the dialogue and stage directions are in a play. A play uses fewer words than a story to let the reader know when and where the action takes place or who the characters are and what they are like. I need to add this information to Scene 1. I'll use my imagination and add interesting details.

Writer's Term
Dialogue and Stage Directions
Dialogue is what characters say to each other.

Stage Directions tell how characters look or what they do on stage.

[DRAFT]

SCENE 1: *Marissa's house*
(sees Ethan and tries not to cry) ← added details in stage directions
Marissa: My life is ruined!
Ethan: Why? What happened?
(rubs her eyes with her sleeve)
Marissa: My mom just told me that we're moving. Oh, Ethan, I don't… I won't…
Ethan: What? Moving? Where?
She starts a new job there next month. ← added details in dialogue
Marissa: Washington! We have to start packing. But I don't want to go!

Write
Read your draft. If necessary, add details to the dialogue and stage directions.

English Language Learners

BEGINNING/INTERMEDIATE
Dialogue Write the following dialogue on the board:

ACTOR 1: Little pig, little pig, let me in!
ACTOR 2: Not by the hairs on my chinny chin chin!

After students practice the lines several times, give them directions for *how* to say the sentences. For example, use the following emotions: excited, frightened, angry. Demonstrate.

ADVANCED/ADVANCED HIGH
Dialogue and Stage Directions Conduct the Dialogue activity above. After students practice the dialogue with the assigned emotion several times, give them stage directions to practice. For example, if they are excited, show the actors how to jump up and down or shake their head as they deliver their lines. Teach the term *stage directions*.

Revise

Focus on Organization

The Rubric Says The script has a clear beginning, middle, and end.

Writing Strategy Let the readers know what's happening right away.

I looked back at the rubric. The play should begin with as much information as possible so that the reader knows where the play takes place and learns something about the characters. It should also tell what the play is going to be about and the problem the characters are facing.

Writer's Term

Beginning
The **beginning** of a play grabs the reader's attention. It makes the reader eager for the play to unfold.

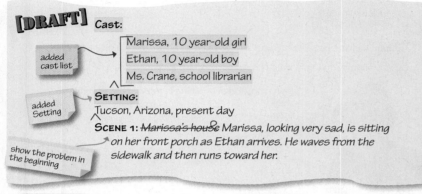

[DRAFT] Cast:

added cast list →
Marissa, 10 year-old girl
Ethan, 10 year-old boy
Ms. Crane, school librarian

added Setting →
SETTING:
Tucson, Arizona, present day
SCENE 1: ~~Marissa's house~~ Marissa, looking very sad, is sitting

show the problem in the beginning →
on her front porch as Ethan arrives. He waves from the sidewalk and then runs toward her.

Analyze

Look at Jack's revisions. How do his changes inform the reader?

Write

Look at your draft again. Be sure to tell where the story takes place and list the characters. Also, make sure to present the problem in the beginning.

Play 89

Collaborative Conferencing

PEER TO PEER Have partners read their drafts aloud to each other. Students give their partner positive feedback on an element of the play that they liked, and they ask one or two questions about details that may be missing from the play.

PEER GROUPS Divide students into groups of four. Each student is assigned one of four elements to look for in each group member's draft: characters list, setting, stage directions, or problem. For each draft, students make one comment or question about their assigned element.

TEACHER-LED Meet with pairs of students. Have students cooperate to read both plays aloud, each taking some of the roles. Read the setting and stage directions yourself. Help students discuss what details might be missing from their plays, prompting them with questions if necessary.

Write
Play

Student Objectives

• Revise the beginning. *(p. 89)*

Revise

Focus on Organization

Provide Information Read Jack's words on page 89 aloud. Explain that students need to grab the reader's interest and set the scene right from the start.

Direct students' attention to the draft excerpt at the bottom of the page. Point out that the highlighted text provides the reader with information that must be understood at the beginning of the play. Have students review their plays to make sure the beginning contains enough information to clearly set the scene.

Writer's Term

Beginning Certain information must be given in the beginning of a play: where and when the story is taking place, who the main characters are, and what is going on as the play opens. The beginning of the play should be interesting, informative, and to the point.

CCSS Common Core State Standards (pp. Z20–Z30))
Writing: W.4.3a, W.4.3b, W.4.3d, W.4.3e, W.4.4, W.4.5, W.4.10
Language: L.4.3c, L.4.6
Speaking and Listening: SL.4.1a, SL.4.1b, SL.4.1c, SL.4.1d, SL.4.3, SL.4.6

Play T89

Write
Play

Week 3 • Day 2

Student Objectives

- Revise to use punctuation for effect. *(p. 90)*

Revise

Focus on Sentence Fluency

Punctuation Enhances Meaning

Remind students that when they talk, they naturally use questions and exclamations as well as statements. Likewise, realistic dialogue uses a variety of sentence types.

Then direct students' attention to Jack's draft excerpt at the bottom of the page. Note that he changed punctuation to make a statement into an exclamation but that he had to change words as well as punctuation to create a question.

✏ Writer's Term

Sentence Types While a mix of sentence types forms realistic and engaging writing, overuse of interrogative or exclamatory sentences can have the opposite effect. Too many exclamations within a short space sound artificial and odd to the audience if the character is not in a life-threatening situation. Similarly, repeated questions sound unrealistic and can be tiring.

Online Writing Center

 Provides **interactive proofreading activities** for each genre.

Revise   Focus on Sentence Fluency

The Rubric Says	A variety of sentence types helps the dialogue flow smoothly.
Writing Strategy	Choose punctuation for effect.

As I read my draft aloud, I found a part that just didn't flow. The rubric reminds me to use a variety of sentence types. I'll use different types of sentences and punctuation to show emotion and help move the play along.

✏ Writer's Term

Sentence Types

A **declarative** sentence gives information.

An **interrogative** sentence asks a question.

An **exclamatory** sentence shows strong feeling.

changed statement to an exclamation to add emotion

 [DRAFT]

Ethan: Well it's no desert. Tucson's far from an ocean gets almost no rain and hardly changes with the seasons. I hear it rains a lot in Washington, and everything's green in the summer. Do you think I bet Tacoma's air smells like the sea?

changed statement to a question to add interest

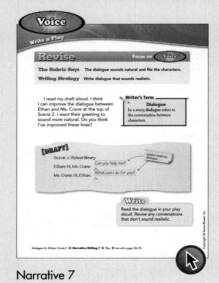

Write

Read your draft aloud. Revise the dialogue so it is expressive and flows smoothly.

90 Narrative Writing

Optional Revising Lessons

Voice

Write a Play

Revise   Focus on Voice

The Rubric Says The dialogue sounds natural and fits the characters.

Writing Strategy Write dialogue that sounds realistic.

I read my draft aloud. I think I can improve the dialogue between Ethan and Ms. Crane at the top of Scene 2. I want their greeting to sound more natural. Do you think I've improved these lines?

Writer's Term
Dialogue
In a story, dialogue refers to the conversation between characters.

[DRAFT]

SCENE 2: School library

Ethan: Hi, Ms. Crane. Can you help me?

Ms. Crane: Hi, Ethan. What can I do for you?

Added realistic dialogue

Write
Read the dialogue in your play aloud. Revise any conversations that don't sound realistic.

Strategies for Writers Grade 4 ■ Narrative Writing 7 ■ Play ■ Use with pages 88–90.

Narrative 7

Word Choice

Write a Play

Revise   Focus on Word Choice

The Rubric Says Concrete words and phrases describe the events precisely.

Writing Strategy Use exact words.

My teacher explained that stage directions help actors know what to do and how to say their lines. They also provide information about the characters, setting, and plot for the reader. But they won't do any good unless I use exact words to tell the actors what to do. I see where I can add some stage directions to Scene 2. See if you think the words explain the action clearly.

Writer's Term
Stage directions
Stage directions tell the characters and stage crew what to do. They also help explain the characters, setting, and plot.

[DRAFT]

Ms. Crane: Yes, she did mention moving when she returned her books. She seemed pretty upset, and she didn't stay to visit like she usually does. Let's see if we can find some facts about Tacoma that might make her feel better.

(They use the library's computer to search for information on Tacoma.)

Ethan: Wow! There are several books and articles right here.

(Both walk to shelves under the window.)

Added exact words to explain action.

Analyze
Look at Jack's revision. Do the stage directions explain the characters, setting, and plot?

Write
Look over your draft. Revise your stage directions to use exact words to explain the action.

Strategies for Writers Grade 4 ■ Narrative Writing 8 ■ Play ■ Use with pages 88–90.

Narrative 8

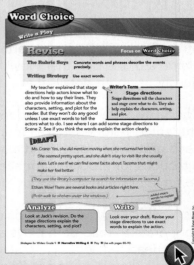

Go to ➡ **Strategies for Writers** at **www. sfw.z-b.com**

Edit — Focus on Conventions

The Rubric Says	The writing contains no errors. All commas are used correctly.
Writing Strategy	Check to make sure commas are used correctly.

I'm finally ready to check my spelling, capitalization, and grammar. The rubric reminds me to check that I used commas correctly. I need to add commas in the part I just revised.

Writer's Term
Commas

Commas are used to separate items in a list of three or more items. The last comma goes before the the word **and** or the word **or.**

Commas are used after introductory words such as **Yes, No,** or **Well.** Place commas around a person's name when the person is being spoken to.

Ethan: Well, it's no desert! Tucson's far from an ocean, gets almost no rain, and hardly changes with the seasons. I hear it rains a lot in Washington, and everything's green in summer. Do you think the air smells like the sea?

added necessary commas

added necessary comma

Marissa: But, Ethan, I like it here!

[DRAFT]

Analyze

Read your draft carefully. Did you use commas correctly? Look at the edits Jack made to his sentences. Is his punctuation correct? Does it help you tell how the characters should speak?

Write — Conventions

Look at your draft again. Be sure to tell where the story takes place and list the characters. Also make sure to present the problem in the beginning.

For more practice with commas, use the exercises on the next two pages.

Play **91**

Related Grammar Practice

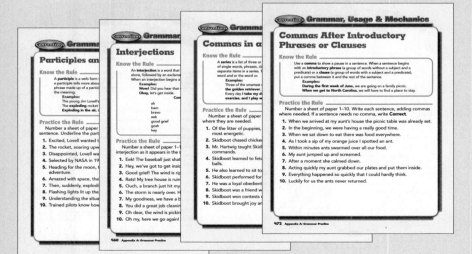

Student Edition pages 447, 460, 471, 472

Go to ➡ **Appendix A: Grammar Practice**

Student Objectives

• Edit for correct comma usage. (*p. 91*)

Edit

Focus on Conventions

Use Commas Correctly Explain to students that it is now time to correct errors in conventions.

Explain that commas serve several purposes. They are used to separate several items in a list of three or more things. In dialogue, commas may be used to signal when the speaker briefly pauses. Commas are used to set off introductory words, such as *yes, no,* or *well.* They are also used to separate the name of a person being addressed from the rest of the sentence.

Writer's Term

Commas Explain to students that commas provide a visual break between words and can indicate that a speaker should pause. Often the meaning of a sentence can be changed dramatically by a comma. Compare these two sentences: *Let's walk Fido* and *Let's walk, Fido.*

CCSS **Common Core State Standards** (pp. Z20–Z30)
Writing: W.4.4, W.4.5, W.4.6, W.4.10
Language: L.4.1f, L.4.2a, L.4.2d, L.4.3b, L.4.6

Play **T91**

Conventions
Mini-Lesson

Student Objectives

- Learn how to use commas to separate items in a series. (p. 92)

Commas in a Series

Write on the board: *You're my best friend because you make me laugh, you never judge me, and you are generous.*

Circle each comma. Ask a volunteer to read the sentence aloud. Explain that each comma makes the reader pause slightly and distinguishes the items in the series.

Now write this sentence on the board: *You're my best, friend because you make, me laugh you never, judge me and you are, generous.*

Ask a volunteer to read this sentence aloud. Ask how the second sentence sounded different from the first one. (Possible response: The commas are not in the right place, so the student paused in the wrong places.) Explain that misplaced commas easily confuse readers and mix up the meaning of a sentence.

Write practice sentences, such as *I need milk bread and coffee from the store* and *Choose whether you want to take a walk go to the movies or stay home,* and ask volunteers to insert commas in the sentences. Have students complete page 92 for more practice using commas in a series.

Online Writing Center

GAMES Provides **interactive grammar games** and **practice activities** in student eBook.

Commas in a Series

Know the Rule

A series is a list of three or more words or phrases. Commas are used to separate the items in a series. The last comma in a series goes before the word *and* or the word *or*.

Example:
Pike Place Market in Seattle sells fish, produce, cheese, **and** herbs.

Practice the Rule

Number a sheet of paper 1–10. Rewrite each sentence correctly, and insert commas where they belong.

1. The market buzzes with the activities of merchants, shoppers, and visitors.
2. Farmers come to sell their fresh berries, greens, herbs, and vegetables.
3. Pike Place Market closes only for Thanksgiving, Christmas, and New Year's Day.
4. Diners can go there to eat breakfast, lunch, or dinner.
5. Fruits grown in Washington State include apples, cherries, plums, and peaches.
6. Cheese is made using milk from a cow, goat, or sheep.
7. Fish found in Washington include salmon, trout, and sturgeon.
8. The fish are caught in lakes, rivers, and oceans.
9. Bakeries at the market sell pastries, cheesecakes, breads, and muffins.
10. You can buy creamed honey spreads made from wildflowers, huckleberries, raspberries, or cherries.

Related Grammar Practice

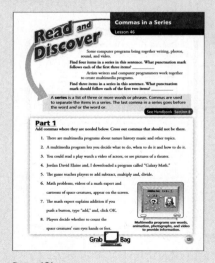

Page 121

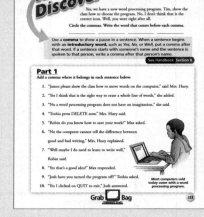

Page 123

 Go to G.U.M. Student Practice Book

Commas After Introductory Words

Know the Rule

Use a **comma** to show a pause in a sentence. When a sentence begins with an **introductory word**, such as *Yes, No,* or *Well,* put a comma after that word. If a sentence includes someone's name and the sentence is spoken to that person, use one or two commas to separate the person's name from the rest of the sentence.

Examples:
Nick, have you ever been to Washington?
Yes, I've been to many beautiful places in Washington.

Practice the Rule

Number a sheet of paper 1–10. Rewrite each sentence correctly, and insert commas where they belong.

1. Keri, didn't you go hiking in Mt. Rainier National Park?
2. No, my family and I went on trails in and around Mt. Olympus.
3. Rita, you wouldn't believe the beautiful views along the way!
4. Well, I would really like to go to the San Juan Islands someday.
5. Yes, that would be a great place to go whale watching.
6. Rudi, have you ever gone on a river cruise down the Columbia River?
7. No, but I hope to someday.
8. Well, I think Washington is the most beautiful place in the world.
9. For once, Keri, I agree with you.
10. I appreciate that, Rudi!

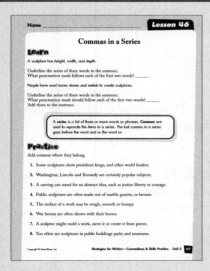

Page 97

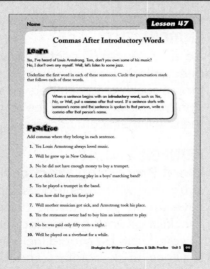

Page 99

Mini-Lesson

Student Objectives

• Learn how to use commas to separate introductory words. *(p. 93)*

Commas After Introductory Words

Commas signal to the reader to pause slightly. Explain to students that a comma should be placed between an introductory word, such as *yes, no,* or *well,* and the rest of the sentence. If a person is addressed at the beginning of a sentence, a comma is used to separate the name from the rest of the sentence.

Write the following sentences on the board: *Well I think we are locked out of the house! Phillipe do you have a spare key? No I don't even have my cell phone.*

Ask for volunteers to tell you where to place the missing commas. Read each completed sentence aloud so students can hear the pause at each comma. (Well, I think we are locked out of the house! Phillipe, do you have a spare key? No, I don't even have my cell phone.) Discuss each example to make sure students understand why each comma was necessary. Have students complete the exercises on page 93 for more practice using commas after introductory words.

CCSS **C**ommon **C**ore **S**tate **S**tandards (pp. Z20–Z30)
Writing: W.4.6
Language: L.4.6

Write
Play

Student Objectives

- Discuss preparation for publishing and presentation. (p. 94)
- Use a final editing checklist to publish their work. (p. 94)

Publish +Presentation

Perform the Play Discuss Jack's decision to have his classmates perform his play, as well as the possibility of creating a podcast or videotape.

Remind students that a play is written with the intention that it will be performed by actors for an audience. They have worked hard on their plays, and there is no better feeling than seeing their characters come to life on a stage or at the front of the classroom. Make time for each play to be performed for the class.

Read through Jack's publishing checklist. Be sure students understand that the checklist relates to the writing traits and strategies they have been using. Have students make a checklist of their own. Allow time in class for students to check over their plays using their checklists.

Strategies for Writers Online
Go to **www.sfw.z-b.com** for additional online resources for students, teachers, and parents.

Publish +Presentation

Publishing Strategy	Publish copies of my play for classmates to perform.
Presentation Strategy	Use a computer to format the play.

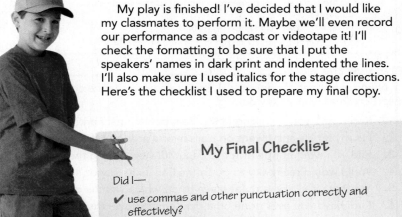

My play is finished! I've decided that I would like my classmates to perform it. Maybe we'll even record our performance as a podcast or videotape it! I'll check the formatting to be sure that I put the speakers' names in dark print and indented the lines. I'll also make sure I used italics for the stage directions. Here's the checklist I used to prepare my final copy.

My Final Checklist

Did I—

✔ use commas and other punctuation correctly and effectively?

✔ edit and proofread carefully?

✔ include the title of the play and my name at the top?

✔ make a neat final copy in play format?

Write
Use Jack's checklist to prepare your final copy. Ask your classmates to act out your play.

Differentiating Instruction

ENRICHMENT
Be a Producer/Director Have students act as producer/director for their play. Students should gather appropriate props, coach cast members on saying their lines with expression and moving around the stage, and make any alterations to the script that seem necessary as the cast rehearses the play.

REINFORCEMENT
Word-Processing Practice Pair students who are struggling with word processing with students who already have strong computer/word-processing skills. Create a checklist of word-processing features you want each pair to cover. The list should include setting margins, indenting lines, using boldface and italics, selecting line spacing, saving and retrieving a file, and printing a file.

Destiny, Here I Come!
by Jack

CHARACTERS:

Marissa, ten-year-old girl

Ethan, ten-year-old boy

Ms. Crane, school librarian

SETTING: *Tucson, Arizona, present day*

SCENE 1: *Marissa, looking very sad, is sitting on her front porch as Ethan arrives. He waves from the sidewalk and then runs toward her.*

Marissa: (*sees Ethan and tries not to cry*) My life is ruined!

Ethan: Why? What happened?

Marissa: (*rubs her eyes with her sleeve*) My mom just told me that we're moving. Oh, Ethan, I don't... I won't...

Ethan: (*very surprised*) What? Moving? Where?

Marissa: Washington! She starts a new job there next month. We have to start packing. (*stomps her foot with each word*) But I don't want to go!

Ethan: Which city are you moving to?

Marissa: Tacoma. I guess it's pretty big, but not as big as Tucson, my mom said.

Ethan: Well, it's no desert! Tucson's far from an ocean, gets almost no rain, and hardly changes with the seasons. I hear it rains a lot in Washington, and everything's green in the summer. Do you think Tacoma's air smells like the sea?

Marissa: But, Ethan, I like it here! I don't want to lose all my friends! (*runs into the house, leaving Ethan standing alone on the porch*)

Ethan: (*thinks out loud*) I must find a way to help Marissa!

SCENE 2: *School library. Ethan heads straight for Ms. Crane's desk.*

Ethan: Hi, Ms. Crane. Can you help me?

Play **95**

Write
Play

Week 3 • Day 5

Student Objectives

- Use a play rubric. *(pp. 78–79)*
- Share a published play. *(pp. 95–97)*

Presentation Strategy Take a moment to review a play's format with students. Remind them that setting details are in italics, stage directions are in italics and within parentheses, speakers' names are in bold print, and each new line of dialogue is indented. Students should also use white space to slightly separate each scene and set neat side margins. These features make the play easier to read and study for a performance.

Encourage students to use word processing to type their plays. Use the classroom computer to review useful features for play format, such as setting margins, using the tab button, and setting text in bold print.

Have students refer to the rubric on pages 78–79 as you read aloud "Destiny, Here I Come!" on pages 95–97. When finished, ask students what score they would assign Jack for each trait. Be sure students can support their answers with examples from the play. Take a vote to see how well Jack did overall in the eyes of your class. Remind students to refer to the rubric to assess their own plays.

CCSS **C**ommon **C**ore **S**tate **S**tandards (pp. Z20–Z30)
Writing: W.4.4, W.4.6, W.4.10
Speaking and Listening: SL.4.4, SL.4.5

Reflecting on a Play

Ask students to think back on this assignment as a whole. Encourage them to share how they feel about the process and experience of writing a play. You might ask:

- How different was writing a play from other writing assignments you have done?

- Did you find working with the play format difficult?

- What was the easiest part of this assignment for you?

- What part of the play-writing process was the most challenging?

- Will you ever write another play? If so, what will you do differently?

Have students write their answers to these questions in their journals, or have them discuss their reflections as a class or in small groups.

Ms. Crane: Hi, Ethan. What can I do for you?

Ethan: I'd like to find out everything I can about Tacoma, Washington. My friend Marissa is moving there.

Ms. Crane: Yes, she mentioned that yesterday when she returned her books. She seemed pretty upset about it. Let's see if we can find some facts about Tacoma that might cheer her up.

(They use the library's computer to search for information on Tacoma.)

Ethan: Wow! There are several books and articles here.

(Both walk to shelves under the windows.)

Ms. Crane: Here's a book on Tacoma's railroad and coal-mining days and another on its early lumber and fishing industries.

Ethan: Thanks, Ms. Crane!

Ms. Crane: *(reaches for a travel magazine behind the checkout desk)* And here's a recent article about Tacoma titled "City of Destiny." Will these give you a good start?

Ethan: *(looks through the materials and smiles)* Absolutely! This is awesome! Thanks, Ms. Crane!

SCENE 3: *Marissa's house, after school the next day*

Ethan: *(knocks on front door, soft at first, then louder)* Marissa, are you home?

Marissa: It's you! You came back! I thought maybe when I left you on the porch you'd never... *(clears throat)* I'm just packing some of my stuff. It'll take me awhile, in case you wanted to go and do something.

Ethan: That's okay. I just came over to see how you were doing. Guess what? I've been busy, too.

Marissa: Doin' what?

Ethan: Well, first I want to say that I think you're very lucky!

Marissa: Why?

Ethan: Because Tacoma is a great place to live, that's why! But here's the best part. You will find your destiny!

Marissa: What are you talking about?

Ethan: I'm talking about Tacoma! It's called City of Destiny!

Marissa: What's destiny?

Ethan: Destiny means following your path, Marissa.

Marissa: *(her eyes light up a little)* Well, I guess I like that idea. But how do you know Tacoma's called City of Destiny?

Ethan: Oh, I found out some really cool things about the city.

Marissa: OK, Mr. Knows-a-Lot, what exactly did you find out that might change my mind about moving?

Ethan: Well, did you know that in the late 1800s the Northern Pacific Railway connected the Great Lakes to Puget Sound right there in Tacoma? That's when they started calling it City of Destiny.

Marissa: *(looks surprised and pleased)* Cool...

Ethan: A lot of new settlers headed out there then. The city began booming with industry. Sawmills, coal mines, lumberyards, and salmon canneries opened and hired a lot of people. Tacoma's an important port city. It still exports and imports many goods.

Marissa: *(looking more interested)* What else did you find out about Tacoma?

Ethan: Well, Tacoma got its name from its first settlers, Native Americans. *Tacobet* is their name for Mt. Rainier. It means "mother of the waters."

Marissa: Wow, maybe *your* destiny will bring you to Tacoma, Ethan! Thank you for all the great info! I guess moving won't be so bad after all. Can you stay for supper? I'll ask! *(she runs inside and calls out happily)* Mom! Ethan says I'm ready to follow my destiny!

Analyze

Use the rubric on pages 78–79 to evaluate Jack's play. Use that rubric to score your own play, too.

CCSS **Common Core State Standards** (pp. Z20–Z30)
Writing: W.4.4, W.4.10
Language: L.4.3c
Speaking and Listening: SL.4.1a, SL.4.1b, SL.4.1c, SL.4.1d, SL.4.3, SL.4.6

Next Generation Narrative Assessment Planner

WEEK 1

Day 1
Analyze
Part 1: Close Reading

Student Objectives
- Understand the directions for a next generation assessment.
- Analyze a text source and a student response.
- Find causes and effects.

Student Activities
- Review and write about taking assessments.
- Read and discuss Part 1 directions. (*pp. 98–99*)
- Read and discuss Source 1. (*pp. 100–101*)

Day 2
Analyze
Part 1: Close Reading

Student Objectives
- Analyze a text source and a student response.
- Identify sensory details.
- Analyze a text source and a student response.
- Compare and contrast elements of a text.

Student Activities
- Read and discuss Source 2. (*pp. 102–103*)
- Read and discuss Source 3. (*pp. 104–105*)

Day 3
Analyze
Part 2: Writing to Multiple Sources

Student Objectives
- Understand the directions for a next generation assessment.
- Understand the scoring guide for a next generation assessment.

Student Activities
- Read and discuss Part 2 directions. (*pp. 106–107*)
- Read and discuss the scoring guide. (*pp. 108–109*)

WEEK 2

Day 1
Write
Revise: Organization, Voice

Student Objectives
- Revise for use of transitions.
- Revise for first-person point of view.

Student Activities
- Read and discuss **Revise: Focus on Organization.** (*p.114*)
- Read and discuss **Revise: Focus on Voice.** (*p. 115*)

Day 2
Write
Revise: Word Choice
Edit: Conventions

Student Objectives
- Revise for concrete words and sensory details.
- Check the grammar, spelling, capitalization, and punctuation.

Student Activities
- Read and discuss **Revise: Focus on Word Choice.** (*p. 116*)
- Read and discuss **Edit: Focus on Conventions.** (*p. 117*)

Note: Optional Revising Lessons are located at **www.sfw.z-b.com**

Day 3
Review
Publish Final Draft

Student Objectives
- Review a final draft.
- Practice taking a timed assessment.

Student Activities
- Read and discuss final draft. (*pp. 118–119*)

Day 4

Write
Prewrite: Ideas, Organization

Student Objectives
- Respond to the assignment.
- Choose a graphic organizer.

Student Activities
- Read and discuss **Prewrite: Focus on Ideas.** (p. 110)
- Read and discuss **Prewrite: Focus on Organization**. (p. 111)

Day 5

Write
Draft: Ideas

Student Objectives
- State the topic in the opening sentence.
- Organize events logically.

Student Activities
- Read and discuss **Draft: Focus on Ideas**. (pp. 112–113)
- Draft a narrative writing test with a focus on topic sentence and sensory details.(pp. 112–113)

Day 4

Practice
Next Generation Assessment

Student Objectives
- Practice taking a timed, next generation narrative assessment.

Student Activities
- Complete **Zaner-Bloser Next Generation Assessment** Part 1: Close Reading

Day 5

Practice
Next Generation Assessment

Student Objectives
- Practice taking a timed, next generation narrative assessment.

Student Activities
- Complete **Zaner-Bloser Next Generation Assessment** Part 2: Writing to Multiple Sources

To complete the chapter in fewer days, combine the learning objectives and activities in a way that supports students as they write.

Differentiating Instruction

For additional Differentiating Instruction activities, see Strategies for Writers Differentiated Instruction Activities at www.sfw.z-b.com.

English Language Learners

Comprehension Mini-Lesson

ZB Next Generation Assessment Practice
Narrative assessment practice appears on the *Strategies for Writers* website at **www.sfw.z-b.com**.

 Strategies for Writers Online
Go to **www.sfw.z-b.com** for additional online resources for students, teachers, and parents.

Online Writing Center

Provides IWB resources, assessments, interactive games and practice activities, videos, eBooks, and a virtual file cabinet.

Analyze
Part 1 Directions

Student Objectives

- Understand the directions for a next generation assessment. (pp. 98–99)

Narrative Writing Review In this chapter, students will apply what they have learned about narrative writing to the challenge of taking a narrative writing test. Tell them to take a few minutes to write about what they have learned about narrative writing. Then ask volunteers to share their responses with the class.

Taking Assessments Engage students in a discussion of their experiences with taking tests or assessments. Ask questions such as the following to facilitate discussion:

- What do you remember about taking an assessment? (Possible responses: It had a prompt. I had a time limit.)

- How might you prepare yourself to take a writing assessment? (Possible responses: Read the directions carefully. Write a draft first. Eat a good breakfast.)

- What advice would you offer someone who is about to take a writing test? (Possible responses: Plan your time carefully. Make sure you understand the directions.)

▶ Strategies for Writers Online
Go to **www.sfw.z-b.com** for additional online resources for students, teachers, and parents.

PART 1

Next Generation Narrative Assessment

Writing and reading are connected. You can respond to what you read through writing. Or you can use what you read as a model for writing. This assessment connects reading and writing. In the reading part, you read literature or informational texts and answer questions about what you read. Then in the writing part, you write an adventure story using what you read.

Now let's analyze each part of this test, so you can really see what the assessment looks like.

PART 1: Close Reading

Your Task
You will examine three sources about pioneers and the Gold Rush. Then you will answer three questions about what you have learned. In Part 2, you will write an adventure story set during the time of the California Gold Rush.

Steps to Follow
In order to plan and write your adventure story, you will do all of the following:
1. Examine three sources.
2. Make notes about the information from the sources.
3. Answer three questions about the sources.

Directions for Beginning
You will have 45 minutes to complete Part 1. You will now examine three sources. Take notes because you may want to refer to your notes while writing your adventure story. You can re-examine any of the sources as often as you like. Answer the questions in the spaces provided.

Preparing Students for Next Generation Assessments

Each Next Generation Assessment chapter prepares students to take a performance-based next generation writing assessment. Students will analyze the assignment and a model assessment and learn strategies for taking next generation assessments.

On the last two days of the second week, students take the *Next Generation Assessment Practice* online or as a written text. Explain to students that although the model narrative assessment focuses on writing an adventure story they will write a different genre when they take their practice assessment. In a real test-taking situation, students will not know ahead of time which genre they will be asked to write.

Your Task This section of the directions gives information about the whole test. You will have two parts to complete. In Part 1, you will read and answer questions. In Part 2, you will write an adventure story.

Steps to Follow This section reviews the task as a list. It tells how many sources you will examine. You also find out how many questions you have to answer. In this assessment, you will have to examine three sources and answer three questions.

Directions for Beginning This section gives information about Part 1 only—the reading part. You'll need to decide how you want to take notes. Will you write them on a piece of paper or use a note tool online? This section also tells how long you'll have to complete your task. These directions tell you that you have 45 minutes. Divide the time by three, since there are three sources, to figure out how much time to spend on each source.

TEST TIP

I preview the text before I start reading. I look at the title and the first sentence of each paragraph. This helps me know what I will read. Then I can plan how to take notes.

Next Generation Assessment **99**

Differentiating Instruction

Enrichment
Note-Taking Instruction Remind students that there are different note-taking strategies. Provide a variety of graphic organizers that students can use to take notes. Discuss with students how to use each one. Show students a digital note-taking tool they can use. Draw a diagram that shows how the tool works and ask students to help you label it.

Next Generation Assessment Tell students that they will be taking different types of assessments in school. Explain that writing assessments used to focus mainly on writing from personal experiences. Add that assessments now include reading passages or watching videos and writing about them. Help students analyze the following three parts of the directions for Part 1: Close Reading:

Your Task The *Your Task* section gives students an overview of what will happen in both Parts 1 and 2 of the assessment.

Steps to Follow The *Steps to Follow* section provides students with steps that they will have to take before they start writing. Remind students that they will be expected to use evidence from the sources they analyze. Discuss with students how to take notes, either manually or digitally.

Directions for Beginning The *Directions for Beginning* section focuses on what students will have to do in Part 1. Tell students that this is the section that explains how much time they have to complete Part 1. Remind them that it is important to plan how much time they can spend reading or watching each source. Assist students with figuring how much time they should take.

CCSS **Common Core State Standards** (pp. Z20–Z30)
Writing: , W.4.3a, W.4.10
Speaking and Listening: SL.4.1a, SL.4.1c, SL.4.1d

Analyze
Source 1: Text

Student Objectives

- Analyze a text source and a student response. *(pp. 100–101)*
- Identify causes and effects. *(p. 101)*

Close Reading Defined In a close reading, students read and then reread a text purposefully. Students are provided with text-dependent questions that require them to think about what the author's purpose was, what the words mean, and what the structure of the text tells the reader. Close reading goes beyond simple recall and requires students to think more deeply and critically about what they are reading.

Tell students that they will learn a process they can use when taking an assessment. Add that there are two steps in this close reading process: *First Reading* and *Second Reading*.

First Reading Ask students to read Source 1 independently to understand the main idea. As they read, have students use sticky notes to identify confusing words or ideas. Then discuss the main idea. Have students share their confusing words or ideas.

▶ **Strategies for Writers Online**
Go to **www.sfw.z-b.com** for additional online resources for students, teachers, and parents.

Source 1: Text

From *The American Adventure: The Gold Rush*
By Sally Senzell Isaacs

Sutter's Mill

In 1839, few people talked about California. It was part of Mexico. Just a few thousand people lived there, mostly American Indians and Mexican families who owned ranches. There were some outsiders, U.S. citizens and Europeans, who moved to California to start a new life. John Sutter was one of them.

John Sutter had been a businessman in Switzerland. He loved to make and spend money. By 1834, he owed money to so many people that he decided to run away. He eventually landed in the Sacramento River valley of California. Sutter dreamed of starting a new settlement that would grow into a busy town. He thought people would be moving to California, and he would sell them food, clothing, and lumber to build their homes.

Sutter's new settlement grew. He started with a building surrounded with high walls for security. Later he added other buildings. The area became known as Sutter's Fort. Sutter hired American Indians to work for him, and they planted fruit trees and wheat fields. They also built a flour mill for turning wheat into flour. As Sutter had hoped, the fort attracted travelers and settlers. He soon decided he needed a sawmill to saw trees into lumber. Sutter hired a carpenter named James Marshall to choose a place for the sawmill and oversee the construction. Marshall found a site by the American River, about 50 miles (80 kilometers) from the fort in an area called Coloma.

On January 24, 1848, Marshall spotted a shiny metal in the muddy water. He picked it up and examined it. He thought it might be gold. In the pouring rain, Marshall rode his horse to Sutter's Fort to show the discovery to his boss. He demanded that Sutter lock the doors, then he uncovered his discovery. The two men performed several tests to find out what metal Marshall had found. The answer was "Gold!"

Comprehension Mini-Lesson

Cause and Effect

Teach Tell students that a cause is the reason that something happens and an effect is what happened as a result of the cause. One effect may have several causes, and a cause may have several effects. Explain that clue words, such as *because* and *as a result* can signal a cause-and-effect relationship. Not all texts, however, have clue words. Readers can ask themselves questions to determine cause-and-effect relationships. Asking *What happened?* leads readers to effects. Asking *Why or How did that happen?* leads readers to causes.

Model/Practice Model finding causes and effects. Use the following example: *I was late for school. I'll never forget to set my alarm again!* The first question we ask is, "What

To Tell If It Is Gold

Marshall knew that gold could be beaten into a different shape without breaking. He also knew that strong chemicals could not change it. He did these tests:

• He hammered the metal with a rock. It flattened but did not break.
• He went to the camp's housekeeper, Jennie Wimmer, and asked her to drop the metal in the pot of lye she was boiling to wash clothes. After several hours, the gold was shiny as ever.

> **Why were people attracted to Sutter's Fort? Use evidence from the text to support your answer.**

 To answer this question, I need to think about what caused people to be attracted to Sutter's Fort. I will reread that part of the text to look for reasons why people would want to come there.

B *I* **U** abc ≡ ≡ ≡ ≡ ≣ ≣ ↺ ↻ A▾ A▾ ✂ 📋 📋 ✓

My Response

Sutter's Fort had high walls for security, which would make people feel safe. There were also wheat fields, fruit trees, and a flour mill inside the fort. The settlers could make bread and other kinds of food from flour. People would be attracted to the fort if they knew there was plenty of food to eat.

Analyze

How well did Jack use evidence from the text to support his answer? Is there anything he can add?

Second Reading Ask students to reread the text, looking for evidence to answer the text-dependent question listed on page 101: *Why were people attracted to Sutter's Fort? Use evidence from the text to support your answer.* Then discuss students' answers to encourage deeper comprehension. Make sure students support their answers with evidence from the text.

Analyze Response Tell students to review Jack's response and compare it to their own. Ask them to write answers to the questions in the **Analyze** box, and then have them share their answers with a partner. Ask volunteers to share their responses with the class.

---

happened?" I was late for school. Then we can ask, "Why was I late?" I was late because I forgot to set my alarm. Being late for school is the effect. The cause is not setting my alarm. Determining what happened and why helps me understand the text.

Apply Check for understanding by asking the following question: *What questions do readers ask themselves to determine causes and effects?* (What happened? Why or how did that happen?) Then display the following sentences: *Burning paper blew out of a campfire and set some dry grass on fire. The wind fanned the flames and the fire raced up a hill. A hiker more than a mile away saw the smoke and called 9-1-1 on his cell phone. Firefighters arrived very quickly. They were able to put out the grass fire before it burned out of control.* Discuss the various causes and effects.

CCSS **C**ommon **C**ore **S**tate **S**tandards (pp. Z20–Z30)
Writing: W.4.10
Speaking and Listening: SL.4.1a, SL.4.1c, SL.4.1d, SL.4.3

Analyze
Source 2: Text

Week 1 • Day 2

Student Objectives

- Analyze a text source and a student response. (*pp. 102–103*)
- Identify sensory details. (*p. 103*)

First Reading Ask students to read Source 2 independently to understand the main idea. As they read, have students use sticky notes to identify confusing words or ideas. Then discuss the main idea. Have students share their confusing words or ideas.

Strategies for Writers Online
Go to **www.sfw.z-b.com** for additional online resources for students, teachers, and parents.

Source 2: Text

From *Westward by Wagon Train*
by Jeff Hendricks

The journey west often began in the towns of Independence and St. Joseph, Missouri, and Council Bluffs, Iowa. These jumping-off spots served as meeting points for pioneers who wished to form a wagon train.

The sight of a line of wagons crossing an ocean of grass often taller than a man on horseback gave rise to the term prairie schooner. The covered wagons reminded pioneers of sailing ships. The tall grass also caused problems. It often got snagged in the wheels of the wagons and had to be cleared out. Small children could be lost in the grass, causing their parents much worry.

Several hundred miles out, the pioneers arrived at the Platte River. They followed it for the next 450 miles. The Platte ran through the high plains in what is now the state of Nebraska and halfway into what is now Wyoming. But the river was very muddy and not much good for drinking or bathing.

During this stretch, pioneers saw funny, furry animals they called prairie dogs. The "prairie dog towns" of the high plains made the children laugh. The pioneers also came across their first herds of buffalo. These great beasts shook the ground as they walked and raised huge clouds of dust.

The pioneers marked their progress using huge rock formations they could see from far away. These included Chimney Rock and Scotts Bluff. In time, the pioneers would reach Fort Laramie. At this military outpost they could rest for a few days and restock their provisions. They could even leave mail that would be delivered to friends and relatives back east.

After that, the travelers would begin to climb into the Rocky Mountains. A major milestone was reaching Independence Rock. Settlers would carve or paint their names on this huge rock. Independence Rock earned its name because it was hoped that a wagon train would reach it on or before the Fourth of July. From there, the travelers continued through the Rocky Mountains, finally reaching South Pass.

Up to this point, the trail was not very difficult. The route to South Pass was broad and easily navigated. Travelers often did not even know they had

---

Comprehension Mini-Lesson

Identify Sensory Details

Teach Tell students that details are the pieces of information that support or tell more about the topic. Sensory details appeal to a reader's senses. Writers can tell how something looks, smells, sounds, tastes, or feels. These details help readers create a picture in their minds about what they are reading.

Model/Practice Model using sensory details. Use the following example: *I can describe macaroni and cheese using the words* gloppy *or* creamy. Help students understand that *gloppy* makes the pasta sound unappealing. Discuss other examples: a gloomy day or a sunny day; an emerald shirt or a green shirt. Students should understand that details tell more, but that certain details make it easier to create clear pictures in the reader's mind.

reached the top of the pass. But reaching the pass signaled that they had crossed into the highest mountain range on the continent.

Soon after crossing the pass, pioneers started leaving the wagon train. Some branched off to the southwest for the Great Salt Lake region. Others headed southwest to take the Old Spanish Trail to California. For the rest, the journey continued along the Oregon Trail. They crossed desert country to another military outpost, Fort Hall in Idaho.

At this stage, the pioneers had traveled nearly 1,200 miles from Missouri. Several days west of Fort Hall, the travelers made one final choice—whether to head to California or Oregon. Families would often choose the fertile farming valleys of Oregon. Rogues and fortune hunters were drawn to California, especially after gold was discovered.

Whichever path the pioneers chose, there were still many challenges to overcome to reach their final destinations.

> **What details help you picture what it was like to be part of a wagon train?**

 I will go back and reread the part that describes traveling with a wagon train. As I read, I will keep track of details I can use in my answer.

B *I* U abc ≡ ≡ ≡ ≡ ≡ ≡ ⬅ ➡ A˅ A˅ ✂ 📋 📋 ABC

My Response
The wagons looked like sailing ships. Prairie grass stretched out on all sides like an ocean. The grass was taller than a man on horseback. It was so thick that children could get lost in it.

Analyze
How well did Jack use details from the text in his answer? Are there any details he can add?

Second Reading Ask students to reread the text, looking for evidence to answer the text-dependent question listed on page 103: *What details help you picture what it was like to be part of a wagon train?* Then discuss students' answers to encourage deeper comprehension. Make sure students support their answers with evidence from the text.

Analyze Response Tell students to review Jack's response and compare it to their own. Ask them to write answers to the questions in the **Analyze** box, and then have them share their answers with a partner. Ask volunteers to share their responses with the class.

Apply Check for understanding by asking the following questions: *What are sensory details? How are they helpful to readers?* (Details that appeal to the senses: touch, taste, hearing, smell, sight. They help readers form pictures about what they are reading.) Then display the following sentences: *The grass was green. The river smelled strange. The dessert tasted good.* Have students add details that tell more about the grass, river, and dessert by appealing to the senses.

CCSS Common Core State Standards (pp. Z20–Z30)
Writing: W.4.10
Speaking and Listening: SL.4.1a, SL.4.1c, SL.4.1d, SL.4.3

Analyze
Source 3: Text

Week 1 • Day 2

Student Objectives

- Analyze a text source and a student response. (pp. 104–105)
- Compare and contrast elements of a text. (p. 105)

First Reading Ask students to read Source 3 independently to understand the main idea. As they read, have students use sticky notes to identify confusing words or ideas. Then discuss the main idea. Have students share their confusing words or ideas.

Strategies for Writers Online
Go to **www.sfw.z-b.com** for additional online resources for students, teachers, and parents.

Source 3: Text

The Rush of Success
By Esther Call

A carpenter named James Marshall discovered gold in California while he was working at Sutter's Mill in January 1848. He looked down and saw something glinting in the water. It was gold! His discovery was published in the local newspaper in the middle of March. The announcement was ignored. It wasn't until a merchant named Sam Brannan publicized the discovery that swarms of people came to search for gold.

In 1848, five thousand miners arrived to strike it rich on the banks of the American River. During his State of the Union address, President James K. Polk told the country that the supply of gold was plentiful and widespread. After that, more than 50,000 people arrived at the American River by the end of 1849. At the peak of the Gold Rush in 1851, about 125,000 people mined in California.

It wasn't easy to strike it rich after thousands of people arrived to try. While people did get rich by mining for gold, many people were also successful selling goods and services to the miners. Mining towns were named for their harsh environments: Last Chance, Rough and Ready, and Poverty Bar. Providing goods and services helped to make the miners' lives a little easier.

Sam Brannan, the man who first publicized the Gold Rush, built a general store at Sutter's settlement. After gold was found, he wanted to attract business. He walked through the streets of San Francisco with a bottle of gold dust shouting, "Gold! Gold from the American River!" His general store sold goods to all the people who came in response to his advertisement. Brannan became the first millionaire in California.

Because miners had to squat when panning for gold, they needed pants that would not rip. Levi Strauss was a tailor from Germany who moved to San Francisco. Initially, he wanted to make tents and wagon covers. However, the miners did not buy them. Then he began using the canvas to make pants. He used copper rivets to make the pants sturdy. Then he found a blue denim material from France called genes. Miners called the pants "jeans" or "Levis." Strauss made a fortune selling these pants.

Comprehension Mini-Lesson

Compare and Contrast
Teach Tell students that readers compare and contrast elements of a text to determine how they are alike and different. Remind students of words that compare such as: *alike, both, same as.* Some words that contrast are *different, but,* and *only.* These are clues readers look for to determine when a writer is comparing or contrasting two or more things. Display the clue words for students to reference.

Model/Practice Model comparing and contrasting. Use the following example: *I can compare two or more things, such as the height of two students: Chris is tall, but Jamie is short. I can compare today's weather to yesterday's: both days it was sunny.* Help students link comparisons and clue words. Discuss other comparisons students can make, such

Henry Wells and William Fargo were part of a group of men that founded the American Express Company in 1850. After gold was discovered in the West, Wells and Fargo wanted to expand American Express. The company declined. Wells and Fargo knew the miners needed banks, so they created Wells Fargo & Company. The banks weighed the gold and turned the dust and nuggets into money. Banks were located in all the major towns and cities. Miners could do all their business at these banks, including receiving mail and packages. The company built a reputation for honesty and hard work. Soon many people besides the miners were using the bank.

And what happened to James Marshall? Unfortunately, he did not get rich. He could not get a claim in the gold field he discovered. In addition, the sawmill he opened failed because so many of the workers left to seek their own fortunes. He wandered California, eventually settling down and building a small cabin.

> **Compare and contrast ways people found success during the Gold Rush. Use details from the text to support your answer.**

 I remember the part about Levi Strauss and how he found success by selling blue jeans. I will look in the text for other examples of people who found success in different ways.

B I U abc ≡ ≡ ≡ ≣ ⫶⫶ ⫶⫶ ↰ ↱ A⁻ A⁻ ✂ ▦ ▦ ABC

My Response

Some people became rich by discovering gold. Other people, like Sam Brannan and Levi Strauss, sold goods to miners. Wells and Fargo created banks that miners used.

Analyze

Did Jack compare and contrast the ways people found success? Are there any details he can add?

Second Reading Ask students to reread the text, looking for evidence to answer the text-dependent question listed on page 105: *Compare and contrast ways people found success during the Gold Rush. Use details from the text to support your answer.* Then discuss students' answers to encourage deeper comprehension. Make sure students support their answers with evidence from the text.

Analyze Response Tell students to review Jack's response and compare it to their own. Ask them to write answers to the questions in the **Analyze** box, and then have them share their answers with a partner. Ask volunteers to share their responses with the class.

as between themes or topics of books or between ideas. Remind students that comparisons do not have to be judgments, such as what is best or worst. Instead they can explain how two things relate to each other.

Apply Check for understanding by asking the following question: *What is a comparison?* (Possible response: A relationship that describes how two things are alike.) *What does it mean to contrast two things?* (Possible response: to tell how they are different) Give groups of students two or more pictures. Have students create sentences that compare and contrast the images using the clue words. Have students share their sentences.

CCSS **C**ommon **C**ore **S**tate **S**tandards (pp. Z20–Z30)
Writing: W.4.10
Speaking and Listening: SL.4.1a, SL.4.1c, SL.4.1d, SL.4.3

Analyze
Part 2 Directions

Student Objectives

- Understand the directions for a next generation assessment. (pp. 106–107)

Next Generation Assessment

Ask students to read the paragraph at the top of page 106. Then help them analyze the following two parts of the directions for Part 2: Writing to Multiple Sources.

Setup The *Setup* section focuses on what students will do in Part 2. Tell students that this is the section that tells them how much time they have to complete Part 2. Explain that they can plan their time based on the stages of the writing process. Ask students if they agree with the amount of time Jack has assigned to each part of the writing process.

Make sure students understand that they will be allowed to go back to Part 1 to examine the sources again, but they cannot change their answers to the questions in Part 1. Remind them that the more time they spend re-examining sources, the less time they will have to write.

Strategies for Writers Online
Go to **www.sfw.z-b.com** for additional online resources for students, teachers, and parents.

PART 2
Next Generation Narrative Assessment

Now that Part 1 is complete, it's time to write the adventure story. Usually you will complete Part 1 on one day and Part 2 on the next day. The directions for Part 2 are longer than Part 1 and continue on a second page. So remember to read the directions carefully and ask questions if you don't understand.

PART 2: Writing to Multiple Sources

Setup
You will now have 70 minutes to review your notes and sources and plan, draft, and revise an adventure story. You may use your notes and refer to the sources. You may also refer to the answers you wrote to questions in Part 1, but you cannot change those answers. Now read your assignment and the information about how your adventure story will be scored. Then begin your work.

Your Assignment
During the 1800s, many people moved west across the United States. They moved for many different reasons, but one reason was to get rich during the Gold Rush. Your assignment is to write an adventure story set during the California Gold Rush with concrete details and examples from each of the sources you have examined. The audience for your story will be your classmates.

English Language Learners

BEGINNING/INTERMEDIATE

Part 2 Directions Have students look at the *Setup* section. Select a few key words that students will not know. As you say each word, have students point to the word and repeat it. Write the word on the board and say it again. Elicit the meaning of each word or teach its meaning if students cannot provide it. Repeat the process with important words from *Your Assignment*. Finally, simplify the writing prompt. Explain Jack's task so that students will understand what he is doing as he works through the narrative test writing process.

Repeat this process with students before they begin their own next generation narrative assessment.

Setup This section lets you know how much time you have to complete Part 2. You can divide the time into the different parts of the writing process. Here's an example of what Jack plans to do.

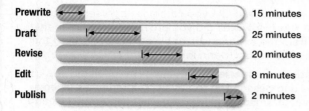

Prewrite	15 minutes
Draft	25 minutes
Revise	20 minutes
Edit	8 minutes
Publish	2 minutes

The directions also tell you that you can go back and examine the sources from Part 1, but the answers can't be changed.

Your Assignment This part explains your writing assignment. The topic of your assignment usually appears in the first few sentences in this section. In this case, it's the first two sentences. Finally, you are given a clue to what kind of voice you should use in your adventure story. Because your audience is your classmates, you should use an entertaining voice.

Your Assignment The *Your Assignment* section provides students with specific information about the topic, genre, and audience for their assignment. Remind students that the topic and genre were introduced in Part 1 of the test. Ask them to go back to the directions for Part 1 to identify the sections where the topic and genre were mentioned.

Point out the following sentence to students from the *Your Assignment* section on page 106: *Your assignment is to write an adventure story set during the California Gold Rush with concrete details and examples from each of the sources you have examined.* Make sure students understand that their writing should be based on information from the sources they have examined, not on their personal experiences.

ADVANCED/ADVANCED HIGH
Part 2 Directions Have students read the *Your Assignment* section and write three to six words or phrases that they think are most important. Then have each student compare with a partner and discuss the meanings of the words and phrases. After they have discussed their ideas, help them verify actual meanings using dictionaries. Further assist them by offering examples of your own. Have the partners outline the task that Jack will follow during the narrative test writing process.

Have students repeat this process before they start their own next generation narrative assessment.

CCSS **Common Core State Standards** (pp. Z20–Z30)
Writing: W.4.8

Analyze
Part 2
Scoring Guide

Week 1 • Day 3

Student Objectives

• Understand the scoring guide for a next generation assessment. *(pp. 108–109)*

Analyze the Scoring Guide Direct students' attention to the Scoring Guide on page 108. Tell students that the scoring guide helps them plan and evaluate their writing. Help students understand how the scoring guide is similar to the rubrics they have seen by asking questions such as the following:

Which section

• focuses on describing events? (second)

• focuses on using logical organization? (first)

• reminds you to appeal to the reader's senses? (second)

• encourages you to improve your sentence fluency? (first)

• reminds you to edit your writing? (third)

Scoring Guide

Your adventure story will be scored on the following criteria:

1. **Focus and organization** How well did you engage the reader by describing a situation and introducing the narrator? How well did your ideas flow using effective transitions? How well did you combine short sentences to improve flow? How well did you provide a conclusion that follows from the experiences or events? How well did the events unfold naturally and logically?

2. **Elaboration of experiences/events** How well did you use dialogue and description to develop experiences, events, and characters? How well did you use concrete words and phrases and sensory details to convey experiences and events precisely? How well did you use first-person point of view to engage your readers?

3. **Conventions** How well did you follow the rules of grammar, punctuation, capitalization, and spelling?

Now you can begin work on your adventure story. Manage your time carefully so that you can:
- plan your story.
- write your story.
- revise and edit for a final draft.

Spell check is available to use.

Type your response in the space provided on the following page. Write as much as you need to fulfill the requirements of the task. You are not limited by the size of the response area on the screen.

108 Narrative Writing

Strategies for Writers Online

Go to **www.sfw.z-b.com** for additional online resources for students, teachers, and parents.

Writing Traits in the Scoring Guide

The second page of the directions tells you how your adventure story will be scored. This scoring guide includes all of the writing traits. You can use what you have learned about the writing traits to help you write an exciting adventure story.

1 Focus and organization

 • How well did you combine short sentences to improve flow?

 • How well did the events unfold naturally and logically with effective transitions?

2 Elaboration of experiences/events

 • How well did you use dialogue and description to develop experiences, events, and characters?

 • How well did you use concrete words and phrases and sensory details to convey experiences and events precisely?

 • How well did you use first-person point of view to engage your readers?

3 Conventions

 • How well did you follow the rules of grammar, punctuation, capitalization, and spelling?

Before you start Part 2, review your plan for how you will divide your time. Remember there is no word limit, but don't feel you have to fill the entire space with your thoughts. Now it's time for Jack to start writing his adventure story.

Writing Traits in the Scoring Guide

Direct students' attention to the information about the scoring guide. Tell students that some scoring guides do not include the names of the six traits, but they still relate to each of the traits. Students can use their writing experience to remember the main requirements associated with each trait:

Ideas events unfold naturally; descriptive details are included to help the reader clearly picture the events, characters, and setting

Organization logical organization that includes helpful transitions that guide the reader

Voice a voice that is engaging and sounds appropriate for both purpose and audience

Word Choice language that is precise and supports the writer's purpose

Sentence Fluency sentences that flow well with a variety of patterns and lengths

Conventions conscientious editing for grammar, spelling, capitalization, and punctuation

CCSS **Common Core State Standards** (pp. Z20–Z30)
Speaking and Listening: SL.4.1a, SL.4.1c, SL.4.1d

Write
Prewrite

Week 1 • Day 4

Student Objectives

• Respond to the assignment. (p. 110)

Prewrite

Focus on Ideas

Gather Information Tell students that they will need to gather evidence, such as facts and examples, from the three sources that they examined in Part 1 to find details for their narrative. Remind students that they are allowed to go back and review the sources, but they cannot change their answers to the questions.

Prewrite   Focus on ⬭ Ideas

Writing Strategy   Respond to the assignment.

Prewrite ⟷ [_____] 15 minutes

 Writers gather information to help them write. This is an important step when you write for an assessment. I will look at the assignment again to find information about what I am supposed to write.

From my assignment, I know I'm supposed to write an adventure story. I also know the topic.

topic

> During the 1800s, many people moved west across the United States. They moved for many different reasons, but one reason was to get rich during the Gold Rush. Your assignment is to write an adventure story set during the California Gold Rush with concrete details and examples from each of the sources you have examined.

genre

First, I'm going to write a sentence stating my topic. Then, I'll think about which of the sources will support my topic. I can't remember all the details about the sources, but I just want to see what I remember.

> **My Topic:**
>   Going west was one way to make a fortune.
> **Sources that Support My Topic:**
>   The text about Sutter's Mill and finding gold
>   The text about all the people who made money in different ways
>   during the Gold Rush

110   Narrative Writing

Differentiating Instruction

ENRICHMENT

Reference Historical Fiction Challenge students to define the genre *historical fiction* and list some books they know that fit into that genre. Link the writing assignment in this assessment to the historical fiction genre. Discuss how students can use historical facts in a story.

 Online Writing Center

Provides **interactive graphic organizers** as well as a variety of graphic organizers in PDF format.

Prewrite

Focus on **Organization**

Writing Strategy Choose a graphic organizer.

Prewrite ⟷ ▭ 15 minutes

I need to start organizing my ideas. A good graphic organizer for a story is a Sequence Chain. It will help me organize the events in my story. I may want to go back now and examine the sources in Part 1 again to get ideas for the kinds of events I can include in my story to make it seem real.

My California Gold Rush Adventure

First Event
I left on a wagon train from New York to make my fortune.

Second Event
I arrived at Sutter's Mill and started searching for gold.

Third Event
A friend asked me to watch his things, so I charged him a fee.

Fourth Event
Some rough-looking men came into town.

Fifth Event
I tricked the men into leaving town and kept my friend's things safe.

Analyze

Does the graphic include enough events to make an exciting story? Are there any other events Jack might want to include?

Next Generation Assessment III

Differentiating Instruction

REINFORCEMENT

Using Facts as Details Support students in using facts as details in their stories. Find a detail from one of the three texts, such as how long the pioneers followed the Platte River or when gold was found, and model using it to create an interesting sentence. For example: *Four hundred fifty miles is a long time to wade through grass on a horse and go without a bath.*

Write
Prewrite

Week 1 • Day 4

Student Objectives

- Choose a graphic organizer. (p. 111)

Prewrite

Focus on

Analyze Graphic Organizer After students have reviewed Jack's Sequence Chain, have them write responses to the questions in the **Analyze** box. Then have them share their responses with a partner. Ask volunteers to share their responses with the class. Tell students that in a test-taking situation a graphic organizer may not be given to them. Explain that they will need to choose one on their own that best suits their assignment. Encourage students to fill in a graphic organizer completely to help them draft their stories.

CCSS **Common Core State Standards** (pp. Z20–Z30)
Writing: W.4.3a, W.4.6, W.4.8, W.4.10
Speaking and Listening: SL.4.1a, SL.4.1c, SL.4.1d

Write
Draft

Student Objectives

- State the topic in the opening sentence. *(pp. 112–113)*
- Organize events logically. *(pp. 112–113)*

Draft

Focus on Ideas

Drafting on Paper Remind students that they may take tests on paper or on a computer. If they take the test on paper, remind them to write on every other line. This leaves space for students to make their corrections when they revise and edit their drafts. Mention that in a timed situation, students will not have time to create a fresh final copy of their writing.

Drafting on a Computer If students take the test on a computer, tell them that they should make sure they know where the Save button is. Encourage students to save often. If they cannot find the Save button, explain that there might be an autosave, but they should check with the adult who is monitoring the test. Point out the wavy lines in Jack's draft. Ask students if they know what the wavy lines mean. (The word is misspelled.)

 Strategies for Writers Online
Go to **www.sfw.z-b.com** for additional online resources for students, teachers, and parents.

Draft
Focus on Ideas

Writing Strategy Remember your purpose as you write, beginning with stating the topic in the first sentence.

Draft ⟷ 25 minutes

 The purpose of my story is to describe an exciting adventure. I'll begin with a good topic sentence. It will tell what the story is about and get readers interested in reading more. I'll use my Sequence Chain as a guide for organizing the events in my story.

> *my topic sentence*
>
> B *I* U abc
>
> Going west was one way to make a fortune. Gold was found in the American River. Sam left New York and joined a wagon train in Independence. The long line of wagons looked like ships crossing an ocean of tall grass. We were a happy band of families and single men. Sam hates snakes, so he's glad he didn't see any. Some of the men were rogues, but before long we were helping each other.
>
> I was one of hundreds of men who gathered at Sutter's Mill. I spent hours squatting and panning. And even though I'd read gold was easy to find, I found nothing. Every night I trudged back to my place to hear at least ten people tell stories about the gold they found. Each piece they found was bigger than the last.
>
> One day, a friend talked to me. He was going into town. He didn't want to leave his stuff in his tent. He was afraid

II2 Narrative Writing

English Language Learners

BEGINNING
Sensory Details Write words associated with autumn, such as apples, leaves, wind, grass, air, squirrels, birds, and colors on index cards. Draw a Five Senses Chart with the title Autumn. Ask students to tell which category each word belongs in on the Five Senses Chart. It is possible for a word to fit in more than one category.

INTERMEDIATE
A Strong Opening Sentence Read the following sentences: *The brown leaves crackled under my feet. I stepped on the leaves.* Ask students which paints a clearer picture. Have them identify sensory details in the sentence. (brown and crackled) Have student partners write a sentence that includes sensory details. Monitor that students' use of sensory details is effective and paints a picture for the reader.

B I U abc ≡ ≡ ≡ ≣ ≔ ≔ ↰ ↱ A˅ A˅ ✂ 📋 📋 ABC

that thieves would steal it. He asked me if I would watch his things.

"Sure," I said. I charged ten cents an hour to sit by his tent. There wasn't much to do. Mostly I just chased animals away.

One day a group of rough-looking men marched into camp. I was scared, but I had a job to do. Thinking fast, I walked up to the leader.

"Hey," I said, "could you help me with a problem?"
What kind of problem he asked.

"I just need to chase a sleeping bare out of a tent," I replied. the men looked at each other in a panick. Then they all turned and ran.

That night I had my own story to tell. The next day, I had many more clients. I didn't find gold, but my wits helped me find my fortune.

Analyze

Does the story begin with a strong topic sentence? Do the events in the story all relate to the topic?

Next Generation Assessment II3

Use a Graphic Organizer
Remind students that they should keep their graphic organizer out as they draft and refer to it frequently. If new details occur to students while they draft, they should consider including them, especially if they make their story more interesting to a reader. If students cannot decide where the new details belong on the organizer, they should probably not use them in their writing.

Support a Narrative
After students have reviewed Jack's draft, have them write responses to the questions in the **Analyze** box. Then have them share their responses with a partner. Ask volunteers to share their responses with the class. As students draft during an assessment, tell them to pay attention to organizing events logically. Have them ask themselves:

- Have I stated my topic (purpose for writing) clearly in the beginning sentence?

- Do I include historical details from the sources?

- Do I give interesting details that support the topic?

ADVANCED/ADVANCED HIGH
Sensory Details Briefly review the five senses. Present students with a familiar object or idea, such as autumn. Have partners complete a Five Senses Chart, making sure to include one idea for each of the five senses, if applicable. Prompt them to think about sounds they hear outside, smells in the air, colors they see, special foods they might eat, and how grass or dead leaves might feel beneath their feet. Have students share their charts with a partner and work together to add additional sensory details.

CCSS **Common Core State Standards** (pp. Z20–Z30)
Writing: W.4.3a
Speaking and Listening: SL.4.1a, SL.4.1c, SL.4.1d

Write
Revise

Week 2 • Day 1

Student Objectives

- Revise for use of transitions. (p. 114)

Revise

Focus on

Time Management Point out that Jack had about twenty minutes to revise his draft and that there were three revision tasks. (If you are using the Optional Revising Lessons, you will need to plan accordingly. See page T116.) Tell students that Jack divided his planned revising time into three six- to seven-minute segments and revised for one strategy at a time. Explain to students that they may not have enough time to revise for all traits during an assessment, so they should focus on the traits they know they usually need help with.

Analyze Revision After students have reviewed Jack's revisions, have them write responses to the questions in the **Analyze** box. Then have them share their responses with a partner. Ask volunteers to share their responses with the class.

Strategies for Writers Online
Go to **www.sfw.z-b.com** for additional online resources for students, teachers, and parents.

Revise   Focus on **Organization**

Writing Strategy   Use transitions to guide the reader.

Revise |◄───► | 20 minutes

Now it's time to check my draft against the scoring guide. I want to be sure I've included all the points that will be scored.

The scoring guide reminds me to use transition words and phrases to organize my story. This helps the events unfold naturally, too. Some transitions show the order in which events take place. Some examples are *soon*, *after*, and *a week later*. I'll look for places to add transitions to show when events happened.

> A year after G~~g~~old was found in the American River, Sam left New York and joined a wagon train in Independence. The long line of wagons looked like ships crossing an ocean of tall grass. We were a happy band of families and single men. Sam hates snakes, so he's glad he didn't see any. Some of the men were rogues, but before long we were helping each other.
>
> After several months of travel, I was one of hundreds of men who gathered at Sutter's Mill.

added transitions

Analyze

Do you think the order of events in Jack's story makes sense? Is there anything else he can do to improve the organization?

Revise

Focus on **Voice**

Writing Strategy   Use first-person point of view.

Revise |←→| 20 minutes

Using the first-person point of view (*I, we, me, us*) will help me engage my readers because it sounds as if the narrator is talking directly to them. I found a few places where I should have used the first-person point of view. I'll read the rest of my draft to make sure I've used the first-person point of view throughout my story.

B *I* <u>U</u> abc ≡ ≡ ≡ ≡ ≣ ≣ ↰ ↱ A⁻ A⁻ ✂ ▣ ▦ ✓

A year after gold was found in the American River, ~~Sam~~ I left New York and joined a wagon train in Independence. The long line of wagons looked like ships crossing an ocean of tall grass. We were a happy band of families and single men. ~~Sam hates~~ I hate snakes, so ~~he's~~ I'm glad ~~he~~ I didn't see any. Some of the men were rogues, but before long we were helping each other.

used first-person point of view

Analyze

How does the revision improve Jack's story? Do you think the readers will understand the narrator better?

Next Generation Assessment   **115**

Differentiating Instruction

REINFORCEMENT

Support Voice Remind students that voice is the way the writer "speaks" to the reader. First-person point of view uses the words *I, me, we, us, my* and *our*. Have students practice using first person by choosing a story written in third-person and rewriting one or two paragraphs so they are told from the first-person point of view. Ask students to explain how the change in point of view affected the voice in the story.

Write
Revise

Week 2 • Day 1

Student Objectives

• Revise for first-person point of view. (*p. 115*)

Revise

Focus on **Voice**

Review Voice Remind students that their voice should sound consistent throughout their story, especially with the point of view used. Have them focus on the second half of their story, where writers often lose track of the voice they established at the beginning and become inconsistent.

Analyze Revision After students have reviewed Jack's revisions, have them write responses to the questions in the **Analyze** box. Then have them share their responses with a partner. Ask volunteers to share their responses with the class.

CCSS Common Core State Standards (pp. Z20–Z30)
Writing: W.4.3a, W.4.3c, W.4.5, W.4.10
Speaking and Listening: SL.4.1a, SL.4.1c, SL.4.1d

Write
Revise

Week 2 • Day 2

Student Objectives

- Revise for concrete words and sensory details. *(p. 116)*

Revise

Focus on Word Choice

Review Concrete Words and Sensory Details Tell students that as they revise for word choice they should look for vague words such as *thing, stuff, place, sport,* and *game*. Explain that while these words are sometimes appropriate, often they should be replaced by more concrete words. Remind students that using sensory details helps the reader picture the events in their story.

Tell students that if Jack had extra time left in the revising period, he could have checked for other traits, such as ideas and sentence fluency. When students are taking an assessment, encourage them to use every minute remaining to improve their writing, even if they think they are finished.

Analyze Revision After students have read Jack's revisions, have them write responses to the questions in the **Analyze** box. Then have them share their responses with a partner. Ask volunteers to share their responses with the class.

Online Writing Center

Provides **interactive proofreading activities** for each genre.

Next Generation Assessment

Revise

Focus on Word Choice

Writing Strategy Add concrete words and sensory details.

Revise — 20 minutes

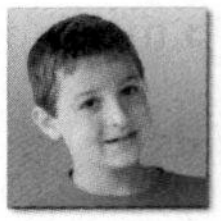

The scoring guide reminds me to use concrete words and phrases to make my writing more interesting. I want my readers to feel as if they are in my adventure story. I'll add some sensory details. Do you think they improve my story?

After several months of travel, I was one of hundreds of men who gathered at Sutter's Mill. Mud covered everything. It smelled of sweat. Clanging and yelling could be heard at all hours. I spent hours squatting and panning. And even though I read gold was easy to find, I found nothing. Every night I trudged back to my ~~place~~ tent to hear at least ten people tell stories about the gold they found. Each piece they found was bigger than the last.

added concrete word

added sensory details

Analyze

Did Jack use sensory details in his story? Are there any other sections of his draft that could use more concrete words or sensory details?

116 Narrative Writing

Optional Revising Lessons

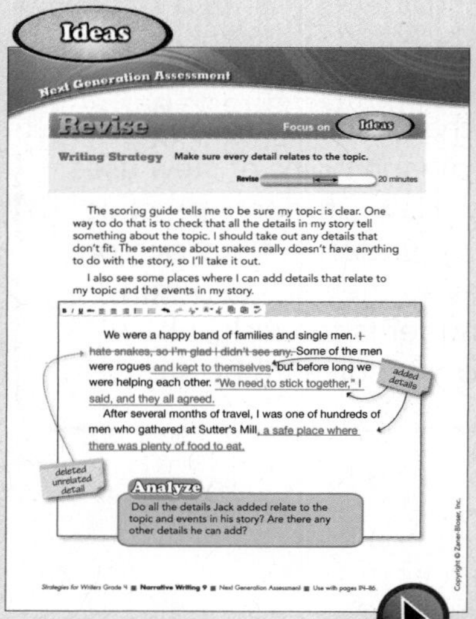

Ideas

Next Generation Assessment

Revise — Focus on Ideas

Writing Strategy Make sure every detail relates to the topic.

Revise — 20 minutes

The scoring guide tells me to be sure my topic is clear. One way to do that is to check that all the details in my story tell something about the topic. I should take out any details that don't fit. The sentence about snakes really doesn't have anything to do with the story, so I'll take it out.

I also see some places where I can add details that relate to my topic and the events in my story.

We were a happy band of families and single men. ~~I hate snakes, so I'm glad I didn't see any.~~ Some of the men were rogues and kept to themselves, but before long we were helping each other. "We need to stick together," I said, and they all agreed.

After several months of travel, I was one of hundreds of men who gathered at Sutter's Mill, a safe place where there was plenty of food to eat.

deleted unrelated detail

added details

Analyze

Do all the details Jack added relate to the topic and events in his story? Are there any other details he can add?

Strategies for Writers Grade 4 ■ Narrative Writing 9 ■ Next Generation Assessment ■ Use with pages 114–86.

Copyright © Zaner-Bloser, Inc.

Narrative 9

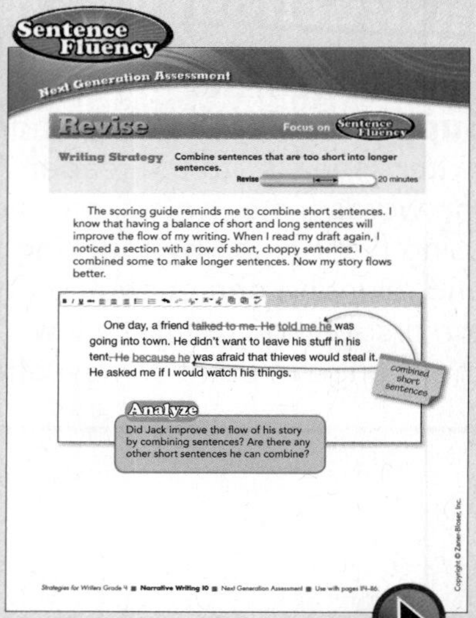

Sentence Fluency

Next Generation Assessment

Revise — Focus on Sentence Fluency

Writing Strategy Combine sentences that are too short into longer sentences.

Revise — 20 minutes

The scoring guide reminds me to combine short sentences. I know that having a balance of short and long sentences will improve the flow of my writing. When I read my draft again, I noticed a section with a row of short, choppy sentences. I combined some to make longer sentences. Now my story flows better.

One day, a friend ~~talked to me. He~~ told me he was going into town. He didn't want to leave his stuff in his tent~~. He~~ because he was afraid that thieves would steal it. He asked me if I would watch his things.

combined short sentences

Analyze

Did Jack improve the flow of his story by combining sentences? Are there any other short sentences he can combine?

Strategies for Writers Grade 4 ■ Narrative Writing 10 ■ Next Generation Assessment ■ Use with pages 114–86.

Copyright © Zaner-Bloser, Inc.

Narrative 10

Go to *Strategies for Writers* at **www.sfw.z-b.com.**

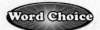

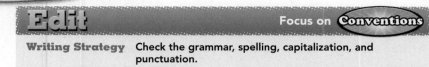

Edit — Focus on Conventions

Writing Strategy Check the grammar, spelling, capitalization, and punctuation.

Edit ————————— 8 minutes

The scoring guide reminds me to use correct grammar and spelling. I also need to check my capitalization and punctuation. I'm glad I planned my time carefully so I have time to check for errors in these important areas. I'll read my draft carefully one more time.

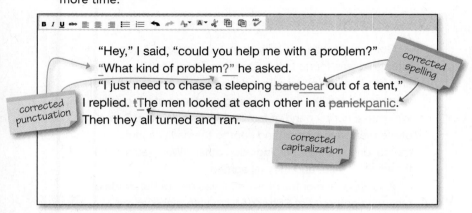

B *I* <u>U</u> abc

"Hey," I said, "could you help me with a problem?"
"What kind of problem?" he asked.
"I just need to chase a sleeping ~~bare~~bear out of a tent,"
I replied. ~~t~~The men looked at each other in a ~~panick~~panic.
Then they all turned and ran.

corrected spelling

corrected punctuation

corrected capitalization

TEST TIP

Reread your writing. As you read, run your finger under each word to make sure it is spelled correctly and is the word you want to use.

Differentiating Instruction

ENRICHMENT

Early Finishers Advanced students often finish tests early. Remind students that they can use the extra time to reread the writing assignment and then carefully read their stories one more time while keeping the writing traits and the writing task in mind.

Write
Edit

Week 2 • Day 2

Student Objectives

- Check the grammar, spelling, capitalization, and punctuation. (p. 117)

Edit

Focus on Conventions

Editing Explain that while a story written for an assessment in a short period of time will rarely be perfect, students should correct as many errors as possible. Assessment graders know that students are writing quickly and watching the clock, so a few errors may slip through. However, assessment graders also look for evidence that students took the time to edit. When they see misspelled words crossed out and correctly spelled words inserted instead, assessment graders know that students are paying attention to editing. If students are taking assessments online, they may not be able to show their edits. If they see wavy lives still remaining in their writing, this means that they have misspelled words. Tell them to check the spelling of these words by using the spell-check feature.

CCSS **Common Core State Standards** (pp. Z20–Z30)
Writing: 4.2d, W.4.3a, W.4.3b, W.4.3d, W.4.6. W.4.10
Language: L.4.2a, L.4.2d
Speaking and Listening: SL.4.1a, SL.4.1c, SL.4.1d

Review
Final Draft

Week 2 • Days 3–5

Student Objectives

• Review a final draft.

• Practice taking a timed assessment. (pp. 118–119)

Publish

Publishing an Assessment

Review Jack's final draft with students. If students take an online assessment, they should always use the spell-check feature one more time before they submit their work. If they take an assessment on paper, they should read through their work one final time before they submit it.

Write About What You Learned
Ask students to write about taking a next generation assessment, including the steps you have to take and how to manage your time. When they are done, lead a discussion about what they wrote using questions such as the following:

• What is the difference between Part 1 and Part 2? (Possible response: Part 1 is reading texts. Part 2 is writing using details from the texts you read in Part 1.)

• Do you have to remember everything you read in Part 1 when you write your assignment in Part 2? (Possible response: No. You can go back to Part 1 to reread a source, but you can't change your answer.)

 Strategies for Writers Online
Go to **www.sfw.z-b.com** for additional online resources for students, teachers, and parents.

Publish

Writing Strategy Submit the final draft of your adventure story.

Publish ▭▭▭▭▭▭▭▭▭ ⏮ 2 minutes

 I am almost finished with my assessment. I used information in the scoring guide and the writing traits to complete my adventure story. Now, I am going to reread my story one more time to make sure it makes sense. Then I will submit my final draft.

> B *I* U abc ≡ ≡ ≡ ≣ ≔ ≔ ↩ ↪ A▾ A▾ ✂ 📋 📋 ABC
>
> Going west was one way to make a fortune. A year after gold was found in the American River, I left New York and joined a wagon train in Independence. The long line of wagons looked like ships crossing an ocean of tall grass. We were a happy band of families and single men. Some of the men were rogues and kept to themselves, but before long we were helping each other. "We need to stick together, " I said, and they all agreed.
>
> After several months of travel, I was one of hundreds of men who gathered at Sutter's Mill, a safe place where there was plenty of food to eat. Mud covered everything. It smelled of sweat. Clanging and yelling could be heard at all hours. I spent hours squatting and panning. And even though I'd read gold was easy to find, I found nothing. Every night I trudged back to my tent to hear at least ten

Differentiating Instruction

REINFORCEMENT
Make the Most of It To reduce students' anxiety about running out of time, advise them to combine the edit and publishing phases. Then tell them to split the time into manageable chunks. Have students spend two to three minutes scanning their drafts for spelling errors, two to three minutes looking for capitalization and punctuation errors, and then two to three minutes looking for the errors they commonly make.

people tell stories about the gold they found. Each piece they found was bigger than the last.

One day, a friend told me he was going into town. He didn't want to leave his stuff in his tent because he was afraid that thieves would steal it. He asked me if I would watch his things.

"Sure," I said. I charged ten cents an hour to sit by his tent. There wasn't much to do. Mostly I just chased animals away.

One day a group of rough-looking men marched into camp. I was scared, but I had a job to do. Thinking fast, I walked up to the leader.

"Hey," I said, "could you help me with a problem?"

"What kind of problem?" he asked.

"I just need to chase a sleeping bear out of a tent," I replied. The men looked at each other in a panic. Then they all turned and ran.

That night I had my own story to tell. The next day I had many more clients. I didn't find gold, but my wits helped me find my fortune.

Now It's **Your Turn**

Don't forget all the advice Jack gave you during his assessment. Now, it's your turn to practice taking a narrative assessment.

Next Generation Assessment **119**

Next Generation Assessment Practice ___

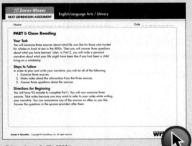

Student Edition

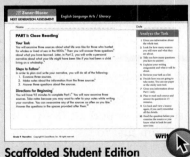

Scaffolded Student Edition

Teacher Edition

- Where do you look to find out what you need to include in your writing? (Possible response: Your Assignment and the Scoring Guide tell you what you need to write.)

Now It's Your Turn

Tell students that they will practice taking a next generation narrative assessment in real time. If time permits, students should complete the assessment over a two-day period. Go to **www. sfw.z-b.com** or the **Strategies for Writers Online Writing Center** to download the **Next Generation Assessment Practice** for narrative writing.

There are two student versions of the assessment. One assessment contains scaffolded support as students take the assessment. The other assessment does not have scaffolded support. Choose which version of the assessment you want your class to take. Review the teacher version of the assessment before giving it to students.

CCSS **C**ommon **C**ore **S**tate **S**tandards ((pp. Z20–Z30)
Writing: W.4.4, W.4.5, W.4.6, W.4.10
Speaking and Listening: SL.4.1c, SL.4.1d

Next Generation Assessment **T119**

Informative/Explanatory writing

Compare-and-Contrast Essay

This genre introduces students to informative/explanatory writing as they examine the similarities and differences between two items and write a compare-and-contrast essay.

Prewrite   Do research and take notes on two things to compare and contrast.
Make an Attribute Chart to show similarities and differences.

Draft   Name two clear topics for comparison and treat them the same.

Revise   Begin with a strong compare-and-contrast lead.
Use a knowledgeable and enthusiastic tone.
Clearly explain domain-specific vocabulary.

Edit   Make sure that homophones are used correctly.

Publish   Display the essay on the classroom bulletin board.

Research Report

This genre gives students a chance to sharpen their research skills as they learn how to gather and share information about interesting topics in a research report.

Prewrite   Narrow a topic and take notes.
Use a Web to organize notes.

Draft   Use the Web to plan the introduction, body, and conclusion of the report.

Revise   Use a formal tone and facts to sound knowledgeable.
Use appositives to explain nouns clearly and precisely.
Use varying sentence lengths that include simple and compound sentences.

Edit   Check the capitalization and correct use of titles.

Publish   Publish the report on the school's website.

How-To Essay

This genre allows students to share something they know how to do while learning strategies for writing an instructive how-to essay.

Prewrite   Choose something to do or make. List all the important steps.
Make an Outline to organize the steps from first to last.

Draft   Use a natural, informative voice.

Revise   Delete information that is not related to the process.
Use specific nouns and strong verbs.
Make sure sentence beginnings are varied and guide the reader.

Edit   Check that all pronouns are used correctly.

Publish   Publish the essay in a class how-to book.

Professional Development Podcasts and Screencasts
Go to **www.sfw.z-b.com** to access the variety of professional development **podcasts** and **screencasts**.

Unit Overview

Summary SCIENCE CONNECTION

Pages T188A–T213

Students will practice the important cross-curricular skill of summarizing by reading an article and writing a summary of its main points.

Prewrite Read an article to summarize. Take notes about the main points.
Make a Five-Column Chart to organize the main points.

Draft Use precise words and strong verbs to explain domain-specific vocabulary.

Revise Make sure all details support the main ideas.
Organize the main points logically with the most important idea first.
Write clear and direct sentences.

Edit Check for double negatives. Make sure verbs are used correctly.

Publish Post the summary on the class website.

Next Generation Informative/Explanatory Assessment

Pages T214A–T235

Students will learn and practice how to take a next generation informative/explanatory assessment. They will learn to read and analyze the directions for each part of the assessment, plan their time effectively, and follow the steps of the writing process to write an informative/explanatory piece that includes evidence from sources they have examined.

Prewrite Respond to the assignment.
Choose a graphic organizer.

Draft Begin with a topic sentence.

Revise Sum up my report in the conclusion.
Use facts to sound knowledgeable.
Choose words and phrases to convey ideas precisely.

Edit Check the grammar, spelling, capitalization, and punctuation.

Online Writing Center

iPad® and IWB Ready

Complete Digital Writing Instruction!

- My Writing Pad
- Interactive Rubrics
- Anchor Papers
- Graphic Organizers

- Content-Area Writing Prompts
- Grammar Games
- Proofreading Activities
- Instructional Videos

- Virtual File Cabinet
- eBooks
- Assessments

For information, go to www.sfw.z-b.com.

21st Century Literacies
Technology, Digital Media & Writing

by **Julie Coiro, Ph.D.,** University of Rhode Island & **Sara B. Kajder, Ph.D.,** Shady Side Academy

 **INQUIRE** First Locate, Then Evaluate

Reading Within Search Engine Results

One of the most challenging aspects of online reading is understanding how to evaluate a long list of Internet search results to determine which link, if any, to pursue. Here are some tips to share with students to determine which link is best:

- **Read the description, not just the link.** Some students skim only the blue underlined titles that appear in the beginning of a search list entry without realizing the description that follows contains helpful clues. Encourage students to stop and notice that the keywords from their search are often bolded within the descriptions. They can avoid clicking on a link that's not useful by reading the available descriptions to more accurately predict if the information will meet their research needs.

- **Know how to read the parts of a website address.** A great deal of information can be gleaned from the dots, slashes, abbreviations, and words contained in the website address, or URL, that appears below descriptions in many lists of search results. Show students how website addresses can be broken down into parts, with each part providing identification of the path leading to the website host, as follows:

http://	kids. discovery.com/	activities/	science experiments
type of protocol	domain name, or host	path or directory to the file	name and type of file

- **Use the clues to try a different search.** If nothing useful is found in the first 10–20 sites listed, try a new search with different keywords. Encourage students to think about words that appeared in the descriptions or within the websites they visited.

Evaluating Reliability

As children begin using the Internet as a source for information, it is important that they realize websites do not go through the same editing process as books. An important strategy to discuss with students involves evaluating the **reliability** of the information that they find online.

A reliable website is one created by a person or a group of people with a reputation for publishing high-quality, truthful information. All quality websites should have an "About Us" or "Who We Are" page that tells more about the authors, their qualifications, their contact information, and their purpose for creating the site. You may wish to explore several websites as a class activity.

To begin, select two or three websites, using a digital projector to view each site with your students. Scroll up and down the site's home page to look for the "About Us" link. Once you have found the link, discuss the answers to questions such as:

- Who created the information?

- What is the purpose of this website?

- When was the information at this site updated?

- What qualifications does the author have?

- Is the information at this website worthy of being used in your own informative/explanatory writing? Why or why not?

Encourage students to consider this series of questions each time they visit a website. The answers will often provide the insights students need to critically evaluate whether the information is reliable and useful for their writing projects.

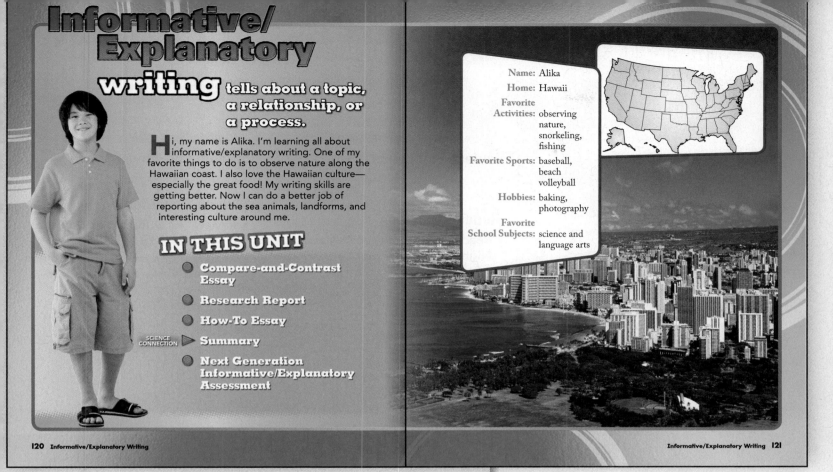

Informative/Explanatory writing tells about a topic, a relationship, or a process.

Hi, my name is Alika. I'm learning all about informative/explanatory writing. One of my favorite things to do is to observe nature along the Hawaiian coast. I also love the Hawaiian culture—especially the great food! My writing skills are getting better. Now I can do a better job of reporting about the sea animals, landforms, and interesting culture around me.

IN THIS UNIT

- Compare-and-Contrast Essay
- Research Report
- How-To Essay
- SCIENCE CONNECTION ▷ Summary
- Next Generation Informative/Explanatory Assessment

Name: Alika

Home: Hawaii

Favorite Activities: observing nature, snorkeling, fishing

Favorite Sports: baseball, beach volleyball

Hobbies: baking, photography

Favorite School Subjects: science and language arts

To differentiate instruction and maximize student achievement, use the Differentiated Instruction Activities available at **www.sfw.z-b.com.**

Created by Amy Humphreys, Ed.M., these engaging activities can be used to meet a wide range of learner needs. Each activity uses a combination of visual, written, oral, and kinesthetic elements, and deliberately leverages the power of collaboration and conversation so students learn to think like writers in fun and engaging ways.

Meet Your Writing Partner, Alika

The writing partner for this chapter is Alika, a boy from Hawaii, who loves to observe nature along the Hawaiian coast. You may wish to explore with students how living in Hawaii might affect Alika's interests, hobbies, and decisions; and how these in turn might influence his choice of writing topics. Encourage students to use their own background knowledge, interests, and personalities as they write, as well. Informative/ Explanatory writing explores many real-world topics, and your students will have many interesting, unique, and authentic ideas to explain.

Compare-and-Contrast Essay Planner

WEEK 1

Day 1
Introduce
Compare-and-Contrast Essay

Student Objectives
- Review the elements of a compare-and-contrast essay.
- Consider purpose and audience.
- Learn the traits of informative/explanatory writing.

Student Activities
- Read and discuss **What's in a Compare-and-Contrast Essay?** (p. 122)
- Read and discuss **Why Write a Compare-and-Contrast Essay?** (p. 123)
- Read **Linking Informative/Explanatory Writing Traits to a Compare-and-Contrast Essay.** (p. 124)

Day 2
Analyze
Close Reading of the Model

Student Objectives
- Read a model compare-and-contrast essay.

Student Activities
- Read **"As Different as Day and Night."** (p. 125)

Day 3
Analyze
Introduce the Rubric

Student Objectives
- Learn to read a rubric.

Student Activities
- Review **"As Different as Day and Night."** (p. 125)
- Read and discuss the **Compare-and-Contrast Essay rubric.** (pp. 126–127)

WEEK 2

Day 1
Write
Prewrite: Ideas

Student Objectives
- Read and understand a prewriting strategy.

Student Activities
- Read and discuss **Prewrite: Focus on Ideas.** (p. 132)
- Apply the prewriting strategy.

Day 2
Write
Prewrite: Organization

Student Objectives
- Make an Attribute Chart to organize ideas.

Student Activities
- Read and discuss **Prewrite: Focus on Organization.** (p. 133)
- Apply the prewriting strategy to create an Attribute Chart.

Day 3
Write
Draft: Ideas

Student Objectives
- Use an Attribute Chart to begin writing.

Student Activities
- Read and discuss **Draft: Focus on Ideas.** (p. 134)
- Apply the drafting strategy by using an Attribute Chart to write a draft.

WEEK 3

Day 1
Write
Revise: Voice

Student Objectives
- Revise for a knowledgeable and enthusiastic voice.

Student Activities
- Read and discuss **Revise: Focus on Voice.** (p. 137)
- Reflect on the model draft.
- Apply the revising strategy.
- Participate in a peer conference.

Day 2
Write
Revise: Word Choice

Student Objectives
- Revise for correct use of domain-specific vocabulary.

Student Activities
- Read and discuss **Revise: Focus on Word Choice.** (p. 138)
- Apply the revising strategy.

Note: Optional Revising Lessons are located at **www.sfw.z-b.com.**

Day 3
Write
Edit: Conventions

Student Objectives
- Edit for correct use of homophones.

Student Activities
- Read and discuss **Edit: Focus on Conventions.** (p. 139)
- Reflect on the model draft.
- Apply the editing strategy.

Note: Teach the Conventions mini-lessons (pp. 140–141) if needed.

TI22A Informative/Explanatory Writing

Day 4	Day 5
Analyze Close Reading for the Traits	**Analyze** Close Reading for the Traits

Student Objectives
- Read a model compare-and-contrast essay.
- Use the compare-and-contrast essay rubric.
- Use the model compare-and-contrast essay to study Ideas, Organization, and Voice.

Student Activities
- Review **"As Different as Day and Night."** *(p. 125)*
- Read and discuss **Using the Rubric to Analyze the Model.** *(pp. 128–129)*

Student Objectives
- Read a model compare-and-contrast essay.
- Use the compare-and-contrast essay rubric.
- Use the model compare-and-contrast essay to study Word Choice, Sentence Fluency, and Conventions.

Student Activities
- Review **"As Different as Day and Night."** *(p. 125)*
- Read and discuss **Using the Rubric to Analyze the Model.** *(pp. 130–131)*

Day 4	Day 5
Write Draft	**Write** Revise: Organization

Student Objectives
- Complete a draft.

Student Activities
- Finish a draft. *(p. 135)*
- Participate in a peer conference.

Student Objectives
- Revise for a strong lead.

Student Activities
- Read and discuss **Revise: Focus on Organization.** *(p. 136)*

Day 4	Day 5
Write Publish: +Presentation	**Write** Publish: +Presentation

Student Objectives
- Discuss preparation for publishing and presentation.
- Use a final editing checklist to publish their work.

Student Activities
- Read and discuss **Publish: +Presentation.** *(p. 142)*
- Apply the publishing strategy.

Student Objectives
- Use a compare-and-contrast essay rubric.
- Share a published compare-and-contrast essay.

Student Activities
- Share their work.
- Use the rubric to reflect upon and evaluate the model and their own writing. *(pp. 126–127, 143)*

To complete the chapter in fewer days, combine the learning objectives and activities in a way that supports students as they write.

Resources at-a-Glance

Grammar, Usage & Mechanics

Differentiating Instruction

For additional Differentiating Instruction activities, see Strategies for Writers *Differentiated Instruction Activities at* **www.sfw.z-b.com.**

English Language Learners

Collaborative Conferencing

Tech Tips

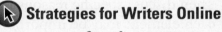 **Strategies for Writers Online**

Go to **www.sfw.z-b.com** for additional online resources for students, teachers, and parents.

Online Writing Center

Provides IWB resources, assessments, interactive games and practice activities, videos, eBooks, and a virtual file cabinet.

Introduce
Compare-and-Contrast Essay

Student Objectives

- Review the elements of a compare-and-contrast essay. *(p. 122)*
- Consider purpose and audience. *(p. 123)*
- Learn the traits of informative/ explanatory writing. *(p. 124)*

What's a Compare- and-Contrast Essay?

Help students understand that a compare-and-contrast essay explores similarities and differences between two or more items. Discuss with students reasons they might need to write a compare-and-contrast essay. Be sure that students understand that the words *compare* and *contrast*, though often used together, have different meanings.

What's in a Compare- and-Contrast Essay?

Read and discuss with students the elements of a compare-and-contrast essay.

Then discuss specific reasons that each element may be important when writing a compare-and-contrast essay.

Strategies for Writers Online

Go to **www.sfw.z-b.com** for additional online resources for students, teachers, and parents.

What's a Compare-and-Contrast Essay?

A compare-and-contrast essay tells how two or more things are alike (compare) and different (contrast).

What's in a Compare-and-Contrast Essay?

Two (or more) Topics
A topic is what I'm writing about. A compare-and-contrast essay usually has at least two topics. I could compare and contrast my pet bird and my pet dog.

Comparisons
When I compare two things, I tell the ways that they are alike or similar.

Contrasts
When I contrast two things, I tell how they are different.

122   Informative/Explanatory Writing

Informative/Explanatory Text Exemplars (Compare-and-Contrast Essay)

Chinery, Michael. *Animal Habitats: Compare Where Reptiles, Mammals, Sharks, Birds and Insects Live and How They Adapt to Their Environments.* **Anness, 2008.** In this factual text, Chinery explains how different animals adapt to their environments. Over 200 photographs accompany the text, making this an informative and enjoyable read.

Haywood, John. *Home, Family & Everyday Life Through the Ages.* **Anness, 2008.** Haywood teaches students how drastically the everyday life of people around the world has changed over the years. In addition to the information provided, several projects and hands-on activities accompany the text.

Why write a Compare-and-Contrast Essay?

There are lots of reasons for writing a compare-and-contrast essay. Here are two good reasons.

To Inform
I can explain something that's new to my reader by comparing and contrasting it with something that's familiar to the reader. I might teach my classmates about seasons in Alaska by comparing and contrasting them with seasons in Hawaii.

To Evaluate
If I compare and contrast two things fairly and without bias, my reader can decide which one he or she thinks is better.

Why write a Compare-and-Contrast Essay?

Point out that all writing has a purpose and is aimed at a specific audience. These authentic purposes help authors shape their writing. Someone writing to inform may explain something new to the reader by comparing and contrasting it with something that is familiar to the reader. A writer who is writing to evaluate can compare and contrast two things fairly and without bias to let the reader decide which one he or she thinks is better. Encourage students to share their own reasons for writing compare-and-contrast essays. Ask them to discuss how these reasons will affect the tone and focus of their writing.

Simon, Seymour. *Crocodiles & Alligators*. Harper-Collins, 2001. *Crocodiles & Alligators* compares the appearance and habits of the two species. Simon uses a combination of facts and photographs to describe these fascinating crocodilians.

Bidner, Jenni. *Is My Cat a Tiger? How Your Pet Compares to Its Wild Cousins*. Lark Books, 2007. Bidner uses text and illustrations to explain the similarities between domestic and wild cats. Students will learn how cats evolved and how their pet's instinctual behaviors are comparable to those of others in their feline family.

CCSS **Common Core State Standards** (pp. Z20–Z30)
Language: L.4.3c
Speaking and Listening: SL.4.1a, SL.4.1b, SL.4.1c, SL.4.1d, SL.4.3, SL.4.6

Introduce

Compare-and-Contrast Essay

Linking Informative/ Explanatory Writing Traits to a Compare-and-Contrast Essay

Read page 124 aloud to help students understand that they will follow Alika as he models using the writing process and the informative/explanatory writing traits together. A good compare-and-contrast essay will be built around a clear topic and main ideas supported by facts and examples. It should have a strong introduction, body, and conclusion and use transitions to connect ideas between well-organized paragraphs. It will use a voice and tone that is appropriate for the purpose and audience. Ask students to decide on a score for each trait, being sure they can provide support for their score. At the end of the discussion, take a vote on the score for each trait to see whether the class comes to a consensus.

Online Writing Center

Provides six **interactive anchor papers** for each text type.

Linking Informative/Explanatory Writing Traits to a Compare-and-Contrast Essay

In this chapter, you will write about how two things are the same and different. This type of informative/explanatory writing is called a compare-and-contrast essay. Alika will guide you through the stages of the writing process: Prewrite, Draft, Revise, Edit, and Publish. In each stage, Alika will show you important writing strategies that are linked to the Informative/Explanatory Writing Traits below.

Informative/Explanatory Writing Traits

 Ideas
- clear topic and main ideas
- details, information, and examples that answer the reader's questions about the topic

 Organization
- a strong introduction, body, and conclusion
- well-organized paragraphs
- transitions that connect ideas

 Voice
- a voice and tone that are appropriate for the purpose and audience

 **Word Choice**
- precise words
- domain-specific vocabulary that is used correctly and explained as necessary

 Sentence Fluency
- clear, direct sentences that flow smoothly

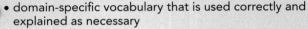 **Conventions**
- no or few errors in grammar, usage, mechanics, and spelling

Before you write, read Taisha Moore's compare-and-contrast essay on the next page. Then use the compare-and-contrast essay rubric on pages 126–127 to decide how well she did. (You might want to look back at What's in a Compare-and-Contrast Essay? on page 122, too!)

Informative/Explanatory Writing Traits in a Compare-and-Contrast Essay

 Ideas The writer builds the essay around a clear topic and main ideas. The main ideas are supported by information and examples that answer the reader's questions.

 **Organization** The paragraphs in the essay are well organized and include a strong introduction, body, and conclusion. Transitions signal comparisons and contrasts.

 **Voice** A knowledgeable-sounding voice and a formal tone are appropriate for the audience and purpose of a compare-and-contrast essay.

As Different as Day and Night

by Taisha Moore

Which two objects in the sky are as different as day and night? One answer to this question is "the sun and the moon." The sun is a bright daytime light. The moon is a beautiful and changing light in the night sky.

two topics

The sun and the moon are both bright objects, but the sun is a star. Earth and the other planets in the solar system revolve around the sun. All life on Earth depends on the sun. Plants need the sun to grow, and animals and people need the sun's heat and light. Unlike the sun, the moon is a satellite. It revolves around Earth. Life on Earth does not depend on the moon, but the moon affects many things on Earth, including the tides.

comparison

Both the sun and the moon seem to change or to move in the sky. The sun seems to rise and set. The moon appears in different places at different times of the year and even at different times of the night.

The moon has a 29-day cycle. Phases of the moon make its circular shape look different at different times of the month. It sometimes looks like a thin crescent, half of a moon, or a full moon. We see only the part of the moon that is lit by sunlight. The sun doesn't have a cycle.

contrast

The moon and the sun also differ in how far away they are from Earth. About one quarter of a million miles away, the moon is Earth's closest neighbor in space. That is one reason we see it so easily. On the other hand, the sun is 93 million miles away. Only its brightness makes it easy to see.

There is no life on either the sun or the moon. The sun has a boiling, busy, bubbling surface. The center of the sun can get as hot as 27 million degrees Fahrenheit. The moon, on the other hand, has no activity. It has no air, no clouds, and no water.

The sun provides our daytime light, and the moon sometimes lights up the darkness. We sometimes use the sun as our symbol for "day" and the moon as our symbol for "night."

Source: Simon, Seymour. *Our Solar System.* New York: Collins, 2007.

Compare-and-Contrast Essay **125**

Word Choice The writer uses precise language and domain-specific vocabulary to make an essay sound knowledgeable.

Sentence Fluency Clear, direct sentences are used to make the writing flow smoothly.

Conventions The writer carefully edits his or her work prior to publishing. Correct use and spelling of words, particularly homophones, enhances the clarity of the writing in a compare-and-contrast essay.

Analyze
Close Reading of the Model

Week 1 • Day 2

Student Objectives

• Read a model compare-and-contrast essay. *(p. 125)*

Read the Model

Read "As Different as Day and Night" aloud to the class. Ask students to listen for a clear topic and main ideas supported by information and examples. Also ask them to notice how the essay is organized. Invite students to think about and discuss how the writer's knowledgeable voice affects how they connect with the writer.

Elements of a Compare-and-Contrast Essay

Have students refer to What's in a Compare-and-Contrast Essay? on page 122 as you refer to the model. Discuss the notes written on the model to enhance students' understanding of the terms.

CCSS **C**ommon **C**ore **S**tate **S**tandards (pp. Z20–Z30)
Writing: W.4.6
Language: L.4.3c
Speaking and Listening: SL.4.1a, SL.4.1b, SL.4.1c, SL.4.1d, SL.4.2, SL.4.3, SL.4.6

Analyze
Introduce the Rubric

Student Objectives

• Learn to read a rubric.
  (pp. 126–127)

Introduce the Rubric

Explain the Rubric Explain that a rubric is a tool for planning, improving, and assessing a piece of writing. Tell students that a rubric helps a writer focus on key elements, or traits, in writing (**Ideas, Organization, Voice, Word Choice, Sentence Fluency, Conventions,** and **Presentation**).

Explain the 6-point system. Point out that the columns on page 126 represent a good paper that might need some polishing but that the columns on page 127 represent writing that needs considerable improvement.

Discuss the Rubric Guide students in a discussion of the rubric. Read the descriptors that go with each trait. Discuss the difference between columns to be sure students fully understand the point system. Tell students to keep the rubric in mind when they write their own compare-and-contrast essay and again when they revise it.

Online Writing Center

Provides a variety of **interactive rubrics,** including 4-, 5-, and 6-point models.

Compare-and-Contrast Essay Rubric

Use this rubric to analyze the model. Then use it to plan and score your own compare-and-contrast essay.

	6	5	4
Ideas	Two topics for comparison are clear. Good examples clearly compare and contrast the topics.	Two topics for comparison are clear. Most examples clearly compare and contrast the topics.	Two topics for comparison are present. The examples do not compare equally.
Organization	The essay is organized by similarities and differences. A strong lead gets the reader's attention.	Similarities and differences are organized. The lead could be stronger.	Most of the time similarities and differences are organized. The lead is not strong.
Voice	The writer's voice sounds knowledgeable. It is clear that the writer wants to inform the reader.	The writer's voice sounds knowledgeable and informative most of the time.	The writer's voice sounds knowledgeable and informative some of the time.
Word Choice	Domain-specific vocabulary is used correctly. It is clearly defined or explained.	Domain-specific vocabulary is used. One or two words are not defined or explained.	Domain-specific vocabulary is used correctly. Many words are not explained or they are not explained well.
Sentence Fluency	Sentences vary in length and type. Effective transitions create a smooth flow.	Most sentences vary in length and type. One or two transitions are needed to improve the flow.	Many sentences share the same length and type. More or better transitions would improve the flow.
Conventions	All homophones are correct. The meaning is clear.	Some homophones are incorrect, but they do not interfere with meaning.	There are a few errors with homophones, but the reader can figure out the meaning.

✛ Presentation   Each paragraph is indented.

126 Informative/Explanatory Writing

CCSS Common Core State Standards

Compare-and-Contrast Essay

Strategies for Writers was designed to incorporate the Common Core State Standards throughout every unit. By presenting the standards in multiple applications, your students' exposure to them will be ensured.

The lessons for compare-and-contrast essay reflect the writing standards for Informative/Explanatory Writing. Ideas and Organization align with standards **W.4.2** and **W.4.2a,** which address choosing and organizing the topics. The concept of beginning with a strong lead and organizing topics around similarities and differences translates to the focus of the essay. Standard **W.4.2b** addresses developing the topic with facts and details, the focus of Ideas and Voice.

3	2	1	
The topics for comparison are clear, but examples are unbalanced and/or vague.	The topics are not stated clearly. Examples are misleading or missing.	The topics are not clear. Examples seem to be unrelated.	**Ideas**
Similarities and differences are not well organized. The lead is very weak.	Similarities and differences are not clear or organized. The lead is weak or absent.	The essay is not organized. The writing is very difficult to understand.	**Organization**
The writer's voice sounds inconsistent, insecure, or vague. The reader feels confused.	The writer's voice is weak and may not be appropriate.	The writer's voice is very weak or absent. The reader cannot tell what the writer knows.	**Voice**
Some domain-specific vocabulary is used incorrectly. Explanations are poor or incomplete.	Domain-specific vocabulary is used incorrectly. Explanations are missing.	Domain-specific vocabulary is not used.	**Word Choice**
Sentences share the same length and type. Transitions are not used.	Several sentences are incomplete. Transitions are confusing or incorrect.	Sentences are incomplete or incorrect. The essay is difficult to read.	**Sentence Fluency**
Noticeable errors with homophones confuse the reader.	Many errors with homophones make it hard to read and understand the text.	The writing contains many errors. It is very difficult to read.	**Conventions**

See Appendix B for 4-, 5-, and 6-point informative/explanatory rubrics.

The rubrics and writing strategies for Sentence Fluency and Word Choice also reflect the Informative/Explanatory standards. Writing standard **W.4.2c** emphasizes creating sentence variety by using linking words, the theme of the Sentence Fluency rubric. Writing Standard **W.4.2d** focuses on using precise language and domain-specific vocabulary.

The language standards are addressed during editing and skills practice. There are also multiple opportunities to address the speaking and listening standards. Most importantly, this chapter will help students produce clear and coherent writing (**W.4.4**), improve writing (**W.4.5**), and use technologies to publish and present finished pieces (**W.4.6**).

Find Evidence in the Model

Small-Group Collaboration Assign students to small groups and tell them to evaluate the model using the rubric. Assign one person in each group to record the group's findings and one person to report the findings to the class. Instruct students to score the model for each trait based on evidence in the text. Remind students to read closely to identify examples to support their high or low scores. Note: Although the models were written to score high in each trait, students should not assume each trait would receive a 6, the top score.

Teacher-Led Discussion Bring the class back together, and have the reporters present their findings and scores. Prompt groups to provide evidence and examples for their scores from the model as needed.

Additional Rubrics

Appendix B includes 4-, 5-, and 6-point rubrics that can be used with any piece of informative/ explanatory writing. The rubrics are also available as blackline masters in the back of this Teacher Edition.

CCSS **C**ommon **C**ore **S**tate **S**tandards (pp. Z20–Z30)
Writing: W.4.6
Language: L.4.3c
Speaking and Listening: SL.4.1a, SL.4.1b, SL.4.1c, SL.4.1d, SL.4.2, SL.4.3, SL.4.6

Analyze
Close Reading for the Traits

Week 1 • Day 4

Student Objectives

- Read a model compare-and-contrast essay. *(p. 125)*
- Use the compare-and-contrast essay rubric. *(pp. 126–127)*
- Use the model compare-and-contrast essay to study **Ideas, Organization,** and **Voice.** *(pp. 128–129)*

Find Evidence in the Model

Evaluate the Model Have volunteers read aloud each section on pages 128-129. Determine whether students agree with each point in Alika's assessment. Use the questions below to initiate the discussion. Be sure students can back up their answers with specific examples from the essay.

Discuss Audience, Task, Purpose Ask students one or more of the following questions as they analyze the model:

- **Audience** Who is the audience? (Possible response: readers of a science magazine)

- **Task** How does Taisha Moore share the information about her topic? (Possible response: She includes facts and details to explain how the sun and moon are similar and different.)

- **Purpose** What is Taisha's purpose for writing this report? (Possible response: to compare and contrast the sun and the moon)

Using the Rubric to Analyze the Model

Compare-and-Contrast Essay

Did you notice that the model on page 125 points out some key elements of a compare-and-contrast essay? As she wrote "As Different as Day and Night," Taisha Moore used these elements to help her compare and contrast the moon and the sun. She also used the 6-point rubric on pages 126–127 to plan, draft, revise, and edit the writing. A rubric is a great tool to evaluate writing during the writing process.

Now let's use the same rubric to score the model. To do this, we'll focus on each trait separately, starting with Ideas. We'll use the top descriptor for each trait (column 6), along with examples from the model, to help us understand how the traits work together. How would you score Taisha on each trait?

Ideas
- Two topics for comparison are clear.
- Good examples clearly compare and contrast the topics.

Taisha makes the topics clear in the first two sentences of her essay. She compares and contrasts the sun and the moon. She uses good, clear examples in each paragraph. In the following paragraph, Taisha talks about differences in distance.

The moon and the sun also differ in how far away they are from Earth. About one quarter of a million miles away, the moon is Earth's closest neighbor in space. That is one reason we see it so easily. On the other hand, the sun is 93 million miles away. Only its brightness makes it easy to see.

128 Informative/Explanatory Writing

English Language Learners

BEGINNING

Same and Different Show a photo of a car and a truck and ask, *Does a car have wheels?* When students answer *yes,* model the sentence *A car has wheels.* Point to the truck and ask, *Does a truck have wheels?* Model the sentence *A truck has wheels.* Point to the wheels in both pictures and model the sentence *This is the same.* Repeat for *different* using a different attribute.

INTERMEDIATE

Compare and Contrast Show a photo of a car and a truck and say, *Let's compare. What is the same?* Students might notice that both are vehicles, have four wheels, have headlights, and so on. Model answers in complete sentences and have students repeat. List answers on the board. Say, *When we compare, we tell how things are the same.* Repeat the activity for *contrast.*

Organization
- The essay is organized by similarities and differences.
- A strong lead gets the reader's attention.

The similarities and differences are well organized. Each paragraph compares and contrasts different features of the sun and moon. Taisha's lead—the first sentence—asks an interesting question. It got my attention right away.

Which two objects in the sky are as different as day and night?

Voice
- The writer's voice sounds knowledgeable.
- It is clear that the writer wants to inform the reader.

Taisha's voice sounds knowledgeable about her topic. She gives facts about the similarities and differences of the sun and the moon. It is clear that her purpose is to inform the reader. In this paragraph, Taisha gives information about the light of the sun and the moon.

The sun and the moon are both bright objects, but the sun is a star. Earth and the other planets in the solar system revolve around the sun. All life on Earth depends on the sun. Plants need the sun to grow, and animals and people need the sun's heat and light. Unlike the sun, the moon is a satellite. It revolves around Earth. Life on Earth does not depend on the moon, but the moon affects many things on Earth, including the tides.

Compare-and-Contrast Essay **129**

Discuss the Traits Ask students one or more of the following questions to discuss the traits in the model:

Ideas Does Taisha Moore present her topic clearly and provide relevant examples in her essay? (Possible responses: Yes, Taisha makes her topics for comparison clear in the first two sentences: the sun and the moon. She supports her main ideas with information and examples in each paragraph.)

Organization How does Taisha organize her essay? (Possible responses: Taisha organizes her paragraphs by similarities and differences. Each paragraph compares or contrasts different features of the sun and moon.)

Voice Does Taisha use a voice that is appropriate for the purpose and audience? (Possible response: Yes, Taisha uses a knowledgeable voice to get her message across.)

ADVANCED
Similarities and Differences Show two similar (but slightly different) photos or use a spot-the-differences activity from a children's magazine. Have partners make a list of the similarities and differences between the pictures. Have students say sentences that compare or contrast the pictures. For example, *It is raining in the first photo. In the second photo it is sunny.*

ADVANCED HIGH
Transition Words Teach students several transition words or phrases that can be used to show compare and contrast; for example, *different, but, however, in contrast, same, similar, similarly, and, too,* and so on. Then repeat the Advanced ELL activity above. Ask students to use a transition word or phrase to connect the two sentences, as in *It is raining in the first photo, but in the second photo it is sunny.*

CCSS **Common Core State Standards** (pp. Z20–Z30)
Language: L.4.3c, L.4.6
Speaking and Listening: SL.4.1a, SL.4.1b, SL.4.1c, SL.4.1d, SL.4.3, SL.4.6

Analyze
Close Reading for the Traits

Week 1 • Day 5

Student Objectives

- Read a model compare-and-contrast essay. *(p. 125)*
- Use the compare-and-contrast essay rubric. *(pp. 126–127)*
- Use the model compare-and-contrast essay to study **Word Choice, Sentence Fluency,** and **Conventions.** *(pp. 130–131)*

Discuss the Traits Ask students one or more of the following questions to discuss the traits in the model:

Word Choice Does Taisha clearly use and explain all content-related words so that readers can understand her essay? (Possible response: Taisha uses domain-specific vocabulary to explain the similarities and differences of the sun and the moon.) Which terms did she explain? (Possible response: She clearly defines and explains the phases of the moon.)

Sentence Fluency Which part of the model flows especially smoothly? (Possible response: The second paragraph flows very smoothly.) What makes the sentences flow? (Possible response: Taisha does a good job of varying sentence lengths and using transitions.)

Conventions Does Taisha use homophones correctly? (Yes, Taisha uses homophones correctly to make her meaning clear to the reader.)

Strategies for Writers Online
Go to **www.sfw.z-b.com** for additional online resources for students, teachers, and parents.

Using the Rubric to Analyze the Model
Compare-and-Contrast Essay

 **Word Choice**
- **Domain-specific vocabulary is used correctly.**
- **It is clearly defined or explained.**

Taisha uses content-related words to explain the similarities and differences of the sun and the moon. In this paragraph, Taisha clearly defines and explains the phases of the moon.

> The moon has a 29-day cycle. Phases of the moon make its circular shape look different at different times of the month. It sometimes looks like a thin crescent, half of a moon, or a full moon. We see only the part of the moon that is lit by sunlight. The sun doesn't have a cycle.

 **Sentence Fluency**
- **Sentences vary in length and type.**
- **Effective transitions create a smooth flow.**

The writer uses a variety of sentences in her essay. Some are short, simple sentences. Some are longer and complex. Taisha also uses transitions effectively. *Both, on the other hand, unlike,* and *but* create a good flow in the essay.

> The center of the sun can get as hot as 27 million degrees Fahrenheit. The moon, on the other hand, has no activity. It has no air, no clouds, and no water.

130 Informative/Explanatory Writing

Tech Tips
Search Engines

Use Keywords Finding information online begins with smart use of keywords, something students need to revisit each time they use a search engine. Take time to discuss what makes a keyword search effective. How specific or broad do your keywords need to be? Students benefit from reminders, but also from a critical discussion of the choices they make. Collaborate with students to design a chart or reference poster of effective keyword strategies to display as a resource.

Conventions
- All homophones are correct.
- The meaning is clear.

Taisha uses homophones correctly. In this example, she does not confuse *its* (belonging to it) with *it's* (the contraction for *it is*). By using words correctly, Taisha makes her meaning clear to the reader.

On the other hand, the sun is 93 million miles away. Only its brightness makes it easy to see.

✚Presentation   Each paragraph is indented.

My Turn!
Now I'm going to write my own compare-and-contrast essay! Follow along to see how I use good writing strategies. I will use the model and the rubric to help me, too.

Differentiating Instruction

ENRICHMENT
Use the Rubric Have partners score the model essay using the top descriptors (column 6) for each trait on page 126. Then have them share and defend their scores for each trait.

REINFORCEMENT
Understand the Traits Make a transparency of the rubric on page 126. Highlight the Ideas trait in column 6. Then say: *The first part of the Ideas trait in this column says the compare-and-contrast essay should have two clear topics.* Point out Taisha's topics in the first paragraph: the sun and the moon. Then say: *The second part says that good examples clearly compare and contrast the topics.* Help students identify the examples in each paragraph. Continue to model the other traits.

✚Presentation   Discuss why Presentation is equally as important as the other traits. Stress the importance of neatness. An essay should be clearly handwritten in pen or typed, and paragraphs should be indented (using the tab key if typed). Discuss how white space can be used to organize text, especially to clearly separate paragraphs. Good margins make the line lengths comfortable to read, and a centered title stands out on a page. Encourage students to think about how good formatting aids the reader.

Think About the Traits

Once students have thoroughly discussed the model, ask them which traits they think are most important in a compare-and-contrast essay and have them explain why. (**Possible responses: Organization is very important because if the essay is not organized by similarities and differences, then it makes no sense. Voice is more important because it establishes a knowledgeable tone and makes it clear that the writer's purpose is to inform the reader.**)

CCSS **Common Core State Standards** (pp. Z20–Z30)
Writing: W.4.6
Language: L.4.3c
Speaking and Listening: SL.4.1a, SL.4.1b, SL.4.1c, SL.4.1d, SL.4.3, SL.4.6

Write
Compare-and-Contrast Essay

Week 2 • Day 1

Student Objectives

• Read and understand a prewriting strategy. (p. 132)

Prewrite

Focus on Ideas

Gather Information From Print and Digital Sources Read page 132 aloud. Draw students' attention to Alika's notes and to the facts and statistics. Discuss that students will need to do research to collect information about their topics. Students should use at least two sources to find new information. Ask students where someone could gather details like these if the person didn't know them already. **(Possible responses: talk with an expert, look in a book, or research the topic online)**

Take Notes on Source Information Point out Alika's notes on page 132. Explain that note cards are an effective way to keep track of information. They can be sorted as needed to organize the information. Tell students that they will be asked to include a list of their sources at the end of their essays.

Online Writing Center

Provides **interactive graphic organizers** as well as a variety of graphic organizers in PDF format.

Prewrite   Focus on Ideas

The Rubric Says	Two topics for comparison are clear. Good examples clearly compare and contrast the topics.
Writing Strategy	Choose two things to compare and contrast. Make notes about both things.

When my teacher asked us to write a compare-and-contrast essay, I decided to compare sharks and whales. Sharks are really interesting fish, and whales are the biggest creatures in the ocean. I've already read a lot about both of them. My teacher said to use at least two sources to find out new information and verify what I know about sharks and whales. I listed everything I learned during my research.

What I Know About Sharks and Whales

Sharks	Whales
• are fish	• make sounds—humpbacks "sing"
• breathe through gills	• are mammals
• 6 inches to about 40 feet long	• have great eyesight, great hearing
• do not make sounds	• have lungs and blowholes
• very good hearing and vision	• can be 10 feet to 100 feet long
• excellent sense of smell	• hardly any sense of smell
	• huge!

Write

Brainstorm a list of topics that you would like to compare and contrast. Select the pair that you think will be the most interesting. Jot down some notes.

132 Informative/Explanatory Writing

English Language Learners

BEGINNING/INTERMEDIATE

Attributes Hold up a classroom object, such as an eraser, and say, *Tell me about this eraser.* Write students' answers on the board, such as *rubber, pink,* and *soft.* Say, *These are attributes of the eraser.* Have students repeat the sentence. Hold up another classroom object and ask, *What are the attributes of this (paper clip)?* Repeat for several objects.

ADVANCED/ADVANCED HIGH

Attribute Chart You may use the information from the Attribute Chart on student page 133 for this activity or you may choose to use a chart that you create. Write the chart on the board. Include the Subject (Shark/Whale) and all of the information in the Attribute column. On index cards, write the attributes that are specific to each subject—*fish, underwater with gills,* and so on. Have partners organize the index cards on the correct spot on the chart.

Prewrite

Focus on **Organization**

The Rubric Says The essay is organized by similarities and differences.

Writing Strategy Make an Attribute Chart to show similarities and differences.

The rubric reminds me that I need to organize my ideas. For example, sharks breathe underwater, but whales have to come up for air. How sharks and whales breathe is an attribute. I took the ideas on my list and made an Attribute Chart.

Writer's Term ___

Attribute Chart
An **attribute** (at•ruh•byoot) is a quality of something. An **Attribute Chart** organizes information about how two things are alike or different.

Attribute Chart

Shark	Attribute	Whale
fish	kind of animal	mammal
underwater with gills	how it breathes	above water with lungs and blowhole
6 inches to 40 feet	its length	10 to 100 feet
none	sounds it makes	many sounds
great vision and hearing	hearing and vision	great vision and hearing
excellent	sense of smell	poor

Analyze
Look at Alika's notes and the Attribute Chart. How will the attributes in the chart help him write a good compare-and-contrast essay?

Write
Look at your notes on the topics that you chose to compare and contrast. What attributes do the two topics have in common? How are they different? Use your notes to make an Attribute Chart.

Compare-and-Contrast Essay **133**

Collaborative Conferencing

PEER TO PEER Have pairs of students exchange organizers. Tell them to ask themselves these questions as they review them: *Is there information the writer could add to help me better understand the topics? Are the attributes clear?* Tell partners to write one or two comments on a sticky note and return the Attribute Chart to the writer.

PEER GROUPS Organize students into small groups. Instruct them to discuss the importance of organizing their notes into a focused Attribute Chart. Have students read their Attribute Charts aloud. Encourage other students to take turns offering one suggestion.

TEACHER-LED Conference with individual students about their Attribute Charts. Before they speak with you, encourage students to think of questions to ask about points they found difficult in creating the chart.

Write
Compare-and-Contrast Essay

Week 2 • Day 2

Student Objectives

- Make an Attribute Chart to organize ideas. *(p. 133)*

Prewrite

Focus on **Organization**

Categorize Information Read the definition of an Attribute Chart in the Writer's Term box on page 133. (Go to **www.sfw.z-b. com** for the downloadable graphic organizers.) Point out that Alika used an Attribute Chart to organize his notes. Ask students to study the organizer and identify the attributes. Then ask how an Attribute Chart can be an effective tool when writing a compare-and-contrast essay. (Possible response: A writer can easily compare and contrast information about two topics.)

Writer's Term ___

Attribute Chart An attribute is a characteristic, feature, or quality of something. For example, *color* is an attribute of hair and eyes. An Attribute Chart takes information about two things and organizes it visually to show how two things are alike or different.

CCSS **C**ommon **C**ore **S**tate **S**tandards (pp. Z20–Z30)
Writing: W.4.2a, W.4.2b, W.4.4, W.4.5, W.4.6, W.4.7, W.4.8, W.4.10
Language: L.4.3c, L.4.6
Speaking and Listening: SL.4.1a, SL.4.1b, SL.4.1c, SL.4.1d, SL.4.3

Compare-and-Contrast Essay **T133**

Write
Compare-and Contrast Essay

Week 2 • Day 3

Student Objectives

• Use an Attribute Chart to begin writing. (*p. 134*)

Draft

Focus on Ideas

Begin a Draft Read page 134 aloud. Remind students that drafting gives them a chance to get ideas on paper without having to worry about making mistakes. Be sure that students understand that they will use their Attribute Charts to guide them through the drafting process.

Draw Evidence From Text Ask students to read Alika's draft on page 135. Discuss whether Alika included the information from his Attribute Chart to compare and contrast his topics. Point out that Alika repeatedly refers to the rubric on page 126 as he writes. Remind students to use the rubric to guide their own writing. Assure them that they will go through each step of the writing process to create their final copy. Review the proofreading marks with students. Tell them that these marks will be helpful as they revise and edit their drafts.

Write a Compare-and-Contrast Essay

Draft

Focus on **Ideas**

The Rubric Says	Two topics for comparison are clear.
Writing Strategy	Name both topics and treat them the same.

Now I'm ready to write. I'll use my Attribute Chart to write a draft. I need to remember that a compare-and-contrast essay shows both differences and similarities.

The rubric reminds me that both topics need to be clearly stated. I should treat both topics equally, too. That means neither topic should get more attention or have more examples than the other. For example, if I talk about how whales and sharks are different, I should be sure to say as much about whales as I do about sharks.

As I'm writing, I'll do the best I can with grammar and spelling, but I won't worry about mistakes. I'll fix them later. Here is part of my draft.

134 Informative/Explanatory Writing

Differentiating Instruction

ENRICHMENT

Evaluate Sources Remind students that they need to research their topics. Have students evaluate different types of sources and create a chart explaining the sources' strengths and weaknesses. Students might list *personal interview* as a source and then explain when an interview would be effective. Have them include at least four types of sources on their charts. Place these charts in the classroom research center.

REINFORCEMENT

Recognize Reliable Sources Work with a small group to discuss the research needed for compare-and-contrast essays. Gather a variety of materials (books, magazines, textbooks) and discuss their effectiveness. Invite students to add different types of sources they have used to the list. Together, make a list of reliable Internet sites.

[DRAFT]

Whales and Sharks

I am going to compare and contrast sharks and whales.

A tiny shark is only six inches long! Its called a dwarf shark.

The smallest whale is about ten feet long.

two topics

comparison

Whales and sharks are alike in many ways. They are usually both very large. Whales are larger than sharks. Whales and sharks both have excellent hearing and vision. However, sharks have a terrific sense of smell. Whales have almost no sense of smell at all.

contrast

Whales and sharks have other differences, to. A big difference is that sharks are fish. They breathe underwater through gills. Whales are mammals, so they have lungs. They have to rise to the surface of the water to breathe through blowholes.

Analyze

Read Alika's draft. Does he give equal attention to both topics?

Write

Use your Attribute Chart to write a draft of your compare-and-contrast essay. Remember to state both topics clearly. Also, be sure to treat both topics equally.

Compare-and-Contrast Essay 135

Write
Compare-and-Contrast Essay

Week 2 • Day 4

Student Objectives

• Complete a draft. *(p. 135)*

Continue Drafting It is important that students are given ample time to draft their essays. As conferencing is important throughout the writing process, be sure to plan time for peer-to-peer, peer group, or teacher-led conferences. Remind students that this is the time to get their ideas down on paper in a creative and engaging way. Assure them that they will have plenty of time to fix any mistakes later.

Use Your Own Words Tell students to always use their own words when drafting. Explain that using another writer's words *as your own* is called plagiarism, and it is not acceptable. To help students avoid plagiarism, encourage them to write down the main ideas from sources instead of taking notes word for word.

Collaborative Conferencing

PEER TO PEER Have pairs of students exchange drafts. Ask students to read the drafts to determine if the writer gave equal attention to each topic. Have them write their comments or questions on sticky notes and affix them on their partner's draft.

PEER GROUPS Have students work in groups of four. Have students pass their draft to the student on the right. Each student writes one comment on a sticky note and passes the draft along to the right. The review ends when everyone has received his or her own draft with three comments.

TEACHER-LED Schedule conferences with pairs of students to exchange drafts. Have them read the drafts for specific traits. Coach them in giving and receiving constructive feedback.

CCSS Common Core State Standards (pp. Z20–Z30)
Writing: W.4.2a, W.4.2b, W.4.4, W.4.5, W.4.6, W.4.7, W.4.8, W.4.10
Language: L.4.3c
Speaking and Listening: SL.4.1a, SL.4.1b, SL.4.1c, SL.4.1d, SL.4.3, SL.4.6

Write
Compare-and-Contrast Essay

Week 2 • Day 5

Student Objectives

• Revise for a strong lead. *(p. 136)*

Revise

Focus on  Organization

Add a Strong Lead Discuss the importance of making sure that the essay introduces the topic with a strong lead that gets the audience's attention right away. Have one volunteer read the draft excerpt without the revisions and another volunteer read the revised excerpt. Then ask:

• Which type of lead did he choose? **(question lead)**

• In what way is Alika's lead a combination of both types of leads? **(It asks a question and, at the same time, gives surprising details about the topics.)**

Finally, point out that Alika's new lead invites readers to learn about the similarities and differences between sharks and whales.

✏️ Writer's Term _____

Lead The lead should convey the writer's purpose by introducing the topic(s) in a catchy way. Writers often write several leads before choosing the best one.

 Strategies for Writers Online
Go to **www.sfw.z-b.com** for additional online resources for students, teachers, and parents.

Write a Compare-and-Contrast Essay

Revise   Focus on **Organization**

The Rubric Says   A strong lead gets the reader's attention.

Writing Strategy   Begin with a compare-and-contrast lead that gets the reader's attention.

After I wrote my first draft, I checked it against the rubric. The rubric tells me that I need to think about my audience. I want to get the reader interested in my topics right away. That means I have to start with a great compare-and-contrast sentence, or lead!

> **Writer's Term _____**
> **Lead**
> A **lead** is the first sentence of a piece of writing. A good lead grabs the reader's attention and makes him or her want to read more. A lead can be a question or a surprising statement.
>
> **Question Lead:** Do you know which of the five senses is the shark's best and the whale's worst?
>
> **Surprise Lead:** Not everyone knows that a shark can be six inches long or that a whale can sing!

[DRAFT]

Have you ever heard of a six-inch shark or a ten-foot whale? ∧ I am going to compare and contrast sharks and whales. A tiny shark is only six inches long! Its called a dwarf shark. The smallest whale is about ten feet long.

 added catchy lead

> **Write**
> Read your draft. Your lead should grab the reader's attention. Use a question or surprising statement as your lead.

English Language Learners

BEGINNING/INTERMEDIATE
Homophones Use photos or demonstrations to convey the meanings of several homophone pairs; for example, *ring/ wring; right/write; hair/hare; meet/meat*. Write the words on the board. Point to the words in each pair and have students repeat them. Ask, *Do they sound the same?* Tell students that the words are *homophones*. Have students repeat the word. Check students' understanding by presenting several more homophone and non-homophone pairs.

ADVANCED/ADVANCED HIGH
Homophones Write the following sentence on the board: *The principle rote the review on the bored.* Tell students that the underlined words are part of a homophone pair and are possibly used incorrectly in the sentence. Demonstrate using a dictionary to check homophone spellings. Check the definition of each homophone and select the spelling for the word with the appropriate definition.

Revise

Focus on **Voice**

The Rubric Says The writer's voice sounds knowledgeable. It is clear that the writer wants to inform the reader.

Writing Strategy Share my knowledge and enthusiasm about the topics.

The rubric reminds me to sound knowledgeable about the topics and to inform the reader. I should think about the purpose of my essay as I revise. I should also think about my audience. I want to inform and engage the reader. I want to sound like an expert on the topics so that the reader will believe the information. If I share my enthusiasm for the topics, then the reader will be interested, too. I'll add some details to share more of my knowledge, and I'll look for places to express my excitement about the topics.

[DRAFT]

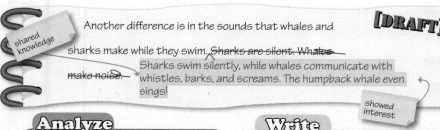

shared knowledge

Another difference is in the sounds that whales and sharks make while they swim. ~~Sharks are silent. Whales make noise.~~ Sharks swim silently, while whales communicate with whistles, barks, and screams. The humpback whale even sings!

showed interest

Analyze

Look at Alika's revisions. How does he show his knowledge and interest in the topics?

Write

Read your draft again. Add details and other interesting information to show your knowledge and enthusiasm about the topics.

Compare-and-Contrast Essay **137**

Collaborative Conferencing

PEER TO PEER Have pairs of students exchange drafts. As they read, have partners focus on answering this question: *Does the writer sound knowledgeable and enthusiastic throughout the draft?* After reading, have students jot down their comments and point out any parts in the drafts that need improvement.

PEER GROUPS Have students form small groups. Tell students to take turns reading sections of their own drafts aloud. Have group members suggest areas that need to sound more knowledgeable or enthusiastic.

TEACHER-LED Conference with individual students. Point out places in their drafts where details could be added to improve the writer's voice.

Week 3 • Day 1

Student Objectives

• Revise for a knowledgeable and enthusiastic voice. (*p. 137*)

Revise

Focus on Voice

Keep Audience in Mind Have students read page 137. Explain the importance of connecting with the audience. Have one volunteer read the draft excerpt without the revisions and another volunteer read the revised excerpt. Then discuss the revision. Ask:

• How did Alika improve his connection with the audience? **(The added details make him sound more knowledgeable and enthusiastic.)**

Remind students that the purpose for writing an essay is to share what they have learned about their topics. The best way for them to connect with their audience is to use an informative, engaging voice.

CCSS **C**ommon **C**ore **S**tate **S**tandards (pp. Z20–Z30)
Writing: W.4.2a, W.4.2b, W.4.4, W.4.5, W.4.10
Language: L.4.1g, L.4.2d, L.4.3c, L.4.4a, L.4.6
Speaking and Listening: SL.4.1a, SL.4.1b, SL.4.1c, SL.4.1d, SL.4.3, SL.4.6

Write
Compare-and-Contrast Essay

Week 3 • Day 2

Student Objectives

• Revise for correct use of domain-specific vocabulary. *(p. 138)*

Revise

Focus on  Word Choice

Define/Explain Domain-Specific Vocabulary Read page 138 aloud. Remind students that the rubric says that domain-specific vocabulary should be used correctly and be explained or defined. Stress to students that in a compare-and-contrast essay it is important to use precise language to explain words that the reader might not know. Otherwise the reader may get lost or lose interest. Remind students that words related to their topics (domain-specific vocabulary) should be used in their essays, but these words should be carefully explained for the reader. Encourage students to review their compare-and-contrast essays and define or explain any vocabulary that needs further clarification.

Revise   Focus on Word Choice

The Rubric Says   Domain-specific vocabulary is used correctly. It is clearly defined or explained.

Writing Strategy   Explain words that readers might not know.

I read my draft again. There are precise words that I have to use to explain the similarities and differences between sharks and whales. The rubric reminds me that domain-specific vocabulary, or words about my topics, need to be used correctly. I won't assume that my readers know what the words mean. I will provide an explanation or definition for the ones I use in my essay.

[DRAFT]

Whales and sharks have other differences, to. A big difference is that sharks are fish. They breathe underwater through gills. Whales are mammals, so they have lungs. They have to rise to the surface of the water to breathe through blowholes.

defined vocabulary word

They breathe through one or two nostrils at the top of their head called blowholes.

Write

Use precise words about each topic in your essay. Be sure to define or explain what they mean.

138   Informative/Explanatory Writing

Optional Revising Lessons

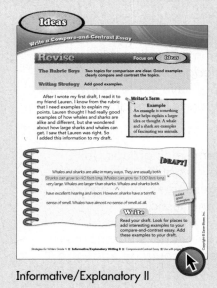

Informative/Explanatory 11

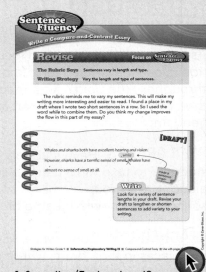

Informative/Explanatory 12

The Rubric Says   All homophones are correct. The meaning is clear.

Writing Strategy   Make sure that homophones are used correctly.

Now I need to check for errors. I always check spelling, punctuation, and capitalization. I'll also make sure that I've used every homophone correctly. Here's the end of my draft.

Writer's Term ✏️

Homophones

Homophones are words that sound the same but have different spellings and meanings.

[DRAFT]

Both whales and sharks are fascinating ~~animals~~ animals. ~~Its~~ It's not surprising that ~~their~~ they're the subjects of poems, stories, and compare-and-contrast essays!

corrected homophones

Analyze

Look at Alika's edits. Are all spelling, punctuation, and capitalization problems fixed? Are homophones used correctly?

Write   **Conventions**

Edit your draft for spelling, punctuation, and capitalization. Make sure that you have used every homophone correctly.

For more practice identifying and using homophones correctly, use the exercises on the next two pages.

Compare-and-Contrast Essay **139**

Related Grammar Practice

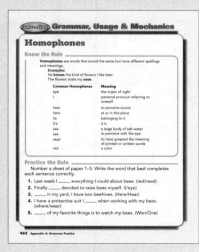

Student Edition page 462

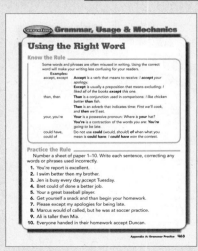

Student Edition page 463

Go to ➡️ **Appendix A: Grammar Practice**

Write
Compare-and-Contrast Essay

Student Objectives

- Edit for correct use of homophones. *(p. 139)*

Edit

Focus on **Conventions**

Check Homophones Have students read Alika's words on page 139. Ask students to notice the corrected homophones in his draft. Have students read their drafts, paying attention to homophones. Remind students that computers have a spell-check option; however, it will not catch commonly misused words like homophones. Use the mini-lessons on pages T140 and T141 for students having trouble with using homophones correctly. Have students complete the exercises on pages 140 and 141.

✏️ **Writer's Term**

Homophones It is especially important to check the spelling of homophones used in writing since the computer's spell checker cannot tell which homophone the writer meant to use.

CCSS **Common Core State Standards** (pp. Z20–Z30)
Writing: W.4.2b, W.4.2d, W.4.4, W.4.5, W.4.6, W.4.10
Language: L.4.1g, L.4.2a, L.4.2d, L.4.3a, L.4.4a, L.4.4c, L.4.6

Compare-and-Contrast Essay **TI39**

Conventions

Mini-Lesson

Student Objectives

- Use homophones correctly.
  (p. 140)

Homophones

Have students review the Know the Rule box on page 140. Then read aloud the following sentence: *Their books are over there.* Ask students to identify the homophones they heard in the sentence. **(their, there)** Then ask students if you used the homophones correctly. **(There is no way to know because you read the sentence aloud.)** While homophone mistakes are not evident in speech, they are very evident in writing. Using homophones incorrectly in writing can be very confusing for the reader.

Have partners practice writing sentences containing pairs of homophones. To model this idea, write an example sentence on the board: *It's too early for the birds to leave the nest.*

You may wish to write a checklist of easily confused homophone pairs on the board as a reference for students. Once students have completed their sentences, have them write the sentences on the board. Discuss any errors.

Online Writing Center

Provides **interactive grammar games** and **practice activities** in student eBook.

Conventions Grammar, Usage & Mechanics

Homophones

Know the Rule

> **Homophones** are words that sound alike but have different spellings and meanings.
>
> **Your** is a possessive pronoun that means "belonging to you."
> **You're** is a contraction made from the words "you are."
>
> **Their** is a possessive pronoun that means "belonging to them."
> **There** is an adverb that means "in that place."
> **They're** is a contraction made from the words "they are."
>
> **Its** is a possessive pronoun that means "belonging to it."
> **It's** is a contraction made from the words "it is" or "it has."
>
> **Two** is a number. **Too** means "also" or "more than enough."
> **To** often means "towards."

Practice the Rule

Number a piece of paper 1–10. Write the word in parentheses that completes each sentence correctly.

1. My class went (two/too/**to**) a natural history museum.
2. We went to a whale exhibit (their/**there**/they're).
3. We learned that a whale isn't a fish; (its/**it's**) a mammal.
4. A whale has a blowhole on the top of (**its**/it's) head.
5. Whales use (**their**/there/they're) blowholes to breathe air.
6. A whale's flipper is a little like (**your**/you're) hand.
7. We found that there are (**two**/too/to) kinds of whales.
8. The whale that (your/**you're**) looking at is a baleen whale.
9. Large amounts of seawater go into (**their**/there/they're) mouths.
10. The baleen hangs (their/**there**/they're) like a loose fringe curtain.

Related Grammar Practice

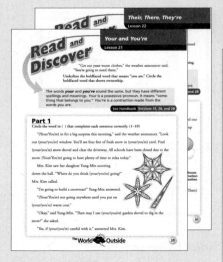

Pages 59, 61, 63, 73, 75

Go to **G.U.M. Student Practice Book**

More Homophones

Know the Rule

> **Homophones** are frequently confused because they sound alike. Remember, though, that they are spelled differently. When you use homophones in your writing, be sure to check the spelling. The spell checker on a computer cannot tell which homophone you meant to use.

Practice the Rule

Number a piece of paper 1–10. Read each sentence. If the sentence uses the wrong homophone, write the correct one. If the sentence uses the correct homophone, write **Correct**.

1. Whales swim differently than fish due. do
2. Fish move there tails from side to side. their
3. Whales move their tails up and down. Correct
4. A whale's tale must be very strong. tail
5. They're largest muscles are in their tails. Their
6. They are able too travel great distances. to
7. They are known for there long-distance migrations. their
8. Whales travel from cool waters two warm waters. to
9. The gray whale travels up to 14,000 miles round trip. Correct
10. Its one of the longest migrations of any mammal. It's

Compare-and-Contrast Essay **141**

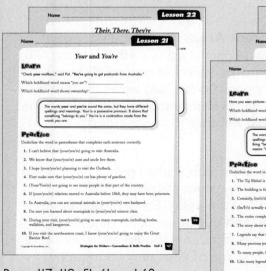
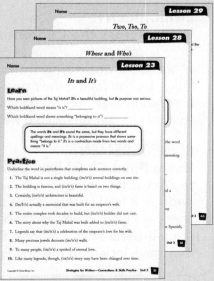

Pages 47, 49, 51, 61, and 63

Go to ➡ Grammar Practice Masters

Conventions

Mini-Lesson

Student Objectives

- Use homophones correctly. (p. 141)

More Homophones

Have students review the Know the Rule box on page 141. Then write the following sentences on the board:

- *Alex, when is your paper <u>do</u>?*
- *I have <u>two</u> finish it by Monday.*
- *<u>Due</u> you have all your research completed?*
- *No, <u>they're</u> is still work to do.*
- *What topic did you choose <u>too</u> research?*
- *I picked an interesting topic on how an animal uses its <u>tale</u>.*

Ask volunteers to identify the homophone that is used incorrectly in each sentence. Take responses and write the corrections on the board. (**due, to, Do, there, to, tail**) Again remind students that it is important to use homophones correctly in writing because mistakes can be very confusing for the reader.

CCSS **C**ommon **C**ore **S**tate **S**tandards (pp. Z20–Z30)
Writing: W.4.6
Language: L.4.1g, L.4.2d, L.4.4a, L.4.6

Compare-and-Contrast Essay **T141**

Write
Compare-and-Contrast Essay

Week 3 • Day 4

Student Objectives

- Discuss preparation for publishing and presentation. *(p. 142)*
- Use a final editing checklist to publish their work. *(p. 142)*

Publish +Presentation

Publishing Strategy Ask students if they like Alika's choice for sharing his essay on the classroom bulletin board. Write additional publishing options on the board, such as school website or class book. Then ask students to consider the options. Which would they prefer? Why? Jot down responses. Tell students that they are using compare-and-contrast skills to make their decisions.

Have a volunteer read Alika's checklist. Remind students that it relates to the editing strategies they have been practicing. Have them use it to perform a final evaluation before publishing their work.

Tell students to include their source(s) at the bottom of their essay. Ask them to list the author, title, and publisher information, as Alika did, or provide students with the school's style for listing sources.

 Strategies for Writers Online
Go to **www.sfw.z-b.com** for additional online resources for students, teachers, and parents.

Publish   +Presentation

Publishing Strategy   Display my essay on the classroom bulletin board.

Presentation Strategy   Indent every paragraph.

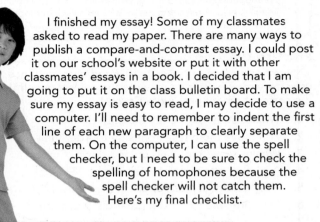

I finished my essay! Some of my classmates asked to read my paper. There are many ways to publish a compare-and-contrast essay. I could post it on our school's website or put it with other classmates' essays in a book. I decided that I am going to put it on the class bulletin board. To make sure my essay is easy to read, I may decide to use a computer. I'll need to remember to indent the first line of each new paragraph to clearly separate them. On the computer, I can use the spell checker, but I need to be sure to check the spelling of homophones because the spell checker will not catch them. Here's my final checklist.

My Final Checklist

Did I—

- ✔ use homophones correctly?
- ✔ use neat handwriting or word processing?
- ✔ indent every paragraph?
- ✔ check for spelling, grammar, and punctuation?
- ✔ provide a list of sources?

Write

Make a checklist to review your own compare-and-contrast essay. Be sure to check your essay carefully before publishing it. Then make a final copy to post on your classroom bulletin board.

Differentiating Instruction

ENRICHMENT

Write Across the Content Areas   Challenge students to write another compare-and-contrast essay on their topics. Alika wrote about whales and sharks. He could expand his knowledge by comparing their depictions in two works of art or by comparing their hunting habits or migration routes. Encourage students to consult reliable websites for more ideas.

REINFORCEMENT

Use a Final Checklist   Meet with a small group of students to discuss the checklists. Have students work together to perform a final evaluation of the essay. Encourage them to check spelling, grammar, and punctuation. Remind them to double-check homophones. Students should also make sure they have indented the first line of each new paragraph.

Whales and Sharks
by Alika

Have you ever heard of a six-inch shark or a ten-foot whale? The smallest shark is only six inches long! It's called a dwarf shark. The smallest whale is about ten feet long.

Whales and sharks are alike in many ways. They are usually both very large. However, whales are larger than sharks. Sharks can grow to 40 feet long, but whales can grow to 100 feet long. Whales and sharks both have excellent hearing and vision. However, sharks have a terrific sense of smell, while whales have almost no sense of smell at all.

Whales and sharks have other differences, too. A big difference is that sharks are fish. They breathe underwater through gills. Whales are mammals, so they have lungs. They have to rise to the surface of the water to breathe. They breathe through one or two nostrils at the top of their head called blowholes.

Another difference is in the sounds that whales and sharks make while they swim. Sharks swim silently, while whales communicate with whistles, barks, and screams. The humpback whale even sings!

Both whales and sharks are fascinating animals. It's not surprising that they're the subjects of poems, stories, and compare-and-contrast essays!

Source: MacQuitty, Miranda. *Ocean.* New York: DK Children, 2008.

Analyze

Use the rubric to evaluate Alika's essay and your own essay.

Compare-and-Contrast Essay **143**

Tech Tips

Online Tools

Use Digital Info-Graphic Tools Writers often use visual tools to help them develop their writing. As students work on the compare-and-contrast essay, asking them to visually represent their argument aids in creating balance. It also helps them manage the information with which they are working. Consider the merits of using a digital info-graphic tool to organize ideas, like those available on the ReadWrite-Think website. Or build a similar mapping/sequencing tool using Google Forms or Docs. This exercise is as much about student writing as it is about using digital information.

See **www.sfw.z-b.com** for further information about and links to these websites and tools.

Write
Compare-and-Contrast Essay

Week 3 • Day 5

Student Objectives

- Use a compare-and-contrast essay rubric. *(pp. 126–127)*
- Share a published compare-and-contrast essay. *(p. 143)*

Presentation Strategy Remind students that anything posted to the classroom bulletin board must be neat and readable. They should indent the first line of each new paragraph. If students choose to use the computer, they should use the tab key to indent paragraphs.

Reflecting on a Compare-and-Contrast Essay

Have students refer to the rubric on pages 126–127 as they read Alika's final copy on page 143. Have all his revisions and edits strengthened the essay? What score should he receive for each writing trait? Finally, have students reflect on the assignment as a whole. Ask:

- What was your favorite part of this assignment?
- What will you do differently in your next essay?

CCSS **Common Core State Standards** (pp. Z20–Z30)

Writing: W.4.4, W.4.6, W.4.8, W.4.10
Language: L.4.2d, L.4.3c, L.4.4a
Speaking and Listening: SL.4.1a, SL.4.1b, SL.4.1c, SL.4.1d, SL.4.3, SL.4.6

Compare-and-Contrast Essay **T143**

Research Report Planner

WEEK 1

Introduce
Research Report

Student Objectives
- Review the elements of a research report.
- Consider purpose and audience.
- Learn the traits of informative/ explanatory writing.

Student Activities
- Read and discuss **What's in a Research Report?** (p. 144)
- Read and discuss **Why Write a Research Report?** (p. 145)
- Read **Linking Informative/Explanatory Writing Traits to a Research Report.** (p. 146)

Analyze
Close Reading of the Model

Student Objectives
- Read a model research report.

Student Activities
- Read **"Fixing the Leaning Tower of Pisa."** (p. 147)

Analyze
Introduce the Rubric

Student Objectives
- Learn to read a rubric.

Student Activities
- Review **"Fixing the Leaning Tower of Pisa."** (p. 147)
- Read and discuss the **Research Report Rubric.** (pp. 148–149)

WEEK 2

Write
Prewrite: Ideas

Student Objectives
- Read and understand a prewriting strategy.

Student Activities
- Read and discuss **Prewrite: Focus on Ideas.** (p. 154)
- Apply the prewriting strategy.

Write
Prewrite: Organization

Student Objectives
- Make a Web to organize notes.

Student Activities
- Read and discuss **Prewrite: Focus on Organization.** (p. 155)
- Apply the prewriting strategy to create a Web.

Write
Draft: Organization

Student Objectives
- Use a Web to begin writing.

Student Activities
- Read and discuss **Draft: Focus on Organization.** (p. 156)
- Apply the drafting strategy by using a Web to write a draft.

WEEK 3

Write
Revise: Word Choice

Student Objectives
- Revise to use appositives.

Student Activities
- Read and discuss **Revise: Focus on Word Choice.** (p. 159)
- Reflect on the model draft.
- Apply the revising strategy.
- Participate in a peer conference.

Write
Revise: Sentence Fluency

Student Objectives
- Revise to include both simple and compound sentences.

Student Activities
- Read and discuss **Revise: Focus on Sentence Fluency.** (p. 160)
- Reflect on the model draft.
- Apply the revising strategy.

Note: Optional Revising Lessons are located at **www.sfw.z-b.com.**

Write
Edit: Conventions

Student Objectives
- Edit for correct use of uppercase letters.

Student Activities
- Read and discuss **Edit: Focus on Conventions.** (p. 161)
- Reflect on the model draft.
- Apply the editing strategy.

Note: Teach the Conventions mini-lessons (pp. 162–163) if needed.

Analyze
Close Reading for the Traits

Student Objectives
- Read a model research report.
- Use the research report rubric.
- Use the model research report to study Ideas, Organization, and Voice.

Student Activities
- Review **"Fixing the Leaning Tower of Pisa."** *(p. 147)*
- Read and discuss **Using the Rubric to Analyze the Model.** *(pp. 150–151)*

Analyze
Close Reading for the Traits

Student Objectives
- Read a model research report.
- Use the research report rubric.
- Use the model research report to study Word Choice, Sentence Fluency, and Conventions.

Student Activities
- Review **"Fixing the Leaning Tower of Pisa."** *(p. 147)*
- Read and discuss **Using the Rubric to Analyze the Model.** *(pp. 152–153)*

Write
Draft

Student Objectives
- Complete a draft.

Student Activities
- Finish a draft. *(p. 157)*
- Participate in a peer conference.

Write
Revise: Voice

Student Objectives
- Revise to use a formal tone and plenty of facts.

Student Activities
- Read and discuss **Revise: Focus on Voice.** *(p. 158)*

Write
Publish: +Presentation

Student Objectives
- Discuss preparation for publishing and presentation.
- Use a final editing checklist to publish their work.

Student Activities
- Read and discuss **Publish: +Presentation.** *(p. 164)*
- Apply the publishing strategy.

Write
Publish: +Presentation

Student Objectives
- Use a research report rubric.
- Share a published research report.

Student Activities
- Share their work.
- Use the rubric to reflect upon and evaluate the model and their own writing. *(pp. 148–149, 165)*

To complete the chapter in fewer days, combine the learning objectives and activities in a way that supports students as they write.

Resources at-a-Glance

Grammar, Usage & Mechanics

Differentiating Instruction

For additional Differentiating Instruction activities, see Strategies for Writers *Differentiated Instruction Activities at* **www.sfw.z-b.com.**

English Language Learners

Collaborative Conferencing

Tech Tips

 Strategies for Writers Online

Go to **www.sfw.z-b.com** for additional online resources for students, teachers, and parents.

Online Writing Center

Provides IWB resources, assessments, interactive games and practice activities, videos, eBooks, and a virtual file cabinet.

Introduce
Research Report

Student Objectives

- Review the elements of a research report. (p. 144)
- Consider purpose and audience. (p. 145)
- Learn the traits of informative/explanatory writing. (p. 146)

What's a Research Report?

Tell students that a research report is a piece of writing that examines a topic and tells ideas and information from sources in a clear way. Explain that research reports include the facts and details the writer has found from multiple sources such as books, websites, and videos. Discuss with students reasons they might need to write a research report. Clarify with students that opinions do not belong in a research report.

What's in a Research Report?

Read and discuss with students the three elements of a research report. (introduction, ideas and concrete facts, concluding statement/section). Reiterate the importance of using sources to find information and domain-specific language in a research report.

 Strategies for Writers Online
Go to **www.sfw.z-b.com** for additional online resources for students, teachers, and parents.

What's a Research Report?

A research report is a piece of writing that gives facts and details about a topic.

What's in a Research Report?

Introduction
In the introduction, I tell the audience what my topic is and why it is interesting. I get the attention of my readers and make them curious to find out more.

Body
The body is the longest part of my report. I develop the idea I presented in the introduction. The body is where I add plenty of facts and details. If I'm writing about sand dunes, I might tell how dunes are formed, what they look like, and how high they get.

Conclusion
My conclusion summarizes the most important information about my topic.

144 *Informative/Explanatory Writing*

Informative/Explanatory Text Exemplars (Research Report)

Berger, Melvin. *Discovering Mars: The Amazing Story of the Red Planet*. Scholastic, 1992. CCSS Berger includes a variety of photos, illustrations, and facts about Mars in this nonfiction text. This exploration of the red planet is sure to keep students informed and interested.

Hakim, Joy. *A History of Us: The First Americans, Prehistory–1600*. Oxford University Press, 2005. CCSS *The First Americans, Prehistory–1600* is part of the *A History of Us* series. In it, Hakim describes the discovery of America, Native American life, and the adventures of well-known explorers.

Why write a Research Report?

There are many reasons to write a research report. Here are three reasons.

To Inform
People in many different careers make research reports to provide information. Police make research reports to tell how an investigation is going. People in business make research reports about training programs for new workers.

To Entertain
Many people enjoy learning about topics that interest them. Nonfiction writers may publish research reports in magazines, newspapers, and books.

To Change
Research reports are often used to support a certain viewpoint when people want to convince others to make changes. Research reports that show how certain animals are becoming extinct have led to the Endangered Species Act.

Why write a Research Report?

Read and discuss with students the reasons for writing a research report listed on page 145. Point out that all writing has a purpose and is aimed at a specific audience. These authentic purposes help authors shape their writing. Someone writing to inform may explain something to the reader by providing information and supporting it with facts and details. A writer whose purpose is to entertain can provide interesting information to help readers enjoy learning about new topics. Someone writing to effect change may write a research report to support a certain viewpoint to convince others to make changes. Encourage students to share their own reasons for writing research reports. Ask them to discuss how these reasons will affect the tone and focus of their writing.

Nelson, Kadir. *We Are the Ship: The Story of Negro League Baseball.* Jump at the Sun, 2008. 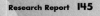 The history of Negro League baseball is skillfully described by Kadir. From the creation of the league to the addition of a black player to a white team, *We Are the Ship: The Story of Negro League Baseball* clearly illustrates the struggles and triumphs of African Americans during that time.

Hall, Leslie. "Seeing Eye to Eye." National Geographic Explorer. September 2009. 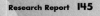 Hall explains how both animals and humans use their eyes to observe the world around them. She also describes the many amazing ways light affects sight.

CCSS **Common Core State Standards** (pp. Z20–Z30)
Language: L.4.3c
Speaking and Listening: SL.4.1a, SL.4.1b, SL.4.1c, SL.4.1d, SL.4.3, SL.4.6

Introduce
Research Report

Linking Informative/ Explanatory Writing Traits to a Research Report

Read page 146 aloud to help students understand that they will follow Alika as he models using the writing process and the informative/ explanatory writing traits together. A good research report will be built around a clear topic and main ideas supported by information and examples that answer the reader's questions. It should have a strong introduction, body, and conclusion and use transitions to connect ideas between well-organized paragraphs. It will use a voice and tone that are appropriate for the purpose and audience.

Linking Informative/Explanatory Writing Traits to a **Research Report**

In this chapter, you will write to share what you have learned about a topic. This type of informative/explanatory writing is called a research report. Alika will guide you through the stages of the writing process: Prewrite, Draft, Revise, Edit, and Publish. In each stage, Alika will show you important writing strategies that are linked to the Informative/Explanatory Writing Traits below.

Informative/Explanatory Writing Traits

	• a clear topic and main ideas • details, information, and examples that answer the reader's questions about the topic
	• a strong introduction, body, and conclusion • well-organized paragraphs • transitions that connect ideas
	• a voice and tone that are appropriate for the purpose and audience
	• precise words • domain-specific vocabulary that is used correctly and explained as necessary
	• clear, direct sentences that flow smoothly
	• no or few errors in grammar, usage, mechanics, and spelling

Before you write, read Jason Yang's research report on the next page. Then use the research report rubric on pages 148–149 to decide how well he did. (You might want to look back at What's in a Research Report? on page 144, too!)

Informative/Explanatory Writing Traits in a Research Report

 Ideas The writer builds the report around a clear topic and main ideas. The main ideas are supported by information and examples that answer the reader's questions.

 **Organization** The paragraphs in the report are well organized and include a strong introduction, body, and conclusion. Transitions link the ideas.

 **Voice** A knowledgeable-sounding voice and a formal tone are appropriate for the audience and purpose of a research report.

Fixing the Leaning Tower of Pisa

by Jason Yang

Research MODEL Report

Pisa is a city in Italy. This city has become famous for its leaning bell tower, an architectural mistake. In fact, the bell tower is known as the Leaning Tower of Pisa. It began to lean soon after it was built 800 years ago.

introduction

The Leaning Tower of Pisa is a very special place. Made of white marble with 207 columns, the tower is very beautiful. It is also very heavy. Most of the walls are nine to ten feet thick. With its thick walls and marble, the tower weighs about 16,000 tons.

body paragraphs

Many attempts have been made to straighten the tower. The south side of the tower leans, so the most common solution has been to put weights on the north side. This has never worked. People also tried putting concrete around the base of the tower. Then they attached cables to support the tower. At one time, 80 tons of concrete were poured into the foundation, but that solution didn't work either. People have also suggested putting huge weights against the tower to hold it upright.

In 1990 the tower was leaning so much that it had to be closed. A committee was formed to solve the problem.

Finally an attempt to save the Leaning Tower of Pisa worked. It seemed to be an unlikely plan at first. It involved moving sand. Led by a chief engineer named Dr. Paolo Heiniger, work crews removed almost 80 tons of soil from under the tower. They took away the soft sand that had caused the tower to lean in the first place. As they did, they slowly moved the south side of the tower toward the north.

Today the tower still leans. The top is still more than 15 feet out over the base. Nevertheless, this is less than the 17 feet of "lean" in 1990. It is also a big enough improvement to reopen the tower. Besides, people didn't really want the tower to stop leaning. They just didn't want it to fall.

conclusion

Sources

Barter, James. *The Tower of Pisa.* San Diego: Lucent Books, 2001.
Jarvis, Marybeth. *Leaning Tower of Pisa.* Danbury, CT: Children's
  Press, 1991.

Word Choice The writer uses precise, clear language to make the research report sound knowledgeable.

Sentence Fluency The lengths and types of sentences in the research report vary. This gives the text rhythm and flow.

Conventions A good writer carefully edits his or her work prior to publishing. Correct grammar, spelling, usage, and mechanics enhance the clarity of the writing in a research report.

Analyze
Close Reading of the Model

Week 1 • Day 2

Student Objectives

• Read a model research report. *(p. 147)*

Read the Model

Read "Fixing the Leaning Tower of Pisa" aloud to the class. Ask students to listen for a clear topic and main ideas supported by information and examples and to notice how the report is organized. **(introduction, body paragraphs, conclusion)** Also ask students to think about and discuss how a knowledgeable voice affects how they connect with the writer.

Elements of a Research Report

Have students refer to "What's in a Research Report?" on page 144 as you refer to the model. Discuss the notes written on the model to enhance students' understanding of the terms.

Point out the list of sources at the bottom of the research report. Explain to students that it is important to list the sources of the information they use to write their reports.

CCSS **C**ommon **C**ore **S**tate **S**tandards (pp. Z20–Z30)
Writing: W.4.6
Language: L.4.3c
Speaking and Listening: L.4.1a, SL.4.1b, SL.4.1c, SL.4.1d, SL.4.2, SL.4.3, SL.4.6

Analyze
Introduce the Rubric

Week 1 • Day 3

Student Objectives

- Learn to read a rubric. (pp. 148–149)

Introduce the Rubric

Explain the Rubric Explain that a rubric is a tool for planning, improving, and assessing a piece of writing. Tell students that a rubric helps a writer focus on key elements, or traits, in writing (**Ideas, Organization, Voice, Word Choice, Sentence Fluency, Conventions,** and **Presentation**).

Explain the 6-point system. Point out that the columns on page 148 represent a good paper that might need some polishing but that the columns on page 149 represent writing that needs considerable improvement.

Discuss the Rubric Guide students in a discussion of the rubric. Read the descriptors that go with each trait. Discuss the difference between columns to be sure students fully understand the point system. Tell students to keep the rubric in mind when they write their own research report and again when they revise it.

Online Writing Center

Provides a variety of **interactive rubrics,** including 4-, 5-, and 6-point models.

Research Report Rubric

Use this rubric to analyze the model. Then use it to plan and score your own research report.

	6	5	4	
Ideas	The report focuses on one topic. All details and facts are related and accurate.	The report focuses on one topic. Most of the details and facts are related.	The report focuses on one topic. Some of the information is vague or not related to the topic.	
Organization	The report has a strong introduction, body, and conclusion. The conclusion sums up the report in a memorable way.	The report has an introduction, body, and conclusion. The conclusion sums up the report.	The report has an introduction, body, and conclusion. The introduction and conclusion are not strong.	
Voice	The writer's voice sounds knowledgeable. It is clear the writer cares about the topic.	The writer's voice sounds knowledgeable and informative most of the time.	The writer's voice sounds knowledgeable some of the time. The writer seems to care about the topic.	
Word Choice	Precise words are used correctly and explained clearly.	Precise words are used correctly and explained most of the time.	Many of the writer's words are precise and correctly used. Some are not explained.	
Sentence Fluency	The writing flows because sentence lengths and types vary.	Most sentences vary in length and type.	Some sentences are the same length and type. More variety would make the writing flow better.	
Conventions	All capitalization and titles are correct. The report is easy to read.	There are a few errors in capitalization or titles, but they do not interfere with meaning.	Minor errors in capitalization and titles are noticeable and distracting.	

+ Presentation The report is prepared on the computer with a limited number of clear fonts.

CCSS Common Core State Standards

Research Report

Strategies for Writers was designed to incorporate the Common Core State Standards throughout every unit. By presenting the standards in multiple applications, your students' exposure to them will be ensured.

The writing standards that support the traits of Ideas and Organization are **W.4.2a,** and **W.4.2b,** which address choosing, organizing, and supporting the topic. Standard **W.4.2e** highlights providing a concluding statement. Standard **W.4.2d** addresses using precise language and domain-specific vocabulary to explain the topic and supports the trait of Word Choice.

3	2	1	
The report does not focus on one topic. Some details and facts may be inaccurate.	The focus is vague. Information and details are very general and not based on facts.	The topic is not clear. Many details and facts are not related to the topic.	**Ideas**
The report has an introduction, body, and conclusion. The conclusion does not sum up the report.	The introduction and body are weak or incomplete. The conclusion does not sum up the report.	The report does not have an introduction, body, or conclusion.	**Organization**
The writer's voice is inconsistent and vague at times. The reader is confused.	The writer's voice may be inappropriate for the purpose and audience. The voice is hard to identify.	The writer's voice is very weak or absent.	**Voice**
Some of the words are too general. Their meaning is sometimes unclear to the reader.	Some words are repetitive or unrelated. Their meaning is not explained.	Many words are too general and incorrectly used.	**Word Choice**
Many sentences are the same in length and type. They do not flow well together.	Sentences are too brief or too wordy. Reading is choppy and awkward.	Sentences are incomplete or incorrect. The report is difficult to read.	**Sentence Fluency**
Frequent errors in capitalization, titles, and other conventions confuse the reader.	Many errors in capitalization and titles make the text difficult to read and understand. The writer shows lack of control over conventions.	The writing contains many errors in capitalization and titles. It is very difficult to read.	**Conventions**

See Appendix B for 4-, 5-, and 6-point informative/explanatory rubrics.

Find Evidence in the Model

Small-Group Collaboration
Assign students to small groups to check the model for each trait. One person in each group should be responsible for recording one or two strong examples per trait as described by the rubric. Ask students to score each trait accordingly for the model. They should be able to support the score given with valid points. Note that although the models were written to score high against the rubric, students should not assume each trait would receive a 6. Encourage each group to thoroughly discuss each trait before assigning each score.

Teacher-Led Discussion Bring the class back together and ask one person from each group to report their findings to the class. The point of this exercise is not to score the model, but rather to practice identifying and evaluating the traits within a piece of writing.

Additional Rubrics

Appendix B includes 4-, 5-, and 6-point rubrics that can be used with any piece of informative/explanatory writing. The rubrics are also available as blackline masters in the back of this Teacher Edition.

Another writing standard addressed in the research report rubric is **W.4.2c,** which emphasizes using words and phrases to link ideas.

The language standards are addressed during editing and skills practice. There are also multiple opportunities to address the speaking and listening standards. Most importantly, this chapter will help students produce clear and coherent writing (**W.4.4**), improve their writing (**W.4.5**), and use technologies to publish and present finished pieces (**W.4.6**).

CCSS Common Core State Standards (pp. Z20–Z30)
Writing: W.4.6
Language: L.4.3c
Speaking and Listening: SL.4.1a, SL.4.1b, SL.4.1c, SL.4.1d, SL.4.2, SL.4.3, SL.4.6

Analyze
Close Reading for the Traits

Student Objectives

- Read a model research report. *(p. 147)*
- Use the research report rubric. *(pp. 148–149)*
- Use the model research report to study **Ideas, Organization,** and **Voice.** *(pp. 150–151)*

Find Evidence in the Model

Evaluate the Model Have volunteers read aloud each section on pages 150–151. Determine whether students agree with each point in Alika's assessment. Use these questions below to initiate the discussion. Be sure students can back up their answers with specific examples from the report.

Discuss Audience, Task, Purpose Ask students one or more of the following questions as they analyze the model:

- **Audience** Who is the audience? (Possible response: all readers)

- **Task** How does the writer share the information and research he did on the topic? (Possible response: He uses facts from sources in a clear way.)

- **Purpose** What is the writer's purpose for writing this report? (Possible response: To inform the readers)

Using the Rubric to Analyze the Model
Research Report

Did you notice that the model on page 147 points out some key elements of a research report? As he wrote "Fixing the Leaning Tower of Pisa," Jason Yang used these elements to help him tell what he learned about the famous tower in Pisa, Italy. He also used the 6-point rubric on pages 148–149 to plan, draft, revise, and edit the writing. A rubric is a great tool to evaluate writing during the writing process.

Now let's use the same rubric to score the model. To do this, we'll focus on each trait separately, starting with Ideas. We'll use the top descriptor for each trait (column 6), along with examples from the model, to help us understand how the traits work together. How would you score Jason on each trait?

Ideas
- The report focuses on one topic.
- All details and facts are related and accurate.

I really enjoyed reading this report. Jason tells us about the Leaning Tower of Pisa and shares interesting facts about it. He gives a lot of details to help the reader understand his topic. This is a good example of a paragraph with some of those important facts.

> The Leaning Tower of Pisa is a very special place. Made of white marble with 207 columns, the tower is very beautiful. It is also very heavy. Most of the walls are nine to ten feet thick. With its thick walls and marble, the tower weighs about 16,000 tons.

English Language Learners

BEGINNING
Topic Write the following sentence on the board: *A camel is a desert animal.* Ask, *What is this sentence about?* Tell students that *camel* is the topic of the sentence. Say *topic,* write it on the board, and have students repeat. Repeat the activity and have students determine the topic of several other sentences.

INTERMEDIATE
Topic Explain that a topic is what a report is about. Write a topic sentence on the board. Give students strips of paper with sentences that may or may not go with this topic sentence. Students read the sentence to the class and tell whether it should be included in the paragraph. Using the correct sentences, write a paragraph on the board that goes with the topic sentence.

Organization
- The report has a strong introduction, body, and conclusion.
- The conclusion sums up the report in a memorable way.

Jason's introduction caught my attention right away, and I wanted to keep reading. I really like the conclusion, too. The Leaning Tower of Pisa, "an architectural mistake," is one place I'd like to visit someday!

Today the tower still leans. The top is still more than 15 feet out over the base. Nevertheless, this is less than the 17 feet of "lean" in 1990. It is also a big enough improvement to reopen the tower. Besides, people didn't really want the tower to stop leaning. They just didn't want it to fall.

Voice
- The writer's voice sounds knowledgeable.
- It is clear the writer cares about the topic.

I learned a lot about the Leaning Tower of Pisa from this report. Jason sounds knowledgeable. It's clear he had carefully researched the topic. Here is a good example—the writer explains how people tried to fix the tower.

Finally an attempt to save the Leaning Tower of Pisa worked. It seemed to be an unlikely plan at first. It involved moving sand. Led by a chief engineer named Dr. Paolo Heiniger, work crews removed almost 80 tons of soil from under the tower. They took away the soft sand that had caused the tower to lean in the first place. As they did, they slowly moved the south side of the tower toward the north.

Research Report 151

Discuss the Traits Ask students one or more of the following questions to discuss the traits in the model:

Ideas Does Jason Yang have a clear topic and good examples in his report? (Possible responses: Yes, the topic, the Leaning Tower of Pisa, is clearly defined. Jason includes examples in the body paragraphs to answer the reader's questions.)

Organization What organization does Jason use to structure his report? (Possible response: Jason organizes his report with a strong introduction, body, and conclusion.)

Voice Does Jason use a voice that is appropriate for the purpose and audience? (Possible response: Yes, Jason uses a knowledgeable voice to get his message across.)

ADVANCED
Relevant Facts Students must decide if a fact is relevant to the main idea. Give students the main idea, such as *There are many different kinds of energy resources*, and list several facts and non-facts, such as *Nonrenewable energy comes from coal and oil; Wind is a renewable form of energy; We can use the sun's energy*, and so on. Have students circle the facts that are relevant to the main idea.

ADVANCED HIGH
Credible Sources Have students use print and credible online resources to find several relevant facts that support a topic that you provide, such as *We need to use more renewable energy sources*. Have students write their findings on a Main Idea Table and use that information to write a paragraph.

CCSS **Common Core State Standards** (pp. Z20–Z30)
Writing: W.4.2b, W.4.8
Language: L.4.3c, L.4.6
Speaking and Listening: SL.4.1a, SL.4.1b, SL.4.1c, SL.4.1d, SL.4.3, SL.4.6

Analyze
Close Reading for the Traits

Week 1 • Day 5

Student Objectives

- Read a model research report. *(p. 147)*
- Use the research report rubric. *(pp. 148–149)*
- Use the model research report to study **Word Choice, Sentence Fluency,** and **Conventions.** *(pp. 152–153)*

Discuss the Traits Ask students one or more of the following questions to discuss the traits in the model:

Word Choice Does Jason use precise words to clearly explain his topic and provide additional information? (Possible response: Jason uses precise words to explain the topic.) Which words does he explain? (Possible response: He uses the appositive *an architectural mistake* to give additional meaning to *This city has become famous for its leaning bell tower, an architectural mistake.*)

Sentence Fluency Which part of the model flows especially smoothly? (Possible response: the third paragraph) What makes the sentences flow? (Possible response: Jason varies sentence lengths and types to give the text rhythm and flow.)

Conventions Does Jason use capitalization and titles correctly? (Yes, Jason uses capitalization and titles correctly.)

Strategies for Writers Online
Go to **www.sfw.z-b.com** for additional online resources for students, teachers, and parents.

Using the Research Report Rubric to Analyze the Model

 **Word Choice**
- Precise words are used correctly and explained clearly.

In this report, Jason uses appositives to add more information about the nouns in his sentences. In the sentence below, *an architectural mistake* is an appositive that provides more information about the tower.

This city has become famous for its leaning bell tower, an architectural mistake.

 **Sentence Fluency**
- The writing flows because sentence lengths and types vary.

The writer used a variety of sentence lengths and types. Here is an example of how the writer used both simple and compound sentences to give the text rhythm and flow.

Many attempts have been made to straighten the tower. The south side of the tower leans, so the most common solution has been to put weights on the north side. This has never worked.

152 Informative/Explanatory Writing

Tech Tips
Online Tools

Create Bibliographies Online Unless teachers are the "voice in their ear" from the very start of the research process, students will often capture incomplete bibliographic information as they use online sources to support their work. Online tools like BibMe help students capture their sources and shape the citation into the proper formatting. Consider using this to build a class repository of sources and citations so that students have a model collection to refer to.

See **www.sfw.z-b.com** for further information about and links to these websites and tools.

Conventions
- All capitalization and titles are correct.
- The report is easy to read.

Jason did a good job editing his paper. He capitalized the first word of every sentence, all the proper nouns, and the one abbreviation of a person's title.

Led by a chief engineer named Dr. Paolo Heiniger, work crews removed almost 80 tons of soil from under the tower. They took away the soft sand that had caused the tower to lean in the first place.

+Presentation The report is prepared on the computer with a limited number of clear fonts.

My Turn!
Now it's my turn to write a research report! I'll use the rubric and good writing strategies to help me. Follow along to see how I do it.

Differentiating Instruction

ENRICHMENT
Objective and Subjective Explain that *subjective* refers to feelings and opinions. *Objective* refers to facts and knowledge. Research reports are based on facts. Writers of research reports should avoid subjective words like *best* or *awesome*. Have students work in pairs to brainstorm words that are subjective rather than objective. Have groups share lists.

REINFORCEMENT
Narrow the Topic Help students learn to choose topics that are specific enough to cover in a report. Discuss why the underlined topic in each pair would make the better research topic: food or <u>Indian food</u>, New York City skyscrapers or <u>the Empire State Building</u>, dogs or <u>guide dogs</u>.

+Presentation Discuss why Presentation is equally as important as the other traits. Stress the importance of neatness. Reports should be clearly handwritten in pen or typed, and paragraphs should be indented (using the tab key if typed). Discuss how white space can be used to organize text, especially to clearly separate paragraphs. Good margins make the line lengths comfortable to read, and a centered title stands out on a page. Preparing the report on the computer will enable students to use formatting features to enhance the appearance of the report.

Think About the Traits

Once students have thoroughly discussed the model, ask them which traits they think are most important in a research report and have them explain why. (Possible response: Organization is very important because if the report does not contain a strong introduction, body paragraphs, and conclusion, the reader will probably lose interest. Voice is important because it establishes a formal tone and communicates that the writer knows and cares about the topic.)

CCSS **Common Core State Standards** (pp. Z20–Z30)
Writing: W.4.6, W.4.8
Language: L.4.3c, L.4.6
Speaking and Listening: SL.4.1a, SL.4.1b, SL.4.1c, SL.4.1d, SL.4.3, SL.4.6

Write
Research Report

Week 2 • Day 1

Student Objectives

• Read and understand a prewriting strategy. *(p. 154)*

Prewrite

Focus on Ideas

Narrow Topic Read page 154 aloud. Discuss the general topic for the report. (volcanoes) Ask what topic Alika chose. (living near a volcano) Then ask how Alika narrowed the general topic. **(He skimmed an encyclopedia article and found one aspect of volcanoes that interested him.)**

Gather Information from Print and Digital Sources Discuss how students will need to do research to collect information and facts. Tell students that they will use at least two sources for their reports. Ask which sources writers might use for a report. **(experts on a topic, books, videos, internet)**

Take Notes on Source Information Point out Alika's notes. Tell students that, like Alika, they will take notes on note cards.

Online Writing Center

Provides **interactive graphic organizers** as well as a variety of graphic organizers in PDF format.

Prewrite   Focus on Ideas

The Rubric Says   The report focuses on one topic.

Writing Strategy   Narrow a topic and take notes.

My teacher asked us to write a research report on something about volcanoes. We had to narrow the topic from volcanoes in general to something specific.

First I skimmed an encyclopedia article about volcanoes to narrow my topic. One thing about volcanoes that interests me most is living near one.

Then I found a book that told more about my topic. As I read the book, I took notes on what people keep in mind if they live near a volcano.

Erickson, Jon. *Volcanoes and Earthquakes.* New York: Tab Books, 2008.

Living Near Volcanoes

escape plans	emergency supplies	dangers
routes to take	flashlight	blasts
higher land	radio	ash
away from wind	batteries	lava
place to meet	food and water	
	can opener	
	first-aid kit	

Write

Do some research and narrow your topic. Then make a list of important things to remember about your topic.

154   Informative/Explanatory Writing

English Language Learners

BEGINNING/INTERMEDIATE

Web Graphic Organizer Draw a Web on the board. In the center circle, write *Types of Energy*. Ask students to give examples of the different types of energy they know about. Then write their answers, such as *coal, geothermal, solar, wind, oil,* and *natural gas,* in the surrounding circles. Mention that types of energy could be separated into renewable and nonrenewable on the Web.

ADVANCED/ADVANCED HIGH

Organizing Details Have students use a Web to organize details about their selected topics. They should write the topic in the center circle. Each of the next layer of circles can be the main idea of each paragraph in the essay. Supporting details would be added to the next layer of circles. Once students have researched a few main ideas and supporting details, have them use their notes to give a brief oral presentation to the class.

Prewrite

Focus on **Organization**

The Rubric Says The report has a strong introduction, body, and conclusion.

Writing Strategy Use a Web to organize the notes.

I know from the rubric that every main idea needs information to back it up. I'll use a Web to organize my report. I can put the topic in the center. The categories from my notes will go in the next set of circles. Then the details for each category will go in smaller circles connected to the categories.

Web

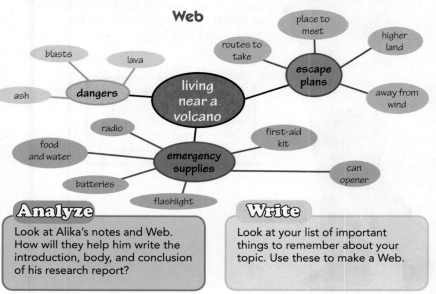

Analyze

Look at Alika's notes and Web. How will they help him write the introduction, body, and conclusion of his research report?

Write

Look at your list of important things to remember about your topic. Use these to make a Web.

Research Report **155**

Collaborative Conferencing

PEER TO PEER Have students exchange organizers. Instruct partners to ask the following questions as they review them: *What information could the writer add to the Web to help me better understand the main ideas? Do the details answer my questions?* Tell partners to write one or two comments on a sticky note and return the Web to the writer.

PEER GROUPS Have students form small groups of three or four to provide feedback on improving their organizers. Have students share their notes and webs. Encourage other students to take turns offering helpful suggestions.

TEACHER-LED Conference with individual students about their Webs. Before they speak with you, encourage students to think of questions to ask about points they found difficult in creating the Web.

Write
Research Report

Week 2 • Day 2

Student Objectives

- Make a Web to organize notes. (p. 155)

Prewrite

Focus on **Organization**

Categorize Information Read page 155. Explain that writers use a variety of organizers to get started writing. Alika used a Web to help organize his notes. (Go to **www.sfw.z-b.com** for the downloadable graphic organizer.) Ask students why he put the words *living near a volcano* in the center of his Web. (It's his topic!) Then ask how the Web will help Alika write a report. (Alika can use the Web to list the main idea and details for each paragraph in the body of the report.)

Writer's Term ___

Source A source is any published material from which information is gathered. Sources can be literary (novels, stories, plays) or informational (encyclopedias, websites, articles). Credible and accurate sources should always be used when including facts in writing.

CCSS **Common Core State Standards** (pp. Z20–Z30)
Writing: W.4.2a, W.4.2b, W.4.4, W.4.5, W.4.6, W.4.7, W.4.8, W.4.10
Language: L.4.3c L.4.6
Speaking and Listening: SL.4.1a, SL.4.1b, SL.4.1c, SL.4.1d, SL.4.3, SL.4.6

Write
Research Report

Week 2 • Day 3

Student Objectives

- Use a Web to begin writing. (p. 156)

Draft

Focus on Organization

Group Related Information in Paragraphs Read page 156 aloud. Remind students that writing a draft gives them a chance to get ideas on paper without having to worry about making mistakes. Encourage students that as they draft their introduction, body, and conclusion, they should group related facts together in the same paragraph.

Develop Topic With Facts and Concrete Details Remind students that as they draft they should include the facts and details they researched from their sources. Encourage them to stay away from including their opinions about the topic and to rely on the evidence from their research.

Writer's Term

Paragraph Each paragraph should have a topic sentence that expresses one main idea. The remaining sentences should support the main idea with facts, definitions, and examples related to the topic.

Online Writing Center

 Provides an **interactive writing pad** for drafting, revising, editing, and publishing.

TI56 Informative/Explanatory Writing

Draft — Focus on Organization

The Rubric Says	The report has a strong introduction, body, and conclusion. The conclusion sums up the report in a memorable way.
Writing Strategy	Use my graphic organizer to plan my paragraphs.

It's time to write my first draft. I know from the rubric that my report should have an introduction, body, and conclusion. I'll use my Web to organize my paragraphs. The introduction and conclusion will both be about the information in the center of the Web—living near a volcano. The dark orange, blue, and purple circles will be the paragraph topics in the body of the report. The lighter colored circles will be the details for each paragraph topic.

Writer's Term

Paragraph
A **paragraph** is a group of sentences that share a common topic or purpose and focus on a single main idea or thought.

156 Informative/Explanatory Writing

Differentiating Instruction

ENRICHMENT

Extend Vocabulary Tell students that *volcano* comes from Vulcano, an island in the Mediterranean Sea. People once believed that Vulcano was the chimney of the forge of Vulcan—the blacksmith of the Roman gods. The lava from volcanoes was thought to pour from Vulcan's forge as he fashioned thunderbolts for Jupiter, king of the gods. Challenge students to find other myths about volcanoes.

REINFORCEMENT

Recognize Reliable Sources Help students list different types of sources they think might be useful for their reports, including the Internet. Discuss each resource and how effective it might be for students.

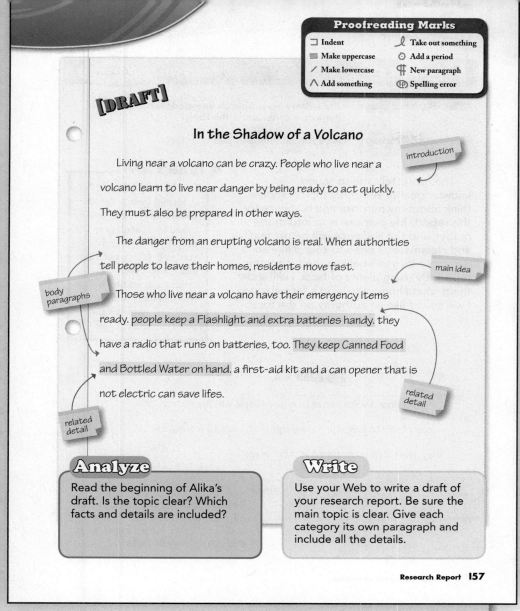

Proofreading Marks

⌐ Indent   ℓ Take out something
≡ Make uppercase   ⊙ Add a period
/ Make lowercase   ⌗ New paragraph
∧ Add something   ⑤℗ Spelling error

[DRAFT]

In the Shadow of a Volcano

introduction

Living near a volcano can be crazy. People who live near a volcano learn to live near danger by being ready to act quickly. They must also be prepared in other ways.

main idea

The danger from an erupting volcano is real. When authorities tell people to leave their homes, residents move fast.

body paragraphs

Those who live near a volcano have their emergency items ready. people keep a Flashlight and extra batteries handy. they have a radio that runs on batteries, too. They keep Canned Food and Bottled Water on hand. a first-aid kit and a can opener that is not electric can save lifes.

related detail

related detail

Analyze

Read the beginning of Alika's draft. Is the topic clear? Which facts and details are included?

Write

Use your Web to write a draft of your research report. Be sure the main topic is clear. Give each category its own paragraph and include all the details.

Collaborative Conferencing

PEER TO PEER Have partners exchange drafts to read. Tell students to think of two or three questions they would like to ask to clarify information or supply missing details. Have them write their questions on sticky notes and affix them to the appropriate places on their partner's draft.

PEER GROUPS Have students work in groups of three or four. Tell students to take turns reading their draft aloud. The other students should comment by telling their favorite part of the draft and point out one place where they thought information was missing.

TEACHER-LED Schedule conferences with pairs of students. Have them read each other's editorial and coach them in giving and receiving constructive feedback.

Write
Research Report

Student Objectives

• Finish a draft. *(p. 157)*

Continue Drafting It is important that students are given ample time to draft research reports. As conferencing is important throughout the writing process, be sure to also plan time for peer-to-peer, peer group, or teacher-led conferences. Remind students that this is the time for getting their ideas down on paper in a creative and engaging way. Assure them that they will have plenty of time to fix any mistakes later.

Use Your Own Words Tell students to always use their own words when drafting. Explain that using another writer's words *as your own* is called plagiarism, and it is not acceptable. To help students avoid plagiarism, encourage them to write down the main ideas from sources instead of taking notes word for word.

CCSS Common Core State Standards (pp. Z20–Z30)
Writing: W.4.2a, W.4.2e, W.4.4, W.4.5, W.4.6, W.4.7, W.4.8, W.4.10
Language: L.4.3c, L.4.6
Speaking and Listening: SL.4.1a, SL.4.1b, SL.4.1c, SL.4.1d, SL.4.3, SL.4.6

Write
Research Report

Week 2 • Day 5

Student Objectives

- Revise to use a formal tone and plenty of facts. *(p. 158)*

Revise

Focus on Voice

Use a Formal Voice Read page 158 aloud. Discuss the importance of making sure that the report sounds knowledgeable and factual. By using a formal tone, the writer will sound like an expert on the topic. Have one volunteer read the draft excerpt without the revision and then another volunteer read it with the revision. Point out how much more knowledgeable Alika's writing sounds after he revised one word! Ask students to consider how Alika's revision improves his voice. (Alika sounds more like an expert. Readers are more likely to trust his information.) Remind students to look for places to use a formal voice and additional facts in their research reports.

✏️ Writer's Term _____

Formal Tone The choice of language, tone, point of view, and style all affect a writer's voice. A research report is a formal piece of writing; the voice should sound knowledgeable and objective.

▶ Strategies for Writers Online

Go to **www.sfw.z-b.com** for additional online resources for students, teachers, and parents.

Revise
Focus on Voice

The Rubric Says The writer's voice sounds knowledgeable. It is clear the writer cares about the topic.

Writing Strategy Use a formal tone and plenty of facts.

The rubric tells me to sound knowledgeable about my topic. I should think about my purpose and audience for this report. My purpose is to inform the reader, and the audience will be my teacher and classmates. I need to sound like an expert so they will believe the facts in my report. By using plenty of facts, I will show them what I know. By using a formal tone, I will sound like an authority on the topic.

✏️ Writer's Term _____

Formal Tone
A **formal tone** is the way you would sound if you talked to an adult or to people you don't know very well. It is respectful and polite. When speaking or writing with a formal tone, you use complete sentences and avoid casual language.

> **[DRAFT]**
>
> used formal tone
>
> risky
> Living near a volcano can be ~~crazy~~. People who live near a
> volcano learn to live near danger by being ready to act quickly.
> They must also be prepared in other ways.

Write

Read your draft. Think about your purpose and audience. Revise your writing to use a formal tone and add plenty of facts.

158 Informative/Explanatory Writing

English Language Learners

BEGINNING/INTERMEDIATE
Capitalization Write a student's name on the board, but do not capitalize it. Ask, *What's wrong?* Correct the capitalization error. Say, *This is a person's name. We must capitalize it.* Repeat for place names, book titles, days, and months.

ADVANCED/ADVANCED HIGH
Using Appositives On the board, write *Hydroelectricity is the main source of power.* Ask students if they know what *hydroelectricity* is. Revise the sentence to *Hydroelectricity, or energy created by water, is the main source of power.* Tell students that the new information helps the reader understand the vocabulary and is called an appositive. Have students write sentences using appositives for *solar energy* and *biofuel*.

Revise

Focus on **Word Choice**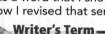

The Rubric Says	Precise words are used correctly and explained clearly.
Writing Strategy	Use appositives to explain nouns the reader may not know.

When using words that are specific to my topic, I can do a favor for the reader by providing more detail about the words. An appositive is one way to do this for nouns. I checked my report. My second paragraph has a word that I should explain. Take a look at how I revised that sentence.

> **Writer's Term** _____
>
> **Appositives**
> An **appositive** is a word or phrase that follows a noun and helps identify or describe it.

[DRAFT]

 added appositive

The danger from an erupting volcano is real. When authorities ∧ , the officials in control, tell people to leave their homes, residents move fast.

Analyze

Look at Alika's revision. How does the appositive he added help the reader?

Write

Read your draft again. Add appositives where needed to provide more detail.

Research Report **159**

Collaborative Conferencing

PEER TO PEER Have pairs of students exchange drafts. After reading the draft, each student offers helpful feedback on different ways to add appositives to describe nouns and strengthen Word Choice.

PEER GROUPS Separate students into small groups. Have them take turns reading sections of their drafts aloud. Then ask group members to suggest places to add appositives to describe nouns in order to strengthen Word Choice.

TEACHER-LED Conference with individual students about their drafts. Point out places where students can strengthen Word Choice by adding appositives to better describe nouns.

Write
Research Report

Student Objectives
- Revise to use appositives. *(p. 159)*

Revise

Focus on

Use Appositives to Explain Nouns Read page 159 aloud. Discuss the importance of explaining nouns and proper nouns that may be unfamiliar to readers. One way to do this is to use appositives, or words or phrases that explain nouns.

It is important to use appositives to explain nouns the reader may not know. Otherwise, readers may lack necessary information to understand the report. Have one volunteer read the draft without the revisions, and then another volunteer read the revised draft. Point out that Alika's writing is clearer after he added an appositive to explain the noun *authorities*.

> **Writer's Term** _____
>
> **Appositives** often help to combine short, choppy sentences. For example, *Alika studied volcanoes. He is a student in fourth grade.* Revised: *Alika, a student in fourth grade, studied volcanoes.* Use commas to set off appositives from the rest of the sentence.

CCSS **Common Core State Standards** (pp. Z20–Z30)
Writing: W.4.2b, W.4.2d, W.4.4, W.4.5, W.4.7, W.4.10
Language: L.4.2a, L.4.3a, L.4.3c, L.4.4a, L.4.6
Speaking and Listening: SL.4.1a, SL.4.1b, SL.4.1c, SL.4.1d, SL.4.3, SL.4.6

Write
Research Report

Week 3 • Day 2

Student Objectives

- Revise to include both simple and compound sentences. (p. 160)

Revise

Focus on

Use a Variety of Sentence Lengths and Types Read page 160 aloud and point out Alika's revisions. Ask students if they think the changes he made improved this part of his draft. Remind students that the rubric says that sentence lengths and types should vary to keep the writing flowing along.

Explain that using a variety of sentences will also keep the audience interested in reading their report. Point out that a string of the same type of sentences can cause readers to lose interest in the writing. By using a mix of sentences, students can avoid this problem. Finally, encourage students to review their drafts for sentence variety. Suggest that they also combine related ideas, using appositives or coordinating conjuctions, such as *or*, *and*, or *but*, to vary the lengths of their sentences. Remind students to use a comma before a coordinating conjuction in a compound sentence.

Revise
Focus on **Sentence Fluency**

The Rubric Says	The writing flows because sentence lengths and types vary.
Writing Strategy	Write both simple and compound sentences.

The rubric reminds me to use a mix of sentence lengths and types. By using a variety of simple and compound sentences, I'll give my text rhythm and flow. I should read my draft out loud and listen for places where short sentences could be combined to make longer ones. I can join sentences using the words *and*, *or*, or *but*.

I read my draft out loud and listened for places where sentences could be combined. I found two short, related sentences in this paragraph. I combined them by using the word *and*.

[DRAFT]

Having an escape plan is important for people who live near a volcano. They decide on a route to take if they have to leave their homes. , and ⌃ They make sure everyone knows the plan.

combined sentences

Write
Check your draft. If needed, combine sentences with *and*, *or*, or *but*.

160 Informative/Explanatory Writing

Optional Revising Lessons

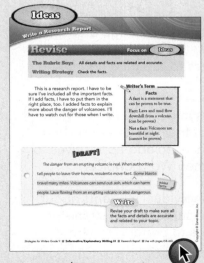

Informative/Explanatory 13   Informative/Explanatory 14

Edit

Focus on Conventions

The Rubric Says   All capitalization and titles are correct.

Writing Strategy   Use uppercase letters correctly.

When I proofread, I always check spelling and punctuation. This time I'm going to pay special attention to capitalization. I want to be sure I've started every sentence with an uppercase letter. I'm also going to check that I've capitalized all proper nouns, all important words in titles, and all abbreviations of personal titles. Finally, I have to make sure that I have not used any uppercase letters that are unnecessary.

> have a radio that runs on batteries, too. They keep Canned Food
>
> and Bottled Water on hand. a first-aid kit and a can opener that is
>
> not electric can save ~~lifes.~~ lives

[DRAFT]

Analyze

Look at Alika's edits. Are all the spelling, capitalization, and punctuation mistakes fixed?

How do Alika's edits improve his writing?

Write   Conventions

Edit your draft for spelling and punctuation. Make sure that all capitalization and titles are correct.

For more practice with capitalization and titles, use the exercises on the next two pages.

Research Report **161**

Related Grammar Practice

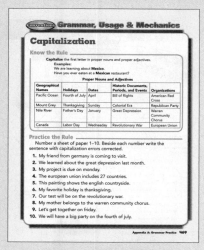

Student Edition page 469

Student Edition page 470

Go to ➡️ Appendix A: Grammar Practice

Student Objectives

• Edit for correct use of uppercase letters. *(p. 161)*

Edit

Focus on Conventions

Check Uppercase Letters Remind students that this is the time to correct mistakes in spelling, punctuation, and capitalization. Then read page 161. Direct students to study Alika's draft. Discuss the changes in the draft excerpt. Suggest that students read their drafts again, paying special attention to how they used uppercase letters. Have they remembered to capitalize the first word of every sentence and all proper nouns? Have they written titles of books, movies, songs, poems, or stories correctly?

Use the mini-lessons on pages T162 and T163 for students having trouble using uppercase letters and writing titles correctly. Then have students complete the exercises on pages 162 and 163.

CCSS **C**ommon **C**ore **S**tate **S**tandards (pp. Z20–Z30)
Writing: W.4.4, W.4.5, W.4.6, W.4.7, W.4.10
Language: L.4.1f, L.4.2a, L.4.2c, L.4.2d, L.4.4a

Research Report **T161**

Mini-Lesson

Student Objectives

• Use uppercase letters correctly. (p. 162)

Capitalization

Discuss the Know the Rule box on page 162. If possible, prepare a Capitalization Rules Chart for display. Explain to students that capitalization is similar to punctuation—it announces the first word of a sentence, proper nouns, titles, and abbreviations.

Point out that most nouns that require capitalization have something in common—they are a specific person, place, or thing. If the person, place, or thing can be made into a plural, it probably should not be capitalized. Write these examples on the board:

• *mother, mothers, Mother Goose*

• *river, rivers, Mississippi River,*

• *kitten, kittens, Fluffy*

Ask why *Mother Goose, Mississippi River,* and *Fluffy* are capitalized. (They each name a specific person, place, or thing.) Remind students that it is important to use capitalization correctly in their research report in order to convey the correct meaning to the reader.

Online Writing Center

Provides **interactive grammar games** and **practice activities** in student eBook.

Capitalization

Know the Rule

Use an **uppercase letter** for
• the first word in every sentence.
• all proper nouns.
• the first word, the last word, and all important words in titles.
• abbreviations of personal titles.

Practice the Rule

Number a piece of paper 1–12. Write each sentence using the correct capitalization. If a sentence is correct, write **Correct**.

1. have you read any books by ms. Margaret Poynter?
2. I got one of her books from the springfield public library.
3. The book is called *volcanoes: The fiery mountains.*
4. I learned about a park in hawaii where you can sometimes see a volcano in action.
5. Like japan, Hawaii has volcanic mountains.
6. volcanoes create many landforms.
7. There is an odd mountain in wyoming called devil's tower.
8. This is a famous landmark in north America.
9. Devil's Tower is made from old lava.
10. This mountain was in the film *Close encounters of the third Kind.*
11. Have you heard of the volcano that erupted in washington?
12. This mountain erupted on may 18, 1980.

Related Grammar Practice

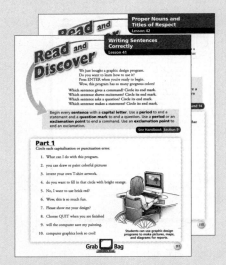

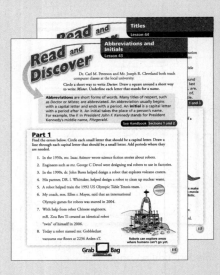

Pages 111, 113, 115, 117

Go to G.U.M. Student Practice Book

Titles

Know the Rule

Underline **book titles** and **movie titles** when you write them by hand. Put them in italics when you use a computer. Use quotation marks around the **titles of songs, poems,** and **stories.** Capitalize the first word, last word, and all the important words of any title. Always capitalize *is, are, was,* and *were* in titles. Do not capitalize *a, an, the, and, to, on, or, of,* or *in* unless that word is the first word or the last word in the title.

Practice the Rule

Number a piece of paper 1–10. Rewrite each title. Use correct punctuation and capitalization.

Type	Title
1. Book	great volcanoes <u>Great Volcanoes</u>
2. Poem	mr. volcano "Mr. Volcano"
3. Song	lava flows "Lava Flows"
4. Movie	the eruption of mount vesuvius <u>The Eruption of Mount Vesuvius</u>
5. Short Story	the story of volcanoes "The Story of Volcanoes"
6. Book	Living near a volcano <u>Living Near a Volcano</u>
7. Poem	ash on the land "Ash on the Land"
8. Book	exploring Pompeii <u>Exploring Pompeii</u>
9. Movie	The Iceland volcano <u>The Iceland Volcano</u>
10. Short Story	One day in summer "One Day in Summer"

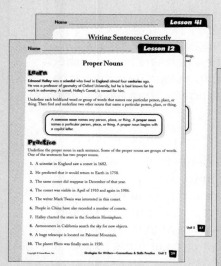

Pages 29, 87, 89, 91, 93

Go to ➡ **Grammar Practice Masters**

Conventions

Mini-Lesson

Student Objectives

• Use titles correctly. *(p. 163)*

Titles

Discuss the Know the Rule box on page 163. Then write the following sentences on the board, being sure to leave out correct capitalization and punctuation of titles:

• *Today I read a poem called sick by Shel Silverstein.*

• *Have you read a book called the great brain?*

• *My family loves to watch old movies, but we especially love the wizard of oz.*

• *My mom's favorite short story is a very famous story called the necklace.*

Ask volunteers where to place uppercase letters and punctuation.

• Today I read a poem called "Sick" by Shel Silverstein.

• Have you read a book called <u>The Great Brain</u>?

• My family loves to watch old movies, but we especially love <u>The Wizard of Oz.</u>

• My mom's favorite short story is a very famous story called "The Necklace."

Remind students to use correct punctuation and capitalization in their research reports. Otherwise, readers can get confused.

CCSS **C**ommon **C**ore **S**tate **S**tandards (pp. Z20–Z30)
Writing: W.4.6
Language: L.4.2a, L.4.6

Write
Research Report

Week 3 • Day 4

Student Objectives

- Discuss preparation for publishing and presentation. *(p. 164)*
- Use a final editing checklist to publish their work. *(p. 164)*

Publish 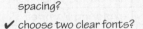 Presentation

Publishing Strategy Ask students if they like Alika's choice for sharing his research report. Ask students to name advantages of presenting their reports online. (Possible responses: Other classes, friends, and family members can read it. The writer can add images or clip art.) Talk about other ways to publish a finished research report. (multimedia presentation, class book, library research display) As a class, choose the best option.

Have a volunteer read Alika's checklist. Remind students that the checklist relates to the editing strategies they have been practicing. Have them use the checklist to perform a final evaluation before publishing their work.

Provide a List of Sources Remind students to include a list of the sources they used to find information about their topics. Provide the citing format guidelines to students to use in their reports.

 Strategies for Writers Online
Go to **www.sfw.z-b.com** for additional online resources for students, teachers, and parents.

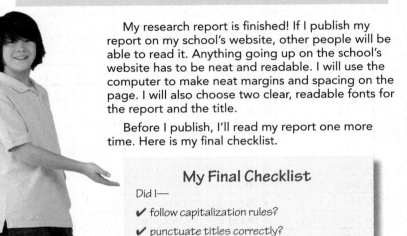

Publish ⁺Presentation

Publishing Strategy	Publish the report on the school's website.
Presentation Strategy	Make good design decisions on the computer.

My research report is finished! If I publish my report on my school's website, other people will be able to read it. Anything going up on the school's website has to be neat and readable. I will use the computer to make neat margins and spacing on the page. I will also choose two clear, readable fonts for the report and the title.

Before I publish, I'll read my report one more time. Here is my final checklist.

My Final Checklist
Did I—

✔ follow capitalization rules?

✔ punctuate titles correctly?

✔ make neat margins and use regular spacing?

✔ choose two clear fonts?

✔ put my name on the report?

✔ provide a list of sources?

Write
Make your own checklist and use it to check your research report. Then publish your research report.

164 Informative/Explanatory Writing

Differentiating Instruction

ENRICHMENT
Copyedit Have pairs of students exchange papers to proofread each other's work. When partners have finished proofreading, have them swap papers again so that each student has his or her own paper again. Then have students discuss and defend their edits.

REINFORCEMENT
Use a Checklist Meet with students to discuss their final checklists. Especially remind them to check to see that they have followed capitalization rules and punctuated titles correctly. If they are typing their reports, students should also make sure that they have used neat margins and spacing, and used no more than two clear fonts to prepare final copies.

In the Shadow of a Volcano
by Alika

Living near a volcano can be risky. People who live near a volcano learn to live near danger by being ready to act quickly. They must also be prepared in other ways.

The danger from an erupting volcano is real. When authorities, the officials in control, tell people to leave their homes, residents move fast. Some blasts travel many miles. Volcanoes can send out ash, which can harm people. Lava flowing from an erupting volcano is also dangerous.

Those who live near a volcano have their emergency items ready. People keep a flashlight and extra batteries handy. They have a radio that runs on batteries, too. They keep canned food and bottled water on hand. A first-aid kit and a can opener that is not electric can save lives.

Having an escape plan is important for people who live near a volcano. They decide on a route to take if they have to leave their homes, and they make sure everyone knows the plan. They always head toward higher ground because lava and mud flow downhill. Also, they try to stay downwind. The wind can carry objects and harmful gas. The plan includes a place for everyone to meet later.

People who live on or near active volcanoes usually adjust to their dangerous neighbors. In the book *Volcanoes and Earthquakes*, Jon Erickson says that people learn to treat volcanoes "as though they were just a normal part of their lives."

Sources
Erickson, Jon. *Volcanoes and Earthquakes.* New York: Tab Books, 2008.
Volcanoes. BrainPOP, 2012. http://www.brainpop.com/science/earthsystem/ volcanoes/

Analyze
Use the rubric to evaluate Alika's report and your own report.

Tech Tips
Websites

Assess Credibility of Online Sources As much as our students might appear to know what they are doing when searching for online information, take time to discuss and evaluate sites together. The RADCAB model moves students through the steps of considering a website's **r**elevance, **a**ppropriateness, **d**etail, **c**urrency, **a**uthority, and **b**ias. Unpack each of these steps over the course of multiple tasks, as each is spelled out in kid-friendly language but requires some smart thinking for readers to internalize and apply. Where the site includes rubrics, you could also work with students to co-construct one appropriate for your class.

Write
Research Report

Week 3 • Day 5

Student Objectives
- Use a research report rubric. (pp. 148–149)
- Share a published research report. (p. 165)

Presentation Strategy Students should take advantage of the formatting features on the computer to make the report neat and presentable. They can also enhance the report by using a display font for the title or adding boldfaced headings.

Reflecting on a Research Report

Have students refer to the rubric on pages 148–149 as they reread Alika's final copy on page 165. Ask students to consider how his revisions and edits strengthened his report. What score should Alika receive for each writing trait?

Next have students reflect on the assignment as a whole. Ask:

- What was your favorite part of this assignment?
- What will you do differently in your next research report?

Allow time for students to share their thoughts.

CCSS **C**ommon **C**ore **S**tate **S**tandards (pp. Z20–Z30)
Writing: W.4.2a, W.4.4, W.4.6, W.4.7, W.4.8, W.4.10
Language: L.4.2a, L.4.3c
Speaking and Listening: SL.4.1a, SL.4.1b, SL.4.1c, SL.4.1d, SL.4.3, SL.4.6

How-To Essay Planner

WEEK 1

Day 1
Introduce
How-To Essay

Student Objectives
- Review the elements of a how-to essay.
- Consider purpose and audience.
- Learn the traits of informative/explanatory writing.

Student Activities
- Read and discuss **What's in a How-To Essay?** (p. 166)
- Read and discuss **Why Write a How-To Essay?** (p. 167)
- Read **Linking Informative/Explanatory Writing Traits to a How-To Essay.** (p. 168)

Day 2
Analyze
Close Reading of the Model

Student Objectives
- Read a model how-to essay.

Student Activities
- Read **"Doing Research for a Town History Report."** (p. 169)

Day 3
Analyze
Introduce the Rubric

Student Objectives
- Learn to read a rubric.

Student Activities
- Review **"Doing Research for a Town History Report."** (p. 169)
- Read and discuss the **How-To Essay Rubric.** (pp. 170–171)

WEEK 2

Day 1
Write
Prewrite: Ideas

Student Objectives
- Read and understand a prewriting strategy.

Student Activities
- Read and discuss **Prewrite: Focus on Ideas.** (p. 176)
- Apply the prewriting strategy.

Day 2
Write
Prewrite: Organization

Student Objectives
- Make an Outline to organize ideas.

Student Activities
- Read and discuss **Prewrite: Focus on Organization.** (p. 177)
- Apply the prewriting strategy to create an Outline.

Day 3
Write
Draft: Voice

Student Objectives
- Use an Outline to begin writing.

Student Activities
- Read and discuss **Draft: Focus on Voice.** (p. 178)
- Apply the drafting strategy by using an Outline to write a draft.

WEEK 3

Day 1
Write
Revise: Word Choice

Student Objectives
- Revise to use precise words that help readers picture the process.

Student Activities
- Read and discuss **Revise: Focus on Word Choice.** (p. 181)
- Reflect on the model draft.
- Apply the revising strategy.
- Participate in a peer conference.

Day 2
Write
Revise: Sentence Fluency

Student Objectives
- Revise to vary sentence beginnings that guide the reader.

Student Activities
- Read and discuss **Revise: Focus on Sentence Fluency.** (p.182)
- Reflect on the model draft.
- Apply the revising strategy.

Note: Optional Revising Lessons are located at **www.sfw.z-b.com.**

Day 3
Write
Edit: Conventions

Student Objectives
- Edit for correct use of pronouns.

Student Activities
- Read and discuss **Edit: Focus on Conventions.** (p. 183)
- Reflect on the model draft.
- Apply the editing strategy.

Note: Teach the Conventions mini-lessons (pp. 184–185) if needed.

Analyze
Close Reading for the Traits

Student Objectives
- Read a model how-to essay.
- Use the how-to essay rubric.
- Use the model how-to essay to study Ideas, Organization, and Voice.

Student Activities
- Review **"Doing Research for a Town History Report."** (p. 169)
- Read and discuss **Using the Rubric to Analyze the Model.** (pp. 172–173)

Analyze
Close Reading for the Traits

Student Objectives
- Read a model how-to essay.
- Use the how-to essay rubric.
- Use the model how-to essay to study Word Choice, Sentence Fluency, and Conventions.

Student Activities
- Review **"Doing Research for a Town History Report."** (p. 169)
- Read and discuss **Using the Rubric to Analyze the Model.** (pp. 174–175)

Write
Draft

Student Objectives
- Complete a draft.

Student Activities
- Finish a draft. (p. 179)
- Participate in a peer conference.

Write
Revise: Ideas

Student Objectives
- Revise to remove details that are not related to the process.

Student Activities
- Read and discuss **Revise: Focus on Ideas.** (p. 180)

Write
Publish: +Presentation

Student Objectives
- Discuss preparation for publishing and presentation.
- Use a final editing checklist to publish their work.

Student Activities
- Read and discuss **Publish: +Presentation.** (p. 186)
- Apply the publishing strategy.

Write
Publish: +Presentation

Student Objectives
- Use a how-to essay rubric.
- Share a published how-to essay.

Student Activities
- Share their work.
- Use the rubric to reflect upon and evaluate the model and their own writing. (pp. 170–171, 187)

Resources at-a-Glance

Grammar, Usage & Mechanics

Differentiating Instruction
For additional Differentiating Instruction activities, see Strategies for Writers *Differentiated Instruction Activities at* **www.sfw.z-b.com.**

English Language Learners

Collaborative Conferencing

Tech Tips

 Strategies for Writers Online

Go to **www.sfw.z-b.com** for additional online resources for students, teachers, and parents.

Online Writing Center

Provides IWB resources, assessments, interactive games and practice activities, videos, eBooks, and a virtual file cabinet.

To complete the chapter in fewer days, combine the learning objectives and activities in a way that supports students as they write.

Introduce
How-To Essay

Student Objectives

- Review the elements of a how-to essay. *(p. 166)*
- Consider purpose and audience. *(p. 167)*
- Learn the traits of informative/ explanatory writing. *(p. 168)*

What's a How-To Essay?

Read aloud the definition for a how-to essay on the top of page 166. Then ask volunteers to respond and share their reasons for writing this type of essay in the past. **(Possible responses: to give written instructions on how to do something; to list materials and explain the steps for making or building something)** Point out that anytime writers explain a process in writing, they are using the how-to essay genre.

What's in a How-To Essay?

Discuss specific reasons why each element is essential to writing a credible how-to essay. Confirm students' understanding of these elements by reading aloud the definitions on page 166.

Strategies for Writers Online
Go to **www.sfw.z-b.com** for additional online resources for students, teachers, and parents.

What's a How-To Essay?

A how-to essay explains how to do or make something.

What's in a How-To Essay?

Materials
These are the things I will need to do my project. I might explain how to make a birdhouse. My materials for that project would be pieces of wood, a saw, a ruler, a pencil, and a hammer and nails.

Steps
Steps tell what you have to do to complete the task. To explain my project, I have to tell you the steps in order.

166 Informative/Explanatory Writing

Informative/Explanatory Text Exemplars (How-To Essay)

Espeland, Pamela. *See You Later, Procrastinator! (Get It Done).* **Free Spirit Publishing, 2007.** Espeland describes both the reasons and solutions for procrastination. She encourages the development of good habits and stresses the importance of maintaining those habits.

Fox, Janet S. *Get Organized Without Losing It.* **Free Spirit Publishing, 2006.** Fox recommends several ways to get students organized. From useful strategies to suggested supplies, *Get Organized Without Losing It* offers a variety of options to support disorganized youth.

Why write a How-To Essay?

People write how-to essays for a lot of different reasons. Here are two important ones.

To Inform
Sometimes I want to share what I know how to do with others. I can write the instructions in a how-to essay.

People have written how-to essays on many topics, from studying for a test to coaching a basketball team. If you want to know how to do something, you can probably find a how-to essay in a book or on the Internet.

To Entertain
My readers may want the instructions in a how-to essay for entertainment. I may write a how-to essay about origami so readers can enjoy making paper animals and flowers. I may write a how-to essay about building a birdhouse. The reader may build one in order to enjoy watching birds from the window.

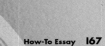

How-To Essay **167**

Kaufman, Richard. *Knack Magic Tricks: A Step-by-Step Guide to Illusions, Sleight of Hand, and Amazing Feats.* **Knack, 2010.** This step-by-step guide explains how to perform magic tricks through the use of text and photographs. The instructions provided are easy to follow and the "magic" is sure to engage readers.

Nissenberg, Sandra K. *The Everything Kids' Cookbook 2nd Edition: From Mac 'n Cheese to Double Chocolate Chip Cookies – 90 Recipes to Have Some Finger-lickin' Fun.* **Adams Media, 2008.** With 90 recipes to choose from, students have the opportunity to prepare a variety of different foods and drinks. Not only does this kid-friendly cookbook include tasty recipes, but it also presents students with safety tips and nutrition facts.

Why write a How-To Essay?

Discuss page 167 with students. As students participate in the discussion, remind them to speak in a way that is appropriate and productive for a classroom discussion.

Point out that all writing has a purpose and a specific audience. These authentic purposes help authors shape their writing. Someone writing to inform may want to share required steps for learning a skill. A writer whose purpose is to entertain may want to explain how to create fun projects. Ask students to consider their own reasons for writing how-to essays in the past. Were they writing to inform or entertain their audience? Ask them how their reasons will affect the tone and focus of their writing. **(Possible responses: To give instructions on a serious topic, such as test-taking strategies, the writer would use a serious, formal tone. To give instructions on a lighter topic, such as a kite-making project, the writer would probably use a lighter, more casual tone.)** Conclude by telling students that they are going to study and practice strategies for writing a how-to essay.

CCSS **Common Core State Standards** (pp. Z20–Z30)
Language: L.4.3c
Speaking and Listening: SL.4.1a, SL.4.1b, SL.4.1c, SL.4.1d, SL.4.3, SL.4.6

Introduce
How-To Essay

Linking Informative/ Explanatory Writing Traits to a How-To Essay

Read page 168 aloud to help students understand that they will follow Alika as he models using the writing process and the informative/explanatory writing traits together.

As they follow Alika, students will see how the Informative/ Explanatory Writing Traits have been adapted and applied to writing a how-to essay. They will see that this type of essay gives information and, therefore, has many factors in common with other types of informative/explanatory writing. However, the particular audience and purpose of a how-to essay determine how the traits are used.

Online Writing Center

Provides six **interactive anchor papers** for each text type.

Linking Informative/Explanatory Writing Traits to a How-To Essay

In this chapter, you will write to explain how to do something. This type of informative/explanatory writing is called a how-to essay. Alika will guide you through the stages of the writing process: Prewrite, Draft, Revise, Edit, and Publish. In each stage, Alika will show you important writing strategies that are linked to the Informative/Explanatory Writing Traits below.

Informative/Explanatory Writing Traits

- clear topic and main ideas
- details, information, and examples that answer the reader's questions about the topic

- a strong introduction, body, and conclusion
- well-organized paragraphs
- transitions that connect ideas

- a voice and tone that are appropriate for the purpose and audience

- precise words
- domain-specific vocabulary that is used correctly and explained as necessary

- clear, direct sentences that flow smoothly

- no or few errors in grammar, usage, mechanics, and spelling

Before you write, read Carlos Ortiz's how-to essay on the next page. Then use the how-to essay rubric on pages 170–171 to decide how well he did. (You might want to look back at What's in a How-To Essay? on page 166, too!)

Informative/Explanatory Writing Traits in a How-To Essay

 **Ideas** The essay tells how to do or make something. All details are related to the process.

 **Organization** There is a strong introduction, body, and conclusion. All the steps in the essay are well-organized.

 **Voice** The writer uses a voice that is appropriate for the purpose and the audience. Using a natural and informative tone is the best way to achieve this in a how-to essay.

Doing Research for a Town History Report

How-To MODEL Essay

by Carlos Ortiz

What was your town like when it was brand-new? Many towns have an interesting history. Research your town's history and write a report that tells about the "early days."

A good place to begin your report is with the founding of the town. Before you start your research, you should make a list of questions you want to answer. Here are some important questions: Where is the town located? When was the town built? Who were the first people who lived there? Why did they think this was a good place to start a community? What were their plans for the future?

There are many places to look for this information. <u>Start</u> by visiting the town hall or the library. Some towns also have a local history museum. <u>Town records and old newspapers</u> are great sources of information. *step*

materials

After you have <u>collected a lot of facts</u> about the early days of your town, you can look for pictures to put in your report. <u>Maps and photographs</u> can show how the town has grown and how buildings have changed. *step*

materials

While you do your research, make sure to write down the sources for all your facts and stories. A good research report ends with a list of all the sources the writer used.

Don't start writing your report just yet, though! The next step is likely to be the most fun. Seek out the "living memory" of your town. A town's "living memory" is the oldest members of the community. They have seen a lot during their own lifetimes. They might even remember stories told by their parents or grandparents. Maybe some of their ancestors helped settle the town.

Finally, it's time to <u>write</u> your report. By this time you should be quite an expert on your town's early days. *final step*

How-To Essay **169**

Word Choice The essay uses precise language (specific nouns and strong verbs) to help the reader "see" the process.

Sentence Fluency Sentence beginnings are varied and help the essay flow smoothly.

Conventions The writer should always proofread carefully prior to publishing. Correct use and spelling of words, particularly pronouns, enhances the clarity of the writing in a how-to essay.

Analyze
Close Reading of the Model

Week 1 • Day 2

Student Objectives

- Read a model how-to essay. *(p. 169)*

Read the Model

Read "Doing Research for a Town History Report" aloud to the class. Ask students to listen for a clear topic (how to do something or make something) and main ideas supported by details that are related to the process. Encourage them to notice how the essay is organized. Also ask students to think about and discuss how a natural and informative voice affects how they connect with the writer.

Elements of a How-To Essay

Have students refer to What's in a How-To Essay? on page 166 as you refer to the model. Discuss the notes written on the model to enhance students' understanding of the terms. Then discuss what is likely to happen if someone tries to follow the instructions in a how-to essay in which necessary materials or steps are missing.

CCSS Common Core State Standards (pp. Z20–Z30)
Writing: W.4.6
Language: L.4.3c
Speaking and Listening: SL.4.1a, SL.4.1b, SL.4.1c, SL.4.1d, SL.4.2, SL.4.3, SL.4.6

Analyze
Introduce the Rubric

Week 1 • Day 3

Student Objectives

• Learn to read a rubric.
  (pp. 170–171)

Introduce the Rubric

Explain the Rubric Explain that a rubric is a tool for planning, improving, and assessing a piece of writing. Tell students that a rubric helps a writer focus on key elements, or traits, in writing (**Ideas, Organization, Voice, Word Choice, Sentence Fluency, Conventions,** and **Presentation**).

Explain the 6-point system. Point out that the columns on page 170 represent a good paper that might need some polishing but that the columns on page 171 represent writing that needs considerable improvement.

Discuss the Rubric Guide students in a discussion of the rubric. Read the descriptors that go with each trait. Discuss the difference between columns to be sure students fully understand the point system. Tell students to keep the rubric in mind when they write their own how-to essay and again when they revise it.

How-To Essay Rubric

Use this rubric to analyze the model. Then use it to plan and score your own how-to essay.

	6	**5**	**4**	
Ideas	The essay tells how to do or make something. All details are related to the process.	The essay tells how to do or make something. Most of the details are related to the process.	The essay tells how to do or make something. One or two details seem unrelated to the process.	
Organization	All the steps are labeled and in the right order. Appropriate transitions guide the reader by linking the sentences.	Most of the steps are labeled and in the right order. Most transitions guide the reader by linking the sentences.	Some steps may be out of order. Some transitions guide the reader by linking the sentences.	
Voice	The writer's voice sounds natural and informative. It is clear that the writer cares about the topic.	The writer's voice sounds natural and informative most of the time. The writer cares about the topic.	The writer sounds too formal or is not informative in places. The reader cannot always tell that the writer cares about the topic.	
Word Choice	The writer uses precise language (specific nouns and strong verbs) that help the reader "see" the process.	More specific nouns or stronger verbs are needed to help the reader "see" the process.	Some verbs and nouns are specific and used appropriately. A few may be vague, but they are not distracting.	
Sentence Fluency	Sentence beginnings are varied and helpful to the reader.	Sentence beginnings are mostly varied and helpful to the reader.	A few sentence beginnings are repetitive.	
Conventions	All pronouns are used correctly.	Most pronouns are used correctly. Errors do not distract the reader.	A few pronouns are used incorrectly, but the errors do not interfere with meaning.	

✚ Presentation All paragraphs are indented.

CCSS Common Core State Standards

How-To Essay

Strategies for Writers was designed and written to incorporate the Common Core State Standards throughout every unit. By presenting the standards in as many applications as possible, your students' exposure to them will be ensured.

The lessons for the how-to essay are based principally on the writing standards for Informative/Explanatory writing. The rubrics and writing strategies reflect the writing standard **W.4.2**. This standard focuses on conveying ideas and information clearly through facts, good organization, precise language, and domain-specific vocabulary in an informative/explanatory piece of writing.

Online Writing Center

Provides a variety of **interactive rubrics,** including 4-, 5-, and 6-point models.

	3	2	1	
	The essay tries to explain how to do or make something. Some details are unclear or unnecessary.	The essay tries to explain how to do or make something, but key steps are vague or missing.	The topic is not clear. The details seem to be unrelated.	**Ideas**
	Steps are not in the right order. Transitions are needed to guide the reader by linking the sentences.	Most steps are not labeled or in the right order. Transitions are confusing or missing.	Steps are not in order. The writing is hard to follow.	**Organization**
	The writer's voice sounds distant or unsure some of the time. It is not clear that the writer cares about the topic.	The voice may not be appropriate for the purpose and audience. The reader cannot tell the writer's attitude toward the subject.	The voice is very weak or absent. The reader cannot get a sense of the writer's purpose.	**Voice**
	Many imprecise nouns and vague verbs confuse the process.	Too many general words keep the reader from picturing the process in some parts.	The words are too general or repetitive. The reader cannot picture the process.	**Word Choice**
	Some sentence beginnings are not varied.	Sentence beginnings are not varied or helpful.	Sentences are incomplete or incorrect.	**Sentence Fluency**
	There are several errors with pronouns. The reader is confused.	Frequent errors with pronouns make it hard to read and understand the text.	The writing contains major errors. It is very difficult to read.	**Conventions**

See Appendix B for 4-, 5-, and 6-point informative/explanatory rubrics.

The language standards for grade 4 students are addressed during editing and skills practice. There are also multiple opportunities to address the speaking and listening standards. Most importantly, this chapter will help students produce clear and coherent writing (**W.4.4**), improve writing (**W.4.5**), and use technologies to publish and present finished pieces (**W.4.6**).

Find Evidence in the Model

Small-Group Collaboration
Assign students to small groups and tell them to evaluate the model using the rubric. Assign one person in each group to record the group's findings and one person to report the findings to the class. Instruct students to score the model for each trait based on evidence in the text. Remind students to read closely to identify examples to support their high or low scores. Note: Although the models were written to score high in each trait, students should not assume each trait would receive a 6, the top score.

Teacher-Led Discussion Bring the class back together, and have the reporters present their findings and scores. Prompt groups to provide evidence and examples for their scores from the model as needed.

Additional Rubrics

Appendix B includes 4-, 5-, and 6-point rubrics that can be used with any piece of informative/ explanatory writing. The rubrics are also available as blackline masters in the back of this Teacher Edition.

CCSS **Common Core State Standards** (pp. Z20–Z30)
Writing: W.4.6
Language: L.4.3c
Speaking and Listening: SL.4.1a, SL.4.1b, SL.4.1c, SL.4.1d, SL.4.2, SL.4.3, SL.4.6

Analyze
Close Reading for the Traits

Week 1 • Day 4

- Read a model how-to essay. (p. 169)
- Use the how-to essay rubric. (pp. 170–171)
- Use the model how-to essay to study **Ideas, Organization,** and **Voice.** (pp. 172–173)

Find Evidence in the Model

Evaluate the Model Have volunteers read aloud each section on pages 172–173. Determine whether students agree with each point in Alika's assessment. Use the questions below to initiate the discussion. Be sure students can back up their answers with specific examples from the essay.

Discuss Audience, Task, Purpose Ask students one or more of the following questions as they analyze the model:

- **Audience** Who is the audience? (Possible response: other students)

- **Task** How does Carlos Ortiz share information about his topic? (Possible response: He includes the steps and materials needed.)

- **Purpose** What is Carlos's purpose for writing this report? (Possible response: to inform his readers about how to do research)

 **Strategies for Writers Online**
Go to **www.sfw.z-b.com** for additional online resources for students, teachers, and parents.

How-To Essay

Using the Rubric to Analyze the Model

Did you notice that the model on page 169 points out some key elements of a how-to essay? As he wrote "Doing Research for a Town History Report," Carlos Ortiz used these elements to help him explain how to do research. He also used the 6-point rubric on pages 170–171 to plan, draft, revise, and edit the writing. A rubric is a great tool to evaluate writing during the writing process.

Now let's use the same rubric to score the model. To do this, we'll focus on each trait separately, starting with Ideas. We'll use the top descriptor for each trait (column 6), along with examples from the model, to help us understand how the traits work together. How would you score Carlos on each trait?

 **Ideas**
- The essay tells how to do or make something.
- All details are related to the process.

This essay gave me lots of good information on how to do research for a town history report. The writer explains all the important steps for gathering materials. All the details he includes, like the ones below, tell me something about writing a good town history report.

While you do your research, make sure to write down the sources for all your facts and stories. A good research report ends with a list of all the sources the writer used.

English Language Learners

BEGINNING

How-To Write *how-to* on the board. Ask a student to come to the front of the classroom. Tell him or her, *Show us **how** you write your name.* The student should write his or her name on the board. Ask other students to perform other tasks, such as *Show us **how** you tie your shoes/brush your teeth/smile/snap your fingers.* After each student demonstrates a task, say, *Thank you for showing us **how to** do that.*

INTERMEDIATE

How-To Write *how-to* on the board. Select a student and say, *Show me how to clap your hands.* After the student claps, ask the class to repeat the sentence. Write *Show me how to ____.* on the board. Have students ask a partner to show them how to do something and then switch roles. Switch partners and repeat.

 **Organization**
- All the steps are labeled and in the right order.
- Appropriate transitions guide the reader by linking the sentences.

Carlos writes all the steps in order. His essay is easy to follow because he makes sure the reader knows what to do first to research a town. In this example, he tells the reader to begin by visiting the town hall or the library.

There are many places to look for this information. Start by visiting the town hall or the library. Some towns also have a local history museum. Town records and old newspapers are great sources of information.

After you have collected a lot of facts about the early days of your town, you can look for pictures to put in your report.

 **Voice**
- The writer's voice sounds natural and informative.
- It is clear that the writer cares about the topic.

I can tell that Carlos cares about learning his town's history. His voice sounds natural all the way through, and he sounds like an expert on writing research reports. The introduction is a good example. He seems to be talking directly to me.

What was your town like when it was brand-new? Many towns have an interesting history. Research your town's history and write a report that tells about the "early days."

How-To Essay 173

Discuss the Traits Ask students one or more of the following questions to discuss the traits in the model:

Ideas Does Carlos explain how to do something? Are all the details related? (Possible responses: Yes, Carlos makes his topic clear in the first paragraph. His essay is about how to find interesting details about a town. All of the details in the essay belong to the topic.)

Organization How does Carlos organize his essay? (Possible responses: Carlos organizes his essay by putting the steps for finding a town's history in order. The steps are clear and easy to follow. He uses helpful transition words to guide the reader.)

Voice Does Carlos use a voice that is appropriate for the purpose and audience? (Possible responses: Yes, Carlos uses a natural and informative voice. It's clear that he likes his topic. He speaks directly to the reader.)

ADVANCED

How-To Have students follow along as you show them how to do something simple, such as make a paper airplane or animal. Use deliberate, simple steps as you describe the task, including order words such as *first, next, then,* and so on. When you are finished, have students work with a partner to restate the steps of the task in order.

ADVANCED HIGH

How-To Have partners tell each other how to make their favorite snack. Suggest they include a list of ingredients and the materials necessary to make the snack. When they are finished describing the task, have the partners write the recipe.

CCSS **Common Core State Standards** (pp. Z20–Z30)
Writing: W.4.2c
Language: L.4.3c, L.4.6
Speaking and Listening: SL.4.1a, SL.4.1b, SL.4.1c, SL.4.1d, SL.4.3, SL.4.4, SL.4.6

Analyze
Close Reading for the Traits

Week 1 • Day 5

Student Objectives

- Read a model how-to essay. (p. 169)
- Use the how-to essay rubric. (pp. 170–171)
- Use the model how-to essay to study **Word Choice, Sentence Fluency,** and **Conventions.** (pp. 174–175)

Discuss the Traits Ask students one or more of the following questions to discuss the traits in the model:

Word Choice Does Carlos use precise language to help the reader see the process? Which specific nouns and strong verbs did he use to help visualize the steps? (Possible responses: Carlos uses a strong verb, *collected*, in the fourth paragraph to paint a clear picture. He also uses specific nouns such as *maps* and *photographs* to tell what kinds of pictures he means.)

Sentence Fluency Which part of the model uses sentence beginnings that are especially varied and helpful to the reader? How is it helpful? (Possible response: The beginnings of his sentences help the reader follow the ideas.)

Conventions Does Carlos use pronouns and antecedents correctly? (Possible response: Yes, Carlos uses them correctly.)

Strategies for Writers Online
Go to **www.sfw.z-b.com** for additional online resources for students, teachers, and parents.

Using the How-To Essay Rubric to Analyze the Model

- The writer uses precise language (specific nouns and strong verbs) that help the reader "see" the process.

Reading the essay, I could picture the different steps in researching a town history report. In this paragraph, *collected* is a strong verb that paints a clearer picture than if Carlos had used a weak verb like *gotten*. The words *maps and photographs* are specific and tell what kinds of pictures he means.

> After you have collected a lot of facts about the early days of your town, you can look for pictures to put in your report. Maps and photographs can show how the town has grown and how buildings have changed.

- Sentence beginnings are varied and helpful to the reader.

The writer helped me follow the steps by giving helpful information at the beginnings of the sentences. Here's a good example. Notice how the words at the beginning of each sentence help the reader follow along.

> A good place to begin your report is with the founding of the town. Before you start your research, you should make a list of questions you want to answer. Here are some important questions: Where is the town located? When was the town built? Who were the first people who lived there?

Tech Tips
Online Tools

Use Multimodal Texts Asking students to work from a model text for how-to essays might take you online to view VoiceThreads, YouTube videos, or other multimodal texts that use image, sound, movement, and text to communicate what students are typically asked to do with words only. Finding these kinds of texts requires specific keyword searches and using "advanced search" options within your browser. Be sure to search for video, slide show (e.g., .ppt files), or audio when searching. When viewing, note how different modes communicate meaning.

See **www.sfw.z-b.com** for further information about and links to these websites and tools.

 • All pronouns are used correctly.

Every word in the essay is spelled correctly. All the sentences begin with an uppercase letter and end with the correct punctuation. When Carlos uses a pronoun in place of a noun, he uses it correctly.

A town's "living memory" is the oldest members of the community. They have seen a lot during their own lifetimes. They might even remember stories told by their parents or grandparents.

✛ Presentation All paragraphs are indented.

My Turn!

Now it's my turn to write a how-to essay! I'll use the rubric and good writing strategies to help me. Read along to see how I do this.

ENRICHMENT

Use the Rubric to Score a Model Have partners score the model essay on page 169 using the top descriptors (column 6) for each trait in the rubric on pages 170–171. Have them share and defend their scores for each trait.

REINFORCEMENT

Understand the Traits Make a transparency of the rubric on page 170. Highlight the Ideas trait in column 6. Then say: *The Ideas trait says the how-to essay should tell how to do or make something.* Point out Carlos's topic in the first paragraph: Research your town's history. Then say: *The second part says that all details relate to the process.* Help students identify the details in each paragraph. Continue to model the other traits.

✛ Presentation Discuss why Presentation is equally as important as the other traits. Stress the importance of neatness. An essay should be clearly handwritten in pen or typed, and paragraphs should be indented (using the tab key if typed). Discuss how white space can be used to organize text, especially to clearly separate paragraphs. Good margins make the line lengths comfortable to read, and a centered title stands out on a page. If needed, work with students to demonstrate word-processing features. Encourage them to think about how good formatting aids the reader.

Think About the Traits

Once students have thoroughly discussed Carlos Ortiz's model how-to essay, ask them which traits they think are most important in a how-to essay and have them explain why. (Possible response: Organization is very important because if the steps in the essay are not labeled and in the right order, then it makes no sense. Word Choice is very important because by using precise language the writer helps the reader "see" the process.)

CCSS **Common Core State Standards** (pp. Z20–Z30)
Writing: W.4.6
Language: L.4.3c
Speaking and Listening: SL.4.1a, SL.4.1b, SL.4.1c, SL.4.1d, SL.4.3, SL.4.6

Write
How-To Essay

Week 2 • Day 1

Student Objectives

• Read and understand a prewriting strategy. *(p. 176)*

Prewrite

Focus on Ideas

Narrow Topic Tell students that they will be choosing a topic for their own how-to essay. Stress the importance of choosing a topic they like and one with several clear steps. For example, a topic such as "How to Play Baseball" is too broad. A topic like "How to Grip a Baseball Bat" is more focused, and a clear and complete description of the steps involved is possible.

Take Notes Point out Alika's notes on page 176. Explain to students that, like Alika, they should use note cards to take notes about their topic. Point out that Alika will probably include more details about his topic as he starts to write.

Organizing Information
Emphasize that writing can be organized in many ways, and one way is to list the steps from first to last. An Outline can help writers organize information in this way.

Online Writing Center

 Provides **interactive graphic organizers** as well as a variety of graphic organizers in PDF format.

T176 Informative/Explanatory Writing

Write a How-To Essay

Prewrite
Focus on **Ideas**

The Rubric Says	The essay tells how to do or make something.
Writing Strategy	Choose something to do or make. Make a list of all the important steps.

My teacher asked us to think of something we can do or make. I thought about the chocolate brownies my Grandma taught me to make. I decided my essay would explain how to make these great brownies! I'm sure lots of the kids in my class would like to try making them. To get started, I should make a list of all the important steps.

Important Steps for Making Brownies

• Melt butter, semisweet chocolate, and milk chocolate chips.
• Use a saucepan.
• Put in eggs and vanilla (beat the eggs).
• Add brown sugar and honey.
• Add flour and salt.
• Put in the macadamia nuts.

• Spread the batter in a baking pan, and bake for 30 minutes.
• You need a square baking pan.
• Put a little butter and parchment paper in the bottom of the pan.
• Cool brownies before you cut them into squares.

Write
Brainstorm a list of things that you like to do or make. Pick one that you think would be interesting to write about in a how-to essay. Then make a list of all the important steps.

176 Informative/Explanatory Writing

English Language Learners

BEGINNING/ INTERMEDIATE
Specific vs. Broad On the board, write *games, making a free throw, basketball, shooting the ball.* Discuss the meanings of any words students don't know. Draw a pyramid on the board. Ask students, *What is the biggest topic?* When students answer *games,* write it at the bottom of the pyramid and erase it from the original list. Then ask, *Now what?* Introduce the terms *broad* and *specific.*

ADVANCED/ ADVANCED HIGH
Outlines On the board, write an outline with the following headings: I. Introduction; II. Body; III. Conclusion. Have partners write a list of steps about how to make something. Then have them organize the steps into the Body section of the outline. After that, they should write a brief introduction and conclusion.

Prewrite

Focus on **Organization**

The Rubric Says	All the steps are labeled and in the right order.
Writing Strategy	Make an outline to list the steps from first to last.

The rubric says that my steps need to be in order. I can use an outline to put my list of steps for making brownies in order, from first to last.

Outline

I. **Introduction**
   I make chocolate brownies that taste like Hawaii to me.

II. **Body**
   A. Butter and line the bottom of a square baking pan with parchment paper.
   B. Melt butter, semisweet chocolate, and milk chocolate chips together in a saucepan.
   C. Add brown sugar and honey.
   D. Put in beaten eggs and vanilla.
   E. Add flour, salt, and nuts.
   F. Spread the batter in a baking pan and bake for 30 minutes.

III. **Conclusion**
   Let the brownies cool, and then cut them into squares and eat them.

Writer's Term
Outline
An **outline** is a writing plan that lists the main ideas next to roman numerals. It lists the details next to letters.

Analyze

Look at Alika's notes and his outline. How do they help him organize the information?

Write

Look at the list of important steps that you made. Use an outline to organize your steps. Put them in order, from first step to last step.

How-To Essay **177**

Collaborative Conferencing

PEER TO PEER Have students exchange organizers. Have partners ask these questions as they review them: *Is there information the writer could add to help me better understand the writer's topic? Are all the steps listed in order?* Tell partners to write one or two comments on a sticky note and return the Outline to the writer.

PEER GROUPS Have students form small groups of three or four to provide feedback on improving their organizers. Have students share their notes and outlines. Encourage other students to take turns offering helpful suggestions.

TEACHER-LED Conference with individual students about their Outlines. Before they speak with you, encourage students to think of questions to ask about points they found difficult in creating the outline.

Write
How-To Essay

Week 2 • Day 2

Student Objectives

• Make an Outline to organize ideas. (*p. 177*)

Prewrite

Focus on

Organize Ideas Point out that an outline includes an introduction, body, and conclusion. Each letter in the body represents a step for making brownies. Discuss why it is important that students put steps in order. (**Possible response: By putting the steps in order, a writer can identify important information, where it goes in the essay, and what information might be missing.**) Then ask why an Outline is an effective tool for planning a how-to essay. (**Possible response: An Outline is a writing plan that helps organize the essay. An Outline organizes information into an introduction, a body, and a conclusion.**)

(Go to **www.sfw.z-b.com** for the downloadable graphic organizer.)

Writer's Term

Outline An Outline lists the main ideas of an essay. It shows the order of the steps, the relative importance of each, and the relationship between each step. An Outline is also helpful for pointing out information that doesn't belong and should be removed.

CCSS **Common Core State Standards** (pp. Z20–Z30)
Writing: W.4.2a, W.4.2b, W.4.2e, W.4.4, W.4.5, W.4.6, W.4.8, W.4.10
Language: L.4.6

Write
How-To Essay

Week 2 • Day 3

Student Objectives

• Use an Outline to begin writing. (p. 178)

Draft

Focus on Voice

Organize Information Read page 178 aloud. Review the term *draft*, making sure that students realize that it is a "rough" form of a written document. Remind students that drafting offers a chance to write down ideas without having to worry about mistakes. Be sure students understand that they will use their Outlines to guide them through the drafting process.

Use a Friendly Voice Direct students to read Alika's draft on page 179. Discuss why he is using a friendly, natural voice. (Baking brownies is fun, so he wants his voice to be relaxed but still informative.)

Develop a Logical Order Discuss the other notes written on the draft. Point out that Alika uses his Outline to put his steps in order and refers to the rubric on page 170 as he writes.

Note: Proofreading marks are shown on page 179 to facilitate marking changes in the draft.

Draft

Focus on **Voice**

The Rubric Says	The writer's voice sounds natural and informative. It is clear that the writer cares about the topic.
Writing Strategy	Use a friendly, natural voice so that the reader can picture the process.

Now it's time to write the first draft of my how-to essay. I'll use my outline to keep the steps in my essay organized. I know from the rubric that I need to use a voice that sounds natural and informative. I'll keep my writing voice sounding friendly and natural by "talking" to my reader directly. I will also include useful information so I sound like an expert on the topic.

I always do my best with spelling and grammar, but I won't worry about mistakes right now. I'll get a chance to fix them later. The beginning of my draft is on the next page.

178 Informative/Explanatory Writing

Differentiating Instruction

ENRICHMENT

Use Logical Order At the top of a sheet of paper, write a starter sentence for a familiar process, such as borrowing a book from the library. Pass it to a student who writes down the next logical step and folds the paper so only the last sentence shows. Have the student pass it on. Continue until all have contributed. Unfold and read the "essay" aloud. Discuss connections (or misconnections) between the steps.

REINFORCEMENT

Visualize the Steps Have students close their eyes and visualize beginning a task. Say: *You're beginning your task. What materials or tools do you need? What will you do first? What do you need to complete step two?* Continue this process until the task is complete.

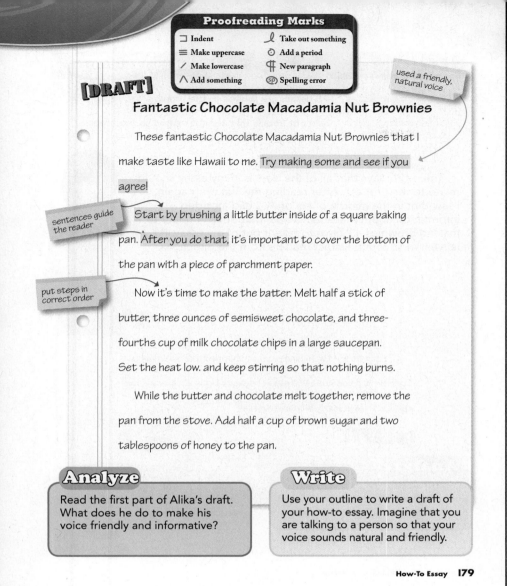

Proofreading Marks

⌐ Indent   ℓ Take out something
≡ Make uppercase   ⊙ Add a period
/ Make lowercase   ¶ New paragraph
∧ Add something   ⑤℗ Spelling error

[DRAFT]

used a friendly, natural voice

Fantastic Chocolate Macadamia Nut Brownies

These fantastic Chocolate Macadamia Nut Brownies that I make taste like Hawaii to me. Try making some and see if you agree!

sentences guide the reader

Start by brushing a little butter inside of a square baking pan. After you do that, it's important to cover the bottom of the pan with a piece of parchment paper.

put steps in correct order

Now it's time to make the batter. Melt half a stick of butter, three ounces of semisweet chocolate, and three-fourths cup of milk chocolate chips in a large saucepan. Set the heat low. and keep stirring so that nothing burns.

While the butter and chocolate melt together, remove the pan from the stove. Add half a cup of brown sugar and two tablespoons of honey to the pan.

Analyze

Read the first part of Alika's draft. What does he do to make his voice friendly and informative?

Write

Use your outline to write a draft of your how-to essay. Imagine that you are talking to a person so that your voice sounds natural and friendly.

How-To Essay **179**

Collaborative Conferencing

PEER TO PEER Have students exchange their drafts to determine if the writer used a friendly, natural voice to help readers picture the process. Tell students to think of two other questions they would like to ask about the steps. Have them write their questions on sticky notes and affix them to their partner's draft.

PEER GROUPS Have students form groups of four and pass their draft to the student on their right. That student writes one comment on a sticky note affixed to the draft and passes the draft to the right. The review ends when everyone has received his or her own draft back with three comments.

TEACHER-LED Conference with pairs of students. Have them read each other's drafts. Coach them in giving and receiving constructive feedback.

Write
How-To Essay

Student Objectives

• Complete a draft. *(p. 179)*

Continue Drafting It is important that students are given ample time to draft how-to essays. As conferencing is important throughout the writing process, be sure to also plan time for peer-to-peer, peer group, or teacher-led conferences. Remind students that this is the time for getting their ideas down on paper in a creative and engaging way. Assure them that they will have plenty of time to fix any mistakes later.

Before students meet in conferences, remind them of how to speak to one another appropriately. The words should be clearly spoken, and students should be respectful of one another.

CCSS **C**ommon **C**ore **S**tate **S**tandards (pp. Z20–Z30)
Writing: W.4.2a, W.4.4, W.4.5, W.4.6, W.4.10

Write
How-To Essay

Student Objectives

- Revise to remove details that are not related to the process. (p. 180)

Revise

Focus on (Ideas)

Remove Unrelated Details Direct students to page 180, and read the introduction aloud. Discuss the importance of making sure that the essay includes only details that are related to the process. Have one volunteer read the draft excerpt without the revisions, and then another volunteer read it with the revision. Ask students to identify the information that Alika deleted.

Then discuss the writer's reason for taking out unrelated information from the essay. (Possible responses: Unrelated information distracts the reader or could be confusing to the reader.) Point out how much more focused Alika's writing is after he removed the unrelated information. Remind students that all of the details in their essay should relate to their process. Direct them to read through their drafts and remove unnecessary information.

 Strategies for Writers Online
Go to **www.sfw.z-b.com** for additional online resources for students, teachers, and parents.

Revise   Focus on (Ideas)

The Rubric Says	All details are related to the process.
Writing Strategy	Take out details that are not related to the process.

The rubric says that all of the details in my essay should relate to the process. After reading my first draft again, I saw that in the middle of my draft, I had included information about macadamia nuts that doesn't relate to making brownies. I'll have to take it out of my essay. If I leave it in, it could distract readers from the directions.

Finally stir in two-thirds cup of chopped macadamia nuts.
~~I don't chop the nuts too much because I love a big, crunchy~~
~~piece of nut in every bite of brownie!~~

deleted unnecessary information

[DRAFT]

Analyze
Look at Alika's revision. Why did he delete the information?

Write
Read your draft again. Delete any details that are not related to the process.

English Language Learners

BEGINNING/ INTERMEDIATE
Pronouns Point to a pile of books on your desk. Write and say, *The books are on my desk.* Erase *The books* and ask, *Which is correct,* It *or* They? Repeat the activity with the subjects *The pile of books, The book,* and *Susan's book.* Remember to also change the verbs, if applicable.

ADVANCED/ ADVANCED HIGH
Relevant Facts Students must decide if information is relevant to the topic. Give students the main idea, such as *Paper hats are easy to make,* and list several related and unrelated ideas, such as *it takes only a few steps to make a hat, they look funny when you wear them, you can use newspaper for your hat,* and so on. Have students circle the information that is relevant to the topic.

Revise
Focus on **Word Choice**

The Rubric Says The writer uses precise language (specific nouns and strong verbs) that help the reader "see" the process.

Writing Strategy Use words that help readers picture the process.

I know from the rubric that I should use specific nouns and strong verbs. Precise words help the reader understand the process. A word like *batter* instead of *brownies* is more helpful for the beginning of the process. A word like *spread* gives a better picture of how to put the batter in the pan.

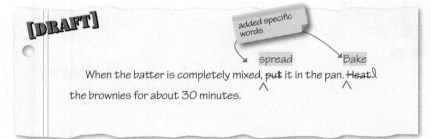

[DRAFT]

added specific words

spread   Bake

When the batter is completely mixed, ~~put~~ it in the pan. ~~Heat~~

the brownies for about 30 minutes.

Analyze
Look at Alika's revisions. How do they help the reader picture the process?

Write
Read your draft. Add specific nouns and strong verbs to help your reader picture the process.

How-To Essay **181**

Collaborative Conferencing

PEER TO PEER Have pairs of students exchange drafts. After reading the draft, have each student suggest two or three words that could be more precise. Writers should consult print or online word resources for replacement words.

PEER GROUPS Have students form small groups. Ask them to take turns reading sections of their drafts aloud. Group members should suggest specific nouns and strong verbs to help readers picture the process.

TEACHER-LED Conference with individual students about their drafts. Point out places where specific nouns and strong verbs could be added to strengthen Word Choice throughout the essay.

Write
How-To Essay

Week 3 • Day 1

Student Objectives

• Revise to use precise words that help readers picture the process. (*p. 181*)

Revise

Focus on **Word Choice**

Use Precise Words Direct students to page 181, and read the introduction aloud. Explain to students that specific nouns and strong verbs help readers "see" the process. Have one volunteer read the draft excerpt without the revisions, and then another volunteer read the revised excerpt. Ask students to identify the information that Alika added.

Then ask why writers should be sure to include specific nouns and strong verbs in their how-to essays. (Possible responses: Specific nouns and strong verbs help readers "see" the process. Exact words make it easier for the reader to understand the different steps.) Point out how much clearer Alika's writing is after he added *spread* and *Bake*. Remind students that they should be sure to use precise words in their essays. Have students read through their drafts and replace vague words with specific ones.

CCSS **Common Core State Standards** (pp. Z20–Z30)
Writing: W.4.2b, W.4.2d, W.4.4, W.4.5, W.4.10
Language: L.4.3a, L.4.6

Write
How-To Essay

Week 3 • Day 2

Student Objectives

- Revise to vary sentence beginnings that guide the reader. *(p. 182)*

Revise

Focus on Sentence Fluency

Vary Sentence Beginnings Read the introduction to page 182 aloud. Remind students that the rubric says that sentence beginnings should be varied and helpful to the reader. Stress to students that in a how-to essay it is important that the audience be able to follow the steps of the process that the writer is describing. The writer can guide the audience by giving helpful information at the beginning of the sentences. This makes it easier for the reader to follow along. Otherwise, readers may become confused in the middle of the process.

Explain that words like *now* and *first* are easier to find if they are put at the beginning of sentences. They also help to link ideas together and make the writing flow smoothly. Encourage students to review their drafts and add sentence beginnings that guide the reader.

Online Writing Center

Provides **interactive proofreading activities** for each genre.

Revise

Focus on **Sentence Fluency**

The Rubric Says Sentence beginnings are varied and helpful to the reader.

Writing Strategy Make sure sentence beginnings guide the reader.

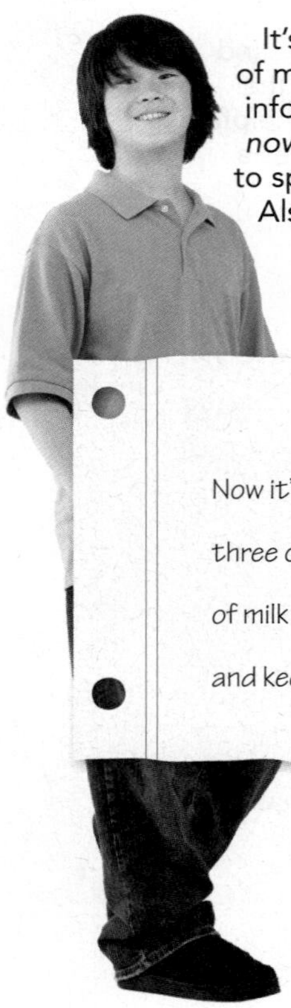

It's important that the reader is able to follow the steps of my essay. I can guide the reader by placing helpful information at the beginnings of the sentences. Words like *now* and *first* show the order of the steps. They are easier to spot if I put them at the beginning of the sentences. Also, they make my writing sound smooth.

[DRAFT]

added helpful word

Now it's time to make the batter. First Melt half a stick of butter, three ounces of semisweet chocolate, and three-fourths cup of milk chocolate chips in a large saucepan. Set the heat low, and keep stirring so that nothing burns.

fixed punctuation

Write

Read your draft. If needed, revise your sentences so that they guide the reader through the process.

Optional Revising Lessons

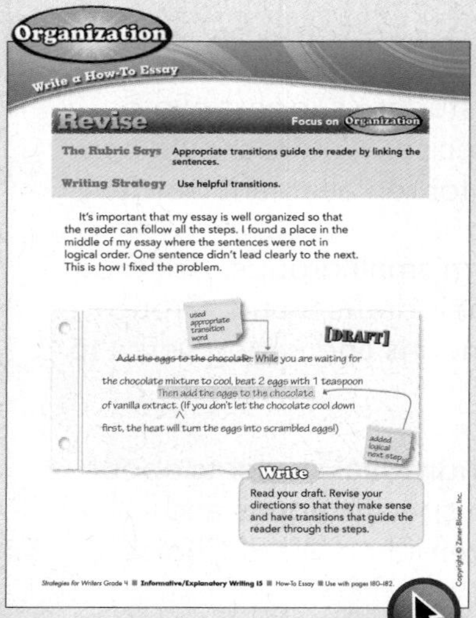
Organization

Write a How-To Essay

Revise — Focus on Organization

The Rubric Says Appropriate transitions guide the reader by linking the sentences.

Writing Strategy Use helpful transitions.

It's important that my essay is well organized so that the reader can follow all the steps. I found a place in the middle of my essay where the sentences were not in logical order. One sentence didn't lead clearly to the next. This is how I fixed the problem.

[DRAFT]

used appropriate transition word

~~Add the eggs to the chocolate.~~ While you are waiting for the chocolate mixture to cool, beat 2 eggs with 1 teaspoon of vanilla extract. Then add the eggs to the chocolate. (If you don't let the chocolate cool down first, the heat will turn the eggs into scrambled eggs!)

added logical next step

Write

Read your draft. Revise your directions so that they make sense and have transitions that guide the reader through the steps.

Strategies for Writers Grade 4 ■ Informative/Explanatory Writing 15 ■ How-To Essay ■ Use with pages 180–182.

Copyright © Zaner-Bloser, Inc.

Informative/Explanatory 15

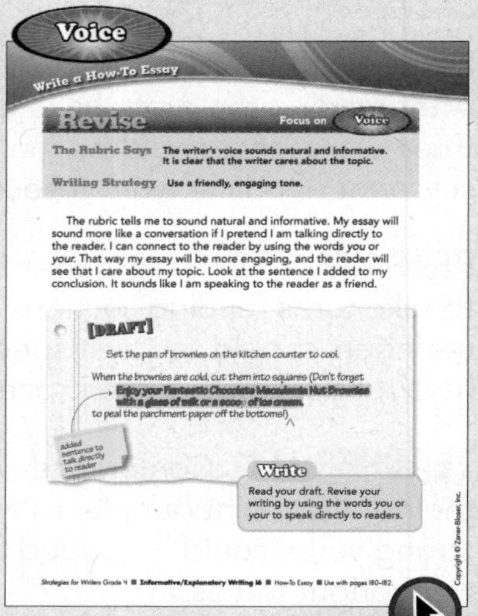
Voice

Write a How-To Essay

Revise — Focus on Voice

The Rubric Says The writer's voice sounds natural and informative. It is clear that the writer cares about the topic.

Writing Strategy Use a friendly, engaging tone.

The rubric tells me to sound natural and informative. My essay will sound more like a conversation if I pretend I am talking directly to the reader. I can connect to the reader by using the words *you* or *your*. That way my essay will be more engaging, and the reader will see that I care about my topic. Look at the sentence I added to my conclusion. It sounds like I am speaking to the reader as a friend.

[DRAFT]

Set the pan of brownies on the kitchen counter to cool. When the brownies are cold, cut them into squares (Don't forget to peal the parchment paper off the bottome!) Enjoy your Fantastic Chocolate Macadamia Nut Brownies with a glass of milk or a scoop of ice cream.

added sentence to talk directly to reader

Write

Read your draft. Revise your writing by using the words *you* or *your* to speak directly to readers.

Strategies for Writers Grade 4 ■ Informative/Explanatory Writing 16 ■ How-To Essay ■ Use with pages 180–182.

Copyright © Zaner-Bloser, Inc.

Informative/Explanatory 16

Go to ***Strategies for Writers*** **at www.sfw.z-b.com**

Edit — Focus on Conventions

The Rubric Says All pronouns are used correctly.

Writing Strategy Check that all pronouns are used correctly.

The rubric tells me that I need to check my essay for errors. I'm going to check spelling, punctuation, and capitalization first. Then I'm going to make sure that I've used all the pronouns correctly.

Writer's Term

Pronouns
A **pronoun** can replace a noun naming a person, place, or thing. Pronouns include **I, me, you, we, us, he, she, it, they,** and **them.**

corrected pronoun

set the pan of brownies on the kitchen counter to cool. When the brownies are cold, cut it into squares (Don't forget to peal the parchment paper off the bottoms!) **them** ... **peel**

[DRAFT]

Analyze
Look at Alika's edits. Are all pronouns used correctly?

Write — Conventions
Edit your draft for spelling, punctuation, and capitalization. Check that you have used all pronouns correctly.

For more practice using pronouns correctly, use the exercises on the next two pages.

How-To Essay **183**

Related Grammar Practice

Student Edition page 464

Go to Appendix A: Grammar Practice

Write
How-To Essay

Student Objectives
- Edit for correct use of pronouns. (p. 183)

Edit

Focus on Conventions

Check Pronouns Have students read Alika's thoughts on page 183. Discuss the changes that he made in punctuation and capitalization in his draft. Ask them to notice the corrected pronoun in Alika's draft. Have students read their drafts again, paying attention to pronouns. Use the mini-lessons on pages T184 and T185 for students having trouble using pronouns correctly. Have students complete the exercises on pages 184 and 185.

Writer's Term

Pronouns A pronoun must match the noun it replaces (the antecedent) in person, case, and number. Interrogative and indefinite pronouns do not have specific antecedents. Examples: _Who watched the Super Bowl? Everyone watched the game._

CCSS Common Core State Standards (pp. Z20–Z30)
Writing: W.4.2c, W.4.4, W.4.5, W.4.6, W.4.10
Language: L.4.2a, L.4.2d, L.4.6

How-To Essay **T183**

Mini-Lesson

Student Objectives

• Use pronouns correctly. *(p. 184)*

Subject and Object Pronouns

Have students review the Know the Rule box on page 184. Then write the following sentence on the board:

• *David pitched the baseball.*

Ask students who or what is performing the action in the sentence. (David) What is the action? (pitched) Who or what is receiving the action? (baseball) Ask students what pronoun they would use to replace the word *David*. (He) Then ask what pronoun they would use to replace the words *baseball*. (it) Next have students write two or three simple sentences that do not include pronouns. Have them exchange papers with a partner and rewrite their partner's sentences, changing the nouns to the correct subject or object pronouns. Discuss the changes with students. You may wish to write lists of subject and object pronouns on the board as a reference for students.

Online Writing Center

Provides **interactive grammar games** and **practice activities** in student eBook.

Subject and Object Pronouns

Know the Rule

A **pronoun** is a word that can take the place of one or more nouns in a sentence. A **subject pronoun** takes the place of one or more nouns in the subject of a sentence.

Use the pronouns *I, we, he, she,* and *they* as subjects in sentences.

An **object pronoun** follows action verbs or prepositions, such as *to, at, for, of,* and *with.*

Use the pronouns *me, us, him, her,* and *them* as objects in sentences. The pronoun *you* is used as a subject or an object. The pronoun *it* can be a subject or an object.

Practice the Rule

Number a sheet of paper 1–8. Write a pronoun that can take the place of the underlined word or words in each sentence.

1. <u>My friend Paulo and I</u> live in a small town on the island of Maui. We
2. Every Saturday morning, <u>Paulo and I</u> run over to the bakery owned by Mr. and Mrs. Lee. we
3. <u>The Lees</u> make the best fresh bread and pastries on Maui! They
4. Mrs. Lee uses family recipes, and <u>Mrs. Lee</u> bakes a mango bread that is delicious. she
5. <u>Mango bread</u> is made using fresh mangoes and macadamia nuts. It
6. Mr. Lee runs the bakery shop, and <u>Mr. Lee</u> always has a loaf of mango bread waiting for me on Saturdays. he
7. Paulo always buys papaya muffins and takes <u>the papaya muffins</u> home to his mother. them
8. Sometimes Paulo eats one of <u>the papaya muffins</u> before he gets home. They're so good! them

Related Grammar Practice

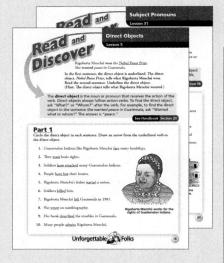

Pages 15, 85, 87, 89, 91

Go to **G.U.M. Student Practice Book**

Pronoun Antecedents

Know the Rule

A **pronoun** must match the noun it replaces. A singular pronoun must be used in place of a singular noun. A plural pronoun must be used in place of a plural noun.
Examples:
Mr. Singh teaches music. **He** also plays the piano.
The students think Mr. Singh is great! **They** all love music.

Practice the Rule

Number a sheet of paper 1–10. Write the correct pronoun to complete each sentence.

1. My sister loves to bake. _____ decided to take a baking class. She
2. The teacher, Tim, is a pastry chef. _____ works at a fancy restaurant. He
3. My sister brought home apple tarts from class. _____ were delicious! They
4. Next the class made a pineapple cake. My sister said _____ had three layers. it
5. My brother and I were hoping to taste a piece, but _____ didn't get to try it. we
6. I hope my sister makes cookies sometime. _____ are easy to make. They
7. I like walnuts in my cookies, but my sister is allergic to _____. them
8. Oatmeal cookies are good with raisins in _____. them
9. A cherry pie would be good, too. _____ is my favorite dessert. It
10. Maybe I should eat a piece of fruit. _____ would be better for me! It

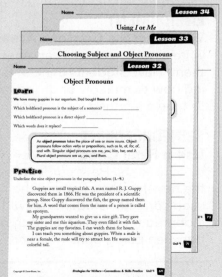

Pages 15, 67, 69, 71, 73

Go to ➡ *Grammar Practice Masters*

Mini-Lesson

Student Objectives

- Use pronoun antecedents correctly. *(p. 185)*

Pronoun Antecedents

Have students review the Know the Rule box on page 185. Write the following sentences on the board:

- *Mrs. Nichols teaches art. She also runs in marathon races.*

- *The other teachers think Mrs. Nichols is both creative and athletic. They enjoy art shows and races!*

Ask volunteers to identify the subject pronoun in each sentence. (She, They) Tell students that the noun the pronoun replaces or identifies is called an *antecedent*. Then ask a volunteer to identify the antecedent for each pronoun. (*Mrs. Nichols* is the antecedent of *She; teachers* is the antecedent of *They*) Stress to students that when they use pronouns, a singular noun can only be replaced by a singular pronoun, and a plural noun can only be replaced by a plural pronoun. By using pronouns correctly, writers can make sure their meaning is clear. You may wish to write lists of singular and plural pronouns on the board as a reference for students.

CCSS **C**ommon **C**ore **S**tate **S**tandards (pp. Z20–Z30)
Writing: W.4.6
Language: L.4.4a, L.4.6

Write
How-to Essay

Student Objectives

- Discuss preparation for publishing and presentation. (p. 186)
- Use a final editing checklist to publish their work. (p. 186)

Publish +Presentation

Publishing Strategy Ask students if they like Alika's choice for sharing his essay in a class how-to book. Ask students to suggest ways Alika could enhance his presentation. (**Possible responses: add sketches of the materials, illustrate the steps, include photographs of the process, etc.**) Explain to students that there are several ways of making a book. If students have previously made class books, ask them to share what they learned in the process.

Have a student read Alika's final checklist. Remind students that the checklist relates to the editing strategies they have been practicing. Have them use the checklist or one you provide to perform a final evaluation before publishing their work.

Strategies for Writers Online
Go to **www.sfw.z-b.com** for additional online resources for students, teachers, and parents.

Publish +Presentation

Publishing Strategy   Publish the essay in a class how-to book.

Presentation Strategy   Indent every paragraph.

I've completed my how-to essay! Now I have to decide how to publish it. I chose the topic of making brownies because I thought kids in my class would like to try making their own. Other kids want to share their how-to essays, too. We decided to put all our essays together in a class how-to book. The book will go in the class library.

I want to be sure my classmates can follow the directions, so I will indent each paragraph. This makes it easy to see where a new step or idea starts. Also, I'll put a little extra space between the paragraphs so the reader can easily find his or her place after looking away. Before I publish my how-to essay, I'm going to check it over one last time. Here's the final checklist I'll use.

My Final Checklist

Did I—

✔ proofread carefully for capitalization, punctuation, and grammar?

✔ use pronouns correctly?

✔ indent every paragraph?

✔ put an extra space between paragraphs?

Write
Make your own checklist and use it to check your how-to essay. Then publish your how-to essay.

Differentiating Instruction

ENRICHMENT
Write Across Content Areas Encourage students to write a how-to essay in another content area that interests them. Have students think of favorite topics, such as explaining how to multiply or divide to solve word problems or how to tune a stringed instrument.

REINFORCEMENT
Use a Final Checklist Meet with a small group to discuss the checklists. Have students perform a final evaluation of the how-to essay. Remind them to check that pronouns are used correctly. Students should also make sure they have indented the first line of each paragraph and left extra space between paragraphs.

Fantastic Chocolate Macadamia Nut Brownies
by Alika

These Fantastic Chocolate Macadamia Nut Brownies that I make taste like Hawaii to me. Try making some, and see if you agree!

Before you make the brownie batter, you have to heat the oven to 350 degrees. Then brush a little butter inside of an eight-inch square baking pan. After you do that, cover the bottom of the pan with a piece of parchment paper.

Now it's time to make the batter. First melt half a stick of butter, three ounces of semisweet chocolate, and three-fourths cup of milk chocolate chips in a large saucepan. Set the heat low and keep stirring so that nothing burns.

After the butter and chocolate melt together, remove the pan from the stove. Then add half a cup of brown sugar and two tablespoons of honey to the pan. Mix everything well so that there aren't any lumps! Once that is done, let the mixture cool for a few minutes.

While you are waiting for the chocolate mixture to cool, beat two eggs with one teaspoon of vanilla extract. Then add the eggs to the chocolate. (If you don't let the chocolate cool down first, the heat will turn the eggs into scrambled eggs!)

Now sift one cup flour along with half a teaspoon of salt into the chocolate. Mix it all together gently. Finally stir in two-thirds cup of chopped macadamia nuts.

When the batter is completely mixed, spread it in the pan. Bake the brownies for about 30 minutes.

Set the pan of brownies on the kitchen counter to cool. When the brownies are cold, cut them into squares. (Don't forget to peel the parchment paper off the bottoms!) Enjoy your Fantastic Chocolate Macadamia Nut Brownies with a glass of milk or a scoop of ice cream.

Analyze

Use the rubric to evaluate Alika's essay. Are the traits of a good how-to essay there? Check your own how-to essay with the rubric, too.

How-To Essay **187**

Student Objectives

- Use a how-to essay rubric. *(pp. 170–171)*
- Share a published how-to essay. *(p. 187)*

Presentation Strategy Encourage students to enhance their presentations with drawings, photographs, or other appropriate graphics. Remind students that they should indent every paragraph to make it easier to see where a new step or idea starts. They should also be sure to leave space between paragraphs to make their essay easy to read.

Reflecting on a How-To Essay

Ask students to consider how Alika's revisions and edits strengthened his essay. What score should Alika receive for each writing trait?

Next have students reflect on the assignment as a whole. Ask:

- What was your favorite part of this assignment?
- What will you do differently in your next how-to essay?

Allow time for students to share their thoughts.

Tech Tips

Digital Images

Use Online Photo Repositories Challenge students to create their own multimodal version of their how-to essay. Use an online photo repository like Flickr to help students find classroom-appropriate, Creative Commons images that can be sequenced to tell their how-to steps. Spend time discussing citation and attribution, search techniques for locating images, and how to follow the Creative Commons license in order to acknowledge the owner or creator of each image. As much as you focus on how the resulting image sequences mirror (or enrich) the how-to essay, discuss how we credit artists when using or reusing their work.

See **www.sfw.z-b.com** for further information about and links to these websites and tools.

CCSS **Common Core State Standards** (pp. Z20–Z30)
Writing: W.4.2a, W.4.2b, W.4.4, W.4.6, W.4.10
Language: L.4.2a, L.4.3c
Speaking and Listening: SL.4.1a, SL.4.1b, SL.4.1c, SL.4.1d, SL.4.3, SL.4.6

Summary Planner

Day 1	Day 2	Day 3
Introduce Summary	**Analyze** Close Reading of the Model	**Analyze** Introduce the Rubric

WEEK 1

Day 1 — Introduce: Summary

Student Objectives
- Review the elements of a summary.
- Consider purpose and audience.
- Learn the traits of informative/explanatory writing.

Student Activities
- Read and discuss **What's in a Summary?** (p. 188)
- Read and discuss **Why Write a Summary?** (p. 189)
- Read **Linking Informative/Explanatory Writing Traits to a Summary.** (p. 190)

Day 2 — Analyze: Close Reading of the Model

Student Objectives
- Read a model summary.

Student Activities
- Read **"What Is Photosynthesis?"** (pp. 191–193)

Day 3 — Analyze: Introduce the Rubric

Student Objectives
- Learn to read a rubric.

Student Activities
- Review **"What Is Photosynthesis?"** (pp. 191–193)
- Read and discuss the **Summary Rubric.** (pp. 194–195)

WEEK 2

Day 1 — Write: Prewrite: Ideas

Student Objectives
- Read and understand a prewriting strategy.

Student Activities
- Read and discuss **Prewrite: Focus on Ideas.** (p. 200–202)
- Apply the prewriting strategy.
- Participate in a peer conference.

Day 2 — Write: Prewrite: Organization

Student Objectives
- Make a Five-Column Chart to organize ideas.

Student Activities
- Read and discuss **Prewrite: Focus on Organization.** (p. 203)
- Apply the prewriting strategy to create a Five-Column Chart.

Day 3 — Write: Draft: Word Choice

Student Objectives
- Use a Five-Column Chart to begin writing.

Student Activities
- Read and discuss **Draft: Focus on Word Choice.** (p. 204)
- Apply the drafting strategy by using a Five-Column Chart to write a draft.

WEEK 3

Day 1 — Write: Revise: Organization

Student Objectives
- Revise to put the most important idea first.

Student Activities
- Read and discuss **Revise: Focus on Organization.** (p. 207)
- Apply the revising strategy.
- Participate in a peer conference.

Day 2 — Write: Revise: Sentence Fluency

Student Objectives
- Revise to include clear and direct sentences.

Student Activities
- Read and discuss **Revise: Focus on Sentence Fluency.** (p. 208)
- Apply the revising strategy.

Note: Optional Revising Lessons are located at **www.sfw.z-b.com.**

Day 3 — Write: Edit: Conventions

Student Objectives
- Edit to eliminate double negatives and use verbs correctly.

Student Activities
- Read and discuss **Edit: Focus on Conventions.** (p. 209)
- Apply the editing strategy.

Note: Teach the Conventions mini-lessons (pp. 210–211) if needed.

Day 4
Analyze
Close Reading
for the Traits

Student Objectives

- Read a model summary.
- Use the summary rubric.
- Use the model summary to study Ideas, Organization, and Voice.

Student Activities

- Review **"What Is Photosynthesis?"** (pp. 191–193)
- Read and discuss **Using the Rubric to Analyze the Model.** (pp. 196–197)

Day 5
Analyze
Close Readng
for the Traits

Student Objectives

- Read a model summary.
- Use the summary rubric.
- Use the model summary to study Word Choice, Sentence Fluency, and Conventions.

Student Activities

- Review **"What Is Photosynthesis?"** (pp. 191–193)
- Read and discuss **Using the Rubric to Analyze the Model.** (pp. 198–199)

Day 4
Write
Draft

Student Objectives

- Complete a draft.

Student Activities

- Finish a draft. (p. 205)
- Participate in a peer conference.

Day 5
Write
Revise: Ideas

Student Objectives

- Revise to make sure that all details support the main ideas.

Student Activities

- Read and discuss **Revise: Focus on Ideas.** (p. 206)

Day 4
Write
Publish: +Presentation

Student Objectives

- Discuss preparation for publishing and presentation.
- Use a final editing checklist to publish their work.

Student Activities

- Read and discuss **Publish: +Presentation.** (p. 212)
- Apply the publishing strategy.

Day 5
Write
Publish: +Presentation

Student Objectives

- Use a summary rubric.
- Share a published summary.

Student Activities

- Share their work.
- Use the rubric to reflect upon and evaluate the model and their own writing. (pp. 194–195, 213)

To complete the chapter in fewer days, combine the learning objectives and activities in a way that supports students as they write.

Resources at-a-Glance

Grammar, Usage & Mechanics

Differentiating Instruction

For additional Differentiating Instruction activities, see Strategies for Writers *Differentiated Instruction Activitiee at* **www.sfw.z-b.com.**

English Language Learners

Collaborative Conferencing

Tech Tips

 Strategies for Writers Online

Go to **www.sfw.z-b.com** for additional online resources for students, teachers, and parents.

Online Writing Center

Provides IWB resources, assessments, interactive games and practice activities, videos, eBooks, and a virtual file cabinet.

Introduce
Summary

Student Objectives

- Review the elements of a summary. (p. 188)
- Consider purpose and audience. (p. 189)
- Learn the traits of informative/ explanatory writing. (p. 190)

What's a Summary?

Read aloud the definition of a summary on page 188. Help students understand that a summary is a shorter piece of writing that tells the main points of a longer piece of writing. Point out that they often use their own words to restate important ideas in a story or article. Explain that an oral summary restates the main points of a reading selection. Then talk about reasons they might need to write a summary. Tell students that they will learn writing strategies to help them write a summary.

What's in a Summary?

Read and discuss with students the four elements of a summary listed on page 188. Then discuss why each element is important to writing a summary.

 Strategies for Writers Online
Go to **www.sfw.z-b.com** for additional online resources for students and teachers.

What's a Summary?

A summary is a shorter piece of writing that tells the main points of a longer piece of writing.

What's in a Summary?

Main Ideas
A summary should explain the main ideas of an original piece of writing. The purpose of a good summary is to help the reader understand and remember the main ideas.

Supporting Details
A summary should include important details from the original piece. All details should support the main ideas.

Organization
Summaries should state the most important point first so the reader knows what the summary explains.

Length
Because a summary is shorter than the original piece of writing, the writer has to be careful not to use too many extra words.

188 Informative/Explanatory Writing

Informative/Explanatory Text Exemplars (Summary)

How Things Work Encyclopedia. DK Publishing, 2009. The *How Things Work Encyclopedia* explains the technology behind many common items including televisions and car engines. With simple text and various photographs, the book does a great job of describing what goes on inside these familiar inventions.

Anderson, Robert. *National Geographic Countries of the World: Italy.* National Geographic Children's Books, 2009. *National Geographic Countries of the World: Italy* describes Italy's history, culture, and geography. In addition to the text, Anderson includes charts, maps, and timelines to enhance this fact-filled resource.

Why write a Summary?

There are many reasons to write a summary. In fact, you will probably write summaries in most of your classes. Here are three important reasons to write them.

To Inform
Summaries are a great way to share information. I can write a summary to inform others about a book or an article I've read, a speech that I've heard, or a movie I've seen.

To Understand
Summarizing is a good way to make sure I understand someone else's ideas. If I can pick out all the main ideas, then I know I understand what the author is trying to get across.

To Research
Summarizing could be really useful when I'm doing research. When I'm starting a project, I read a lot of different reference materials before I focus on my topic. If I write a summary of each reference article, I can keep track of things.

Why write a Summary?

Read and discuss with students the reasons for writing a summary listed on page 189. Point out that all writing has a purpose and is aimed at a specific audience. These authentic purposes help authors shape their writing. For example, someone writing to inform may share information about something he or she has seen, heard, or read. Someone whose purpose is to try to understand new ideas may write a summary to make sure he or she understands what the author is trying to get across. A writer who needs to do research may write summaries of several reference articles in order to keep track of information he or she is gathering. Encourage students to share their own reasons for writing summaries. Ask students to consider the purpose and audience for each reason.

Janssen, Sarah. *The World Almanac for Kids 2012*. World Almanac, 2011. Janssen has incorporated facts, photos, and features into this detailed reference book. Including information on the environment, movies and television, sports, and technology, *The World Almanac for Kids 2012* is sure to inform students while still holding their interest.

Stevens, Kathryn. *Stringed Instruments*. Child's World, 2002. Stevens includes interesting information about stringed instruments in this nonfiction text. The appearance, sound, and functionality of violins, guitars, harps, and pianos are described in a language appropriate for young students.

CCSS **C**ommon **C**ore **S**tate **S**tandards (pp. Z20–Z30)
Language: L.4.3c
Speaking and Listening: SL.4.1a, SL.4.1b, SL.4.1c, SL.4.1d, SL.4.3, SL.4.6

Introduce
Summary

Linking Informative/ Explanatory Writing Traits to a Summary

Read page 190 aloud to help students understand that they will follow Alika as he models using the writing process and the informative/explanatory writing traits together.

As they follow Alika, students will see how the Informative/ Explanatory Writing Traits have been adapted and applied to writing a summary. They will see that a summary has many factors in common with other types of informative/explanatory writing. However, the particular audience and purpose of a summary determine how the traits are used.

Online Writing Center

 Provides six **interactive anchor papers** for each text type.

Linking Informative/Explanatory Writing Traits to a **Summary**

In this chapter, you will briefly tell about an article you have read. This type of informative/explanatory writing is called a summary. Alika will guide you through the stages of the writing process: Prewrite, Draft, Revise, Edit, and Publish. In each stage, Alika will show you important writing strategies that are linked to the Informative/Explanatory Writing Traits below.

Informative/Explanatory Writing Traits

- clear topic and main ideas
- details, information, and examples that answer the reader's questions about the topic

- a strong introduction, body, and conclusion
- well-organized paragraphs
- transitions that connect ideas

- a voice and tone that are appropriate for the purpose and audience

- precise words
- domain-specific vocabulary that is used correctly and explained as necessary

- clear, direct sentences that flow smoothly

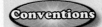
- no or few errors in grammar, usage, mechanics, and spelling

Before you write, read Mitchell Martino's summary of an article about photosynthesis. Then use the summary rubric on pages 194–195 to decide how well he did. (You might want to look back at What's in a Summary? on page 188, too!)

Informative/Explanatory Writing Traits in a Summary

 **Ideas** The writer builds the summary around a clear topic and main ideas. Only the most important main ideas and details are included in a summary.

 **Organization** The paragraphs in the summary are well organized. A logical order makes the summary easy to follow.

 **Voice** To ensure that the reader is engaged throughout the summary, it's important to use the appropriate voice and tone. Using a formal tone is the best way to achieve this in a summary.

What Is Photosynthesis?

by Leah Flora
Summary by Mitchell Martino

Summary MODEL

[note: main ideas]

All living things need food to live and grow. People do this by eating food. Plants do this by making their own food in a process called photosynthesis.

[note: organization]

Plants need three things to make food—energy, carbon dioxide, and water. Plants get energy from the sunlight, carbon dioxide from the air, and water from the soil. With these three ingredients, plants can perform photosynthesis, which means "putting together with light." *Photo* means "light" and *synthesis* means "putting together."

[note: supporting details]

All the action happens in the leaves of green plants. Plants are green because of chlorophyll. The green chlorophyll is inside structures called chloroplasts. The chloroplasts collect energy from sunlight. (That's the "light" part of *photosynthesis*.) Carbon dioxide enters the underside of leaves through tiny holes called stomata, and water from the roots moves up the plant through tubes called xylem. With energy from sunlight, the chloroplasts combine the carbon dioxide and water. (That's the "putting together" part.) As a result, plants create sugars, or food, as well as give off oxygen during the process of photosynthesis.

We need plants to survive. Plants store some of the food they make, and that's how fruits, such as apples, and vegetables, such as carrots, give our own bodies energy. Because plants also give off oxygen, we have fresh air to breathe. Life on this planet would not be possible without plants.

[note: one-page length]

Summary **191**

 **Word Choice** The writer uses domain-specific vocabulary to explain the main ideas clearly and precisely.

 **Sentence Fluency** Clear, direct sentences are used to make the writing flow smoothly.

 **Conventions** The writer carefully edits his or her work prior to publishing. Correct use and spelling of words, particularly verbs and negatives, enhances the clarity of the writing in a summary.

Analyze
Close Reading of the Model

Week 1 • Day 2

Student Objectives

- Read a model summary. (pp. 191–193)

Read the Model

Read the summary of the article "What Is Photosynthesis?" aloud to the class. After reading, point out the title and read the introduction again. Be sure students can identify the topic of the summary. (photosynthesis) Also direct students to look at how the writer organized the summary. Be sure students understand that the main points are organized logically.

Elements of a Summary

Have students refer to What's in a Summary? on page 188 as you refer to the model. Discuss the notes written on the model to enhance students' understanding of the terms. Model giving an oral summary of text the class has read recently. Tell students your purpose is to share information. Then invite volunteers to share their experiences with reading a text and summarizing an author's main points.

CCSS **C**ommon **C**ore **S**tate **S**tandards (pp. Z20–Z30)
Writing: W.4.6
Language: L.4.3c
Speaking and Listening: SL.4.1a, SL.4.1b, SL.4.1c, SL.4.1d, SL.4.2, SL.4.3, SL.4.6

What Is Photosynthesis?
by Leah Flora

Food for Thought

Does a plant eat? You might be thinking, "That's silly. Of course plants don't eat food!" Not so fast! You may be surprised to learn that plants convert light, gas, and water to make their own food.

You Are What You Eat

No doubt you've heard this old saying, and it still holds true. People and many other animals, including fish and birds, consume parts of plants, like the roots, the stems, the flowers, and the leaves. They also eat the seeds, fruits, and vegetables that are produced by plants every day.

It's no secret that our bodies depend on plants. We need them in order to breathe and remain healthy. Many green plants contain the nutrients we use in vitamins and medicines.

Photo Op

In order to be food for us, plants first produce food for themselves. The process of making their food is called *photosynthesis* (foh • toh • **sin** • thih • sis). *Photo* means "light" and *synthesis* means "putting together."

Using three things—energy from sunlight, carbon dioxide from the air, and water from the soil—plants manufacture their own food.

A Little Sunlight, Please

Plants' food manufacturing process takes place in the leaves of green plants in special cell structures called *chloroplasts*. This part of the plant cell contains *chlorophyll* molecules that are called *photoreceptors*. These light-sensitive molecules absorb the sun's energy as sunlight shines on the surface of the leaves. Chlorophyll gives leaves their green color.

Breath of Fresh Air

On the underside of leaves are tiny openings called *stomata*. Carbon dioxide, an invisible gas, is a *byproduct* of human and animal respiration. The carbon dioxide we exhale into the air is taken in through the stomata on plant leaves.

CO_2 by Any Other Name

To complete the cycle, plants take up rainwater and the nutrients in the soil through their roots. The water travels upward through tubes

192 Informative/Explanatory Writing

Books for Professional Development

Fitzgibbon, Kathleen. *Teaching With Wikis, Blogs, Podcasts & More*. New York: Scholastic, 2010. For those who are new to the world of wikis, blogs, and other online tools, Fitzgibbon's book is a valuable resource that shows how using digital resources helps teachers and students alike thrive in today's classroom. This book, filled with quick tips and practical ideas for melding technology with everyday teaching, includes innovative ways to publish student work.

Wormeli, Rick. *Summarization in Any Subject: 50 Techniques to Improve Student Learning*. Alexandria, VA: ASCD, 2004. Here you will find a classroom-tested collection of written, spoken, artistic, and kinesthetic summarization techniques for both individual and group activities across the content areas. These techniques are easily adjustable to any curriculum and are presented with ample directions and examples.

 Strategies for Writers Online
Go to **www.sfw.z-b.com** for additional online resources for students, teachers, and parents.

called *xylem* to reach the leaves. Even the tallest trees pull water to their leaves against gravity! When the water reaches the leaves, those efficient chloroplasts "put together" the water and carbon dioxide (CO_2). This process forms sugars, which are the food for the plant. Tubes called *phloem* carry and store the sugars inside the plant.

Thank a Plant

It's good that plants and people share the planet! Both plants and people benefit from the process of photosynthesis. Not only do plants make food (sugars) for their own use, but through their leaves they release the oxygen we breathe. Plants also produce something else that is important to our survival—fruits, grains, and vegetables! So, the next time you take a bite from a juicy apple, munch a carrot stick, or dream under the shade of an oak tree, remember to thank a plant!

Gilmore, Barry. Plagiarism: *Why It Happens and How to Prevent It.* **Portsmouth, NH: Heinemann, 2008.** With the digital revolution, the availability of online source material has further increased teachers' concerns about plagiarism in the classroom. Gilmore's book provides classroom-tested strategies for increasing students' understanding of plagiarism, setting expectations for academic honesty, and reducing or eliminating plagiarism.

Overmeyer, Mark. *When Writing Workshop Isn't Working: Answers to Ten Tough Questions, Grades 2–5.* **Portland, ME: Stenhouse, 2005.** This book is a valuable reference for teachers working with students struggling with writing. It contains easy-to-follow directions, a user-friendly format, and answers to questions such as *How do I help students develop stronger voice and word choice skills?*

CCSS **Common Core State Standards** (pp. Z20–Z30)
Language: L.4.3c
Speaking and Listening: SL.4.1a, SL.4.1b, SL.4.1c, SL.4.1d, SL.4.2, SL.4.3, SL.4.6

Analyze
Introduce the Rubric

Week 1 • Day 3

Student Objectives
- Learn to read a rubric. (pp. 194–195)

Introduce the Rubric

Explain the Rubric Explain that a rubric is a tool for planning, improving, and assessing a piece of writing. Tell students that a rubric helps a writer focus on key elements, or traits, in writing (**Ideas, Organization, Voice, Word Choice, Sentence Fluency, Conventions,** and **Presentation**).

Explain the 6-point system. Point out that the columns on page 194 represent a good paper that might need some polishing but that the columns on page 195 represent writing that needs considerable improvement.

Discuss the Rubric Guide students in a discussion of the rubric. Read the descriptors that go with each trait. Discuss the difference between columns to be sure students fully understand the point system. Tell students to keep the rubric in mind when they write their own summary and again when they revise it.

Online Writing Center

Provides a variety of **interactive rubrics,** including 4-, 5-, and 6-point models.

Summary **Rubric**

Use this rubric to analyze the model. The use it to plan and score your own summary.

	6	5	4
Ideas	The topic is clear. Only main ideas and supporting details are included.	The topic is clear. Most main ideas are supported.	The topic is clear. Some details do not support the main ideas.
Organization	The main points are given in logical order. The summary is easy to follow.	Most main points are given in a logical order. Most of the summary is easy to follow.	A few main points are in logical order. The summary is not easy to follow in places.
Voice	The tone is consistent and appropriate for the purpose and the audience.	The tone is consistent and appropriate most of the time.	The tone is appropriate in the beginning, but it fades.
Word Choice	Domain-specific vocabulary is used and explained. Strong verbs help the reader understand the topic.	Domain-specific words are used and explained. Most of the verbs are strong and helpful.	Several domain-specific words may be used incorrectly or need explanations. Most of the verbs are strong and helpful.
Sentence Fluency	Sentences are clear and direct.	Most sentences are clear and direct.	A few sentences are not clear.
Conventions	The writing contains no errors. There are no double negatives. Verbs are correct.	A few errors are present but do not confuse the reader. There are no double negatives.	Several errors confuse the reader. Double negatives or incorrect verbs stop the reader.
+Presentation	The summary is neat and legible.		

194 Informative/Explanatory Writing

CCSS **Common Core State Standards**
Summary

Strategies for Writers was designed and written to incorporate the Common Core State Standards throughout every unit. By presenting the standards in as many applications as possible, your students' exposure to them will be ensured.

The lessons for the summary are based principally on the writing standards for Informative/Explanatory writing. The rubrics and writing strategies reflect the writing standard **W.4.2**. This standard focuses on conveying ideas and information clearly through facts, good organization, precise

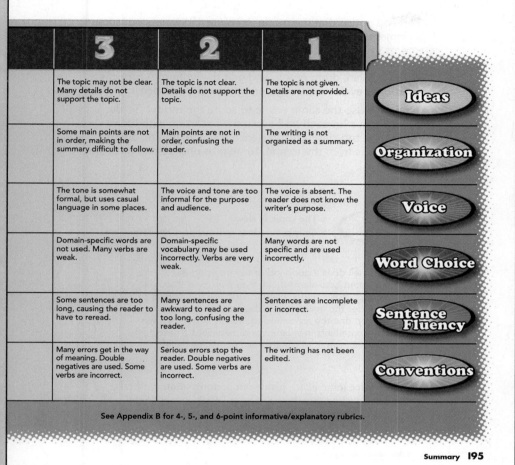

3	2	1	
The topic may not be clear. Many details do not support the topic.	The topic is not clear. Details do not support the topic.	The topic is not given. Details are not provided.	**Ideas**
Some main points are not in order, making the summary difficult to follow.	Main points are not in order, confusing the reader.	The writing is not organized as a summary.	**Organization**
The tone is somewhat formal, but uses casual language in some places.	The voice and tone are too informal for the purpose and audience.	The voice is absent. The reader does not know the writer's purpose.	**Voice**
Domain-specific words are not used. Many verbs are weak.	Domain-specific vocabulary may be used incorrectly. Verbs are very weak.	Many words are not specific and are used incorrectly.	**Word Choice**
Some sentences are too long, causing the reader to have to reread.	Many sentences are awkward to read or are too long, confusing the reader.	Sentences are incomplete or incorrect.	**Sentence Fluency**
Many errors get in the way of meaning. Double negatives are used. Some verbs are incorrect.	Serious errors stop the reader. Double negatives are used. Some verbs are incorrect.	The writing has not been edited.	**Conventions**

See Appendix B for 4-, 5-, and 6-point informative/explanatory rubrics.

Find Evidence in the Model

Small-Group Collaboration
Assign students to small groups and tell them to evaluate the model using the rubric. Assign one person in each group to record the group's findings and one person to report the findings to the class. Instruct students to score the model for each trait based on evidence in the text. Remind students to read closely to identify examples to support their high or low scores. Note: Although the models were written to score high in each trait, students should not assume each trait would receive a 6, the top score.

Teacher-Led Discussion Bring the class back together, and have the reporters present their findings and scores. Prompt groups to provide evidence and examples for their scores from the model as needed.

Additional Rubrics

Appendix B includes 4-, 5-, and 6-point rubrics that can be used with any piece of informative/explanatory writing. The rubrics are also available as blackline masters in the back of this Teacher Edition.

language, and domain-specific vocabulary in an informative/explanatory piece of writing.

The language standards for grade 4 students are addressed during editing and skills practice. In addition, there are multiple opportunities to address the speaking and listening standards during the writing process. Most importantly, this chapter will help students produce clear and coherent writing (**W.4.4**), improve their writing (**W.4.5**), and use technologies to publish and present their finished pieces (**W.4.6**).

CCSS **Common Core State Standards** (pp. Z20–Z30)
Writing: W.4.6
Language: L.4.3c
Speaking and Listening: SL.4.1a, SL.4.1b, SL.4.1c, SL.4.1d, SL.4.2, SL.4.3, SL.4.6

Analyze
Close Reading for the Traits

Week 1 • Day 4

Student Objectives

- Read a model summary. *(pp. 191–193)*
- Use the summary rubric. *(pp. 194–195)*
- Use the model summary to study **Ideas, Organization,** and **Voice.** *(pp. 196–197)*

Find Evidence in the Model

Evaluate the Model Have volunteers read aloud pages 196–197. Determine whether students agree or disagree with each point in Alika's assessments. Use the questions below to initiate the discussion. Be sure students can back up their answers with specific examples from the model.

Discuss Audience, Task, Purpose Ask students one or more of the following questions as they analyze the model:

- **Audience** Who is the audience? (Possible response: all readers)

- **Task** How does Mitchell Martino summarize the article? (Possible response: He includes the main ideas and supporting details from the article.)

- **Purpose** What is Mitchell's purpose for writing this report? (Possible responses: To inform the readers)

Summary

Using the Rubric to Analyze the Model

Did you notice that the model on page 191 points out some key elements of a summary? As he wrote, Mitchell used these elements to help him summarize how plants make food and how plants are food for us. He also used the 6-point rubric on pages 194–195 to plan, draft, revise, and edit the writing. A rubric is a great tool to evaluate writing during the writing process.

Now let's use the same rubric to score the model. To do this, we'll focus on each trait separately, starting with Ideas. We'll use the top descriptor for each trait (column 6), along with examples from the model, to help us understand how the traits work.

Ideas
- The topic is clear.
- Only main ideas and supporting details are included.

I think Mitchell does a good job of summarizing the article. The article is about how plants make their own food through the process of photosynthesis. Even though the summary is shorter, it includes the main ideas in the article.

I also noticed that the article included information that we use nutrients from plants in vitamins and medicines. These details would not have fit Mitchell's main points, so he left them out.

With these three ingredients, plants can perform photosynthesis, which means "putting together with light." *Photo* means "light" and *synthesis* means "putting together."

English Language Learners

BEGINNING
The 5 W's Locate a photograph of scientists working in a laboratory. On the board write *what, who, when, why,* and *where.* Point to the picture and ask, *What is happening?* When a student gives an answer, repeat it, and write it on the board. Repeat for *who, when, where,* and *why.* Review the list. Ask, *What is happening? Who is there?* and so on. Demonstrate how to answer in a complete sentence.

INTERMEDIATE
The 5 W's Read a short nonfiction text that clearly answers the 5 W's. Write on the board *what, who, when, why,* and *where.* As volunteers take turns filling out the information on the board, those at their seats fill in a 5 W's chart. Review the 5 W's chart by asking, *What happened? Who was there?* and so on. Have students ask each other.

Organization
- The main points are given in logical order.
- The summary is easy to follow.

Mitchell organizes his main points logically. His summary is very easy to follow. We're studying the parts of plants in science class. The summary really helped me understand how green plants make food for themselves and for us.

The chloroplasts collect energy from sunlight. (That's the "light" part of *photosynthesis*.) Carbon dioxide enters the underside of leaves through tiny holes called stomata, and water from the roots moves up the plant through tubes called xylem.

Voice
- The tone is consistent and appropriate for the purpose and the audience.

I know that Mitchell read the article carefully because he definitely sounds knowledgeable. I think he wants the reader to know that his information is accurate. He sounds enthusiastic about sharing what he's learned, but he uses a formal tone.

All living things need food to live and grow. People do this by eating food. Plants do this by making their own food in a process called photosynthesis.

Summary **197**

Discuss the Traits Ask students one or more of the following questions to discuss the traits in the model:

Ideas Does Mitchell have a clear topic? (Yes; he states it in the first paragraph.) What is his topic? (photosynthesis) Do the details support his main ideas about the topic? (yes)

Organization How does Mitchell organize his summary? (He uses logical order.) Is his summary easy to follow? (yes)

Point out that Mitchell organized his summary with an introduction, body, and conclusion. The introduction explains the topic of the summary, the body supports the topic, and the conclusion sums it all up. He was careful to take the information from Leah Flora's article and organize it in a logical way.

Voice Does Mitchell use an appropriate voice for his purpose and audience? (Possible responses: Yes; Mitchell uses a formal, knowledgeable voice. He sounds enthusiastic about sharing what he's learned.)

ADVANCED

Identifying the 5 W's Tell students about a scientific discovery such as the discovery of penicillin. Write on the board *what, who, when, why* and *where*. Ask, *What happened in my story? Who was there?* and so on. Write students' answers. Have partners tell each other about a time they were scared, or have them tell a funny adventure story. Have one student fill in the 5 W's chart for their partner's story.

ADVANCED HIGH

Identifying the 5 W's Ask each student to read an article from the school newspaper. After students have read their piece, have them fill in a 5 W's chart. Then have them trade selections and 5 W's charts with a partner. The partner should read the selection and review the chart for mistakes.

CCSS Common Core State Standards (pp. Z20–Z30)
Language: L.4.3c, L.4.6
Speaking and Listening: SL.4.1a, SL.4.1b, SL.4.1c, SL.4.1d, SL.4.3, SL.4.4, SL.4.6

Summary **T197**

Analyze
Close Reading for the Traits

Week 1 • Day 5

Student Objectives

- Read a model summary. *(pp. 191–193)*
- Use the summary rubric. *(pp. 194–195)*
- Use the model summary to study **Word Choice, Sentence Fluency,** and **Conventions.** *(pp. 198–199)*

Discuss the Traits Ask students one or more of these questions to discuss the traits in the model:

 Word Choice Does Mitchell use and explain words related to the topic so that readers can understand his summary? **(Possible responses: Mitchell uses many of the words from Leah Flora's article. For example, he uses and explains the words *photosynthesis* and *chloroplasts*. He also uses the verbs *perform*, *combine*, and *collect* correctly. The meaning is clear.)**

Sentence Fluency Are the sentences clear and focused? **(Possible responses: The sentences in the introduction state the topic and prepare the reader to learn about photosynthesis. The sentences in the body explain the process. The sentences in the conclusion tell how plants help people.)** What makes the sentences flow? **(Possible response: They are written in a clear and direct style.)**

▶ Strategies for Writers Online

Go to **www.sfw.z-b.com** for additional online resources for students, teachers, and parents.

Using the Rubric to Analyze the Model
(Summary)

 **Word Choice**
- Domain-specific vocabulary is used and explained.
- Strong verbs help the reader understand the topic.

I noticed that Mitchell uses and explains many of the words from the article in his summary. If I hadn't read Ms. Flora's article, I would need these words to understand photosynthesis. Mitchell uses strong verbs, such as *perform, combine, create,* and *collect.* They really help me understand the process.

As a result, plants create sugars, or food, as well as give off oxygen during the process of photosynthesis.

 **Sentence Fluency**
- Sentences are clear and direct.

Mitchell's sentences are clear and focused all the way through the summary. They support his purpose for writing. The sentences in the introduction state the topic and prepare the reader to learn about photosynthesis. The sentences in the body of the summary explain the process. The sentences in the conclusion tell how plants help us.

Because plants also give off oxygen, we have fresh air to breathe. Life on this planet would not be possible without plants.

Tech Tips
Online Resources

Avoid Plagiarism Avoiding plagiarism when writing a summary can be difficult for students. Discuss this throughout the unit as students write and examine the writing of others. Investigate kid-friendly and kid-directed sites that offer examples of appropriate summaries. Grow this into a PowerPoint-based game where students examine different examples and help identify those that are plagiarized from a common or known text, and those that follow the rules appropriately. Use humor here, but emphasize the importance of this exercise.

Conventions
- The writing contains no errors.
- There are no double negatives.
- Verbs are correct.

I didn't notice any errors in the summary. All subjects and verbs agree, too. I'm sure that Mitchell used a dictionary to check the spelling and usage of unfamiliar words. In this example, the word *chloroplasts* is plural, so he was careful to use a plural verb, *combine*.

With energy from sunlight, the chloroplasts combine the carbon dioxide and water.

Presentation The summary is neat and legible.

My Turn!
Now it's my turn to write a summary. I'll use the rubric and good writing strategies to help me. Read on to see how I do it.

Summary **199**

Differentiating Instruction

ENRICHMENT
Use the Rubric Have students work in pairs to score the model summary on pages 191–193 using the top descriptors (column 6) for each trait in the rubric on pages 194–195. Have them share and defend their scores for each trait.

REINFORCEMENT
Understand the Traits Make a transparency of the rubric on pages 194–195. Highlight the Ideas trait. Then say: *The Ideas trait says the summary should have a clear topic.* Then point out the topic in the title and the first paragraph. Then say: *The second part says only main ideas and supporting details are included.* Help students identify the main idea and supporting details in each paragraph. Continue to model the other traits.

Presentation Point out that the trait of Presentation is equally as important as the other traits. Discuss why presentation is important. (It can make a difference as to whether readers want to read a piece of writing. It's the reader's first impression of the writer.) Text should be clearly handwritten in pen or typed using a clear font. Remind students to indent paragraphs (using the tab key if typed). Talk about how white space can be used to organize text, especially to clearly separate paragraphs. Good margins make the line lengths comfortable to read, and a centered title stands out on a page.

Think About the Traits

Once students have thoroughly discussed Mitchell Martino's model summary, ask them which traits they think are most important in a summary and have them explain why. (Possible response: Organization is very important because if the main points of the summary are not logical and easy to follow, it will make no sense to the readers. Voice is important because it establishes a formal tone and makes it clear that the writer's purpose is to inform the reader.)

CCSS **Common Core State Standards** (pp. Z20–Z30)
Writing: W.4.6
Language: L.4.3c
Speaking and Listening: SL.4.1a, SL.4.1b, SL.4.1c, SL.4.1d, SL.4.3, SL.4.6

Write
Summary

Week 2 • Day 1

Student Objectives

- Read and understand a prewriting strategy. *(pp. 200–202)*

Prewrite

Focus on Ideas

Narrow Topic Read the introduction to page 200 aloud and discuss how Alika decided to write about levers. Explain that Alika had studied simple machines in science, so he already had some information about his topic. Also mention that he finds the topic interesting so he found an article about it.

Gather Information from Print and Digital Sources Before students read "Machines Work" on pages 200–201, read the title and the headings. Explain that these features often yield clues as to the topic of an article.

Take Notes on Source Information Ask students to read the whole article and make notes on the author's big ideas. (They can later compare their notes to Alika's on page 202.) Explain that careful note-taking is especially important when preparing to write a summary.

 Strategies for Writers Online
Go to **www.sfw.z-b.com** for additional online resources for students, teachers, and parents.

Write a Summary

Prewrite — Focus on Ideas

The Rubric Says	The topic is clear. Only main ideas and supporting details are included.
Writing Strategy	Read an article and take notes about the main points.

My teacher asked us to read an article and write a summary of it. I chose an article on simple machines because we studied them in science. As I read, I found the main points in the article. On page 202, you will see the notes I took as I read.

Machines Work
by J. Johar-Newton

Machines Make Life Easier

Beep! Beep! Beep! Your alarm clock sounds and you reach to turn it off. As you stretch your arms and roll out of bed, you wonder what's for breakfast. Scrambled eggs? Cereal? You walk out to the kitchen and hear coffee percolating and toast popping out of the toaster. As you sit down at the table, you wonder: What would my day be like without machines? No alarm clock to wake me up. No stove or microwave to heat up food. No toast. Without machines, you would have to do a lot more work just to make it through breakfast!

Simple Machines

The machines you used this morning are complex with multiple parts working together, and they made work easier for you. But what is work? In science, work is the result of applying a force over a distance to move an object. A force is a push or a pull. Most simple machines reduce the amount of force needed to move an object. That makes work easier for you!

In this article, you will learn about one of the six types of simple machines: levers. There are three classes of levers.

Levers: A Class Act

The lever is an inflexible bar that moves on a fixed point called a fulcrum. Take, for example, a paint can with a tightly sealed lid. You can try to pry off the lid with your fingers, but you would need a great deal of force. Using a screwdriver as a lever can make the work of removing the lid easier.

First-Class Levers

In a first-class lever such as this, the fulcrum, where the screwdriver touches the rim of the can, is between the input and the output forces. As you apply an

200 Informative/Explanatory Writing

English Language Learners

BEGINNING

Topic Write this sentence on the board: *Tennessee is a state in the southern U.S.* Ask, *What is this sentence about?* Tell students that Tennessee is the topic of the sentence. Say *topic* and write it on the board. Repeat the activity and have students determine the topic of several other sentences.

INTERMEDIATE

Topic Write a topic sentence on the board. Give students strips of paper with sentences that may or may not go with this topic sentence. Students read the sentence to the class and tell whether it should be included in the paragraph. Using the correct sentences, write a paragraph on the board that goes with the topic sentence. Students will use information about the topic as they write a summary.

input force by pushing on one end of the lever, the lever pivots on the fulcrum. The other end of the lever moves in the opposite direction,

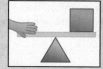

First-class lever

and the output force pops off the lid. The distance your hand moves is longer than the distance the lid moves. The work of getting the lid off was made easier. You put in a smaller amount of force over a longer distance and got a greater amount of force over a smaller distance. Seesaws, claw hammers, and crowbars are other examples of first-class levers.

Second-Class Levers

One type of second-class lever is a nutcracker. In second-class levers, the fulcrum—where the two handles, or levers, are joined—is at one end. The

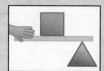

Second-class lever

input force is at the other end, where your hand is, with the output force in between. As you squeeze your hand inward, the levers turn around the fulcrum. The levers move in the same inward direction and exert an output force that cracks the nut's hard shell. The work of cracking the nut was made easier. You put in a smaller amount of force over a longer distance and got a greater amount of force over a smaller distance in return. Wheelbarrows and staplers are other examples of second-class levers.

Third-Class Levers

In a third-class lever, such as a baseball bat, the fulcrum, or pivot point, is at one end—in this case, your elbow. Your forearm becomes

Third-class lever

part of the lever. The output force is at the other end, the end of the bat. The input force is in between, where your hands supply the force to swing the bat. As in a second-class lever, the input and output forces act in the same direction. In a third-class lever, however, a greater input force is needed over a smaller distance. In return, you get a smaller output force applied over a longer distance. The output force also acts with a greater speed, which is helpful when hitting a moving target. Tennis rackets, golf clubs, and fishing rods are other examples of third-class levers.

Natural Levers

Natural levers can be found inside our bodies. Our elbows, arms, knees, and jaw help us move objects every day.

As part of the family of simple machines, levers help us by making work and play easier. Look around you. What levers do you see? What levers have you used today?

Key

△ fulcrum

▢ output force

✋ input force

Summary **201**

ADVANCED

Domain-Specific Vocabulary Ask, *What is vocabulary?* Students should know that *vocabulary* is words. Often the words are related. On the board, draw a Network Tree or a Web graphic organizer. Write *vocabulary* in the center circle. On the next layer, write *Science, Math, Social Studies, English*. Write a few different science topics around the Science circle, and say, *This is specific vocabulary.* Continue adding details to one science topic.

ADVANCED HIGH

Using Powerful Verbs After students have written their first drafts, have them circle all the verbs they used in the first paragraph. Then have a partner read the paragraph and change each of the circled verbs to a stronger one. Have the partners discuss why they made each change. Monitor that students' changes were appropriate.

CCSS **Common Core State Standards** (pp. Z20–Z30)
Writing: W.4.2d, W.4.4, W.4.5, W.4.8, W.4.9b, W.4.10
Language: L.4.6

Take Notes on Source Information

Read the introduction on page 202. Point out that before Alika begins to summarize the article, he needs to list the author's main points. Read Alika's notes aloud. Point out that he listed the author's big ideas in logical order. To write his summary, Alika will use only the details from the article that support the main points. Remind students that his summary will be shorter than the article because it does not include all the details.

Have students select and read articles on topics they find interesting. Tell them that this will help them share the information in an enthusiastic way. As needed, assist them in selecting short articles from resources in your classroom or on the Internet. Set aside time for them to read and take notes on their articles.

To summarize the article "Machines Work," I first need to find the author's main points. Then I'll choose only the details that support them. Here are my notes. Did you pick out the same big ideas?

Notes on "Machines Work"

✔ Machines help us do work.

✔ Work happens when a force (push or pull) moves something over a distance.

✔ Simple machines are simple. Can reduce force you exert. Makes work easier.

✔ There are 6 simple machines. One is the lever. It's a bar that pivots on a fulcrum, fixed point.

    ✔ First-class lever needs a small force over a long distance to get a large force over a short distance. Input force and output force are in opposite directions. Examples include screwdrivers used to open lids, seesaws, claw hammers, crowbars.

✔ Second-class lever needs a small force over a long distance to get a large force over a short distance. Input and output forces are in same direction. Examples include nutcrackers, wheelbarrows, and staplers.

✔ Third-class lever needs a large force over a short distance to get a small force over a long distance. Input and output forces are in same direction. You gain speed. Examples include baseball bats, tennis rackets, golf clubs, and fishing rods.

Write

Choose an article about a science topic that interests you. Read the article and take notes on the main points.

202 Informative/Explanatory Writing

Collaborative Conferencing

PEER TO PEER Have pairs exchange the notes they took on "Machines Work." Ask them to evaluate their partner's notes by asking, *Do the notes list the main points in logical order?* Then have students refer to Alika's notes on page 202 to compare notes.

PEER GROUPS Have students form groups of three or four. Ask them to discuss "Machines Work" and agree on the big ideas in the article. Students should then compare notes to see if they are similar and complete. In addition, have them compare their notes to Alika's on page 202.

TEACHER-LED Schedule conferences with individual students. Before they meet with you, encourage them to reread "Machines Work" and to think of questions to ask you about finding the main points and supporting details in the article.

Online Writing Center

Provides **interactive graphic organizers** as well as a variety of graphic organizers in PDF format.

Prewrite

Focus on Organization

The Rubric Says The main points are given in logical order.

Writing Strategy Use a Five-Column Chart to organize the main points.

I need to organize my notes in a clear way so that I can put them in a logical order in my summary. This way my summary will be easy to follow. I'll use a Five-Column Chart to categorize ideas about levers. Each heading identifies a main point about levers. Each row gives details about a different class of lever. You can see my Five-Column Chart below.

Five-Column Chart

Type of Lever and Examples	Placement of Fulcrum and Forces	Direction of Forces	Input Force/ Distance	Output Force/ Distance
First-class levers: screwdriver used to take off paint can lid, seesaw, claw hammer used to pry nails	Fulcrum between input and output forces	Opposite	Small/Long	Great/Short
Second-class levers: nutcracker, wheelbarrow, stapler	Fulcrum on one end, output force, input force	Same	Small/Long	Great/Short
Third-class levers: baseball bat, tennis racket, golf club, fishing rod	Fulcrum on one end, input force, output force	Same	Great/Short	Small/Long Output force is fast!

Analyze

How will Alika's Five-Column Chart help him write a summary?

Write

Look at your notes. Organize them in a Five-Column Chart.

Summary **203**

Write
Summary

Week 2 • Day 2

Student Objectives

• Make a Five-Column Chart to organize ideas. (p. 203)

Prewrite

Focus on

Categorize Information Explain that writers use a variety of organizers to get started writing. Alika used a Five-Column Chart to help him organize his notes. (Go to **www.sfw.z-b.com** for the downloadable graphic organizer.) Remind students that there are various organizers they can use, but using a Five-Column Chart to organize the main points and important details will help them to write a clear, well-organized summary. Together, study the organizer and have students identify the main points Alika selected.

Writer's Term

Categorize Information can be categorized by deciding into what group or general division information belongs.

CCSS **Common Core State Standards** (pp. Z20–Z30)
Writing: W.4.2a, W.4.2b, W.4.4, W.4.5, W.4.6, W.4.8, W.4.9b, W.4.10
Language: L.4.3c, L.4.6
Speaking and Listening: SL.4.1a, SL.4.1b, SL.4.1c, SL.4.1d, SL.4.3, SL.4.6

Summary **T203**

Write
Summary

Week 2 • Day 3

Student Objectives

• Use a Five-Column Chart to begin writing. *(p. 204)*

Draft

Focus on

Begin a Draft Remind students that writing a draft gives them a chance to get ideas on paper without having to worry about making mistakes. Be sure that students understand that they will use their Five-Column Chart to guide them through the drafting process. Read page 204 aloud. Ask students to read Alika's draft on pages 204–205. Have students compare Alika's draft to his Five-Column Chart.

Point out that Alika included the information from his Five-Column Chart to organize his summary about levers. He also used precise words and strong verbs to explain his topic. Explain that Alika refers to the rubric on page 194 as he writes.

Draw Evidence From the Text

Discuss that students will need to read through their article to find evidence to support the information they put in their Five-Column Chart.

Online Writing Center

 Provides an **interactive writing pad** for drafting, revising, editing, and publishing.

T204 Informative/Explanatory Writing

Draft

Focus on **Word Choice**

The Rubric Says	Domain-specific vocabulary is used and explained. Strong verbs help the reader understand the topic.
Writing Strategy	Use precise words and strong verbs.

I will need to use and explain some of the words from the article. For example, I will definitely use *lever* and *fulcrum*. I'll also choose strong verbs to help explain how simple machines work. One strong verb is clearer than using several vague, or unclear, words. I will keep this in mind while drafting, but I will focus on getting my ideas down first.

After I write down all of the important ideas, I will go back to the summary and revise with a focus on wording. As I draft, I will do my best not to make spelling, grammar, punctuation, or capitalization errors, but I know that I'll have a chance to fix them later when I edit.

Machines Work [DRAFT]

Machines help us every day. Some machines are very complex; others are more simple. In science terms, work is the result of applying a force over a distance to move an object, which makes the work of moving the object much easier. Simple machines are tools that help make our work easier.

Differentiating Instruction

ENRICHMENT

Summarize Informational Text Invite students to give short, oral summaries of their favorite nonfiction texts, perhaps some they've already shared with classmates or reading buddies. Prompt them with this sentence starter: *My favorite nonfiction book (article) is about….* Remind them to explain any words related to their topic. Ask listeners to jot down the title, big ideas, and memorable details for each summary.

REINFORCEMENT

Organize the Information Have students write the information for the graphic organizer on sticky notes. This way, they can experiment with the best order of information, moving it from column to column easily.

[DRAFT]

One of the six simple machines is called a lever. A lever is an inflexible bar that pivots on a fixed point called a fulcrum. The position of the fulcrum, the input force, and the output force determine whether the lever is a first-, second-, or third-class lever. Each lever has its own advantages.

precise words

strong verbs

A first-class lever, such as a seesaw, has the fulcrum located between the input and output forces. My cousin fell off a seesaw and broke her wrist. A smaller input force is applied over a longer distance, resulting in a greater output force applied over a shorter distance. The input and the output forces act in opposite directions. When you use a screwdriver to pry off a paint can lid, you are using a first-class lever to make work easier. Seesaws, claw hammers, and crowbars are examples of first-class levers.

precise words

Analyze

Read the beginning of Alika's draft. Did he choose precise words that help the reader understand the topic?

Write

Use your notes and chart to draft your summary. Choose precise words and strong verbs to explain the main points.

Summary **205**

Collaborative Conferencing

PEER TO PEER Have partners exchange drafts. Ask: *Has the writer used precise words and strong verbs?* Have students think of several questions they would like to ask to clarify vocabulary. Then have them write their questions on sticky notes and affix them on their partner's draft.

PEER GROUPS Form groups of four. Have students pass their draft to the student on the right to read. That student writes one comment on a sticky note on the draft and passes the draft along to the right. In the end, students should receive their own draft with three helpful comments.

TEACHER-LED Conference with pairs of students. Have them exchange drafts. Ask them to read for Ideas (see *Ideas* descriptor on page 194). Coach them in giving and receiving constructive feedback.

Write
Summary

Week 2 • Day 4

Student Objectives

• Complete a draft. *(p. 205)*

Continue Drafting It is important that students are given ample time to draft summaries. As conferencing is important throughout the writing process, be sure to also plan time for peer-to-peer, peer group, or teacher-led conferences. Remind students that this is the time to get their ideas down on paper in a creative and engaging way. Assure them that they will have plenty of time to fix any mistakes later.

Paraphrase Information Tell students to always use their own words when drafting. Explain that one way to use their own words is to focus on the main ideas of the facts they've researched. Encourage them to write down the main points of the facts instead of writing down the notes they took word for word. Tell students that this is called paraphrasing the text.

Note that using another writer's words as their own is called plagiarism. Tell the students that plagiarism is not acceptable.

CCSS **C**ommon **C**ore **S**tate **S**tandards (pp. Z20–Z30)
Writing: W.4.2a, W.4.2d, W.4.4, W.4.5, W.4.6, W.4.9b, W.4.10
Language: L.4.3a, L.4.3c, L.4.6
Speaking and Listening: SL.4.1b, SL.4.1c, SL.4.1d, SL.4.3, SL.4.4, SL.4.6

Write
Summary

Week 2 • Day 5

Student Objectives
- Revise to make sure all details support the main ideas. *(p. 206)*

Revise

Focus on [Ideas]

Remove Unimportant Details
Point out that during revising, repetitive and nonsupporting (unrelated) details should be removed.

Have a volunteer read the draft excerpt without the revisions, and then another volunteer read the revised excerpt. Make sure students can identify the main idea. **(first-class lever)** Point out how Alika's writing is much clearer and easier to follow after he removed details that don't support the main idea. Finally, remind students that their summary should include only main ideas and supporting details from the article.

✏ Writer's Term

Supporting Details Details that work to clarify, explain, describe, or expand upon the main topic are supporting details. These details provide important information the reader needs in order to understand the main ideas.

 Strategies for Writers Online
Go to **www.sfw.z-b.com** for additional online resources for students, teachers, and parents.

T206 Informative/Explanatory Writing

Revise
Focus on [Ideas]

The Rubric Says	Only main ideas and supporting details are included.
Writing Strategy	Make sure all details support the main ideas.

The rubric reminds me to check my draft to make sure all my details support my ideas. I noticed that in my paragraph about first-class levers, I used *seesaw* as an example in both the first and last sentences.

I also deleted the sentence about my cousin because this detail does not support the main idea.

Writer's Term
✏ **Supporting Details**
Supporting details provide important information the reader needs to understand the main ideas.

[DRAFT]
A first-class lever, ~~such as a seesaw,~~ has the fulcrum located between the input and output forces. ~~My cousin fell off a seesaw and broke her wrist.~~ A smaller input force is applied over a longer distance, resulting in a greater output force applied over a shorter distance. The input and the output forces act in opposite directions. When you use a screwdriver to pry off a paint can lid, you are using a first-class lever to make work easier. Seesaws, claw hammers, and crowbars are examples of first-class levers.

removed repetitive detail

removed non-supporting detail

Write
Read your draft carefully. Delete any details that do not support your main ideas.

206 Informative/Explanatory Writing

English Language Learners

BEGINNING/INTERMEDIATE
Negative Words Show students a picture of a child playing. Ask, *What is the child doing?* After asking several questions about the photo, begin asking some *yes/no* questions for which the answer is *no*. For example, *Is the child a boy?* When students answer *no*, model the complete sentence, *The child is not a boy.* Underline *not*. Repeat the activity to introduce other negative words, such as *doesn't, isn't, no, none, nobody,* and so on. Point to the underlined words and say, *These are negative words.*

ADVANCED/ ADVANCED HIGH
Double Negatives Have partners brainstorm a list of negative words, such as *no, none, nobody, nothing, not, nowhere, no one, doesn't, didn't, wasn't, weren't, aren't, isn't.* Remind students that they may use only one negative word in a sentence.

Revise

Focus on  Organization

The Rubric Says   The main points are given in logical order.

Writing Strategy   Put the most important idea first.

The author's most important point needs to be stated at the beginning of my summary. I read my introduction again and decided that the first two sentences didn't really state the main idea. So I crossed them out and moved the last sentence in the paragraph to the beginning. Do you think my revision improves my introduction?

[DRAFT]

Simple machines are tools that help make our work easier. ~~Machines help us every day. Some machines are very complex; others are more simple.~~ In science terms, work is the result of applying a force over a distance to move an object, which makes the work of moving the object much easier.

put most important idea first

Analyze
Look at Alika's revision. Did he improve the order of ideas in the introduction? In what way?

Write
Revise your draft so that your summary begins with the most important idea and that other important ideas follow logically.

Summary **207**

Collaborative Conferencing

PEER TO PEER   Have pairs of students exchange their drafts. After reading them, have students offer helpful feedback on different ways to strengthen Organization.

PEER GROUPS   Have students form small groups of three or four. Have them take turns reading their drafts aloud. Have group members suggest areas that may need to be rearranged in a more logical order.

TEACHER-LED   Schedule conferences with individual students. Have them focus on their introductions. Assist them, as needed, in putting their most important idea first.

Write
Summary

Week 3 • Day 1

Student Objectives

- Revise to put the most important idea first. *(p. 207)*

Revise

Focus on  Organization

Put the Most Important Idea First
Read the introduction to page 207 aloud. Have one volunteer read the draft excerpt without the revision, and then another volunteer read the revised excerpt. Point out that Alika improved it by removing the first two sentences and moving the main idea to the first sentence. Ask students why he deleted the first two sentences. **(Possible response: Alika's topic is simple machines.)**

Have students read their own introductions to make sure their lead sentence is the main idea of the summary. Remind students to use their Five-Column Chart to present the main ideas in the order they are presented in their article. Organizing their writing in this way will make the summary easier for the reader to follow.

CCSS **C**ommon **C**ore **S**tate **S**tandards (pp. Z20–Z30)
Writing: W.4.2a, W.4.2b, W.4.4, W.4.5, W.4.9b, W.4.10
Language: L.4.3c, L.4.6
Speaking and Listening: SL.4.1a, SL.4.1b, SL.4.1c, SL.4.1d, SL.4.3, SL.4.6

Write
Summary

Week 3 • Day 2

Student Objectives

- Revise to include clear and direct sentences. (p. 208)

Revise

Focus on Sentence Fluency

Revise Long, Confusing Sentences Read page 208 aloud. Remind students that the rubric says that sentences need to be clear and direct. Stress to students that long, confusing sentences make the summary unclear and hard for readers to understand. Clear, direct sentences help the summary flow smoothly and support the purpose for writing. Encourage students to review their summaries and revise any long or confusing sentences.

Revise

Focus on **Sentence Fluency**

The Rubric Says Sentences are clear and direct.

Writing Strategy Write clear sentences.

I know from the rubric that my sentences need to be clear and direct. When I read my draft again, I noticed that the beginning of my paragraph about second-class levers was long and confusing. I revised it by breaking it into two sentences. Do you think I improved my writing?

[DRAFT]

A second-class lever has the fulcrum on one end, the input and force on the other, the output force in between, and the forces in this kind of lever act in the same direction.

revised long, confusing sentence

Write

Check your draft for long or confusing sentences and clarify them.

208 Informative/Explanatory Writing

Optional Revising Lessons

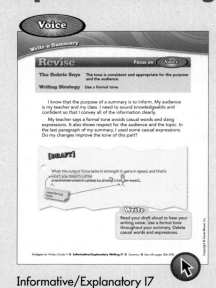

Informative/Explanatory 17

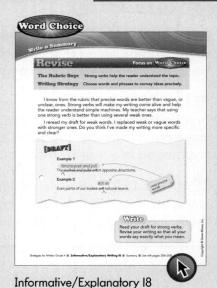

Informative/Explanatory 18

Go to ➡ *Strategies for Writers* at **www.sfw.z-b.com**

The Rubric Says   The writing contains no errors. There are no double negatives. Verbs are correct.

Writing Strategy   Check for double negatives. Make sure verbs are used correctly.

This is my chance to correct any mistakes I made while writing my draft. First I checked my spelling, capitalization, and punctuation to make sure my writing is correct. Then I reread my draft to look for double negatives and verb errors. I found some! Here are my edits.

Writer's Term _____

Negatives

A **negative** is a word that means "no" or "not." Do not use two negatives in the same sentence.

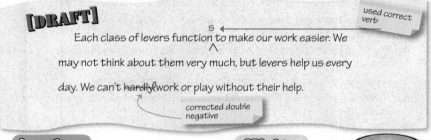

[DRAFT]
                                                                    used correct
                                                                    verb
                                                s
Each class of levers function to make our work easier. We
                            ^
may not think about them very much, but levers help us every

day. We can't ~~hardly~~ work or play without their help.

                    corrected double
                    negative

Analyze

How do Alika's edits make his writing easier to understand?

Write   **Conventions**

Edit your writing carefully. Be on the lookout for errors you make easily. Be sure you have not used double negatives.

For more practice in fixing double negatives and subject-verb errors, use the exercises on the next two pages.

Summary **209**

Related Grammar Practice _____

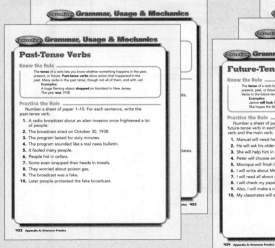

Student Edition pages 452, 453   Student Edition pages 454, 455, 456

Go to ➡ **Appendix A: Grammar Practice**

Student Objectives

• Edit to eliminate double negatives and use verbs correctly. *(p. 209)*

Edit

Focus on

Edit for Correct Use of Verbs and Negatives Have students read Alika's words on page 209. Then direct them to study the draft excerpt. Ask students to notice the corrections in Alika's model draft. Have students read their drafts carefully, paying special attention to verbs and negatives. Use the mini-lessons on pages T210 and T211 for students having problems with negatives and verb usage. Have students complete the exercises on pages 210 and 211 in their books.

Writer's Term _____

Negatives When two negatives are used in the same sentence, a double negative occurs. Using two negatives in the same sentence is incorrect. Some adverbs that end in *-ly* such as *hardly* and *barely* are also negative in meaning.

CCSS Common Core State Standards (pp. Z20–Z30)
Writing: W.4.4, W.4.5, W.4.6, W.4.9b, W.4.10
Language: L.4.1f, L.4.2a, L.4.2d, L.4.6

Conventions

Mini-Lesson

Student Objectives

• Recognize negatives. *(p. 210)*

Negatives

Have students review the Know the Rule box on page 210. Then read aloud the following sentences:

• I am *not* planning to go to any movies this weekend.

• I am *not* planning to go to no movies this weekend.

Ask students to identify the negatives in the sentences. (not; not, no)

Ask students which sentence has a double negative. (The second sentence has a double negative. It uses *not* and *no* in the same sentence.)

Explain to students that double negatives are very noticeable in both speaking and writing and are not acceptable in formal speech. Double negatives are confusing for the reader; avoid using two negatives in the same sentence.

You may wish to write a list of negatives on the board as a reference for students. Then have students complete page 210. Go over the answers and correct any errors.

Online Writing Center

 Provides **interactive grammar games** and **practice activities** in student eBook.

Negatives

Know the Rule

A **negative** is a word that means "no" or "not." The words *no, not, nothing, none, never, nowhere,* and *nobody* are negatives. The word *not* is found in contractions such as *don't* or *wasn't.* Do not use two negatives, called a double negative, in the same sentence.

Practice the Rule

Number a separate sheet of paper 1–10. Correctly rewrite the sentences that have double negatives. If the sentence is correct, write **Correct**.
Possible answers are given.

1. Who can work or play without ~~no~~ simple machines?
2. We couldn't barely move the log a few inches without a lever.
3. There were no simple machines ~~nowhere~~ anywhere to help move the heavy boxes.
4. By using a smaller force over a longer distance, a lever can make work easier for you. **Correct**
5. That rusty wheelbarrow can't ~~barely~~ hold the weight.
6. After smashing his thumb, he won't use ~~no~~ a hammer to crack open a walnut.
7. She didn't mention ~~no~~ scissors as an example of a first-class lever.
8. Everyone agreed that a golf club is a third-class lever. **Correct**
9. The lid ~~hardly~~ didn't budge until she applied an input force.
10. He told the men never to move ~~no~~ heavy loads without using a lever.

Related Grammar Practice

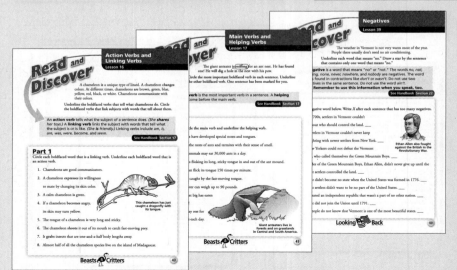

Pages 43, 45, 101

Go to ➡ **G.U.M. Student Practice Book**

Action Verbs and Linking Verbs

Know the Rule

An **action verb** tells what the subject of a sentence does. (*Waves crashed on the beach.*) A **linking verb** links the subject with words that tell what the subject is or is like. (*The waves were powerful.*) Linking verbs include *am, is, are, was, were, become,* and *seem.* Hint: Look for the linking verbs in contractions, too.

Practice the Rule

Number a separate sheet of paper 1–10. Write the verb in each sentence and tell whether it is an action verb or a linking verb.

1. A force is a push or a pull. is—linking
2. The lever pivots around the fulcrum. pivots—action
3. That's not a lever! It's an inclined plane. is—linking; is—linking
4. Each simple machine functions in a helpful way. functions—action
5. The hammer pries the rusty nail from the board. pries—action
6. He used his arm as a lever. used—action
7. Machines with many parts are not simple machines. are—linking
8. The Jaws of Life opened the car door. opened—action
9. Is a pair of pliers a first-class lever? Is—linking
10. The children sped toward the seesaw. sped—action

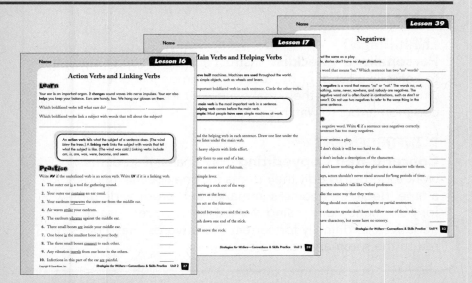

Pages 37, 39, 83

Go to ➡ *Grammar Practice Masters*

Mini-Lesson

Student Objectives

• Use action verbs and linking verbs correctly. *(p. 211)*

Action Verbs and Linking Verbs

Have students review the Know the Rule box on page 211. Then write the following sentences on the board:

• *Aaron jumped into the deep water.*
• *He is a strong and competitive swimmer.*
• *Jose hit a grand slam at his baseball game.*
• *He was the best player for that game.*
• *Aaron and Jose participate in many sports.*
• *They are both skilled athletes.*

Ask volunteers to identify the action verbs and the linking verbs in each sentence. (**Action Verbs: jumped, hit, participate; Linking Verbs: is, was, are**) Remind students that it is important to use action verbs and linking verbs correctly to make sure the meaning of their writing is clear.

You may wish to write a list of action verbs and linking verbs on the board as a reference for students. Then have students complete page 211. Go over their answers and correct any errors.

CCSS Common Core State Standards (pp. Z20–Z30)
Writing: W.4.6
Language: L.4.4a, L.4.6

Write
Summary

Week 3 • Day 4

Student Objectives

- Discuss preparation for publishing and presentation. *(p. 212)*
- Use a final editing checklist to publish their work. *(p. 212)*

Publish + Presentation

Publishing Strategy Ask students if they like Alika's choice for sharing his summary on the class website. Invite students to name other ways they could publish their own summaries. Perhaps one student will want to include his or her summary as part of a display in your language arts classroom, while another will want to include it in a multimedia presentation to the class.

Have a volunteer read Alika's checklist. Remind students that the checklist relates to the editing strategies they have been practicing. Have students use the checklist or one you suggest to perform a final evaluation before publishing their work.

Strategies for Writers Online
Go to **www.sfw.z-b.com** for additional online resources for students, teachers, and parents.

Publish + Presentation

Publishing Strategy	Post the summary to the class website.
Presentation Strategy	Use a clear font and indent paragraphs.

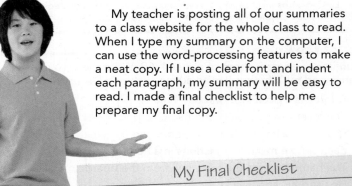

My teacher is posting all of our summaries to a class website for the whole class to read. When I type my summary on the computer, I can use the word-processing features to make a neat copy. If I use a clear font and indent each paragraph, my summary will be easy to read. I made a final checklist to help me prepare my final copy.

My Final Checklist

Did I—

- ✔ check the spelling, punctuation, and capitalization?
- ✔ make sure my summary contains no double negatives?
- ✔ look to see that all verbs are used correctly?
- ✔ use a clear font and indent all paragraphs?
- ✔ provide a list of sources?

Write

Make your own checklist and use it to prepare your final copy. Then publish your summary.

212 Informative/Explanatory Writing

Differentiating Instruction

ENRICHMENT
Personalized Checklist Instruct a small group of students to compile a list of errors that are common in students' writing. Then have them make a poster for the classroom of common errors to watch out for.

REINFORCEMENT
Concentrated Copyediting Have pairs of students work together to edit their drafts for one specific thing at a time. Begin by trading summaries and proofreading only for punctuation or spelling. Next edit for correct use of negatives, and finally for correct use of verbs. Have pairs return the summaries and discuss edits.

☐ 📧 Send 📧 Reply 🗔 Attach 🗔 Print

Machines Work
by J. Johar-Newton
Summary by Alika

Simple machines are tools that help make our work easier. In science terms, work is the result of applying a force over a distance to move an object. A force is a push or a pull. A simple machine can reduce the amount of force needed to move an object, which makes the work of moving the object much easier.

One of the six simple machines is called a lever. A lever is an inflexible bar that pivots on a fixed point called a fulcrum. The position of the fulcrum, the input force, and the output force determine whether the lever is a first-, second-, or third-class lever. Each lever has its own advantages.

A first-class lever has the fulcrum located between the input and output forces. A smaller input force is applied over a longer distance, resulting in a greater output force applied over a shorter distance. The forces push and pull in opposite directions. When you use a screwdriver to pry off a paint can lid, you are using a first-class lever to make work easier. Seesaws, claw hammers, and crowbars are examples of first-class levers.

A second-class lever has the fulcrum on one end, the input force on the other, and the output force in between. The forces in this kind of lever act in the same direction. As in the first-class lever, a smaller input force is applied over a longer distance, and a greater output force is applied over a shorter distance. Wheelbarrows and staplers are examples of second-class levers.

A third-class lever has the fulcrum on one end, the output force on the other, and the input force in between. The forces act in the same direction, but the input force is greater than the output force. In third-class levers, the input force acts over a shorter distance than the output force. What the output force lacks in strength it gains in speed, and that's what you need to drive a ball. Tennis rackets, golf clubs, and fishing rods are examples of third-class levers.

Each class of levers functions to make our work easier. We may not think about them very much, but levers help us every day. Even parts of our bodies act as natural levers. We can't work or play without their help.

Analyze

Use the rubric to evaluate Alika's summary and your own.

Tech Tips

Wikis

Publish Online Publishing content from students' summaries works as an information-literacy exercise when students add their discoveries, ideas, and contributions to a wiki, or "knowledge community" site. In editing an article on a site like Wikipedia or Wikijunior, students need to not only have their facts correct, but they also need to add information in a way that contributes to the existing piece. Sometimes students' writing will be deleted or rejected in the process. Work with students to examine site elements like the edit history to see how the article has evolved and to "listen in" on discussion in the threads. Understanding the community will help students learn how to better contribute.

See **www.sfw.z-b.com** for further information about and links to these websites and tools.

Write
Summary

Week 3 • Day 5

Student Objectives

- Use a summary rubric. *(pp. 194–195)*
- Share a published summary. *(p. 213)*

Presentation Strategy Neat and legible presentation is important when handwriting or typing a piece of writing. However, oral presentation is important, too. If students decide to present their summaries orally, they should remember to speak loudly, clearly, and at an understandable pace.

Reflecting on a Summary

Have students refer to the rubric on pages 194–195 as they reread Alika's final copy on page 213. Did his revisions and edits strengthen his summary? What score would Alika have received for each writing trait?

Next have students reflect on the assignment as a whole. Ask:

- What was your favorite part of this assignment?
- What will you do differently in your next summary?

CCSS **C**ommon **C**ore **S**tate **S**tandards (pp. Z20–Z30)
Writing: W.4.2a, W.4.4, W.4.6, W.4.9b, W.4.10
Language: L.4.2a, L.4.2d, L.4.3c
Speaking and Listening: SL.4.1a, SL.4.1b, SL.4.1c, SL.4.1d, SL.4.3, SL.4.4, SL.4.6

Next Generation Informative/Explanatory Assessment Planner

WEEK 1

Day 1
Analyze
Part 1: Close Reading

Student Objectives
- Understand the directions for a next generation assessment.
- Analyze a text source and a student response.
- Identify cause and effect relationships.

Student Activities
- Review and write about taking assessments.
- Read and discuss Part 1 directions. (pp. 214–215)
- Read and discuss Source 1. (pp. 216–217)

Day 2
Analyze
Part 1: Close Reading

Student Objectives
- Analyze a text source and a student response.
- Draw conclusions.
- Analyze a text source and a student response.
- Ask and answer questions.

Student Activities
- Read and discuss Source 2. (pp. 218–219)
- Read and discuss Source 3. (pp. 220–221)

Day 3
Analyze
Part 2: Writing to Multiple Sources

Student Objectives
- Understand the directions for a next generation assessment.
- Understand the scoring guide for a next generation assessment.

Student Activities
- Read and discuss Part 2 directions. (pp. 222–223)
- Read and discuss the scoring guide. (pp. 224–225)

WEEK 2

Day 1
Write
Revise: Organization, Voice

Student Objectives
- Revise to ensure the conclusion sums up the report.
- Revise to use facts to sound knowledgeable.

Student Activities
- Read and discuss **Revise: Focus on Organization.** (p. 230)
- Read and discuss **Revise: Focus on Voice.** (p. 231)

Day 2
Write
Revise: Word Choice
Edit: Conventions

Student Objectives
- Revise to include precise language.
- Check the grammar, spelling, capitalization, and punctuation.

Student Activities
- Read and discuss **Revise: Focus on Word Choice.** (p. 232)
- Read and discuss **Edit: Focus on Conventions.** (p. 233)

Note: Optional Revising Lessons are located at **www.sfw.z-b.com**

Day 3
Review
Publish Final Draft

Student Objectives
- Review a final draft.
- Practice taking a timed assessment.

Student Activities
- Read and discuss final draft. (pp. 234–235)

Day 4	Day 5
Write Prewrite: Ideas, Organization	**Write** Draft: Ideas

Student Objectives
- Respond to the assignment.
- Choose a graphic organizer.

Student Activities
- Read and discuss **Prewrite: Focus on Ideas.** (p. 226)
- Read and discuss **Prewrite: Focus on Organization.** (p. 227)

Student Objectives
- Begin with a topic sentence.
- Stay on topic.

Student Activities
- Read and discuss **Draft: Focus on Ideas.** (p. 228–229)

Day 4	Day 5
Practice Next Generation Assessment	**Practice** Next Generation Assessment

Student Objectives
- Practice taking a timed, next generation informative/explanatory assessment.

Student Activities
- Complete **Zaner-Bloser Next Generation Assessment** Part 1: Close Reading

Student Objectives
- Practice taking a timed, next generation informative/explanatory assessment.

Student Activities
- Complete **Zaner-Bloser Next Generation Assessment** Part 2: Writing to Multiple Sources

To complete the chapter in fewer days, combine the learning objectives and activities in a way that supports students as they write.

Resources at-a-Glance

Differentiating Instruction

For additional Differentiating Instruction activities, see Strategies for Writers Differentiated Instruction Activities at www.sfw.z-b.com.

English Language Learners

Comprehension Mini-Lesson

ZB Next Generation Assessment Practice

Informative/explanatory assessment practice appears on the *Strategies for Writers* website at **www. sfw.z-b.com**.

 Strategies for Writers Online

Go to **www.sfw.z-b.com** for additional online resources for students, teachers, and parents.

Online Writing Center

Provides IWB resources, assessments, interactive games and practice activities, videos, eBooks, and a virtual file cabinet.

Analyze
Part 1 Directions

Student Objectives

• Understand the directions for a next generation assessment. (*pp. 214–215*)

Informative/Explanatory Writing Review In this chapter, students will apply what they have learned about informative writing to the challenge of taking an informative/explanatory writing test. Tell them to take a few minutes to write about what they have learned about informative/explanatory writing. Then ask volunteers to share their responses with the class.

Taking Assessments Engage students in a discussion of their experiences with taking tests or assessments. Ask questions such as the following to facilitate discussion.

• What do you remember about taking an assessment? (Possible responses: There was a writing prompt. I had a time limit.)

• How might you prepare yourself to take a writing assessment? (Possible responses: eat a good breakfast, read the directions carefully, write a draft first)

• What advice would you offer someone who is about to take a writing test? (Possible responses: Write legibly. Make sure you understand the directions.)

 Strategies for Writers Online
Go to **www.sfw.z-b.com** for additional online resources for students, teachers, and parents.

Next Generation Informative/Explanatory Assessment

You know that writing assessments can often include both reading and writing. It is important to learn how to take this kind of assessment. For the first part of the test, you will read some sources and answer questions. Then, in the second part, you will use information from those sources in your writing. Practice planning your time for each part so you can do your best work.

Now let's analyze each part of this test, so you can really see what the assessment looks like.

PART 1: Close Reading

Your Task
You will examine three sources about the Great Depression. Then you will answer three questions about what you have learned. In Part 2, you will write a report explaining what happened during the Great Depression and how people from different walks of life helped each other.

Steps to Follow
In order to plan and write your report, you will do all of the following:
1. Examine three sources.
2. Make notes about the information from the sources.
3. Answer three questions about the sources.

Directions for Beginning
You will have 45 minutes to complete Part 1. You will now examine three sources. Take notes because you may want to refer to your notes while writing your report. You can re-examine any of the sources as often as you like. Answer the questions in the spaces provided.

Preparing Students for Next Generation Assessments

Each Next Generation Assessment chapter prepares students to take a performance-based next generation writing assessment. Students will analyze the assignment and a model assessment and learn strategies for taking next generation assessments.

On the last two days of the second week, students take the *Next Generation Assessment Practice* online or as a written test. Explain to students that although the model informative/explanatory assessment focuses on writing a report, they will write a different genre when they take their practice assessment. In a real test-taking situation, students will not know ahead of time which genre they will be asked to write.

Your Task This section of the directions gives information about the whole test. You will have two parts to complete. In Part 1, you will read and answer questions. In Part 2, you will write a report.

Steps to Follow This section reviews the task as a list. It tells how many sources you will examine. You also find out how many questions you have to answer. In this assessment, you will have to examine three sources and answer three questions.

Directions for Beginning This section gives information about Part 1 only—the reading part. You'll need to decide how you want to take notes. Will you write them on a piece of paper or use a note tool online? This section also tells how long you'll have to complete your task. These directions tell you that you have 45 minutes. Divide the time by three, since there are three sources, to figure out how much time to spend on each source.

TEST TIP

After I read each source, I write down two or three of the most important ideas. That helps me remember what each source is about when I take the writing part of the assessment.

Next Generation Assessment **215**

Differentiating Instruction

REINFORCEMENT
Planning Your Time Have students work in pairs to determine how much time they would spend reading each source in Part 1, taking notes on it, and answering a comprehension question. Guide them to understand that they should spend about 15 minutes on each source and leave at least 5 minutes to answer the question.

Next Generation Assessment
Tell students that they will be taking different types of assessments in school. Explain that writing assessments used to focus mainly on writing from personal experiences. Add that assessments now include reading passages and writing about them. Help students analyze the following three parts of the directions for Part 1: Close Reading:

Your Task The *Your Task* section gives students an overview of what will happen in both Parts 1 and 2 of the assessment.

Steps to Follow The *Steps to Follow* section provides students with steps that they will have to take before they start writing. Remind students that they will be expected to use evidence from the sources they analyze. Discuss with students how to take notes, either manually or digitally.

Directions for Beginning
The *Directions for Beginning* section focuses on what students will have to do in Part 1. Tell students that this is the section that explains how much time they have to complete Part 1. Remind them that it is important to plan how much time they can spend reading each source. Assist students with figuring how much time they should take.

CCSS **Common Core State Standards** (pp. Z20–Z30)
Writing: W.4.7, W.4.10
Speaking and Listening: SL4.1a, SL.4.1c, SL.4.1d, SL.4.3, SL.4.6

Analyze
Source 1: Text

Week 1 • Day 1

Student Objectives

- Analyze a text source and a student response. (pp. 216–217)
- Identify cause and effect relationships. (p. 217)

Close Reading Defined In a close reading, students read and then reread a text purposefully. Students are provided with text-dependent questions that require them to think about what the author had to say, what the author's purpose was, what the words mean, and what the structure of the text tells the reader. Close reading goes beyond simple recall and requires students to think more deeply and critically about what they are reading.

Tell students that they will learn a process they can use when taking an assessment. Add that there are two steps in this close reading process: *First Reading* and *Second Reading*.

First Reading Ask students to read Source 1 independently to understand the main idea. As they read, have students use sticky notes to identify confusing words or ideas. Then discuss the main idea. Have students share their confusing words or ideas.

 Strategies for Writers Online
Go to **www.sfw.z-b.com** for additional online resources for students, teachers, and parents.

Source 1: Text

The Great Depression
By Owen Anderson

The Great Depression of the 1930s was a time when the United States was in a financial crisis. This crisis touched every area of people's lives.

While the Great Depression was caused by several events and factors, many consider the stock market crash of 1929 as marking its beginning. The stock market is a place where stocks are bought and sold. Stocks are units of ownership in a company. When a company is doing well, their stocks are worth more. When a company is doing poorly, their stocks are worth less. In October of 1929, stock prices fell to record lows. People sold their stocks, causing the market to crash. Feeling panicked, the public rushed to get their money out of banks, causing the banks to fail. Once the banks were closed, people who had not retrieved their money couldn't get it back.

Many people lost their life savings, homes, and farms. With little to no money, people couldn't buy a lot of the things they used to, which hurt companies and industries. Workers were laid off as companies went out of business. At the worst point of the Great Depression, one out of every four Americans was jobless, and nearly half of American families were living in poverty without enough food, proper shelter, or medical care.

At this same time, a severe drought hit the Great Plains. Farmland dried out, and dust storms blew away the topsoil. People had to leave their farms. Nearly 1,300,000 Americans migrated to California, hoping to find work as pickers and farmhands. Some hitchhiked or hopped rides on freight trains. Families traveling by car had to stop to do work to earn money for gas.

During the Great Depression, four million Americans roamed the country looking for food and work. People tried to help each other as much as possible. When parents couldn't feed their kids, other families would take the children in. One man remembered 19 people living in his six-room house. Another told of neighbors bringing coal in a wheelbarrow to help his family of nine stay warm. In Ohio, a businessman put an ad in the newspaper using a fake name. All he asked was for people to write and tell him about their hardships. He read each letter and sent checks to 150 families. He never shared his real name; he simply wanted to help others.

216   Informative/Explanatory Writing

Comprehension Mini-Lesson

Cause and Effect

Teach Remind students that a cause is why something happened and an effect is what happened as a result of a cause. One effect may have several causes, and a cause may have several effects. Sometimes causes must be inferred from effects. For example, show students two books. Say: *I read only the first chapter of this book, but I read the other book in one day.* Then have students infer a cause for each action. (Possible response: You didn't like the first book, but you did like the second one.) Remind students that they can infer causes and effects by asking: *Why might this have happened?* or *Why did this probably happen?* As you discuss cause and effect relationships, make sure that the relationships you identify are causal and not sequential.

Of the four million Americans looking for food and work, at least 250,000 were teenagers. Shopkeepers would offer teens scraps of meat and vegetables, which they would cook together in one pot and share. Some homeowners offered food, a place to sleep, or perhaps a dollar for a meal. Many of these young migrant workers would travel by hopping on and off freight trains. They created a system of signs to tell others where they might find help. One sign meant they could sleep in the barn. Another let them know they could do chores in exchange for food.

As hard as times were, there was a spirit of determination, grit, and pride. People stuck together and made the best of things.

> **What were some effects of the Great Depression on people's lives? Use examples from the text to support your answer.**

 The question asks about effects of the Great Depression. An effect is what happens as the result of a cause. I'll reread the text and look for details about what happened during the Great Depression.

B *I* U abc ≡ ≡ ≡ ≡ ⋮≡ ≡ ↩ ↪ A⁻ A⁻ ✂ 📋 📋 ABC

My Response

Many people suffered during the Great Depression. They lost their jobs because a lot of companies went out of business. They had to travel around the country to find food and work. People even lost their homes, farms, and money they had saved all their lives.

Analyze

How well did Alika explain some effects of the Great Depression? What other effects could he include in his answer?

Second Reading Ask students to reread the text, looking for evidence to answer the text-dependent question listed on page 217: *What were some effects of the Great Depression on people's lives? Use examples from the text to support your answer.* Then discuss students' answers to encourage deeper comprehension. Make sure students support their answers with evidence from the text.

Analyze Response Tell students to review Alika's response and compare it to their own. Ask them to write answers to the questions in the **Analyze** box, and then have them share their answers with a partner. Ask volunteers to share their responses with the class.

Model/Practice Model finding cause-and-effect relationships. Draw a square on the board. Then draw two more squares below it. Finally, draw arrows pointing downward from the top square to the other two squares. Write the following effects in the bottom two squares (one in each square): *I ate many fresh vegetables all summer. I had fresh flowers on my kitchen table all summer.* Ask students to think of a possible cause for the two effects. (Possible cause: I grew many plants in my garden.) Have pairs write down two effects of one cause and trade their papers with another student pair, who must think of a possible cause.

Apply Read aloud a short paragraph that includes several unstated cause-and-effect relationships. Have students show the relationships they find.

CCSS **C**ommon **C**ore **S**tate **S**tandards (pp. Z20–Z30)
Writing: W.4.9b, W.4.10
Language: L.4.3c
Speaking and Listening: SL.4.1a, SL.4.1c, SL.4.1d, SL.4.2, SL.4.3, SL.4.6

Analyze
Source 2: Text

Week 1 • Day 2

Student Objectives

- Analyze a text source and a student response. *(pp. 218–219)*
- Draw conclusions. *(p. 219)*

First Reading Ask students to read Source 2 independently to understand the main idea. As they read, have students use sticky notes to identify confusing words or ideas. Then discuss the main idea. Have students share their confusing words or ideas.

Strategies for Writers Online
Go to **www.sfw.z-b.com** for additional online resources for students, teachers, and parents.

Source 2: Text

"Seeing Through Dorothea's Eyes"
by Sudipta Bardhan

In 1919, camera in hand, Dorothea Lange traveled to San Francisco. She set up her own portrait studio and became successful photographing the rich and famous. Ten years later, when the Great Depression began, things changed for everyone, including Lange.

People all over the country lost their jobs. Businesses closed, and fewer people could afford Lange's portraits. Her business suffered, but she saw this as a mixed blessing. She realized that she wasn't very happy only creating portraits for pay.

Lange struggled to decide what to do next. She took a vacation to help her make a decision. Walking alone in the mountains, she remembered the pictures she had filed away in her heart from her childhood, of bustling markets and hard-working immigrants. Suddenly, she knew what to do.

"I had to take pictures and concentrate upon people, only people," she said. "All kinds of people, people who paid me and people who didn't."

Lange wandered the streets of San Francisco, just as she had done as a child in New York City. She watched people around her going about their lives. One day, she took a photo of people waiting in a bread line. She hung that photo in her studio with the portraits, and realized that it was more powerful than all of the work she had done before.

The state of California soon hired Lange to photograph the living conditions of migrant farm workers. She traveled out of San Francisco to the camps where migrants from the Midwest came to try to find work. In one camp, she came across a woman and her family on the brink of starvation. "I saw and approached the hungry and desperate mother. She said that they had been living on frozen vegetables from the surrounding fields, and birds that the children killed."

Lange was appalled by the way these families were living. She took photographs of the woman and her children, and of other people in the camp. When people saw those photographs, they were shocked as well. In fact, the federal government rushed 20,000 pounds of food to the workers in that camp, mainly because Lange had brought attention to them.

218 Informative/Explanatory Writing

Comprehension Mini-Lesson

Draw Conclusions

Teach Tell students that a conclusion is a decision you reach after thinking carefully about something. Explain that readers often have to draw conclusions about the information in a text, especially if the relationship between two or more ideas isn't clearly stated. To draw a conclusion, readers think about what they know and make a decision based on the information in the text. They check to make sure the conclusion they drew makes sense.

Model/Practice Model drawing conclusions. Remind students of the story *The Three Little Pigs.* Draw a conclusion about the third little pig: *I know that the third pig builds a house out of bricks that wasn't blown down. I conclude that the pig is very smart because he found a strong building material.* Model drawing other conclusions about the pigs,

The pictures Dorothea Lange took during the Great Depression captured people's despair and their hopelessness. But the photos also captured their pride and honor. She saw in these people a determination that even the Great Depression could not take away. Using her camera, Lange kept a record of people who would have otherwise been forgotten. When President Franklin Roosevelt began a program to help those people most affected by the Depression, Dorothea Lange's photographs played an important role in bringing aid to many migrant workers.

Throughout her life, Lange believed that "a camera is an instrument that teaches people how to see." She hung her camera around her neck almost every day. The pictures she made decades ago are still teaching us to see that beauty can always be found in the strength and determination of the human spirit.

> Why were Lange's pictures of the migrants more powerful than her other portaits? Use evidence from the text in your answer.

I don't see the answer in the text, so I have to draw a conclusion. To do this, I have to put together several pieces of information to answer the question.

B *I* U abc ≡ ≡ ≡ ≡ ≡ ≡ ⬅ ➡ A▾ A▾ ✂ 📋 📋 ✓

My Response

The pictures changed how people viewed the migrants. Food was sent to people she photographed. Her pictures showed the migrants' despair and determination.

Analyze

> How well did Alika use evidence from the text in his answer? Is there anything he can add?

Second Reading Ask students to reread the text, looking for evidence to answer the text-dependent question listed on page 219: *Why were Lange's pictures of the migrants more powerful than her other portraits? Use evidence from the text in your answer.* Then discuss students' answers to encourage deeper comprehension. Make sure students support their answers with evidence from the text.

Analyze Response Tell students to review Alika's response and compare it to their own. Ask them to write answers to the questions in the **Analyze** box, and then have them share their answers with a partner. Ask volunteers to share their responses with the class.

---

such as the third is kind because he lets his brothers stay with him and the first is lazy because he builds his house too quickly.

Apply Provide additional familiar tales and have students draw conclusions about characters or events in each. Have students share the evidence they used to arrive at each conclusion.

CCSS **C**ommon **C**ore **S**tate **S**tandards (pp. Z20–Z30)
Writing: W.4.9b, W.4.10
Language: L.4.3c
Speaking and Listening: SL4.1a, SL.4.1c, SL.4.1d, SL.4.3, SL.4.6

Analyze
Source 3: Text

Week 1 • Day 2

Student Objectives

- Analyze a text source and a student response. *(pp. 220–221)*
- Ask and answer questions. *(p. 221)*

First Reading Ask students to read Source 3 independently to understand the main idea. As they read, have students use sticky notes to identify confusing words or ideas. Then discuss the main idea. Have students share their confusing words or ideas.

Source 3: Text

Seven-Cent Cotton and Forty-Cent Meat
By Anonymous

Seven-cent cotton and forty-cent meat,
How in the world can a poor man eat?
Flour up high and cotton down low,
How in the world can we raise the dough?
Clothes worn out, shoes run down,
Old slouch hat with a hole in the crown.
Back nearly broken and fingers all sore,
Cotton gone down to rise no more.

Seven-cent cotton and eight-dollar pants,
Who in the world has got a chance?
We can't buy clothes and we can't buy meat;
Too much cotton and not enough to eat.
Can't help each other, what shall we do?
I can't explain it so it's up to you.
Seven-cent cotton and two-dollar hose,
Guess we'll have to do without any clothes.

Seven-cent cotton and forty-cent meat,
How in the world can a poor man eat?
Mules in the barn, no crops laid by,
Corn crib empty and the cow's gone dry.
Well water low, nearly out of sight,
Can't take a bath on Saturday night.
No use talking, any man is beat
With seven-cent cotton and forty-cent meat.

Seven-cent cotton and forty-cent meat
How in the world can a poor man eat?
Poor getting poorer all around here;
Kids coming regular every year.

→

220 Informative/Explanatory Writing

Comprehension Mini-Lesson

Ask and Answer Questions

Teach Remind students that as they read a text, it is important to ask themselves questions about what they are reading. This will help them evaluate whether they understand what they are reading. Tell them that this is something that needs to be done periodically while they are reading, not just at the end of a chapter. Explain that they will find this strategy especially helpful while reading nonfiction, like the books they use in science and social studies classes.

Model/Practice Think about a book you are currently reading. Say to students, *I'm reading a book about dogs. The text talks about dogs that have jobs. I stopped and asked myself what I thought the author meant by jobs. Then I reread the next sentence and found the answer to my*

Strategies for Writers Online
Go to **www.sfw.z-b.com** for additional online resources for students, teachers, and parents.

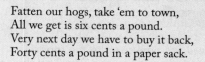

Fatten our hogs, take 'em to town,
All we get is six cents a pound.
Very next day we have to buy it back,
Forty cents a pound in a paper sack.

We'll raise our cotton, we'll raise our meat.
We'll raise everything we eat.
We'll raise our chickens, pigs, and corn;
We'll make a living just as sure as you're born.
Farmers getting stronger every year,
Babies getting fatter all around here.
No use talking, Roosevelt's the man,
To show the world that the farmer can.

How does the poem illustrate the problems farmers faced during the Great Depression? Use evidence from the poem in your answer.

This question asks me how the poem illustrates the problems farmers faced. I will reread the poem with this question in mind and look for an answer.

B *I* U abc ☰ ☰ ☰ ☰ ☷ ☷ ↰ ↱ A▾ A▾ ✂ ▣ ▤ ABC

My Response

Farmers were poor. They did not make enough money selling cotton and hogs to buy enough food and clothes for themselves. Their clothes were wearing out.

Analyze

How well did Alika answer the question? Is there any other evidence he could have used?

Next Generation Assessment **221**

question. Explain to students that they should ask themselves questions the entire time they are reading a text.

Apply Ask students to read a page in a nonfiction book and ask themselves questions as they read. Then ask volunteers to explain how this helped them understand the text better.

Second Reading Ask students to reread the text, looking for evidence to answer the text-dependent question listed on page 221: *How does the poem illustrate the problems farmers faced during the Great Depression? Use evidence from the poem in your answer.* Then discuss students' answers to encourage deeper comprehension. Make sure students support their answers with evidence from the text.

Analyze Response Tell students to review Alika's response and compare it to their own. Ask them to write answers to the questions in the **Analyze** box, and then have them share their answers with a partner. Ask volunteers to share their responses with the class.

CCSS **Common Core State Standards** (pp. Z20–Z30)
Writing: W.4.9b, W.4.10
Language: L.4.3c
Speaking and Listening: SL4.1a, SL.4.1c, SL.4.1d, SL.4.3, SL.4.6

Analyze
Part 2 Directions

Student Objectives

- Understand the directions for a next generation assessment. (pp. 222–223)

Next Generation Assessment

Ask students to read the paragraph at the top of page 222. Then help them analyze the following two parts of the directions for Part 2: Writing to Multiple Sources.

Setup The *Setup* section focuses on what students will do in Part 2. Tell students that this is the section that tells them how much time they have to complete Part 2. Explain that they can plan their time based on the stages of the writing process. Ask students if they agree with the amount of time Alika has assigned to each part of the writing process.

Make sure students understand that they will be allowed to go back to Part 1 to examine the sources again, but they cannot change their answers to the questions in Part 1. Remind them that the more time they spend re-examining sources, the less time they will have to write.

Strategies for Writers Online

Go to **www.sfw.z-b.com** for additional online resources for students, teachers, and parents.

Next Generation Informative/Explanatory Assessment

Now that Part 1 is complete, it's time to write the report. Usually you will complete Part 1 on one day and Part 2 on the next day. The directions for Part 2 are longer than Part 1 and continue on a second page. So remember to read the directions carefully and ask questions if you don't understand.

PART 2: Writing to Multiple Sources

Setup
You will now have 70 minutes to review your notes and sources, plan, draft, and revise a report. You may use your notes and refer to the sources. You may also refer to the answers you wrote to questions in Part 1, but you cannot change those answers. Now read your assignment and the information about how your report will be scored. Then begin your work.

Your Assignment
The Great Depression was a very difficult time in America, but it was also a time when people helped others. Your assignment is to write a report explaining what happened during the Great Depression and how people from different walks of life helped each other. Support your topic with concrete details and examples from each of the sources you have examined. The audience for your report will be the adults and students in your school.

English Language Learners

BEGINNING/INTERMEDIATE

Part 2 Directions Have students look at the *Setup* section. Select a few key words that students will not know. As you say each word, have students point to the word and repeat it. Write the word on the board and say it again. Elicit the meaning of each word or teach its meaning if students cannot provide it. Repeat the process with important words from *Your Assignment*. Finally, simplify the writing prompt. Explain Alika's task so that students will understand what he is doing as he works through the informative/explanatory test writing process.

Repeat this process with students before they begin their own next generation informative/explanatory assessment.

Setup This section lets you know how much time you have to complete Part 2. You can divide the time into the different parts of the writing process. Here's an example of what Alika plans to do.

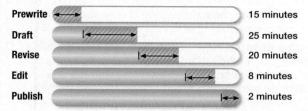

Prewrite	15 minutes
Draft	25 minutes
Revise	20 minutes
Edit	8 minutes
Publish	2 minutes

The directions also tell you that you can go back and examine the sources from Part 1, but the answers can't be changed.

Your Assignment This part explains your writing assignment. The topic of your assignment usually appears in the first few sentences in this section. In this case, it's the first two sentences. Finally, you are given a clue to what kind of voice you should use in your report. Because your audience is the adults and students in your school, you should sound serious and knowledgeable.

Your Assignment The *Your Assignment* section provides students with specific information about the topic, genre, and audience for their assignment. Remind students that the topic and genre were introduced in Part 1 of the test. Ask them to go back to the directions for Part 1 to identify the sections where the topic and genre were mentioned.

Point out the following sentence to students from the *Your Assignment* section on page 222: *Your assignment is to write a report explaining what happened during the Great Depression and how people from different walks of life helped each other.* Make sure students understand that their writing should be based on information from the sources they have examined, not on their personal experiences.

ADVANCED/ ADVANCED HIGH
Part 2 Directions   Have students read the *Your Assignment* section and write three to six words or phrases that they think are most important. Then have each student compare with a partner and discuss the meanings of the words and phrases. After they have discussed their ideas, help them verify actual meanings using dictionaries. Further assist them by offering examples of your own. Have the partners outline the task that Alika will follow during the informative/explanatory test writing process.

Have students repeat this process before they start their own next generation informative/explanatory assessment.

CCSS **C**ommon **C**ore **S**tate **S**tandards (pp. Z20–Z30)
Writing: W.4.2a, W.4.7, W.4.10
Speaking and Listening: SL4.1a, SL.4.1c, SL.4.1d

Analyze
Part 2
Scoring Guide

Week 1 • Day 3

Student Objectives

• Understand the scoring guide for a next generation assessment. *(pp. 224–225)*

Analyze the Scoring Guide Direct students' attention to the Scoring Guide on page 224. Tell students that the scoring guide helps them plan and evaluate their writing. Help students understand how the scoring guide is similar to the rubrics they have seen by asking questions such as the following:

Which section

• focuses on presenting clear ideas? (second)

• reminds you to stay on topic? (first)

• helps you improve your tone and inform the reader? (second)

• encourages you to use a variety of sentences? (first)

• reminds you to edit your writing? (third)

Scoring Guide

Your report will be scored on the following criteria:

1. **Focus and organization** How well did you introduce your topic? How well did you use a variety of sentences? How well did you group related information in paragraphs? How well did you stay on topic throughout the report? How well did your conclusion sum up the information you presented?

2. **Elaboration of topic** How well did you develop the topic with relevant facts, definitions, concrete details, quotations, or other information and examples? How well did you clearly express ideas using precise language and domain-specific vocabulary that was appropriate for your audience and purpose? How knowledgeable did you sound about your topic?

3. **Conventions** How well did you follow the rules of grammar, punctuation, capitalization, and spelling?

Now you can begin work on your report. Manage your time carefully so that you can:

• plan your report.
• write your report.
• revise and edit for a final draft.

Spell check is available to use.

Type your response in the space provided on the following page. Write as much as you need to fulfill the requirements of the task. You are not limited by the size of the response area on the screen.

Strategies for Writers Online
Go to **www.sfw.z-b.com** for additional online resources for students, teachers, and parents.

Writing Traits in the Scoring Guide

The second page of the directions tells you how your report will be scored. This scoring guide includes all of the writing traits. You can use what you have learned about the writing traits to help you write an interesting report.

1 Focus and organization

- How well did you use a variety of sentences?

- How well did your conclusion sum up the information you presented?

2 Elaboration of topic

- How well did you develop the topic with relevant facts, definitions, concrete details, quotations, or other information and examples?

- How knowledgeable did you sound about your topic?

- How well did you clearly express ideas using precise language and domain-specific vocabulary?

3 Conventions

- How well did you follow the rules of grammar, punctuation, capitalization, and spelling?

Before you start Part 2, review your plan for how you will divide your time. Remember there is no word limit, but don't feel you have to fill the entire space with your thoughts. Now it's time for Alika to start writing his report.

Writing Traits in the Scoring Guide

Direct students' attention to the information about the scoring guide. Tell students that some scoring guides do not include the names of the six traits, but they still relate to each of the traits. Students can use their writing experience to remember the main requirements associated with each trait:

Ideas a clearly stated topic, supported by facts and other evidence from credible sources

Organization logical organization that includes helpful transitions that guide the reader

Voice a voice that sounds knowledgeable and appropriate for both purpose and audience

Word Choice language that is precise and supports the writer's purpose

Sentence Fluency sentences that flow well with a variety of patterns and lengths

Conventions conscientious editing for grammar, spelling, capitalization, and punctuation

CCSS **Common Core State Standards** (pp. Z20–Z30)
Writing: W.4.2b
Speaking and Listening: SL4.1a, SL.4.1c, SL.4.1d

Write
Prewrite

Week 1 • Day 4

Student Objectives

• Respond to the assignment.
  (p. 226)

Prewrite

Focus on Ideas

Gather Information Tell students that they will need to gather evidence, such as facts and examples, from the three sources that they examined in Part 1 to support their topic. Remind students that they are allowed to go back and review the sources, but they cannot change their answers to the questions.

Online Writing Center

Provides **interactive graphic organizers** as well as a variety of graphic organizers in PDF format.

T226 Informative/Explanatory Writing

Prewrite   Focus on Ideas

Writing Strategy   Respond to the assignment.

Prewrite ←→ [   ] 15 minutes

Writers gather information to help them write. This is an important step when you write for an assessment. I will look at the assignment again to find information about what I am supposed to write.

From my assignment, I know I'm supposed to write a report. I also know the topic.

> *topic*
>
> The Great Depression was a very difficult time in America, but it was also a time when people helped others. Your assignment is to write a report explaining what happened during the Great Depression and how people from different walks of life helped each other.
>
> *genre*

First, I'm going to write a topic sentence. Then, I'll think about which of the sources will support my topic sentence. I can't remember all the details about the sources, but I just want to see what I remember.

> **My Topic Sentence:**
>   The Great Depression was a time of hardship and helping others.
> **Sources that Support My Topic Sentence:**
>   The text about the Great Depression
>   The poem about the farmers

226 Informative/Explanatory Writing

Differentiating Instruction

ENRICHMENT
Create Your Own Assignment Challenge students to write their own report assignment, using the model assignment on page 222 to guide them. Then have them exchange assignments and respond by writing a clear topic statement such as Alika wrote on page 226.

Prewrite

Focus on **Organization**

Writing Strategy Choose a graphic organizer.

Prewrite ◀▬▶ 15 minutes

I need to start organizing my ideas. A good graphic organizer for a report is a Web. It will help me organize important details from the sources in Part 1 to support my topic. I can go back now and examine the sources again so I can get more specific.

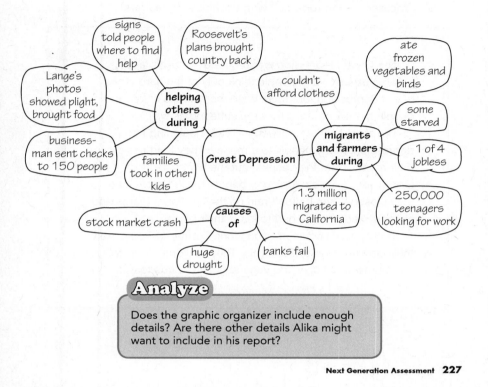

- signs told people where to find help
- Roosevelt's plans brought country back
- ate frozen vegetables and birds
- Lange's photos showed plight, brought food
- couldn't afford clothes
- some starved
- **helping others during**
- businessman sent checks to 150 people
- **migrants and farmers during**
- 1 of 4 jobless
- families took in other kids
- **Great Depression**
- 1.3 million migrated to California
- 250,000 teenagers looking for work
- stock market crash
- **causes of**
- banks fail
- huge drought

Analyze

Does the graphic organizer include enough details? Are there other details Alika might want to include in his report?

Differentiating Instruction

REINFORCEMENT

Break Down Your Assignment Read Aloud *Your Assignment* on page 222. Ask students to explain in their own words what it means. If needed, guide them to restate the directions. One way might be to break down the assignment into a bulleted list and go over each point carefully. Encourage them to use this strategy in their own assessment writing.

Write
Prewrite

Week 1 • Day 4

Student Objectives

- Choose a graphic organizer. *(p. 227)*

Prewrite

Focus on  Organization

Analyze Graphic Organizer After students have reviewed Alika's Web, have them write responses to the questions in the **Analyze** box. Then have them share their responses with a partner. Ask volunteers to share their responses with the class. Tell students that in a test-taking situation a graphic organizer may not be given to them. Explain that they will need to choose one on their own that best suits their assignment. Encourage students to fill in a graphic organizer completely to help them draft their reports.

CCSS **C**ommon **C**ore **S**tate **S**tandards (pp. Z20–Z30)
Writing: W.4.2a, W.4.8, W.4.9b, W.4.10
Speaking and Listening: SL4.1a, SL.4.1c, SL.4.1d

Write
Draft

Week 1 • Day 5

Student Objectives

- Begin with a topic sentence.
- Stay on topic. (pp. 228–229)

Draft

Focus on Ideas

Drafting on Paper Remind students that they may take tests on paper or on a computer. If they take the test on paper, remind them to write on every other line. This leaves space for students to make their corrections when they revise and edit their drafts. Mention that in a timed situation, students will not have time to create a fresh final copy of their writing.

Drafting on Computer If students take the test on a computer, tell them that they should make sure they know where the Save button is. Encourage students to save often. If they cannot find the Save button, explain that there might be an autosave, but they should check with the adult monitoring the test. Point out the wavy lines in Alika's draft. Ask students if they know what the wavy lines mean. (The word is misspelled.)

 Strategies for Writers Online
Go to **www.sfw.z-b.com** for additional online resources for students, teachers, and parents.

Draft   Focus on Ideas

Writing Strategy Begin with a topic sentence.

Draft |◄━━━━━━━━━━| 25 minutes

 I'll begin my report with a topic sentence. This will be the most important part of the introduction. Then I'll use my Web as a guide. As I write the rest of my report, I'll group related information together and also stay focused on the topic so I won't confuse my readers.

> **The Great Depression was a time of hardship and helping others.** Most people think only of the hard times of the Depression, but there were many times when people helped others who were suffering as well.
>
> The stock market crashed in 1929, beginning the depression. Many people lost money. They tried to get their money from their banks, but the banks had lost money too. They couldn't pay people back. Before long they closed. Then it didn't rain on the farmland. Plants and animals died. People had to leave their farms.
>
> Many people could not find work. Farmers who had left their farms moved to California. They couldn't afford to eat. Some could only find vegetables and birds to eat.

topic sentence

English Language Learners

BEGINNING

Identify Facts Read a simple nonfiction text about bears. After reading, write *Bears are animals*. Ask, *Is this always true?* and then say *Facts are always true*. Say "facts" and have students repeat. Show pictures from the book to encourage students to give more simple facts about bears that they might know from other sources. Record responses. Then read sentences one at a time and have students repeat.

INTERMEDIATE

Word Choice Remind students that when they speak or write, they should try to use powerful verbs. Write the following verbs on the board: *said, declared, exclaimed, cried, stated, answered,* and *uttered*. Have students work in pairs to place words in order from boring and weak to strong and convincing. Allow them to use a dictionary for support.

B *I* U abc ≡ ≡ ≡ ≡ ≣ ≣ ↰ ↱ A⌄ A⌄ ✂ 🗐 🗎 ✓

Even as people were struggling, others tried to help. One businessman sent checks to 150 family's. Families took in each other's children. Some people rode the rails, looking for food or work.

The goverment helped people. Food was sent to the camps. President Roosevelt put together plans.

The depression was terrible for the country. Then it ended.

Analyze

Does the first sentence introduce the topic well? Do all the details in the report relate to the topic?

ADVANCED/ADVANCED HIGH
Using Precise and Vivid Words Explain what you mean by *vague words* as compared to *precise words*. Ask students to help you generate a list of vague words that they speak or hear in everyday conversation. (possible responses: pretty, good, nice, goes). Have them work in pairs to think of more precise words that they might use instead. (possible responses: attractive, outstanding, kind, declares or dashes, depending upon use) Have them share their suggestions for precise words with the class.

Use a Graphic Organizer Remind students that they should keep their graphic organizer out as they draft and refer to it frequently. If new evidence occurs to students while they draft, they should consider including it, especially if it supports their topic. If students cannot decide where the new evidence belongs on the organizer, they should probably not use it in their writing.

Support a Topic After students have reviewed Alika's draft, have them write responses to the questions in the **Analyze** box. Then have them share their responses with a partner. Ask volunteers to share their responses with the class. As students draft during an assessment, tell them to pay attention to presenting and supporting their topic clearly. Have them ask themselves:

- Have I stated my topic sentence (purpose for writing) clearly in the introduction?

- Do I include historical details from the sources?

- Do I give interesting details that support the topic?

CCSS **C**ommon **C**ore **S**tate **S**tandards (pp. Z20–Z30)
Writing: W.4.2a, W.4.2b, W.4.9b, W.4.10
Language: L.4.3a, L.4.6
Speaking and Listening: SL.4.1a, SL.4.1c, SL.4.1d

Write
Revise

Student Objectives

- Revise to ensure the conclusion sums up the report. *(p. 230)*

Revise

Focus on

Time Management Point out that Alika had about twenty minutes to revise his draft and that there were three revision tasks. (If you are using the Optional Revising Lessons, you will need to plan accordingly. See page T232.) Tell students that Alika divided his planned revising time into three six- to seven-minute segments and revised for one strategy at a time. Explain to students that they may not have enough time to revise for all traits during an assessment, so they should focus on the traits they know they usually need help with.

Analyze Revision After students have reviewed Alika's revision, have them write responses to the questions in the **Analyze** box. Then have them share their responses with a partner. Ask volunteers to share their responses with the class.

Strategies for Writers Online
Go to **www.sfw.z-b.com** for additional online resources for students, teachers, and parents.

Revise   Focus on **Organization**

Writing Strategy   Sum up my report in the conclusion.

Revise |←——→| 20 minutes

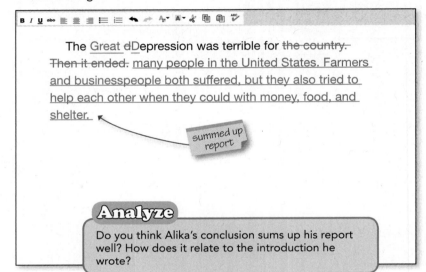

Now, it's time to check my draft against the scoring guide. I want to be sure I've included all the points that will be scored.

The scoring guide reminds me to sum up my report in the conclusion. I know that the conclusion should relate to the introduction but sum up the report a little differently. The conclusion is the last thing readers will read and remember, so it has to be good!

The Great dDepression was terrible for ~~the country. Then it ended.~~ many people in the United States. Farmers and businesspeople both suffered, but they also tried to help each other when they could with money, food, and shelter.

summed up report

Analyze

Do you think Alika's conclusion sums up his report well? How does it relate to the introduction he wrote?

Revise

Focus on **Voice**

Writing Strategy Use facts to sound knowledgeable.

Revise |←——→| 20 minutes

The scoring guide tells me to be sure I sound knowledgeable about my topic. I need to sound like an expert on the Great Depression. One way to do that is to use facts. There are a lot of numbers in the sources I read. These are important facts that I will add to my report.

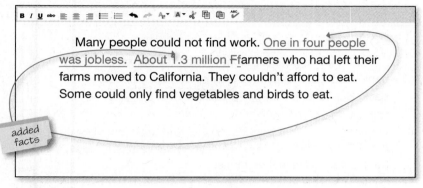

Many people could not find work. One in four people was jobless. About 1.3 million Ffarmers who had left their farms moved to California. They couldn't afford to eat. Some could only find vegetables and birds to eat.

added facts

Analyze

How do the facts Alika added make him sound knowledgeable about his topic? What other facts could he add to his report?

Differentiating Instruction

REINFORCEMENT

Support Voice Remind students that voice is the way the writer "speaks" to the reader. Facts inform the reader. To sound knowledgeable, a writer includes many facts about the topic. Read Alika's report aloud, using a serious tone of voice. Ask students how the facts he included make him sound knowledgeable about the topic.

Write
Revise

Week 2 • Day 1

Student Objectives

- Revise to use facts to sound knowledgeable. *(p. 231)*

Revise

Focus on

Review Voice Remind students that their voice should sound knowledgeable throughout an informative/explanatory piece of writing. When taking an assessment, students should make sure they include facts and other evidence from the sources they read in order to sound knowledgeable.

Analyze Revision After students have reviewed Alika's revisions, have them write responses to the questions in the **Analyze** box. Then have them share their responses with a partner. Ask volunteers to share their responses with the class.

CCSS **C**ommon **C**ore **S**tate **S**tandards (pp. Z20–Z30)
Writing: W.4.2e, W.4.9b, W.4.10
Speaking and Listening: SL.4.1a, SL.4.1b, SL.4.1c, SL.4.1d

Write
Revise

Student Objectives

- Revise to include precise language. *(p. 232)*

Revise

Focus on Word Choice

Review Precise Language Read aloud the Writing Strategy and the introduction on page 232. Discuss the importance of replacing vague words with more precise words. Ask volunteers to explain why Alika replaced the words he did and how his revisions help make his ideas clearer. Tell students that if Alika had time left in the revising period, he could have checked for other traits, such as Ideas and Sentence Fluency. When students are taking an assessment, encourage them to use every minute remaining to improve their writing, even if they think they are finished.

Analyze Revision After students have read Alika's revisions, have them write responses to the questions in the **Analyze** box. Then have them share their responses with a partner. Ask volunteers to share their responses with the class.

Next Generation Assessment

Revise

Focus on **Word Choice**

Writing Strategy Choose words and phrases to convey ideas precisely.

Revise ◄══════► 20 minutes

 The scoring guide reminds me to use precise language in my report. This will make my report easy to read and understand. I'll read my draft again. I noticed that there are several places where I could replace a vague word or phrase with a more precise word or phrase.

> They tried to get their money from their banks, but the banks had lost money too. They couldn't pay people back. Before long they failed ~~closed~~. Then a severe drought swept through the Great Plains. ~~it didn't rain on the farmland.~~ Crops were ruined and livestock died of thirst. ~~Plants and animals died.~~ Farmers and their families ~~People~~ had to leave their farms.

added precise language

Analyze

Do these word changes make the language more precise? Could other parts of his draft use more precise language?

Optional Revising Lessons

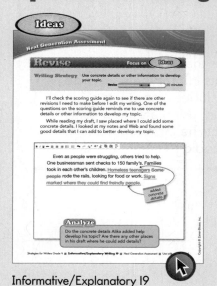

Informative/Explanatory 19

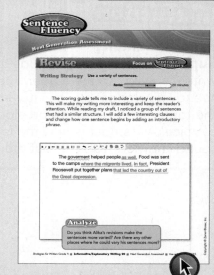

Informative/Explanatory 20

Go to ➡ **Strategies for Writers** at **www.sfw.z-b.com.**

Writing Strategy Check the grammar, spelling, capitalization, and punctuation.

Edit |←—→| 8 minutes

The scoring guide reminds me to use correct grammar and spelling. I also need to check my capitalization and punctuation. That's a lot to do, but I scheduled enough time to check for errors in these important areas. I'll read my draft carefully one more time.

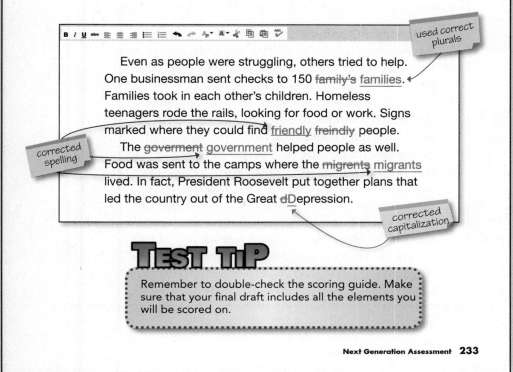

used correct plurals

Even as people were struggling, others tried to help. One businessman sent checks to 150 ~~family's~~ families. Families took in each other's children. Homeless teenagers rode the rails, looking for food or work. Signs marked where they could find friendly ~~freindly~~ people. The ~~goverment~~ government helped people as well. Food was sent to the camps where the ~~migrents~~ migrants lived. In fact, President Roosevelt put together plans that led the country out of the Great ~~d~~Depression.

corrected spelling

corrected capitalization

TEST TIP

Remember to double-check the scoring guide. Make sure that your final draft includes all the elements you will be scored on.

Differentiating Instruction

REINFORCEMENT

Learning to Plan With only eight minutes to edit, less proficient writers may become anxious during the editing stage of the writing process. Advise students to break down the task into more manageable chunks. Looking for one or two types of errors at a time may help students be successful.

Write
Edit

Week 2 • Day 2

Student Objectives

• Check the grammar, spelling, capitalization, and punctuation. *(p. 233)*

Edit

Focus on Conventions

Editing Explain that while a report written for an assessment in a short period of time will rarely be perfect, students should correct as many errors as possible. Assessment graders know that students are writing quickly and watching the clock, so a few errors may slip through. However, assessment graders also look for evidence that students took the time to edit. When they see misspelled words crossed out and correctly spelled words inserted instead, assessment graders know that students are paying attention to editing. If students are taking assessments online, they may not be able to show their edits. If they see wavy lives still remaining in their writing, this means that they have misspelled words. Tell them to check the spelling of these words by using the spell-check feature.

CCSS **Common Core State Standards** (pp. Z20–Z30)
Writing: W.4.2b, W.4.6, W.4.9b, W.4.10
Language: L.4.2a, L.4.2d, L.4.3a, L.4.6
Speaking and Listening: SL.4.1a, SL.4.1b, SL.4.1c, SL.4.1d

Review
Final Draft

Week 2 • Days 3–5

Student Objectives

- Review a final draft.
- Practice taking a timed assessment. *(pp. 234–235)*

Publish

Publishing an Assessment

Review Alika's final draft with students. If students take an online assessment, they should always use the spell-check feature one more time before they submit their work. If they take an assessment on paper, they should read through their work one final time before they submit it.

Write About What You Learned

Ask students to write about taking a next generation assessment, including the steps you have to take and how to manage your time. When they are done, lead a discussion about what they wrote using questions such as the following:

- What is the difference between Part 1 and Part 2? (Possible response: Part 1 is reading texts. Part 2 is writing using the information you learned in Part 1.)

- What can you do to remember details from each source? (Possible response: Use notes or a graphic organizer to help keep track of the details.)

 Strategies for Writers Online
Go to **www.sfw.z-b.com** for additional online resources for students, teachers, and parents.

Publish

Publishing Strategy   Submit the final draft of your research report.

Publish ▭▭▭▭▭▭▭▭▭▭ ⏩ 2 minutes

 I am almost finished with my assessment. I used information in the scoring guide and the writing traits to complete my report. Now, I will read the report once more to make sure all the details I included were related to my topic. Then I will submit my final draft.

> The Great Depression was a time of hardship and helping others. Most people think only of the hard times of the Depression, but there were many times when people helped others who were suffering as well.
>
> The stock market crashed in 1929, beginning the Depression. Many people lost money. They tried to get their money from their banks, but the banks had lost money too. They couldn't pay people back. Before long they failed. Then a severe drought swept through the Great Plains. Crops were ruined and livestock died of thirst. Farmers and their families had to leave their farms.
>
> Many people could not find work. One in four people was jobless. More than 1.3 million farmers who had left their farms moved to California. They couldn't afford to eat. Some could only find vegetables and birds to eat.

234   *Informative/Explanatory Writing*

Differentiating Instruction

ENRICHMENT
Reaching the Finish Line Students who often finish writing tests early may fall into the habit of simply waiting for the testing period to be over. Remind them to use the remaining time to improve their writing. Have them look back at the list of traits on page 225 and revise for Ideas and Sentence Fluency, too.

Even as people were struggling, others tried to help. One businessman sent checks to 150 families. Families took in each other's children. Homeless teenagers rode the rails, looking for food or work. Signs marked where they could find friendly people.

The government helped people as well. Food was sent to the camps where the migrants lived. In fact, President Roosevelt put together plans that led the country out of the Great Depression.

The Great Depression was terrible for many people in the United States. Farmers and businesspeople both suffered, but they also tried to help each other when they could with money, food, and shelter.

Now It's Your Turn

Don't forget all the advice Alika gave you. Now, it's your turn to practice taking an informative/explanatory assessment.

Next Generation Assessment Practice

Student Edition

Scaffolded Student Edition

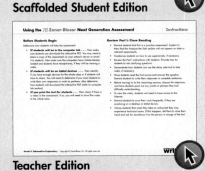

Teacher Edition

• Where do you look to find out what you need to include in your writing? (Possible response: Your Assignment and the Scoring Guide tell you what you need to write.)

Now It's Your Turn

Tell students that they will practice taking a next generation informative/ explanatory assessment in real time. If time permits, students should complete the assessment over a two-day period. Go to **www. sfw.z-b.com** or the **Strategies for Writers Online Writing Center** to download the **Next Generation Assessment Practice** for informative/ explanatory writing.

There are two student versions of the assessment. One assessment contains scaffolded support as students take the assessment. The other assessment does not have scaffolded support. Choose which version of the assessment you want your class to take. Review the teacher version of the assessment before giving it to students.

CCSS **C**ommon **C**ore **S**tate **S**tandards (pp. Z20–Z30)
Writing: W.4.4, W.4.5, W.4.9b, W.4.10
Speaking and Listening: SL.4.1a, SL.4.1c, SL.4.1d

Opinion writing

Opinion Essay

Pages T238A–T263

This genre opens the door to opinion writing by encouraging students to develop and support an opinion with reasons that will convince others.

Prewrite Form an opinion on a topic.
List and organize strong reasons and factual details that support the opinion.

Draft State the opinion in an introduction, provide reasons and supporting details in the body, and restate the opinion in the conclusion.

Revise Use effective transition words and phrases to guide the reader.
Keep purpose in mind and stay connected with the audience.
Use neutral words to express opinion.

Edit Check the use of adverbs.

Publish Present essay as a speech.

Editorial

Pages T264A–T285

In this genre, students will further develop their opinion writing skills as they explore how to write an editorial.

Prewrite Write an opinion on an issue. List reasons for the opinion.
Use a Main-Idea Table to organize the opinion and reasons.

Draft Organize the information in a logical order.

Revise Use a convincing tone and first-person point of view.
Choose words and phrases to convey ideas precisely, and combine sentences.

Edit Make sure that past-tense verbs are formed correctly.

Publish Publish the editorial in the class newspaper.

Friendly Letter

Pages T286A–T307

In this genre, students will extend their opinion writing skills as they learn and apply strategies for writing a friendly letter that expresses an opinion.

Prewrite Decide what to write about and research facts about the issue.
Use a Network Tree to organize facts and reasons.

Draft Use first-person point of view and casual language.

Revise Add facts to support the reasons.
Replace loaded words with neutral ones.
Combine short, choppy sentences to make the writing flow.

Edit Use punctuation correctly.

Publish Address an envelope and mail the letter.

Professional Development Podcasts and Screencasts

Go to **www.sfw.z-b.com** to access the variety of professional development **podcasts** and **screencasts**.

Unit Overview

Response to Literature ◄ LITERATURE CONNECTION
Pages T308A–T329

In this genre, students will state and support their opinions on books they have read.

Prewrite Decide on a topic. Make a list of details.
Use a Four-Paragraph Organizer to plan the response.

Draft Use exact words.

Revise Include information from the book, such as quotations.
Use transitions to show how ideas are related.
Combine sentences.

Edit Check the use of all pronouns.

Publish Present the response to literature as part of a class-published book.

Next Generation Opinion Assessment
Pages T330A–T351

Students will learn and practice how to take a next generation opinion assessment. They will learn to read and analyze the directions for each part of the assessment, plan their time effectively, and follow the steps of the writing process to write an opinion piece that includes evidence from sources they have examined.

Prewrite Respond to the assignment.
Choose a graphic organizer.

Draft State an opinion in the opening sentence. Make sure everything in the essay supports the opinion.

Revise Make sure you provide a concluding statement that is related to the information presented.
Use a sincere, convincing voice that matches the purpose of your editorial.
Use precise language that is appropriate for your audience and purpose.

Edit Check the grammar, spelling, capitalization, and punctuation.

Online Writing Center

iPad® and IWB Ready

Complete Digital Writing Instruction!

- My Writing Pad
- Interactive Rubrics
- Anchor Papers
- Graphic Organizers

- Content-Area Writing Prompts
- Grammar Games
- Proofreading Activities
- Instructional Videos

- Virtual File Cabinet
- eBooks
- Assessments

For information, go to www.sfw.z-b.com

21st Century Literacies
Technology, Digital Media & Writing

by **Julie Coiro, Ph.D.**, University of Rhode Island & **Sara B. Kajder, Ph.D.**, Shady Side Academy

 **INQUIRE** **First Locate, Then Evaluate**

Reading Within Websites

Model for students the following strategy to help them learn to stop, think, and anticipate where important information about a website's content might be found.

1. Read the title of the page and the title of the website in the margin at the top of the window.

2. To get a big picture of the information within the site, scan menu choices by holding your mouse over the navigational or topical menus that often appear along the sides of the frame or across the top of the window, but don't click yet.

3. Make predictions about where each of the major links may lead and anticipate a link's path through multiple levels of a website.

4. Explore interactive features of dynamic images (animated images or images that change as a viewer holds the mouse over them), pop-up menus, and scroll bars that may reveal additional levels of information.

5. Identify the creator of the website and when it was last updated. You can often find this information by clicking on a button labeled "About This Site." Consider what this information indicates about the site.

6. Notice and try out any electronic supports the site has, such as an organizational site map or internal search engine.

7. Make a judgment about whether to explore the site further. If the site looks worthwhile, decide which areas of the site to explore first.

After several demonstrations, have students practice these strategies in their own online reading.

Evaluating Author's Perspective

One aspect of reading critically involves the ability to detect the author's perspective.

One strategy for helping students understand the concepts of bias and perspective involves helping them distinguish between facts, opinions, and point of view. A classroom discussion about opinion writing techniques can provide an excellent context within which to introduce these ideas. Your students are bound to have different opinions about various topics, so you may wish to highlight these differences by selecting a topic that some students really like and others really don't. Ask students to write three factual, non-opinionated statements about the topic. Then ask them to write three sentences that give their opinion and attempt to persuade others to agree with their opinion. Encourage students to share their sentences with the class while others try to guess whether they're facts or opinions. Categorize the sentences that reflect one point of view (e.g., *I like broccoli.*) versus another (e.g., *I don't like broccoli.*), and explain that both are valid but come from different perspectives. Thus, the ideas are biased toward one perspective or another. Explain that a more complete explanation of this topic would include sentences that represent both perspectives.

Tell students that many websites are written from only one perspective. This is important to know so students do not base their whole thinking about an issue on one person's point of view. If they feel they are not getting "the whole story" from one website, they should look for another website that offers a different perspective.

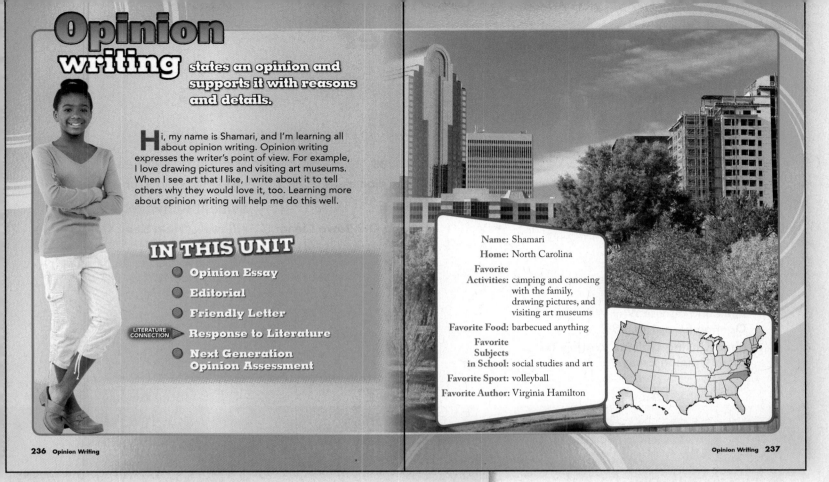

Opinion writing states an opinion and supports it with reasons and details.

Hi, my name is Shamari, and I'm learning all about opinion writing. Opinion writing expresses the writer's point of view. For example, I love drawing pictures and visiting art museums. When I see art that I like, I write about it to tell others why they would love it, too. Learning more about opinion writing will help me do this well.

IN THIS UNIT

- **Opinion Essay**
- **Editorial**
- **Friendly Letter**
- LITERATURE CONNECTION ▶ **Response to Literature**
- **Next Generation Opinion Assessment**

Name:	Shamari
Home:	North Carolina
Favorite Activities:	camping and canoeing with the family, drawing pictures, and visiting art museums
Favorite Food:	barbecued anything
Favorite Subjects in School:	social studies and art
Favorite Sport:	volleyball
Favorite Author:	Virginia Hamilton

To differentiate instruction and maximize student achievement, use the Differentiated Instruction Activities available at **www.sfw.z-b.com.**

Created by Amy Humphreys, Ed.M., these engaging activities can be used to meet a wide range of learner needs. Each activity uses a combination of visual, written, oral, and kinesthetic elements, and deliberately leverages the power of collaboration and conversation so students learn to think like writers in fun and engaging ways.

Meet Your Writing Partner, Shamari

The writing partner for this chapter is Shamari, a girl from North Carolina. You may wish to explore with students how Shamari's preferences, hobbies, interests, and personality connect with her choices of writing topics. Explain to students that Shamari will use what she knows to make decisions about her topics—a process that helps make her writing special and real. Encourage students to use their own background knowledge, interests, and personalities as they write as well. Opinion writing is based on forming and articulating personal opinions, and your students will have many interesting and authentic points to make.

Opinion Essay Planner

WEEK 1

Day 1
Introduce
Opinion Essay

Student Objectives
- Review the elements of an opinion essay.
- Consider purpose and audience.
- Learn the traits of opinion writing.

Student Activities
- Read and discuss **What's in an Opinion Essay?** (p. 238)
- Read and discuss **Why Write an Opinion Essay?** (p. 239)
- Read **Linking Opinion Writing Traits to an Opinion Essay.** (p. 240)

Day 2
Analyze
Close Reading of the Model

Student Objectives
- Read a model opinion essay.

Student Activities
- Read **"Help Keep Our Town Clean!"** (p. 241)

Day 3
Analyze
Introduce the Rubric

Student Objectives
- Learn to read a rubric.

Student Activities
- Review **"Help Keep Our Town Clean!"** (p. 241)
- Read and discuss the **Opinion Essay Rubric.** (pp. 242–243)

WEEK 2

Day 1
Write
Prewrite: Ideas

Student Objectives
- Read and understand a prewriting strategy.

Student Activities
- Read and discuss **Prewrite: Focus on Ideas.** (p. 248)
- Apply the prewriting strategy.

Day 2
Write
Prewrite: Organization

Student Objectives
- Make an Order-of-Importance Organizer to list reasons in order.

Student Activities
- Read and discuss **Prewrite: Focus on Organization.** (p. 249)
- Apply the prewriting strategy.
- Participate in a peer conference.

Day 3
Write
Draft: Ideas

Student Objectives
- Use an Order-of-Importance Organizer to begin writing.

Student Activities
- Read and discuss **Draft: Focus on Ideas.** (p. 250)
- Apply the drafting strategy.

WEEK 3

Day 1
Write
Revise: Voice

Student Objectives
- Revise to use a sincere voice.

Student Activities
- Read and discuss **Revise: Focus on Voice.** (p. 255)
- Reflect on the model draft.
- Apply the revising strategy.
- Participate in a peer conference.

Day 2
Write
Revise: Word Choice

Student Objectives
- Revise to replace loaded words with neutral ones.

Student Activities
- Read and discuss **Revise: Focus on Word Choice.** (p. 256)
- Apply the revising strategy.

Note: Optional Revising Lessons are located at **www.sfw.z-b.com**

Day 3
Write
Edit: Conventions

Student Objectives
- Edit for correct use of adverbs.

Student Activities
- Read and discuss **Edit: Focus on Conventions.** (p. 257)
- Reflect on the model draft.
- Apply the editing strategy.

Note: Teach the Conventions mini-lessons (pp. 258–259) if needed.

Day 4

Analyze
Close Reading for the Traits

Student Objectives
- Read a model opinion essay.
- Use the opinion essay rubric.
- Use the model opinion essay to study Ideas, Organization, and Voice.

Student Activities
- Review **"Help Keep Our Town Clean!"** (p. 241)
- Read and discuss **Using the Rubric to Analyze the Model.** (pp. 244–245)

Day 5

Analyze
Close Reading for the Traits

Student Objectives
- Read a model opinion essay.
- Use the opinion essay rubric.
- Use the model opinion essay to study Word Choice, Sentence Fluency, and Conventions.

Student Activities
- Review **"Help Keep Our Town Clean!"** (p. 241)
- Read and discuss **Using the Rubric to Analyze the Model.** (pp. 246–247)

Day 4

Write
Draft

Student Objectives
- Complete a draft.

Student Activities
- Finish a draft. (pp. 251–253)
- Participate in a peer conference.

Day 5

Write
Revise: Organization

Student Objectives
- Revise to use transition words to guide the reader.

Student Activities
- Read and discuss **Revise: Focus on Organization.** (p. 254)
- Reflect on a model draft.
- Apply the revising strategy.

Day 4

Write
Publish: +Presentation

Student Objectives
- Discuss preparation for publishing and presentation.
- Use a final editing checklist to publish their work.

Student Activities
- Read and discuss **Publish: +Presentation.** (p. 260)
- Apply the publishing strategy.

Day 5

Write
Publish: +Presentation

Student Objectives
- Use an opinion essay rubric.
- Share a published opinion essay.

Student Activities
- Share their work.
- Use the rubric to reflect upon and evaluate the model and their own writing. (pp. 242–243; 261–263)

To complete the chapter in fewer days, combine the learning objectives and activities in a way that supports students as they write.

Resources at-a-Glance

Grammar, Usage & Mechanics

Differentiating Instruction

For additional Differentiating Instruction activities, see Strategies for Writers *Differentiated Instruction Activities at* **www.sfw.z-b.com.**

English Language Learners

Collaborative Conferencing

Tech Tips

 Strategies for Writers Online

Go to **www.sfw.z-b.com** for additional online resources for students, teachers, and parents.

Online Writing Center

Provides IWB resources, assessments, interactive games and practice activities, videos, eBooks, and a virtual file cabinet.

Introduce
Opinion Essay

Week 1 • Day 1

Student Objectives

- Review the elements of an opinion essay. *(p. 238)*
- Consider purpose and audience. *(p. 239)*
- Learn the traits of opinion writing. *(p. 240)*

What's an Opinion Essay?

Discuss with students the definition of an opinion essay. Provide examples of well-written opinion essays and ask students to identify the writer's point of view and reasons. Then ask them to think about whether the writer supported the reasons with facts and examples that support the reasons. Finally, point out that anytime they write an essay to convince readers to agree with their opinion, they are using the opinion essay genre.

What's in an Opinion Essay?

Read and discuss with students the elements of an opinion essay listed on page 238. Discuss why each element is important to keep in mind while writing a convincing essay.

 Strategies for Writers Online
Go to **www.sfw.z-b.com** for additional online resources for students, teachers, and parents.

What's an Opinion Essay?

An opinion essay states my opinion and has reasons and details to support my point of view.

What's in an Opinion Essay?

Opinion
That's what I think about my topic. I can't prove that my opinion is right, but I can explain it and support it with reasons and information. For instance, I think my class should take a trip to the university art museum. It's full of beautiful paintings and sculptures!

Reasons
Reasons tell why I believe in my opinion. To help the audience understand my point of view, my reasons need to be backed up by accurate facts and details.

Introduction
The first paragraph of my essay will be my introduction. I'll get my reader interested in my topic and state my opinion.

Conclusion
That's my last paragraph. In my conclusion, I'll restate my opinion and sum up my reasons for supporting it.

238 Opinion Writing

Opinion Text Exemplars (Opinion Essay)

Laidlow, Rob. *Wild Animals in Captivity.* **Fitzhenry and Whiteside, 2008.** Laidlow uses facts and examples to describe the inhumane practices of most zoos. Using specific guidelines expressed by the author, students are encouraged to analyze the way animals are treated at the zoos they visit.

Erickson, Russell E. *A Toad for Tuesday.* **Houghton Mifflin, 2001.** On his way to visit his aunt, Warton the toad encounters an owl. With just five days to convince the owl not to eat him, Warton must use his persuasive skills to befriend the hungry bird.

Why write an Opinion Essay?

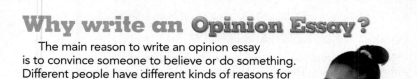

The main reason to write an opinion essay is to convince someone to believe or do something. Different people have different kinds of reasons for writing an opinion essay.

To Express an Opinion
I might write an opinion essay to members of the parent-teacher organization to ask them to consider my point of view about sponsoring a class trip.

A librarian might post an opinion essay for people who visit the library. He or she may provide facts and details to invite them to meet an author.

An applicant to a special program sometimes writes an opinion essay using clearly organized reasons to present himself or herself as the best candidate.

Opinion Essay **239**

Amsel, Sheri. *365 Ways to Live Green for Kids: Saving the Environment at Home, School, or at Play – Every Day!* Adams Media, 2009. Amsel encourages kids to reduce, reuse, and recycle in her book *365 Ways to Live Green for Kids: Saving the Environment at Home, School, or at Play – Every Day!* With reasons for decreasing pollution and eating organic foods, as well as ways to protect plants and animals, this book is sure to persuade students to become more earth-friendly.

Dray, Philip. *Yours for Justice, Ida B. Wells: The Daring Life of a Crusading Journalist.* Peachtree, 2008. Ida B. Wells was a journalist who fought tirelessly to end violence against African Americans. She also spoke out against Jim Crow laws and fought to end segregation.

Why write an Opinion Essay?

Read aloud and discuss with students the reasons for writing an opinion essay listed on page 239. Point out that all writing has a purpose and is aimed at a specific audience. Encourage students to discuss how having authentic purposes helps authors shape their writing. For example, someone writing to express an opinion on a topic will make sure the reasons are clearly stated. A writer who is writing to express an opinion on a book or movie will include examples and direct quotations to convince the reader. And a person who is writing to be considered for a job will include prior experience, a list of skills, and other relevant details to convince the reader that the writer is the right person for the position.

Encourage students to think about their own reasons for writing opinion pieces and how these reasons will affect the focus and tone of their writing. Conclude the discussion by explaining to students that they are going to study and practice strategies for writing a good opinion essay.

CCSS **C**ommon **C**ore **S**tate **S**tandards (pp. Z20–Z30)
Language: L.4.3c
Speaking and Listening: SL.4.1a, SL.4.1b, SL.4.1c, SL.4.1d, SL.4.3, SL.4.6

Opinion Essay **T239**

Introduce
Opinion Essay

Linking Opinion Writing Traits to an Opinion Essay

Read the introduction to page 240 aloud to help students understand that they will follow Shamari as she models using the writing process and the opinion writing traits together.

All good opinion writing will have examples of the traits shown on page 240. However, as students progress through the unit, they will see how the Opinion Writing Traits are adapted and applied to writing an opinion essay.

In this chapter, you will try to convince your audience to agree with your opinion. This type of writing is called an opinion essay. Shamari will guide you through the stages of the writing process: Prewrite, Draft, Revise, Edit, and Publish. In each stage, Shamari will show you important writing strategies that are linked to the Opinion Writing Traits below.

Opinion Writing Traits

Ideas	• a clear opinion • strong reasons that are supported by facts and details
Organization	• a clear, logical organization • an introduction, body, and conclusion • transitions that connect opinions and reasons
Voice	• a voice and tone that are appropriate for the audience and purpose
 **Word Choice**	• fair and balanced language • specific words and phrases
 **Sentence Fluency**	• a variety of sentence patterns that make the writing flow
 **Conventions**	• no or few errors in spelling, grammar, punctuation, and capitalization

Before you write, read Bob West's opinion essay on the next page. Then use the opinion essay rubric on pages 242–243 to decide how well he did. (You might want to look back at What's in an Opinion Essay? on page 238, too!)

Opinion Writing Traits in an Opinion Essay

 **Ideas** The writer's opinion is clearly stated and supported with strong reasons. The writer includes supporting facts and examples.

 **Organization** The essay includes a strong introduction that states the writer's opinion. In the body, reasons (main ideas) and evidence (supporting details) are organized by order of importance. Helpful transition words and phrases guide the reader. The conclusion restates the writer's opinion.

 **Voice** The writer establishes and maintains a convincing, sincere voice and a formal style that suits the writer's purpose and audience.

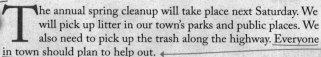

HELP KEEP OUR TOWN CLEAN!

Opinion MODEL Essay

by Bob West

introduction

The annual spring cleanup will take place next Saturday. We will pick up litter in our town's parks and public places. We also need to pick up the trash along the highway. Everyone in town should plan to help out. ← *opinion*

The main reason for needing so many people is that the town has a huge amount of litter. Paper, bags, and bottles need to be picked up along the roads. The public boat landing needs to be cleaned up. The litter around Swan Pond is destroying the beauty of the woods and water. The small parks department cannot do all of this work. To do a good job, many people are needed. Teams of four people will be assigned to small sections of highways, parks, and other sites. The cleanup committee is hoping to have a hundred cleanup teams. If we all help, the town won't have to raise extra money for cleanup. *transition words*

reasons

Another reason everyone should join in is to build community spirit. Teams of people who work together will get to know each other. They will feel needed in their town. Some people will become more aware of the litter problem. Once they know about it, they will discourage littering. They may want to talk about the problem with others. Our town will become a clean place. People who have worked hard to clean up won't want to see litter in their beautiful town again.

We should all gladly help out next Saturday. We have a huge litter problem, and it is up to us to solve it. The people who do the work will also benefit by building community spirit. As Mayor Willis has said, "When we take care of our town, we take care of ourselves." *conclusion*

Opinion Essay **241**

Word Choice The writer uses convincing language, avoiding loaded words that might offend the audience.

Sentence Fluency A variety of sentence patterns makes the writing flow well and holds the reader's attention throughout the essay.

Conventions The writer has edited the essay carefully. All adverbs are used correctly.

Analyze
Close Reading of the Model

Student Objectives

- Read a model opinion essay. (p. 241)

Read the Model

Ask students to listen for the writing traits as you read "Help Keep Our Town Clean!" aloud. Ask students to note how the essay is organized. Also ask students to think about how the writer reaches out to the reader. They should agree that the writing voice supports the writer's purpose and connects with the reader.

Elements of an Opinion Essay

Have students refer to What's in an Opinion Essay?" on page 238 as you refer to the model on page 241. Discuss the notes written on the model to enhance students' understanding of the terms. Ask students to find additional examples in the text to support their analysis of the model.

CCSS **C**ommon **C**ore **S**tate **S**tandards (pp. Z20–Z30)
Writing: W.4.6
Language: L.4.3c
Speaking and Listening: SL.4.1a, SL.4.1b, SL.4.1c, SL.4.1d, SL.4.2, SL.4.3, SL.4.6

Analyze
Introduce the Rubric

Week 1 • Day 3

Student Objectives

- Learn to read a rubric. (pp. 242–243)

Introduce the Rubric

Explain the Rubric Explain that a rubric is a tool for planning, improving, and assessing a piece of writing. Tell students that a rubric helps a writer focus on key elements, or traits, in writing (**Ideas, Organization, Voice, Word Choice, Sentence Fluency, Conventions,** and **Presentation**).

Point out that column 6 describes a very good opinion essay, one that has received the highest score in all categories. This is what students should strive for in their own writing.

Discuss the Rubric When students score their paper for each trait, they should first decide whether it falls on the left of the rubric (uses the trait well) or on the right (needs improvement in using the trait). By examining the paper more closely, students can refine the score to a single number.

Opinion Essay Rubric

Use this rubric to analyze the model. Then use it to plan and score your own opinion essay.

	6	5	4	
Ideas	The writer's opinion is clear. The ideas are supported by plenty of strong details.	The writer's opinion is clear. The essay has some strong details.	The writer's opinion is clear. Strong details are needed.	
Organization	The reasons are organized in a clear order that supports the writer's purpose. Transition words make the essay easy to follow.	One or two reasons may be out of order. The writer uses some transition words.	Some reasons are not organized in a clear way. The writer uses some transition words.	
Voice	The writer's voice sounds sincere and has a serious tone that matches the writer's purpose. It connects with the reader.	The writer's voice sounds sincere and has a serious tone most of the time. It mostly connects with the reader.	The writer has a voice, but it may not always sound sincere or connect with the reader.	
Word Choice	The writer's language is fair and balanced. No loaded words or phrases are used.	The writer's language is fair almost all the time. One or two loaded words should be replaced.	The writer's language is fair most of the time. The writer uses some loaded words.	
Sentence Fluency	A variety of sentence patterns makes the essay flow.	Most sentence patterns are varied. Most of the essay flows naturally.	Some variety in sentence beginnings and structure adds interest.	
Conventions	Adverbs are used correctly. The meaning is clear.	Most adverbs are used correctly. The meaning is clear.	Some minor errors with adverbs exist, but they do not distract the reader.	

✛ Presentation White space and text are balanced. The pages are numbered.

242 Opinion Writing

CCSS Common Core State Standards

Opinion Essay

Strategies for Writers was designed and written to weave the Common Core State Standards throughout every unit. For Opinion writing, the standards inform the unit's writing rubrics, objectives, and strategies. By presenting the standards in as many applications as possible, your students' exposure to them will be ensured. As a result, students are more likely to employ the standards' language in writing opinion pieces as well as in discussions about writing.

The lessons for Opinion Essay are based principally on the writing standards for Opinion writing. The rubrics and writing

Online Writing Center

 Provides a variety of **interactive rubrics,** including 4-, 5-, and 6-point models.

T242 Opinion Writing

3	2	1	
The writer's opinion is not clear enough. Details are too few in number or weak.	The writer provides a general opinion. Only one or two details are provided.	The writer's opinion is not provided. The details are missing.	Ideas
Several reasons are out of order. More or better transition words are needed.	The reasons are not organized. Transition words are missing.	There is no clear organization. Transition words are not used.	Organization
The writer's voice sounds sincere only some of the time. It sometimes does not connect with the reader.	The voice is inconsistent and may be inappropriate for the purpose and audience. The reader is confused or distracted.	The voice is very weak or absent. The writer does not sound sincere or connect with the reader.	Voice
Much of the language is biased. Several loaded words are used.	Most of the words are emotional and biased. Some may offend the reader.	Word choice does not seem thought out. Words are biased and poorly used.	Word Choice
Few sentence patterns are present. The sentences do not flow naturally.	Sentence beginnings, length, and structure are not varied. The writing is choppy and awkward.	Sentences are incomplete or incorrect. The essay is very difficult to read.	Sentence Fluency
Several errors in the use of adverbs confuse the reader.	Many serious errors impair readability and meaning. Adverbs are vague, confusing, or missing.	The writing contains many major errors in the use of adverbs. It is very difficult to read.	Conventions

See Appendix B for 4-, 5-, and 6-point opinion rubrics.

Find Evidence in the Model

Small-Group Collaboration
Assign students to small groups and ask them to check the model on page 241 for each trait. One person in each group should be responsible for recording one or two strong examples of the trait as described by the rubric. Ask students to score each trait accordingly for the model. They should be able to support their scores. Note that although the models were written to score high in each trait, students should not assume each trait would receive a 6, the top score. Encourage students to discuss each trait thoroughly before assigning each score.

Teacher-Led Discussion Bring the class back together and ask one person from each group to report their findings to the class. The point of this exercise is to practice identifying and evaluating the traits within a piece of writing.

Additional Rubrics

Appendix B includes 4-, 5-, and 6-point rubrics that can be used with any piece of opinion writing. The rubrics are also available as blackline masters in the back of this Teacher Edition.

strategies reflect the writing standard **W.4.1**, which focuses on introducing and supporting a point of view with reasons and information.

The language standards for grade 4 students are addressed during editing and skills practice. In addition, there are multiple opportunities to address the speaking and listening standards during the writing process. Most importantly, this chapter will help your students produce coherent writing (**W.4.4**), improve their writing (**W.4.5**), and use technologies to publish their finished pieces (**W.4.6**).

CCSS **Common Core State Standards** (pp. Z20–Z30)
Writing: W.4.6
Language: L.4.3c
Speaking and Listening: SL.4.1a, SL.4.1b, SL.4.1c, SL.4.1d, SL.4.2, SL.4.3, SL.4.6

Analyze
Close Reading for the Traits

Week 1 • Day 4

Student Objectives

- Read a model opinion essay. (p. 241)
- Use the opinion essay rubric. (pp. 242–243)
- Use the model opinion essay to study **Ideas, Organization,** and **Voice**. (pp. 244–245)

Find Evidence in the Model

Evaluate the Model Have volunteers read aloud each section on pages 244–245. Use the questions below to initiate the discussion. Be sure students can back up their answers with specific examples from the opinion essay.

Discuss Audience, Task, Purpose Ask students one or more of the following questions as they analyze the model:

- **Audience** Who is the audience? (Possible response: all readers)

- **Task** How does the writer show his opinion? (Possible responses: The writer states his opinion in the first paragraph, gives his reasons in the body, and states his opinion again in the conclusion of his essay.)

- **Purpose** What is the writer's purpose for writing this essay? How do you know? (Possible response: to persuade the reader to help him clean up the area; He gives reasons for why the trash needs to be cleaned up.)

Opinion Essay

Using the Rubric to Analyze the Model

Did you notice that the model on page 241 points out some key elements of an opinion essay? As he wrote "Help Keep Our Town Clean!" Bob West used these elements to help him convince others to agree with his opinion. He also used the 6-point rubric on pages 242–243 to plan, draft, revise, and edit the writing. A rubric is a great tool to evaluate writing during the writing process.

Now let's use the same rubric to score the model. To do this, we'll focus on each trait separately, starting with Ideas. We'll use the top descriptor for each trait (column 6), along with examples from the model, to help us understand how the traits work together. How would you score Bob on each trait?

Ideas
- The writer's opinion is clear.
- The ideas are supported by plenty of strong details.

Bob does a good job of clearly stating his opinion in the essay's introduction: Everyone in town should help out with the spring cleanup. Then Bob presents strong details that support his reasons that people should get involved in the annual cleanup.

The main reason for needing so many people is that the town has a huge amount of litter. Paper, bags, and bottles need to be picked up along the roads. The public boat landing needs to be cleaned up. The litter around Swan Pond is destroying the beauty of the woods and water. The small parks department cannot do all of this work. To do a good job, many people are needed.

English Language Learners

BEGINNING

Facts and Opinions Read a simple text about fish. After reading, write *Fish are animals.* Ask, *Is this always true?* and then say, *Facts are always true.* Say the word *facts* and have students repeat. Write *Fish are pretty.* Ask, *Is this always true?* and then say, *An opinion is what we think about something.* Say the word *opinion* and have students say it. Confirm understanding with other fact/opinion examples.

INTERMEDIATE

Fact and Opinion Use the Beginning ELL activity above to illustrate the meanings of *fact* and *opinion*. Draw a Fact and Opinion Chart on the board with *School* as the topic. Ask a student to make a statement about school and then have other students determine whether the statement is fact or opinion.

Organization
- The reasons are organized in a clear order that supports the writer's purpose.
- Transition words make the essay easy to follow.

In the body of the essay, Bob presents two important reasons for his opinion. He starts with his main reason and uses *Another reason* to begin the next paragraph. The essay is easy to follow.

> The main reason for needing so many people is that the town has a huge amount of litter.

> Another reason everyone should join in is to build community spirit.

Voice
- The writer's voice sounds sincere and has a serious tone that matches the writer's purpose.
- It connects with the reader.

Bob makes it clear that he's sincere about his opinion. He gives plenty of details that support his point of view. In his conclusion, he uses the word *we* to connect with the reader. This made me feel like part of the same community as Bob.

> We should all gladly help out next Saturday. We have a huge litter problem, and it is up to us to solve it.

Opinion Essay **245**

Discuss the Traits Ask students one or more of the following questions to discuss the traits in the model.

Ideas Does the writer state a clear opinion? (Possible responses: The writer states a clear opinion about everyone helping clean up the town. His ideas made me want to keep reading.)

Organization Is the essay organized into three parts (introduction, body, and conclusion)? (Possible responses: The essay leads with a strong introduction that states the problem, a body with strong reasons, and a conclusion that restates the writer's opinion. Ideas are easily followed from beginning to end.)

Voice Does the writer maintain a sincere tone? (Possible responses: The writer sounds sincere and serious. He reaches out to the audience by asking them to participate in the spring cleanup day.)

ADVANCED

Opinion and Reasons Read an editorial in the school newspaper. Write the author's opinion on the board. Have partners highlight the reasons the author gives for that opinion. In small groups have students share the reasons they found. Have them write a short paragraph about *school dress code*, giving their opinion and reasons for their opinion.

ADVANCED HIGH

Opinion and Reasons Introduce a Fact and Opinion Chart. Assign a topic, such as *Internet Safety*, to each pair of students. Have partners complete the Fact and Opinion Chart and then have the pair write a letter to their peers that makes a strong suggestion in support of a position. After their letters are complete, have students read their letters to the class. Then ask the class to vote on which arguments were presented most convincingly.

CCSS **C**ommon **C**ore **S**tate **S**tandards (pp. Z20–Z30)
Language: L.4.3c, L.4.6
Speaking and Listening: SL.4.1a, SL.4.1b, SL.4.1c, SL.4.1d, SL.4.3, SL.4.4, SL.4.6

Analyze
Close Reading for the Traits

Week 1 • Day 5

Student Objectives

- Read a model opinion essay. (p. 241)
- Use the opinion essay rubric. (pp. 242–243)
- Use the model opinion essay to study **Word Choice, Sentence Fluency,** and **Conventions.** (pp. 246–247)

Discuss the Traits Ask students one or more of the following questions to discuss the traits in the model:

Word Choice How does the writer use words and phrases effectively? (Possible responses: He uses exact words and phrases such as *teams of four people, cleanup committee,* and *cleanup teams* to express his opinion and convince others to help clean up the town. He avoids using any language that might sound like he's blaming the reader for the problem.)

Sentence Fluency What evidence in the essay shows how the writer varied sentence patterns to keep the essay flowing along? (Possible response: The writer begins sentences in different ways to keep the writing flowing along.)

Conventions Does the writer use words, including adverbs, correctly? (Yes, Bob uses the adverbs and the words *good* and *well* correctly.)

Strategies for Writers Online
Go to **www.sfw.z-b.com** for additional online resources for students, teachers, and parents.

Using the Rubric (Opinion Essay) to Analyze the Model

- The writer's language is fair and balanced.
- No loaded words or phrases are used.

Words like *litterbug* and *slob* are examples of loaded words, or words with extra meanings. Bob doesn't use loaded words. Instead, he just explains how the cleanup can help people.

> Some people will become more aware of the litter problem. Once they know about it, they will discourage littering. They may want to talk about the problem with others.

- A variety of sentence patterns makes the essay flow.

Bob uses a variety of long and short, simple and complex sentences throughout his essay. This made his essay flow and helped me to follow his thinking.

> The small parks department cannot do all of this work. To do a good job, many people are needed. Teams of four people will be assigned to small sections of highways, parks, and other sites. The cleanup committee is hoping to have a hundred cleanup teams. If we all help, the town won't have to raise extra money for cleanup.

246 Opinion Writing

Tech Tips
Blogs

Share Writing on Blogs Engage student writers in posting an opinion essay in a class blog like Kidblog. Not only will this allow students to "publish," but it also allows students to receive and respond to comments from other readers. Sites like Kidblog promote dialog about high-interest topics and additional research suggestions, furthering students' reading as well as their writing. Using a class login (e.g., Miss Smith's Fourth Grade) will also help provide anonymity when needed.

See **www.sfw.z-b.com** for further information about and links to these websites and tools.

Conventions
- Adverbs are used correctly.
- The meaning is clear.

I read through the essay again. I had no trouble catching Bob's meaning. Bob also uses adverbs correctly. In these sentences, the adverbs *hard* and *gladly* describe verbs.

People who have worked hard to clean up won't want to see litter in their beautiful town again.

We should all gladly help out next Saturday.

+Presentation White space and text are balanced. The pages are numbered.

My Turn!

Now it's my turn to write an opinion essay. Follow along to see how I use the rubric and good writing strategies to help me.

+Presentation Explain to students that Presentation is just as important as any of the other traits. Neatness is always a priority, and text should be clearly handwritten or typed. White space should be balanced with text and used to create neat margins and keep lines of text readable. Paragraphs should be indented, or space should be left between block paragraphs. The title of the essay should be centered at the top of the first page.

Think About the Traits

After students have thoroughly discussed the model essay, ask them which traits they think are the most important in an opinion essay and have them explain why.
(Possible response: Ideas are very important in an opinion essay because if an opinion and reasons are not stated clearly, the writer's purpose for writing may be misunderstood.)

Differentiating Instruction

ENRICHMENT

Identify Issues of Concern Have small groups brainstorm a list of issues they care about. Then have them compare lists. Ask them to prioritize the shared issues on the list by deciding which are most important. Have students present the top three issues to the class and give their reasons for including them on their final list of potential topics.

REINFORCEMENT

Understand Elements of an Opinion Essay Some students may benefit from seeing additional samples of opinion essays. Find some in your school or local newspaper to share with students. Have them work in pairs to identify the writer's opinion and reasons. They should also note the facts and details that support the writer's point of view.

CCSS **Common Core State Standards** (pp. Z20–Z30)
Writing: W.4.6
Language: L.4.3c, L.4.6
Speaking and Listening: SL.4.1a, SL.4.1b, SL.4.1c, SL.4.1d, SL.4.3, SL.4.6

Write
Opinion Essay

Week 2 • Day 1

Student Objectives

- Read and understand a prewriting strategy. *(p. 248)*

Prewrite

Focus on Ideas

Brainstorm Topics Read page 248 aloud. Brainstorm a list of potential school-related topics. **(Possible responses: a later school start time, a new item on the school lunch menu, a revised dress code or homework policy)** Ask students to choose one topic from the list and state an opinion on the topic they choose. Then have them list at least three reasons that support their point of view. Explain that Shamari plans to state her opinion in her introduction. Also point out that she will probably use the two strongest reasons in her essay.

Gather Information from Print and Digital Sources Explain to students that to support an opinion, writers often research a topic for current, factual information.

✎ Writer's Term

Opinion Point out that an *opinion* should be supported by credible reasons. Otherwise, the writer's point of view may not be taken seriously.

⟶ Online Writing Center

Provides **interactive graphic organizers** as well as a variety of graphic organizers in PDF format.

Prewrite

Focus on Ideas

The Rubric Says The writer's opinion is clear. The ideas are supported by plenty of strong details.

Writing Strategy Decide on an opinion. List reasons for the opinion.

My teacher gave us a list of possible topics for an opinion essay. The topic I'm most interested in is whether our school should stay open until 6:00 P.M. I've always wanted the school to stay open later.

I listed all the reasons I could think of for keeping the school open later. That was my strategy for getting started.

Writer's Term

Opinion
An **opinion** is a belief that is based on reasons. Unlike a fact, an opinion cannot be proven to be true.

> **My Opinion:** The school building should stay open until 6:00 P.M.
>
> **Reasons to Support My Opinion**
> 1. There could be more after-school activities and clubs.
> 2. Students can wait inside for a ride home.
> 3. Activities can last longer, and students can get back into the building after outdoor activities.
> 4. The band and other groups could meet later.

Write
Choose a topic that you find interesting for an opinion essay. Decide what your opinion is, and then list some reasons that support your opinion.

248 Opinion Writing

English Language Learners

BEGINNING/INTERMEDIATE

Opinions and Reasons Write *School Dress Code.* Ask, *Is this a good idea?* Invite discussion. List students' opinions. Then review the meaning of opinion. Then ask, *Why is/isn't it a good idea?* After you have discussed and written the answers, circle them and say, *These are the reasons for your opinion.* Repeat with another example.

ADVANCED/ADVANCED HIGH

Order of Importance Repeat the Beginning/Intermediate ELL activity above. Then introduce the Order-of-Importance Organizer. Review the meanings of *most important, next in importance,* and *least important.* Have partners work together to arrange their reasons for/against a school dress code in an Order-of-Importance Organizer.

Prewrite

The Rubric Says   The reasons are organized in a clear order that supports the writer's purpose.

Writing Strategy   Use an Order-of-Importance Organizer.

The rubric reminds me to use strong reasons to support my opinion. An Order-of-Importance Organizer will help me list my reasons in order. I have decided to organize them from most important to least important.

Writer's Term

Order-of-Importance Organizer
An **Order-of-Importance Organizer** shows reasons in order of their importance. Usually, the most important reason goes first, and the least important reason goes last.

Order-of-Importance Organizer

Most Important:
Students can wait inside for a ride home.

Next in Importance:
Activities can last longer, and students can get back into the building after outdoor activities.

Next in Importance:
The band and other groups could meet later.

Least Important:
There could be more after-school activities and clubs.

Analyze
Look at Shamari's notes and graphic organizer. How will they help Shamari write a good opinion essay?

Write
Look at your notes. Use an Order-of-Importance Organizer to put your reasons in order.

Opinion Essay **249**

Collaborative Conferencing

PEER TO PEER Have students exchange organizers. As they read, have them ask the following questions: *Is the organizer complete? Do the reasons appear to be listed in order?* Have readers make comments on sticky notes and return with the organizer.

PEER GROUPS Separate students into small groups of three or four. Have each group state one or two reasons for using an Order-of-Importance Organizer to write a draft essay. Then ask them to share and revise their reasons, based on feedback from other groups.

TEACHER-LED Schedule conferences with students. To demonstrate how important the organizer is to writing a good essay, create one for one of the issues on their list, arranging reasons in random order. Discuss how not prioritizing reasons would weaken an essay.

Write
Opinion Essay

Week 2 • Day 2

Student Objectives

• Make an Order-of-Importance Organizer to list reasons in the best order. *(p. 249)*

Prewrite

Focus on  Organization

Prioritize Ideas and Evidence
Explain that writers use different types of organizers to organize their ideas. Shamari used an Order-of-Importance Organizer to help organize the reasons she had listed in her notes. (Go to **www.sfw.z-b.com** for the downloadable graphic organizer.) Have students study the organizer to see how Shamari organized the reasons. Tell students that an Order-of-Importance Organizer can be an effective tool when writing an opinion essay.

Writer's Term
Main Idea The Main Idea of an essay is the most important thought about the topic. The main idea is supported by facts and details that explain and support the writer's opinion.

CCSS **C**ommon **C**ore **S**tate **S**tandards (pp. Z20–Z30)
Writing: W.4.1a, W.4.1b, W.4.1c, W.4.4, W.4.5, W.4.6, W.4.8, W.4.10
Language: L.4.3c, L.4.6
Speaking and Listening: SL.4.1a, SL.4.1b, SL.4.1c, SL.4.1d, SL.4.3, SL.4.6

Write
Opinion Essay

Week 2 • Day 3

Student Objectives

- Use an Order-of-Importance Organizer to begin writing. (p. 250)

Draft

Focus on Ideas

Begin a Draft Read page 250 aloud. Be sure students understand that they will use their organizer to write their draft.

Point out that students should not be overly concerned with grammar and spelling at this point. If they are doing their writing in class, plan and facilitate time for writing, conferences, and reflection.

Draw Evidence From Text or Experience Discuss with students that they will need to do research to collect information and facts.

Writer's Term
Reasons Supporting details for a writer's reasons should be accurate. Using up-to-date information and checking facts are the writer's responsibility. Information that is used to support the writer's point of view should be verified before it is included in an opinion essay.

Online Writing Center

Provides an **interactive writing pad** for drafting, revising, editing, and publishing.

Draft
Focus on (Ideas)

The Rubric Says	The writer's opinion is clear. The ideas are supported by plenty of strong details.
Writing Strategy	Make sure the opinion and reasons are clear.

Now I can start writing. In order to convince others to believe in my opinion, I need to make sure they understand what my opinion is. I also need to be sure that all my reasons strongly support my opinion. That means I should state my opinion clearly and openly in the first paragraph. Then I should support it with my two most important reasons in the next two paragraphs. In my final paragraph, I'll restate my opinion in a sincere way that convinces my readers.

As I write my draft, I'll do the best I can with spelling and grammar, but I won't worry about mistakes right now. I'll have a chance to fix them later. My draft begins on page 252.

Writer's Term
Reasons
Good **reasons** support a writer's opinion. Strong details and facts that support the writer's reasons can convince others to agree with the writer.

250 Opinion Writing

Differentiating Instruction

ENRICHMENT
Give Good Reasons In small groups, have students state their opinion and present their reasons in order of importance. For each reason, students should give one or two facts that support it. Members of each group should then give their opinion on whether the writer's reasons are well supported. Encourage students to include at least three well-supported reasons in their drafts.

REINFORCEMENT
State the Opinion Have students state their opinions verbally and then write them down. Refer students to Shamari's opinion statement on page 248 to write their own. Review their opinion statements to make sure they are clear and focused. Remind students that they should state their opinion in the introduction.

My Opinion (first paragraph)
The school building should stay open until 6:00 P.M.

My Reasons

Reason 1 (next paragraph)
Students can wait inside for a ride home.

Reason 2 (next paragraph)
Activities can last longer, and students can get back into the building after outdoor activities.

My Restatement (final paragraph)
Adams School should keep its doors open until 6:00 P.M.

Collaborative Conferencing

PEER TO PEER Have partners exchange drafts to read. Tell students to think of two or three questions they would like to ask to clarify information or supply missing details. Have them write their questions on sticky notes and affix them to the appropriate places on their partner's draft.

PEER GROUPS Have students work in groups of four. Students pass their draft to the student on the right to read. That student writes one comment or suggestion on a sticky note affixed to the draft and passes the draft along to the right. The review ends when everyone has received his or her own draft back with three comments.

TEACHER-LED Schedule conferences with pairs of students. Have them read each other's draft and coach them in giving and receiving constructive criticism.

Write
Opinion Essay

Week 2 • Day 4

Student Objectives

• Complete a draft. *(pp. 251–253)*

Continue Drafting It is important that students are given ample time to draft their essays. As conferencing is important throughout the writing process, be sure to plan time for peer-to-peer, peer group, or teacher-led conferences. Remind students that this is the time to get their ideas down on paper in a creative and engaging way. Assure them that they will have plenty of time to fix any mistakes later.

Note: To facilitate editing, proofreading marks are provided as a reference on page 253.

Paraphrase Information Tell students to always use their own words when drafting. Explain that one way to use your own words is to focus on the main ideas of the facts they've researched. Encourage them to write down the main points of the facts instead of writing down the notes they took word for word.

CCSS **Common Core State Standards** (pp. Z20–Z30)
Writing: W.4.1a, W.4.1b, W.4.1d, W.4.4, W.4.5, W.4.6, W.4.10
Language: L.4.3c, L.4.6
Speaking and Listening: SL.4.1a, SL.4.1b, SL.4.1c, SL.4.1d, SL.4.3, SL.4.4, SL.4.6

State the Opinion in the Introduction Remind students to refer to Shamari's introduction as they write their own drafts. Encourage students to state their opinion clearly in the introduction. This lets the audience know the writer's purpose and prepares the reader for the writer's message.

[DRAFT]

Keep the Doors Open

Adams School is a busy place. The first teachers arrive very early in the morning. There is activity all day long. The doors are locked at 4:30 P.M. Because many people need to use the building after that, the school should stay open until 6:00 P.M.

opinion stated in first paragraph

The most important reason is that sometimes students have to wait for a ride home. Often students have school clubs and activities. They might have sports or band practice. It's stupid to think that all parents get out of work before 5:00 P.M. Miserable, overtired kids who need to wait for a ride should not have to stand outside the building, especially when it is cold, rainy, or dark. If students could wait inside, they could use their time good. They could do homework or read quietly in the school liberry. They could sit comfortable and talk softly with their friends in a warm place.

strongest reason in first argument paragraph

252 Opinion Writing

Strategies for Writers Online

Go to **www.sfw.z-b.com** for additional online resources for students, teachers, and parents.

Proofreading Marks

⌐ Indent   ℓ Take out something
≡ Make uppercase   ⊙ Add a period
/ Make lowercase   ¶ New paragraph
∧ Add something   ⓢⓟ Spelling error

[DRAFT]

The second reason the doors should be open is for
students who have activities there. After school ends, many
activities take place in and around the school building. Some go
on after 4:30 P.M. Many sports teams practice on the school fields.
Some practices end after 5:00 P.M. Sometimes students need to
go back into the school after practice. Right now they can't do
that. Also, some activities that take place inside the school are cut
short because the building closes so early.

next strongest reason in second argument paragraph

Adams School should keep its doors open until 6:00 P.M.
Many students are still using the school building or grounds at
4:30 P.M. keeping the school open an hour and a half later
would make life easier for them and sometimes for the
adults in their lifes, too.

opinion restated in last paragraph

Analyze

Read Shamari's draft. What
reasons did she give for her
opinion? Do you think she gave
enough reasons to support her
opinion well? Why or why not?

Write

Use your Order-of-Importance
Organizer to write a draft of your
opinion essay. Remember to
clearly state your opinion and
use plenty of strong details to
support it.

Opinion Essay 253

**Restate the Opinion in the
Conclusion** As students complete
their drafts, remind them to restate
their opinion in the conclusion.
Point out the notes written on
Shamari's draft. Recommend that
they restate their opinion in the
first sentence of the last paragraph.
Doing so will also help them focus
their conclusions.

CCSS **Common Core State Standards** (pp. Z20–Z30)
Writing: W.4.1a, W.4.1b, W.4.1d, W.4.4, W.4.5, W.4.10

Opinion Essay T253

Write
Opinion Essay

Week 2 • Day 5

Student Objectives

- Revise to use transition words to guide the reader. *(p. 254)*

Revise

Focus on

Link Opinion and Reasons After writing their drafts, read aloud page 254. Point out Shamari's changes and discuss each one. Do her transition words and phrases help the reader follow her ideas?

Then review the model opinion essay on page 241 and point out the following helpful phrases in the body paragraphs: *The main reason, To do a good job, If we all help, Once they know about it.* Make sure students understand that using transition phrases such as these helps to connect ideas and makes it easier for the reader to follow the essay.

Ask students to check their writing carefully for places where transition words and phrases could help link their ideas. Encourage students to try out several examples from the model in their own drafts. Refer students to the list of transitions on page 487.

 Strategies for Writers Online
Go to **www.sfw.z-b.com** for additional online resources for students, teachers, and parents.

Revise
Focus on **Organization**

The Rubric Says	Transition words make the essay easy to follow.
Writing Strategy	Use transition words to guide the reader.

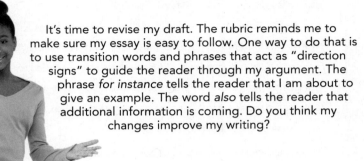

It's time to revise my draft. The rubric reminds me to make sure my essay is easy to follow. One way to do that is to use transition words and phrases that act as "direction signs" to guide the reader through my argument. The phrase *for instance* tells the reader that I am about to give an example. The word *also* tells the reader that additional information is coming. Do you think my changes improve my writing?

[DRAFT]

If students could wait inside, they could use their time good.
For instance,
~~They~~ could do homework or read quietly in the school liberry.
also
They could sit comfortable and talk softly with their friends in
a warm place.

added transition words

Write

Read your draft. Revise your draft to include transition words that help the reader follow your essay.

254 Opinion Writing

English Language Learners

BEGINNING/INTERMEDIATE

Transition Words and Phrases Refer to students' reasons for supporting (or not supporting) a school dress code. Teach several ways to introduce each reason; for example, *The most important reason is that…, Another reason is…, A final reason that I like a dress code is…,* and so on. Have students practice using these transition phrases as they say their reasons to each other.

ADVANCED/ADVANCED HIGH

Editing for Adverb Usage Review what an adverb is and give several examples, including adverbs that do not end with *-ly*. After students have written their first drafts, have them circle all the adverbs they used. Then have them trade with a partner who will read the draft and check that each adverb is appropriate. Then have the partners discuss why they made each change.

Revise

Focus on Voice

The Rubric Says	The writer's voice sounds sincere and has a serious tone that matches the writer's purpose. It connects with the reader.
Writing Strategy	Keep the audience in mind as you revise.

I read my draft again. The rubric tells me to sound sincere and serious. I should also connect to the reader. To do that, I need to think about my purpose and audience. My audience is students and others at my school. My purpose is to convince them that the building needs to stay open longer for students to use. I added two sentences that speak directly to the audience about things they care about. Keeping my audience in mind helped me strengthen my introduction.

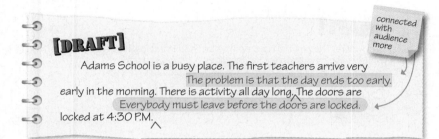

connected with audience more

[DRAFT]

Adams School is a busy place. The first teachers arrive very ~~early in the morning. There is activity all day long.~~ The doors are locked at 4:30 P.M.

The problem is that the day ends too early.

Everybody must leave before the doors are locked.

Analyze
Look at Shamari's changes. What makes her writing sound sincere? How does she establish a serious tone in her opening paragraph?

Write
Read your draft. Revise your writing to connect with your audience, from beginning to end.

Opinion Essay **255**

Collaborative Conferencing

PEER TO PEER Have partners exchange drafts. After reading, ask each student to offer feedback on how to strengthen the piece. If needed, have students consult the model essay, the rubric, and the analysis as they revise for organization, voice, and word choice.

PEER GROUPS Have students form small groups. Have each student read aloud a section of his or her draft. Ask each group member to offer one suggestion on how to strengthen it. Have writers consult the revising lesson pages in their book to inform their revision.

TEACHER-LED Schedule conferences to read each student's draft. Point out strengths and weaknesses. Talk about ways to improve the draft and inform the revision. If a student seems stalled or discouraged, revisit steps in the process to make improvements and keep going.

Write
Opinion Essay

Week 3 • Day 1

Student Objectives
- Revise to use a sincere voice. (p. 255)

Revise

Focus on Voice

Keep the Audience in Mind
Remind students that audience and purpose determine the writer's voice in every piece of writing. Discuss how those two factors influence the writer's voice in a text message, a science report, and a picture book for young children.

Read page 255 aloud. Point out the changes that Shamari made to her draft. Ask students to discuss how the revisions improve the draft. **(Possible responses: Shamari's revisions give information readers need to understand the problem.)** Remind students that they should use a sincere voice that sounds serious and focused. As they present the problem or issue, they should also remember to provide information the reader needs to understand the problem. Doing so shows respect for the reader and the message.

CCSS **Common Core State Standards** (pp. Z20–Z30)
Writing: W.4.1c, W.4.4, W.4.5, W.4.10
Language: L.4.3a, L.4.3c, L.4.6
Speaking and Listening: SL.4.1a, SL.4.1b, SL.4.1c, SL.4.1d, SL.4.3, SL.4.6

Write
Opinion Essay

Week 3 • Day 2

Student Objectives

- Revise to replace loaded words with neutral ones. *(p. 256)*

Revise

Focus on Word Choice

Use Neutral Words Explain to students that using loaded or negative words will not convince the audience. In fact, these types of words can alienate readers. On the other hand, using neutral words throughout an opinion essay helps convince the audience that the writer has thoughtfully formed an opinion that can be defended with strong reasons and facts.

As students revise for **Word Choice**, remind them to consult print and online word resources such as dictionaries, thesauruses, and glossaries.

✎ Writer's Term ____

Loaded Words can offend readers and undermine the writer's argument. Instead of convincing the audience, negative language sends a negative message.

Online Writing Center

Provides **interactive proofreading activities** for each genre.

Write an Opinion Essay

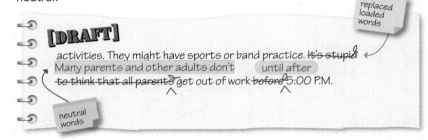

Revise

Focus on **Word Choice**

The Rubric Says	The writer's language is fair and balanced. No loaded words or phrases are used.
Writing Strategy	Replace loaded words with neutral words.

When I reread the rubric, I realized I had to check my opinion essay for loaded words. I want to use strong reasons and details that explain my opinion to my readers. I don't want to trick them by using words with added meanings. I'll replace loaded words with words that are more neutral.

✎ Writer's Term ____

Loaded Words

Loaded words carry extra meaning. For example, a shack and a house are both places in which to live, but the word **shack** makes the place seem shabby. It creates a feeling that is different from **house**.

replaced loaded words

[DRAFT]

activities. They might have sports or band practice. ~~It's stupid~~
Many parents and other adults don't   until after
~~to think that all parents~~ get out of work ~~before~~ 5:00 P.M.

neutral words

Analyze

Look at Shamari's revisions. How do neutral words strengthen her opinion?

Write

Check your draft again. Revise your writing to replace any loaded words with neutral words.

256 Opinion Writing

Optional Revising Lessons ____

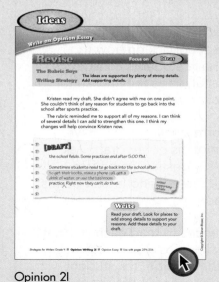

Opinion 21

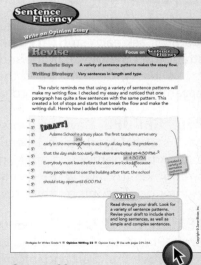

Opinion 22

Go to ➡ **Strategies for Writers** at **www.sfw.z-b.com**

Edit

Focus on Conventions

The Rubric Says   Adverbs are used correctly. The meaning is clear.

Writing Strategy   Check that adverbs are used correctly.

I know from the rubric that I need to check my essay for errors. First I'll check spelling, punctuation, and capitalization. Next I'll check to see that I used each adverb correctly.

Writer's Term

Adverbs

Adverbs are words that describe verbs. Many adverbs end in *-ly*. However, some common adverbs, including **fast, later, well,** and **once,** do not.

[DRAFT]

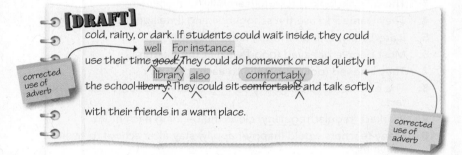

cold, rainy, or dark. If students could wait inside, they could

use their time ~~good~~ well For instance, They could do homework or read quietly in

the school ~~liberry~~ library also They could sit ~~comfortable~~ comfortably and talk softly

with their friends in a warm place.

corrected use of adverb

corrected use of adverb

Analyze

Look at Shamari's edits. How well did she proofread her writing and use adverbs correctly? What other changes, if any, are still needed in her draft?

Write   Conventions

Edit your draft to check that you have used all adverbs correctly.

For more practice using adverbs correctly, use the exercises on the next two pages.

Opinion Essay **257**

Related Grammar Practice

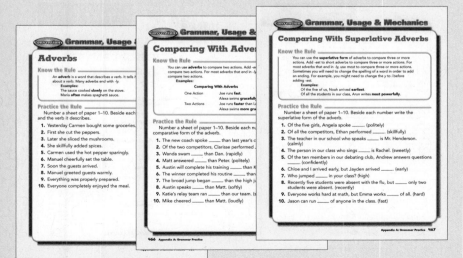

Student Edition pages 457, 466, 467

Go to ➡ **Appendix A: Grammar Practice**

Write
Opinion Essay

Student Objectives

• Edit for correct use of adverbs. *(p. 257)*

Edit

Focus on Conventions

Check Adverbs Review the difference between revising (improving text) and editing (correcting text). Tell students that this is the time to go back and correct mistakes in spelling, punctuation, grammar, and capitalization. Remind students to look for the kinds of errors they frequently make.

Use the mini-lessons on pages T258–T259 for students having problems with using adverbs correctly.

Writer's Term

Adverbs Using adverbs correctly requires practice. A common error is splitting an infinitive with an adverb that ends in *-ly*. (Example: *You need to quickly run to catch the bus.*) Using adverbs correctly in speaking will help students use them correctly in writing, too.

CCSS **Common Core State Standards** (pp. Z20–Z30)
Writing: W.4.4, W.4.5, W.4.6, W.4.10
Language: L.4.1g, L.4.2a, L.4.2d, L.4.3a, L.4.4c, L.4.6

Opinion Essay **T257**

Conventions

Mini-Lesson

Student Objectives

• Use adverbs correctly. *(p. 258)*

Adverbs

Read and discuss the information about adverbs at the top of page 258. Write the words *how* and *when* on the board. Ask students to explain why you have written these words. **(These are the questions that adverbs answer.)** After the word *how*, write these examples: *easily, quietly, secretly, slowly, quickly.* After the word *when*, write: *now, then, later, soon, yesterday, finally.* Explain that these are examples of adverbs.

Next write the following sentence on the board: *Amy secretly baked a cake.* Ask students to identify the verb and adverb in the sentence. **(The verb is *baked*. The adverb is *secretly*.)** Ask:

• **Which question about the verb does the adverb answer? (how)**

Write: *Amy finally baked a cake.*

• **What is the adverb and which question about the verb does it answer? (The adverb is *finally*. It answers the question *when*.)**

Note that the verb in each sentence is the same. Discuss how the meaning of the sentence is changed by the adverb.

Online Writing Center

Provides **interactive grammar games** and **practice activities** in student eBook.

Adverbs

Know the Rule

> **Adverbs** are describing words. An adverb describes a verb. Adverbs tell how or when. Many adverbs end in *-ly*. The words *well* and *fast* are also adverbs.

Practice the Rule

Number a piece of paper 1–12. Read each sentence below. On your paper, write the word that correctly completes each sentence.

1. Last year, the closing time for the school was (usual/**usually**) three o'clock.
2. This year, those hours were (quiet/**quietly**) changed.
3. The officials looked (careful/**carefully**) at many things.
4. They wanted to use the school building (intelligent/**intelligently**).
5. (**Late**/Lately) one afternoon, a meeting was held.
6. Most people behaved (good/**well**) at the meeting.
7. They listened (polite/**politely**) to each speaker.
8. The officials (surprising/**surprisingly**) discovered some interesting facts.
9. Workers (regular/**regularly**) clean the building each night.
10. Many teachers would (happy/**happily**) stay after school to oversee activities.
11. The town officials (final/**finally**) decided to let local groups use the building after school hours.
12. Our teacher (excited/**excitedly**) told us the news the next day.

Related Grammar Practice

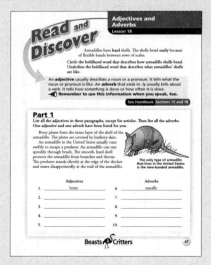

Page 47

Page 67

 Go to G.U.M. Student Practice Book

Good and Well

Know the Rule

Good is an adjective that describes a noun. **Well** is an adverb that describes a verb.

Example:
The lunchroom offers **good** food. However, some students do not eat **well** at school.

Practice the Rule

Number a piece of paper 1–10. Write the correct adjective (**good/well**) to complete the sentence.

1. My soccer team played _____ last week. well
2. The fans had a _____ time watching us win. good
3. Afterward, my sister said she had never seen us play so _____. well
4. The whole team went out to see a _____ movie. good
5. My favorite actor played the "_____ guy." good
6. The tickets cost a lot, but it was money _____ spent. well
7. Next, we went to a _____ pizza restaurant. good
8. They have a _____ selection of toppings there. good
9. We ate _____ that night. well
10. Finally, everyone went home for a _____ night's sleep. good

---

Mini-Lesson

Student Objectives

• Use *good* and *well* correctly. (p. 259)

Good and *Well*

Read aloud the example sentence in Know the Rule on page 259. Point out that *good* and *well* are easily confused describing words. Explain that *good* is an adjective; it is never used as an adverb. When used as an adverb, *well* can describe a verb, an adjective, or another adverb. Do the first practice sentence together and point out that *well* tells *how*.

Note: *Well* is an adjective when it is used to describe one's health, such as *He feels well*.

Page 41

Adjectives and Adverbs — Lesson 18

Learn

Tornadoes are **violent** storms. Their winds rotate **rapidly**.

Underline the boldfaced word that describes how a tornado's winds rotate. Circle the boldfaced word that describes what kind of storm tornadoes are.

An **adjective** usually describes a noun or a pronoun. It tells what the noun or pronoun is like. An **adverb** that ends in *-ly* usually tells about a verb. It tells how something is done or how often it is done.

Practice

Decide whether each boldfaced word is an adjective or an adverb. Write **ADJ** if it is an adjective. Write **ADV** if it is an adverb.

1. A tornado usually follows a **narrow** path.
2. Unlike hurricanes, which move **slowly**, tornadoes are fast.
3. Hurricanes are **huge** storms that form over the Atlantic Ocean.
4. Tornadoes **normally** form over land.
5. A **broad** area of the United States is called Tornado Alley.
6. **Many** tornadoes strike this area during spring and summer.
7. During the summer, the National Weather Service **carefully** watches this part of the country.
8. The National Weather Service **swiftly** issues warnings about bad storms.
9. Sometimes it warns people about **severe** thunderstorms.
10. Such storms can **quickly** produce tornadoes.

Copyright © Zaner-Bloser, Inc.   *Strategies for Writers—Conventions & Skills Practice* Unit 2

Page 55

Good and Well — Lesson 25

Learn

We planned **well** for our trip to the Arctic. I wrote a **good** report about igloos.

Which boldfaced word describes a noun? _____

Which boldfaced word describes a verb? _____

Good is an adjective that describes a noun. **Well** is an adverb that describes a verb.

Practice

Circle the word that the word in parentheses is describing. Decide whether that word is a noun or a verb. Then underline the word in parentheses that completes each sentence correctly.

1. Everyone wanted to get a (good/well) look at an igloo.
2. We saw several (good/well) examples near fishing holes.
3. Igloos must be built (good/well) in order to keep out the cold.
4. An igloo makes a (good/well) shelter for people.
5. Of course, the structure must be built (good/well).
6. An experienced builder can make a (good/well) igloo in less than an hour.
7. The snow must be compressed (good/well) so that it sticks together.
8. Blocks of snow are arranged in a circle to make a (good/well) base.
9. If blocks are not placed (good/well), the entire structure may fall.
10. Even in fierce weather, an igloo provides (good/well) shelter.

Copyright © Zaner-Bloser, Inc.   *Strategies for Writers—Conventions & Skills Practice* Unit 2

Go to ➡ Grammar Practice Masters

CCSS **Common Core State Standards** (pp. Z20–Z30)
Writing: W.4.6
Language: L.4.1g, L.4.4a, L.4.6

Write
Opinion Essay

Week 3 • Day 4

Student Objectives

- Discuss preparation for publishing and presentation. *(p. 260)*
- Use a final editing checklist to publish their work. *(p. 260)*

Publish +Presentation

Publishing Strategy Read aloud page 260 and discuss with students the publishing option. As an alternative to publishing their essays as speeches, explore options, such as publishing the essays in school newspapers, in student magazines, or on your school website.

Then point out Shamari's plans for preparing her final copy. **(setting neat margins, making sure to leave spaces between lines, and numbering pages)** Ask students why these formatting considerations are important as they prepare their own essays to read as speeches. **(readability, following text on page as it's read)** Finally, read the checklist aloud. Suggest that students refer to it as they prepare final copies of their opinion essays.

Provide a List of Sources Remind students to include a list of the sources they used to find information about their topics. Provide the citing format guidelines to students to use in their essay.

Strategies for Writers Online
Go to **www.sfw.z-b.com** for additional online resources for students, teachers, and parents.

Publish +Presentation

Publishing Strategy	Give my essay as a speech on "Sound Off Day."
Presentation Strategy	Use good margins and number the pages.

My opinion essay is finished. Now it's time to publish. Every student in class wrote his or her own essay, so we thought it would be good if everyone could hear all the opinions. That's why we decided to have a "Sound Off Day" when all the students could give their essays as speeches and record them as podcasts. Before I publish my essay, I'll check to be sure I left enough space around the text so that it is easy to read out loud. I'll also number my pages so they don't get lost or out of order. I'll use this final checklist to prepare my final copy.

My Final Checklist

Did I—

✓ check my spelling and punctuation?
✓ use adverbs correctly?
✓ use good margins?
✓ number the pages?
✓ put my name on the paper?

Write

Make a checklist to check your opinion essay. Then make a final copy. Practice reading your essay aloud before presenting it.

260 Opinion Writing

Differentiating Instruction

ENRICHMENT
Add Captions Have students find photos and illustrations that relate to their opinion essay. Then have them write short captions identifying each visual. Tell students their captions should be accurate and interesting. Have an experienced word processor show others how to incorporate the visuals and captions in the essays.

REINFORCEMENT
Proofread After students edit their drafts, have them put their writing away for a day. Then have students exchange drafts to proofread each other's work for one specific kind of error. Encourage students to work with at least three different peer editors. When they have finished, have writers verify the edits and make their corrections.

SOUND OFF DAY

Keep the Doors Open
by Shamari

Adams School is a busy place. The first teachers arrive very early in the morning, and there is activity all day long. The problem is that the day ends too early. Everybody must leave before the doors are locked at 4:30 P.M. Because many people need to use the building after that, the school should stay open until 6:00 P.M.

1

Write
Opinion Essay

Student Objectives

- Use an opinion essay rubric. (*pp. 242–243*)
- Share a published opinion essay. (*pp. 261–263*)

Presentation Strategy Remind students of the importance of neatness when creating their final draft. Point out the many word-processing features computers have to offer. It's easy to set neat margins, use the tab key to indent paragraphs, double-space text, and select one or two clear fonts. Depending on the topic, students may want to create visuals to enhance the main ideas in their presentation. If students present their opinion essays aloud, be sure they speak slowly and clearly, yet with expression.

Tech Tips
Online Tools

Collaborate Online Writing an opinion essay typically requires addressing counterarguments held by opposing thinkers. Use an interactive writing space like Google Docs to exchange students' opinions on a topic. As the lead learner, you can post a comment for students working on laptops to respond to in real-time. Your class could also collaborate with another class by asking them to respond to the opinion statements offered. The goal here is to facilitate students' interaction with diverse perspectives and to gain new ways of thinking that should ultimately strengthen their own opinion writing.

See **www.sfw.z-b.com** for further information about and links to these websites and tools.

CCSS **C**ommon **C**ore **S**tate **S**tandards (pp. Z20–Z30)
Writing: W.4.4, W.4.6, W.4.10
Language: L.4.2d
Speaking and Listening: SL.4.4, SL.4.5

Reflecting on an Opinion Essay

Read aloud the questions in the Analyze box on page 263. Refer students to the opinion essay rubric on pages 242–243 to evaluate Shamari's essay. Ask:

• How did you use the rubric as you wrote your essay?

Have students record their responses in a journal or in their notes on the chapter.

Have students turn and talk to a partner to share their responses to these questions:

• What is the strongest part of your essay?

• What advice would you give to someone who is about to write an opinion essay?

After students have shared with partners, ask volunteers to share their answers with the class.

2

The most important reason is that sometimes students have to wait for a ride home. Often students have school clubs and activities. They might have sports or band practice. Many parents and other adults don't get out of work until after 5:00 P.M. Students who need to wait for a ride should not have to stand outside the building, especially when it is cold, rainy, or dark. If students could wait inside, they could use their time well. For instance, they could do homework or read quietly in the school library. They also could sit comfortably and talk softly with their friends in a warm place.

The second reason the doors should be open is for students who have activities there. After school ends, many activities take place in and around the school building. Some go on after 4:30 P.M. For example, many sports teams practice on the school fields. Some practices end after 5:00 P.M. Sometimes students need

Strategies for Writers Online
Go to **www.sfw.z-b.com** for additional online resources for students, teachers, and parents.

3

to go back into the school after practice to get their books, make a phone call, get a drink of water, or use the bathroom. Right now they can't do that. Also, some activities that take place inside the school are cut short because the building closes so early. This happened just last week. Mr. Azar's class was practicing for the holiday play. The cast needed more practice time, but everyone had to leave by 4:30 P.M.

Adams School should keep its doors open until 6:00 P.M. Many students are still using the school building or grounds at 4:30 P.M. Keeping the school open an hour and a half later would make life easier for them and sometimes for the adults in their lives, too.

Analyze

Use the rubric to evaluate Shamari's essay. Are all the traits of a good opinion essay there? Now use the rubric to evaluate your opinion essay.

CCSS **Common Core State Standards** (pp. Z20–Z30)
Writing: W.4.4, W.4.10
Language: L.4.3c
Speaking and Listening: SL.4.1a, SL.4.1b, SL.4.1c, SL.4.1d, SL.4.3, SL.4.6

Editorial Planner

WEEK 1

Day 1
Introduce
Editorial

Student Objectives
- Review the elements of an editorial.
- Consider purpose and audience.
- Learn the traits of opinion writing.

Student Activities
- Read and discuss **What's in an Editorial?** (p. 264)
- Read and discuss **Why Write an Editorial?** (p. 265)
- Read **Linking Opinion Writing Traits to an Editorial.** (p. 266)

Day 2
Analyze
Close Reading of the Model

Student Objectives
- Read a model editorial.

Student Activities
- Read **"Students Deserve Healthy Foods."** (p. 267)

Day 3
Analyze
Introduce the Rubric

Student Objectives
- Learn to read a rubric.

Student Activities
- Review **"Students Deserve Healthy Foods."** (p. 267)
- Read and discuss the **Editorial Rubric.** (pp. 268–269)

WEEK 2

Day 1
Write
Prewrite: Ideas

Student Objectives
- Read and understand a prewriting strategy.

Student Activities
- Read and discuss **Prewrite: Focus on Ideas.** (p. 274)
- Apply the prewriting strategy.

Day 2
Write
Prewrite: Organization

Student Objectives
- Use a Main-Idea Table to organize the opinion and reasons.

Student Activities
- Read and discuss **Prewrite: Focus on Organization.** (p. 275)
- Apply the prewriting strategy.
- Participate in a peer conference.

Day 3
Write
Draft: Organization

Student Objectives
- Organize information in a logical order.

Student Activities
- Read and discuss **Draft: Focus on Organization.** (p. 276)
- Apply the drafting strategy.

WEEK 3

Day 1
Write
Revise: Word Choice

Student Objectives
- Revise to choose words and phrases to convey ideas precisely.

Student Activities
- Read and discuss **Revise: Focus on Word Choice.** (p. 279)
- Reflect on the model draft.
- Apply the revising strategy.
- Participate in a peer conference.

Day 2
Write
Revise: Sentence Fluency

Student Objectives
- Revise to mix together simple and compound sentences.

Student Activities
- Read and discuss **Revise: Focus on Sentence Fluency.** (p. 280)
- Apply the revising strategy.

Note: Optional Revising Lessons are located at **www.sfw.z-b.com.**

Day 3
Write
Edit: Conventions

Student Objectives
- Edit for correct use of past-tense verbs.

Student Activities
- Read and discuss **Edit: Focus on Conventions.** (p. 281)
- Reflect on the model draft.
- Apply the editing strategy.

Note: Teach the Conventions mini-lessons (pp. 282–283) if needed.

Day 4	Day 5

Analyze
Close Reading for the Traits

Analyze
Close Reading for the Traits

Student Objectives
- Read a model editorial.
- Use the editorial rubric.
- Use the model editorial to study Ideas, Organization, and Voice.

Student Objectives
- Read a model editorial.
- Use the editorial rubric.
- Use the model editorial to study Word Choice, Sentence Fluency, and Conventions.

Student Activities
- Review **"Students Deserve Healthy Foods."** *(p. 267)*
- Read and discuss **Using the Rubric to Analyze the Model.** *(pp. 270–271)*

Student Activities
- Review **"Students Deserve Healthy Foods."** *(p. 267)*
- Read and discuss **Using the Rubric to Analyze the Model.** *(pp. 272–273)*

Day 4	Day 5

Write
Draft

Write
Revise: Voice

Student Objectives
- Complete a draft.

Student Objectives
- Revise to use a convincing tone and first-person point of view.

Student Activities
- Finish a draft. *(p. 277)*
- Participate in a peer conference.

Student Activities
- Read and discuss **Revise: Focus on Voice.** *(p. 278)*
- Apply the revising strategy.

Day 4	Day 5

Write
Publish: +Presentation

Write
Publish: +Presentation

Student Objectives
- Discuss preparation for publishing and presentation.
- Use a final editing checklist to publish their work.

Student Objectives
- Use the editorial rubric.
- Share a published editorial.

Student Activities
- Read and discuss **Publish: +Presentation.** *(p. 284)*
- Apply the publishing strategy.

Student Activities
- Share their work.
- Use the rubric to reflect upon and evaluate the model and their own writing. *(pp. 268–269; 285)*

To complete the chapter in fewer days, combine the learning objectives and activities in a way that supports students as they write.

Resources at-a-Glance

Grammar, Usage & Mechanics

Differentiating Instruction

For additional Differentiating Instruction activities, see Strategies for Writers *Differentiated Instruction Activities at* **www.sfw.z-b.com.**

English Language Learners

Collaborative Conferencing

Tech Tips

 Strategies for Writers Online

Go to **www.sfw.z-b.com** for additional online resources for students, teachers, and parents.

Online Writing Center

Provides IWB resources, assessments, interactive games and practice activities, videos, eBooks, and a virtual file cabinet.

Introduce
Editorial

Student Objectives

- Review the elements of an editorial. (p. 264)
- Consider purpose and audience. (p. 265)
- Learn the traits of opinion writing. (p. 266)

What's an Editorial?

Discuss with students the definition of an editorial. Provide examples of well-written editorials, and ask students to share their views on convincing ones they have read. Ask them to state the writer's point of view. Then ask them to think about whether the writer supported the opinion with details that helped to convince them. Finally, point out that anytime they write to convince readers to agree with their opinion, they are using the editorial genre.

What's in an Editorial?

Read and discuss with students the elements of an editorial listed on page 264. Explain that these organizational elements—Introduction, Body, and Conclusion—are common to various genres, such as editorials and book or movie reviews. Then discuss why each element is important to keep in mind while writing a convincing editorial.

 Strategies for Writers Online
Go to **www.sfw.z-b.com** for additional online resources for students, teachers, and parents.

What's an Editorial?

It's an article I write for a newspaper or magazine that expresses my opinion about a topic. My topic should interest readers of that publication.

What's in an Editorial?

Introduction
That's my first paragraph. I'll get the reader interested in my topic right away. Then I'll state my opinion. One thing I feel strongly about is that my school needs a student newspaper! My friends and I want to take photographs and write articles about life at school.

Body
The body is where I convince the reader that my opinion is correct. I'll give reasons for my opinion and offer examples that support it. I'll also give facts and information that support my reasons.

Conclusion
That's my last paragraph. I'll restate my opinion and summarize my reasons and facts.

Opinion Text Exemplars (Editorial)

Dunn, John M. *Voices from the Civil War: Northerners.* Blackbirch Press, 2003. Dunn describes the circumstances of the Civil War from the perspective of the Northerners. By including artifacts from primary sources, *Voices from the Civil War: Northerners* allows students to understand the war from several different viewpoints.

Dunn, John M. *Voices from the Civil War: Southerners.* Blackbirch Press, 2003. Dunn describes the circumstances of the Civil War from the perspective of the Southerners. By including artifacts from primary sources, *Voices from the Civil War: Southerners* allows students to understand the war from several different viewpoints.

Why write an Editorial?

There are many reasons to write an editorial. Here are some reasons I thought of.

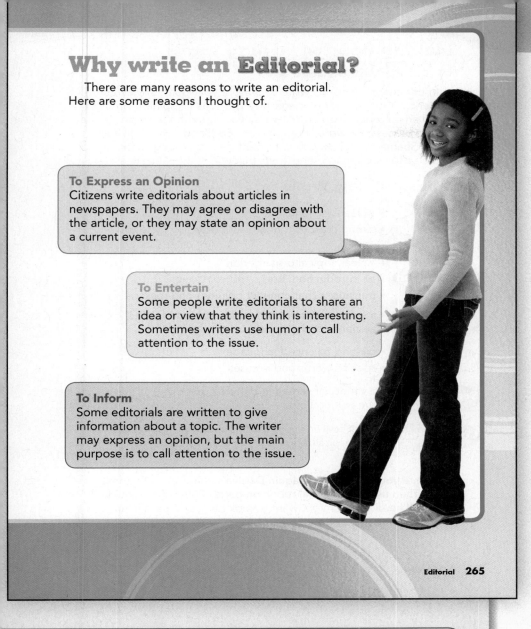

To Express an Opinion
Citizens write editorials about articles in newspapers. They may agree or disagree with the article, or they may state an opinion about a current event.

To Entertain
Some people write editorials to share an idea or view that they think is interesting. Sometimes writers use humor to call attention to the issue.

To Inform
Some editorials are written to give information about a topic. The writer may express an opinion, but the main purpose is to call attention to the issue.

Why write an Editorial?

Read aloud and discuss with students the reasons for writing an editorial listed on page 265. Point out that all writing has a purpose and is aimed at a specific audience. Encourage students to discuss how having authentic purposes helps authors shape their writing. For example, someone writing to express an opinion on an issue or a current event will make sure the reasons are clearly stated. A writer who is writing to entertain may use humorous details and examples to convince the reader. And a writer who is writing to inform will include clear reasons and details to convince the reader that the issue is important.

Encourage students to think about their own reasons for writing editorials and how these reasons will affect the focus and tone of their writing. Conclude the discussion by explaining to students that they are going to study and practice strategies for writing a good editorial.

Oxlade, Chris and Anita Ganeri. *Down the Drain: Conserving Water.* Heinemann-Raintree, 2005. *Down the Drain: Conserving Water* describes the many ways people use water and explains why conserving it is so important. Oxlade also helps students gain a perspective on how much water they themselves use by encouraging them to record their daily usage in a journal.

Jory, John. *Thanks and Have Fun Running the Country: Kids' Letters to President Obama.* McSweeney's Publishing, 2009. *Thanks and Have Fun Running the Country: Kids' Letters to President Obama* presents President Obama with advice from youth around the US. Including suggestions regarding the economy, education, and politics, the words of these children leave our 44th president with a lot to consider.

CCSS **C**ommon **C**ore **S**tate **S**tandards (pp. Z20–Z30)
Language: L.4.3c
Speaking and Listening: SL.4.1a, SL.4.1b, SL.4.1c, SL.4.1d, SL.4.3, SL.4.6

Introduce
Editorial

Linking Opinion Writing Traits to an Editorial

Read the introduction to page 266 aloud to help students understand that they will follow Shamari as she models using the writing process and the opinion writing traits together. As they follow Shamari, students will see how the Opinion Writing Traits have been adapted and applied to writing an editorial. They will see that an editorial has many factors in common with other types of opinion writing. However, the particular audience and purpose of an editorial determine how the traits are used.

In this chapter, you will write to present your point of view to readers of a newspaper or magazine. This type of opinion writing is called an editorial. Shamari will guide you through the stages of the writing process: Prewrite, Draft, Revise, Edit, and Publish. In each stage, Shamari will show you important writing strategies that are linked to the Opinion Writing Traits below.

Opinion Writing Traits

Ideas	• a clear opinion • strong reasons that are supported by facts and details
Organization	• a clear, logical organization • an introduction, body, and conclusion • transitions that connect opinions and reasons
Voice	• a voice and tone that are appropriate for the audience and purpose
 Word Choice	• fair and balanced language • specific words and phrases
Sentence Fluency	• a variety of sentence patterns that make the writing flow
Conventions	• no or few errors in spelling, grammar, punctuation, and capitalization

Before you write, read Joaquin Dasilva's editorial on the next page. Then use the editorial rubric on pages 268–269 to decide how well he did. (You might want to look back at What's in an Editorial? on page 264, too!)

Opinion Writing Traits in an Editorial

 **Ideas** The writer's opinion is clearly stated and supported with strong reasons. The writer includes relevant details that support each reason.

 **Organization** The introduction states the writer's opinion. The body presents reasons in order of importance. Helpful transitions guide the reader. A concluding statement or section restates the writer's opinion.

 **Voice** The writer establishes and maintains a convincing, sincere voice and a formal style that supports the writer's purpose and connects with the audience.

Students Deserve Healthy Foods

strong introduction

by Joaquin Dasilva

Just eat right. This sounds simple, but it's not always as easy as it sounds, especially when we're in school. As students, what can we do to help ourselves develop healthy eating habits? First we need to remove vending machines that sell junk food and change soda machine choices to water and low-sugar juices. Then we need to work with teachers, staff, and parents to develop a healthy eating program at school. **the issue** **opinion**

Why are good eating habits so important? What we eat affects our health now and will continue to affect us in the future. When we eat snack foods and sugary sodas too often, we eat too much fat, sugar, and salt. This type of diet causes many students to gain weight. Children who have poor eating habits tend to have less energy and to get tired quickly. They don't exercise enough and may have trouble paying attention in class. Maybe in the past people thought eating sweets did not harm children, but now we know better.

Vending machines encourage students to eat junk. Most of the foods sold in vending machines are bad for our health. The cafeteria should offer us more fresh foods, such as fruits and vegetables. Vending machines make unhealthy snack foods and high-sugar drinks easily available to us. Many kids are in a hurry to eat because they are hungry or they have a short lunch period. Often students would rather buy junk food than wait in a long cafeteria line for healthier choices. We need to get rid of these snack vending machines and fill soda machines with low-sugar juices and water. It also would help to organize lunch lines in the cafeteria so they are shorter and move more quickly. **body**

Students, teachers, staff, and parents should work together to plan a healthy eating program. The program would eliminate unhealthy foods and give us more healthy choices. We need more fresh fruits, vegetables, and salads. We should have sandwiches on whole-grain breads with lean meats like turkey, chicken, ham, and tuna fish. We should also have low-fat dairy products like yogurt and low-fat cheeses. Fried foods such as French fries, fried chicken, and fish sticks should be replaced with baked potatoes, chicken, or fish.

Eating right in school may not always be simple, but it's a challenge we can meet! Together, we can make our school a "Healthy Food Zone." **strong conclusion**

Editorial 267

Word Choice The writer uses specific and precise words to convince the reader. Unfamiliar words are explained for the reader.

Sentence Fluency A variety of sentence patterns makes the writing flow well and holds the reader's attention throughout the editorial.

Conventions The writer has edited carefully. All verbs are used correctly.

Student Objectives

• Read a model editorial. *(p. 267)*

Read the Model

Ask students to listen for the writing traits as you read "Students Deserve Healthy Foods" aloud. Ask students to note how the editorial is organized. Also ask students to think about how the writer speaks directly to the reader. They should agree that the writer's sincere and knowledgeable voice supports the writer's purpose and connects with the reader.

Elements of an Editorial

Have students refer to What's in an Editorial? on page 264 as you refer to the model on page 267. Discuss the notes written on the model to enhance students' understanding of the terms. Ask students to find additional examples in the text to support their analysis of the model.

CCSS Common Core State Standards (pp. Z20–Z30)
Writing: W.4.6
Language: L.4.3c
Speaking and Listening: SL.4.1a, SL.4.1b, SL.4.1c, SL.4.1d, SL.4.2, SL.4.3, SL.4.6

Analyze
Introduce the Rubric

Student Objectives

- Learn to read a rubric. (pp. 268–269)

Introduce the Rubric

Explain the Rubric Explain that a rubric is a tool for planning, improving, and assessing a piece of writing. Tell students that a rubric helps a writer focus on key elements, or traits, in writing (**Ideas, Organization, Voice, Word Choice, Sentence Fluency, Conventions,** and **Presentation**).

Point out that column 6 describes a very good editorial, one that has received the highest score in all categories. This is what students should strive for in their own writing.

Discuss the Rubric When students score their paper for each trait, they should first decide whether it falls on the left of the rubric (uses the trait well) or on the right (needs improvement in using the trait). By examining the paper more closely, students can refine the score to a single number.

Online Writing Center

Provides a variety of **interactive rubrics,** including 4-, 5-, and 6-point models.

Editorial Rubric

Use this rubric to analyze the model. Then use it to plan and score your own editorial.

	6	5	4
Ideas	The editorial expresses an opinion on one issue. Reasons offer facts and details that clarify and support the opinion.	The editorial expresses an opinion that could be stated more clearly. The reason is supported by facts and details.	The editorial expresses an opinion. Some of the reasons may not support the opinion.
Organization	The editorial has a strong introduction, body, and conclusion. The introduction grabs the reader's attention.	The editorial has an introduction, body, and conclusion. The introduction is fairly strong.	The introduction, body, and conclusion are noticeable but unoriginal.
Voice	The writer uses a convincing tone. First-person point of view connects with the reader.	The tone is convincing most of the time. The writer uses the first-person point of view.	The writer's tone is appropriate but not always convincing. The writer uses first-person point of view.
Word Choice	Words are focused and support the opinion.	Many words support the opinion.	The writing is basically clear. Some words do not relate to the opinion.
Sentence Fluency	Sentences are clear and flow naturally.	Most sentences are clear and flow naturally.	Some sentence beginnings are repetitive.
Conventions	Past-tense verbs are formed correctly. The meaning is clear.	Most past-tense verbs are formed correctly. The meaning is clear.	The writer shows good control of verb tenses. Minor errors do not confuse the reader.

✛ Presentation The editorial is formatted neatly on the computer.

CCSS Common Core State Standards
Editorial

Strategies for Writers was designed and written to weave the Common Core State Standards throughout every unit. For Opinion writing, the standards inform the unit's writing rubrics, objectives, and strategies. By presenting the standards in as many applications as possible, your students' exposure to them will be ensured. As a result, students are more likely to employ the standards' language in writing opinion pieces as well as in discussions about writing.

The lessons for Editorial are based principally on the writing standards for Opinion writing. The rubrics and writing

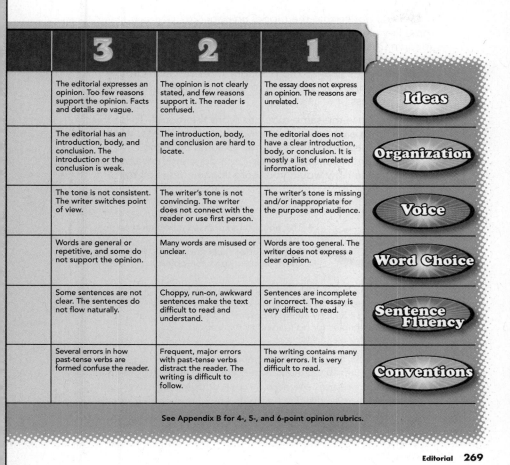

	3	2	1	
	The editorial expresses an opinion. Too few reasons support the opinion. Facts and details are vague.	The opinion is not clearly stated, and few reasons support it. The reader is confused.	The essay does not express an opinion. The reasons are unrelated.	Ideas
	The editorial has an introduction, body, and conclusion. The introduction or the conclusion is weak.	The introduction, body, and conclusion are hard to locate.	The editorial does not have a clear introduction, body, or conclusion. It is mostly a list of unrelated information.	Organization
	The tone is not consistent. The writer switches point of view.	The writer's tone is not convincing. The writer does not connect with the reader or use first person.	The writer's tone is missing and/or inappropriate for the purpose and audience.	Voice
	Words are general or repetitive, and some do not support the opinion.	Many words are misused or unclear.	Words are too general. The writer does not express a clear opinion.	Word Choice
	Some sentences are not clear. The sentences do not flow naturally.	Choppy, run-on, awkward sentences make the text difficult to read and understand.	Sentences are incomplete or incorrect. The essay is very difficult to read.	Sentence Fluency
	Several errors in how past-tense verbs are formed confuse the reader.	Frequent, major errors with past-tense verbs distract the reader. The writing is difficult to follow.	The writing contains many major errors. It is very difficult to read.	Conventions

See Appendix B for 4-, 5-, and 6-point opinion rubrics.

Find Evidence in the Model

Small-Group Collaboration
Assign students to small groups and ask them to check the model for each trait. One person in each group should be responsible for recording one or two strong examples of the trait as described by the rubric. Ask students to score each trait accordingly for the model. They should be able to support their scores. Note that although the model was written to score high in each trait, students should not assume each trait would receive a 6, the top score. Encourage students to discuss each trait thoroughly before assigning each score.

Teacher-Led Discussion Bring the class back together and ask one person from each group to report their findings to the class. The point of this exercise is to practice identifying and evaluating the traits within a piece of writing.

Additional Rubrics

Appendix B includes 4-, 5-, and 6-point rubrics that can be used with any piece of opinion writing. The rubrics are also available as blackline masters in the back of this Teacher Edition.

strategies reflect the writing standard **W.4.1,** which focuses on introducing and supporting a point of view with reasons and information.

The language standards for grade 4 students are addressed during editing and skills practice. In addition, there are multiple opportunities to address the speaking and listening standards during the writing process. Most importantly, this chapter will help your students produce coherent writing (**W.4.4**), improve their writing (**W.4.5**), and use technologies to publish their finished pieces (**W.4.6**).

CCSS **C**ommon **C**ore **S**tate **S**tandards (pp. Z20–Z30)
Writing: W.4.6
Language: L.4.3c
Speaking and Listening: SL.4.1a, SL.4.1b, SL.4.1c, SL.4.1d, SL.4.2, SL.4.3, SL.4.6

Analyze
Close Reading for the Traits

Week 1 • Day 4

Student Objectives

- Read a model editorial. *(p. 267)*
- Use the editorial rubric. *(pp. 268–269)*
- Use the model editorial to study **Ideas**, **Organization**, and **Voice**. *(pp. 270–271)*

Find Evidence in the Model

Evaluate the Model Have volunteers read aloud each section on pages 270–271. Determine whether students agree with each point in Shamari's assessment. Use the questions below to initiate the discussion. Be sure students can back up their answers with specific examples from the editorial.

Discuss Audience, Task, Purpose Ask students one or more of the following questions as they analyze the model:

- **Audience** Who is the audience? (Possible response: school officials, readers of the school newspaper)

- **Task** How does the writer show his opinion? (Possible responses: The writer states his opinion at the end of the first paragraph.)

- **Purpose** What is the writer's purpose for writing this essay? How do you know? (Possible response: to persuade his school to offer more healthful food options; He explained his reasons in the body of the editorial.)

Using the Rubric to Analyze the Model
(Editorial)

Did you notice that the model on page 267 points out some key elements of an editorial? As he wrote his editorial, Joaquin Dasilva used these elements to help him convince others to agree with his opinion. He also used the 6-point rubric on pages 268–269 to plan, draft, revise, and edit the writing. A rubric is a great tool to evaluate writing during the writing process.

Now let's use the same rubric to score the model. To do this, we'll focus on each trait separately, starting with Ideas. We'll use the top descriptor for each trait (column 6), along with examples from the model, to help us understand how the traits work together. How would you score Joaquin on each trait?

Ideas
- The editorial expresses an opinion on one issue.
- Reasons offer facts and details that clarify and support the opinion.

Joaquin clearly states his opinion. He then provides examples that support and clarify it. Look at his paragraph about planning a healthy eating program. Joaquin provides a lot of good examples for his readers to think about.

Students, teachers, staff, and parents should work together to plan a healthy eating program. The program would eliminate unhealthy foods and give us more healthy choices. We need more fresh fruits, vegetables, and salads. We should have sandwiches on whole-grain breads with lean meats like turkey, chicken, ham, and tuna fish.

270 Opinion Writing

English Language Learners

BEGINNING

Editorials Provide several different publications that include editorials. Point out the editorial in each. Say *editorial* and have students repeat. Say, *An editorial is a writer's opinion about something.* Have students trade publications and locate the editorials. Review the meaning of *opinion* using examples.

INTERMEDIATE

Organizing an Editorial Post a simple editorial on an overhead transparency or interactive whiteboard. Say *editorial* and have students repeat. Point out the introduction, body, and conclusion. Say each word and have students repeat. Ask a volunteer to circle the topic and underline the opinion in the introductory paragraph. Then, using a different color, have another student underline the reasons in each paragraph in the body. Finally, ask a student to find where the opinion is restated in the final paragraph.

Organization
- The editorial has a strong introduction, body, and conclusion.
- The introduction grabs the reader's attention.

Joaquin expresses his opinion in the editorial's introduction. The body of his editorial is well organized around the issue. Joaquin's introduction hooks readers by stating the problem in a way they can relate to.

> Just eat right. This sounds simple, but it's not always as easy as it sounds, especially when we're in school.

Voice
- The writer uses a convincing tone.
- First-person point of view connects with the reader.

Joaquin uses words like *we* and *our health* to connect with his audience—other students. His choice of words creates a convincing tone. Here's a good example.

> Most of the foods sold in vending machines are bad for our health. The cafeteria should offer us more fresh foods, such as fruits and vegetables. Vending machines make unhealthy snack foods and high-sugar drinks easily available to us.

Editorial **271**

Discuss the Traits Ask students one or more of the following questions to discuss the traits in the model.

Ideas Does the writer state a clear opinion? (Possible responses: The writer states a clear opinion about providing healthy foods in the school. His reasons are based on fact.)

Organization Is the editorial organized into three parts (introduction, body, and conclusion)? (Possible responses: The editorial leads with a strong introduction that states the issue and the writer's opinion on it. The body of the editorial presents the writer's reasons in logical order. The concluding statement calls the reader to action.)

Voice Does the writer use a sincere, convincing voice? (Possible responses: Joaquin sounds knowledgeable and enthusiastic. He uses a first-person point of view to connect with the reader.)

ADVANCED/ADVANCED HIGH

Strong Introductions Demonstrate *attention-grabbing* by doing something unexpected, such as snapping your fingers. Say, *I just grabbed your attention.* Write *attention-grabbing introduction* on the board. Under the topic *Exercise,* write the following introductions: *Exercise is food for your body and soul; Jumping jacks, jogging, and gymnastics; You should exercise; Is your health important to you?* Ask students to rank the introductions according to how interesting they are. Remind students to use simple phrases, questions, or single words to capture the attention of the audience.

Write several more topics on the board and have students write a snappy introductory phrase or sentence for each one. Then read as a class, discuss the merits of each, and vote for the best introduction for each topic.

CCSS Common Core State Standards (pp. Z20–Z30)
Language: L.4.3c, L.4.6
Speaking and Listening: SL.4.1a, SL.4.1b, SL.4.1c, SL.4.1d, SL.4.3, SL.4.6

Analyze
Close Reading for the Traits

Week 1 • Day 5

Student Objectives

- Read a model editorial. *(p. 267)*
- Use the editorial rubric. *(pp. 268–269)*
- Use the model editorial to study **Word Choice, Sentence Fluency,** and **Conventions.** *(pp. 272–273)*

Discuss the Traits Ask students one or more of the following questions to discuss the traits in the model.

Word Choice How does the writer use precise, fair words? (Possible responses: Joaquin uses specific words and phrases such as *healthy eating habits, low-sugar juices, exercise,* and *junk food* to express and support his opinion.)

Sentence Fluency What evidence in the editorial shows how the writer varied sentences for interest? (Possible response: The writer uses a variety of simple and compound sentences. The questions are focused and engage the reader directly.)

Conventions What evidence in the editorial shows how the writer proofread carefully? (Possible responses: I can tell Joaquin proofread his writing carefully. There are no errors in spelling or grammar, so it's easy to understand. Also, the verbs are used correctly.)

Strategies for Writers Online
Go to **www.sfw.z-b.com** for additional online resources for students, teachers, and parents.

Using the Editorial Rubric to Analyze the Model

 • Words are focused and support the opinion.

Joaquin phrases everything in a way that supports his opinion. He chooses his words and phrases for effect. In this paragraph, he wants the audience to understand why poor eating habits are bad for children. This information supports his opinion that the school should serve healthful foods.

Why are good eating habits so important? What we eat affects our health now and will continue to affect us in the future. When we eat snack foods and sugary sodas too often, we eat too much fat, sugar, and salt. This type of diet causes many students to gain weight. Children who have poor eating habits tend to have less energy and to get tired quickly. They don't exercise enough and may have trouble paying attention in class.

 • Sentences are clear and flow naturally.

Each sentence should lead smoothly and naturally into the next one. Joaquin does a good job of creating flow. For example, after he explains why vending machines are a problem in school, he follows with a solution to the problem.

Many kids are in a hurry to eat because they are hungry or they have a short lunch period. Often students would rather buy junk food than wait in a long cafeteria line for healthier choices. We need to get rid of these snack vending machines and fill soda machines with low-sugar juices and water. It also would help to organize lunch lines in the cafeteria so they are shorter and move more quickly.

272 Opinion Writing

Tech Tips
Podcasts

Create a Podcast Recasting a piece of writing into another mode (e.g., audio or movement) changes what the writer is able to communicate. Have students recast a piece of editorial writing into a podcast while keeping a specific audience in mind. Challenge students to do more than just record a reading of their written work—the podcast has a specific audience and performance aspect. Keep reflection at the forefront of the work. How does using a document to create a podcast impact what writers can share? How does revisiting the written draft after recording the audio impact what writers include?

Conventions
- Past-tense verbs are formed correctly.
- The meaning is clear.

Joaquin uses correct spelling, capitalization, and punctuation. His writing is easy to understand. When Joaquin uses a past-tense verb, he uses it correctly.

Maybe in the past people thought eating sweets did not harm children, but now we know better.

✛Presentation The editorial is formatted neatly on the computer.

My Turn!
Now it's my turn to write an editorial. Follow along to see how I use the rubric and good writing strategies to help me.

✛Presentation Explain to students that Presentation is just as important as any of the other traits. Neatness is always a priority, and text should be clearly handwritten in pen or typed, using only a few readable fonts. White space should be used to create neat margins and to keep lines of text readable. Paragraphs should be indented (using the tab key if typed), or space should be left between blocked paragraphs. The title of the editorial should be centered at the top of the first page.

Think About the Traits

Once students have thoroughly discussed the model, ask them which traits they think are the most important in an editorial and have them explain why. (Possible response: Word Choice is a very important trait because using precise words and phrases helps convince readers to agree with the writer's opinion.)

Differentiating Instruction

ENRICHMENT
Understand Presentation Organize students in small groups. Provide several sample travel ads in print or online. Ask students to discuss the importance of presentation. Have students review each ad's basic design elements, such as the use of headings, photographs, captions, color, and other visuals. Have them assess each element's effectiveness as an enhancement to (or distraction from) the text.

REINFORCEMENT
Use a Computer To prepare students for publishing their editorials, schedule computer lab sessions during which students can work with and learn how to use the various word-processing functions of the computer. Determine the level of students' ability to use the computer and match instruction to the needs.

CCSS **Common Core State Standards** (pp. Z20–Z30)
Writing: W.4.6
Language: L.4.3c
Speaking and Listening: SL.4.1a, SL.4.1b, SL.4.1c, SL.4.1d, SL.4.3, SL.4.6

Write Editorial

Week 2 • Day 1

Student Objectives

- Read and understand a prewriting strategy. *(p. 274)*

Prewrite

Focus on Ideas

Gather Information from Print and Digital Sources Read page 274 aloud. Display several travel magazines or find them online. Brainstorm a list of potential topics with students. (vacation destinations, their home state(s), local attractions, historical locations) Ask students to choose their favorite location from the list. Then have them list at least three reasons that they can use to recommend (or not recommend) the location to others.

Take Notes on Source Information Point out Shamari's notes. Tell students that, like Shamari, they will use note cards to take notes.

Writer's Term

Reasons Point out that each reason should support the opinion. In other words, a good reason is logical, accurate, and credible. If weak or unrelated reasons are presented, they may confuse, rather than convince, the reader.

Write an Editorial

Prewrite
Focus on **Ideas**

The Rubric Says The editorial expresses an opinion on one issue.

Writing Strategy Write an opinion on an issue. List reasons for the opinion.

My teacher asked us to imagine that we have been hired to write an editorial for a travel magazine. Our job will be to convince people to visit a special place for vacation. In my opinion, North Carolina is the best place for a vacation!

I'll write down my opinion and a list of the best reasons I know for visiting North Carolina.

Writer's Term

Reasons
Reasons are the explanations behind an opinion.

My Opinion: North Carolina is the perfect place for a vacation.

Reasons That Support My Opinion:
the Great Smoky Mountains
the Piedmont Region; historic Stagville
the people are great, too

Things to do: camping, hiking, horseback riding, white-water rafting, swimming, fishing, sailing, shopping, golf, go to a theme park

Write

Choose a topic for an editorial. Write down your opinion about the topic. Then jot down a list of reasons that support your opinion.

274 Opinion Writing

English Language Learners

BEGINNING/INTERMEDIATE

Brainstorming Write *Vacation Places* on the board, and invite students to name places they have visited or would like to visit. Quickly write their answers on the board and encourage them to keep the ideas coming. Tell them this is called *brainstorming* and that all ideas are good ideas when they are brainstorming. Then have partners choose a place and brainstorm reasons that it is the best place for a vacation.

ADVANCED/ADVANCED HIGH

Main-Idea Table Draw a table on the board. Write *Healthy After School Snacks* on the tabletop. Along the legs, write students' ideas for healthy snacks. Repeat the activity with another topic, such as *Things to Do at the Beach.* Introduce a Main-Idea Table, and have students use it to organize ideas for their editorials.

The Rubric Says	The editorial has a strong introduction, body, and conclusion.
Writing Strategy	Use a Main-Idea Table to organize the opinion and reasons.

Now I need to organize my notes. The Main-Idea Table will help me organize my information into an introduction, body, and conclusion. The main idea will be in the introduction and conclusion. The supporting details will be in the body of the editorial.

Writer's Term

Main Idea
A **Main Idea** is the most important thought about a topic that is supported by details.

Main-Idea Table

Main Idea: North Carolina is the perfect place for a vacation.		
Supporting Detail Great Smoky Mountains —camping, hiking, riding, rafting	**Supporting Detail** Piedmont Region— Stagville, shopping, golf, theme park	**Supporting Detail** the people— warm, kind, welcome visitors

Analyze
Look at Shamari's notes and the graphic organizer. How will they help her write a good editorial?

Write
Look at your notes. Use a Main-Idea Table to put your opinion and list of reasons in order.

Editorial **275**

Collaborative Conferencing

PEER TO PEER Have partners exchange organizers. Tell students to ask the following question as they read them: *Is the main idea well supported by at least three strong reasons?* Have partners write their comments on a sticky note and return the organizer with their feedback.

PEER GROUPS Separate students into small groups of three or four. Have each group state one or two reasons for using a Main-Idea Table to write an editorial. Then ask them to share their reasons and revise them based on feedback from other groups.

TEACHER-LED Schedule prewriting conferences with individuals or pairs of students. To demonstrate how important the organizer is to writing a good editorial, create a Main-Idea Table with only one reason. Discuss how not supporting one's opinion would weaken the editorial.

Write
Editorial

Week 2 • Day 2

Student Objectives
• Use a Main-Idea Table to organize the opinion and reasons. *(p. 275)*

Prewrite

Focus on **Organization**

Organize Ideas Explain that writers use different types of organizers to organize their ideas. Shamari used a Main-Idea Table to help her organize the reasons she had already written down in her notes. (Go to **www.sfw.z-b.com** for the downloadable graphic organizer.) Have students study the organizer, and then ask how a Main-Idea Table can be an effective tool when writing an opinion piece. (Possible response: A Main-Idea Table helps a writer state the main idea and support it with strong details.) If students cannot think of at least three strong reasons to write on their organizers, have them consider a different topic.

Writer's Term

Main Idea The Main Idea is the most important thought about a topic. It is supported by details. The main idea is found in the introduction of an editorial.

CCSS **Common Core State Standards** (pp. Z20–Z30)
Writing: W.4.1a, W.4.1b, W.4.1d, W.4.4, W.4.5, W.4.6, W.4.8, W.4.10
Language: L.4.3c, L.4.6 .
Speaking and Listening: SL.4.1a, SL.4.1b, SL.4.1c, SL.4.1d, SL.4.3, SL.4.6

Write
Editorial

Week 2 • Day 3

Student Objectives

- Organize information in a logical order. (p. 276)

Draft

Focus on  Organization

Draft an Editorial Be sure students understand that they will use their organizer to write their draft. The "table" will be used for the introduction, and each "leg" will become a paragraph.

Students need not be concerned with writing a perfect draft. Explain that students will go through the writing process to create their final copy. Editing is part of the process.

Note: Proofreading marks are provided as a reference on page 277.

Writer's Term

Introduction, Body, and Conclusion A well-written editorial is one that is well organized from top to bottom. The introduction engages the reader's interest. The body supports the opinion by providing solid reasons in a logical order. A strong conclusion restates the opinion and summarizes the writer's main points.

Online Writing Center

 Provides an **interactive writing pad** for drafting, revising, editing, and publishing.

Draft
Focus on **Organization**

The Rubric Says The editorial has a strong introduction, body, and conclusion.

Writing Strategy Organize the information in a logical order.

It's time to start writing! I'm going to use my Main-Idea Table to write a draft. The rubric reminds me to organize my notes into an introduction, body, and conclusion. I will state the main idea in the introduction and again in the conclusion. The details in the table are the reasons. They will form the body of the editorial and connect the introduction to the conclusion.

As I write my draft, I'll do the best I can with spelling and grammar, but I won't worry about mistakes right now. I'll have a chance to fix them later. Read the beginning of my draft on the next page.

Writer's Term
Introduction, Body, and Conclusion
The **introduction** is the first paragraph, and it states the main idea.
The **body** is the part that provides reasons and supporting details.
The **conclusion** is the last paragraph of a paper. It ties up loose ends and summarizes main points.

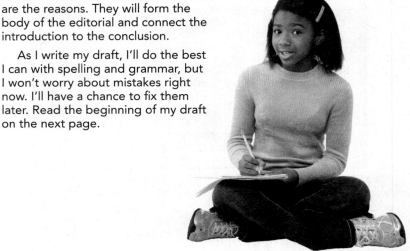

276 Opinion Writing

Differentiating Instruction

ENRICHMENT
Research a Topic Challenge students to investigate the cultural side of their community, city, or state. What does it offer the music lover? Where can a resident or visitor enjoy art or dance? What museums could people visit? Ask students to create a poster advertising one or more events with the goal of enticing families to attend.

REINFORCEMENT
Read an Opinion Piece Pass out copies of a short, well-organized article on a topic related to a destination. Ask students to read the title and predict what the piece is about. After reading, ask students to identify the writer's opinion. Then ask students to identify the writer's reasons. Read the writer's conclusion and talk about what makes it strong.

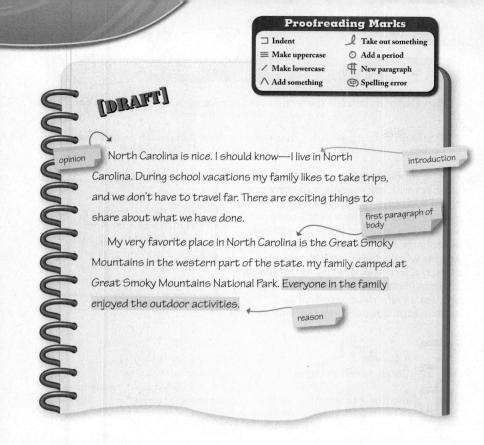

Proofreading Marks

⌐ Indent
≡ Make uppercase
/ Make lowercase
∧ Add something

ℓ Take out something
⊙ Add a period
¶ New paragraph
(SP) Spelling error

[DRAFT]

opinion → North Carolina is nice. I should know—I live in North Carolina. During school vacations my family likes to take trips, and we don't have to travel far. There are exciting things to share about what we have done.

introduction

first paragraph of body

My very favorite place in North Carolina is the Great Smoky Mountains in the western part of the state. my family camped at Great Smoky Mountains National Park. Everyone in the family enjoyed the outdoor activities.

reason

Analyze
Read Shamari's draft. What opinion did she state in the introduction? What reason does she give to support her opinion?

Write
Use your Main-Idea Table to write a draft of your editorial. Organize your writing into an introduction, body, and conclusion.

Editorial **277**

Collaborative Conferencing

PEER TO PEER Have partners exchange drafts to read. Tell students to think of two or three questions they would like to ask to clarify information or supply missing details. Have them write their questions on sticky notes and affix them to the appropriate places on their partner's draft.

PEER GROUPS Have students work in groups of four. Students pass their editorial to the student on the right to read. That student writes one comment or suggestion on a sticky note affixed to the draft and passes it along to the right. The review ends when everyone has received his or her own editorial back with three comments.

TEACHER-LED Schedule conferences with pairs of students. Have them read each other's editorial and coach them in giving and receiving constructive criticism.

Student Objectives
• Complete a draft. *(p. 277)*

Continue Drafting It is important that students are given ample time to plan and draft their editorials. As conferencing is important throughout the writing process, be sure to plan time for peer-to-peer, peer group, or teacher-led conferences. Remind students that this is the time to get their ideas down on paper in a creative and engaging way. Assure them that they will have plenty of time to fix any mistakes later.

CCSS **C**ommon **C**ore **S**tate **S**tandards (pp. Z20–Z30)
Writing: W.4.1a, W.4.1b, W.4.1d, W.4.4, W.4.5, W.4.6, W.4.10
Language: L.4.3c, L.4.6
Speaking and Listening: SL.4.1a, SL.4.1b, SL.4.1c, SL.4.1d, SL.4.3, SL.4.4, SL.4.6

Write
Editorial

Week 2 • Day 5

Student Objectives

• Revise to use a convincing tone and first-person point of view. (p. 278)

Revise

Focus on Voice

Improve Voice Read aloud the information at the top of page 278. Discuss how Shamari's revisions add a sincere, believable tone to her editorial. Also discuss how using first-person point of view strengthens her connection to the reader. Have students look for places where they can improve voice in their drafts.

Writer's Term _____

Tone The tone set by the writer affects the reader directly. A knowledgeable, sincere voice assists the writer in two ways: 1) It convinces the reader that the writer is interested and invested in the topic; 2) It sets an appropriate tone that conveys the writer's purpose.

 Strategies for Writers Online
Go to **www.sfw.z-b.com** for additional online resources for students, teachers, and parents.

Revise   Focus on **Voice**

The Rubric Says	The writer uses a convincing tone. First-person point of view connects with the reader.
Writing Strategy	Use a convincing tone and first-person point of view.

The rubric reminds me that I should connect with my readers and convince them to accept my opinion. The best way to do that is with the words I choose to express my opinion. If the tone of my editorial is sincere and believable, the reader will probably accept my ideas. I should also speak directly to the reader by using first-person point of view (*I, me, we, us*). I want people to feel as enthusiastic about North Carolina as I do!

Writer's Term _____

Tone

Tone is the way writing sounds. It shows the writer's attitude toward the subject of his or her writing. A writer's tone can be serious, funny, formal, personal, and so forth.

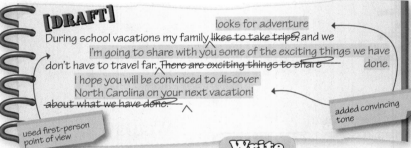

[DRAFT]

During school vacations my family ~~likes to take trips?~~ looks for adventure and we ~~don't have to travel far. There are exciting things to share~~ I'm going to share with you some of the exciting things we have done.

I hope you will be convinced to discover North Carolina on your next vacation! ~~about what we have done.~~

used first-person point of view

added convincing tone

Write

Read your draft. Look for ways to to change your tone so that it is more convincing. Revise your draft to use first-person point of view.

278 Opinion Writing

English Language Learners

BEGINNING/INTERMEDIATE

First-Person Point of View Review usage of the first-person pronouns *I, we, me, us, my,* and *our.* Give several simple examples, such as *Our family likes to go camping. We go camping every summer. Our parents always take us to a new place.* Write other examples, but do not include the pronouns. Have Beginning ELLs fill in the appropriate pronouns, and have Intermediates check for mistakes.

ADVANCED/ADVANCED HIGH

Convincing Tone Have partners trade drafts and look for places where the writer's tone could be stronger or more convincing. As you monitor, identify two or three examples of weak tone and discuss ways to strengthen them as a class. For example, students might suggest changing *I think you'll like camping in the valley* to *I know you'll find camping in the valley to be an experience of a lifetime!*

Revise
Focus on Word Choice

The Rubric Says   Words are focused and support the opinion.

Writing Strategy   Choose words and phrases to convey ideas precisely.

The rubric says that all the words in my editorial should support my opinion. I read through my draft again. In my last paragraph, I found some information that has nothing to do with my topic. I'll take that out now.

[DRAFT]

~~deleted unnecessary words~~

Please accept my invitation to visit my home state, North Carolina. ~~I was born in the city of Raleigh.~~ Come and experience the special places my family has thoroughly enjoyed. There are so many more to discover!

Analyze
Look at Shamari's revision. How did deleting the unnecessary words improve her draft?

Write
Read your draft again. Revise your writing to take out any information that doesn't support your opinion.

Editorial   **279**

Collaborative Conferencing

PEER TO PEER   Have partners exchange drafts. After reading, ask each student to offer feedback on how to strengthen the piece. If needed, have students consult the model editorial, the rubric, and the analysis for revising voice, word choice, and sentence fluency.

PEER GROUPS   Have students form small groups. Have each student read aloud a section of his or her draft. Ask each group member to offer one suggestion on how to strengthen it. Have writers consult the revising lesson pages in their book to inform their revision.

TEACHER-LED   Schedule conferences to read each student's draft. Point out strengths and weaknesses. Talk about ways to improve the draft and inform the revision. If a student seems stalled or discouraged, revisit steps in the process to make improvements and keep going.

Write
Editorial

Week 3 • Day 1

Student Objectives
• Revise to choose words and phrases to convey ideas precisely. (p. 279)

Revise

Focus on Word Choice

Choose Precise Words   Read page 279 aloud. Point out the changes that Shamari made to her draft. Ask students to discuss how the revisions improve the draft. **(Possible response: Shamari took out personal information that is not related directly to the topic.)** Talk about how including unnecessary information (filler) in the editorial actually weakens the writing.

Have students read their drafts to make sure all their words and phrases are necessary. Also remind them to check their conclusions to make sure they are focused, restate the opinion, and tie up loose ends.

CCSS **C**ommon **C**ore **S**tate **S**tandards (pp. Z20–Z30)
Writing: W.4.1b, W.4.1d, W.4.4, W.4.5, W.4.10
Language: L.4.3a, L.4.3c, L.4.6
Speaking and Listening: SL.4.1a, SL.4.1b, SL.4.1c, SL.4.1d, SL.4.3, SL.4.6

Write
Editorial

Week 3 • Day 2

Student Objectives

• Revise to mix together simple and compound sentences. (p. 280)

Revise

Focus on

Vary Sentence Patterns Read aloud the top of page 280. Then ask a volunteer to read the before and after versions of the draft. Ask students to listen for the improvements. Do Shamari's sentences now flow naturally? Are her ideas easier to follow?

Encourage writing partners to exchange drafts and read for sentence fluency. Ask readers to place a small sticky note on two or more sentences in a row that share the same pattern. Tell the writers to vary the sentence patterns at those points to improve the flow.

Revise

Focus on **Sentence Fluency**

The Rubric Says   Sentences are clear and flow naturally.

Writing Strategy   Combine sentences.

I asked a friend to read my paragraph out loud. While I listened, I noticed some problems. The paragraph about meeting the people of North Carolina seems difficult to read. The ideas are mixed up. I could combine sentences to make my ideas clear. Now both my ideas and my sentences will flow well.

[DRAFT]

~~You get to meet wonderful people here. That's~~ last but not ~~,~~ you get to meet wonderful people like my family and me least when you take a vacation in North Carolina. ~~For example, there's my family and me.~~ North Carolinians are proud to live in such a beautiful state.

revised for clarity and flow

Write

Read your draft out loud so you can hear how your writing sounds. Edit any sentences that do not flow smoothly.

280 Opinion Writing

Optional Revising Lessons

Opinion 23

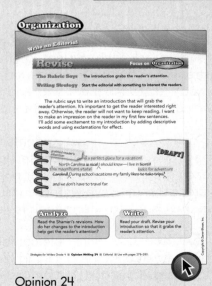

Opinion 24

The Rubric Says — Past-tense verbs are formed correctly. The meaning is clear.

Writing Strategy — Make sure that past-tense verbs are formed correctly.

The rubric reminds me that I need to check my editorial for errors. I'll begin by checking my spelling, punctuation, and capitalization. Next I'll look over my draft to make sure that I used past-tense verbs correctly.

Writer's Term
Past-Tense Verbs
Past-tense verbs show that an action happened in the past. For example: *While we stayed on the Outer Banks, we swam in the ocean.* The verbs **stayed** and **swam** are past-tense verbs.

[DRAFT]

than one hundred and fifty years ago. It is ~~was~~ very interesting to
see how people ~~have~~ had to make so many of the things they used.
It was also very sad to see how enslaved people ~~live~~ lived.

corrected verb tense

Analyze
How did Shamari's edits improve the flow of her sentences? How did she use past-tense verbs correctly?

Write — Conventions
Edit your draft for spelling, punctuation, and capitalization. Make sure that you have used all past-tense verbs correctly.

For more practice with past-tense verbs, use the exercises on the next two pages.

Editorial **281**

Related Grammar Practice

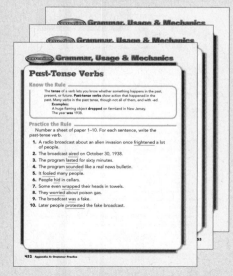

Student Edition pages 452, 453, 454

Student Edition pages 456, 461

Go to ➡ Appendix A: Grammar Practice

Write
Editorial

Student Objectives
- Edit for correct use of past-tense verbs. (p. 281)

Edit

Focus on Conventions

Check Past-Tense Verbs Review the difference between revising (improving text) and editing (correcting text). Tell students that this is the time to go back and correct mistakes in spelling, punctuation, grammar, and capitalization.

Direct students' attention to the Writer's Term box. Discuss the information about past-tense verbs. Ask students to read Shamari's draft and identify her edits. Finally, have them check their editorials for correct use of past-tense verbs.

Use the mini-lessons on pages T282–T283 for students having problems using verb forms correctly.

Writer's Term
Past-Tense Verbs The past-tense forms of common irregular verbs, such as *do, know, make, speak,* and *write,* must be memorized and practiced, especially for students whose first language is not English. Oral practice will help them develop an ear for the correct past-tense forms.

CCSS **Common Core State Standards** (pp. Z20–Z30)
Writing: W.4.4, W.4.5, W.4.6, W.4.10
Language: L.4.1f, L.4.2a, L.4.2d, L.4.6

Conventions

Mini-Lesson

Student Objectives

- Use past-tense verbs correctly. (p. 282)

Past-Tense Verbs

Read the information in Know the Rule at the top of page 282. Explain that *lived* and *spoke* are examples of the *simple past*—verbs that tell about an action that happened at a specific time in the past. Model using each verb in a sentence, such as *We lived in Ohio for five years. She spoke about her trip to Asia.* Clarify that for simple past, regular verbs add *-ed* to the base form (*talk/talked*). If the base word ends with *e*, drop the *e* and add *-ed* (*move/moved*). Verbs ending in a consonant plus *y* change the *y* to *i* before adding *-ed* (*carry/carried*). Verbs ending in a short vowel followed by a single consonant often double the consonant and add *-ed* (*stop/stopped*). Explain that the simple past-tense verb form is the same for all persons: *I stopped, you stopped, he/she/it stopped, we stopped, they stopped.*

Explain that some past-tense verbs have irregular forms that will have to be memorized. *Speak* is one of those verbs. (See page T283 for a mini-lesson on irregular verbs.)

Online Writing Center

Provides **interactive grammar games** and **practice activities** in student eBook.

Past-Tense Verbs

Know the Rule

A **past-tense verb** shows an action that happened in the past. Many past-tense verbs end in *-ed* (*live/lived*). Irregular verbs change spelling in their past-tense form (*speak/spoken*). Make sure the tense of each verb agrees with the time in which the action takes place.

Practice the Rule

Number a piece of paper 1–12. Read each sentence below. On your paper, write the correct past-tense form of the verb in parentheses.

1. Last year, my family (visit) the Great Smoky Mountains National Park. visited
2. What an incredible vacation we (have)! had
3. We hiked, (swim), had picnics, and visited historic sites. swam
4. We also enjoyed beautiful scenery and (see) lots of wildlife. saw
5. I even (learn) a little about the history of the park. learned
6. We (begin) our day with a visit to Cades Cove. began
7. We (start) out early in the morning. started
8. Long ago, this beautiful forest valley (is) part of the Cherokee Nation. was
9. Europeans (settle) in the area in 1818. settled
10. Sadly, in time, they (force) most of the Cherokee people to leave. forced
11. Bison, elk, mountain lions, and wolves once (live) in the valley, too, but now are gone. lived
12. However, when we visited, we (see) whitetail deer, a young black bear, and some wild turkeys. saw

Related Grammar Practice

Page 77

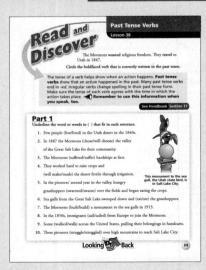

Page 99

 G.U.M. Student Practice Book

Irregular Verbs

Know the Rule

Irregular verbs change their spelling in their past-tense form.
Examples:
I **begin** my guitar lessons today. I **began** playing guitar last year.
I **write** in my journal every day. I **wrote** about my birthday party
yesterday. We may **lose** the game today. We **lost** against the same
team last week.

Practice the Rule

Number a piece of paper 1–10. Write the correct past-tense form of
the irregular verb.

1. For my assignment, I (write) about visiting the Great Smoky
   Mountains National Park. wrote
2. I (begin) by writing about our drive to Clingman's Dome. began
3. Our trip took a long time because we (lose) our way a couple of
   times. lost
4. My father (begin) to get nervous when he couldn't find the
   parking lot. began
5. Then I (write) about how we had to walk the last half-mile to the top. wrote
6. My brother (lose) his camera when he tripped, but luckily we
   managed to find it. lost
7. While we looked out at the view, the clouds (begin) to roll in. began
8. So we (begin) to walk back to where we had parked our car. began
9. I almost (lose) my shoe in the mud! lost
10. Finally I (write) about how we made it back to our car just as it
    started to pour. wrote

Editorial 283

Conventions

Mini-Lesson

Student Objectives

• Form irregular verbs correctly.
  (p. 283)

Irregular Verbs

Read the information in Know
the Rule at the top of page 283.
Explain that *began, wrote,* and *lost*
are examples of the *simple past*—
verbs that tell about an action that
happened at a specific time in the
past. However, these verbs do not
form the simple past by adding *-ed*.
Instead, they have their own unique,
irregular past-tense forms. Then
write the following verbs on the
board: *have, do, sing, know, see, eat.*
Explain that these are also examples
of irregular verbs. Irregular verbs
can form the past tense in many
different ways (*had, did, sang, knew,
saw, ate*). Encourage students to
consult word resources for the past-
tense forms of irregular verbs.

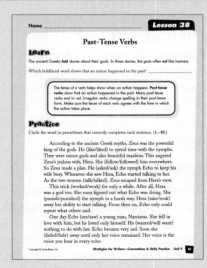

Page 65

Page 81

CCSS Common Core State Standards (pp. Z20–Z30)
Writing: W.4.6
Language: L.4.2d, L.4.6

Write
Editorial

Week 3 • Day 4

Student Objectives

- Discuss preparation for publishing and presentation. (p. 284)
- Use a final editing checklist to publish their work. (p. 284)

Publish +Presentation

Publishing Strategy Read aloud page 284 and discuss with students the publishing options. As an alternative to publishing their editorials in a class newspaper, have students explore other options, such as publishing them in school and local newspapers, in student magazines, or on the school website.

Then point out Shamari's plans for preparing her final copy. (setting neat margins, making sure to leave space between lines, and using clear fonts) (Ask students why these formatting considerations are important as they prepare their own final copies for publication. (easy to read) Finally, read the checklist aloud. Suggest that students refer to it as they prepare final copies of their editorials.

Provide a List of Sources Remind students to include a list of any sources they used to find information about their topics. Provide the citing format guidelines for students to reference, as needed.

 Strategies for Writers Online
Go to **www.sfw.z-b.com** for additional online resources for students, teachers, and parents.

Publish +Presentation

Publishing Strategy	Publish my editorial in the class newspaper.
Presentation Strategy	Make good design decisions on the computer.

My editorial is finished! It's time to think about ways of publishing it. There are lots of ways to publish an editorial: in newspapers, magazines, and online, to name a few. Since I'd like to give everyone in my class a chance to read my editorial, I'll publish it in the first issue of our class newspaper.

The computer can help me present my work in a very neat and readable way. I will use the computer to make neat margins and spacing on the page. I will also choose clear fonts. I'll use the computer's spell checker, but I should check my spelling, too. Before publishing it, I will read my editorial one last time. Here's the final checklist I'll use.

My Final Checklist

Did I—

✔ form past-tense verbs correctly?
✔ use clear fonts?
✔ make neat margins and spacing?
✔ put my name on the paper?

Write

Make a checklist. Check your editorial against it. Then make a final draft. Submit your editorial to the editor of your class newspaper or website for publication.

Differentiating Instruction

ENRICHMENT
Explore Issues By forming an opinion on an issue, developing reasons, and finding facts to support it, students clarify their thinking. Also editorials open opportunities for discussion on a variety of topics. Encourage students to create an online student-friendly forum and publish their opinions regularly.

REINFORCEMENT
Check Spelling If students are typing their final copies, discuss simple spelling errors that spell checkers may miss. Point out that it is the writer's responsibility to spell every word correctly. After performing a spell check, have students print a copy and exchange editorials with a writing partner for a final spelling check. Refer students to print or online word resources to make their final corrections.

Welcome to North Carolina!

by Shamari

North Carolina is a perfect place for a vacation! I should know—I live in this magnificent state! During school vacations my family looks for adventure, and we don't have to travel far. I'm going to share with you some of the exciting things we have done. I hope you will be convinced to discover North Carolina on your next vacation!

My favorite place in North Carolina is the Great Smoky Mountains in the western part of the state. My family camped at Great Smoky Mountains National Park. Everyone in the family enjoyed hiking parts of the Appalachian Trail. There's horseback riding in the mountain forests and white-water rafting on the Nantahala River.

The Piedmont Region in central North Carolina is where most of our cities are located. There's a fun theme park, great shopping, and nice golf courses. There are fascinating historic sites like the plantation in Stagville. On our visit, we learned about life on a plantation more than one hundred and fifty years ago. It was very interesting to see how people had to make so many of the things they used. It was also very sad to see how enslaved people lived. I'm sure glad life is very different in North Carolina now!

Last but not least, when you take a vacation in North Carolina, you get to meet wonderful people like my family and me. North Carolinians are proud to live in such a beautiful state. We are warm and kind, and we always welcome visitors.

Please accept my invitation to visit my home state, North Carolina. Come and experience the special places my family has thoroughly enjoyed. There are many more to discover!

Analyze

Use the rubric to evaluate Shamari's editorial. Are all the traits of a good editorial there? Now use the rubric to evaluate your editorial.

Editorial **285**

Tech Tips

Blogs, Podcasts

Share Work Online Sharing work online opens writers to feedback from an audience that reads, views, listens to, and engages with their work. Remember that students need help understanding how to work with that feedback and engage with the online audience, whether the feedback is highly critical or simply parents sharing their pride in a student's accomplishment. Talk with students about how they filter and understand feedback received on blog posts, podcasts, or other posted writing, and how they provide others with helpful comments or "ratings."

Write
Editorial

Week 3 • Day 5

Student Objectives

- Use an editorial rubric. (pp. 268–269)
- Share a published editorial. (p. 285)

Presentation Strategy Remind students of the importance of neatness when creating their final draft. Point out the many word-processing features computers have to offer. It's easy to set neat margins, use the tab key to indent paragraphs, double-space text, and select one or two clear fonts. Depending on the topic, students may want to create or find illustrations or other visuals to enhance their presentation.

Reflecting on an Editorial

Read aloud the questions in the Analyze box on page 285. Then refer students to the editorial rubric on pages 268–269 to score Shamari's editorial. Ask:

- How did you use the rubric as you wrote your editorial?

CCSS **Common Core State Standards** (pp. Z20–Z30)
Writing: W.4.4, W.4.6, W.4.10
Language: L.4.2d, L.4.3c, L.4.4c
Speaking and Listening: SL.4.1a, SL.4.1b, SL.4.1c, SL.4.1d, SL.4.3, SL.4.6

Editorial **T285**

Friendly Letter Planner

WEEK 1

Day 1
Introduce
Friendly Letter

Student Objectives
- Review the elements of a friendly letter.
- Consider purpose and audience.
- Learn the traits of opinion writing.

Student Activities
- Read and discuss **What's in a Friendly Letter?** (p. 286)
- Read and discuss **Why Write a Friendly Letter?** (p. 287)
- Read **Linking Opinion Writing Traits to a Friendly Letter.** (p. 288)

Day 2
Analyze
Close Reading of the Model

Student Objectives
- Read a model friendly letter.

Student Activities
- Read **"Dear Chase."** (p. 289)

Day 3
Analyze
Introduce the Rubric

Student Objectives
- Learn to read a rubric.

Student Activities
- Review **"Dear Chase."** (p. 289)
- Read and discuss the **Friendly Letter Rubric.** (pp. 290–291)

WEEK 2

Day 1
Write
Prewrite: Ideas

Student Objectives
- Read and understand a prewriting strategy.

Student Activities
- Read and discuss **Prewrite: Focus on Ideas.** (p. 296)
- Apply the prewriting strategy.

Day 2
Write
Prewrite: Organization

Student Objectives
- Use a Network Tree to organize facts and reasons.

Student Activities
- Read and discuss **Prewrite: Focus on Organization.** (p. 297)
- Apply the prewriting strategy.
- Participate in a peer conference.

Day 3
Write
Draft: Voice

Student Objectives
- Use first-person point of view and casual language.

Student Activities
- Read and discuss **Draft: Focus on Voice.** (p. 298)
- Apply the drafting strategy.

WEEK 3

Day 1
Write
Revise: Word Choice

Student Objectives
- Revise to replace loaded words with neutral ones.

Student Activities
- Read and discuss **Revise: Focus on Word Choice.** (p. 301)
- Reflect on the model draft.
- Apply the revising strategy.
- Participate in a peer conference.

Day 2
Write
Revise: Sentence Fluency

Student Objectives
- Revise to combine short, choppy sentences to make the writing flow.

Student Activities
- Read and discuss **Revise: Focus on Sentence Fluency.** (p. 302)
- Apply the revising strategy.

Note: Optional Revising Lessons are located at **www.sfw.z-b.com**

Day 3
Write
Edit: Conventions

Student Objectives
- Edit for correct use of punctuation.

Student Activities
- Read and discuss **Edit: Focus on Conventions.** (p. 303)
- Reflect on the model draft.
- Apply the editing strategy.

Note: Teach the Conventions mini-lessons (pp. 304–305) if needed.

Day 4	Day 5
Analyze **Close Reading** **for the Traits**	**Analyze** **Close Reading** **for the Traits**

Student Objectives
- Read a model friendly letter.
- Use the friendly letter rubric.
- Use the model friendly letter to study Ideas, Organization, and Voice.

Student Activities
- Review **"Dear Chase."** *(p. 289)*
- Read and discuss **Using the Rubric to Analyze the Model.** *(pp. 292–293)*

Student Objectives
- Read a model friendly letter.
- Use the friendly letter rubric.
- Use the model friendly letter to study Word Choice, Sentence Fluency, and Conventions

Student Activities
- Review **"Dear Chase."** *(p. 289)*
- Read and discuss **Using the Rubric to Analyze the Model.** *(pp. 294–295)*

Day 4	Day 5
Write **Draft**	**Write** **Revise: Ideas**

Student Objectives
- Complete a draft.

Student Activities
- Finish a draft. *(p. 299)*
- Participate in a peer conference.

Student Objectives
- Revise to add facts to support the reasons.

Student Activities
- Read and discuss **Revise: Focus on Ideas.** *(p. 300)*
- Apply the revising strategy.

Day 4	Day 5
Write **Publish: +Presentation**	**Write** **Publish: +Presentation**

Student Objectives
- Discuss preparation for publishing and presentation.
- Use a final editing checklist to publish their work.

Student Activities
- Read and discuss **Publish: +Presentation.** *(p. 306)*
- Apply the publishing strategy.

Student Objectives
- Use a friendly letter rubric.
- Send a published friendly letter.

Student Activities
- Share their work.
- Use the rubric to reflect upon and evaluate the model and their own writing. *(pp. 290–291; 307)*

To complete the chapter in fewer days, combine the learning objectives and activities in a way that supports students as they write.

Resources at-a-Glance

Grammar, Usage & Mechanics

Differentiating Instruction

For additional Differentiating Instruction activities, see Strategies for Writers *Differentiated Instruction Activities at* **www.sfw.z-b.com.**

English Language Learners

Collaborative Conferencing

Tech Tips

 Strategies for Writers Online

Go to **www.sfw.z-b.com** for additional online resources for students, teachers, and parents.

Online Writing Center

Provides IWB resources, assessments, interactive games and practice activities, videos, eBooks, and a virtual file cabinet.

Introduce
Friendly Letter

Student Objectives

- Review the elements of a friendly letter. (p. 286)
- Consider purpose and audience. (p. 287)
- Learn the traits of opinion writing. (p. 288)

What's a Friendly Letter?

Ask volunteers to tell about friendly letters, notes, and e-mails they have written. Ask about their recipients and their purposes for writing. Talk about the various kinds of friendly writing, including announcements, invitations, thank-you notes, and newsletters.

What's in a Friendly Letter?

In the context of the kinds of letters students have just shared, ask them to identify these elements of a friendly letter:

- personal tone
- organization
- five parts (heading, greeting, body, closing, and signature)

Confirm students' understanding of the elements by reading aloud the definitions on page 286.

Strategies for Writers Online

Go to **www.sfw.z-b.com** for additional online resources for students, teachers, and parents.

What's a Friendly Letter?

I like writing friendly letters to my family members and friends. When I express an opinion in the letter, I try to convince the person who reads the letter to agree with me.

What's in a Friendly Letter?

Personal Tone
In a friendly letter, I want to use a personal tone. My letter should sound like I am talking to the reader in a conversation. I'll use first-person point of view and sound casual yet polite.

Organization
I want to be organized and convincing. I'll state my opinion in an introduction, support it with facts and reasons in the body, and restate it in a conclusion.

Five Parts
A friendly letter has certain words and pieces of information in a particular place on the page. The five parts of a friendly letter are the heading, greeting, body, closing, and signature.

Opinion Text Exemplars (Friendly Letter)

Leedy, Loreen. *Messages in the Mailbox: How to Write a Letter.* Holiday House, 1994. *Messages in the Mailbox* discusses different types of letters and how to write them. Readers can learn how to compose friendly letters, business letters, and letters of complaint, along with other forms of correspondence.

Cleary, Beverly. *Dear Mr. Henshaw.* HarperCollins Publishers, 2000. *Dear Mr. Henshaw* tells the story of the correspondence between Leigh and Mr. Henshaw, his favorite author. Through these letters, Leigh soon realizes that he wants to become a writer himself.

Why write a Friendly Letter?

There are a lot of reasons to write a friendly letter. Here are three reasons for writing a friendly letter.

To Express an Opinion
I may write a friendly letter to convince a friend or family member to come visit me or to watch a movie I saw.

To Resolve a Disagreement
If a friend and I disagree about something, a friendly letter can help resolve the issue.

To Entertain
Sometimes it's fun to debate about something. I can carry on a debate long distance by writing my opinions in a friendly letter.

Why write a Friendly Letter?

Good writers always have a purpose and an audience. In the case of friendly letters, the audience usually consists of one reader, the intended recipient of the letter. Both purpose and audience influence how the writer crafts his or her writing.

Conclude by telling students that they are going to study and practice strategies for writing a friendly letter that expresses and supports the writer's opinion on a topic.

Hesse, Karen. *Letters From Rifka*. Square Fish, 2009.
In letters to her cousin, Rifka, a young Jewish girl, chronicles her family's escape from Russia to America. Rifka and her family surmount many obstacles on their journey, including bands of Russian soldiers, disease, and a storm at sea.

Armstrong, Jennifer. *Thomas Jefferson: Letters From a Philadelphia Bookworm*. WinslowHouse International, 2000. In a series of fictionalized letters, 12-year-old Amelia Hornsby corresponds with President Thomas Jefferson about life in the early 1800s, including the Lewis and Clark expedition and life at Monticello. The letters capture Jefferson's personality, describing his many interests in farming, engineering, and politics.

CCSS **Common Core State Standards** (pp. Z20–Z30)
Language: L.4.3c
Speaking and Listening: SL.4.1a, SL.4.1b, SL.4.1c, SL.4.1d, SL.4.3, SL.4.6

Introduce
Friendly Letter

Linking Opinion Writing Traits to a Friendly Letter

Read page 288 aloud to help students understand that they will follow Shamari as she models using the writing process and the opinion writing traits together. A good friendly letter will convey the writer's opinion and speak directly to the recipient.

As they follow Shamari, students will see how the Opinion Writing Traits have been adapted and applied to writing a friendly letter. They will see that a friendly letter can be used to express an opinion and, therefore, has many factors in common with other types of opinion writing. However, the particular audience and purpose of a friendly letter determine how the traits are used.

Linking Opinion Writing Traits to a *Friendly Letter*

In this chapter, you will write a letter to convince someone you know to agree with your opinion. This type of opinion writing is called a friendly letter. Shamari will guide you through the stages of the writing process: Prewrite, Draft, Revise, Edit, and Publish. In each stage, Shamari will show you important writing strategies that are linked to the Opinion Writing Traits below.

Opinion Writing Traits

Ideas	• a clear opinion • strong reasons that are supported by facts and details
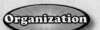 **Organization**	• a clear, logical organization • an introduction, body, and conclusion • transitions that connect opinions and reasons
 **Voice**	• a voice and tone that are appropriate for the audience and purpose
 **Word Choice**	• fair and balanced language • specific words and phrases
Sentence Fluency	• a variety of sentence patterns that make the writing flow
 **Conventions**	• no or few errors in spelling, grammar, punctuation, and capitalization

Before you write, read Samuel Taylor's friendly letter on the next page. Then use the friendly letter rubric on pages 290–291 to decide how well he did. (You might want to look back at What's in a Friendly Letter? on page 286, too!)

Opinion Writing Traits in a Friendly Letter

 **Ideas** The writer expresses an opinion on a topic and gives good reasons that support the writer's viewpoint. The writer's purpose for writing is clear to the reader.

 **Organization** The letter is well organized and easy for the reader to follow. Transition words and phrases connect all of the writer's ideas. The letter has five parts: heading, greeting, body, closing, and signature.

 **Voice** The writer uses a friendly, convincing voice and the first-person point of view to connect with the recipient. The writer's voice sets a personal tone.

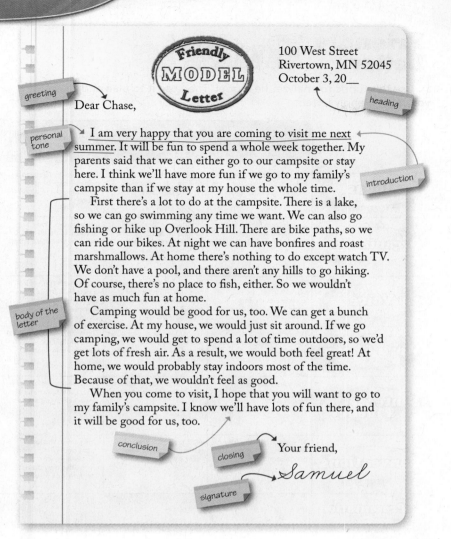

Friendly MODEL Letter

100 West Street
Rivertown, MN 52045
October 3, 20___

heading

greeting
Dear Chase,

personal tone
I am very happy that you are coming to visit me next summer. It will be fun to spend a whole week together. My parents said that we can either go to our campsite or stay here. I think we'll have more fun if we go to my family's campsite than if we stay at my house the whole time.

introduction

First there's a lot to do at the campsite. There is a lake, so we can go swimming any time we want. We can also go fishing or hike up Overlook Hill. There are bike paths, so we can ride our bikes. At night we can have bonfires and roast marshmallows. At home there's nothing to do except watch TV. We don't have a pool, and there aren't any hills to go hiking. Of course, there's no place to fish, either. So we wouldn't have as much fun at home.

body of the letter

Camping would be good for us, too. We can get a bunch of exercise. At my house, we would just sit around. If we go camping, we would get to spend a lot of time outdoors, so we'd get lots of fresh air. As a result, we would both feel great! At home, we would probably stay indoors most of the time. Because of that, we wouldn't feel as good.

When you come to visit, I hope that you will want to go to my family's campsite. I know we'll have lots of fun there, and it will be good for us, too.

conclusion

closing
Your friend,

Samuel

signature

Friendly Letter   **289**

Word Choice   The writer uses fair and balanced language throughout the letter. The writer does not use loaded words in the message.

Sentence Fluency   A variety of sentence patterns holds the reader's interest. The flow of ideas is uninterrupted.

Conventions   The writer has edited the letter carefully. Five parts of a friendly letter, abbreviations, and initials are used correctly.

Analyze
Close Reading of the Model

Week 1 • Day 2

Student Objectives

- Read a model friendly letter. (p. 289)

Read the Model

Read "Dear Chase" aloud. Ask students to listen for the personal tone used throughout the letter. Also ask them to notice how the parts of the letter are organized. Tell students to think about how the writer speaks directly to the reader. They should agree that the writer's sincere and friendly voice supports the writer's purpose and connects with the reader.

Elements of a Friendly Letter

Have students refer to What's in a Friendly Letter? on page 286 as you refer to the model on page 289. Use the notes on the model to discuss the various elements of a friendly letter that expresses the writer's opinion. Make sure students can identify each part of a friendly letter: heading, greeting, body, closing, signature.

CCSS **Common Core State Standards** (pp. Z20–Z30)
Writing: W.4.6
Language: L.4.3c
Speaking and Listening: SL.4.1a, SL.4.1b, SL.4.1c, SL.4.1d, SL.4.2, SL.4.3, SL.4.6

Analyze
Introduce the Rubric

Week 1 • Day 3

Student Objectives

- Learn to read a rubric. (pp. 290–291)

Introduce the Rubric

Explain the Rubric Explain that a rubric is a tool for planning, improving, and assessing a piece of writing. Tell students that a rubric helps a writer focus on key elements, or traits, in writing (**Ideas, Organization, Voice, Word Choice, Sentence Fluency, Conventions,** and **Presentation**).

Point out that column 6 describes a very good friendly letter, one that has received the highest score in all categories. This is what students should strive for in their own writing.

Discuss the Rubric When students score their paper for each trait, they should first decide whether it falls on the left of the rubric (uses the trait well) or on the right (needs improvement in using the trait). By examining the paper more closely, students can refine the score to a single number.

Online Writing Center

Provides a variety of **interactive rubrics,** including 4-, 5-, and 6-point models.

T290   Opinion Writing

Friendly Letter Rubric

Use this rubric to analyze the model. Then use it to plan and score your own friendly letter.

	6	5	4
Ideas	The letter clearly states an opinion. Strong, convincing facts support the reasons.	The letter clearly states an opinion. Many facts support the reasons.	The letter clearly states an opinion. Somewhat convincing facts support the reasons.
Organization	Introduction, body, and conclusion are clear. Focused transition words connect ideas.	Introduction, body, and conclusion are clear. One or two more or better transition words would help connect ideas.	Introduction, body, and conclusion are clear. Ordinary transition words are used.
Voice	The writer uses a personal, friendly tone. The voice is appropriate for the purpose and audience.	The writer's tone of voice is personal, friendly, and appropriate for the purpose and audience most of the time.	The writer's tone of voice is personal, friendly, and appropriate for the purpose and audience some of the time.
Word Choice	The writer's language is fair. No loaded words are used.	The writer's language is fair and balanced most of the time. One loaded word may be present.	The writer's language is fair some of the time. One or two words are loaded.
Sentence Fluency	The sentences vary in length and structure. They flow naturally.	Most of the sentences are varied and flow naturally.	Some of the sentences are varied and flow naturally. A few sentences are too short.
Conventions	All five parts of the friendly letter are present and punctuated correctly.	All five parts of the friendly letter are present, and most are punctuated correctly.	One part of the letter might be missing. There are a few punctuation errors, but they do not interfere with meaning.

✚ Presentation   The letter has all five parts placed neatly and correctly.

290   Opinion Writing

CCSS Common Core State Standards
Friendly Letter

Strategies for Writers was designed and written to weave the Common Core State Standards throughout every unit. For Opinion writing, the standards inform the unit's writing rubrics, objectives, and strategies. By presenting the standards in as many applications as possible, your students' exposure to them will be ensured. As a result, students are more likely to employ the standards' language in writing opinion pieces as well as in discussions about writing.

The lessons for Friendly Letter are based principally on the writing standards for Opinion writing. The rubrics and writing

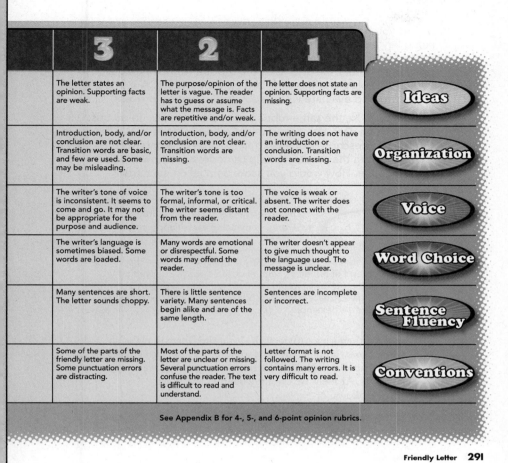

	3	2	1	
	The letter states an opinion. Supporting facts are weak.	The purpose/opinion of the letter is vague. The reader has to guess or assume what the message is. Facts are repetitive and/or weak.	The letter does not state an opinion. Supporting facts are missing.	**Ideas**
	Introduction, body, and/or conclusion are not clear. Transition words are basic, and few are used. Some may be misleading.	Introduction, body, and/or conclusion are not clear. Transition words are missing.	The writing does not have an introduction or conclusion. Transition words are missing.	**Organization**
	The writer's tone of voice is inconsistent. It seems to come and go. It may not be appropriate for the purpose and audience.	The writer's tone is too formal, informal, or critical. The writer seems distant from the reader.	The voice is weak or absent. The writer does not connect with the reader.	**Voice**
	The writer's language is sometimes biased. Some words are loaded.	Many words are emotional or disrespectful. Some words may offend the reader.	The writer doesn't appear to give much thought to the language used. The message is unclear.	**Word Choice**
	Many sentences are short. The letter sounds choppy.	There is little sentence variety. Many sentences begin alike and are of the same length.	Sentences are incomplete or incorrect.	**Sentence Fluency**
	Some of the parts of the friendly letter are missing. Some punctuation errors are distracting.	Most of the parts of the letter are unclear or missing. Several punctuation errors confuse the reader. The text is difficult to read and understand.	Letter format is not followed. The writing contains many errors. It is very difficult to read.	**Conventions**

See Appendix B for 4-, 5-, and 6-point opinion rubrics.

strategies reflect the writing standard **W.4.1,** which focuses on introducing and supporting a point of view with reasons and information.

The language standards for grade 4 students are addressed during editing and skills practice. In addition, there are multiple opportunities to address the speaking and listening standards during the writing process. Most importantly, this chapter will help your students produce coherent writing (**W.4.4**), improve their writing (**W.4.5**), and use technologies to publish their finished pieces (**W.4.6**).

Find Evidence in the Model

Small-Group Collaboration Assign students to small groups and ask them to check the model for each trait. One person in each group should be responsible for recording one or two strong examples of the trait as described by the rubric. Ask students to score each trait accordingly for the model. They should be able to support their scores. Note that although the model was written to score high in each trait, students should not assume each trait would receive a 6, the top score. Encourage students to discuss each trait thoroughly before assigning each score.

Teacher-Led Discussion Bring the class back together and ask one person from each group to report their findings to the class. The point of this exercise is to practice identifying and evaluating the traits within a piece of writing.

Additional Rubrics

Appendix B includes 4-, 5-, and 6-point rubrics that can be used with any piece of opinion writing. The rubrics are also available as blackline masters in the back of this Teacher Edition.

CCSS **Common Core State Standards** (pp. Z20–Z30)
Writing: W.4.6
Language: L.4.3c
Speaking and Listening: SL.4.1a, SL.4.1b, SL.4.1c, SL.4.1d, SL.4.2, SL.4.3, SL.4.6

Analyze
Close Reading for the Traits

Student Objectives

- Read a model friendly letter. (p. 289)
- Use the friendly letter rubric. (pp. 290–291)
- Use the model friendly letter to study **Ideas, Organization,** and **Voice.** (pp. 292–293)

Find Evidence in the Model

Evaluate the Model Have volunteers read aloud each section on pages 292–293. Determine whether students agree with each point in Shamari's assessment. Use the questions below to initiate the discussion. Be sure students can back up their answers with specific examples from the friendly letter.

Discuss Audience, Task, Purpose Ask students one or more of the following questions as they analyze the model:

- **Audience** Who is the audience? (Possible response: Samuel's friend, Chase)

- **Task** How does the writer show his knowledge of friendly letters? (Possible response: The writer uses the correct form for a friendly letter.)

- **Purpose** What is the writer's purpose for writing this essay? How do you know? (Possible response: to inform the reader; The letter includes information about camping.)

Using the Rubric to Analyze the Model
Friendly Letter

Did you notice that the model on page 289 points out some key elements of a friendly letter? As he wrote his letter, Samuel Taylor used these elements to help him introduce his opinion to others. He also used the 6-point rubric on pages 290–291 to plan, draft, revise, and edit the writing. A rubric is a great tool to evaluate writing during the writing process.

Now let's use the same rubric to score the model. To do this, we'll focus on each trait separately, starting with Ideas. We'll use the top descriptor for each trait (column 6), along with examples from the model, to help us understand how the traits work together. How would you score Samuel on each trait?

Ideas
- The letter clearly states an opinion.
- Strong, convincing facts support the reasons.

Samuel states his opinion clearly in the introduction—the first paragraph of his letter. Samuel doesn't just tell Chase that staying at the campsite would be more fun than staying at home. He gives Chase a lot of good reasons why he thinks this is true. Here's an example.

> First there's a lot to do at the campsite. There is a lake, so we can go swimming any time we want. We can also go fishing or hike up Overlook Hill. There are bike paths, so we can ride our bikes. At night we can have bonfires and roast marshmallows.

292 Opinion Writing

English Language Learners

BEGINNING

Parts of a Friendly Letter Post a friendly letter. Circle the following parts of a letter: Heading, Greeting, Body, Closing, and Signature. Say each word and have students repeat. Then check students' understanding by pointing to each part and having the group say its name. Then do individual concept checking.

INTERMEDIATE

Parts of a Friendly Letter Review the parts of a friendly letter. Also review the placement of each element and paragraph indentations. Brainstorm possible greetings, such as *Dear Joaquin* or *Dear Cousin,* and possible closings, such as *Your friend, Your cousin, Yours truly,* or *Sincerely.*

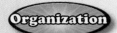

Organization
- Introduction, body, and conclusion are clear.
- Focused transition words connect ideas.

Samuel's letter has a clear introduction, body, and conclusion. Each paragraph leads into the next. I've learned that focused transition words help tie ideas together. Samuel uses transition words such as *so, as a result,* and *because of* to show the connections between his ideas.

> If we go camping, we would get to spend a lot of time outdoors, so we'd get lots of fresh air. As a result, we would both feel great! At home, we would probably stay indoors most of the time. Because of that, we wouldn't feel as good.

Voice
- The writer uses a personal, friendly tone.
- The voice is appropriate for the purpose and audience.

In writing, I know that tone reveals your attitude toward your topic and your reader. Samuel chose just the right tone for his letter. I could tell that he was writing to a friend. His language was casual and friendly and set a personal tone that showed respect for his friend Chase.

> I am very happy that you are coming to visit me next summer. It will be fun to spend a whole week together. My parents said that we can either go to our campsite or stay here.

Discuss the Traits Ask students one or more of the following questions to discuss the traits in the model:

Ideas Does the writer state a clear opinion? (Possible responses: The writer states a clear opinion about going to his family's campsite. He gives strong reasons to convince his friend.)

Organization What organization does Samuel use? How does he use transitions? (Possible responses: The letter is well organized into five parts. He uses transition words such as *First, At night,* and *Of course* to connect his ideas.)

Voice How would you describe Samuel's voice? (Possible responses: personal, friendly, and convincing)

ADVANCED
Audience and Purpose Ask students who the audience is for a friendly letter. Most likely it will be a friend or family member. Then ask, *Why would you write a friendly letter to persuade?* Allow students time to brainstorm ideas. Remind students that the purpose of this friendly letter will be to try to convince someone to agree with an opinion.

ADVANCED HIGH
Cause and Effect Suggest students use cause and effect to convey a convincing tone. Write on the board *Watts Bar Lake is the best place to go because it has great fishing. Watts Bar Lake has great fishing so it's the best place to go.* Explain that cause-and-effect sentences can be written in cause/effect or effect/cause order. Review transition words and phrases, such as *due to, as a result, therefore, since,* and *because of.*

CCSS Common Core State Standards (pp. Z20–Z30)
Writing: W.4.1c
Language: L.4.3c, L.4.6
Speaking and Listening: SL.4.1a, SL.4.1b, SL.4.1c, SL.4.1d, SL.4.3, SL.4.6

Analyze
Close Reading for the Traits

Week 1 • Day 5

Student Objectives

- Read a model friendly letter. *(p. 289)*
- Use the friendly letter rubric. *(pp. 290–291)*
- Use the model friendly letter to study **Word Choice, Sentence Fluency,** and **Conventions.** *(pp. 294–295)*

Discuss the Traits Ask students one or more of the following questions to discuss the traits in the model:

 **Word Choice** How does the writer use fair and balanced language? (Possible responses: Samuel uses casual, polite language to connect with his reader. Samuel's words are fair.)

Sentence Fluency What evidence in the friendly letter shows how the writer varied sentence lengths to keep the writing flowing? (Possible responses: Although the letter is short, Samuel wrote sentences of different lengths to make the writing flow. The writing is not choppy.)

Conventions What evidence in the letter shows how the writer punctuated correctly? (Possible responses: I can tell that Samuel proofread his letter carefully. His punctuation is correct. All five parts of a friendly letter are used correctly.)

Strategies for Writers Online
Go to **www.sfw.z-b.com** for additional online resources for students, teachers, and parents.

Using the Rubric to Analyze the Model
Friendly Letter

 **Word Choice**
- The writer's language is fair.
- No loaded words are used.

Samuel uses fair language to explain why he would rather go camping when his friend comes to visit. He doesn't use loaded words to try to convince Chase. His language is honest and straightforward.

> When you come to visit, I hope that you will want to go to my family's campsite. I know we'll have lots of fun there, and it will be good for us, too.

 **Sentence Fluency**
- The sentences vary in length and structure.
- They flow naturally.

In his letter, Samuel uses a variety of long and short, simple and compound sentences. Each sentence begins differently, too. This made his writing flow and his letter interesting to read.

> At home there's nothing to do except watch TV. We don't have a pool, and there aren't any hills to go hiking. Of course, there's no place to fish, either. So, we wouldn't have as much fun at home.

294 Opinion Writing

Tech Tips

Networks

Use ePals Network Students need to write real texts for authentic audiences. Consider breaking down classroom boundaries by using the global ePals network to connect students with digital pen pals. Doing so requires using the website to contact a classroom teacher and setting up either a class account or individual student e-mail addresses. Take time to establish guidelines, setting parameters on everything from how often you'll correspond to what the limits are for sharing personal information. Providing an audience is important, but so is helping writers know how to work in smart and safe ways.

See **www.sfw.z-b.com** for further information about and links to these websites and tools.

Conventions
- All five parts of the friendly letter are present and punctuated correctly.

If you look again at the letter on page 289, you'll see that the parts of Samuel's letter have been labeled. He included all five parts of a friendly letter: the heading, the greeting, the body of the letter, the closing, and the signature. Also, he was careful to use capital letters and commas correctly in all the parts and to end each sentence with correct punctuation.

✛Presentation The letter has all five parts placed neatly and correctly.

My Turn!
Now it's my turn to write a friendly letter. I'll use what I've learned from studying the model. Follow along as I use the rubric and good writing strategies to help me.

Friendly Letter **295**

✛Presentation Explain to students that Presentation is just as important as any of the other traits. Neatness is always a priority, and text should be clearly handwritten in pen or typed. White space should be used to create neat margins and to keep lines of text readable. Paragraphs should be indented (using the tab key if typed), or space should be left between block paragraphs. In a letter, all five parts should be present, and they should be neat and be punctuated correctly.

Think About the Traits

Once students have thoroughly discussed the model, ask them which traits they think are the most important in a friendly letter and have them explain why. **(Possible response: Voice is a very important trait because using a friendly, polite voice will help to convince the reader.)**

Differentiating Instruction

ENRICHMENT
Express Yourself Encourage students to express and support their opinions online. Have them create their own class newsletter wherein they can propose changes, offer solutions, or make suggestions on a variety of topics. Tell them to anticipate opposing viewpoints and assist them in crafting and posting their communications in a fair and balanced way. Also point out the value of thinking through their opinions before writing and posting online.

REINFORCEMENT
Understand Elements of a Friendly Letter Some students may benefit from seeing additional samples of short, well-written letters. Find some in young readers' books or magazines to share with students. Have them work in pairs to identify the writer's tone and organization in each sample.

CCSS **Common Core State Standards** (pp. Z20–Z30)
Writing: W.4.6
Language: L.4.3c
Speaking and Listening: SL.4.1a, SL.4.1b, SL.4.1c, SL.4.1d, SL.4.3, SL.4.6

Write
Friendly Letter

Week 2 • Day 1

Student Objectives

- Read and understand a prewriting strategy. *(p. 296)*

Prewrite

Focus on **Ideas**

Gather Information About a Topic
Read page 296 aloud. Then have students propose possible topics for their letters and list them on the board. Ask students to choose their favorites and decide on the purpose for writing (express an opinion on the topic) and the recipient (family member or close friend). After they have made their choices, encourage students to use the Internet to find at least three facts about their topic that they can use to support their opinion. Explain that Shamari has listed facts in her notes.

✏️ **Writer's Term** _____

Fact Point out that a fact is a true statement. This means that it is verifiable information. In opinion writing, writers use supporting facts to convince an audience.

Online Writing Center

Provides **interactive graphic organizers** as well as a variety of graphic organizers in PDF format.

Prewrite
Focus on **Ideas**

The Rubric Says	The letter clearly states an opinion.
Writing Strategy	Decide what to write about and research facts about the issue.

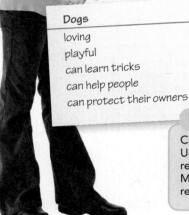

My teacher asked us to write a letter to convince someone about something. I have the perfect topic. My parents said we could have a pet. My grandparents are going to get it for us, but they haven't decided on a puppy or a kitten. My dad helped me find a couple of books and websites on the Internet with information about cats and dogs. I took notes from these sources.

Writer's Term ⌐

Fact
A **fact** is a statement that can be proven to be true. Facts support a writer's reasons.

Dogs	Cats
loving	loving, but also independent
playful	playful, but mostly as kittens
can learn tricks	don't learn tricks easily
can help people	don't help people
can protect their owners	don't protect their owners

Write

Choose a topic for a friendly letter. Use print or Internet resources to research facts about the issue. Make a list of important things to remember about the topic.

296 Opinion Writing

English Language Learners

BEGINNING/INTERMEDIATE
Facts and Opinions Read a simple text about dance. After reading, write *Dancing is a physical activity.* Ask, *Is this always true?* and then say, *Facts are always true.* Say *facts* and have students repeat. Write *Dancing is fun.* Ask, *Is this always true?* and then say, *An opinion is what we think or feel about something.* Say *opinion* and have students say it. Confirm understanding with other fact/opinion examples.

ADVANCED/ADVANCED HIGH
Network Tree Review the terms *opinion, reason,* and *fact.* Ask groups of three to work together to create a Network Tree about the following opinion: *Dancing is an excellent way to exercise.* When they are finished, have them trade with another group who should verify the facts using a credible resource.

Prewrite

Focus on **Organization**

The Rubric Says Introduction, body, and conclusion are clear.

Writing Strategy Use a Network Tree to organize facts and reasons.

I know from the rubric that my letter must have an introduction, body paragraphs, and a conclusion. I think adding a puppy to our family would be better for us than a kitten. I'll use a Network Tree to organize my notes and plan my letter.

Writer's Term

Network Tree
A Network Tree organizes information. The writer's opinion goes at the top of the tree. Reasons for the opinion go on the next level. Facts and other details go on the lowest level.

Network Tree

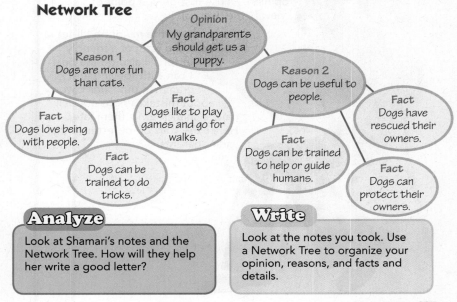

Opinion
My grandparents should get us a puppy.

Reason 1
Dogs are more fun than cats.

Reason 2
Dogs can be useful to people.

Fact
Dogs love being with people.

Fact
Dogs like to play games and go for walks.

Fact
Dogs can be trained to do tricks.

Fact
Dogs can be trained to help or guide humans.

Fact
Dogs have rescued their owners.

Fact
Dogs can protect their owners.

Analyze
Look at Shamari's notes and the Network Tree. How will they help her write a good letter?

Write
Look at the notes you took. Use a Network Tree to organize your opinion, reasons, and facts and details.

Friendly Letter **297**

Collaborative Conferencing

PEER TO PEER Have students exchange their organizers. Direct them to ask these questions as they review them: *Is the writer's opinion clear? Do the details support it?* Tell partners to write their comments on a sticky note and return the organizer with their feedback.

PEER GROUPS Separate students into small groups of three or four. Have each group state one or two reasons for using a Network Tree to express an opinion in a letter. Then ask them to share their reasons and revise them based on feedback from other groups.

TEACHER-LED Schedule prewriting conferences with students. To demonstrate how important the organizer is to writing a good letter, create one that leaves out the supporting fact(s) for one reason. Discuss how not supporting it would weaken the writer's opinion.

Write
Friendly Letter

Student Objectives

• Use a Network Tree to organize facts and reasons. (p. 297)

Prewrite

Focus on **Organization**

Organize Ideas Explain that writers use different types of organizers to organize their ideas. Have students study the organizer and then ask how a Network Tree can be an effective tool when writing an opinion piece. **(Possible response: A Network Tree helps a writer state an opinion and support it with strong details.)** (Go to **www.sfw.z-b.com** for the downloadable graphic organizer.) If students cannot think of supporting facts for each reason, suggest that they learn more about their topic.

Writer's Term

Network Tree This organizer shows how the writer's reasons and facts "grow" out of the writer's opinion. The visual organization of ovals and connecting lines helps writers arrange their ideas.

CCSS Common Core State Standards (pp. Z20–Z30)
Writing: W.4.1a, W.4.1b, W.4.1d, W.4.4, W.4.5, W.4.6, W.4.8, W.4.10
Language: L.4.3c, L.4.6
Speaking and Listening: SL.4.1a, SL.4.1b, SL.4.1c, SL.4.1d, SL.4.3, SL.4.6

Write
Friendly Letter

Week 2 • Day 3

Student Objectives

• Use first-person point of view and casual language. *(p. 298)*

Draft

Focus on Voice

Draft a Friendly Letter Read page 298 aloud. Begin by asking what it means to draft a friendly letter. Be sure students understand that they will use their organizer to write their draft. Also remind them to use the first-person point of view and casual language to speak directly to their reader.

Point out that, like Shamari, students should not be overly concerned with correctness at this point. The main thing is to get their ideas down on paper. If they are doing their writing in class, plan and facilitate time for writing, conferences, and reflection. Explain that students will go through the writing process to create their final copy of writing. Editing is part of the process.

Note: To facilitate editing, proofreading marks are provided as a reference on page 299.

Online Writing Center

 Provides an **interactive writing pad** for drafting, revising, editing, and publishing.

Draft

Focus on **Voice**

The Rubric Says The writer uses a personal, friendly tone. The voice is appropriate for the purpose and audience.

Writing Strategy Use first-person point of view and casual language.

My audience is my grandparents, and my purpose is to convince them to get a dog for our family. I want my own voice to come through. Yet, I also have to remember that I am writing to adults. Since this will be a letter to my grandparents, I'll keep my language casual but polite. Because my letter will express my personal opinion, I'll use first-person point of view (*I, me, we, us*).

As I write my draft, I'll set it up in the form of a friendly letter. I'll also do the best I can with spelling and grammar, but I won't worry about mistakes right now. I'll have a chance to fix them later. Here's the start of my letter to my grandparents.

298 Opinion Writing

Differentiating Instruction

ENRICHMENT

Instant Communications Explain to students that in 1639, a tavern in Boston was the only official mail drop in the American colonies for letters from Europe. Mail was either picked up by the recipient or delivered on foot or horseback. It could take months to get a letter to the recipient. Invite students to discuss the advantages (and disadvantages) of using technology to send instant messages.

REINFORCEMENT

Clarify Opinions Have students state their opinions verbally, and then write them down. Review the statements to make sure they are clear. If needed, assist students in clarifying their opinions. To help students focus and organize their letters, remind them to state their opinion in the first paragraph.

1000 martin st
Raleigh, Nc 27601
march 16, 20___

Dear Grandma and Grandpa

    I am very grateful that you are going to get a pet for our
family. Mom and dad said we could have either a puppy or a
kitten. I think you should get us a puppy. Dogs are much more fun
than cats. They are also more useful than cats.

personal tone

first-person point of view

    Dogs have always make better pets than cats because dogs
are more fun. Dogs go on walks with people and play games like
fetch. They can learn tricks like lying down and rolling over. A dog
will wag its tail, bark, and jump around. Dogs are very loving
animals. A dog will put its head on your lap or nuzzle you to be
petted. Cats are useless. Cats do not go for walks. They don't
play games. They don't learn tricks very easily. They don't jump
around. They don't join in the fun. Cats can be loving, but a cat
has to be in the mood to be stroked or petted.

Analyze
Read the beginning of Shamari's draft. How did she use a personal tone that shows respect for the reader?

Write
Use your Network Tree to write a draft of your friendly letter. Set the right tone by choosing your words thoughtfully.

Collaborative Conferencing

PEER TO PEER Have partners exchange letters. Tell students to think of two or three questions they would like to ask to clarify information or supply missing details. Have them write their questions on sticky notes and affix them to the appropriate places on their partner's letter.

PEER GROUPS Have students work in groups of four. Students pass their letters to the student on the right to read. That student writes one comment or suggestion on a sticky note affixed to the draft and passes the letter along to the right. The review ends when everyone has received his or her own letter back with three comments.

TEACHER-LED Schedule conferences with pairs of students. Have them read each other's letter and coach them in giving and receiving constructive criticism.

Write
Friendly Letter

Week 2 • Day 4

Student Objectives
• Complete a draft. *(p. 299)*

Continue Drafting It is important that students are given ample time to plan and draft their friendly letters. As conferencing is important throughout the writing process, be sure to plan time for peer-to-peer, peer group, or teacher-led conferences. Remind students that this is the time to get their ideas down on paper in a creative and engaging way. Assure them that they will have plenty of time to fix any mistakes later.

CCSS **Common Core State Standards** (pp. Z20–Z30)
Writing: W.4.1a, W.4.1b, W.4.4, W.4.5, W.4.6, W.4.10
Language: L.4.3c
Speaking and Listening: SL.4.1a, SL.4.1b, SL.4.1c, SL.4.1d, SL.4.3, SL.4.4, SL.4.6

Write
Friendly Letter

Week 2 • Day 5

Student Objectives

• Revise to add facts to support the reasons. (p. 300)

Revise

Focus on Ideas

Add Facts Read page 300 aloud and discuss Shamari's thoughts about adding facts to her draft. Direct students to study the excerpt and identify the facts she has added. Discuss how they support her reason. Ask students to explain why it's useful to have plenty of supporting facts in an opinion piece of writing. **(Possible response: Facts help to support the writer's reasons and to convince the reader to share the writer's opinion.)** Have students look for places in their friendly letters where they can add facts to support their reasons.

Strategies for Writers Online
Go to **www.sfw.z-b.com** for additional online resources for students, teachers, and parents.

T300   Opinion Writing

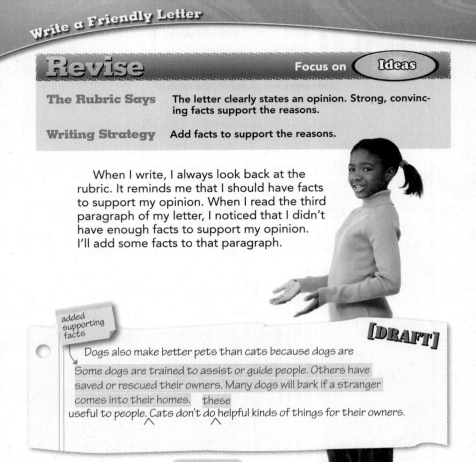

Write a Friendly Letter

Revise   Focus on Ideas

The Rubric Says   The letter clearly states an opinion. Strong, convincing facts support the reasons.

Writing Strategy   Add facts to support the reasons.

When I write, I always look back at the rubric. It reminds me that I should have facts to support my opinion. When I read the third paragraph of my letter, I noticed that I didn't have enough facts to support my opinion. I'll add some facts to that paragraph.

added supporting facts

[DRAFT]

Dogs also make better pets than cats because dogs are

Some dogs are trained to assist or guide people. Others have saved or rescued their owners. Many dogs will bark if a stranger comes into their homes.   these

useful to people. Cats don't do helpful kinds of things for their owners.

Write
Read your draft. Look for places to add facts that support your reasons. Add these facts to your draft.

300   Opinion Writing

English Language Learners

BEGINNING/INTERMEDIATE
Using Sources to Find Facts Ask students where they can learn facts about a subject. Give partners an index card with a question written on it. For example, *What are four types of dancing?* Have them use reliable print and online resources to research and write an answer to the question. Ask them to record the source where they found the answer.

ADVANCED/ADVANCED HIGH
Loaded Words Ask students to draw an animal and a beast. Ask them to compare the two drawings. Then ask students, *Is a beast an animal?* When they answer *yes*, tell them that *beast* is a loaded word and causes the reader to imagine something less appealing. Challenge students to come up with other examples.

Revise  Focus on Word Choice

The Rubric Says   The writer's language is fair. No loaded words are used.

Writing Strategy   Replace loaded words with neutral ones.

The rubric reminds me to use fair language. I've learned that loaded words can cause strong emotions in the reader. Sometimes the use of loaded words can distract or upset the reader. If I use loaded words, the reader may even stop reading. When I reread my draft, I noticed a loaded word I should replace with a neutral one.

[DRAFT]

very different

Cats are ~~useless~~. Cats do not go for walks. They don't play games. They don't learn tricks very easily. They don't jump around.

They don't join in the fun.

replaced loaded word

Analyze
Look at Shamari's revision. How does using neutral language help make her letter more convincing?

Write
Read your draft. Revise your draft by finding loaded words and replacing them with neutral ones.

Friendly Letter **301**

Collaborative Conferencing

PEER TO PEER Have partners exchange letters. After reading, ask each student to offer feedback on how to strengthen their drafts. If needed, have students consult the model letter, the rubric, and the analysis for ideas, word choice, and sentence fluency.

PEER GROUPS Have students form small groups. Have each student read aloud a section of his or her letter. Ask each group member to offer one suggestion on how to strengthen it. Have writers consult the revising lesson pages in their book to inform their revision.

TEACHER-LED Schedule conferences to read each student's draft. Point out strengths and weaknesses. Talk about ways to improve the draft and inform the revision. If a student seems stalled or discouraged, revisit steps in the process to make improvements and keep going.

Write
Friendly Letter

Week 3 • Day 1

Student Objectives

- Revise to replace loaded words with neutral ones. *(p. 301)*

Revise

Focus on Word Choice

Use Fair Language Read the introduction to page 301. Have a volunteer read aloud the excerpt without the change. Then have a volunteer read aloud the excerpt with the change. Point out that *very different* expresses an observation without sounding negative or biased. Have students check their drafts for places to replace negative words with neutral ones that don't offend the reader. Encourage them to consult print or online word resources to find good replacement words.

CCSS **Common Core State Standards** (pp. Z20–Z30)
Writing: W.4.1b, W.4.4, W.4.5, W.4.6, W.4.8, W.4.10
Language: L.4.3a, L.4.3c, L.4.4c, L.4.6
Speaking and Listening: SL.4.1a, SL.4.1b, SL.4.1c, SL.4.1d, SL.4.3, SL.4.6

Write
Friendly Letter

Week 3 • Day 2

Student Objectives

- Revise to combine short, choppy sentences to make the writing flow. *(p. 302)*

Revise

Focus on

Vary Sentence Lengths Read the top of page 302 aloud. Then read the unrevised draft excerpt. Ask:

- What makes the writing boring? (Almost all the sentences start with *They* and share the same sentence pattern.)

Then read the draft again with the revisions. Ask:

- How did Shamari improve the flow in this part? (by combining closely related ideas to vary sentence lengths)

Have students read their own drafts and combine short, choppy sentences. Remind students to combine ideas that go together naturally.

Online Writing Center

 Provides **interactive proofreading activities** for each genre.

Revise
Focus on **Sentence Fluency**

The Rubric Says	The sentences vary in length and structure. They flow naturally.
Writing Strategy	Combine short, choppy sentences to make the writing flow.

I reread my draft out loud. This time I listened for a smooth flow. I found a lot of short, choppy sentences in my second paragraph. If I combine some of them, that will add variation and make my writing flow.

[DRAFT]

petted. Cats are very different. Cats do not go for walks. They don't play games. *or* They don't learn tricks very easily. They don't jump around. *and* They don't join in the fun.

combined short, choppy sentences

Write

Read through your draft. Revise it by combining short, choppy sentences to make your writing flow.

302 Opinion Writing

Optional Revising Lessons

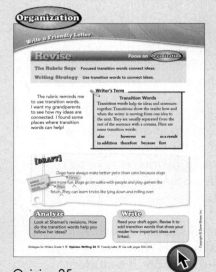

Opinion 25

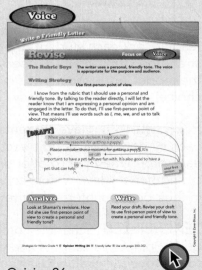

Opinion 26

Go to ➡ *Strategies for Writers* at www.sfw.z-b.com

Edit — Focus on Conventions

I'll check my spelling, capitalization, and punctuation. Then I'll check that my letter has all five parts. My letter won't make a very good impression if it has a lot of errors in it.

Writer's Term

Punctuating a Friendly Letter

Capitalize	Use Commas
• street	• between day and year
• city	
• state	• between city and state
• month	
• words in greeting	• after greeting
• closing	• after closing
• signature	

[DRAFT]

uppercase letters

1000 martin st
Raleigh, Nc 27601

march 16, 20___

period needed

Analyze

Look at how Shamari edited her writing to use capitalization and punctuation correctly. Has she fixed all the errors in capitalization and punctuation correctly?

Write — Conventions

Edit your draft for spelling, capitalization, and punctuation. Check that you have included all five parts of a friendly letter.

For more practice with friendly letters and abbreviations, use the exercises on the next two pages.

Friendly Letter **303**

Related Grammar Practice

Student Edition page 468

Student Edition page 475

Go to ▶ **Appendix A: Grammar Practice**

Write
Friendly Letter

Week 3 • Day 3

Student Objectives

• Edit for correct use of punctuation. (p. 303)

Edit

Focus on Conventions

Check Abbreviations Review the difference between revising (improving text) and editing (correcting text). Tell students that this is the time to go back and correct mistakes in spelling, punctuation, grammar, and capitalization.

Direct attention to the Writer's Term box and read the information. Ask students to explain Shamari's edits to the heading. Then have them check their capitalization and punctuation.

Use the mini-lessons on pages T304–T305 for students having problems using punctuation correctly.

Writer's Term

Punctuating a Friendly Letter
The United States Postal Service uses two-letter abbreviations for the names of U.S. states and possessions. The letters are capitalized without punctuation or spaces between letters. See **www.usps.com**.

CCSS **Common Core State Standards** (pp. Z20–Z30)
Writing: W.4.4, W.4.5, W.4.6, W.4.10
Language: L.4.2a, L.4.2d, L.4.6

Mini-Lesson

Student Objectives

• Use the five parts of a friendly letter correctly. (p. 304)

Friendly Letter Parts

Read and discuss the Know the Rule section on page 304. Before having students do the practice, create the outline of a friendly letter on the board, drawing lines that represent the five parts of a friendly letter in their correct positions. Tell students that you are about to write a short thank-you letter to an individual (a special guest, speaker, or author), but you need help filling in the blanks correctly. One part at a time, ask students where you should place the heading, greeting, body, closing, and signature.

Next provide students with copies of a friendly-letter outline with write-on lines that represent the five parts. Ask students to think of a time when someone did something especially kind for them. Direct students to use their outlines to write a brief thank-you note to the individual. If they don't know their recipient's address, supply a generic address for them to use. Once they have finished filling in the form, have students exchange forms and check for correct placement of the five parts.

Online Writing Center

Provides **interactive grammar games** and **practice activities** in student eBook.

Parts of a Friendly Letter

Know the Rule

A friendly letter has five parts.
- The **heading** gives your address and the date. Use a comma to separate the name of a city or town from the name of a state. Use another comma to separate the month and the day from the year.
- The **greeting** includes the name of the person you are writing to. It begins with an uppercase letter and ends with a comma.
- The **body** of the letter is your message.
- The **closing** is a friendly way to say goodbye. It begins with an uppercase letter and ends with a comma.
- The **signature** is your name.

A letter's envelope has two parts.
- The **address** of the person receiving the letter.
- The **return address** of the person sending the letter.

Note: When addressing an envelope, use all uppercase letters and no punctuation.

Practice the Rule

Number a piece of paper 1–7. Read the letter and envelope below and on the next page. Write the name of each numbered part of this friendly letter.

heading **1.** 32 Lake St.
Duluth, MN 50800
November 12, 20___

2. Dear Samuel, greeting

3. body Thanks for inviting me to visit. I really had a great time. I liked meeting your parents, and staying at the campsite was a lot of fun. Maybe you can come to Duluth for a visit sometime soon.

closing **4.** Your friend,

signature **5.** Chase

Related Grammar Practice

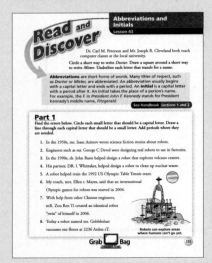

Page 115

Go to ➡ **G.U.M. Student Practice Book**

6. CHASE SIMONS **return address**
32 LAKE ST
DULUTH MN 50800

address 7. SAMUEL TAYLOR
100 WEST ST
RIVERTOWN MN 52045

U.S. POSTAGE

Abbreviations and Initials

Know the Rule

Abbreviations are short forms of words. In a letter, you might use abbreviations for a title (*Mr.*) and a street name (*Elm St.*). An **initial** is an uppercase letter with a period after it. An initial takes the place of a name. For example, *D.J. Connors* stands for *David Jacob Connors.*

Practice the Rule

Number a piece of paper 1–10. Match the abbreviations and initials to their written-out forms. Write the letter of the abbreviation or initial.

1. Doctor Lewis	h	**a.**	J.F.K.
2. Saint Mary's Hospital	b, g	**b.**	St.
3. Broad Road	e	**c.**	Mr.
4. Market Street	b, g	**d.**	Sr.
5. Warren Avenue	j	**e.**	Rd.
6. Mister Jackson	c	**f.**	Blvd.
7. Cleveland Boulevard	f	**g.**	St.
8. Clive Staples Lewis	i	**h.**	Dr.
9. John Fitzgerald Kennedy	a	**i.**	C.S.
10. Frank Mahoney, Senior	d	**j.**	Ave.

Friendly Letter **305**

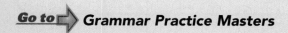

Student Objectives

• Use abbreviations correctly. (p. 305)

Abbreviations and Initials

Read and discuss the Know the Rule section on page 305. Before having students do the practice, create the outline of an envelope on the board, drawing lines that represent the location of the return address, the recipient address, and the postage area. Ask students for their help to fill in the blanks correctly. Remind them to refer to the Know the Rule on this page to help them use abbreviations and initials correctly.

Next provide students with copies of an envelope outline with lines that represent the addresses. If needed, supply a generic address for them to use. Once they have finished, ask student volunteers to exchange their forms and check for correctness.

CCSS **C**ommon **C**ore **S**tate **S**tandards (pp. Z20–Z30)
Writing: W.4.6
Language: L.4.2a, L.4.2d, L.4.6

Write
Friendly Letter

Week 3 • Day 4

Student Objectives

• Discuss preparation for publishing and presentation. *(p. 306)*

• Use a final editing checklist to publish their work. *(p. 306)*

Publish +Presentation

Publishing Strategy Read page 306 and discuss Shamari's choice for publishing her friendly letter. Ask students to discuss the advantages of sending a letter by mail instead of using e-mail. Ask students to consider other publishing options for other types of letters in which they express an opinion.

Direct their attention to Shamari's checklist for publishing her friendly letter. Remind students that her checklist is based on the writing strategies in this chapter. Ask students to consider why neat handwriting is included on the list. **(The letter will be easy to read.)** Neatness also reveals how the writer feels about his or her letter. Have students use the checklist to prepare their final copies. Remind them to sign their letters.

 Strategies for Writers Online
Go to **www.sfw.z-b.com** for additional online resources for students, teachers, and parents.

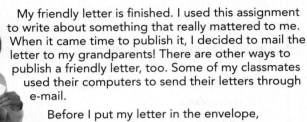

Publish +Presentation

Publishing Strategy	Address an envelope and ask my parents to mail my letter.
Presentation Strategy	Check all the parts of the letter.

My friendly letter is finished. I used this assignment to write about something that really mattered to me. When it came time to publish it, I decided to mail the letter to my grandparents! There are other ways to publish a friendly letter, too. Some of my classmates used their computers to send their letters through e-mail.

Before I put my letter in the envelope, I looked it over one last time. In addition to making sure my letter has all five parts, I made sure it was written neatly and carefully. Here is my final checklist.

My Final Checklist

Did I—

✔ make sure my letter has all five parts?

✔ correctly punctuate all five parts of my letter?

✔ use abbreviations and initials correctly?

✔ use my best handwriting or careful word processing?

Write
Make a checklist to check your friendly letter. Then make a final copy. Address an envelope to the person to whom you are writing, and then mail the letter.

306 Opinion Writing

Differentiating Instruction

ENRICHMENT

Form a Pen-Pal Group Writing letters is a good way to explore a wide range of topics. Letters open dialogue on issues students care about and provide a way to learn more. Encourage students to think about forming an inter- or intra-school pen pal organization and write letters regularly.

REINFORCEMENT

Proofread After students have edited their letters, have them put their writing away for a day. Then have students exchange letters to proofread each other's work for one specific kind of error (five parts, abbreviations and initials, spelling, capitalization, punctuation). Encourage students to work with at least three different peer editors. When they have finished proofreading, have writers verify the edits and make their final corrections.

1000 Martin St.
Raleigh, NC 27601
March 16, 20___

Dear Grandma and Grandpa,

I am very grateful that you are going to get a pet for our family. Mom and Dad said we could have either a puppy or a kitten. I think you should get us a puppy. Dogs are much more fun than cats. Dogs are also more useful than cats.

Dogs have always made better pets than cats because dogs are more fun. First, dogs go on walks with people and play games like fetch. Also, they can learn tricks like lying down and rolling over. A dog will wag its tail, bark, and jump around. In addition, dogs are very loving animals. A dog will put its head on your lap or nuzzle you to be petted. However, cats are very different. Cats do not go for walks. They don't play games or learn tricks very easily. They don't jump around and join in the fun. Cats can be loving, but a cat has to be in the mood to be stroked or petted.

Dogs also make better pets than cats because dogs are useful to people. Some dogs are trained to assist or guide people. Others have saved or rescued their owners. Many dogs will bark if a stranger comes into their homes. Cats don't do these helpful kinds of things for their owners.

When you make your decision, I hope you will consider my reasons for getting a puppy. It's important to have a pet we can have fun with. It's also good to have a pet that can help us.

Love,

Shamari

Analyze

Use the rubric to evaluate Shamari's friendly letter. Are all the traits of a good friendly letter there? Then evaluate your friendly letter against the rubric.

Friendly Letter 307

Tech Tips

Digital Tools

Use Digital Tools Choosing digital tools is as much about what you have to say as who you are seeking to engage. Consider taking the friendly letter into a multimodal space by asking students to construct a digital postcard using a tool like Postalz. Keep audience at the forefront of students' thinking as you consider which images would have the best impact, how to balance allowing the image to do some of the communicating alongside your written words, and how the confined space of the postcard limits how much can be written.

See **www.sfw.z-b.com** for further information about and links to these websites and tools.

Write
Friendly Letter

Week 3 • Day 5

Student Objectives

• Use a friendly letter rubric. (pp. 290–291)
• Send a published friendly letter. (p. 307)

Presentation Strategy Review the reason for each of the five parts, as necessary. Then remind students of the importance of a neat appearance. If students prepare the letter on a computer, they should set neat margins, use the tab key to indent paragraphs, double-space the text, and select one or two neat fonts. Depending on their topic, students may want to include pictures or illustrations to enhance their letter.

After they have prepared their final copies, encourage students to send the letters.

Reflecting on a Friendly Letter

Instruct students to turn to a partner and talk about their experience in writing a friendly letter. Use these questions to prompt discussion:

• How did you use the rubric when you wrote your letter?
• What is the strongest part of your letter? Why?

CCSS **C**ommon **C**ore **S**tate **S**tandards (pp. Z20–Z30)
Writing: W.4.4, W.4.6, W.4.10
Language: L.4.3c
Speaking and Listening: SL.4.1a, SL.4.1b, SL.4.1c, SL.4.1d, SL.4.3, SL.4.6

Response to Literature Planner

WEEK 1

Day 1
Introduce
Response to Literature

Student Objectives
- Review the elements of a response to literature.
- Consider purpose and audience.
- Learn the traits of opinion writing.

Student Activities
- Read and discuss **What's in a Response to Literature?** (p. 308)
- Read and discuss **Why Write a Response to Literature?** (p. 309)
- Read and discuss **Linking Opinion Writing Traits to a Response to Literature.** (p. 310)

Day 2
Analyze
Close Reading of the Model

Student Objectives
- Read a model response to literature.

Student Activities
- Read **"A Magic Tree House Book with a Message."** (p. 311)

Day 3
Analyze
Introduce the Rubric

Student Objectives
- Learn to read a rubric.

Student Activities
- Review **"A Magic Tree House Book with a Message."** (p. 311)
- Read and discuss the **Response to Literature Rubric.** (pp. 312–313)

WEEK 2

Day 1
Write
Prewrite: Ideas

Student Objectives
- Decide on a topic.
- Make a list of details.

Student Activities
- Read and discuss **Prewrite: Focus on Ideas.** (p. 318)
- Apply the prewriting strategy.

Day 2
Write
Prewrite: Organization

Student Objectives
- Use a Four-Paragraph Organizer to plan the response.

Student Activities
- Read and discuss **Prewrite: Focus on Organization.** (p. 319)
- Apply the prewriting strategy.
- Participate in a peer conference.

Day 3
Write
Draft: Word Choice

Student Objectives
- Use exact words.

Student Activities
- Read and discuss **Draft: Focus on Word Choice.** (p. 320)
- Apply the drafting strategy.

WEEK 3

Day 1
Write
Revise: Organization

Student Objectives
- Revise to use transitions to show how ideas are related.

Student Activities
- Read and discuss: **Revise: Focus on Organization.** (p. 323)
- Reflect on the model draft.
- Apply the revising strategy.
- Participate in a peer conference.

Day 2
Write
Revise: Sentence Fluency

Student Objectives
- Revise to combine sentences.

Student Activities
- Read and discuss: **Revise: Focus on Sentence Fluency.** (p. 324)
- Reflect on the model draft.
- Apply the revising strategy.

Note: Optional Revising Lessons are located at **www.sfw.z-b.com**

Day 3
Write
Edit: Conventions

Student Objectives
- Edit for correct use of pronouns.

Student Activities
- Read and discuss **Edit: Focus on Conventions.** (p. 325)
- Reflect on the model draft.
- Apply the editing strategy.

Note: Teach the Conventions mini-lessons (pp. 326–327) if needed.

Day 4	Day 5
Analyze Close Reading for the Traits	**Analyze** Close Reading for the Traits
Student Objectives • Read a model response to literature. • Use the response to literature rubric. • Use the model response to literature to study Ideas, Organization, and Voice. **Student Activities** • Review **"A Magic Tree House Book with a Message."** (p. 311) • Read and discuss **Using the Rubric to Analyze the Model.** (pp. 314–315)	**Student Objectives** • Read a model response to literature. • Use the response to literature rubric. • Use the model response to literature to study Word Choice, Sentence Fluency, and Conventions. **Student Activities** • Review **"A Magic Tree House Book with a Message."** (p. 311) • Read and discuss **Using the Rubric to Analyze the Model.** (pp. 316–317)

Day 4	Day 5
Write Draft	**Write** Revise: Ideas
Student Objectives • Complete a draft. **Student Activities** • Finish writing a draft. (p. 321) • Participate in a peer conference.	**Student Objectives** • Revise to include information from the book, such as quotations. **Student Activities** • Read and discuss **Revise: Focus on Ideas.** (p. 322) • Reflect on the model draft. • Apply the revising strategy.

Day 4	Day 5
Write Publish: +Presentation	**Write** Publish: +Presentation
Student Objectives • Discuss preparation for publishing and presentation. • Use a final editing checklist to publish their work. **Student Activities** • Read and discuss **Publish: +Presentation.** (p. 328) • Apply the publishing strategy.	**Student Objectives** • Use a response to literature rubric. • Share a published response to literature. **Student Activities** • Share their work. • Use the rubric to reflect upon and evaluate the model and their own writing. (pp. 312–313; 329)

To complete the chapter in fewer days, combine the learning objectives and activities in a way that supports students as they write.

Resources at-a-Glance

Grammar, Usage & Mechanics

Differentiating Instruction

For additional Differentiating Instruction activities, see Strategies for Writers *Differentiated Instruction Activities at www.sfw.z-b.com.*

English Language Learners

Collaborative Conferencing

Tech Tips

 Strategies for Writers Online

Go to **www.sfw.z-b.com** for additional online resources for students, teachers, and parents.

Online Writing Center

Provides IWB resources, assessments, interactive games and practice activities, videos, eBooks, and a virtual file cabinet.

Introduce
Response to Literature

Student Objectives

- Review the elements of a response to literature. *(p. 308)*
- Consider purpose and audience. *(p. 309)*
- Learn the traits of opinion writing. *(p. 310)*

What's a Response to Literature?

Discuss the definition of a response to literature. Explain that the purpose of this type of opinion writing is to convince others to read a book that the writer has read and recommends. Point out that this chapter will help students express and support their opinion, using examples from the book.

What's in a Response to Literature?

Read and discuss the definitions for each element of a response to literature on page 308. Ask students how the elements are related and important to writing a response to literature. **(Possible responses: The summary provides important details about the book. The theme is the book's main message. The supporting evidence backs up the writer's opinion.)**

Strategies for Writers Online

Go to **www.sfw.z-b.com** for additional online resources for students, teachers, and parents.

What's a Response to Literature?

It's an opportunity to share my opinion of a book I've read. My response will be a book review that includes a short description of the plot and characters, the author's main message, and my opinion of the book.

What's in a Response to Literature?

Summary
A response to literature should include a summary of the book. A summary is a brief description of the plot and the important characters. It usually does not reveal the ending of the book, especially if it's a surprise.

Theme
The theme of a book is the author's main point or message to the reader. Sometimes the reader has to figure it out. Sometimes the author tells exactly what it is.

Supporting Evidence
The writer's opinion needs to be supported with information from the book, such as details and direct quotations. Some information can be paraphrased, or put into the writer's own words. Writers can also use their own knowledge to support their opinion.

Opinion Text Exemplars (Response to Literature)

James, Elizabeth. *How to Write Terrific Book Reports*. HarperCollins, 1998. *How to Write Terrific Book Reports* helps students prepare a written or oral book report. It contains tips from selecting a book to taking notes, including using card catalogs to generate reports in the form of articles or diary entries.

Romaneck, Greg. *Civil War Books for Younger Readers: 350 Critical Reviews and Summaries*. AuthorHouse, 2006. Romaneck provides a synopsis of a multitude of Civil War books offered to young readers. Each page includes a summary, a brief review, and publication information for each of 350 books.

Why write a Response to Literature?

There are many reasons to respond to literature. Here are three I can think of. Can you add another?

To Express an Opinion
Sometimes I am very excited about a book I've read. I like to write about it to convince readers to agree with my opinion and get them to read the book. Then we can discuss the book among ourselves.

To Inform
I often learn so much new information from a great book! Writing a book review is a good way to give my friends the opportunity to learn new things, too.

To Understand
When I write a book review, I learn a lot about what I am thinking and feeling. Sometimes I even surprise myself!

Why write a Response to Literature?

Read and discuss with students the reasons for writing a response to literature listed on page 309. Point out that all writing has a purpose and is aimed at a specific audience. These authentic purposes help writers shape their writing. Someone writing to express an opinion wants to convince the audience to read the book. A person writing to inform may share factual information. A person writing to understand will share personal feelings and reflections and include details from the book as evidence for those feelings and reflections. Encourage students to think about their own reasons for writing a response to literature and how they will convey their purpose to their audience.

Davidson, Margaret. *Louis Braille: The Boy Who Invented Books for the Blind*. Scholastic Paperbacks, 1991. This biography introduces students to Louis Braille, the inventor of the printing system used by the blind. After becoming blind at a young age, Braille worked to create a way for people like himself to read.

Campbell, Janis. *Authors by Request: An Inside Look at Your Favorite Writers*. Beyond Words Publishing, 2002. Campbell provides readers with several short biographies of popular children's book authors. The life and works of writers such as Avi and Lois Lowry are detailed in this engaging reference book.

CCSS **C**ommon **C**ore **S**tate **S**tandards (pp. Z20–Z30)
Language: L.4.3c
Speaking and Listening: SL.4.1a, SL.4.1b, SL.4.1c, SL.4.1d, SL.4.3, SL.4.6

Introduce
Response to Literature

Linking Opinion Writing Traits to a Response to Literature

Read the introduction to page 310 aloud to help students understand that they will follow Shamari as she models using the writing process and the opinion writing traits together. A good response will state the writer's opinion and support the writer's reasons with direct quotes and examples.

As they follow Shamari, students will see how the Opinion Writing Traits have been adapted and applied to writing a response to literature. They will see that a response to literature has many factors in common with other types of opinion writing. However, the particular audience and purpose of a response to literature determine how the traits are used.

Linking Opinion Writing Traits to a **Response to Literature**

In this chapter, you will write to convince your readers to agree with your opinion about a book. This type of opinion writing is called a response to literature. Shamari will guide you through the stages of the writing process: Prewrite, Draft, Revise, Edit, and Publish. In each stage, Shamari will show you important writing strategies that are linked to the Opinion Writing Traits below.

Opinion Writing Traits

Ideas
- a clear opinion
- strong reasons that are supported by facts and details

Organization
- a clear, logical organization
- an introduction, body, and conclusion
- transitions that connect opinions and reasons

Voice
- a voice and tone that are appropriate for the audience and purpose

Word Choice
- fair and balanced language
- specific words and phrases

Sentence Fluency
- a variety of sentence patterns that make the writing flow

Conventions
- no or few errors in spelling, grammar, punctuation, and capitalization

Before you write, read Toshio Mori's response to literature on the next page. Then use the response to literature rubric on pages 312–313 to decide how well he did. (You might want to look back at What's in a Response to Literature? on page 308, too!)

Opinion Writing Traits in a Response to Literature

Ideas The response clearly states and supports the writer's opinion. Details from the book or story support the writer's reasons.

Organization The writer's ideas are organized logically. Effective transitions guide the reader through the response.

Voice The writer uses a convincing voice and formal tone that suits the writer's purpose and audience.

A Magic Tree House Book with a Message

by Toshio Mori

I just finished reading two Magic Tree House books by Mary Pope Osborne. Each book takes Jack and his sister Annie on an adventure. In *Pirates Past Noon*, they go back in time to the days of the Caribbean pirates. In *Tigers at Twilight*, they explore a jungle in India. I enjoyed reading both books. In my opinion, *Tigers at Twilight* sends an important message. The title means that time is running out for the tigers. The book helped me to care about what happens to them.

theme

In *Tigers at Twilight*, Annie and Jack are amazed at the beautiful jungle, with playful monkeys, colorful peacocks, and small deer. Then they find out that the jungle is also home to many large wild animals. One tiger came too close, and Jack and Annie had to escape on an elephant! Later, they found out that the tiger they saw was being hunted. Read the book to find out how they help the tiger.

summary

Tigers at Twilight is filled with interesting facts about jungle animals, like how much a wild tiger eats and how a python can "swallow an animal the size of a full-grown deer." Unfortunately, poachers—people who hunt illegally—kill too many animals.

Did you know that once animals become extinct they're gone forever? Their future depends on what we do today! Read *Tigers at Twilight* to learn how we can work together to save them.

supporting evidence

Word Choice The words are specific. Examples from the book are accurately quoted.

Sentence Fluency A variety of well-written sentences keeps the reader's interest and makes the response flow smoothly.

Conventions The writer has edited the response carefully. Pronouns are used correctly.

Analyze
Close Reading of the Model

Student Objectives

- Read a model response to literature. *(p. 311)*

Read the Model

Read aloud "A Magic Tree House Book with a Message" on page 311. Ask students to listen for the writer's opinion and supporting evidence as you read. Point out the theme, summary, and supporting evidence. Also ask students to think about how the formal writing style conveys the writer's purpose and assures the audience that the writer knows the book well.

Elements of a Response to Literature

Have students refer to What's in a Response to Literature? on page 308 as you refer to the model response. Point out the notes written on the model to enhance students' understanding of the terms. Be sure to talk about how the writer avoids plagiarism by referring to the book and using quotation marks for words that belong to the author of the book. Tell students that they will now use the model to analyze the traits of a good response to literature.

CCSS **C**ommon **C**ore **S**tate **S**tandards (pp. Z20–Z30)
Writing: W.4.6
Language: L.4.3c
Speaking and Listening: SL.4.1a, SL.4.1b, SL.4.1c, SL.4.1d, SL.4.2, SL.4.3, SL.4.6

Analyze
Introduce the Rubric

Week 1 • Day 3

Student Objectives

- Learn to read a rubric. *(pp. 312–313)*

Introduce the Rubric

Explain the Rubric Explain that a rubric is a tool for planning, improving, and assessing a piece of writing. Tell students that a rubric helps a writer focus on key elements, or traits, in writing (**Ideas, Organization, Voice, Word Choice, Sentence Fluency, Conventions,** and **Presentation**).

Point out that column 6 describes a very good response to literature, one that has received the highest score in all categories. This is what students should strive for in their own writing.

Discuss the Rubric When students score their paper for each trait, they should first decide whether it falls on the left of the rubric (uses the trait well) or on the right (needs improvement in using the trait). By examining the paper more closely, students can refine the score to a single number.

Online Writing Center

Provides six **interactive anchor papers** for each text type.

Response to Literature Rubric

Use this rubric to analyze the model. Then use it to plan and score your own response to literature.

	6	5	4
Ideas	The writer's opinion is clearly stated. Reasons are supported by strong evidence (quotations, paraphrases, facts, or details).	The writer's opinion is clearly stated. Most evidence is strong and supports the reasons.	The writer's opinion is stated. Some evidence does not support the reasons.
Organization	The book review is organized logically. Transition words are used effectively.	The parts of the book review are in order. Most transition words are used effectively.	Most parts of the book review are in order. Transition words are used but not effectively.
Voice	The writer uses a formal tone that sounds knowledgeable and convincing.	The writer uses a formal tone that sounds knowledgeable most of the time.	The writer sounds convincing in the beginning and then fades somewhat.
Word Choice	Specific nouns and strong verbs are used to convince the reader.	Specific nouns and strong verbs convince the reader most of the time.	A few of the words are vague and should be replaced.
Sentence Fluency	A variety of sentence patterns makes the writing flow smoothly.	Most sentences are varied. Most of the writing flows smoothly.	Several sentences in a row share the same pattern.
Conventions	The writing has been edited carefully. Pronouns are used correctly.	A few errors are present but do not confuse the reader. Pronouns are used correctly.	Several errors confuse the reader. One or two pronouns may be used incorrectly.

+ Presentation The use of multimedia strengthens the message.

CCSS Common Core State Standards

Response to Literature

Strategies for Writers was designed and written to weave the Common Core State Standards throughout every unit. For Opinion writing, the standards inform the unit's writing rubrics, objectives, and strategies. By presenting the standards in as many applications as possible, your students' exposure to them will be ensured. As a result, students are more likely to employ the standards' language in writing opinion pieces as well as in discussions about writing.

The lessons for Response to Literature are based principally on the writing standards for Opinion writing. The rubrics and writing strategies reflect the writing standard **W.4.1,** which

3	2	1	
The writer's opinion is stated. Supporting evidence may be unimportant or unrelated.	The writer's opinion is not clear or is weak. Supporting evidence is weak.	An opinion is not stated. Supporting evidence is missing.	**Ideas**
Some parts of the book review appear to be out of order. Transition words are confusing or missing.	Some parts of the book review are missing. Few if any transition words are used.	The writing is not organized. Transition words are not used.	**Organization**
The writer sounds uninformed and unconvincing in many places.	The tone does not match the writer's purpose. It may be too informal to convince.	Voice is very weak or absent. The audience does not know the writer's purpose.	**Voice**
Several words are general and overused. They dull the message.	Many words are too general or unconvincing. The reader may lose interest.	Words are very basic and limited. Some are used incorrectly.	**Word Choice**
Too many sentences share the same pattern. The writing is choppy.	Sentences are too short or irregular.	Sentences are poorly constructed. Some are incomplete.	**Sentence Fluency**
Many errors confuse the reader. Some pronouns are used incorrectly.	Serious errors stop the reader. Pronouns are used incorrectly.	The writing has not been edited.	**Conventions**

See Appendix B for 4-, 5-, and 6-point opinion rubrics.

Response to Literature **313**

Find Evidence in the Model

Small-Group Collaboration
Assign students to small groups and ask them to check the model for each trait. One person in each group should be responsible for recording one or two strong examples of the trait as described by the rubric. Ask students to score each trait accordingly for the model. They should be able to support their scores. Note that although the model was written to score high in each trait, students should not assume each trait would receive a 6, the top score. Encourage students to discuss each trait thoroughly before assigning each score.

Teacher-Led Discussion Bring the class back together and ask one person from each group to report their findings to the class. The point of this exercise is to practice identifying and evaluating the traits within a piece of writing.

Additional Rubrics

Appendix B includes 4-, 5-, and 6-point rubrics that can be used with any piece of opinion writing. The rubrics are also available as blackline masters in the back of this Teacher Edition.

focuses on introducing and supporting a point of view with reasons and information.

The language standards for grade 4 students are addressed during editing and skills practice. In addition, there are multiple opportunities to address the speaking and listening standards during the writing process. Most importantly, this chapter will help your students produce coherent writing (**W.4.4**), improve their writing (**W.4.5**), and use technologies to publish their finished pieces (**W.4.6**).

CCSS **Common Core State Standards** (pp. Z20–Z30)
Writing: W.4.6
Language: L.4.3c
Speaking and Listening: SL.4.1a, SL.4.1b, SL.4.1c, SL.4.1d, SL.4.2, SL.4.3, SL.4.6

Analyze
Close Reading for the Traits

Week 1 • Day 4

Student Objectives

- Read a model response to literature. *(p. 311)*
- Use the response to literature rubric. *(pp. 312–313)*
- Use the model response to literature to study **Ideas, Organization,** and **Voice.** *(pp. 314–315)*

Find Evidence in the Model

Evaluate the Model Read aloud each section on pages 314–315. Discuss as a class whether students agree or disagree with Shamari's assessments of the model. Use the questions below to initiate the discussion. Be sure students can back up their answers with specific examples from the report.

Discuss Audience, Task, Purpose Ask students one or more of the following questions as they analyze the model:

- **Audience** Who is the audience? (Possible response: all readers)

- **Task** How does the writer show his opinion? (Possible response: The writer states his opinion in the first paragraph.)

- **Purpose** What is the writer's purpose for writing this report? How do you know? (Possible response: to persuade the reader to read this book; He gives reasons why others should read this book.)

Using the Rubric to Analyze the Model
Response to Literature

Did you notice that the model on page 311 points out some key elements of a response to literature? As he wrote "A Magic Tree House Book with a Message," Toshio used these elements to help him write his book review. He also used the 6-point rubric on pages 312–313 to plan, draft, revise, and edit the writing. A rubric is a great tool to evaluate writing during the writing process.

Now let's use the same rubric to score the model. To do this, we'll focus on each trait separately, starting with Ideas. We'll use the top descriptor for each trait (column 6), along with examples from the model, to help us understand how the traits work together. How would you score Toshio on each trait?

Ideas

- The writer's opinion is clearly stated.
- Reasons are supported by strong evidence (quotations, paraphrases, facts, or details).

Toshio states his opinion in the introduction of his book review. He tells why the second book is important. He supports his opinion with evidence from the book in the body of the review.

> In my opinion, *Tigers at Twilight* sends an important message. The title means that time is running out for the tigers. The book helped me to care about what happens to them.

> *Tigers at Twilight* is filled with interesting facts about jungle animals, like how much a wild tiger eats and how a python can "swallow an animal the size of a full-grown deer." Unfortunately, poachers—people who hunt illegally—kill too many animals.

314 Opinion Writing

English Language Learners

BEGINNING

Review Read a very simple fiction story to students, for example, "Cinderella." Ask, *Did you like the story?* Help students answer in complete sentences. Then ask *yes/no* questions, such as *Was Cinderella a kind girl? Did you like the witch?* As students' ability allows, introduce open-ended questions, such as *Why didn't you like the witch?*

INTERMEDIATE

Summary and Theme Read the same fiction story to students. Have partners list the characters and the important plot points. As a class, discuss the theme of the story. Write a few themes for the story on the board, and have students discuss which one best describes the author's message. For "Cinderella," you might use *Be kind and good things will happen; Rich princes make good husbands; It's easy to go from rags to riches.*

Organization
- The book review is organized logically.
- Transition words are used effectively.

Toshio gives his opinion in the introduction. He summarizes the book and gives supporting evidence in the body. Toshio uses transition words, such as *then* and *later*, to make the book review easy to follow. His conclusion invites the audience to read the book.

Then they find out that the jungle is also home to many large wild animals. One tiger came too close, and Jack and Annie had to escape on an elephant! Later, they found out that the tiger they saw was being hunted.

Voice
- The writer uses a formal tone that sounds knowledgeable and convincing.

You can tell that Toshio liked reading and learning from *Tigers at Twilight*. He shares some of the things he learned and invites his audience to read the book, too. However, he keeps his language formal throughout the book review.

Did you know that once animals become extinct they're gone forever? Their future depends on what we do today! Read *Tigers at Twilight* to learn how we can work together to save them.

Discuss the Traits Ask students one or more of the following questions to discuss the traits in the model:

Ideas Does the writer state an opinion clearly and use examples from the book to support the reasons? (Possible response: Yes, it's clear that in Toshio's opinion *Tigers at Twilight* sends an important message.)

Organization Is the review organized in a way that guides the reader? (Possible response: The response is well organized, and transition words make it easy to follow.)

Voice Is a formal tone maintained? (Possible response: Toshio sounds knowledgeable and speaks directly to the reader.)

ADVANCED
Paraphrasing Read a language- and grade-level-appropriate story. Cut apart the paragraphs and give to students. Tell them to rewrite the paragraph in their own words. Then have a volunteer read the paraphrased article to class. Teach the word *paraphrase* to students. Say the word, write it on the board, and have students repeat.

ADVANCED HIGH
Stating Opinions Have students practice giving clear opinions. Offer a topic, such as *adventure movies*, and have students talk about whether they enjoy adventure movies. Ask them to list their reasons for liking or not liking adventure movies. Have them use this information to write a three- or four-sentence introduction that clearly states their opinion. Have them trade papers and check for strong statements of opinion.

CCSS **C**ommon **C**ore **S**tate **S**tandards (pp. Z20–Z30)
Writing: W.4.1a, W.4.8
Language: L.4.3c, L.4.6
Speaking and Listening: SL.4.1a, SL.4.1b, SL.4.1c, SL.4.1d, SL.4.3, SL.4.4, SL.4.6

Analyze

Close Reading for the Traits

Week 1 • Day 5

Student Objectives

- Read a model response to literature. *(p. 311)*
- Use the response to literature rubric. *(pp. 312–313)*
- Use the model response to literature to study **Word Choice, Sentence Fluency,** and **Conventions**. *(pp. 316–317)*

Discuss the Traits Ask students one or more of the following questions to discuss the traits in the model:

Word Choice How does the writer use exact words? (Possible responses: Toshio uses many specific words that are related to the topic. He shows courtesy for the reader when he defines an unfamiliar word.)

Sentence Fluency What evidence in the report shows how the writer varied sentences to keep the text flowing smoothly? (Possible responses: Toshio writes a variety of sentences, including asking a question. The writing flows well.)

Conventions How does the writer use correct grammar, mechanics, and spelling? (Possible responses: It's obvious that the response was carefully edited. There are no pronoun errors to confuse the reader.)

▶ Strategies for Writers Online

Go to **www.sfw.z-b.com** for additional online resources for students, teachers, and parents.

Response to Literature

Using the Rubric to Analyze the Model

Word Choice
- Specific nouns and strong verbs are used to convince the reader.

Toshio names specific animals that Annie and Jack saw in the jungle. He also uses specific words from the book as supporting evidence. I'm glad he defined the word *poachers* to help me understand what it means.

> Unfortunately, poachers—people who hunt illegally—kill too many animals.

Sentence Fluency
- A variety of sentence patterns makes the writing flow smoothly.

Toshio's book review had sentences of different types and lengths. They kept the book review flowing smoothly. I like the conclusion. It contains three very different types of sentences. Each sentence is punctuated for effect.

> Did you know that once animals become extinct they're gone forever? Their future depends on what we do today! Read *Tigers at Twilight* to learn how we can work together to save them.

Tech Tips

Online Tools

Make Digital Posters Work together as a class to transform a written book review or response to literature into a digital (and multimodal) poster using Glogster. With this online tool, you can embed media into a single "page." If doing this for the first time, work with video and images located online, and take time to evaluate how those sources affect the meaning or impact of the larger review poster. Publishers' book trailers, media from film versions of texts, and so on are good sources. Discuss how the choice and arrangement of media speaks to a particular audience. Then spend some time discussing the audience this sort of multimodal review addresses.

See **www.sfw.z-b.com** for further information about and links to these websites and tools.

Conventions
- The writing has been edited carefully.
- Pronouns are used correctly.

Toshio is careful to spell, punctuate, and capitalize correctly in his book review. This example also shows that he used pronouns correctly.

Each book takes Jack and his sister Annie on an adventure. In *Pirates Past Noon*, they go back in time to the days of the Caribbean pirates. In *Tigers at Twilight*, they explore a jungle in India. I enjoyed reading both books.

✛Presentation The use of multimedia strengthens the message.

My Turn!
Now it's my turn to write a response to literature. I'll use the rubric and good writing strategies to help me.

✛Presentation Explain to students that Presentation is just as important as any of the other traits. Neatness is always a priority, and text should be typed. White space should be used to create neat margins and to space correctly the lines of text in each part of the review. Paragraphs should be indented and space should be left between paragraphs for ease of reading. Multimedia presentations should include an attractive visual display, such as illustrations or computer-generated slides, montage, or video.

Think About the Traits

Once students have thoroughly discussed the model response to literature, ask them which traits they think are the most important in a response and have them explain why. **(Possible response: Voice is very important because the writer needs to sound confident and knowledgeable to convince the reader.)**

Differentiating Instruction

ENRICHMENT
Add Visuals Challenge students to create or find visuals that would enhance the response on page 311. Have students present the enhancements to the class. Then have them discuss how visuals heighten the reader's interest in a response.

REINFORCEMENT
Link the Traits to the Model Assist students in linking each trait to the model. For example, read aloud the top descriptor (column 6) for Ideas: *The writer's opinion is clearly stated. Reasons are supported by strong evidence (quotations, paraphrases, facts, or details).* Make sure students can point out the opinion and identify the evidence in the model. Then ask students if they agree that the writer earns a top score for the trait of Ideas.

CCSS **C**ommon **C**ore **S**tate **S**tandards (pp. Z20–Z30)
Writing: W.4.6
Language: L.4.3c
Speaking and Listening: SL.4.1a, SL.4.1b, SL.4.1c, SL.4.1d, SL.4.3, SL.4.6

Write
Response to Literature

Week 2 • Day 1

Student Objectives

- Decide on a topic. *(p. 318)*
- Make a list of details.

Prewrite

Focus on Ideas

Gather Information from Digital and Print Sources Read page 318 aloud. Have students list stories they have read, including ones they have read together in class.

Be sure students have access to the stories, either as handheld books or online. Give them time to refresh their memories of the plot lines, characters, and themes. Have them choose their favorite story on their list. Then have them list the details from that story, as Shamari did.

Take Notes on Source Information Have students record book details they want to use in their responses on note cards.

Writer's Term

Opinion An informed opinion means that it can be backed up by facts and specific examples. Writers need to be prepared to defend their opinions by using strong, verifiable details that convince their audience.

Online Writing Center

 Provides **interactive graphic organizers** as well as a variety of graphic organizers in PDF format.

Prewrite
Focus on (Ideas)

The Rubric Says The writer's opinion is clearly stated.

Writing Strategy Decide on a topic. Make a list of details.

My class has read several books by the same author, Jerry Spinelli. Now my teacher wants us to write a book review about our favorite book. That's easy to decide! I know which one I liked the best.

I'll state my opinion and make some notes to help me get ideas for my essay.

Writer's Term
Opinion
Your **opinion** is what you believe about something. When you state an opinion, be prepared to give reasons for why you think as you do.

Fourth Grade Rats
by Jerry Spinelli
My opinion: <u>Fourth Grade Rats</u> is a great book because it
1. is fun to read
2. makes you laugh
3. teaches an important lesson about growing up

 Write

Choose a book you can recommend to others. Make notes about the book, and tell why it is your favorite.

318 Opinion Writing

English Language Learners

BEGINNING/INTERMEDIATE
Word Choice Remind students that when they draft, they should use strong verbs. Write the following verbs on the board: *like, enjoy, love, adore, admire, favor.* Have students work in pairs using the Continuum Scale to place words in order from boring and weak to strong and convincing.

ADVANCED/ADVANCED HIGH
Using Appositives On the board, write *Some tribes traded wampum for goods.* Ask students if they know what *wampum* is. Revise the sentence to *Some tribes traded wampum—a type of money—for goods.* Tell students that the new information helps the reader understand the vocabulary and is called an appositive. Have students write sentences using appositives for *maize* and *flint.*

The Rubric Says The book review is organized logically.

Writing Strategy Use a Four-Paragraph Organizer to plan the response.

The rubric reminds me to organize my book review logically. A Four-Paragraph Organizer will help me put the proper information in each paragraph.

Writer's Term

Supporting Evidence
Supporting Evidence is a fact or set of facts a writer uses to support an opinion.

Four-Paragraph Organizer

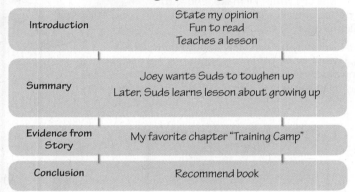

Introduction	State my opinion Fun to read Teaches a lesson
Summary	Joey wants Suds to toughen up Later, Suds learns lesson about growing up
Evidence from Story	My favorite chapter "Training Camp"
Conclusion	Recommend book

Analyze
Look at the graphic organizer. How will it help Shamari write her book review?

Write
Use your notes to make a Four-Paragraph Organizer. Arrange ideas into the four parts of a book review.

Response to Literature **319**

Collaborative Conferencing

PEER TO PEER Have partners exchange their organizers. Tell students to ask the following question as they read them: *What is the book's message or theme?* Tell partners to write their comments on a sticky note and return the organizer with their feedback.

PEER GROUPS Separate students into small groups of three or four. Have each group state one or two reasons for using a Four-Paragraph Organizer to draft a response to literature. Then ask them to share their reasons and revise them based on feedback from other groups.

TEACHER-LED Schedule prewriting conferences. To demonstrate how important the organizer is to writing a good response, create one for one of the books on their list, leaving out the supporting evidence. Discuss how this would weaken the writer's message.

Write
Response to Literature

Student Objectives

• Use a Four-Paragraph Organizer to plan the response. *(p. 319)*

Prewrite

Focus on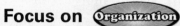

Organize Ideas Explain to students that creating a Four-Paragraph Organizer is a good way to plan the four parts of their response to literature: the introduction, summary, evidence, and conclusion. (Go to **www. sfw.z-b.com** for the downloadable graphic organizers.) Point out the information in each part. Have them use their notes to fill in the organizer. Tell them it's a good idea to include more evidence from the story than they may use in their response. If they cannot find or remember enough details, help them choose another story.

Writer's Term
Supporting Evidence Supporting Evidence is a fact or set of facts the writer uses to support his or her opinion. The supporting evidence is found in the body of a piece of writing.

CCSS **Common Core State Standards** (pp. Z20–Z30)
Writing: W.4.1a, W.4.1b, W.4.1d, W.4.4, W.4.5, W.4.6, W.4.8, W.4.9a, W.4.10
Language: L.4.3a, L.4.3c, L.4.6
Speaking and Listening: SL.4.1a, SL.4.1b, SL.4.1c, SL.4.1d, SL.4.3, SL.4.6

Write
Response to Literature

Week 2 • Day 3

Student Objectives
• Use exact words. (*p. 320*)

Draft

Focus on Word Choice

Draft a Response Read page 320 aloud and ask what it means to draft a response to literature. Be sure students understand that they will use their organizer to write their draft. Explain that students will go through the writing process to create their final copy of writing. Editing is part of the process.

Note: To facilitate editing, proofreading marks are provided as a reference on page 321.

Writer's Term
Word Choice Clear writing uses precise words. Moreover, well-chosen words show that the writer knows and cares about the topic. The conscientious writer consults print and online word resources to find just the "right" word and keeps a word journal to expand his or her writing vocabulary.

Online Writing Center
Provides an **interactive writing pad** for drafting, revising, editing, and publishing.

Draft
Focus on Word Choice

The Rubric Says	Specific nouns and strong verbs are used to convince the reader.
Writing Strategy	Use exact words.

I'm ready to write my draft. I'll use my graphic organizer to get my ideas on paper. The rubric says to use specific nouns and strong verbs. My teacher says that choosing exact words for effect will capture the attention of my audience and hold their interest. If I can't think of the best words as I write, I'll make a note to find better ones in a dictionary or thesaurus later.

As I write my book review about *Fourth Grade Rats*, I won't worry too much about making mistakes. I'll do my best with grammar and spelling, but I know I can fix my mistakes when I edit my writing. Here's my draft.

Writer's Term
Word Choice
Good writers choose words that mean exactly what they want to say and give the right effect. Use specific nouns and strong action verbs in your writing.

Differentiating Instruction

ENRICHMENT
Post It Ask for volunteers to prepare a large, colorful Four-Paragraph Organizer poster for use in class. Tell students to include the parts shown on page 319. Encourage students to refer to it whenever they respond to literature, whether in discussion groups or in writing.

REINFORCEMENT
Read a Review Before writing their drafts, provide students with several examples of short, well-written reviews on books for young readers. Then have pairs of students work together to identify the supporting evidence. After they have identified several examples, ask them to determine whether the review convinced them to read the book. Make sure they can defend their opinions.

[DRAFT]

A Rat Grows Up

"First grade babies! Second grade cats! Third grade angels! Fourth grade rats!" *Fourth Grade Rats* by Jerry Spinelli is a great book. It is about growing up. Joey and Suds are best friends. Joey tries to change Suds into a rat. It is fun to read. It teaches an important lesson about peer pressure. ← *writer's opinion*

Joey is proud of his new ratlike ways. Joey wants Suds to follow his example. Suds doesn't really want to change. He *prefers* being an angel! Suds sees how the other kids look up to Joey. All the girls like him. Suds gives in and lets Joey teach them to be a tough, fearless, and rude rat, just like Joey.

Suds and Joey say some very funny things about food. In my favorite chapter "Training Camp," Joey makes Suds toughen up. It's really funny.

strong verb

Analyze

Read the beginning of Shamari's draft. How closely did she follow her organizer?

Write

Use your Four-Paragraph Organizer to write your draft. Remember to use specific nouns and strong verbs to make your ideas clear.

Response to Literature 321

Collaborative Conferencing

PEER TO PEER Have partners exchange drafts to read. Tell students to think of two or three questions they would like to ask to clarify information or supply missing details. Have them write their questions on sticky notes and affix them to the appropriate places on their partner's draft.

PEER GROUPS Have students work in groups of four. Students pass their draft to the student on the right to read. That student writes one comment or suggestion on a sticky note affixed to the draft and passes the draft along to the right. The review ends when everyone has received his or her own draft back with three comments.

TEACHER-LED Schedule conferences with pairs of students. Have them read each other's draft and coach them in giving and receiving constructive criticism.

Write
Response to Literature

Week 2 • Day 4

Student Objectives

• Complete a draft. *(p. 321)*

Continue Drafting It is important that students are given ample time to write their drafts. As conferencing is important throughout the writing process, be sure to also plan time for peer-to-peer, peer group, or teacher-led conferences. Remind students that this is the time to get their ideas down on paper in a creative and engaging way. Assure them that they will have plenty of time to fix any mistakes later.

CCSS **Common Core State Standards** (pp. Z20–Z30)
Writing: W.4.1b, W.4.4, W.4.5, W.4.6, W.4.9a, W.4.10
Language: L.4.3a, L.4.3c, L.4.4c, L.4.6
Speaking and Listening: SL.4.1a, SL.4.1b, SL.4.1c, SL.4.1d, SL.4.3, SL.4.6

Write
Response to Literature

Student Objectives

- Revise to include information from the book, such as quotations. (p. 322)

Revise

Focus on Ideas

Use Quotations Read page 322 aloud. Explain that when Shamari's writing partner read her draft, he wanted to know more about the story. Shamari's solution not only provides specific information from the book but also provides support for her opinion of the book.

Explain that plagiarism means using the author's words as your own. Tell students they must use quotation marks whenever they include a direct quote from the book. Have students read their drafts and add an example or quotation to clarify and support their main points.

Citing Sources Read aloud the Write feature. Then tell students to write each quotation they will use in their drafts on its own note card, along with the quotation's page number. Tell students they will need to cite the page number for each quotation at the end of their report.

 Strategies for Writers Online
Go to **www.sfw.z-b.com** for additional online resources for students, teachers, and parents.

Revise

Focus on **Ideas**

The Rubric Says   Reasons are supported by strong evidence (quotations, paraphrases, facts, or details).

Writing Strategy   Include information from the book, such as quotations.

I asked Darian to read my draft. He thought that I could add some more information from the story so that readers would understand better why I liked the book so much.

The rubric reminds me to use quotations from the book. I'm going to add one that made me laugh out loud. I'll make sure to put the author's words in quotation marks so my readers will know that they aren't mine. This will support my opinion that the book is fun to read.

[DRAFT]

For example, Joey tells Suds that the worse food tastes, "the faster you grow up." Suds replies, "All I gotta do is go find a dead skunk and eat it and poof, I'll be thirty years old."

Suds and Joey say some very funny things about food. ^

added quotations

Write

Read your draft and revise it by adding quotations that support your response to the story. To avoid plagiarism, be sure to use quotation marks to separate the author's words from yours.

322 Opinion Writing

English Language Learners

BEGINNING/INTERMEDIATE

Using Quotations Tell students to think about the book they are reviewing. Ask, *What was your favorite part?* Model how students might include a quote from the book in their writing. For example, *This part was funny. "The wind sent the family flying!"* Review placement of the exclamation point and quotations marks.

ADVANCED/ADVANCED HIGH

Using Different Kinds of Sentences Tell students they can make their writing more interesting by varying the types of sentences they write. Write the following sentences on the board: *The Native American boy gave water to the horse. The young brave led the horse to a pool of sparkling water.* Ask students which sentence sounds more descriptive. Write other plain sentences on the board, and have students suggest ways to make them more interesting.

Revise

Focus on **Organization**

The Rubric Says Transition words are used effectively.

Writing Strategy Use transitions to show how ideas are related.

Transition words connect one idea to another. When I read the rubric for Organization, I checked my draft for transition words. I found places in the summary where I could use temporal words. Do my revisions help show how the ideas are related?

[DRAFT]

At first,
Suds doesn't really want to change. He prefers being an angel!
Then,
Suds sees how the other kids look up to Joey. All the girls like
Finally,
him. Suds gives in and lets Joey teach them to be a tough,

fearless, and rude rat, just like Joey.

added transition words

Analyze
Look at the transition words Shamari added in the revision. How do they improve the draft?

Write
Read your draft again. Add transition words, such as temporal words, that help to connect ideas.

Response to Literature 323

Collaborative Conferencing

PEER TO PEER Have partners exchange drafts. After reading, ask each student to offer feedback on how to strengthen the piece. If needed, have students consult the model response, the rubric, and the analysis for revising ideas, organization, and sentence fluency.

PEER GROUPS Have students form small groups. Have each student read aloud a section of his or her draft. Ask each group member to offer one suggestion on how to strengthen it. Have writers consult the revising lesson pages in their book to inform their revision.

TEACHER-LED Schedule conferences to read each student's draft. Point out strengths and weaknesses. Talk about ways to improve the draft and inform the revision. If a student seems stalled or discouraged, revisit steps in the process to make improvements and keep going.

Write
Response to Literature

Week 3 • Day 1

Student Objectives

- Revise to use transitions to show how ideas are related. *(p. 323)*

Revise

Focus on

Use Transitions Before reading page 323, have students talk about what it means to use transitions to show how ideas are related. List their responses on the board. (Possible responses: Transitions connect ideas. They guide the reader. They signal the reader that ideas are connected. They tell when events happen.)

Read the page and the draft excerpt aloud. Ask students how Shamari's revisions show how her ideas are related. (Possible responses: Her changes help me follow her ideas. The transitions tell when things happened in the story.) Explain that in the revising step, writers can reorganize and connect ideas so they make sense to the reader.

✎ **Writer's Term** _____
Transition Words In addition to guiding the reader through a text, transition words help sentences flow smoothly. See the list of transitions on page 487.

CCSS **Common Core State Standards** (pp. Z20–Z30)
Writing: W.4.1b, W.4.1c, W.4.4, W.4.5, W.4.9a, W.4.10
Language: L.4.1f, L.4.2b L.4.3c, L.4.6
Speaking and Listening: SL.4.1a, SL.4.1b, SL.4.1c, SL.4.1d, SL.4.3, SL.4.6

Write
Response to Literature

Week 3 • Day 2

Student Objectives

- Revise to combine sentences. (p. 324)

Revise

Focus on  Sentence Fluency

Combine Sentences Read page 324 aloud. Talk about Shamari's reasons for making the changes. Students should agree that the revisions eliminate choppiness and improve the flow of the writing.

Then read the Write feature on the page. Point out that using the same kinds of sentences makes for a boring writing pattern. Encourage students to read their drafts aloud to a partner. Tell partners to listen for too many sentences that share the same pattern or length. Refer students to the model on page 311, the rubric on pages 312–313, and the analysis on page 316. Then give them ample time to improve the flow of their writing.

Revise

Focus on **Sentence Fluency**

The Rubric Says A variety of sentence patterns makes the writing flow smoothly.

Writing Strategy Combine sentences.

The rubric reminded me that my sentences should flow smoothly. I read my draft aloud. I noticed right away that my introduction sounded too choppy. So I revised it. Do you think I improved the flow?

[DRAFT]

"First grade babies! Second grade cats! Third grade angels!

Fourth grade rats!" *Fourth Grade Rats* by Jerry Spinelli is a

great book. ~~It is~~ about growing up. Joey and Suds are best

~~until~~ friends. ~~Joey~~ , makes you laugh, and tries to change Suds into a rat. It is fun to read ~~it~~

—making someone change to fit in the group

teaches an important lesson about peer pressure.

combined sentences

Write

Read your draft aloud, listening for places where the writing sounds choppy. Improve the flow of ideas by combining sentences.

324 Opinion Writing

Optional Revising Lessons

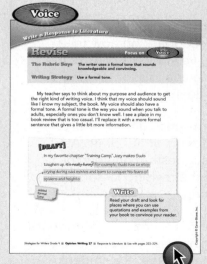

Opinion 27

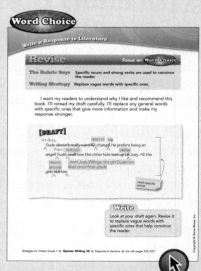

Opinion 28

Go to **Strategies for Writers** at www.sfw.z-b.com

Edit

Focus on Conventions

The Rubric Says	The writing has been edited carefully. Pronouns are used correctly.
Writing Strategy	Check the use of all pronouns.

The rubric reminds me to check my writing carefully. I see a place where I could use pronouns in place of names. I also found an error. I think my changes make my writing clearer.

Writer's Term ____

Pronouns

A **pronoun** is a word that takes the place of one or more nouns. A singular pronoun must replace a singular noun. A plural pronoun must replace a plural noun.

used pronouns correctly

[DRAFT]

I
~~We~~ recommend this book to everyone! You're going to love the

surprise turn at the end of the story. I don't want to spoil it for

you
~~them~~, but both Joey and Suds learn an important lesson about

doing the right thing and what it really means to grow up.

Analyze

Look at Shamari's revisions and edits. What do you think of her sentences? Does she use pronouns correctly?

Write
Conventions

Edit your draft for spelling, punctuation, and capitalization. Check that you have used all pronouns correctly.

For more practice using pronouns correctly, use the exercises on the next two pages.

Response to Literature **325**

Related Grammar Practice ____

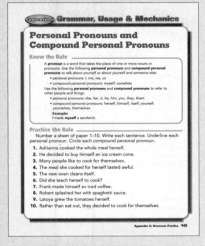

Student Edition page 451

Go to ➡ **Appendix A: Grammar Practice**

Write
Response to Literature

Student Objectives
- Edit for correct use of pronouns. (p. 325)

Edit

Focus on Conventions

Check Pronouns Review the difference between revising (improving text) and editing (correcting text). Tell students that this is the time to go back and correct mistakes in spelling, punctuation, grammar, and capitalization.

Encourage students to use print and online word resources. If they are using word processors, remind them that the spellchecker does not catch every word, especially the spelling of homophones.

Use the mini-lessons on pages T326–T327 for students having problems with using pronouns correctly.

Writer's Term ____

Pronouns Beginning writers may overuse nouns in their writing. This can result in awkward, laborious sentences. Using pronouns efficiently improves the clarity, cadence, and conciseness of one's writing.

CCSS **C**ommon **C**ore **S**tate **S**tandards (pp. Z20–Z30)
Writing: W.4.4, W.4.5, W.4.6, W.4.9a, W.4.10
Language: L.4.1a, L.4.1f L.4.2a, L.4.2d, L.4.4c, L.4.6

Mini-Lesson

Student Objectives

• Use pronouns correctly. (p. 326)

Personal and Possessive Pronouns

Before assigning the practice, have students read the Know the Rule box on page 326. Assist them in matching up personal and possessive pronouns:

Personal	Possessive
I/me	my/mine
you	your/yours
we/us	our/ours
he/him	his
she/her	her/hers
they/them	their/theirs

After completing the practice on this page, have students make a list of pronouns that trip them up from time to time. Remind them to consult the list whenever they are writing to make sure they've used the words correctly.

Online Writing Center

Provides **interactive grammar games** and **practice activities** in student eBook.

T326 Opinion Writing

Personal and Possessive Pronouns

Know the Rule

Personal pronouns can be used in place of names of people and things. **Possessive pronouns** show ownership.

Personal Pronouns
I me you we he him she her they them it

Possessive Pronouns
my your his her its their our ours

Practice the Rule

Number a piece of paper 1–10. Write the pronoun from one of the lists that correctly completes the sentence. Remember to capitalize the first letter if the word begins a sentence.

1. Jeff biked to the library. _____ wanted to check out a book. **He**
2. Jeff found the book and took _____ to the check-out desk. **it**
3. "Can I see _____ library card?" the librarian asked Jeff. **your**
4. Jeff gave the librarian _____ card. **his**
5. Then Jeff saw Lisa. _____ was checking out a book, too. **She**
6. Jeff asked, "What book are _____ going to read?" **you**
7. "*Cliques, Phonies, and Other Baloney*," _____ replied. **she**
8. Jeff had a big smile on _____ face. **his**
9. "I read that book already! Let _____ know what you think!" **me**
10. Jeff and Lisa headed home, eager to read _____ books. **their**

326 Opinion Writing

Related Grammar Practice

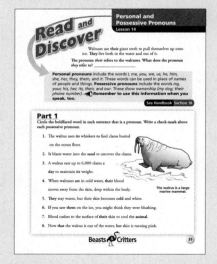

Page 39

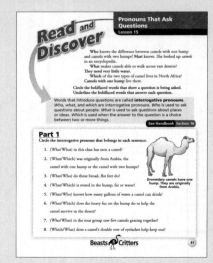

Page 41

Go to ➡ **G.U.M. Student Practice Book**

Relative Pronouns

Know the Rule

Relative pronouns are used to connect one part of a sentence to another part. They make the meaning in the sentence clear. *Who, whose, whom, which,* and *that* are relative pronouns.

Examples:
The students **who** have read *Diary of a Wimpy Kid* love it.
It's the book **that** everyone loves to read.
This book, **which** was published in 2007, is very funny.
I think Jeff Kinney is the author to **whom** you are referring.
He is the author **whose** books are all 224 pages long!

Note: A **relative adverb** (*when, where, why*) sometimes can be used in place of a relative pronoun with a preposition to shorten a sentence and improve the flow, as in this example: *Can you tell me **when** it was published?*

Practice the Rule

Number a piece of paper 1–10. Write the correct relative pronoun to complete each sentence.

1. Every week I go to the library, (that/**which**) is my favorite place to be.
2. *Backpack Stories* is a great book (which/**whose**) author likes to write humorous stories.
3. A book (whom/**that**) I'm interested in is *Adventures in Cartooning*.
4. The girl (**who**/which) recommended it to me loves to draw.
5. Tell me about the books (**that**/who) you recommend.
6. The book (that/**whose**) title interests me is *Bug-a-licious*.
7. It tells about different cultures (whom/**that**) eat bugs.
8. There are people (**who**/whom) think that bugs taste delicious!
9. I like the book *Blueberry Girl,* (who/**which**) has beautiful pictures.
10. Yes, the illustrator of that book is Charles Vess, (that/**who**) is very talented.

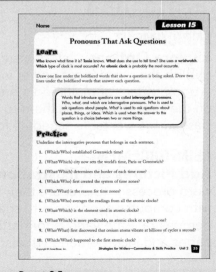

Page 33   Page 35

Go to ➡ Grammar Practice Masters

Student Objectives

• Use relative pronouns correctly. (*p. 327*)

Relative Pronouns

Have students read the Know the Rule on page 327. Then go over the examples for the rule together. Relative pronouns are easily confused, so it's a good idea to provide additional examples before assigning the practice.

I read *Diary of a Young Girl, which* was written by Anne Frank.

The book *that* was written by Anne Frank is still widely read.

Mrs. Paro, *who* loaned me the book, is very kind.

After students feel confident using relative pronouns, assign the practice. Allow them to consult print and online word resources as they make their choices.

CCSS **Common Core State Standards** (pp. Z20–Z30)
Writing: W.4.6
Language: L.4.1a, L.4.1g, L.4.4a, L.4.6

Write
Response to Literature

Student Objectives

- Discuss preparation for publishing and presentation. (p. 328)
- Use a final editing checklist to publish their work. (p. 328)

Publish +Presentation

Publishing Strategy Use Shamari's finished response to discuss publishing and presentation. Ask students to name the presentation elements that make it stand out as a polished piece. (**Possible responses: interesting title; good word processing, indented paragraphs; illustrations**) Tell the class that Shamari's choice is not the only publishing option. Invite students to name other ways they could publish their work.

Have each student use the checklist to prepare the final copy. Encourage them to make a final evaluation of his or her writing before publishing it. Then have students publish copies of their responses in a class book.

Provide a List of Sources

Remind students to include a list of the sources they used to find information about their topics. Provide the citing format guidelines to students to use in their report.

 Strategies for Writers Online
Go to **www.sfw.z-b.com** for additional online resources for students, teachers, and parents.

Publish +Presentation

Publishing Strategy	Present the book review as part of a class-published book.
Presentation Strategy	Make a video to go with the book review.

My book review is finished. I can't wait to publish it! It will be part of a class book called *Our Best Books Ever*. It will be on display in the library for everyone to see.

Before I make a final copy, I have two things to do. One is to find information about the author on the Internet and add it to my review. I think this is great information to share with others who read my review. Then I am going to ask a couple of friends to help me make a video that will be just like a movie trailer. That will really support my claim that *Fourth Grade Rats* is a great book. The video can run on a library computer near the book display.

My teacher says we have to make sure that our reviews are neat and attractive. I'm using a computer to prepare my final copy. I'll set good margins, center the title and my name, and use clear, easy-to-read fonts.

To prepare my final copy, I'll use this checklist.

My Final Checklist
Did I—
- ✔ edit carefully?
- ✔ use pronouns correctly?
- ✔ make a neat final copy?
- ✔ put a title and my name at the top of the page?

Write

Make a checklist to help you prepare your final copy. Accompany your writing with a short video of a favorite scene from the book.

Differentiating Instruction

ENRICHMENT
Explore Options If students explored other ways to publish their responses earlier in the chapter, such as e-book, video, or multimedia presentation, have them vote on the best option. Ask them to present their idea to the class with a workable schedule for completion.

REINFORCEMENT
Add Pictures and Illustrations If students are using a word processor to prepare their final copies, invite those with computer experience to share their finished work and demonstrate the various formatting options for designing pages and incorporating visuals.

A Rat Grows Up
by Shamari

"First grade babies! Second grade cats! Third grade angels! Fourth grade rats!" *Fourth Grade Rats* by Jerry Spinelli is a great book about growing up. Joey and Suds are best friends until Joey tries to change Suds into a rat. It is fun to read, makes you laugh, and teaches an important lesson about peer pressure—making someone change to fit in the group.

Joey is proud of his new ratlike ways, and he wants Suds to follow his example. At first, Suds resists changing. He prefers being an angel! Then, Suds notices how the other kids idolize Joey. All the girls swarm around him, even Judy Billings, the girl Suds has liked since first grade. Finally, Suds gives in and lets Joey teach him to be a tough, fearless, and rude rat, just like Joey.

Suds and Joey say some very funny things about food. For example, Joey tells Suds that the worse food tastes, "the faster you grow up." Suds replies, "All I gotta do is go find a dead skunk and eat it and poof, I'll be thirty years old." In my favorite chapter, "Training Camp," Joey makes Suds toughen up. For example, Suds has to stop crying during sad movies and learn to conquer his fears of spiders and heights.

I recommend this book to everyone! You're going to love the surprise turn at the end of the story. I don't want to spoil it for you, but both Joey and Suds learn an important lesson about doing the right thing and what it really means to grow up.

Analyze

Use the rubric to evaluate Shamari's response to literature and your own response.

Response to Literature **329**

Tech Tips

Websites

Use Online Publishing Sites Several publishers have created online sites for young readers to share reviews and suggested readings with their peers. Scholastic's Share What You're Reading site engages students as readers and writers and presents an authentic opportunity for fairly immediate publishing. Take time to write the actual review outside of the Scholastic site first, as this piece of writing is important enough to draft and consider. Doing so also models a strategy for countering the data loss that can occur when composing directly in the text field on a website.

See **www.sfw.z-b.com** for further information about and links to these websites and tools.

Write
Response to Literature

Student Objectives

- Use a response to literature rubric. *(pp. 312–313)*
- Share a published response to literature. *(p. 329)*

Presentation Strategy Encourage students to use computer programs to make movies or slide shows to accompany their written work. If necessary, arrange time for the technology resource person in your school to instruct students on selected programs. For example, students might ask classmates to act out several very short scenes from the book to create a book trailer, just like the movie trailers that preview a new movie.

Reflecting on a Response to Literature

Ask:

- How has your opinion of the book changed since writing a response to literature?

- What is the best part of your response? Why?

CCSS **C**ommon **C**ore **S**tate **S**tandards (pp. Z20–Z30)

Writing: W.4.4, W.4.6, W.4.9a, W.4.10
Language: L.4.1a, L.4.3c
Speaking and Listening: SL.4.1a, SL.4.1b, SL.4.1c, SL.4.1d, SL.4.3, SL.4.5, SL.4.6

Next Generation Opinion Assessment Planner

WEEK 1

Day 1
Analyze
Part 1: Close Reading

Student Objectives
- Understand the directions for a next generation assessment.
- Analyze a text source and a student response.
- Draw inferences.

Student Activities
- Review and write about taking assessments.
- Read and discuss Part 1 directions. (pp. 330–331)
- Read and discuss Source 1. (pp. 332–333)

Day 2
Analyze
Part 1: Close Reading

Student Objectives
- Analyze a text source and a student response.
- Identify details.
- Analyze a video source and a student response.
- Summarize a video.

Student Activities
- Read and discuss Source 2. (pp. 334–335)
- View and discuss Source 3. (pp. 336–337)

Day 3
Analyze
Part 2: Writing to Multiple Sources

Student Objectives
- Understand the directions for a next generation assessment.
- Understand the scoring guide for a next generation assessment.

Student Activities
- Read and discuss Part 2 directions. (pp. 338–339)
- Read and discuss the scoring guide. (pp. 340–341)

WEEK 2

Day 1
Write
Revise: Organization, Voice

Student Objectives
- Revise to include a concluding statement that is related to the information presented.
- Revise to ensure that the writing has a sincere, convincing voice related to the purpose.

Student Activities
- Read and discuss **Revise: Focus on Organization**. (p. 346)
- Read and discuss **Revise: Focus on Voice**. (p. 347)

Day 2
Write
Revise: Word Choice
Edit: Conventions

Student Objectives
- Revise to include precise language.
- Check the grammar, spelling, capitalization, and punctuation.

Student Activities
- Read and discuss **Revise: Focus on Word Choice**. (p. 348)
- Read and discuss **Edit: Focus on Conventions**. (p. 349)

Note: Optional Revising Lessons are located at **www.sfw.z-b.com**.

Day 3
Review
Publish Final Draft

Student Objectives
- Review a final draft.
- Practice taking a timed assessment.

Student Activities
- Read and discuss final draft. (pp. 350–351)

Day 4	Day 5
Write Prewrite: Ideas, Organization	**Write** Draft: Ideas

Student Objectives
- Respond to the assignment.
- Choose a graphic organizer.

Student Activities
- Read and discuss **Prewrite: Focus on Ideas**. (p. 342)
- Read and discuss **Prewrite: Focus on Organization**. (p. 343)

Student Objectives
- State the opinion in the opening sentence.
- Make sure everything in the editorial supports the opinion.

Student Activities
- Read and discuss **Draft: Focus on Ideas**. (pp. 344–345)

Day 4	Day 5
Practice Next Generation Assessment	**Practice** Next Generation Assessment

Student Objectives
- Practice taking a timed, next generation opinion assessment.

Student Activities
- Complete **Zaner-Bloser Next Generation Assessment** Part 1: Close Reading

Student Objectives
- Practice taking a timed, next generation opinion assessment.

Student Activities
- Complete **Zaner-Bloser Next Generation Assessment** Part 2: Writing to Multiple Sources

To complete the chapter in fewer days, combine the learning objectives and activities in a way that supports students as they write.

Resources at-a-Glance

Differentiating Instruction

For additional Differentiating Instruction activities, see Strategies for Writers Differentiated Instruction Activities at www.sfw.z-b.com.

English Language Learners

Comprehension Mini-Lesson

ZB **Next Generation Assessment Practice**
Opinion assessment practice appears on the *Strategies for Writers* website at **www.sfw.z-b.com**.

 Strategies for Writers Online
Go to **www.sfw.z-b.com** for additional online resources for students, teachers, and parents.

Online Writing Center

Provides IWB resources, assessments, interactive games and practice activities, videos, eBooks, and a virtual file cabinet.

Analyze
Part 1 Directions

Student Objectives

- Understand the directions for a next generation assessment. *(pp. 330–331)*

Opinion Writing Review In this chapter, students will apply what they have learned about opinion writing to the challenge of taking an opinion writing test. Tell them to take a few minutes to write about what they have learned about opinion writing. Then ask volunteers to share their responses with the class.

Taking Assessments Engage students in a discussion of their experiences with taking tests or assessments. Ask questions such as the following to facilitate discussion:

- What do you remember about taking an assessment? (Possible responses: It had a time limit. I ran out of time. It tested all my writing skills.)

- How might you prepare yourself to take a writing assessment? (Possible responses: getting a good night's sleep, having several sharp pencils and an eraser, reading the directions very carefully)

- What advice would you offer someone who is about to take a writing test? (Possible responses: Plan your time. Ask questions.)

 Strategies for Writers Online
Go to **www.sfw.z-b.com** for additional online resources for students, teachers, and parents.

PART 1

Next Generation Opinion Assessment

Writing assessments don't always focus only on writing. Sometimes, they include reading, too. In the reading part, you are asked to read literature or informational texts and answer questions about what you have read. You may have to watch a video and answer a question about it. Then in the writing part, you are asked to write an opinion piece based on what you read.

Now let's analyze each part of this test, so you can really see what the assessment looks like.

PART 1: Close Reading

Your Task
You will examine three sources about people who encouraged others to appreciate and protect birds. Then you will answer three questions about what you have learned. Later, in Part 2, you will write an editorial about choosing a name for a new park that is designed for bird watching.

Steps to Follow
In order to plan and write your editorial, you will do all of the following:
1. Examine three sources.
2. Make notes about the information from the sources.
3. Answer three questions about the sources.

Directions for Beginning
You will have 45 minutes to complete Part 1. You will now examine three sources. Take notes because you may want to refer to your notes while writing your editorial. You can re-examine any of the sources as often as you like. Answer the questions in the spaces provided.

Preparing Students for Next Generation Assessments

Each Next Generation Assessment chapter prepares students to take a performance-based next generation writing assessment. Students will analyze the assignment and a model assessment and learn strategies for taking next generation assessments.

On the last two days of the second week, students take the *Next Generation Assessment Practice* online or as a written test. Explain to students that although the model opinion assessment focuses on writing an editorial, they will write a different genre when they take their practice assessment. In a real test-taking situation, students will not know ahead of time which genre they will be asked to write.

Your Task This section of the directions gives information about the whole test. You will have two parts to complete. In Part 1, you will read and answer questions. In Part 2, you will write an editorial.

Steps to Follow This section reviews the task as a list. It tells how many sources you will examine. You also find out how many questions you have to answer. In this assessment, you will have to examine three sources and answer three questions.

Directions for Beginning This section gives information about Part 1 only—the reading part. You'll need to decide how you want to take notes. Will you write them on a piece of paper or use a note tool online? This section also tells how long you'll have to complete your task. These directions tell you that you have 45 minutes. Divide the time by three, since there are three sources, to figure out how much time to spend on each source.

TEST TIP

To save time, I read the question before I start reading a text or watching a video. You can do this, too. It will help you know what to focus on when you examine a source.

Next Generation Assessment

Tell students that they will be taking different types of assessments in school. Explain that writing assessments used to focus mainly on writing from personal experiences. Add that assessments now include reading passages or watching videos and writing about them. Help students analyze the following three parts of the directions for Part 1: Close Reading:

Your Task The *Your Task* section gives students an overview of what will happen in both Parts 1 and 2 of the assessment.

Steps to Follow The *Steps to Follow* section provides students with steps that they will have to take before they start writing. Remind students that they will be expected to use evidence from the sources they analyze instead of their own personal experiences. Discuss with students how to take notes, either manually or digitally.

Directions for Beginning The *Directions for Beginning* section focuses on what students will have to do in Part 1. Tell students that this is the section that explains how much time they have to complete Part 1. Remind them that it is important to plan how much time they can spend reading or watching each source. Assist students with figuring how much time they should take.

Differentiating Instruction

REINFORCEMENT

Visualize the Task To help visual learners understand the directions for Part 1: Close Reading, model how to draw a diagram that represents each step they will take to complete Part 1. For example, draw three boxes and label them Source 1, Source 2, and Source 3. Ask students to help you complete the diagram to represent the other steps.

CCSS **Common Core State Standards** (pp. Z20–Z30)
Writing: W.4.10
Speaking and Listening: SL.4.1a, SL.4.1b, SL.4.1c, SL.4.1d

Analyze
Source 1: Text

Student Objectives

- Analyze a text source and a student response. *(pp. 332–333)*
- Draw inferences. *(p. 333)*

Close Reading Defined In a close reading, students read and then reread a text purposefully. Students are provided with text-dependent questions that require them to think about what the author had to say, what the author's purpose was, what the words mean, and what the structure of the text tells the reader. Close reading goes beyond simple recall and requires students to think more deeply and critically about what they are reading.

Tell students that they will learn a process they can use when taking an assessment. Add that there are two steps in this close reading process: *First Reading* and *Second Reading*.

First Reading Ask students to read Source 1 independently to understand the main idea. As they read, have students use sticky notes to identify confusing words or ideas. Then discuss the main idea. Have students share their confusing words or ideas.

Strategies for Writers Online
Go to **www.sfw.z-b.com** for additional online resources for students, teachers, and parents.

Source 1: Text

**From *For the Birds: The Life of Roger Tory Peterson*
by Peggy Thomas**

Some people called him a naturalist, artist, photographer, teacher. But he was just Roger. Roger Tory Peterson. And he lived his life for the birds.

In 1943, Roger was drafted into the army. Wearing the plumage of a soldier, Roger moved with his wife, Barbara, to Washington, D.C., where he designed camouflage and illustrated military handbooks. But birds were always on his mind. One day, Roger found a prairie horned lark's nest on the drill field and convinced his captain to change the troop's parade route so the nest would not be disturbed.

Each night he painted bird portraits in the bathroom, because the best light was over the medicine cabinet.

Then the army sent Roger to Florida. For three months, he studied the effects a new pesticide had on birds. Although not much was known about the chemical DDT, Roger warned against its use. It killed insects, a vital food source for birds.

When the war ended, Roger felt that familiar sense of freedom and took flight. He hung over cliffs, submerged himself in swamps, and crouched under canvas to get just the right camera shot. He revised his first field guide and wrote another one for Europe.

By 1954, it was time to make a nest of his own. With his wife and two sons, Roger settled into a house in Old Lyme, Connecticut, surrounded by plenty of wilderness and an abundance of birds. It was there in 1957 that Roger first noticed that something horrible was happening.

"I scanned the marsh through my telescope. I saw the usual number of adults about—but where were the young [ospreys]?"

No osprey eggs hatched that year. Throughout the Northeast, peregrine falcons were also disappearing, and down South, bald eagle nests were empty. Roger and other scientists believed that the cause might be the widespread spraying of DDT, the pesticide he had studied years ago. Someone had to stand up for the birds before they vanished completely.

Comprehension Mini-Lesson

DRAWING INFERENCES

Teach Tell students that readers draw inferences when they come to a conclusion or make a judgment about information in a text. Explain that readers do this by taking what they already know and combining it with what they learn from the text. Discuss that drawing inferences is an important skill because authors do not always directly state information they expect readers to understand; sometimes they may simply hint at the information. Explain that all readers have personal knowledge and experiences they can use to draw inferences while reading and better understand a text.

Model/Practice Model drawing an inference. Use the following example: *One morning while I was getting ready for work, I was listening to the news. I missed the weather*

Along with others, Roger spoke to birders and businessmen, scientists and politicians.

Because he had sparked the world's appreciation for birds, people listened. In 1972, the government banned the use of DDT in the United States.

> **What information do you think Roger Tory Peterson included in his field guides? Use evidence from the text to support your answer.**

 I don't see an exact answer to the question. So I drew an inference from the text. To draw an inference, you need to come up with an answer that makes sense based on the information in the text.

B *I* U abc ≡ ≡ ≡ ≡ ≣ ≣ ↺ ↻ A▾ A▾ ✂ 📋 📋 ABC✓

My Response

I know he was always interested in birds. After the war was over, he spent a lot of time taking pictures of birds. So, I think he included pictures of birds, as well as information about the birds' nests and where the birds lived in his field guides.

Analyze

How well did Shamari use evidence from the text to support her answer? Is there anything she can add?

Second Reading Ask students to reread the text, looking for evidence to answer the text-dependent question listed on page 333: *What information do you think Roger Tory Peterson included in his field guides?* Then discuss students' answers to encourage deeper comprehension. Make sure students support their answers with evidence from the text.

Analyze Response Tell students to review Shamari's response and compare it to their own. Ask them to write answers to the questions in the **Analyze** box, and then have them share their answers with a partner. Ask volunteers to share their responses with the class.

---

report, but at the end of the news, the reporter said, "Don't forget to bring an umbrella." Since I know that you need an umbrella only when it rains, I inferred that it might be rainy that day. I made an inference by combining what I already know with what I learned.

Apply Check for understanding by asking the following question: *How does a reader draw inferences?* (The reader uses clues from the text along with his or her own knowledge to understand what is not directly stated in the text.) Then display the following sentences. *Macy yawned and looked at the clock. It was only 7 P.M. Even so, she got up from the couch and headed upstairs. "I think I'll go to bed early tonight," she said.* Ask: *What inference can you make about Macy?* (Possible response: Macy is very tired.)

CCSS **Common Core State Standards** (pp. Z20–Z30)
Writing: W.4.8, W.4.10
Speaking and Listening: SL.4.1a, SL.4.1b, SL.4.1c, SL.4.1d, SL.4.2

Analyze
Source 2: Text

Week 1 • Day 2

Student Objectives

- Analyze a text source and a student response. *(pp. 334–335)*
- Identify details. *(p. 335)*

First Reading Ask students to read Source 2 independently to understand the main idea. As they read, have students use sticky notes to identify confusing words or ideas. Then discuss the main idea. Have students share their confusing words or ideas.

Strategies for Writers Online

Go to **www.sfw.z-b.com** for additional online resources for students, teachers, and parents.

Source 2: Text

From *On the Frontier with Mr. Audubon*
By Barbara Brenner

October 11, 1820

My name is Joseph Mason.

Most likely you never heard of me. Or of my teacher, Mr. John James Audubon. He is a painter around these parts and teaches drawing to young persons like myself. He also works at the museum here in Cincinnati, where his job is preparing birds for the museum's displays.

Mr. Audubon has a regular passion for birds. He has a notion to paint every bird in America and make a big book or portfolio of them for folks to marvel at. Right now he is planning a trip down the Ohio and Mississippi rivers to search for birds to paint. And now here is where Joseph Mason comes into the picture. John James Audubon has asked me to go with him!

I am to help Mr. Audubon find bird specimens and to do other chores for him as he may need me. In return, he will provide my board and also teach me drawing. I hope to be a painter when I grow up, but while Mr. Audubon's specialty is birds, mine is plants and flowers.

Both Mr. Audubon and I like nothing better than to hunt and fish and tramp through the woods; we are much alike in that. I think that may be why Mr. Audubon chose me to go on this trip with him.

October 20, 1820

Today it rained so hard that we were forced to stay in the cabin. After we drew for a while and Mr. A. showed me some tricks with color and shading, we sat and talked. Mr. Audubon told me some things about his life that he has told no one else. I'm glad he chose me to tell his tale to; Mr. Audubon is a born storyteller. Listening to him is better than reading from the most exciting book.

John James Audubon was born on the island of Santo Domingo. His father, who was a French sea captain, had a plantation there. His mother died very soon after he was born. I think from what he doesn't say that Mr. Audubon's mother and father weren't married. When he was three he went to France, where his father's wife took him for her son and raised him with love and devotion.

Comprehension Mini-Lesson

IDENTIFY DETAILS

Teach Tell students that details are pieces of information that help explain or prove the main idea in a text. Explain that details often help us create a picture in our minds of what is being described in the text. Discuss that a text can have both major and minor details. Explain that major details support the main idea, while minor details tell more specific information about the major details.

Model/Practice Model identifying major and minor details: *In a paragraph I recently read about space travel, the main idea was that space travel has allowed people to discover places beyond Earth. One major detail that supports this idea was that astronauts have explored the moon. This major detail was then supported by these minor details: Neil Armstrong was the first person to walk on the moon, and several astronauts have conducted experiments there. These*

> I think that Mr. Audubon was rich when he was young. He tells me of parties and servants and a house in the country where he first became interested in birds. He said he used to sneak off into the woods to watch birds when he should have been in school. He had a fine collection of birds' nests and eggs by the time he was ten years old.
>
> One thing that happened when he was a little boy seems to have had a deep effect on him. There was a pet monkey in his house. Also a beautiful parrot. One day the monkey killed the bird in a fit of jealousy. Mr. Audubon never forgot it; he was heartbroken for the bird.
>
> "But you kill birds all the time," I said to him. "If you love them so much, why do you kill them?"
>
> "What I kill I use for my work or to feed us," he said. "If I could draw my birds without killing them, I surely would."

How do you know that John James Audubon had a strong interest in birds? Identify two examples from the text.

I could only remember one example from the text. I will need to reread the text to find another example. While I reread, I will also make sure that I remembered the other example correctly.

B *I* U abc ≡ ≡ ≡ ≣ ≔ ≔ ↰ ↱ A⁻ A⁻ ✂ 🗐 🗐 🗹

My Response

He wanted to paint all the birds in America. Also, he created museum displays that had birds in them.

Analyze

How well did Shamari use evidence from the text to support her answer? Is there anything she can add?

---

minor details give me more information about one major detail, which in turn supports the main idea of the passage.

Apply Recall two kinds of details discussed in this lesson: major details and minor details. Have a volunteer explain each type of detail. (Major details support the main idea; minor details support a major detail.) Read aloud the following text or write it on the board: *Hiking is an amazing experience. We hiked all morning to the top of the mountain, where we saw the surrounding mountain range for miles and miles. The mountains contained rolling hills of green spruce trees and rock formations.*

Ask students to identify the main idea in the paragraph. (Hiking is an amazing experience.) Then ask them to identify which major and minor details support it. (Possible response: **Major Detail:** We saw the surrounding mountain range for miles and miles; **Minor Details:** Mountains contained rolling hills of green spruce trees and rock formations.)

Second Reading Ask students to reread the text, looking for evidence to answer the text-dependent question listed on page 335: *How do you know that John James Audubon had a strong interest in birds?* Then discuss students' answers to encourage deeper comprehension. Make sure students support their answers with evidence from the text.

Analyze Response Tell students to review Shamari's response and compare it to their own. Ask them to write answers to the questions in the **Analyze** box, and then have them share their answers with a partner. Ask volunteers to share their responses with the class.

CCSS **Common Core State Standards** (pp. Z20–Z30)
Writing: W.4.8, W.4.10
Speaking and Listening: SL.4.1a, SL.4.1b, SL.4.1c, SL.4.1d, SL.4.2

Analyze
Source 3: Video

Student Objectives

- Analyze a video source and a student response. *(pp. 336–337)*
- Summarize a video. *(pp. 336–337)*

Examining Video Sources Tell students that on some assessments they may be asked to listen to audio or watch a video. Explain that they can use the close reading process that they have learned, but they need to be watchful of how much time they have to complete Part 1. For example, they may not have enough time to watch a video more than once. If students are running out of time, remind them about the Test Tip Shamari gave on page 331 that suggests they read the question first before examining the source.

First Viewing As a class, view Source 3, *Friends of Feathers,* to understand the main idea. If students are using an ebook, ask them to view the video independently. As they watch, have students take notes to identify confusing words or ideas. Then discuss the main idea. Have students share their confusing words or ideas.

 View the video at **www.sfw.z-b.com/video/g4.**

 **Strategies for Writers Online**
Go to **www.sfw.z-b.com** for additional online resources for students, teachers, and parents.

Source 3: Video

View the video at www.sfw.z-b.com/video/g4.

Friends of Feathers

How did the people in the video help protect birds? Write a summary using three details from the video.

TEST TiP

If you aren't sure how to spell a person's name, a place, or a group mentioned in a video, try the best you can to spell it correctly. Your score in Part 1 depends on whether you answer the question correctly, not on how well you can spell proper nouns.

Comprehension Mini-Lesson

SUMMARIZE

Teach Explain to students that summarizing is retelling the most important parts of a text. Note that summaries should be in students' own words. Recall that summaries should be brief and should include only the basic points and main characters of a story or the key ideas and supporting details of a text. Emphasize that summarizing requires students to use many strategies and skills.

Model/Practice Model how to summarize a text. *After I read a chapter or a section of a text, I summarize what I read in my own words. I tell about only the most important points, not every detail or fact. Summarizing helps me better understand and remember what I have read. For example, after I read a chapter about the physical characteristics of*

This question asked me to identify three details from the video. Because I have about 15 minutes to answer this question, I can watch the video again. When I hear a detail that answers the question, I will click the pause button so I can type it in the space provided. I will repeat this plan until I have identified all three details. I think this will help me write my summary quickly.

B *I* U abc ≡ ≡ ≡ ≡ ≣ ≣ ↶ ↷ A▾ A▾ ✂ 📋 📋 ✓

My Response

Many people helped protect birds. Harriet Hemenway and Minna Hall held tea parties and convinced women to stop wearing feathered hats. Also, they formed the Massachusetts Audubon Society, which worked to get laws passed to keep birds safe. And in 1903, Congress passed laws to protect birds.

Analyze

Do you think Shamari's plan was effective? Is there another way to watch the video and save time?

Next Generation Assessment **337**

---

camels, I summarized it by stating that camels have tough skin and woolly fur to protect them from the sand and sun in the desert. This was the most important information in the chapter.

Ask students what type of information they should include in a summary. (Possible response: answers to *who, what, when, where,* and *why* questions.)

Apply Read aloud a short text of your choosing. Pause at certain points, and invite volunteers to summarize the information. Remind students that their summaries should be brief and in their own words. Then, after you have finished reading, have students work in groups to write a brief summary of the entire text.

Second Viewing Ask students to review the video, listening for evidence to answer the text-dependent question listed on page 336: *How did the people in the video help protect birds?* Then discuss students' answers to encourage deeper comprehension. Make sure students support their answers with evidence from the video.

Analyze Response Tell students to review Shamari's response and compare it to their own. Ask them to write answers to the questions in the **Analyze** box, and then have them share their answers with a partner. Ask volunteers to share their responses with the class.

CCSS **Common Core State Standards** (pp. Z20–Z30)
Writing: W.4.8, W. 4.10
Speaking and Listening: SL.4.1a, SL.4.1b, SL.4.1c, SL.4.1d, SL.4.2

Analyze
Part 2 Directions

Student Objectives

- Understand the directions for a next generation assessment. (pp. 338–339)

Next Generation Assessment

Ask students to read the paragraph at the top of page 338. Then help them analyze the following two parts of the directions for Part 2: Writing to Multiple Sources:

Setup The *Setup* section focuses on what students will do in Part 2. Tell students that this is the section that tells them how much time they have to complete Part 2. Explain that they can plan their time based on the stages of the writing process. Ask students if they agree with the amount of time Shamari has assigned to each part of the writing process.

Make sure students understand that when they take an assessment they will be allowed to go back to Part 1 to examine the sources again, but they cannot change their answers to the questions in Part 1. Remind them that the more time they spend re-examining sources, the less time they will have to write.

Strategies for Writers Online
Go to **www.sfw.z-b.com** for additional online resources for students, teachers, and parents.

Next Generation Opinion Assessment

Now that Part 1 is complete, it's time to write the editorial. Usually you will complete Part 1 on one day and Part 2 on the next day. The directions for Part 2 are longer than Part 1 and continue on a second page. So remember to read the directions carefully and ask questions if you don't understand.

PART 2: Writing to Multiple Sources

Setup
You will now have 70 minutes to review your notes and sources, plan, draft, and revise an editorial. You may use your notes and refer to the sources. You may also refer to the answers you wrote to questions in Part 1, but you cannot change those answers. Now read your assignment and the information about how your editorial will be scored. Then begin your work.

Your Assignment
A new park designed for bird watching will be opening in your community soon. The city council is considering naming the park after Roger Tory Peterson, John James Audubon, or Harriet Hemenway and Minna Hall. Your assignment is to write an editorial for the newspaper explaining which of the three choices is best and why. Support your position with concrete details and examples from each of the sources you have examined. The audience for your editorial will be the people in your community.

English Language Learners

BEGINNING/INTERMEDIATE

Part 2 Directions Have students look at the *Setup* section. Select a few key words that students will not know. As you say each word, have students point to the word and repeat it. Write the word on the board and say it again. Elicit the meaning of each word or teach its meaning if students cannot provide it. Repeat the process with important words from *Your Assignment*. Finally, simplify the writing prompt. Explain Shamari's task so that students will understand what she is doing as she works through the opinion test writing process.

Repeat the process with students before they begin their own next generation opinion assessment.

Setup This section lets you know how much time you have to complete Part 2. You can divide the time into the different parts of the writing process. Here's an example of what Shamari plans to do.

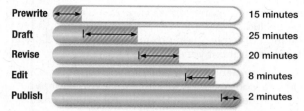

Prewrite	15 minutes
Draft	25 minutes
Revise	20 minutes
Edit	8 minutes
Publish	2 minutes

The directions also tell you that you can go back and examine the sources from Part 1, but the answers can't be changed.

Your Assignment This part explains your writing assignment. The topic of your assignment usually appears in the first few sentences in this section. In this case, it's the first three sentences. Finally, you are given a clue to what kind of voice you should use in your editorial. Because your audience is the people in your community, you should use a serious and knowledgeable voice.

Your Assignment The *Your Assignment* section provides students with specific information about the topic, genre, and audience for their assignment. Remind students that the topic and genre were introduced in Part 1 of the test. Ask them to go back to the directions for Part 1 to identify the sections where the topic and genre were mentioned.

Point out the following sentence to students from the *Your Assignment* section on page 338: *Support your position with concrete details and examples from each of the sources you have examined.* Make sure students understand that their writing should be based on information from the sources they have examined, not on their personal experiences.

ADVANCED/ADVANCED HIGH
Part 2 Directions Have students read the *Your Assignment* section and write three to six words or phrases that they think are most important. Then have each student compare with a partner and discuss the meanings of the words and phrases. After they have discussed their ideas, help them verify actual meanings using dictionaries. Further assist them by offering examples of your own. Have the partners outline the task that Shamari will follow during the opinion test writing process.

Have students repeat this process before they start their own next generation opinion assessment.

CCSS **Common Core State Standards** (pp. Z20–Z30)
Writing: W.4.8
Speaking and Listening: SL.4.1a

Analyze
Part 2
Scoring Guide

Week 1 • Day 3

Student Objectives

- Understand the scoring guide for a next generation assessment. *(pp. 340–341)*

Analyze the Scoring Guide Direct students' attention to the Scoring Guide on page 340. Tell students that the scoring guide helps them plan and evaluate their writing. Help students understand how the scoring guide is similar to the rubrics they have seen by asking questions such as the following:

Which section

- focuses on presenting clear ideas? (second)

- focuses on using logical organization? (first)

- helps you improve your tone and convince the reader? (second)

- encourages you to improve your sentence fluency? (first)

- reminds you to edit your writing? (third)

Scoring Guide

Your editorial will be scored on the following criteria:

1. **Statement of purpose/focus and organization** How well did you introduce your topic? How well did you use different lengths of sentences? How well did you group related information in paragraphs? How well did you provide a concluding statement or section that is related to the information or explanation presented? How well did you stay on topic throughout your editorial?

2. **Elaboration of evidence** How well did you support your opinion with reasons or other examples? How well did you use precise language that is appropriate for your audience and purpose? How well did you use a sincere, convincing voice that matches the purpose of your editorial?

3. **Conventions** How well did you follow the rules of grammar, punctuation, capitalization, and spelling?

Now begin work on your editorial. Manage your time carefully so that you can:
- plan your editorial.
- write your editorial.
- revise and edit for a final draft.

Spell check is available to use.

Type your response in the space provided on the following page. Write as much as you need to fulfill the requirements of the task. You are not limited by the size of the response area on the screen.

340 Opinion Writing

Strategies for Writers Online
Go to **www.sfw.z-b.com** for additional online resources for students, teachers, and parents.

Writing Traits in the Scoring Guide

The second page of the directions tells you how your editorial will be scored. This scoring guide includes all of the writing traits. You can use what you have learned about the writing traits to help you write an effective editorial.

1 Focus and organization

• How well did you use different lengths of sentences?

• How well did you provide a concluding statement?

2 Elaboration of evidence

• How well did you support your opinion with reasons or other examples?

• How well did you use a sincere, convincing voice that matches the purpose of your editorial?

• How well did you use precise language that is appropriate for your audience and purpose?

3 Conventions

• How well did you follow the rules of grammar, punctuation, capitalization, and spelling?

Before you start Part 2, review your plan for how you will divide your time. Remember there is no word limit, but don't feel you have to fill the entire space with your thoughts. Now it's time for Shamari to start writing her editorial.

Writing Traits in the Scoring Guide

Direct students' attention to the information about the scoring guide. Tell students that some scoring guides do not include the names of the six traits, but they still relate to each of the traits. Students can use their writing experience to remember the main requirements associated with each trait:

Ideas a clear point of view, supported by strong reasons and evidence from credible sources

Organization logical organization that includes helpful transitions that guide the reader

Voice a voice that sounds convincing and appropriate for both purpose and audience

Word Choice language that is precise and supports the writer's purpose

Sentence Fluency sentences that flow well with a variety of patterns and lengths

Conventions conscientious editing for grammar, spelling, capitalization, and punctuation

CCSS Common Core State Standards (pp. Z20–Z30)
Writing: W.4.6
Speaking and Listening: SL.4.1a, SL.4.1c, SL.4.1d

Write
Prewrite

Week 1 • Day 4

Student Objectives

• Respond to the assignment.
  (p. 342)

Prewrite

Focus on **Ideas**

Gather Information Tell students that when they take an assessment they will need to gather evidence, such as facts and examples, from the three sources that they examined in Part 1 to support their opinion. Remind students that they will be allowed to go back and review the sources, but they cannot change their answers to the questions.

Prewrite

Focus on Ideas

Writing Strategy Respond to the assignment.

Prewrite ←→ [_____] 15 minutes

 Writers gather information to help them write. This is a key step when you write for an assessment. You can gather a lot of information from the directions. Take another look at the assignment in the directions. The assignment explains what you are supposed to write.

From my assignment, I know I'm supposed to write an editorial. I also know the topic.

> **topic**
> A new park designed for bird watching will be opening in your community soon. The city council is considering naming the park after Roger Tory Peterson, John James Audubon, or Harriet Hemenway and Minna Hall. Your assignment is to write an editorial for the newspaper explaining which of the three choices is best and why.
> **genre**

First, I'm going to write a sentence stating my opinion. Then, I'll think about which of the sources will support my opinion. I can't remember all the details about the sources, but I just want to see what I remember.

My Opinion:
  The park should be named after John James Audubon.
Sources that Support My Opinion:
  The story about John James Audubon and his passion for birds
  The video about Minna Hall and Harriet Hemenway

342 Opinion Writing

Differentiating Instruction

ENRICHMENT

Create Your Assignment Challenge students to write their own opinion assessment assignment, using the model assignment on page 338 to guide them. Then have them exchange assignments and respond by writing a clear opinion statement like Shamari did on page 342.

Online Writing Center

 Provides **interactive graphic organizers** as well as a variety of graphic organizers in PDF format.

Prewrite
Focus on **Organization**

Writing Strategy   Choose a graphic organizer.

Prewrite ←→ [⬚] 15 minutes

I need to start organizing my ideas. A good graphic organizer for an editorial is a Network Tree. It will help me identify evidence from the sources in Part 1 to support my opinion. I may want to go back now and examine the sources again so I can get more specific.

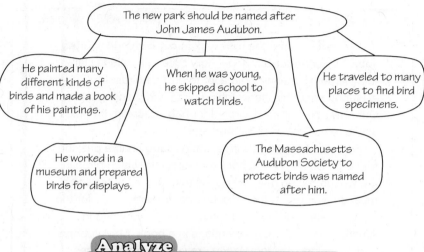

The new park should be named after John James Audubon.

He painted many different kinds of birds and made a book of his paintings.

When he was young, he skipped school to watch birds.

He traveled to many places to find bird specimens.

He worked in a museum and prepared birds for displays.

The Massachusetts Audubon Society to protect birds was named after him.

Analyze

Does the graphic include enough evidence to support Shamari's opinion? Is there anything she left out?

Next Generation Assessment 343

Differentiating Instruction

REINFORCEMENT
Break Down Your Assignment Read aloud *Your Assignment* on page 338. Ask students to explain in their own words what it means. If needed, guide them in restating the directions, possibly by breaking the assignment into a bulleted list so that the meaning is clear. Encourage them to use this strategy whenever they are given an opinion assessment.

Write
Prewrite

Week 1 • Day 4

Student Objectives
• Choose a graphic organizer. *(p. 343)*

Prewrite

Focus on **Organization**

Analyze Graphic Organizer After students have reviewed Shamari's Network Tree, have them write responses to the questions in the **Analyze** box. Then have them share their responses with a partner. Ask volunteers to share their responses with the class. Tell students that in a test-taking situation a graphic organizer may not be given to them. Explain that they will need to choose one on their own that best suits their assignment. Encourage students to fill in a graphic organizer completely to help them draft their writing during an assessment.

CCSS **Common Core State Standards** (pp. Z20–Z30)
Writing: W.4.1a, W.4.1b, W.4.6, W.4.10
Speaking and Listening: SL.4.1a, SL.4.1c, SL.4.1d

Write
Draft

Student Objectives

- State the opinion in the opening sentence.
- Make sure everything in the editorial supports the opinion. *(pp. 344–345)*

Draft

Focus on Ideas

Drafting on Paper Remind students that they may take tests on paper or on a computer. If they take the test on paper, remind them to write on every other line. This leaves space for students to make their corrections when they revise and edit their drafts. Mention that in a timed situation, students will not have time to create a fresh final copy of their writing.

Drafting on a Computer If students take the test on a computer, tell them that they should make sure they know where the Save button is. Encourage students to save often. If they cannot find the Save button, explain that there might be an auto-save, but they should check with the adult monitoring the test. Point out the wavy lines in Shamari's draft. Ask students if they know what the wavy lines mean. (The word is misspelled.)

 Strategies for Writers Online
Go to **www.sfw.z-b.com** for additional online resources for students, teachers, and parents.

Draft   Focus on   Ideas

Writing Strategy State your opinion in the opening sentence. Make sure everything in your editorial supports your opinion.

Draft |◄———————►| 25 minutes

 A good editorial lets the reader know the writer's point of view right away. So I'll state my opinion. Next I'll use my Network Tree as a guide for writing the body of my editorial. It reminds me of the reasons that support my opinion.

my opinion

B I U abc ☰ ☰ ☰ ☷ ☰ ↩ ↪ A⁺ A▾ ✂ 🗐 📋 ✓

We should name the new park in our community after John James Audubon. Roger Tory Peterson, Minna Hall, and Harriet Hemenway did a lot to protect birds. Mr. Audubon spent his life watching birds and painting them. Our new park will be designed for bird watching. It makes sense to name it after Mr. Audubon.

From the time he was little, Mr. Audubon had a passion for birds. He skipped school sometimes to watch birds in the woods. When he grew up, he became a painter and a museum worker. At the museum, he prepared birds for the displays. He really, really wanted to paint every bird in America and include his paintings in a book. Mr. Audubon and his helper, Joseph Mason, traveled to many places to find bird specimens. They spent a lot of time painting and drawing the birds they found.

English Language Learners

BEGINNING

Stating Opinions Using the *Your Assignment* section from the opinion assessment on page 338, ask students to give their opinions. Ask, *Who do you think the new park should be named after?* Help them create a simple sentence to clearly state their opinions. For example, *I think the new park should be named after Roger Tory Peterson.*

INTERMEDIATE

Supporting Opinions Have students work with a partner to reread Shamari's draft and identify the reasons she gives to support her opinion. Have them explain how the reasons support her opinion. Ask questions to generate responses, such as, *What reason does she give? Why does she give that reason?* Remind students that when they write an opinion piece, they must include reasons to support their opinion.

B *I* <u>U</u> abc ≡ ≡ ≡ ≡ ⬅ ➡ A⌄ A⌄ ✂ 📋 📋 ABC✓

Its true that Roger Tory Peterson helped protect birds by warning <u>agenst</u> the use of DDT. Minna Hall and Harriet Hemenway also helped birds They held tea <u>partys</u> and <u>convincd</u> people to stop wearing hats with feathers. They even created a society to protect birds. It was named after Mr. Audubon.

Analyze

Does the editorial begin with a clear statement of Shamari's opinion? Does all the information that follows support her opinion?

Next Generation Assessment 345

ADVANCED/ ADVANCED HIGH

Writing Opinions Have students use the Network Tree that Shamari created to write a paragraph or two. Monitor as they write to make sure they are beginning with the main idea, or what they want to convince their reader to think or do. After students have written their paragraph(s), have them trade with another student. Partners should review the draft and look for specific details. Remind students that the rest of the editorial should include strong sentences that support the writer's opinions.

Use a Graphic Organizer Remind students that during an assessment they should keep their graphic organizer out as they draft and refer to it frequently. If new evidence occurs to students while they draft, they should consider including it, especially if it supports their opinion. If students cannot decide where the new evidence belongs on the organizer, they should probably not use it in their writing.

Support an Opinion After students have reviewed Shamari's draft, have them write responses to the questions in the **Analyze** box. Then have them share their responses with a partner. Ask volunteers to share their responses with the class. As students draft during an assessment, tell them to pay attention to presenting and supporting their reasons logically. Have them ask themselves:

- Have I stated my opinion (purpose for writing) clearly in the beginning sentence?

- Do I present each reason in its own paragraph?

- Do I support each reason with relevant facts and examples?

CCSS **Common Core State Standards** (pp. Z20–Z30)
Writing: W.4.1b, W.4.9b, W.4.10
Speaking and Listening: SL.4.1a, SL.4.1c, SL.4.1d

Write
Revise

Week 2 • Day 1

Student Objectives

- Revise to include a concluding statement that is related to the information presented. *(p. 346)*

Revise

Focus on  Organization

Time Management Point out that Shamari had about twenty minutes to revise her draft and that there were three revision tasks. (If you are using the Optional Revising Lessons, you will need to plan time for these. See page T348.) Tell students that Shamari divided her planned revising time into three six- to seven-minute segments and revised for one strategy at a time. Explain to students that they may not have enough time to revise for all traits during an assessment, so they should focus on the traits they know they usually need help with.

Analyze Revision After students have reviewed Shamari's concluding section, have them write responses to the questions in the **Analyze** box. Then have them share their responses with a partner. Ask volunteers to share their responses with the class.

 Strategies for Writers Online
Go to **www.sfw.z-b.com** for additional online resources for students, teachers, and parents.

Revise   Focus on **Organization**

Writing Strategy   Make sure you provide a concluding statement that is related to the information presented.

Revise |←——→| 20 minutes

Now, it's time to check my draft against the scoring guide. I want to be sure I've included all the points that will be scored.

The scoring guide reminds me to provide a concluding statement or section that is related to the information that I presented. I noticed that I didn't include a concluding section. I just ended with my last piece of evidence. I'll add a few sentences at the end and make sure that they relate to my opinion and the evidence I used.

> Its true that Roger Tory Peterson helped protect birds by warning agenst the use of DDT. Minna Hall and Harriet Hemenway also helped birds They held tea partys and convincd people to stop wearing hats with feathers. They even created a society to protect birds. It was named after Mr. Audubon.
>
> For these reasons, I believe we should name our new park after Mr. Audubon. I can't wait to go bird watching in the John James Audubon Park!

concluding section

Analyze

Do you think Shamari's concluding section makes sense with the rest of her editorial? Is there anything else she could do to improve the organization?

Revise
Focus on **Voice**

Writing Strategy   Use a sincere, convincing voice that matches the purpose of your editorial.

Revise |←——→| 20 minutes

Since the purpose of my editorial is to get my readers to agree with me, I need to sound confident and knowledgeable from beginning to end. When I read my draft again, I noticed that I sounded too casual in my second paragraph.

> **B** *I* <u>U</u> abc ≡ ≡ ≡ ≡ ≔ ≔ ↶ ↷ A▾ A▾ ✂ ▣ ▣ ✓
>
> From ~~the time he was little~~ an early age, Mr. Audubon had a passion for birds. He skipped school sometimes to watch birds in the woods. When he grew up, he became a painter and a museum worker. At the museum, he prepared birds for the displays. He ~~really, really wanted~~ decided to paint every bird in America and include his paintings in a book.
>
> *improved voice*

Analyze

How does the revision improve Shamari's voice? Does she sound more knowledgeable?

Differentiating Instruction

REINFORCEMENT

Support Voice Remind students that voice is the way the writer "speaks" to the reader through his or her writing. To be effective, the writer's voice should suit the purpose and the audience. Help students "hear" Shamari's voice by reading her editorial aloud with expression and phrasing. Students should agree that Shamari's voice speaks directly to the reader in a sincere, convincing way.

Write
Revise

Week 2 • Day 1

Student Objectives

- Revise to ensure that the writing has a sincere, convincing voice related to the purpose. *(p. 347)*

Revise

Focus on   Voice

Review Voice Remind students that their voice should sound convincing all the way through an editorial. When taking an assessment, tell students that their conclusion should sound just as convincing as the introduction.

Analyze Revision After students have read Shamari's revisions, have them write responses to the questions in the **Analyze** box. Then have them share their responses with a partner. Ask volunteers to share their responses with the class.

CCSS **C**ommon **C**ore **S**tate **S**tandards (pp. Z20–Z30)
Writing: W.4.1d, W.4.10
Speaking and Listening: SL.4.1a, SL.4.1c, SL.4.1d

Write
Revise

Student Objectives

- Revise to include precise language. *(p. 348)*

Revise

Focus on

Review Precise Language Read aloud the Writing Strategy and the introduction to page 348. Then ask a volunteer to read Shamari's draft twice, once without the revision, and then with Shamari's changes. Students should agree that Shamari's word choice makes her meaning clearer. Tell students that if Shamari had time left in the revising period, she could have checked for other traits, such as **Ideas** and **Sentence Fluency**. When students are taking an assessment, encourage them to use every minute remaining to improve their writing, even if they think they are finished.

Analyze Revision After students have read Shamari's revisions, have them write responses to the questions in the **Analyze** box. Then have them share their responses with a partner. Ask volunteers to share their responses with the class.

Online Writing Center

Provides **interactive proofreading activities** for each genre.

Revise　　Focus on **Word Choice**

Writing Strategy Use precise language that is appropriate for your audience and purpose.

Revise ◄———► 20 minutes

 The scoring guide reminds me to use precise language that is appropriate for my audience and purpose. I'll read my draft again. I noticed that there are a few places where I could replace a word or phrase with a more precise word or phrase. This will make my editorial easier to read and understand.

> Its true that Roger Tory Peterson helped protect birds by warning agenst the use of DDT, a chemical that was killing birds. Minna Hall and Harriet Hemenway also helped birds They held tea partys and convincd ~~people~~ other women in their community to stop wearing hats with feathers. They even created a society to protect birds called the Massachusetts Audubon Society. It was named after Mr. Audubon.

added precise language

Analyze

Did Shamari use precise language in her revision? Are there any other sections of her draft that could use more precise language?

Optional Revising Lessons

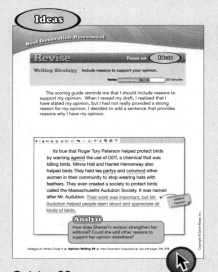

Opinion 29

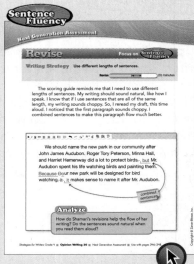

Opinion 30

Go to ➡ *Strategies for Writers* at www.sfw.z-b.com.

Edit — Focus on Conventions

Writing Strategy Check the grammar, spelling, capitalization, and punctuation.

Edit ▭▭▭▭▭▭ ⟷ 8 minutes

The scoring guide reminds me to check and correct my grammar and spelling. To save time, I can use the spell-check feature. I also need to make sure that I've used capitalization and punctuation correctly. It's a good thing that I planned how to use my time. Now I have time to check for errors.

~~Its~~ It's true that Roger Tory Peterson helped protect birds by warning ~~agenst~~ against the use of DDT, a chemical that was killing birds. Minna Hall and Harriet Hemenway also helped birds. They held tea ~~partys~~ parties and ~~convined~~ convinced other women in their community to stop wearing hats with feathers. They even created a society to protect birds called the Massachusetts Audubon Society. It was named after Mr. Audubon.

corrected spelling

corrected punctuation

TEST TIP
Spell-checking doesn't catch all your errors like homophones or misused words. Always reread your writing after you use the spell-check feature.

Differentiating Instruction

ENRICHMENT
Time to Edit Enthusiastic writers who finish early may fall into the habit of waiting for the assessment period to end. Suggest some strategies they can practice, such as reading their writing quietly to themselves to check for voice and fluency, or reading their drafts "backwards" to check for misspellings.

Write
Edit

Week 2 • Day 2

Student Objectives
• Check the grammar, spelling, capitalization, and punctuation. *(p. 349)*

Edit

Focus on Conventions

Editing Review and discuss the corrections Shamari made. Explain that while an editorial written for an assessment in a short period of time will rarely be perfect, students should correct as many errors as possible. Assessment graders know that students are writing quickly and watching the clock, so a few errors may slip through. However, assessment graders also look for evidence that students took time to edit. When they see misspelled words crossed out and correctly spelled words inserted instead, assessment graders know that students are paying attention to editing. If students are taking assessments online, they may not be able to show their edits. If they see wavy lines still remaining in their writing, this means that they have misspelled words. Tell them to check the spelling of these words by using the spell-check feature.

CCSS Common Core State Standards (pp. Z20–Z30)
Writing: W. 4.4, W.4.5, W.4.6, W.4.9b, W.4.10
Language: L.4.2a, L.4.2d, L.4.3a
Speaking and Listening: SL.4.1a, SL.4.1c, SL.4.1d

Review
Final Draft

Week 2 • Days 3–5

Student Objectives

- Review a final draft.
- Practice taking a timed assessment.
  (pp. 350–351)

Publish

Publishing an Assessment

Review Shamari's final draft with students. If students take an online assessment, they should always use the spell-check feature one more time before they submit their work. If they take an assessment on paper, they should read through their work one final time before they submit it.

Write About What You Learned

Ask students to write about taking a next generation assessment, including the steps you have to take and how to manage your time. When they are done, lead a discussion about what they wrote using questions such as the following:

- What is the difference between Part 1 and Part 2? (Possible response: Part 1 is reading texts or watching videos. Part 2 is writing about the things you read or watched in Part 1.)

▶ Strategies for Writers Online
Go to **www.sfw.z-b.com** for additional online resources for students, teachers, and parents.

Publish

Publishing Strategy   Submit the final draft of your editorial.

Publish ▭▭▭▭▭▭▭▭▭ ◂▸ 2 minutes

 I am almost done with my assessment. I used information in the scoring guide and the writing traits to complete my editorial. Now, I am going to use the spell-check feature one more time to make sure I didn't miss any spelling errors. Then I will submit my final draft.

We should name the new park in our community after John James Audubon. Roger Tory Peterson, Minna Hall, and Harriet Hemenway did a lot to protect birds, but Mr. Audubon spent his life watching birds and painting them. Because our new park will be designed for bird watching, it makes sense to name it after Mr. Audubon.

From an early age, Mr. Audubon had a passion for birds. He skipped school sometimes to watch birds in the woods. When he grew up, he became a painter and a museum worker. At the museum, he prepared birds for the displays. He decided to paint every bird in America and include his paintings in a book. Mr. Audubon and his helper, Joseph Mason, traveled to many places to find bird specimens. They spent a lot of time painting and drawing the birds they found.

350   Opinion Writing

Differentiating Instruction

REINFORCEMENT

Make the Most of It   To reduce students' anxiety about running out of time, advise them to combine the edit and publishing phases. Then tell them to split the time into manageable chunks. Have students spend two to three minutes scanning their drafts for spelling errors, two to three minutes looking for capitalization and punctuation errors, and then two to three minutes looking for the errors they commonly make.

It's true that Roger Tory Peterson helped protect birds by warning against the use of DDT, a chemical that was killing birds. Minna Hall and Harriet Hemenway also helped birds. They held tea parties and convinced other women in their community to stop wearing hats with feathers. They even created a society to protect birds called the Massachusetts Audubon Society. It was named after Mr. Audubon. Their work was important, but Mr. Audubon helped people learn about and appreciate all kinds of birds.

For these reasons, I believe we should name our new park after Mr. Audubon. I can't wait to go bird watching in the John James Audubon Park!

Now It's Your Turn

Don't forget all the advice Shamari gave you during her assessment. Now, it's your turn to practice taking an opinion assessment.

- Do you have to remember everything you read in Part 1 when you write your assignment in Part 2? (Possible response: No. You can go back to Part 1 to reread a source, but you can't change your answer.)

- Where do you look to find out what you need to include in your writing? (Possible response: Your Assignment and the Scoring Guide tell you what you need to write.)

Now It's Your Turn

Tell students that they will practice taking a next generation opinion assessment in real time. If time permits, students should complete the assessment over a two-day period. Go to **www. sfw.z-b.com** or the **Strategies for Writers Online Writing Center** to download the **Next Generation Assessment Practice** for opinion writing.

There are two student versions of the assessment. One assessment contains scaffolded support as students take the assessment. The other assessment does not have scaffolded support. Choose which version of the assessment you want your class to take. Review the teacher version of the assessment before giving it to students.

Next Generation Assessment Practice

Student Edition

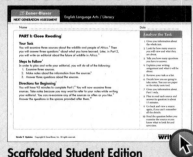

Scaffolded Student Edition

Teacher Edition

CCSS **C**ommon **C**ore **S**tate **S**tandards (pp. Z20–Z30)
Writing: W.4.4, W.4.5, W.4.10
Speaking and Listening: SL.4.1a, SL.4.1c, SL.4.1d

More Writing Practice

Descriptive Elements in the Text Types

CCSS Common Core State Standards

Making the Connection

Writers frequently use descriptive elements in each of the three text types (Narrative, Informative/Explanatory, and Opinion). These descriptive elements add interest and make the writing clearer. In addition, writers sometimes blend the three text types as needed for their task, audience, or purpose. This unit includes the strategies, skills, and practice that will allow students to successfully incorporate descriptive writing in the three text types.

Descriptive Paragraph

Pages T354A–T375

This genre introduces students to descriptive writing, guiding them as they use their five senses to create vivid "word picture" impressions of people, places, or things.

Prewrite   Take some notes about an interesting place. Make a Web to organize the notes.

Draft   Select details that will help the reader "see" the place.

Revise   Use words and phrases that help the reader follow the description. Use first-person point of view to share feelings. Include word pictures to improve the description.

Edit   Make sure plural nouns and articles are correct.

Publish   Publish the description as part of a brochure.

Professional Development Podcasts and Screencasts
Go to **www.sfw.z-b.com** to access the variety of professional development **podcasts** and **screencasts**.

Overview

Character Sketch Narrative

Pages T376A–T397

This genre helps students learn how to describe a real person or a character from a book.

Prewrite	Choose a character from a book and jot down some details about him or her. Use a Spider Map to organize details about the character.
Draft	Organize the information in an introduction, body, and conclusion. Use helpful transitions.
Revise	Let the reader know what you think about the character. Replace clichés with concrete words and phrases. Use short, simple sentences to make a point.
Edit	Make sure there are no run-on sentences.
Publish	Illustrate the character sketch and post a final copy on the class bulletin board or website.

Poetry Review Opinion

Pages T398A–T421

As they explore this genre, students will learn how to write a response to a poem of their choice. They will be encouraged to focus on the feelings and images that the poem evokes.

Prewrite	Jot down some ideas about an interesting poem. Make a Network Tree to organize examples and details.
Draft	Use first person (*I, me, my*) to share thoughts about the poem.
Revise	Use examples from the poem. Use *like* to compare one thing to another. Start sentences in different ways.
Edit	Make sure adjectives are used correctly.
Publish	Read the response aloud to the class.

Poem ◄ MATH CONNECTION Informative/Explanatory

Pages T422A–T443

Students will express their understanding of a math concept in the creative form of a poem.

Prewrite	Choose a topic. Make a list of details. Use a Three-Column Chart to plan the poem.
Draft	Use figurative language.
Revise	Use details that help the reader "see" the subject. Make sure to follow the shape of the poem. Adjust the length of lines for a smooth flow.
Edit	Check prepositions and prepositional phrases.
Publish	Submit the poem to a magazine or online publisher of children's poetry.

21st Century Literacies
Technology, Digital Media & Writing

by **Julie Coiro, Ph.D.,** University of Rhode Island & **Sara B. Kajder, Ph.D.,** Shady Side Academy

 INSPIRE Websites to Spark Ideas

Describing: Art and Nature

The Internet provides immediate access to a range of lesson plans that support students as they observe and respond to the world around them. Even more exciting is that the Internet also links you to a host of stunning art collections to inspire students' descriptive writing.

- **The Art Zone (www.nga.gov/kids/zone/zone. htm),** sponsored by the National Gallery of Art for Kids, is an interactive website where young children can create imaginary landscapes, online collages, motion paintings, or symmetrical designs and then use their best descriptive writing techniques to represent in words their original artistic creation.

- **Pics for Learning (http://pics.tech4learning.com)** includes a growing list of thousands of copyright-friendly images of animals, plants, nature, and more that have been donated by amateur photographers for students and teachers to use in their classrooms.

- **Andy Cook's Landscape Photography Gallery (www.rockymtnrefl.com/galleries.htm)** features high-quality, landscape photographs of Colorado, the Rocky Mountains, and the southwest United States. The photographs load quickly, the website is easy for students to navigate by themselves, and the vibrant colors will surely spark interesting descriptions in their writing.

- **Storybird Collaborative Storytelling (http:// storybird.com)** provides a unique interface in which children select brilliant illustrations drawn by artists and then compose a companion story that is immediately added to an online story collection. The database of illustrations could be a perfect inspiration for art-inspired descriptive writing.

Publishing Poetry

Many children love to write poetry, but some struggle with choosing the right words, while others are unsure of the correct format. Fortunately, the Internet provides many wonderful websites to spark students' creativity and engage them in the process of writing poems. Here are just a few:

- **The Favorite Poem Project (www.favoritepoem. org/project.html),** founded by Robert Pinsky, the 39th Poet Laureate of the United States, seeks to improve poetry's place in American classrooms by encouraging active, engaging lessons that emphasize a direct, vocal connection to poems.

- **Instant Poetry Forms (http://ettcweb.lr.k12.nj.us/ forms/newpoem.htm)** is an award-winning website designed to help kids create dozens of different kinds of poems using interactive fill-in-the blank forms. Students may choose to write an "All About Me Poem," a cinquain, an instant 5W poem, a limerick, and many more.

- **The Dream Flag Project (www.dreamflags.org),** created by sixth grade teachers in Pennsylvania, connects students in grades K–12 to their dreams through poetry and art. Students first read the poetry of Langston Hughes, particularly his dream poems. Then they create their own dream poems on pieces of cloth to share with the online community as a dream flag. To date, more than 40,000 dream flags have been created!

- **Poetry Teachers.com (www.poetryteachers.com)** is all about using humor to inspire a love of poetry by including poetry games, downloadable theater versions of poems for students to perform in class, and some great lesson plans and tips on how to teach funny poetry in the classroom.

More Writing Practice

Descriptive Elements in the Text Types

Why do good writers use Descriptive Elements?

Hi, my name is Marta. I am studying about how to use descriptive elements in my writing. Good writing often includes details about the five senses that help readers picture the way things look, sound, feel, smell, and taste. And, I can use descriptive elements in Narrative, Informative/Explanatory, and Opinion writing! By including description, I'll be a better writer.

Meet Your Writing Partner, Marta

The writing partner for this unit is Marta. Point out that she explains why descriptive elements make good writing. Ask students why including details about the five senses is important to good writing. **(Help readers picture how things, look, sound, feel, smell, and taste.)** Then tell students that they are going to practice using descriptive elements in their own Narrative, Informative/Explanatory, and Opinion Writing.

To differentiate instruction and maximize student achievement, use the Differentiated Instruction Activities available at **www.sfw.z-b.com.**

Created by Amy Humphreys, Ed.M., these engaging activities can be used to meet a wide range of learner needs. Each activity uses a combination of visual, written, oral, and kinesthetic elements, and deliberately leverages the power of collaboration and conversation so students learn to think like writers in fun and engaging ways.

Descriptive Paragraph Planner

WEEK 1

Day 1
Introduce
Descriptive Paragraph

Student Objectives
- Review the elements of a descriptive paragraph.
- Consider purpose and audience.
- Learn the traits of descriptive writing.

Student Activities
- Read and discuss **What's in a Descriptive Paragraph?** (p. 354)
- Read and discuss **Why Write a Descriptive Paragraph?** (p. 355)
- Read **Linking Descriptive Writing Traits to a Descriptive Paragraph.** (p. 356)

Day 2
Analyze
Close Reading of the Model

Student Objectives
- Read a model descriptive paragraph.

Student Activities
- Read **"Our Secret Hiding Place."** (p. 357)

Day 3
Analyze
Introduce the Rubric

Student Objectives
- Learn to read a rubric.

Student Activities
- Review **"Our Secret Hiding Place."** (p. 357)
- Read and discuss the **Descriptive Paragraph Rubric.** (pp. 358–359)

WEEK 2

Day 1
Write
Prewrite: Ideas

Student Objectives
- Read and understand a prewriting strategy.

Student Activities
- Read and discuss **Prewrite: Focus on Ideas.** (p. 364)
- Apply the prewriting strategy.

Day 2
Write
Prewrite: Organization

Student Objectives
- Make a Web to organize notes.

Student Activities
- Read and discuss **Prewrite: Focus on Organization.** (p. 365)
- Reflect on the model Web.
- Apply the prewriting strategy to create a Web.
- Participate in a peer conference.

Day 3
Write
Draft: Ideas

Student Objectives
- Begin writing, using sensory details.

Student Activities
- Read and discuss **Draft: Focus on Ideas.** (p. 366)
- Apply the drafting strategy by using a Web to write a draft.

WEEK 3

Day 1
Write
Revise: Voice

Student Objectives
- Revise for first-person point of view.

Student Activities
- Read and discuss **Revise: Focus on Voice.** (p. 369)
- Reflect on the model draft.
- Apply the revising strategy.
- Participate in a peer conference.

Day 2
Write
Revise: Word Choice

Student Objectives
- Revise for descriptive word choice.

Student Activities
- Read and discuss **Revise: Focus on Word Choice.** (p. 370)
- Reflect on the model draft.
- Apply the revising strategy.

Note: Optional Revising Lessons are located at **www.sfw.z-b.com**

Day 3
Write
Edit: Conventions

Student Objectives
- Edit for accurate use of articles and plural nouns.

Student Activities
- Read and discuss **Edit: Focus on Conventions.** (p. 371)
- Apply the revising strategy.

Note: Teach the Conventions mini-lessons (pp. 372–373) if needed.

Analyze
Close Reading for the Traits

Student Objectives
- Read a model descriptive paragraph.
- Use the descriptive paragraph rubric.
- Use the model descriptive paragraph to study Ideas, Organization, and Voice.

Student Activities
- Review **"Our Secret Hiding Place."** (p. 357)
- Read and discuss **Using the Rubric to Analyze the Model.** (pp. 360–361)

Analyze
Close Reading for the Traits

Student Objectives
- Read a model descriptive paragraph.
- Use the descriptive paragraph rubric.
- Use the model descriptive paragraph to study Word Choice, Sentence Fluency, and Conventions.

Student Activities
- Review **"Our Secret Hiding Place."** (p. 357)
- Read and discuss **Using the Rubric to Analyze the Model.** (pp. 362–363)

Write
Draft

Student Objectives
- Complete a draft.

Student Activities
- Finish the draft.
- Reflect on the model draft. (p. 367)
- Participate in a peer conference.

Write
Revise: Organization

Student Objectives
- Revise for helpful transitions.

Student Activities
- Read and discuss **Revise: Focus on Organization.** (p. 368)
- Reflect on a model draft.
- Apply the revising strategy.

Write
Publish: +Presentation

Student Objectives
- Discuss preparation for publishing and presentation.
- Use a final editing checklist to publish their work.

Student Activities
- Read and discuss **Publish: +Presentation.** (p. 374)
- Apply the publishing strategy.

Write
Publish: +Presentation

Student Objectives
- Use a descriptive paragraph rubric.
- Share a published descriptive paragraph.

Student Activities
- Share their work.
- Use the rubric to reflect upon and evaluate the model and their own writing. (pp. 358–359, 375)

To complete the chapter in fewer days, combine the learning objectives and activities in a way that supports students as they write.

Resources at-a-Glance

Grammar, Usage & Mechanics

Differentiating Instruction
For additional Differentiating Instruction activities, see Strategies for Writers *Differentiated Instruction Activities at* **www.sfw.z-b.com.**

English Language Learners

Collaborative Conferencing

Tech Tips

 Strategies for Writers Online

Go to **www.sfw.z-b.com** for additional online resources for students, teachers, and parents.

Online Writing Center

Provides IWB resources, assessments, interactive games and practice activities, videos, eBooks, and a virtual file cabinet.

Introduce
Descriptive Paragraph

Week 1 • Day 1

Student Objectives

- Review the elements of a descriptive paragraph. *(p. 354)*
- Consider purpose and audience. *(p. 355)*
- Learn the traits of descriptive writing. *(p. 356)*

What's a Descriptive Paragraph?

Discuss the definition of a descriptive paragraph with students. Ask them to think of paragraphs or short stories they have read that had very clear, memorable descriptions. Read the examples aloud and discuss what makes each one memorable or enjoyable to read.

What's in a Descriptive Paragraph?

Read and discuss the elements of a descriptive paragraph with students. Ask students to brainstorm possible topics for a descriptive paragraph, such as a favorite place to relax, a family member, or their first pet.

Discuss sensory details and why they are important in a descriptive paragraph. Point out sensory details in the example paragraphs you read.

 Strategies for Writers Online
Go to **www.sfw.z-b.com** for additional online resources for students, teachers, and parents.

What's a Descriptive Paragraph?

It's a clear, detailed picture in words of a specific person, place, or thing.

What's in a Descriptive Paragraph?

Topic
This is what my paragraph is all about. It could be the day I spent at the beach with my family or a biking trip with my friends. The details I write will support the topic.

Sensory Details
I can bring my paragraph to life with details related to the five senses. By creating word pictures, I can tell my readers how something looks, sounds, smells, feels, or tastes.

354 More Writing Practice

Descriptive Text Exemplars (Descriptive Paragraph)

Lauber, Patricia. *Hurricanes: Earth's Mightiest Storms.* Scholastic, 1996. **CCSS** Lauber describes the formation, tracking, and destruction caused by "Earth's mightiest storms." Complete with text, maps, and photographs, *Hurricanes: Earth's Mightiest Storms* offers readers valuable insight into these violent windstorms.

Kavash, E. Barrie. "Ancient Mound Builders." *Cobblestone.* October 2003. **CCSS** Long ago, people of many different cultures constructed mounds for use as homes, temples, and even tombs. Kavash describes their laborious construction as well as their historical relevance in this informative magazine article.

Why write a Descriptive Paragraph?

Describing is important for all writers. I can think of a lot of reasons to write a descriptive paragraph. Here are a few.

To Entertain
Writers of stories use descriptive paragraphs to make the characters, setting, and action seem real. Good descriptions help the readers picture the story in their minds. The reader can enjoy an amazing imaginary world.

To Inform
Describing is one way to give people information. Describing what you observe is an important activity of scientists. The observations that they write are detailed descriptions of what they see or hear. I can write about something I've seen or heard to share with others.

To Express an Opinion
How a writer describes something can influence a reader's opinion about it. That's why historians try hard to describe events in history without giving an opinion.

Fiction writers have a different goal. They often use opinion words like *beautiful, scary, awful,* and *delicious* to bring emotion to a story. They want to make the readers think and feel a certain way.

Banting, Erinn. *England the Land.* **Crabtree, 2004.**
CCSS The geography, climate, people, and cities of England are all outlined in England the Land. Banting provides readers with a foundation for understanding the many aspects of this regal country.

Simon, Seymour. *Horses.* **HarperCollins, 2006.** CCSS
Simon uses photographs and text to describe the different characteristics of horses. From their evolution to their interactions with one another, *Horses* explains these quadrupeds in a way that young readers will comprehend and enjoy.

Why write a Descriptive Paragraph?

Remind students that all writing has a purpose. Writers write for many reasons and for a variety of audiences. These factors help shape the writing. In the case of a descriptive paragraph, the purpose will affect what types of details the writer chooses to include.

Read page 355 aloud. Discuss the choices a writer might make in writing a descriptive paragraph for different purposes. For example, a writer who wants to entertain will use fun, unusual, or exciting details to describe the topic. A writer who wants to inform will choose details that convey information clearly and give the reader an accurate picture of the topic. When expressing an opinion, a writer will think about exactly what he or she wants to say about the topic and choose words that convey that feeling.

Encourage students to consider their reasons for writing a descriptive paragraph and how these reasons will affect the choices they make as they write.

CCSS **C**ommon **C**ore **S**tate **S**tandards (pp. Z20–Z30)
Language: L.4.3c
Speaking and Listening: SL.4.1a, SL.4.1b, SL.4.1c, SL.4.1d, SL.4.3, SL.4.6

Introduce
Descriptive Paragraph

Linking Descriptive Writing Traits to a Descriptive Paragraph

Have students read page 356. Emphasize that they will follow Marta as she models using the writing process and the descriptive writing traits together.

Discuss with students how each trait applies to a descriptive paragraph. Ask students to imagine how readers would react to reading a paragraph that was lacking in one of the traits—for example, if the paragraph was poorly organized or lacking in sensory details.

Linking Descriptive Writing Traits to a Descriptive Paragraph

In this chapter, you will describe a special place. This type of descriptive writing is called a descriptive paragraph. Marta will guide you through the stages of the writing process: Prewrite, Draft, Revise, Edit, and Publish. In each stage, Marta will show you important writing strategies that are linked to the Descriptive Writing Traits below.

Descriptive Writing Traits

- a clear and complete topic
- sensory details and examples that help the reader "see" what is being described

- well-organized paragraphs that each tell about one main idea
- transitions that guide the reader through the text

- a voice and tone that are appropriate for the purpose and connect with the audience

- precise, descriptive language that creates a picture for the reader

- different kinds of sentences that make the writing flow

- no or few errors in grammar, usage, mechanics, and spelling

Before you write, read Andrea Baum's descriptive paragraph on the next page. Then use the descriptive paragraph rubric on pages 358–359 to decide how well she did. (You might want to look back at What's in a Descriptive Paragraph? on page 354, too!)

Descriptive Writing Traits in a Descriptive Paragraph

 Ideas The writer must choose a topic that is appropriate in scope. Students should choose a single place and focus on an aspect of that place that can be described in the space of a paragraph. Focusing on sensory details will help readers get a clear, complete picture of the place.

 **Organization** The descriptive paragraph should have a clearly stated main idea that is supported by the details. Transitions will help readers move from one detail to the next.

 **Voice** In the descriptive paragraph, students connect with readers through the use of first-person point of view.

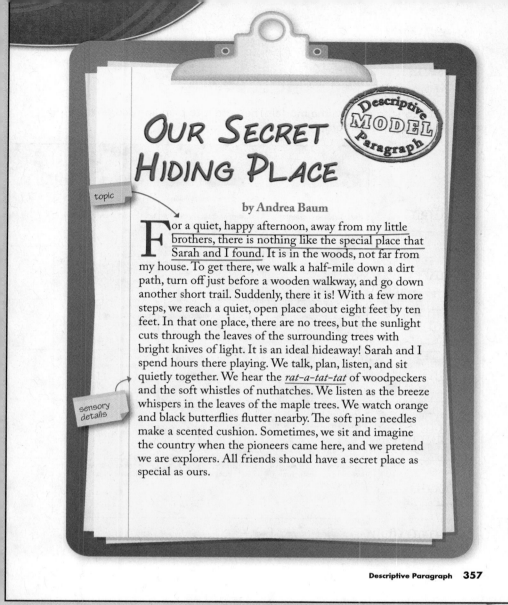

OUR SECRET HIDING PLACE

Descriptive MODEL Paragraph

by Andrea Baum

topic

For a quiet, happy afternoon, away from my little brothers, there is nothing like the special place that Sarah and I found. It is in the woods, not far from my house. To get there, we walk a half-mile down a dirt path, turn off just before a wooden walkway, and go down another short trail. Suddenly, there it is! With a few more steps, we reach a quiet, open place about eight feet by ten feet. In that one place, there are no trees, but the sunlight cuts through the leaves of the surrounding trees with bright knives of light. It is an ideal hideaway! Sarah and I spend hours there playing. We talk, plan, listen, and sit quietly together. We hear the *rat-a-tat-tat* of woodpeckers and the soft whistles of nuthatches. We listen as the breeze whispers in the leaves of the maple trees. We watch orange and black butterflies flutter nearby. The soft pine needles make a scented cushion. Sometimes, we sit and imagine the country when the pioneers came here, and we pretend we are explorers. All friends should have a secret place as special as ours.

sensory details

Descriptive Paragraph   357

Word Choice A descriptive paragraph does not give the reader much room to ramble. Precise words and phrases will help the reader form a clear and complete picture of the place described.

Sentence Fluency Variety in sentence types gives writing a pleasing rhythm and flow. Writing with variety is not only more enjoyable to read, it is easier to follow.

Conventions Too many errors in grammar, usage, mechanics, and spelling make writing confusing and hard to read. The writer's message is easily lost or misunderstood when conventions are not correctly applied.

Analyze
Close Reading of the Model

Week 1 • Day 2

Student Objectives

• Read a model descriptive paragraph. *(p. 357)*

Read the Model

Read "Our Secret Hiding Place" aloud as students follow along in their books. Ask volunteers for their impressions of the place described. Does it sound appealing to them? Why do they think they might like or dislike Andrea's secret place?

Elements of a Descriptive Paragraph

Use the notes on the model to discuss the elements of a descriptive paragraph. Refer students to What's in a Descriptive Paragraph? on page 354 if they need to review the elements. Discuss how the details support the topic of the paragraph, and ask students to find additional sensory details. Make a chart on the board to list the sensory details and the sense each one describes.

CCSS **C**ommon **C**ore **S**tate **S**tandards (pp. Z20–Z30)
Writing: W.4.6
Language: L.4.3c
Speaking and Listening: SL.4.1a, SL.4.1b, SL.4.1c, SL.4.1d, SL.4.2, SL.4.3, SL.4.6

Analyze
Introduce the Rubric

Week 1 • Day 3

Student Objectives

- Learn to read a rubric. (*pp. 358–359*)

Introduce the Rubric

Explain the Rubric Explain that a rubric is a tool for planning, improving, and assessing a piece of writing. Tell students that a rubric helps a writer focus on key elements, or traits, in writing (**Ideas, Organization, Voice, Word Choice, Sentence Fluency, Conventions,** and **Presentation**). Point out that column 6 describes a very good descriptive paragraph, one that has received the highest score in all categories. This is what students should strive for in their own writing.

Discuss the Rubric Guide students in a discussion of the rubric. Read the descriptors that go with each trait and note the progression from the top descriptor to the lowest one. Discuss what sets a level-6 descriptive paragraph apart from a lower-scoring one. Remind students to keep the rubric in mind when they write their own descriptive paragraph and again when they revise it.

Online Writing Center

Provides a variety of **interactive rubrics,** including 4-, 5-, and 6-point models.

T358 More Writing Practice

Descriptive Paragraph Rubric

Use this rubric to analyze the model. Then use it to plan and score your own descriptive paragraph.

	6	5	4	
Ideas	The writer's topic is clear. Sensory details create a clear, focused picture of one place.	The writer's topic is clear. A few more sensory details would help create a clearer picture.	The writer's topic is fairly clear. Sensory details would help create a clearer picture.	
Organization	A clear topic sentence introduces the topic. Well-chosen transitions guide the reader through the description.	A clear topic sentence introduces the topic. Most transitions guide the reader through the description.	A topic sentence introduces the topic. Some transitions guide the reader through the description.	
Voice	The writer's personality comes across clearly. The voice speaks directly to the reader.	The writer's voice is sincere and natural in most places.	The writer's personality comes through. The voice is ordinary in a few places.	
Word Choice	Descriptive language creates a vivid picture for the reader.	Most of the language is descriptive and helps the reader "see" the place.	Some descriptive language is vague or overused.	
Sentence Fluency	A mix of sentence types and lengths makes the writing enjoyable to read.	Most of the writing has a mix of sentence types and lengths.	Some sentences are different types and lengths, but a few more would improve the writing.	
Conventions	Articles and plural nouns are used correctly. The writing is easy to read.	The use of articles and plural nouns is mostly correct.	Few errors in articles and plural nouns are noticeable.	

✛ Presentation The paragraph is neat and legible.

CCSS Common Core State Standards
Descriptive Paragraph

Writing descriptive texts can engage the Common Core State Standards for both Narrative and Informative/Explanatory writing. The Ideas rubric for the descriptive paragraph is drawn from narrative standard **W.4.3,** which mentions sensory details. The Organization rubric reflects both informative/explanatory standard **W.4.2** and narrative standard **W.4.3,** both of which address the importance of linking ideas. The Organization rubric also picks up the

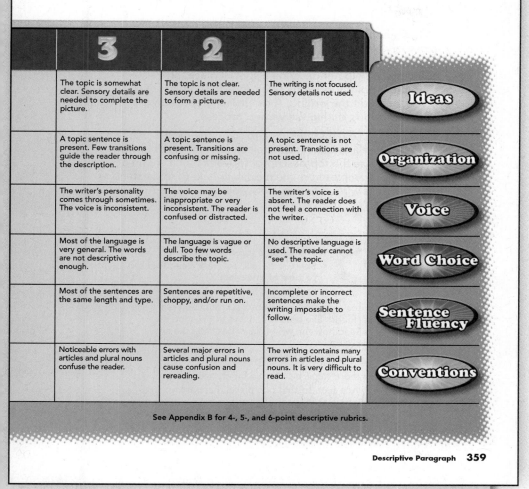

	3	2	1	
	The topic is somewhat clear. Sensory details are needed to complete the picture.	The topic is not clear. Sensory details are needed to form a picture.	The writing is not focused. Sensory details not used.	**Ideas**
	A topic sentence is present. Few transitions guide the reader through the description.	A topic sentence is present. Transitions are confusing or missing.	A topic sentence is not present. Transitions are not used.	**Organization**
	The writer's personality comes through sometimes. The voice is inconsistent.	The voice may be inappropriate or very inconsistent. The reader is confused or distracted.	The writer's voice is absent. The reader does not feel a connection with the writer.	**Voice**
	Most of the language is very general. The words are not descriptive enough.	The language is vague or dull. Too few words describe the topic.	No descriptive language is used. The reader cannot "see" the topic.	**Word Choice**
	Most of the sentences are the same length and type.	Sentences are repetitive, choppy, and/or run on.	Incomplete or incorrect sentences make the writing impossible to follow.	**Sentence Fluency**
	Noticeable errors with articles and plural nouns confuse the reader.	Several major errors in articles and plural nouns cause confusion and rereading.	The writing contains many errors in articles and plural nouns. It is very difficult to read.	**Conventions**

See Appendix B for 4-, 5-, and 6-point descriptive rubrics.

emphasis on introducing the topic from narrative standard **W.4.3**. The Word Choice rubric is drawn principally from informative/explanatory standard **W.4.2,** which explicitly mentions precise language. The Conventions rubric addresses standards **L.4.1** and **L.4.2,** which address command of the conventions of grammar, usage, capitalization, spelling, and punctuation.

Find Evidence in the Model

Small-Group Collaboration Assign a small group of students and tell them to evaluate the model using the rubric. Assign one person in each group to record the group's findings and one person to report the findings to the class. Instruct students to score the model for each trait based on evidence in the text. Remind students to read closely to identify examples to support their high or low scores. Note: Although the models were written to score high in each trait, students should not assume each trait would receive a 6, the top score.

Teacher-Led Discussion Bring the class back together and have the reporters present their findings and scores. Prompt groups to provide evidence and examples for their scores from the model as needed.

Additional Rubrics

Appendix B includes 4-, 5-, and 6-point rubrics that can be used with any piece of descriptive writing. The rubrics are also available as blackline masters in the back of this Teacher Edition.

CCSS **Common Core State Standards** (pp. Z20–Z30)
Writing: W.4.6
Language: L.4.3c
Speaking and Listening: SL.4.1a, SL4.1b, SL.4.1c, SL.4.1d, SL.4.2, SL.4.3, SL.4.6

Analyze
Close Reading for the Traits

Week 1 • Day 4

Student Objectives

- Read a model descriptive paragraph. *(p. 357)*
- Use the descriptive paragraph rubric. *(pp. 358–359)*
- Use the model descriptive paragraph to study **Ideas, Organization,** and **Voice.** *(pp. 360–361)*

Find Evidence in the Model

Evaluate the Model Read each section on pages 360–361 with students. Determine whether students agree with each point in Marta's assessment. Use the questions below to initiate the discussion. Be sure students can back up their answers with specific examples from the paragraph.

Discuss Audience, Task, Purpose Ask students one or more of the following questions as they analyze the model:

- **Audience** Who is the audience? (Possible response: all readers)

- **Task** How does the writer use detail to describe the place? (Possible responses: She uses sensory details in a way that lets the reader see the place.)

- **Purpose** What is the writer's purpose for writing this report? How do you know? (Possible responses: To entertain the reader; the details make the reader want to go to the place.)

Using the Rubric *Descriptive Paragraph* to Analyze the Model

Did you notice that the model on page 357 points out some key elements of a descriptive paragraph? As she wrote "Our Secret Hiding Place," Andrea Baum used these elements to help her describe a special place. She also used the 6-point rubric on pages 358–359 to plan, draft, revise, and edit the writing. A rubric is a great tool to evaluate writing during the writing process.

Now let's use the same rubric to score the model. To do this, we'll focus on each trait separately, starting with Ideas. We'll use the top descriptor for each trait (column 6), along with examples from the model, to help us understand how the traits work together. How would you score Andrea on each trait?

- The writer's topic is clear.
- Sensory details create a clear, focused picture of one place.

Andrea writes a description about a secret hiding place she found with her friend. She uses her senses to describe their special place. Read how the writer describes what their hideaway looks like.

> With a few more steps, we reach a quiet, open place about eight feet by ten feet. In that one place, there are no trees, but the sunlight cuts through the leaves of the surrounding trees with bright knives of light.

360 More Writing Practice

English Language Learners

BEGINNING

The Five Senses Demonstrate the meanings of *sight, sound, touch, taste,* and *smell,* and make sure students understand that each sense corresponds to a certain part of the body. For example, our sense of sight is fulfilled by the eyes. Say a word, such as *sweet, chirp,* or *bright,* and have students point to the body part that we use to perceive the idea of the word. Then model a sentence for students to repeat, such as *I can taste something sweet.*

INTERMEDIATE

Observation Chart Briefly review the five senses. Present students with a familiar object, such as a leaf or a banana. Have partners complete an Observation Chart graphic organizer for the object, making sure to include at least one idea for each of the five senses.

- A clear topic sentence introduces the topic.
- Well-chosen transitions guide the reader through the description.

Andrea introduces the topic right away. Her topic sentence gives the main idea of the paragraph. It also creates a lot of interest in the place. In the paragraph, I notice that Andrea uses transitions like *in the woods, half-mile down,* and *just before.* The words help me follow the description.

> It is in the woods, not far from my house. To get there, we walk a half-mile down a dirt path, turn off just before a wooden walkway, and go down another short trail.

- The writer's personality comes across clearly.
- The voice speaks directly to the reader.

Andrea's personality comes through in her writing. You can tell she likes her secret place and her friend Sarah. You see her secret place from her point of view.

> It is an ideal hideaway! Sarah and I spend hours there playing. We talk, plan, listen, and sit quietly together.

Descriptive Paragraph **361**

Discuss the Traits Ask students one or more of the following questions to discuss the traits in the model:

Ideas What is your favorite sensory detail in the model? Why do you like it? (Possible response: *The soft pine needles make a scented cushion.* The detail reminds me of the scent of the woods, and I like that smell.)

Organization What kinds of information do the transitions give the reader? (where things are and when they happen)

Voice How does Andrea speak directly to the reader? (She speaks as herself, using words like *I* and *we.*)

ADVANCED/ADVANCED HIGH

Place Descriptions As a class, brainstorm different locations in your town, such as a bowling alley, a library, the post office, the movie theater, a swimming pool, a park, and a coffee shop. Assign one place to each pair of students and have them use a Web graphic organizer and brainstorm descriptive words to describe each place. Randomly redistribute the Web graphic organizers to another pair who should then write a few sentences to describe the place using the words on the web. Ask a volunteer to read the description of the place as the rest of the students try to guess the place that is being described.

CCSS **Common Core State Standards** (pp. Z20–Z30)
Writing: W.4.3d
Language: L.4.3a, L.4.3c, L.4.6
Speaking and Listening: SL.4.1a, SL.4.1b, SL.4.1c, SL.4.1d, SL.4.3, SL.4.6

Analyze
Close Reading for the Traits

Week 1 • Day 5

Student Objectives

- Read a model descriptive paragraph. *(p. 357)*
- Use the descriptive paragraph rubric. *(pp. 358–359)*
- Use the model descriptive paragraph to study **Word Choice, Sentence Fluency,** and **Conventions.** *(pp. 362–363)*

Discuss the Traits Ask students one or more of the following questions to discuss the traits in the model:

Word Choice Can you close your eyes and easily imagine yourself in Andrea's secret place? (**Possible response: Yes, because the descriptions are very clear and help me see Andrea's place.**)

Sentence Fluency What makes the model flow smoothly? (**Possible response: the sentences**) What makes the sentences flow? (**Possible response: the sentences varying in length.**)

Conventions What plural nouns does Andrea use in the model paragraph? (**Possible responses:** *woods, steps, trees, leaves, knives*)

Strategies for Writers Online
Go to **www.sfw.z-b.com** for additional online resources for students, teachers, and parents.

Using the Rubric to Analyze the Model
Descriptive Paragraph

Word Choice
- Descriptive language creates a vivid picture for the reader.

Andrea uses interesting descriptive words. She creates word pictures by describing the sights, sounds, and smells of her secret hiding place. I can picture her secret place in my mind!

> We listen as the breeze whispers in the leaves of the maple trees. We watch orange and black butterflies flutter nearby. The soft pine needles make a scented cushion.

Sentence Fluency
- A mix of sentence types and lengths makes the writing enjoyable to read.

The writer uses a variety of sentence types and lengths in her writing. She includes exclamations to add excitement to the paragraph. When she describes the way to her secret place, she starts with a very short sentence. It is an exclamation that shows the excitement of the moment.

> Suddenly, there it is! With a few more steps, we reach a quiet, open place about eight feet by ten feet.

Tech Tips
Digital Media

Use Digital Media As much as 21st century practice involves digital media, it is also about authentic tasks and audience. Students' work can matter outside of our classrooms, and we should strive to put their good work into action as often as possible. As students begin their study of what makes an effective descriptive paragraph, consider popular places in your community where you might post their descriptive passages. Or collaborate with another class of students (use ePals or Global SchoolNet to find partners). The goal is to make their texts useable *and* used.

See **www.sfw.z-b.com** for further information about and links to these websites and tools.

Conventions
- Articles and plural nouns are used correctly. The writing is easy to read.

I read the description very carefully. Every word is spelled correctly. There are no errors in capitalization or punctuation either. The writer uses articles and plural nouns correctly. Look at this example. It has six plural nouns. Can you find them?

> We hear the *rat-a-tat-tat* of woodpeckers and the soft whistles of nuthatches. We listen as the breeze whispers in the leaves of the maple trees. We watch orange and black butterflies flutter nearby.

✛Presentation The paragraph is neat and legible.

Now it's my turn to write a descriptive paragraph! I'll use the 6-point rubric on pages 358–359 and good writing strategies to help me. Follow along to see how I do it.

Descriptive Paragraph **363**

✛Presentation Remind students of the importance of creating a neat, legible copy. Ask students about times they have had to decipher sloppy handwriting or type that was difficult to read. Make sure students understand that readers who are frustrated and impatient will not be a receptive audience for their writing.

Using a computer is an excellent way to create clean, legible text. Encourage students to use a word-processing program and choose one legible font for the text of their paragraph.

Think About the Traits

Once students have thoroughly discussed the model, ask them which traits they think are most important in a descriptive paragraph and have them explain why. (Possible response: Word Choice is an important trait, as precise, descriptive language helps get images across to the reader in few words.)

Differentiating Instruction

ENRICHMENT
Change Point of View Encourage students to identify particular audiences that might find the model description paragraph especially interesting. For example, bird watchers, naturalists, or hikers might be receptive audiences. Then challenge students to write a brief description of Andrea's secret place from the point of view of one of these audience members.

REINFORCEMENT
Support Conventions You may wish to review the targeted conventions. Model the concept of singular vs. plural by using objects in the room such as desks, chairs, and books. Help students observe that the plural is formed by adding -s to the end of the word. Review the articles by helping students identify them in the model paragraph.

CCSS **Common Core State Standards** (pp. Z20–Z30)
Writing: W.4.6
Language: L.4.2d, L.4.3c
Speaking and Listening: SL.4.1a, SL.4.1b, SL.4.1c, SL.4.1d, SL.4.3, SL.4.6

Write
Descriptive Paragraph

Week 2 • Day 1

Student Objectives

- Read and understand a prewriting strategy. (p. 364)

Prewrite

Focus on Ideas

Gather Information Read page 364 aloud as students follow along in their books. Discuss how Marta chose to write about her visit to the Monterey Bay Aquarium. Then have students brainstorm a list of interesting places they have been to and might like to write about.

Take Notes Ask students to look at the notes Marta made. Point out that she may remember more details as she begins to write. Have students choose the place they want to write about and take notes about the place.

Online Writing Center

Provides **interactive graphic organizers** as well as a variety of graphic organizers in PDF format.

T364 More Writing Practice

Write a Descriptive Paragraph

Prewrite
Focus on Ideas

The Rubric Says   The writer's topic is clear. Sensory details create a clear, focused picture of one place.

Writing Strategy   Make some notes about an interesting place you know.

I love visiting Splash Zone at the Monterey Bay Aquarium. I can see and even touch a lot of sea creatures there. My teacher asked us to think of a place we had visited and liked. Right away, I thought of Splash Zone. My strategy will be to jot down notes about what I saw, heard, and smelled.

Notes for My Paragraph

- Splash Zone—best part of the aquarium
- a place for families
- different species of fish
- salty smell of the sea
- can hold starfish
- a beautiful coral reef
- walls of bubbling water
- hear excited children
- a window that puts you next to penguins
- giant clam chair
- sounds of fish eating
- hear "talking" penguins
- walls that feel like coral
- smell of animals
- water play area

Write

Think about an interesting place you know well. What would a visitor want to know about it? Jot down notes about it.

English Language Learners

BEGINNING/INTERMEDIATE

Ideas Show students a photo or a drawing of your favorite place, for example, the beach. Describe how the place looks (bright, clean, colorful); smells (like the ocean or suntan lotion); feels (gritty sand, cool water); sounds (waves crashing, seagulls cawing); and tastes (salty water, sweet tropical fruit). Then have students draw a picture of their favorite place and describe the place to a partner using sensory details.

ADVANCED/ADVANCED HIGH

Topic Sentence Have students read a short informative text that is several paragraphs long. Ask them to identify the topic sentence of each paragraph and underline it. Have them compare with a partner and then as a class. Remind students that the topic sentence is not always the first sentence in the paragraph. Then have students identify the specific details that support the topic sentence in each paragraph.

Prewrite

The Rubric Says   A clear topic sentence introduces the topic. Well-chosen transitions guide the reader through the description.

Writing Strategy   Make a Web to organize your notes.

I know from the rubric that organization is important. To organize my notes, I'm going to make a Web. I'll put the main idea of my paragraph in the middle of my Web. Then I'll use my five senses to put the details in circles around my topic. The Web will make writing my paragraph easier because all of the information will be right there as I write.

Writer's Term

Main Idea and Supporting Details
The **Main Idea** is the most important thought about a topic. **Supporting Details** explain more about the main idea and provide more information about the topic.

Web

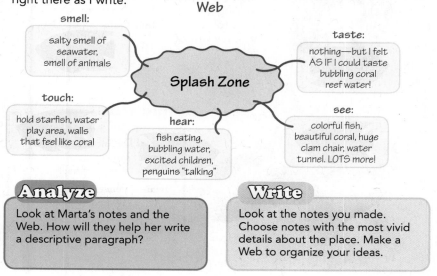

smell:
salty smell of seawater, smell of animals

taste:
nothing—but I felt AS IF I could taste bubbling coral reef water!

Splash Zone

touch:
hold starfish, water play area, walls that feel like coral

hear:
fish eating, bubbling water, excited children, penguins "talking"

see:
colorful fish, beautiful coral, huge clam chair, water tunnel. LOTS more!

Analyze
Look at Marta's notes and the Web. How will they help her write a descriptive paragraph?

Write
Look at the notes you made. Choose notes with the most vivid details about the place. Make a Web to organize your ideas.

Descriptive Paragraph   **365**

Collaborative Conferencing

PEER TO PEER   Have partners exchange Webs. Tell students to ask one question about their partner's Web, such as "What did the starfish feel like when you held it?" Each student can decide whether to include the answer to the question as a detail in his or her Web.

PEER GROUPS   Have groups of three or four students pass their Webs around the group. Students write the detail they find the most interesting on a sticky note attached to each Web.

TEACHER-LED   Work with individual students to hone their Webs. Point out your favorite detail in each student's Web, and then ask questions to elicit additional details.

Write
Descriptive Paragraph

Week 2 • Day 2

Student Objectives

- Make a Web to organize notes. (p. 365)

Prewrite

Focus on **Organization**

Organize Ideas   Explain that writing can be organized in many ways, and one way is to use a Web. (Go to **www.sfw.z-b.com** for the downloadable graphic organizer.) Have a student read the Writer's Term box aloud. Ask students if they have made a Web before. If so, how did the Web help them write? Read the rubric, writing strategy, and Marta's words aloud to students, and then discuss Marta's Web with them. Ask how Marta has organized the details. (by the five senses)

Writer's Term
Main Idea and Supporting Details Remind students that the main idea, or topic, is the most important thought in the paragraph. The main idea is supported by details that explain more about the topic. These details should make the reader want to continue reading the paragraph.

CCSS **C**ommon **C**ore **S**tate **S**tandards (pp. Z20–Z30)
Writing: W.4.3b, W.4.3d, W.4.4, W.4.5, W.4.6, W.4.8, W.4.10
Language: L.4.3a, L.4.3c, L.4.6
Speaking and Listening: SL.4.1a, SL.4.1b, SL.4.1c, SL.4.1d, SL.4.3, SL.4.6

Write
Descriptive Paragraph

Week 2 • Day 3

Student Objectives

- Begin writing, using sensory details. *(pp. 366–367)*

Draft

Focus on Ideas

Draft a Descriptive Paragraph
Discuss the term *draft* with students. Be sure they realize that a draft is an early, "rough" form of a written document. Explain that the purpose of a draft is to get ideas on paper without worrying about making mistakes. For example, Marta is not worried about grammar or spelling mistakes at this time. She knows that she will be changing and correcting her draft several times before it's ready to publish. Point out how Marta keeps going back to the rubric as she writes. Remind students to get in the habit of using the rubrics to help them as they write.

✏️ Writer's Term _____

Topic Sentence and Detail Sentences A topic sentence does not have to appear at the beginning of the paragraph, but it often does. Encourage students to write their topic sentence first, and then develop the detail sentences.

Online Writing Center

 Provides an **interactive writing pad** for drafting, revising, editing, and publishing.

Draft

Focus on **Ideas**

The Rubric Says The writer's topic is clear. Sensory details create a clear, focused picture of one place.

Writing Strategy Select details that will help the reader "see" the place.

Now it's time to write my descriptive paragraph. I'll use the center of my Web to write my topic sentence. Then I'll choose information from the other circles to write detail sentences. I know from the rubric that my topic sentence needs to be so clear that my reader can almost "see" my subject.

I won't worry about checking grammar or spelling right now. I know I'll get a chance to fix any mistakes later when I edit my writing.

✏️ Writer's Term _____

Topic Sentence and Detail Sentences
A **topic sentence** states the main idea of a whole paragraph.

Detail sentences go with, tell about, or give examples of the topic sentence.

366 More Writing Practice

Differentiating Instruction

ENRICHMENT

Write a Mystery Description Challenge students to write a descriptive paragraph about a common item found at home or in the classroom without revealing the name of the item. Each paragraph should include a wealth of sensory details about the item. Have students trade paragraphs with a partner and try to guess the item described.

REINFORCEMENT

Simplify the Web Have students create a simpler form of the Web, focusing on just two or three senses. Students will most likely want to include sight and sound in their Webs; you may work with them to decide which other sense can most easily be used to describe the place they have chosen.

[DRAFT]

detail sentence

Wet, Wild, and Wonderful

topic sentence

No one should miss Splash Zone at the Monterey Bay Aquarium. It is

the best place to learn about a life of sea animals. Where else can

kids sit in a giant clam chair or hear fish eating? Where else is there

a coral reef with bubbling walls of water. I can crawl through

a tunnel. As I crawl, I see sea horses, eeles, reef sharks, and

all kinds of fish. The bubbling water looked cold. Then there are

model starfish and other creatures. In the water play area, kids

can make waves and tide pooles. Then there are the blackfooted

penguins. They hop and swim around there home with rocks by the

water. They talk like donkys. A neat special window makes it seem as

if I suddenly popped up next to them. I can even stand behind a big

wall where I can put my head inside cutout faces on top of

painted penguin bodies. We took pictures. Splash Zone was fun.

detail sentence (×4)

Analyze

Read Marta's draft. Does her topic sentence describe a real place that readers might like to visit? How do the details she included help readers to "see" the place?

Write

Use your notes and Web to write your own draft. Remember to write a clear topic sentence and choose details that will help readers "see" what you describe.

Descriptive Paragraph 367

Collaborative Conferencing

PEER TO PEER Have students exchange drafts with a partner. Tell students to pick out the detail they like best in their partner's draft and to ask one question to clarify something they don't understand or one about a detail they would like to know more about.

PEER GROUPS Have students work in groups of three, taking turns to read their drafts aloud to the group. Have group members comment on which aspect of each place they found easiest to visualize based on the descriptions.

TEACHER-LED Work with pairs of students. Have each student read his or her draft aloud. Facilitate a discussion between students about what aspect of their partner's place they would like to know more about.

Write
Descriptive Paragraph

Week 2 • Day 4

Student Objectives

• Complete a draft.

Continue Drafting Read the model draft aloud as students follow along in their books, or ask student volunteers to read the draft aloud. Review the Writer's Term box on page 366, directing students' attention to the definitions of *topic sentence* and *detail sentences*. Discuss how Marta's topic sentence captures what she wants her readers to know about Splash Zone. Examine with students each detail sentence indicated by the notes. Discuss how each one supports the topic sentence.

It is important that students are given ample time to draft their paragraphs. As conferencing is important throughout the writing process, be sure to also plan time for peer-to-peer, peer group, or teacher-led conferences. Remind students that this is the time for getting their ideas down on paper in a creative and engaging way. Assure them that they will have plenty of time to fix any mistakes later.

CCSS Common Core State Standards (pp. Z20–Z30)

Writing: W.4.3a, W.4.3b, W.4.3d, W.4.4, W.4.5, W.4.6, W.4.10

Language: L.4.3a, L.4.3c, L.4.6

Speaking and Listening: SL.4.1a, SL.4.1b, SL.4.1c, SL.4.1d, SL.4.3, SL.4.6

Write Descriptive Paragraph

Week 2 • Day 5

Student Objectives

- Revise for helpful transitions. (p. 368)

Revise

Focus on Organization

Include Helpful Transitions

Read the rubric descriptor, writing strategy, and Writer's Term box aloud as students follow along in their books. Discuss why transitions are important to a reader. Then have volunteers read the draft excerpt aloud, first without the revisions and then with the revisions. How do these transitions guide the reader? **(Possible response: They help you feel like you are moving from place to place inside Splash Zone.)**

 Writer's Term

Transitions Various types of transition words can be used to link ideas logically. Temporal transitions, such as *first*, *then*, and *next* show sequence. Words such as *unlike*, *just like*, *instead*, and *but* show comparison and contrast. *Nearby*, *farther away*, *next to*, and *beyond* can show transitions from place to place. See page T487 for a list of transitions.

Strategies for Writers Online
Go to **www.sfw.z-b.com** for additional online resources for students, teachers, and parents.

Revise

Focus on **Organization**

The Rubric Says	Well-chosen transitions guide the reader through the description.
Writing Strategy	Use words and phrases that help the reader follow the description.

After I wrote my paragraph, I decided to add transitions. The rubric says that well-chosen transitions guide the reader. Phrases that begin with *at* will help the reader feel as if they are following me through Splash Zone. I can explain where we found the model starfish and the blackfooted penguins.

 Writer's Term

Transitions

Transitions guide the reader from one idea to the next. In a paragraph, transitional words and phrases help link the details in a logical order.

[DRAFT]

At the touch pool,

~~Then~~ there are model starfish and other creatures. In the water play   *added transition*

area, kids can make waves and tide pooles. ~~Then there~~ are the   At the end of Splash Zone

blackfooted penguins. They hop and swim around there home with   *added transition*

rocks by the water.

Write

Read your draft. Revise your draft to add transitions that guide the reader through your description.

English Language Learners

BEGINNING/INTERMEDIATE
Position Transitions Have students refer to the pictures they drew of their favorite places. Ask them to draw themselves in the picture. Then have them describe the items in the picture with respect to their location. For example, draw yourself lying in a hammock in your beach picture. Then say, *Above me, the towering coconut trees sway in the breeze.* Circle *Above me,* and tell students that the words tell where the trees are. Introduce other position words and phrases, such as *nearby, around the corner, to my right,* and so on.

ADVANCED/ADVANCED HIGH
Position Transitions Have partners work together to write a description of the classroom, including transition words that tell about the position of various items in the room, such as the teacher's desk and the computer station. Have volunteers from each pair read the descriptions, and discuss them as a group. On the board, write any words that indicate position.

Revise

Focus on Voice

The Rubric Says The writer's personality comes across clearly. The voice speaks directly to the reader.

Writing Strategy Use first-person point of view to share your feelings.

The rubric says that I should let my personality come through in my writing. I should also speak directly to the reader.

By sharing my feelings about my visit to Splash Zone, the reader will get to know a little bit about my personality. By using first person (*I, me, my, we*), I help the reader share my personal experience.

[DRAFT]

used first-person words

if I suddenly popped up next to them. I can even stand behind

a big wall where I can put my head inside cutout faces on top of

My parents and I looked silly in the picture

we took there. I remember Splash Zone

and laugh whenever I look at the photograph

of my family as penguins!

painted penguin bodies. ~~We took pictures. Splash Zone was fun.~~

Analyze
Look at Marta's revisions. What do they tell you about Marta's personality? What words show that she is writing from the first-person point of view?

Write
Read your draft again. Look for places where you can add personal feelings about your experience. Remember to use *I, me, we,* and *our* to talk about your feelings.

Descriptive Paragraph **369**

Collaborative Conferencing

PEER TO PEER Have partners exchange drafts. Tell students to suggest to their partner one place where a transition would be helpful or to point out a transition they found especially helpful.

PEER GROUPS Have students work in groups of three or four and pass their drafts around the group. Each student uses a pencil to lightly circle a place where a transition could be added or improved or to underline a transition they think works well.

TEACHER-LED Meet with individual students. Ask questions to elicit their personal reactions to the place they describe and coach them on using first-person point of view to convey their personal experiences.

Write
Descriptive Paragraph

Week 3 • Day 1

Student Objectives

• Revise for first-person point of view. (p. 369)

Revise

Focus on Voice

Use First-Person Point of View

Read the rubric descriptor and writing strategy aloud. Ask student volunteers to define first-person point of view. Help students practice the concept by writing sample sentences such as the following on the board and asking students to tell you which ones are in first person:

The aquarium is my favorite place to go.

Maya and Dan went to the zoo last week.

I keep some fish in a tank at home.

Mrs. Suarez rescues animals that have been abandoned.

Read Marta's words and the draft excerpt with students and discuss why using first-person point of view helps Marta connect with the reader.

CCSS **Common Core State Standards** (pp. Z20–Z30)
Writing: W.4.3b, W.4.3c, W.4.3d, W.4.4, W.4.5, W.4.10
Language: L.4.3a, L.4.3c, L.4.6
Speaking and Listening: SL.4.1a, SL.4.1b, SL.4.1c, SL.4.1d, SL.4.3, SL.4.6

Write Descriptive Paragraph

Week 3 • Day 2

Student Objectives

- Revise for descriptive word choice. (p. 370)

Revise

Focus on Word Choice

Create Word Pictures Emphasize that word pictures are very descriptive passages that help the reader visualize what the writer is describing. Have students read Marta's draft and identify the word picture she has added. Discuss ways in which adding this word picture makes the description more interesting and vivid.

Have students look for places in their descriptive paragraphs where they can add word pictures.

Writer's Term

Word Picture A word picture often uses comparisons to help readers create a mental image. The item being described is compared to a familiar image that readers can easily picture. Word pictures usually also use precise language, that is, *amazing, delicious, impressive,* or *skillful* instead of *good*.

Online Writing Center

Provides **interactive proofreading activities** for each genre.

T370 More Writing Practice

Revise

Focus on **Word Choice**

The Rubric Says   Descriptive language creates a vivid picture for the reader.

Writing Strategy   Include word pictures to improve my description.

After I wrote my draft, I decided to write a word picture to support my topic. At Splash Zone, we had a picture taken of us behind the painted penguins with cutout faces. I'll revise my new sentence to make a funny word picture describing that photograph. That way, my audience will be able to "see" how much fun Splash Zone is.

Writer's Term

Word Picture

A **word picture** is a vivid description of something in words. By painting pictures with words, you help the reader imagine the place you are describing.

[DRAFT]

like a family of chubby birds wearing tuxedos

My parents and I looked ~~silly~~ in the picture we took there.

created a word picture

I remember Splash Zone and laugh whenever I look at the photograph of my

family as penguins!

Write

Read your draft. Revise your draft to create word pictures that help the reader imagine what you are describing.

370   More Writing Practice

Optional Revising Lessons

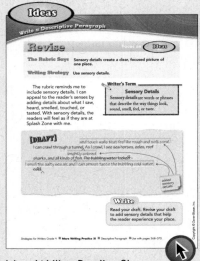

More Writing Practice 3l

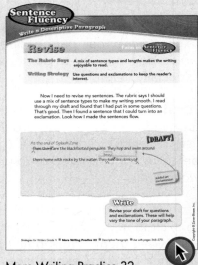

More Writing Practice 32

Go to ➡ **Strategies for Writers** at **www.sfw.z-b.com.**

Edit

The Rubric Says Articles and plural nouns are used correctly.

Writing Strategy Make sure plural nouns and articles are correct.

Next I'll check my spelling, capitalization, and punctuation. Also the rubric reminds me to make sure that all my plural nouns and articles are formed correctly.

Writer's Term

Plural Nouns
A **plural noun** names more than one thing. Add **-s** to most singular nouns to form the plural. Add **-es** to singular nouns that end in **s, x, ch,** or **sh.** Some nouns form the plural in other ways, like *children* or *geese.*

[DRAFT]

No one should miss Splash Zone at the Monterey Bay Aquarium. It is the

the lives

best place to learn about ~~a life~~ of sea animals.

 corrected article and plural noun

Analyze
What do you think of Marta's revisions? Are the plural nouns and articles correct? How do you know?

Write   **Conventions**
Edit your draft for spelling, capitalization, and punctuation. Make sure all your plural nouns and articles are correct.

For more practice with plural nouns and articles, use the exercises on the next two pages.

Descriptive Paragraph **371**

Related Grammar Practice

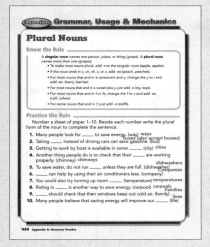

Student Edition page 450

Go to ➡ **Appendix A: Grammar Practice**

Student Objectives
- Edit for accurate use of articles and plural nouns. *(p. 371)*

Edit

Focus on **Conventions**

Check Plural Nouns Tell students that articles are the short words before nouns: *a, an,* and *the.* Discuss why mistakes in using articles and plural nouns can be confusing.

Teach the Conventions mini-lessons on pages T372–T373 if students need help using articles and plural nouns correctly.

Have students begin checking their paragraphs to correct the formation of plural nouns and the use of articles. Remind them that they should also be editing their drafts for spelling, punctuation, and capitalization.

Writer's Term
Plural Nouns Other common plural nouns with irregular formations are *men* and *women.* Some nouns, such as *sheep, moose,* and *fruit,* do not change forms in the plural. Many singular nouns, such as *life,* change the *f* to *v* to form the plural (*lives*).

CCSS **Common Core State Standards** (pp. Z20–Z30)
Writing: W.4.3a, W.4.3b, W.4.3d, W.4.4, W.4.5, W.4.6, W.4.10
Language: L.4.2a, L.4.2d, L.4.3a, L.4.6

Descriptive Paragraph **T371**

Conventions

Mini-Lesson

Student Objectives

• Form plural nouns correctly. (p. 372)

Plural Nouns

Begin by asking students to explain what a noun is. (A noun is a word that names a person, place, thing, or idea.) Review the rules for forming plural nouns. Model each of these rules by writing a singular noun on the board, then asking students to explain how the plural would be formed. Then reverse the process.

Provide students with ten index cards each. Tell them that they will be making their own singular/plural noun flashcards. Each set should include the following: one card each for words ending in *s*, *x*, *ch*, or *sh*; one card each for words ending in *y* or *f*; the remaining four cards for nouns that require only *-s* to form the plural. Model how cards should be made with a singular noun on the front and its plural form on the back. Check completed cards for accuracy. Then have students work with a partner, using their flashcards to practice.

Online Writing Center

Provides **interactive grammar games** and **practice activities** in student eBook.

Conventions **Grammar, Usage & Mechanics**

Plural Nouns

Know the Rule

A **noun** is a word that names a person, place, or thing. A singular noun names one thing. A plural noun names more than one thing. Most singular nouns become plural when you add *-s*.
> **Example: dog/dogs**

If a singular noun ends in *s, x, ch,* or *sh,* add *-es* to make it a plural noun.
> **Example: tax/taxes**

If a singular noun ends in a consonant and *y,* change the *y* to *i* before adding *-es.*
> **Example: daisy/daisies**

Many singular nouns that end in *f* change the *f* to *v* to form the plural.
> **Example: shelf/shelves, hoof/hooves**

However, not all singular nouns that end in *f* do this.
> **Example: roof/roofs, chief/chiefs, cliff/cliffs**

Practice the Rule

Number a separate sheet of paper 1–10. Read each sentence below. Write the plural form of the noun in parentheses.

1. We spent two (week) at a national park. weeks
2. The (beach) had soft white sand. beaches
3. We ate many picnic (lunch) there. lunches
4. One beach was divided into two (half). halves
5. People could swim and have (party) on one side. parties
6. Birds raised their (baby) on the other side. babies
7. Sometimes (fox) would raid a nest. foxes
8. Some people pitched (tent) at a nearby campground. tents
9. Campers were careful not to leave any (mess) behind. messes
10. People always carried their trash and (dish) away. dishes

Related Grammar Practice

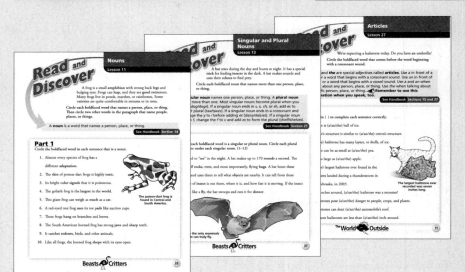

Pages 33, 37, 71

Go to **G.U.M. Student Practice Book**

Articles

Know the Rule

A, *an*, and *the* are special adjectives called **articles**. Use *a* before a word that begins with a consonant sound. Use *an* before a word that begins with a vowel sound. Use *a* and *an* when talking about any one person, place, or thing. Use *the* when talking about specific persons, places, or things.

Examples:

The moon shone brightly until **a** cloud blocked it out.

An ant crawled into **the** tent.

Practice the Rule

Number a separate sheet of paper 1–10. Read each sentence below. Write the correct article (*a*, *an*, *the*) to complete each sentence.

1. Our campsite was by _____ edge of the lake. **the**
2. I had _____ air mattress to put in my tent. **an**
3. We brought wood to build _____ fire. **a**
4. I looked for _____ stick to roast marshmallows. **a**
5. _____ roasted marshmallows were delicious. **The**
6. We kept warm by _____ fire my dad built. **the**
7. During the night, I heard _____ owl in the trees. **an**
8. _____ nighttime animal sounds kept me awake. **The**
9. I saw _____ sun come up in the morning. **the**
10. I helped pack up and take _____ tents down. **the**

Student Objectives

• Use articles correctly. *(p. 373)*

Articles

Read the definition of *articles* with students. Make sure students understand that *the* is used for specific items, while *a* and *an* are used for any item in a group. Demonstrate using classroom commands such as the following:

Please hand me the pencil. (gesturing toward a specific pencil)

Please get me a pencil. (gesturing toward a group of pencils)

Show me the map of the United States.

Show me a map.

Ask volunteers to make up their own commands to demonstrate the different articles.

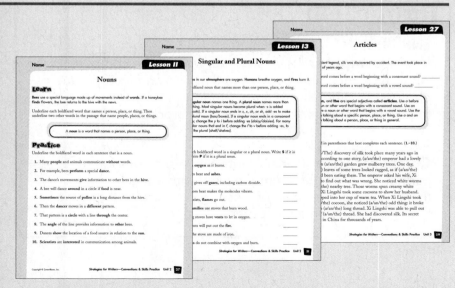

Pages 27, 31, 59

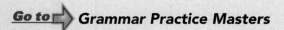

Go to ➡ *Grammar Practice Masters*

CCSS Common Core State Standards (pp. Z20–Z30)
Writing: W.4.6
Language: L.4.2d, L.4.4a, L.4.6

Write
Descriptive Paragraph

Week 3 • Day 4

Student Objectives

- Discuss preparation for publishing and presentation. *(p. 374)*
- Use a final editing checklist to publish their work. *(p. 374)*

Publish +Presentation

Publishing Strategy Show students samples of brochures for theme parks or travel destinations. Explain that the purpose of a brochure is to advertise or promote something. Discuss with students why a brochure is a good publishing choice for Marta's descriptive paragraph. Ask them to suggest the benefits of including photographs or drawings in a brochure. Challenge students to think of other ways Marta could publish her work.

Review Marta's final checklist for publishing, and then have students make a final checklist of their own. Encourage students to include drawings or photographs in their brochures.

Strategies for Writers Online
Go to **www.sfw.z-b.com** for additional online resources for students, teachers, and parents.

Publish   +Presentation

Publishing Strategy	Publish the description as part of a brochure.
Presentation Strategy	Use a limited number of clear fonts.

My descriptive paragraph is done! My next step is to publish it. I think I should publish my description as part of a brochure. In a brochure, I can describe what it's like to be at Splash Zone and invite others to visit, too. Then my classmates will see why they should go! I will prepare my brochure on the computer. The rubric tells me to use clear fonts. Too many fonts will distract from my writing. So I will choose a few fonts that are attractive and easy to read. I will use this checklist to check my descriptive paragraph one more time.

My Final Checklist

Did I—
- ✔ check to make sure all plural nouns are correct?
- ✔ make sure I used articles correctly?
- ✔ use a few clear fonts?
- ✔ put my name on the brochure?

Write

Make a checklist for your own descriptive paragraph. Then make a final copy and publish it as part of a brochure. Make copies of your brochure to share with your classmates.

374 More Writing Practice

Differentiating Instruction

ENRICHMENT

Use a Computer Have students work in the computer lab to type their final copy as well as find and incorporate photos and other illustrations. Students may work as a group to research images to include in their brochures.

REINFORCEMENT

Computer Help Pair students with more computer-literate partners or allow them time to work with a teacher to learn the features of the word-processing program as they type their paragraph on a computer.

Wet, Wild, and Wonderful
by Marta

No one should miss Splash Zone at the Monterey Bay Aquarium. It is the best place to learn about the lives of sea animals. Where else could I sit in a giant clam chair or hear fish eating? Where else could I visit a coral reef with bubbling walls of water? I can crawl through a tunnel and touch walls that feel like rough and soft coral. As I crawl, I see sea horses, eels, reef sharks, and all kinds of brightly colored fish. I smell the salty sea air, and I can almost taste the bubbling, cold water. At the touch pool, I can pick up live and model starfish and other creatures. In the water play area, I can make waves and tide pools. At the end of Splash Zone are the blackfooted penguins. They hop and swim around their rocky home. They bray like donkeys! A special window makes it seem as if I suddenly pop up next to them. I can even stand behind a big wall where I can put my head inside cutout faces on top of painted penguin bodies. My parents and I looked like a family of chubby birds wearing tuxedos in the picture we took there. I remember Splash Zone and laugh whenever I look at the photograph of my family as penguins!

Analyze

Use the rubric to evaluate Marta's paragraph. Then use it to evaluate your own paragraph.

Tech Tips
Online Videos

Use Online Video Series Our students invariably bring a range of literacies and technology know-how that exceeds what we know as teachers. This is an opportunity to leverage that and have students reciprocally teach one another. Ask student groups to apply their descriptive skills to create a "how-to" video modeled from the Common Craft online video series. Post these online, and tag them so others can find them to provide feedback and, perhaps more importantly, to learn. A multimodal description is more complex than a written paragraph and is an interesting extension of what they've learned.

See **www.sfw.z-b.com** for further information about and links to these websites and tools.

Write
Descriptive Paragraph

Week 3 • Day 5

Student Objectives

- Use a descriptive paragraph rubric. *(pp. 358–359)*
- Share a published descriptive paragraph. *(p. 375)*

Presentation Strategy Remind students that a neat, legible paper makes it easier to get their message across to the reader. Messy, cramped, hard-to-read handwriting makes reading a chore and may discourage a reader from reading through to the end.

Tell students that when using a computer, simple common fonts such as Times New Roman or Arial are best. They may wish to use a more decorative font for the title, but it should still be easily readable.

Reflecting on a Descriptive Paragraph

Ask students to share their paragraph with a partner and tell one thing they like about their paragraph and one thing they would do differently next time. Each partner should respond with one positive comment about the paragraph.

CCSS **Common Core State Standards** (pp. Z20–Z30)
Writing: W.4.3a, W.4.4, W.4.6, W.4.10
Language: L.4.3c
Speaking and Listening: SL.4.1a, SL.4.1b, SL.4.1c, SL.4.1d, SL.4.3, SL.4.6

Character Sketch Planner

	Day 1	Day 2	Day 3
WEEK 1	**Introduce** Character Sketch	**Analyze** Close Reading of the Model	**Analyze** Introduce the Rubric

WEEK 1

Day 1 — Introduce: Character Sketch

Student Objectives
- Review the elements of a character sketch.
- Consider purpose and audience.
- Learn the traits of descriptive writing.

Student Activities
- Read and discuss **What's in a Character Sketch?** (p. 376)
- Read and discuss **Why Write a Character Sketch?** (p. 377)
- Read **Linking Descriptive Writing Traits to a Character Sketch.** (p. 378)

Day 2 — Analyze: Close Reading of the Model

Student Objectives
- Read a model character sketch.

Student Activities
- Read **"Johnny Appleseed."** (p. 379)

Day 3 — Analyze: Introduce the Rubric

Student Objectives
- Learn to read a rubric.

Student Activities
- Review **"Johnny Appleseed."** (p. 379)
- Read and discuss the **Character Sketch Rubric.** (pp. 380–381)

WEEK 2

Day 1 — Write: Prewrite: Ideas

Student Objectives
- Read and understand a prewriting strategy.

Student Activities
- Read and discuss **Prewrite: Focus on Ideas.** (p. 386)
- Apply the prewriting strategy.

Day 2 — Write: Prewrite: Organization

Student Objectives
- Make a Spider Map to organize details.

Student Activities
- Read and discuss **Prewrite: Focus on Organization.** (p. 387)
- Reflect on the model Spider Map.
- Apply the prewriting strategy to create a Spider Map.
- Participate in a peer conference.

Day 3 — Write: Draft: Organization

Student Objectives
- Begin writing an introduction, body, and conclusion.

Student Activities
- Read and discuss **Draft: Focus on Organization.** (p. 388)
- Apply the drafting strategy by using a Spider Map to write a draft.

WEEK 3

Day 1 — Write: Revise: Word Choice

Student Objectives
- Revise to eliminate clichés.

Student Activities
- Read and discuss **Revise: Focus on Word Choice.** (p. 391)
- Reflect on the model draft.
- Apply the revising strategy.
- Participate in a peer conference.

Day 2 — Write: Revise: Sentence Fluency

Student Objectives
- Revise for sentence length.

Student Activities
- Read and discuss **Revise: Focus on Sentence Fluency.** (p. 392)
- Reflect on the model draft.
- Apply the revising strategy.

Note: Optional Revising Lessons are located at **www.sfw.z-b.com**

Day 3 — Write: Edit: Conventions

Student Objectives
- Edit to eliminate run-on sentences.

Student Activities
- Read and discuss **Edit: Focus on Conventions.** (p. 393)
- Reflect on the model draft.
- Apply the revising strategy.

Note: Teach the Conventions mini-lessons (pp. 394–395) if needed.

Day 4
Analyze
Close Reading for the Traits

Student Objectives
- Read a model character sketch.
- Use the character sketch rubric.
- Use the model character sketch to study Ideas, Organization, and Voice.

Student Activities
- Review **"Johnny Appleseed."** (p. 379)
- Read and discuss **Using the Rubric to Analyze the Model.** (pp. 382–383)

Day 5
Analyze
Close Reading for the Traits

Student Objectives
- Read a model character sketch.
- Use the character sketch rubric.
- Use the model character sketch to study Word Choice, Sentence Fluency, and Conventions.

Student Activities
- Review **"Johnny Appleseed."** (p. 379)
- Read and discuss **Using the Rubric to Analyze the Model.** (pp. 384–385)

Day 4
Write
Draft

Student Objectives
- Complete a draft.

Student Activities
- Finish the draft.
- Reflect on the model draft. (p. 389)
- Participate in a peer conference.

Day 5
Write
Revise: Voice

Student Objectives
- Revise to express the writer's personality.

Student Activities
- Read and discuss **Revise: Focus on Voice.** (p. 390)
- Reflect on a model draft.
- Apply the revising strategy.

Day 4
Write
Publish: +Presentation

Student Objectives
- Discuss preparation for publishing and presentation.
- Use a final editing checklist to publish their work.

Student Activities
- Read and discuss **Publish: +Presentation.** (p. 396)
- Apply the publishing strategy.

Day 5
Write
Publish: +Presentation

Student Objectives
- Use a character sketch rubric.
- Share a published character sketch.

Student Activities
- Share their work.
- Use the rubric to reflect upon and evaluate the model and their own writing. (pp. 380–381, 397)

To complete the chapter in fewer days, combine the learning objectives and activities in a way that supports students as they write.

Resources at-a-Glance

Grammar, Usage & Mechanics

Differentiating Instruction
For additional Differentiating Instruction activities, see Strategies for Writers *Differentiated Instruction Activities at* **www.sfw.z-b.com.**

English Language Learners

Collaborative Conferencing

Tech Tips

 Strategies for Writers Online

Go to **www.sfw.z-b.com** for additional online resources for students, teachers, and parents.

Online Writing Center

Provides IWB resources, assessments, interactive games and practice activities, videos, eBooks, and a virtual file cabinet.

Introduce
Character Sketch

Student Objectives

- Review the elements of a character sketch. *(p. 376)*
- Consider purpose and audience. *(p. 377)*
- Learn the traits of descriptive writing. *(p. 378)*

What's a Character Sketch?

Have a student volunteer read aloud the definition of a character sketch. Point out that the word *sketch* has different meanings. It can be a quick drawing or a brief description. A character sketch is a brief description of a real or fictional person. A good character sketch allows readers to picture the subject in their minds.

What's in a Character Sketch?

Read and discuss the elements of a character sketch with students. Then ask students to name interesting people whom they know from real life, books, or movies. Ask them to explain why they find these people memorable. Then explain that a character sketch allows a writer to introduce such characters to other people who might find them interesting.

 Strategies for Writers Online
Go to **www.sfw.z-b.com** for additional online resources for students, teachers, and parents.

What's a Character Sketch?

It's a description of a real person or a character in a book.

What's in a Character Sketch?

Appearance
That's what my character looks like. Describing my character will help the reader "see" the person.

Thoughts
That's what my character thinks. Describing what my character thinks will make the person more interesting.

Words
That's what my character says. Describing what a character says makes the person seem real.

Actions
That's what my character does. My character's actions will tell a lot about his or her personality. The actions could be adventuresome like an astronaut in space or thoughtful like an author.

Descriptive Text Exemplars (Character Sketch)

Fry, Jason. *Star Wars Clone Wars Character Encyclopedia*. DK Publishing, 2010. Fry describes over 200 characters from the Star Wars Clone Wars series in this engaging reference book. A diagram and statistics, including the character's species, height, gender, and allegiance, provide readers with an in-depth explanation of each character.

Snider, Brandon T. *DC Comics: The Ultimate Character Guide*. DK Publishing, 2011. This guide describes the many superheroes and villains of DC Comics. Including members such as Superman and Wonder Woman, *DC Comics: The Ultimate Character Guide* provides a brief description of each character.

Why write a Character Sketch?

Describing a person can be fun, but it's also helpful.
Here are some good reasons for writing a character sketch.

To Entertain
People are so interesting! Characters can be quiet or adventuresome, heroes or villains. They make good decisions or bad ones. Exploring the world of people—real and imaginary—is fascinating!

To Inform
Biographers write character sketches to help us get to know the people they are writing about. Reporters may write character sketches of people in the community. I can write a character sketch about an interesting person to share with others.

To Understand
No two people are exactly the same. Writing about real people and characters in books can help us understand others. We can recognize what we have in common. We can learn to appreciate our differences.

Character Sketch **377**

Why write a Character Sketch?

Have students take turns reading aloud the reasons for writing a character sketch on page 377. Remind them that the purpose of a character sketch is to help the reader form a strong mental image of the person. As a class, discuss where students might expect to find a character sketch written for entertainment, information, or understanding. For example, would they be surprised to find an informational character sketch in a fan magazine? Would a character sketch of an imaginary person be out of place in a nonfiction story?

Point out that, like other types of writing students have explored, character sketches are written for a specific audience. Encourage students to keep in mind their own reasons for writing as well as their intended audiences as they develop their character sketches.

Grant, John. *Encyclopedia of Walt Disney's Animated Characters: From Mickey Mouse to Hercules.* **Disney Editions, 1998.** Hundreds of Disney creations are included in John Grant's extensive encyclopedia. From Tinkerbell to Timon and Pumba, students are sure to find their favorite Disney character in this colorful compilation.

Stewart, Mark. *Movie Characters.* **Gareth Stevens Publishing, 2009.** Including characters such as Harry Potter and James Bond, this top ten guide offers readers fun facts about their favorite cast members. Part of the *Ultimate 10: Entertainment* series, *Movie Characters* is one of several books giving readers a glimpse into the world of entertainment.

CCSS **Common Core State Standards** (pp. Z20–Z30)
Language: L.4.3c
Speaking and Listening: SL.4.1a, SL.4.1b, SL.4.1c, SL.4.1d, SL.4.3, SL.4.6

Character Sketch **T377**

Introduce
Character Sketch

Linking Descriptive Writing Traits to a Character Sketch

Have students read page 378. Emphasize that they will follow Marta as she models using the writing process and the descriptive writing traits together.

Discuss with students how each trait applies to a character sketch. Ask students to imagine how readers would react to reading a paragraph that was lacking in one of the traits—for example, if the language was vague or the writer failed to connect with the reader.

Online Writing Center

Provides six **interactive anchor papers** for each text type.

Linking Descriptive Writing Traits to a Character Sketch

In this chapter, you will describe a person. This type of descriptive writing is called a character sketch. Marta will guide you through the stages of the writing process: Prewrite, Draft, Revise, Edit, and Publish. In each stage, Marta will show you important writing strategies that are linked to the Descriptive Writing Traits below.

Descriptive Writing Traits

 Ideas
- a clear and complete topic
- sensory details and examples that help the reader "see" what is being described

 Organization
- well-organized paragraphs that each tell about one main idea
- transitions that guide the reader through the text

 Voice
- a voice and tone that are appropriate for the purpose and connect with the audience

 Word Choice
- precise, descriptive language that creates a picture for the reader

 Sentence Fluency
- different kinds of sentences that make the writing flow

 **Conventions**
- no or few errors in grammar, usage, mechanics, and spelling

Before you write, read Ed Lee's character sketch on the next page. Then use the character sketch rubric on pages 380–381 to decide how well he did. (You might want to look back at What's in a Character Sketch? on page 376, too!)

Descriptive Writing Traits in a Character Sketch

 **Ideas** The writer must choose a topic that is appropriate in scope. Students should focus on aspects of the person that can be described in the space of a short sketch. Abundant sensory details will help readers feel they know the character described.

 **Organization** The character sketch should have a clearly stated main idea that is supported by the details about the person described. Transitions will help readers move from one detail to the next.

 **Voice** An appropriate voice and tone will convey the flavor of the subject's personality and help the reader understand how the writer feels about the subject.

JOHNNY APPLESEED

Character MODEL Sketch

by Ed Lee

Johnny Appleseed is the title of a book by Reeve Lindbergh. It is also the name of the folk hero who is the main character in the book. Johnny Appleseed was a real person, but Appleseed wasn't his real last name. The name given to him at birth was John Chapman. He was later called Johnny Appleseed because he traveled around the country planting apple trees.

appearance → Johnny Appleseed was a thin man with a lean face. He traveled barefoot, sometimes in rain and snow. His clothes were old and worn, but he did not care about how he looked. He cared about what he did with his life.

actions → The life he chose was to plant apple trees across the country. He knew that apples were a very important crop in early America, and they could be grown easily. However, pioneers did not have room to carry small trees with them. Johnny Appleseed carried young, healthy apple trees to families who were settling the western frontier. Sometimes he shared a meal and talked with the families, but he never stayed long in any one place. Wherever he went next, he scattered his precious apple seeds.

Johnny Appleseed was a very gentle man. He walked alone **actions** through unsettled territory filled with wild animals, but he never carried anything to protect himself. He told people that **words** he would never harm a living creature. He was also a very grateful person, and he appreciated the beauty around him. He spoke about his love for the grand, green forests, the vast prairies, and the wide rivers. He spoke about his respect for the rich and fertile land he traveled.

Johnny Appleseed gave a lot to people. The wilderness blossomed with his apple trees. Even so, he did not believe that **thoughts** anyone owed him any special thanks. In our day, people express their thanks by writing books about him. The next time you take a bite of fresh-baked apple pie, think of Johnny Appleseed!

Character Sketch 379

Analyze
Close Reading of the Model

Week 1 • Day 2

Student Objectives

• Read a model character sketch. *(p. 379)*

Read the Model

Read "Johnny Appleseed" aloud as students follow along in their books. Ask volunteers for their reactions to the character sketch. What type of person was Johnny Appleseed? How does the writer feel about Johnny Appleseed?

Elements of a Character Sketch

Use the notes on the model to discuss the elements of a character sketch. Refer students to What's in a Character Sketch? on page 376 if they need to review the elements. Discuss how each type of detail contributes to the overall picture of Johnny Appleseed.

CCSS **Common Core State Standards** (pp. Z20–Z30)
Writing: W.4.6
Language: L.4.3c
Speaking and Listening: SL.4.1a, SL.4.1b, SL.4.1c, SL.4.1d, SL.4.2, SL.4.3, SL.4.6

Analyze
Introduce the Rubric

Week 1 • Day 3

Student Objectives

- Learn to read a rubric. *(pp. 380–381)*

Introduce the Rubric

Explain the Rubric Explain that a rubric is a tool for planning, improving, and assessing a piece of writing. Tell students that a rubric helps a writer focus on key elements, or traits, in writing (**Ideas, Organization, Voice, Word Choice, Sentence Fluency, Conventions,** and **Presentation**). Point out that column 6 describes a very good character sketch, one that has received the highest score in all categories. This is what students should strive for in their own writing.

Discuss the Rubric Guide students in a discussion of the rubric. Read the descriptors that go with each trait, and take a moment to point out the ways the traits support each other. For example, using precise words to paint a picture (**Word Choice**) helps the writer convey descriptive details (**Ideas**). Remind students to keep the rubric in mind when they write their own character sketch and again when they revise it.

Online Writing Center

Provides a variety of **interactive rubrics,** including 4-, 5-, and 6-point models.

Character Sketch Rubric

Use this rubric to analyze the model. Then use it to plan and score your own character sketch.

	6	5	4	
Ideas	The writer's topic is clear. Descriptive details bring the subject to life for the reader.	The writer's topic is clear. Many important details bring the character to life.	The writer's topic is clear. More descriptive details would help the reader.	
Organization	The strong introduction, body, and conclusion fit together well. A variety of helpful transitions guides the reader through the description.	The strong introduction, body, and conclusion fit together. Most transitions help the reader follow the description.	The introduction, body, and conclusion fit together. In one or two places, transitions help the reader follow the description.	
Voice	The writer's personality comes through. The reader can tell the writer knows about and likes the subject.	The writer's personality and feelings come through most of the time.	Some of the writer's personality and feelings come through. The voice is appropriate.	
Word Choice	The words paint a clear picture. Concrete words and phrases help the reader "see" the subject.	Most of the words and phrases are concrete and help the reader "see" the subject.	Some words and phrases are too general. The reader cannot always picture the subject.	
Sentence Fluency	Sentence lengths and structures are varied effectively.	Most of the sentence structures and lengths are varied.	Many of the sentences are the same length and/or structure.	
Conventions	The writing is free from errors. Compound sentences are written correctly. There are no run-on sentences.	There are minor errors in compound sentences and no run-on sentences. Errors do not impair meaning.	There are a few errors in compound sentences and one or two run-on sentences. However, the errors do not confuse the reader.	

+Presentation A title and the writer's name are on the sketch. Paragraphs are indented.

CCSS Common Core State Standards
Character Sketch

Writing descriptive text can engage the Common Core State Standards for both Narrative and Informative/Explanatory writing. The Ideas rubric for the character sketch is drawn from several standards, both informative/explanatory and narrative: **W.4.2** focuses on clearly introducing a topic, **W.4.2** emphasizes concrete details, **W.4.3** focuses on establishing a character, and **W.4.3** mentions the importance of description. With its focus on transitions, the Organization rubric reflects both informative/explanatory standard **W.4.2** and narrative standard **W.4.c**. The Organization rubric also picks up the emphasis on introduction and conclusion from standards

3	2	1	
The writer's topic is unclear in places. Descriptions are not specific, confusing the reader.	The writer's topic is not clear. Few descriptive details help the reader.	The writer's topic is not clear. Details are unrelated or not provided.	**Ideas**
The introduction, body, and conclusion do not fit together well. Transitions, if used, may mislead or confuse the reader.	The introduction, body, and conclusion are not clear. Transitions are not used.	The writing does not have an introduction and/or a conclusion. Transitions are not used.	**Organization**
The writer's personality and feelings are inconsistent and not creatively expressed.	The writer's voice is very weak. It is difficult to sense personality or feelings. The voice may be inappropriate.	The reader cannot sense the writer's personality. The writer seems not to know or care about the subject.	**Voice**
Some of the words and phrases are dull. Some phrases are hard for the reader to understand.	The words and phrases are ordinary. They do not describe the subject well.	Many words or phrases are misused, confusing, and vague. The reader feels lost.	**Word Choice**
Repetitive sentence beginnings and length make text choppy and awkward.	Lack of sentence variety makes text very difficult to read and understand.	Many sentences are incomplete or incorrect. They are difficult to read.	**Sentence Fluency**
Several run-on sentences and incorrect compound sentences make the reader stop to reread.	Too many run-on sentences and incorrect compound sentences confuse the reader.	Many run-on sentences and poor compound sentences make the writing very hard to understand.	**Conventions**

See Appendix B for 4-, 5-, and 6-point descriptive rubrics.

W.4.2, W.4.3, W.4.2, and W.4.3. The Word Choice rubric is drawn principally from narrative standard W.4.3, which focuses on concrete words and phrases. The Conventions rubric addresses standards L.4.1 and L.4.2, which address command of the conventions of grammar, usage, capitalization, spelling, and punctuation.

Find Evidence in the Model

Small-Group Collaboration
Assign a small group of students and tell them to evaluate the model using the rubric. Assign one person in each group to record the group's findings and one person to report the findings to the class. Instruct students to score the model for each trait based on evidence in the text. Remind students to read closely to identify examples to support their high or low scores. Note: Although the models were written to score high in each trait, students should not assume each trait would receive a 6, the top score.

Teacher-Led Discussion Bring the class back together and have the reporters present their findings and scores. Prompt groups to provide evidence and examples for their scores from the model as needed.

Additional Rubrics

Appendix B includes 4-, 5-, and 6-point rubrics that can be used with any piece of descriptive writing. The rubrics are also available as blackline masters in the back of this Teacher Edition.

CCSS **C**ommon **C**ore **S**tate **S**tandards (pp. Z20–Z30)
Writing: W.4.6
Language: L.4.3c
Speaking and Listening: SL.4.1a, SL.4.1b, SL.4.1c, SL.4.1d, SL.4.2, SL.4.3, SL.4.6

Analyze
Close Reading for the Traits

Week 1 • Day 4

Student Objectives

- Read a model character sketch. (p. 379)
- Use the character sketch rubric. (pp. 380–381)
- Use the model character sketch to study **Ideas, Organization,** and **Voice**. (pp. 382–383)

Find Evidence in the Model

Evaluate the Model Read each section on pages 382–383 with students. Determine whether students agree with each point in Marta's assessment. Use the questions below to initiate the discussion. Be sure students back up their answers with specific examples from the model.

Discuss Audience, Task, Purpose Ask students one or more of the following questions as they analyze the model:

- **Audience** Who is the audience? (Possible response: all readers)

- **Task** How does the writer arrange the information about the character ? (Possible responses: He uses a different paragraph to explain each trait of the character.)

- **Purpose** What is the writer's purpose for writing this character sketch? How do you know? (Possible responses: To inform the readers; the report includes facts and details about the character.)

Using the Rubric to Analyze the Model
Character Sketch

Did you notice that the model on page 379 points out some key elements of a character sketch? As he wrote "Johnny Appleseed," Ed Lee used these elements to help him describe a person. He also used the 6-point rubric on pages 380–381 to plan, draft, revise, and edit the writing. A rubric is a great tool to evaluate writing during the writing process.

Now let's use the same rubric to score the model. To do this, we'll focus on each trait separately, starting with Ideas. We'll use the top descriptor for each trait (column 6), along with examples from the model, to help us understand how the traits work together. How would you score Ed on each trait?

Ideas
- The writer's topic is clear.
- Descriptive details bring the subject to life for the reader.

Ed makes it clear right away that he wants to tell his readers about Johnny Appleseed. He gives lots of specific details about his subject. This part tells me about Johnny Appleseed's personality. Details about what he said and did helped me really understand what kind of person he was.

> Johnny Appleseed was a very gentle man. He walked alone through unsettled territory filled with wild animals, but he never carried anything to protect himself. He told people that he would never harm a living creature.

English Language Learners

BEGINNING/ INTERMEDIATE

Identifying Characteristics Read a short story to students. Ask, *Who is the main character?* As a class, complete a Spider Map. Elicit one-word descriptions from students about the character's personality, actions, and appearance. After completing the map, model simple sentences about the character using information from the chart. Then have students repeat.

Organization

- The strong introduction, body, and conclusion fit together well.
- A variety of helpful transitions guides the reader through the description.

The first paragraph introduces us to Johnny Appleseed. The body of the sketch tells us details about Johnny Appleseed's life and why he is remembered. Ed's paragraphs flow together well. Helpful transitions like *In our day* and *The next time* guide the reader all the way through the sketch.

In our day, people express their thanks by writing books about him. The next time you take a bite of fresh-baked apple pie, think of Johnny Appleseed!

Voice

- The writer's personality comes through.
- The reader can tell the writer knows about and likes the subject.

The writer's voice comes through in his description of Johnny Appleseed. He shares with readers what he thinks makes Johnny Appleseed so special. In the last paragraph, the writer shows his respect for his subject.

Johnny Appleseed gave a lot to people. The wilderness blossomed with his apple trees. Even so, he did not believe that anyone owed him any special thanks.

Character Sketch **383**

Discuss the Traits Ask students one or more of the following questions to discuss the traits in the model:

Ideas Which details tell you how dedicated Johnny Appleseed was to his mission? (Possible responses: *Wherever he went, he scattered his precious apple seeds. He spoke about his respect for the rich and fertile land he traveled.*)

Organization What kinds of information do the transitions give the reader? (time order/when things happened)

Voice What word would you use to describe the author's voice? (Possible responses: informative, confident)

ADVANCED/ADVANCED HIGH
Identifying Characteristics Show a photo of a person who students know. Have students ask and answer the following questions to each other: *Who is he or she? What does he or she do? What does he or she look like? What is his or her personality like?* Have students complete a Spider Map and then use the map to describe the person to the group. Write the sentences on the board and have students repeat them. Then ask students to write the sentences on paper. Have students repeat the activity with a fictional character.

CCSS **C**ommon **C**ore **S**tate **S**tandards (pp. Z20–Z30)
Language: L.4.3c
Speaking and Listening: SL.4.1a, SL.4.1b, SL.4.1c, SL.4.1d, SL.4.3, SL.4.6

Analyze
Close Reading for the Traits

Week 1 • Day 5

Student Objectives

- Read a model character sketch. (p. 379)
- Use the character sketch rubric. (pp. 380–381)
- Use the model character sketch to study **Word Choice, Sentence Fluency,** and **Conventions.** (pp. 384–385)

Discuss the Traits Ask students one or more of the following questions to discuss the traits in the model:

 What words does Ed use that help you "see" what he is describing? (Possible responses: *green forests; vast prairies; wide rivers*)

 How does a mix of sentence lengths and structures make reading more enjoyable? (Possible response: It keeps the reading interesting.)

Conventions Why is it important that all compound sentences are written correctly? (Possible response: They are confusing when written incorrectly.)

▶ Strategies for Writers Online
Go to **www.sfw.z-b.com** for additional online resources for students, teachers, and parents.

Using the Rubric to Analyze the Model
Character Sketch

 **Word Choice**
- The words paint a clear picture.
- Concrete words and phrases help the reader "see" the subject.

Ed uses a lot of specific phrases like *a thin man with a lean face* that help the reader picture Johnny Appleseed. Look at these sentences.

> Johnny Appleseed was a thin man with a lean face. He traveled barefoot, sometimes in rain and snow. His clothes were old and worn, but he did not care about how he looked.

Sentence Fluency
- Sentence lengths and structures are varied effectively.

The writer varies the sentence lengths to keep the reader interested. Look at the first paragraph. He uses both long and short sentences to introduce Johnny Appleseed. A variety of sentence lengths helps the writing flow.

> *Johnny Appleseed* is the title of a book by Reeve Lindbergh. It is also the name of the folk hero who is the main character in the book. Johnny Appleseed was a real person, but Appleseed wasn't his real last name. The name given to him at birth was John Chapman.

Tech Tips
Wikis

Use a Wiki Our students are readers within the classroom and their larger peer community. The characters they know are shared, but their experiences, perspectives, and contexts influence their individual readings of those characters. Create a wiki (see for example, Wikispaces or Wikis in Education) in which students post their draft sketches for feedback, input, and shared perspectives across the class or with another audience. Using a wiki also allows for posting images or other texts that challenge or enrich their readings, and for you to follow their changes and edits.

See **www.sfw.z-b.com** for further information about and links to these websites and tools.

Conventions

- The writing is free from errors.
- Compound sentences are written correctly.
- There are no run-on sentences.

I carefully read through the sketch again. All the compound sentences are correct. I looked for run-on sentences, but I couldn't find any.

He was also a very grateful person, and he appreciated the beauty around him. He spoke about his love for the grand, green forests, the vast prairies, and the wide rivers. He spoke about his respect for the rich and fertile land he traveled.

✚Presentation

The title and author's name are on the paper. Each paragraph is indented.

My Turn!

Now it's my turn to write my own character sketch. Follow along to see how I'll use the rubric and good writing strategies.

✚**Presentation** Remind students of the importance of the appearance of a piece of writing. Ask students what might happen to a paper if the title and author's name are not included at the top. **(It could get lost.)** Show an example of writing with no paragraph indents to help students understand how indents help readers see when the writer is moving from one main idea to the next.

Using a computer is an excellent way to create clean text with clear, consistent paragraph indents. Encourage students to use a word-processing program if at all possible.

Think About the Traits

Once students have thoroughly discussed the model, ask them which traits they think are most important in a character sketch and have them explain why. **(Possible response: Word Choice is the most important trait because painting a clear picture of the subject is the goal of a character sketch.)**

Differentiating Instruction

ENRICHMENT

Interview the Character Challenge students to create a character sketch in the form of an interview between a journalist and the character. The questions and answers should reflect the writer's opinion of the character, and the answers should show the character's personality. You may wish to have students work in pairs and perform their interviews for the group.

REINFORCEMENT

Support Transitions Before students begin writing, you may wish to review the types of transitions they might use in their sketches. Mention that some common types of transitions tell when things happened (*first, then, later*), where they happened (*near, at the other end, farther away*), and why they happened (*so, therefore, because*).

CCSS **Common Core State Standards** (pp. Z20–Z30)
Writing: W.4.3c, W.4.6
Language: L.4.3c, L.4.6
Speaking and Listening: SL.4.1a, SL.4.1b, SL.4.1c, SL.4.1d, SL.4.3, SL.4.6

Write
Character Sketch

Week 2 • Day 1

Student Objectives

• Read and understand a prewriting strategy. (p. 386)

Prewrite

Focus on Ideas

Gather Information Read aloud Marta's reasons for choosing Pecos Bill as the subject for her character sketch. Ask students why Pecos Bill will make a good subject for a sketch. Where did Marta find the information she needs for her notes? (a book about Pecos Bill)

Next, direct students' attention to the notes Marta made. Ask what types of information the notes give about Pecos Bill. (his actions and his feelings)

Take Notes on Source Information Tell students to choose a character and jot down some notes about him or her. Remind them that they may add more details later.

Online Writing Center

 Provides **interactive graphic organizers** as well as a variety of graphic organizers in PDF format.

Prewrite   Focus on (Ideas)

The Rubric Says The writer's topic is clear. Descriptive details bring the subject to life for the reader.

Writing Strategy Choose a character from a book and jot down some details about him or her.

When my teacher said we could write about a character from a book, I decided to write about Pecos Bill. He is a funny, wild character from a tall tale. Heroes in tall tales do things that regular people can't do. Everyone would probably enjoy reading about Pecos Bill's fantastic adventures.

First I'll jot down a list of details about Pecos Bill.

My Notes

The Book: Pecos Bill by Steven Kellogg

The Character: Pecos Bill

Details from the Book:

• falls in a river
• grows up with coyotes
• feels like a member of the coyote pack
• always looks happy and smiling
• looks strong
• decides to become a Texan
• tells outlaws he'll turn them into cowboys
• chases and catches a horse named Lightning
• says Lightning can go free
• ropes a tornado
• sure of himself

Write

Think about an interesting book character that you would like to write about. Jot down details about your character.

386 More Writing Practice

English Language Learners

BEGINNING/INTERMEDIATE

Time Transitions On the board, draw a timeline and label *NOW* in the middle of it. On index cards, write the following words and phrases: *long ago, back then, nowadays, soon, recently, two months ago, in the present day, yesterday, in a month's time, someday.* Define any words students do not know. Then, as a group, place the words on the appropriate part of the timeline to show whether they happened in the past, present, or future. Challenge students to add other words or phrases to the timeline.

ADVANCED/ADVANCED HIGH

Self-Descriptions Ask students to describe their appearance, actions, thoughts, and personality. First have them complete a Spider Map. Then have them use the information in the map to write a descriptive paragraph. Ask volunteers to share their paragraphs with the group.

Prewrite

Focus on **Organization**

The Rubric Says	The strong introduction, body, and conclusion fit together well.
Writing Strategy	Use a Spider Map to organize details about the character.

I know that the purpose of a character sketch is to tell all about a character. So I need details about how my character acts, talks, thinks, and looks. I'm going to use a Spider Map to be sure I have those kinds of details. I'll also use the Spider Map to organize them.

Writer's Term

Spider Map
A **Spider Map** organizes information about a topic. The topic goes in the center, the categories go on the spider's "legs," and specific details about the categories are attached to the "legs."

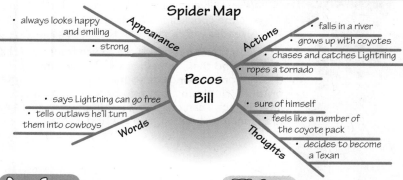

Spider Map

Appearance
• always looks happy and smiling
• strong

Actions
• falls in a river
• grows up with coyotes
• chases and catches Lightning
• ropes a tornado

Pecos Bill

Words
• says Lightning can go free
• tells outlaws he'll turn them into cowboys

Thoughts
• sure of himself
• feels like a member of the coyote pack
• decides to become a Texan

Analyze
Look at the notes and the Spider Map. How will they help Marta write a good character sketch?

Write
Look at your list. Choose the details that best describe your character. Organize these details using a Spider Map.

Character Sketch **387**

Collaborative Conferencing

PEER TO PEER Have partners exchange Spider Maps. Tell students to ask one question about the "leg" that has the fewest details to try to prompt their partner into thinking of an additional detail.

PEER GROUPS Have groups of three or four students pass their Spider Maps around the group. On each map, have students use pencil to either draw a mark over one detail they think is unnecessary or circle a category they think could use another detail.

TEACHER-LED Work with pairs of students. Coach students in offering constructive suggestions for types of details that could be added to each other's Spider Maps.

Write
Character Sketch

Week 2 • Day 2

Student Objectives

• Make a Spider Map to organize details. (p. 387)

Prewrite

Focus on

Categorize Information Have a volunteer read aloud the description of a Spider Map on page 387. (Go to **www.sfw.z-b.com** for the downloadable graphic organizer.) Point out that writing can be organized in many ways. Discuss why a Spider Map is a good graphic organizer for this assignment. (Possible response: It allows the writer to put details into logical categories.)

Writer's Term

Spider Map A Spider Map helps a writer organize information into categories and place all the details where they can be easily found. It also helps a writer keep perspective on the amount of detail in each category. If one "leg" is much longer or shorter than the others, it may be necessary to add or delete details or divide a category.

CCSS **C**ommon **C**ore **S**tate **S**tandards (pp. Z20–Z30)
Writing: W.4.3a, W.4.3b, W.4.3c, W.4.4, W.4.5, W.4.6, W.4.8, W.4.9a, W.4.10
Language: L.4.3c, L.4.6
Speaking and Listening: SL.4.1a, SL.4.1b, SL.4.1c, SL.4.1d, SL.4.3, SL.4.6

Character Sketch **T387**

Write
Character Sketch

Student Objectives

- Begin writing an introduction, body, and conclusion. (pp. 388–389)

Draft

Focus on

Draft a Character Sketch Read page 388 aloud as students follow along in their books. Make sure students understand the function of the introduction, body, and conclusion. Point out that the Spider Map will provide the information for the body of the paragraph. The introduction and conclusion are more loosely linked to the Spider Map: the introduction will tell the reader what the sketch is about, and the conclusion will wrap up the information.

Read the last paragraph again to emphasize the point that students will be able to review their work to add transitions later, in addition to editing to correct errors in spelling, punctuation, capitalization, and grammar.

Online Writing Center

 Provides an **interactive writing pad** for drafting, revising, editing, and publishing.

Draft
Focus on **Organization**

The Rubric Says The strong introduction, body, and conclusion fit together well. A variety of helpful transitions guides the reader through the description.

Writing Strategy Organize the information in an introduction, body, and conclusion. Use helpful transitions.

Now I'm ready to describe my character. I'll use my Spider Map to help me write a draft.

First I need to tell my readers what I am writing about. My introduction should tell the book I read, the character's name, and the reason I chose to write about the character. The body of the sketch is where I will put all the details I have collected.

Finally I will wrap up my description in the conclusion. Maybe I will leave the reader with a question to think about.

The rubric also reminds me to use transitions, like *one day* and *then*, to help readers follow my description. I will include as many as I can as I write my draft. But I can always go back and add them later. In fact, I can check my transitions as well as my grammar, punctuation, and spelling at the end.

388 More Writing Practice

Differentiating Instruction

ENRICHMENT
Expand the Character Sketch Have students write a sketch about a pair or group of characters from one book. The sketch should deal with each character individually and then show how the characters interact with one another.

REINFORCEMENT
Work With a Partner Have students work in pairs to choose a character, take notes, and create a Spider Map. Help students decide how to divide the work of writing the draft. Students may wish to collaborate on the introduction and conclusion but divide up the body so that each student writes about two of the categories in the Spider Map.

⊐ Indent	ℓ Take out something
≡ Make uppercase	⊙ Add a period
/ Make lowercase	⌗ New paragraph
∧ Add something	ⓢⓟ Spelling error

[DRAFT]

Pecos Bill

In the book <u>Pecos Bill</u> by Steven Kellogg, the main character is an interesting person. He is called Pecos Bill because as a child he falls into the Pecos River. That action makes changes that make new actions happen in his whole life.

introduction

A coyote rescues baby Bill from the river in the nick of time. Bill grows up in a family of coyotes. He believes he is a coyote

body

One day Pecos Bill is taking a coyote nap a Texan on a horse discovers him. Bill becomes a Texan instead of a coyote. Always happy and smiling. he grows strong and sure of himself. He wrestles with creetures like a giant rattlesnake. The fiercest outlaws in Texas are amazed. He informs outlaws that he will turn them into honest cowboys they agree! They promise to round up all the steers in Texas for him.

transitions

Then Pecos Bill trys to catch a wild horse named Lightning. Bill chases Lightning from the Arctic Circle to the Grand Canyon. He leaps onto the silver stallion's back and sings to it in its own language. He offers the horse freedom. Lightning decides to stay with Pecos Bill forever.

conclusion

Analyze

Read the draft. Is the sketch organized with an introduction, body, and conclusion?

Write

Use your Spider Map to write your own draft. Remember to organize your information in an introduction, body, and conclusion. Use transitions to guide the reader.

Character Sketch 389

Collaborative Conferencing

PEER TO PEER Have students exchange drafts with a partner. Tell students to label the introduction, body, and conclusion on their partner's sketch. If they have trouble identifying any of the parts, have them ask their partner questions to clarify.

PEER GROUPS Assemble students in small groups. Have students pass their drafts to the left around the group. Group members should write one question about information they would like clarified in each draft on a sticky note and attach it to the draft.

TEACHER-LED Meet with individuals and provide guidance on what should be included in the introduction, body, and conclusion.

Write
Character Sketch

Week 2 • Day 4

Student Objectives

• Complete a draft.

Continue Drafting Read the model draft aloud as students follow along or ask student volunteers to read the draft aloud. Point out the highlighted transitions and discuss how they help the reader move from one idea to another.

Have students compare the parts of the draft to Marta's Spider Map. Discuss with students how Marta has organized her details. (chronological order) Does this organization make sense for a character sketch? (Yes, because telling the character's life in order helps the reader understand what happened to Pecos Bill.)

Finally instruct students to work on their own drafts.

Use Your Own Words Tell students to always use their own words when drafting. Note that using other writer's words *as their own* is called plagiarism. Tell students that plagiarism is not allowable. Explain that one way to use your own words is to focus on the main ideas of the facts they've researched. Encourage them to write down the main points of the facts instead of writing down the notes they took word for word.

CCSS **C**ommon **C**ore **S**tate **S**tandards (pp. Z20–Z30)
Writing: W.4.3a, W.4.3b, W.4.3c, W.4.3e, W.4.4, W.4.5, W.4.6, W.4.9a, W.4.10
Language: L.4.3c, L.4.6
Speaking and Listening: SL.4.1a, SL.4.1b, SL.4.1c, SL.4.1d, SL.4.3, SL.4.6

Write
Character Sketch

Week 2 • Day 5

Student Objectives

• Revise to express the writer's personality. *(p. 390)*

Revise

Focus on 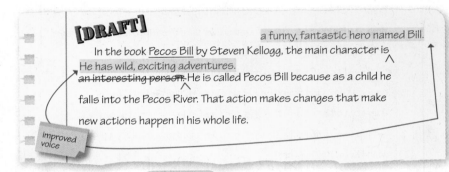 Voice

Express Feelings Read the rubric descriptor and writing strategy aloud as students follow along in their books. Then have volunteers read the draft excerpt aloud, first without the revisions and then with the revisions. Discuss the revisions. What do they tell the reader about the writer's feelings? (Possible response: The writer likes and admires Pecos Bill and she thinks his life story is exciting.) How do the revisions make the reader feel about the subject? (Possible response: They make the reader want to know more about Pecos Bill.) Explain that if they want their readers to become excited about their characters, students must show their own enthusiasm.

With students, brainstorm words and phrases they can use to express their feelings about the characters they chose.

 Strategies for Writers Online
Go to **www.sfw.z-b.com** for additional online resources for students, teachers, and parents.

Revise
Focus on **Voice**

The Rubric Says The writer's personality comes through. The reader can tell the writer knows about and likes the subject.

Writing Strategy Let the reader know what you think about the character.

I know from the rubric that I should let my personality come through in my writing. To do that, I will explain what I think about Pecos Bill. There are other ways to show my voice, too. The details I choose, the kinds of words I use, and the kinds of sentences I write will all combine to show my voice.

[DRAFT]

In the book <u>Pecos Bill</u> by Steven Kellogg, the main character is ~~an interesting person.~~ a funny, fantastic hero named Bill. He has wild, exciting adventures. He is called Pecos Bill because as a child he falls into the Pecos River. That action makes changes that make new actions happen in his whole life.

improved voice

Write

Read your draft. Choose details, words, and sentence types that help your personality come through in your writing.

390 More Writing Practice

English Language Learners

BEGINNING/INTERMEDIATE
Using Quotations Tell students to think about the subject of their character sketch and ask, *What does your subject often say?* Model how students might include the quote in their writing. For example, Ronaldo says, *"I'm living a dream."* Review placement of the comma and quotation marks.

ADVANCED/ ADVANCED HIGH
Using Vivid Words Identify a few vague words that students wrote in their Spider Maps, for example, *strong* or *good*. Challenge partners to come up with more precise words, for example, *powerful* or *magnificent*. Then have each student revise their sensory details to include more vivid descriptive words.

Revise

The Rubric Says   The words paint a clear picture. Concrete words and phrases help the reader "see" the subject.

Writing Strategy   Replace clichés with concrete words and phrases.

I read my draft to myself. I remembered from the rubric that I should use concrete words and phrases in my writing. I looked back and found a place in my draft where I had used a cliché. See what I did to make my writing more specific.

Writer's Term _____

Cliché
A **cliché** is an expression that has been overused. These expressions lose their meaning or freshness. For example, "flat as a pancake" and "good as gold" are clichés.

[DRAFT]

replaced overused expression

just as he is sinking

A coyote rescues baby Bill from the river ~~in the nick of time~~. Bill grows up in a family of coyotes.

 Analyze

Look at the changes. What words replace the cliché? How do they improve Marta's draft?

Write

Read your draft again. Look for clichés. Replace any worn-out words and phrases with specific ones.

Character Sketch   391

Collaborative Conferencing

PEER TO PEER Have partners read their drafts aloud. Each student makes a comment on how his or her partner feels about the subject of his or her sketch (e.g., "You think the character is both smart and funny."). If the comment does not reflect how the writer feels, he or she can revise the draft for Voice.

PEER GROUPS Have students work in groups of three or four and pass their drafts around the group. Each student circles in pencil any clichés he or she sees.

TEACHER-LED Meet with pairs of students. Have students point out what they like best about their partner's essay. Then facilitate a short discussion about the use of Voice in each sketch.

Write
Character Sketch

Week 3 • Day 1

Student Objectives

• Revise to eliminate clichés. (p. 391)

Revise

Focus on Word Choice

Use Concrete Words and Phrases
Discuss why clichés should be avoided in writing. Ask:

• How might a reader feel when a piece of writing is filled with overused expressions? **(Possible responses: bored, disinterested)**

Help students note that Marta did not just avoid using a cliché; she also used words that clarify the action.

Start a classroom list of common clichés (e.g., green with envy, grinning from ear to ear, crying your eyes out) to avoid or use sparingly. Keep the list accessible as a class writing resource.

Writer's Term _____

Clichés are so familiar they can easily slip into writing without the writer noticing. Students may find it easier to locate clichés in their writing if they read their drafts aloud or ask a classmate to read their draft.

CCSS Common Core State Standards (pp. Z20–Z30)
Writing: W.4.3b, W.4.3d, W.4.4, W.4.5, W.4.9a, W.4.10
Language: L.4.2b, L.4.3a, L.4.3c, L.4.5b, L.4.6
Speaking and Listening: SL.4.1a, SL.4.1b, SL.4.1c, SL.4.1d, SL.4.3, SL.4.6

Write
Character Sketch

Week 3 • Day 2

Student Objectives

• Revise for sentence length. (p. 392)

Revise

Focus on

Use Short Sentences Effectively
Write the following on the board: *Paul Bunyan was a very big man who was much larger than other people.* On a separate line, write *Paul Bunyan was a big man. He towered over everybody.* (If necessary, explain that Paul Bunyan is a folklore character, a lumberjack.) Discuss the sentences with students. Ask: *Which is more effective in getting the point across, the long sentence or the pair of short sentences?* **(the short sentences)** Explain that while sentence variety is important, it is sometimes effective to use two or more short sentences in a row to emphasize a point.

Direct students' attention to the draft excerpt on page 392. Have student volunteers read it aloud, once without the revision and once with the revision. Guide students to note that the revision has more impact.

Revise

Focus on  Sentence Fluency

The Rubric Says Sentence lengths and structures are varied effectively.

Writing Strategy Use short, simple sentences to make a point.

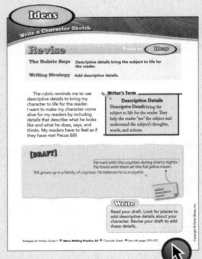

The rubric says to vary sentence lengths and structures effectively. A variety of sentences helps the writing flow. Sometimes you want to get the reader's attention to make a point. A short, simple sentence can do that. I will look for places where I can change a longer sentence to a shorter sentence to make a point.

used short sentence to make a point

He is called Pecos Bill because as a child he falls into the Pecos

That accident changes more than Bill's name. It changes his whole life.

River. ~~That action makes changes that make new actions happen~~
^
~~in his whole life.~~

[DRAFT]

Write

Look for places in your draft where you can add short, simple sentences that make a point.

392 **More Writing Practice**

Optional Revising Lessons

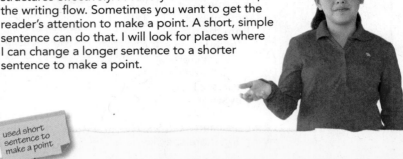

Ideas
Write a Character Sketch

Revise   Focus on **Ideas**

The Rubric Says Descriptive details bring the subject to life for the reader.

Writing Strategy Add descriptive details.

The rubric reminds me to use descriptive details to bring my character to life for the reader. I want to make my character come alive for my readers by including details that describe what he looks like and what he does, says, and thinks. My readers have to feel as if they have met Pecos Bill!

Writer's Term
Descriptive Details
Descriptive Details bring the subject to life for the reader. They help the reader "see" the subject and understand the subject's thoughts, words, and actions.

[DRAFT]

He runs with the coyotes during starry nights. He howls with them at the full yellow moon. Bill grows up in a family of coyotes. He believes he is a coyote.

Write
Read your draft. Look for places to add descriptive details about your character. Revise your draft to add these details.

Strategies for Writers Grade 4 ■ **More Writing Practice 33** ■ Character Sketch ■ Use with pages 390–392.

More Writing Practice 33

Organization
Write a Character Sketch

Revise   Focus on **Organization**

The Rubric Says A variety of helpful transitions guides the reader through the description.

Writing Strategy Add helpful transitions.

I read my draft again. The rubric reminds me to use transitions to guide my reader through my sketch. I found a place that could use some temporal transitions to connect the events. I think my changes help make this part easier to follow. Do you agree?

[DRAFT]

Then Pecos Bill tries to catch a wild horse named Lightning. Bill chases Lightning from the Arctic Circle to the Grand Canyon. He leaps onto the silver stallion's back and sings to it in its own language. He offers the horse freedom.

Write
Revise your draft. Add transitions that help the reader follow the events.

Strategies for Writers Grade 4 ■ **More Writing Practice 34** ■ Character Sketch ■ Use with pages 390–392.

More Writing Practice 34

Go to **Strategies for Writers** at **www.sfw.z-b.com.**

Edit

Focus on (Conventions)

The Rubric Says   Compound sentences are written correctly. There are no run-on sentences.

Writing Strategy   Make sure there are no run-on sentences.

Next I'll check my spelling, capitalization, and punctuation. As I checked my writing, I found a run-on sentence. I'll correct it now by joining the two thoughts in the sentence with a comma and the word *and*.

Writer's Term _____

Run-on Sentences

A **run-on sentence** is made of two sentences that have been run together without a comma and a conjunction. To correct a run-on sentence, turn it into a **compound sentence** by adding a comma and a conjunction, such as **and, or,** or **but,** between the two complete thoughts.

[DRAFT]

corrected run-on sentence

One day Pecos Bill is taking a coyote nap ∧ ,and a Texan on a horse discovers him. Bill becomes a Texan instead of a coyote. Always

Analyze

What do you think of the way Marta revised her sentences? What other ways can a run-on sentence be fixed?

Write   (Conventions)

Edit your draft for spelling, punctuation, and capitalization. Fix any run-on sentences.

For more practice fixing run-on sentences, use the exercises on the next two pages.

Character Sketch **393**

Related Grammar Practice _____

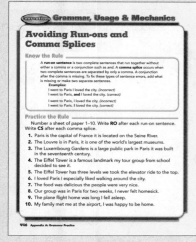

Student Edition page 446

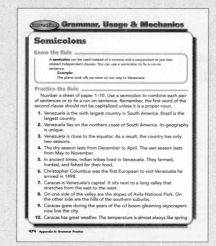

Student Edition page 474

Go to ⟶ **Appendix A: Grammar Practice**

Write
Character Sketch

Week 3 • Day 3

Student Objectives

- Edit to eliminate run-on sentences. *(p. 393)*

Edit

Focus on (Conventions)

Check for Run-on Sentences
Remind students that a period acts as a stop sign, telling the reader when to stop and start the next idea. Tell students that reading sentences aloud can often help them hear run-on sentences that need editing.

Direct students to begin checking their own writing for run-on sentences. Remind them to also edit their drafts for spelling, punctuation, and capitalization.

If some of your students are having trouble identifying and correcting run-on sentences or using compound sentences correctly, you may wish to teach the mini-lessons on pages T394 and T395.

Writer's Term _____

Run-on Sentences Sometimes it makes sense to divide a run-on sentence into two separate, shorter sentences. How a run-on sentence can best be fixed will be dictated by how the ideas in the sentence are related and which solution makes the writing flow better.

CCSS **Common Core State Standards** (pp. Z20–Z30)
Writing: W.4.4, W.4.5, W.4.6, W.4.9a, W.4.10
Language: L.4.1f, L.4.2a, L.4.2c, L.4.2d, L.4.6

Character Sketch **T393**

Conventions
Mini-Lesson

Student Objectives

• Correct run-on sentences. *(p. 394)*

Run-on Sentences

Ask:

• What are the two parts every sentence must have? (a subject and a predicate)

• What must every sentence express? (a complete thought)

Explain that a run-on sentence is a sentence that keeps on going after it should have stopped. A run-on sentence can be rewritten as two or more individual sentences, or the individual ideas can be combined with a coordinating conjunction such as *and*, *but*, or *or*.

Print copies of the following run-on sentence and distribute them to students: *Railroad engineer Casey Jones is a real-life American hero he became a folk hero when he stayed with his train during a crash he applied the brakes he died in the crash he saved many lives his bravery and self-sacrifice made him a hero.*

Have students turn to a partner and, together, decide how to repair the run-on sentence. Then bring students back together and ask several students to share their corrections. Any corrections to the run-on sentence are acceptable if they make sense.

Run-on Sentences

Know the Rule

Begin every sentence with an uppercase letter and end with the correct punctuation mark. There should be no run-on sentences. A **run-on sentence** is two complete thoughts that run together without punctuation and a conjunction.

Example: Her story was long it was very interesting.

Use a comma followed by **and, but,** or **or** to join two sentences to make a compound sentence.

Example: Her story was long, **but** it was very interesting.

Practice the Rule

Number a sheet of paper 1–10. Rewrite each sentence, correcting any errors in capitalization or punctuation. Correct any run-on sentences by adding a comma and a conjunction.

1. on a hot June day in 1778, an important battle was fought.
2. One hero of the battle was Molly Hays most now call her Molly Pitcher.
3. Washington planned to attack the British and Molly knew there would be a terrible battle.
4. the sound of musket and cannon fire soon filled the air.
5. It was a hot summer day men began falling from the heat.
6. Molly saw the problem she heard the men cry for water.
7. Molly spotted a cool stream nearby she filled a pitcher with water.
8. again and again, she brought pitchers of cool water to the thirsty soldiers.
9. Who was the woman who brought the water ?
10. Her family called her Molly Hays the grateful soldiers called her Molly Pitcher.

Related Grammar Practice

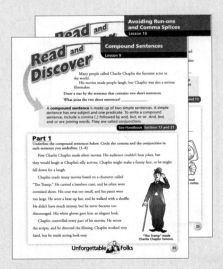

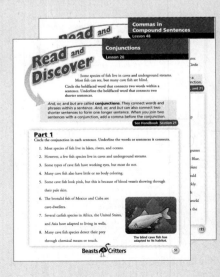

Pages 23, 25, 51, 125

Go to ➡ **G.U.M. Student Practice Book**

Compound Sentences

Know the Rule

A **compound sentence** is made up of two simple sentences. A simple sentence has one subject and one predicate. To write a compound sentence, include a comma (,) followed by **and, but,** or **or. And, but,** and **or** are joining words. They are called conjunctions.

Examples:

I wrote about Annie Oakley, **and** I included information about her childhood.

She was born a long time ago, **but** her story lives on in books, plays, and songs.

I might watch a movie about Annie Oakley, **or** I could read a book about her life.

Practice the Rule

Number a sheet of paper 1–8. Each compound sentence below contains two simple sentences. Write the two sentences and circle the comma and conjunction that join them.

1. Annie Oakley was a famous sharpshooter, and she is remembered in books, movies, and plays.
2. Annie Oakley was born in 1860, and she lived in a log cabin.
3. Her mother named her Phoebe Ann, but her sisters called her Annie.
4. Annie Oakley learned to shoot at nine years of age, and she won her first shooting contest at 16.
5. Annie Oakley beat Frank Butler in a shooting contest, and then she married him.
6. The Butlers traveled to Europe, and they performed for Queen Victoria.
7. Annie Oakley had a difficult childhood, but she was a successful adult.
8. You can learn more about Annie Oakley by reading a biography about her, or you could see the famous play *Annie Get Your Gun*.

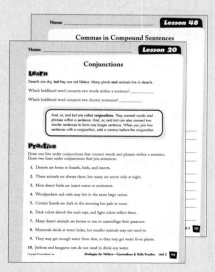

Pages 23, 25, 45, 101

Go to ⟹ Grammar Practice Masters

Mini-Lesson

Student Objectives

- Use compound sentences correctly. (*p. 395*)

Compound Sentences

Remind students that all sentences have a subject and a predicate. Simple sentences have one subject and one predicate. Each part of a compound sentence has its own subject and predicate.

Print out the following and hand it out to students or write it on the board:

I like to watch TV,	*I could relax for a little while.*
Tonight I might stay home,	*I like going to the movies better.*
Sometimes I play at my house,	*she also wants me to have playtime.*
Mom wants me to do my homework,	*sometimes I play next door.*
I could do my math homework first,	*I might go to my friend Rob's house.*

Have students make compound sentences from the parts in the two columns plus the conjunctions *and, but,* and *or.* Some pairs of simple sentences can be combined in more than one way.

CCSS Common Core State Standards (pp. Z20–Z30)
Writing: W.4.6
Language: L.4.1f, L.4.2a, L.4.2c, L.4.6

Write
Character Sketch

Week 3 • Day 4

Student Objectives

- Discuss preparation for publishing and presentation. *(p. 396)*
- Use a final editing checklist to publish their work. *(p. 396)*

Publish ⁺Presentation

Publishing Strategy Discuss Marta's plans for publishing her character sketch. Ask students to suggest the various ways she might choose to portray Pecos Bill (e.g., pencil sketch, full-color drawing, in a particular setting or pose). Ask students to brainstorm ideas for additional pictures she might choose to include, such as photographs of coyotes or the Pecos River.

Review Marta's final checklist. Have students make checklists of their own and use them to prepare their final copy. Encourage students to share their finished work with a parent or family member who would enjoy reading about an interesting character.

Provide a List of Sources Remind students to include a list of the sources they used to find information about their topics. Provide the citing format guidelines to students to use in their character sketch.

 Strategies for Writers Online
Go to **www.sfw.z-b.com** for additional online resources for students, teachers, and parents.

Publish ⁺Presentation

Publishing Strategy	Illustrate the character sketch and post the final copy on the class bulletin board or website.
Presentation Strategy	Put the title and your name on the paper. Indent every paragraph.

I've finished my character sketch! Now I have to decide how to publish it. I think my classmates will want to "see" Pecos Bill in two ways. I will draw a picture of him to go along with my character sketch, and I will post them both on our class bulletin board. Since my sketch will be on the bulletin board, I need to clearly put the title and my name on the paper. The rubric also reminds me to indent each paragraph. That way, my story will be neat and easier to read.

My Final Checklist

Did I—

✔ fix any run-on sentences?

✔ form compound sentences correctly?

✔ put the title and my name on the paper?

✔ indent every paragraph?

Write

Use the checklist to check your own character sketch. Then make a final copy for the class bulletin board. You may want to post it to your class website, too.

Differentiating Instruction

ENRICHMENT

Write a Play Challenge students to turn their sketches into plays that can be performed for the class. Point out that students will need to add dialogue and think about the personalities of the other characters in addition to that of the main character. After converting their sketches into plays, students can direct a group of classmates in a performance.

REINFORCEMENT

Use Dictation If you are publishing students' work on the class website, allow students to dictate their character sketches to you as you type them on the computer. Allow students extra time in the computer lab to receive help scanning and inserting illustrations into their documents.

Pecos Bill
by Marta

In the book <u>Pecos Bill</u> by Steven Kellogg, the main character is a funny, fantastic hero named Bill. He has wild, exciting adventures. He is called Pecos Bill because as a child he falls into the Pecos River. That accident changes more than Bill's name. It changes his whole life.

A coyote rescues baby Bill from the river just as he is sinking, and Bill grows up in a family of coyotes. He runs with the coyotes during starry nights. He howls with them at the full yellow moon. He believes he is a coyote.

One day Pecos Bill is taking a coyote nap, and a Texan on a horse discovers him. Bill becomes a Texan instead of a coyote. He is always happy and smiling, and he grows strong and sure of himself. He wrestles with creatures like a giant rattlesnake. The fiercest outlaws in Texas are amazed. He informs them that he will turn them into honest cowboys, and they agree! They promise to round up all the steers in Texas for him.

Then Pecos Bill tries to catch a wild horse named Lightning. Bill chases Lightning from the Arctic Circle to the Grand Canyon. Finally, he leaps onto the silver stallion's back and sings to it in its own language. Then he offers the horse freedom, but Lightning decides to stay with Pecos Bill forever.

Pecos Bill saves his bride, Slewfoot Sue, by roping a tornado in outer space! He and Sue are blown down to Earth, and they land on his family's wagon in California. What other character in a book has ever had adventures like that?

Analyze
Use the rubric to check the story. Are the traits of a good character sketch there? Then, use the rubric to check your character sketch.

Online Survey Tools

Use Online Survey Tools Gathering responses to students' writing can be challenging, especially when they are posted online. Prepare student writers to share feedback that will help improve a piece while also protecting them from receiving comments that aren't helpful. Consider using an online survey tool such as Google Forms or SurveyMonkey as a tool for collecting responses to student work. This provides both specific prompts for a reader to consider when responding, but it also presents the comments in a searchable, sortable way that will help you and the class consider what worked (or didn't) in individual pieces.

See **www.sfw.z-b.com** for further information about and links to these websites and tools.

Write
Character Sketch

Week 3 • Day 5

Student Objectives

- Use a character sketch rubric. *(pp. 380–381)*
- Share a published character sketch. *(p. 397)*

Presentation Strategy Remind students that neat, clear presentation is important to the reader. Whether the character sketches are published on a bulletin board or a website, they must have the title and author's name at the top so that the reader can identify the writer and the subject of each sketch. Explain that indenting paragraphs makes it easier for the reader to know when the writer is moving from one idea to the next.

Reflecting on a Character Sketch

Divide the class into groups of two or three students. Ask each group to talk about what they like best about their sketch and what they would do differently the next time.

CCSS **C**ommon **C**ore **S**tate **S**tandards (pp. Z20–Z30)
Writing: W.4.4, W.4.6, W.4.9a, W.4.10
Language: L.4.1f, L.4.2c, L.4.3c
Speaking and Listening: SL.4.1a, SL.4.1b, SL.4.1c, SL.4.1d, SL.4.3, SL.4.6

Character Sketch **T397**

Poetry Review Planner

WEEK 1

Day 1
Introduce
Poetry Review

Student Objectives
- Review the elements of a poetry review.
- Consider purpose and audience.
- Learn the traits of descriptive writing.

Student Activities
- Read and discuss **What's in a Poetry Review?** (p. 398)
- Read and discuss **Why Write a Poetry Review?** (p. 399)
- Read **Linking Descriptive Writing Traits to a Poetry Review.** (p. 400)

Day 2
Analyze
Close Reading of the Model

Student Objectives
- Read a model poetry review.

Student Activities
- Read **"My Playful Friend, 'The Wind.'"** (p. 401)

Day 3
Analyze
Introduce the Rubric

Student Objectives
- Learn to read a rubric.

Student Activities
- Review **"My Playful Friend, 'The Wind.'"** (p. 401)
- Read and discuss the **Poetry Review Rubric.** (pp. 402–403)

WEEK 2

Day 1
Write
Prewrite: Ideas

Student Objectives
- Read and understand a prewriting strategy.

Student Activities
- Read and discuss **Prewrite: Focus on Ideas.** (p. 408)
- Apply the prewriting strategy.

Day 2
Write
Prewrite: Organization

Student Objectives
- Make a Network Tree to organize details and examples.

Student Activities
- Read and discuss **Prewrite: Focus on Organization.** (p. 409)
- Reflect on the model Network Tree.
- Apply the prewriting strategy to create a Network Tree.
- Participate in a peer conference.

Day 3
Write
Draft: Voice

Student Objectives
- Begin writing, using first-person point of view.

Student Activities
- Read and discuss **Draft: Focus on Voice.** (p. 410)
- Apply the drafting strategy by using a Network Tree to write a draft.

WEEK 3

Day 1
Write
Revise: Word Choice

Student Objectives
- Revise to include comparisons.

Student Activities
- Read and discuss **Revise: Focus on Word Choice.** (p. 413)
- Reflect on the model draft.
- Apply the revising strategy.
- Participate in a peer conference.

Day 2
Write
Revise: Sentence Fluency

Student Objectives
- Revise for varied sentence beginnings.

Student Activities
- Read and discuss **Revise: Focus on Sentence Fluency.** (p. 414)
- Apply the revising strategy.

Note: Optional Revising Lessons are located at **www.sfw.z-b.com**

Day 3
Write
Edit: Conventions

Student Objectives
- Edit for correct use of adjectives.

Student Activities
- Read and discuss **Edit: Focus on Conventions.** (p. 415)
- Reflect on the model draft.
- Apply the revising strategy.

Note: Teach the Conventions mini-lessons (pp. 416–417) if needed.

Day 4

Analyze
Close Reading
for the Traits

Student Objectives
- Read a model poetry review.
- Use the poetry review rubric.
- Use the model poetry review to study Ideas, Organization, and Voice.

Student Activities
- Review **"My Playful Friend, 'The Wind.'"** (p. 401)
- Read and discuss **Using the Rubric to Analyze the Model.** (pp. 404–405)

Day 5

Analyze
Close Reading
for the Traits

Student Objectives
- Read a model poetry review.
- Use the poetry review rubric.
- Use the model poetry review to study Word Choice, Sentence Fluency, and Conventions.

Student Activities
- Review **"My Playful Friend, 'The Wind.'"** (p. 401)
- Read and discuss **Using the Rubric to Analyze the Model.** (pp. 406–407)

Day 4

Write
Draft

Student Objectives
- Complete a draft.

Student Activities
- Finish the draft.
- Reflect on the model draft. (p. 411)
- Participate in a peer conference.

Day 5

Write
Revise: Ideas

Student Objectives
- Revise to include examples.

Student Activities
- Read and discuss **Revise: Focus on Ideas.** (p. 412)
- Reflect on the model draft.
- Apply the revising strategy.

Day 4

Write
Publish: +Presentation

Student Objectives
- Discuss preparation for publishing and presentation.
- Use a final editing checklist to publish their work.

Student Activities
- Read and discuss **Publish: +Presentation.** (p. 418)
- Apply the publishing strategy.

Day 5

Write
Publish: +Presentation

Student Objectives
- Use a poetry review rubric.
- Share a published poetry review.

Student Activities
- Share their work.
- Use the rubric to reflect upon and evaluate the model and their own writing. (pp. 402–403, 419–421)

To complete the chapter in fewer days, combine the learning objectives and activities in a way that supports students as they write.

Resources at-a-Glance

Grammar, Usage & Mechanics

Differentiating Instruction

For additional Differentiating Instruction activities, see Strategies for Writers *Differentiated Instruction Activities at* **www.sfw.z-b.com.**

English Language Learners

Collaborative Conferencing

Tech Tips

▶ Strategies for Writers Online

Go to **www.sfw.z-b.com** for additional online resources for students, teachers, and parents.

Online Writing Center

Provides IWB resources, assessments, interactive games and practice activities, videos, eBooks, and a virtual file cabinet.

Introduce
Poetry Review

Student Objectives

- Review the elements of a poetry review. *(p. 398)*
- Consider purpose and audience. *(p. 399)*
- Learn the traits of descriptive writing. *(p. 400)*

What's a Poetry Review?

Select a humorous poem to share with students. The poetry of Shel Silverstein or Jack Prelutsky offers good source materials. Read the poem aloud and then ask students what the poem was about. What did they like about it? Encourage them to be specific. Next discuss the definition of a poetry review on page 398.

What's in a Poetry Review?

Read and discuss the elements of a poetry review with students. Tell them to think about the elements in relation to the poem you read aloud. What could they say about the poem that shows evidence of careful reading? What's a central idea they could express about the poem? What examples and details would support that central idea?

 Strategies for Writers Online
Go to **www.sfw.z-b.com** for additional online resources for students, teachers, and parents.

What's a Poetry Review?

It's an essay that describes the writer's experience of reading a poem.

What's in a Poetry Review?

Evidence of Careful Reading
The writer's ideas come from reading a poem carefully. A poetry review focuses on the feelings and images that the poem evokes. Reading a poem about the beauty of nature would make me want to spend time in a garden or at a lake.

Examples and Details
The writer supports his or her central idea with examples and details from the poem.

A Central Idea
The writer expresses a central idea about the poem. The central idea may be whether or not the writer liked the poem, or how the writer felt after reading the poem.

Descriptive Text Exemplars (Poetry Review)

Lasky, Kathryn. *A Voice of Her Own: A Story of Phillis Wheatley, Slave Poet.* **Candlewick, 2005.** This book chronicles the life of Phillis Wheatley, an African girl brought to New England as a slave in 1761 who later became famous as the first black poet of America. Readers will learn about the experiences that influenced Wheatley and about her courage and strength.

Goldstein, Bobbye S. *Inner Chimes: Poems on Poetry.* **Boyds Mills Press, 1992.** Goldstein has compiled 20 beautifully written poems that describe the rewarding and sometimes frustrating act of poetry writing. Including works by famous authors such as Jack Prelutsky, *Inner Chimes: Poems on Poetry* offers young readers insight into the art of poetry.

Why write a Poetry Review?

There are different reasons for writing a poetry review. Here are a few.

To Reflect
Poems can touch me in different ways. Writing about my response to a poem helps me put my feelings into words.

To Entertain
If I really love a poem, I enjoy sharing my response to it with others. My readers may find it interesting to compare my response with theirs.

To Teach a Lesson
Sometimes a poem can teach a lesson. By giving the poem a closer look and writing about it, I can learn something of value.

Poetry Review **399**

Why write a Poetry Review?

Use this opportunity to talk about poetry. Write the following on the board: *words, rhythm, imagination.* Explain to students that these are important elements of poetry. Ask students to suggest reasons why people write poetry. (Possible responses: for fun; to express thoughts or emotions; because they like how poetry sounds or uses language) Explain to students that a poem isn't just the expression of the poet; of equal importance is the response that the poem triggers in the reader. Poems can make you laugh, cry, think, understand, or remember things. In a poetry review, you can share what a poem meant to you as you read it. Read and discuss the reasons for writing a poetry review on page 399. Encourage students to consider their reasons for writing and their audiences as they develop their poetry reviews.

Cooper, Floyd. *Coming Home: From the Life of Langston Hughes.* **Putnam Juvenile, 1998.** *Coming Home: From the Life of Langston Hughes* recounts the childhood circumstances that shaped Hughes's extraordinary life. Learn how Hughes persevered against racism and segregation, as well as a difficult family life, to become one of America's greatest poets.

Kerley, Barbara. *Walt Whitman: Words For America.* **Scholastic Press, 2004.** Walt Whitman was an American poet who captured the American spirit in his poetry. This biography describes Whitman's life as a nurse caring for soldiers during the Civil War. It chronicles how he turned to his poetry to help himself, and the nation, grieve after President Lincoln's assassination.

CCSS **Common Core State Standards** (pp. Z20–Z30)
Language: L.4.3c
Speaking and Listening: SL.4.1a, SL.4.1b, SL4.1c, SL.4.1d, SL.4.3, SL.4.6

Introduce
Poetry Review

Linking Descriptive Writing Traits to a Poetry Review

Have students read page 400. Emphasize that they will follow Marta as she models using the writing process and the descriptive writing traits together.

Discuss with students how each trait applies to a poetry review. Ask students to imagine how readers would react to reading a poetry review that was lacking in one of the traits—for example, if the topic was unclear and it was hard to figure out what poem the writer was talking about.

Linking Descriptive Writing Traits to a Poetry Review

In this chapter, you will write a response to a poem. This type of descriptive writing is called a poetry review. Marta will guide you through the stages of the writing process: Prewrite, Draft, Revise, Edit, and Publish. In each stage, Marta will show you important writing strategies that are linked to the Descriptive Writing Traits below.

Descriptive Writing Traits

 Ideas
- a clear and complete topic
- sensory details and examples that help the reader "see" what is being described

 Organization
- well-organized paragraphs that each tell about one main idea
- transitions that guide the reader through the text

 Voice
- a voice and tone that are appropriate for the purpose and connect with the audience

 Word Choice
- precise, descriptive language that creates a picture for the reader

 Sentence Fluency
- different kinds of sentences that make the writing flow

 **Conventions**
- no or few errors in grammar, usage, mechanics, and spelling

Before you write, read Marcus West's poetry review on the next page. Then use the poetry review rubric on pages 402–403 to decide how well he did. (You might want to look back at What's in a Poetry Review? on page 398, too!)

Descriptive Writing Traits in a Poetry Review

 **Ideas**   Examples of sensory details from the poem will help the reader understand the writer's reactions to the poem.

 **Organization**   The poetry review should have a clearly stated main idea that is supported by details and examples from the poem. Transitions will help readers move from one detail to the next.

 **Voice**   An appropriate voice and tone will help the writer connect with the reader and help the reader understand the writer's feelings about the poem.

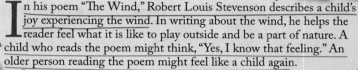

My Playful Friend, "The Wind"

Poetry MODEL Review

by Marcus West

central idea *detail*

In his poem "The Wind," Robert Louis Stevenson describes a child's joy experiencing the wind. In writing about the wind, he helps the reader feel what it is like to play outside and be a part of nature. A child who reads the poem might think, "Yes, I know that feeling." An older person reading the poem might feel like a child again.

feelings

Stevenson makes both the child speaker of the poem and the wind real characters. He makes the wind seem lively and real. He treats it like a person. The child always speaks to the wind directly. He says, "O wind," "O you," and "O blower." Maybe he is teasing the wind a little. In fact, the reader almost expects the wind to answer the child back.

example

In the first and second verses of the poem, the child explains how he knows the wind is there. He says that he saw the wind "toss the kites on high." He also heard it make sounds like the swish of "ladies' skirts across the grass." The child also shows how strong the wind is when he says, "I felt you push."

images

The child knows the wind is there and has seen the things it does. Yet everything the lively wind does is easier to see than the wind itself. Because of this, the child claims that the wind is hiding from him and tells it, "I could not see yourself at all." The child also is curious. He really wants to know who and what the wind is. In the last verse, the child asks whether the wind is "young or old," a "beast," or "just a stronger child than me."

feeling

The rhythm in this poem makes it seem playful. It is easy to imagine a little boy or girl outside, pretending the wind is a friend. The rhythm goes *tah–DUM, tah–DUM*, like a child skipping. Each two lines end with words that rhyme, like a child's song. The last two lines are the same in each verse. Children often say words over and over as they play. The poet uses rhythm, rhyme, and repeated words to make the reader feel as free as the wind and happy as a child.

Poetry Review **401**

Word Choice Precise, descriptive words and phrases will help the reader understand exactly the images and feelings the reviewer wants to convey about the poem.

Sentence Fluency Variety in sentence types gives writing a pleasing rhythm and flow. Writing with variety is not only more enjoyable to read, it is easier to follow.

Conventions Clear, accurate spelling, punctuation, capitalization, and grammar combine to reinforce the writer's message.

Analyze
Close Reading of the Model

Week 1 • Day 2

Student Objectives

• Read a model poetry review. (p. 401)

Read the Model

Before students read "My Playful Friend, 'The Wind'," read the poem "The Wind" to students (Robert Louis Stevenson, from *A Child's Garden of Verses* [1895]). Ask students to close their eyes and listen carefully to what they can "see" the wind do. Then have students read the model poetry review and discuss whether they agree with the writer. Ask them what examples from the poem they might add to the ones the writer chose.

Elements of a Poetry Review

Use the notes on the model to discuss the elements of a poetry review. Refer students to What's in a Poetry Review? on page 398 if they need to review the elements. Discuss how each element helps the reviewer get his opinion across to the reader.

CCSS **Common Core State Standards** (pp. Z20–Z30)
Writing: W.4.6
Language: L.4.3c
Speaking and Listening: SL.4.1a, SL.4.1b, SL.4.1c, SL.4.1d, SL.4.2, SL.4.3, SL.4.6

Analyze
Introduce the Rubric

Week 1 • Day 3

Student Objectives

- Learn to read a rubric.
  (pp. 402–403)

Introduce the Rubric

Explain the Rubric Explain that a rubric is a tool for planning, improving, and assessing a piece of writing. Tell students that a rubric helps a writer focus on key elements, or traits, in writing (**Ideas, Organization, Voice, Word Choice, Sentence Fluency, Conventions,** and **Presentation**). Point out that column 6 describes a very good poetry review, one that has received the highest score in all categories. This is what students should strive for in their own writing.

Discuss the Rubric Guide students in a discussion of the rubric. Read the descriptors for each trait. Discuss the differences between the descriptors for each score. Note that descriptors for scores less than 6 use words such as *most* and *some* to express that the traits are not fully used. The top descriptors state that the traits are expressed throughout the writing. Tell students to keep the rubric in mind when they write their own poetry review and again when they revise it.

Online Writing Center

 Provides a variety of **interactive rubrics,** including 4-, 5-, and 6-point models.

Poetry Review Rubric

Use this rubric to analyze the model. Then use it to plan and score your own poetry review.

	6	5	4	
Ideas	The topic is introduced clearly. The review has a central idea, and several examples offer support.	The topic is introduced clearly. The review has a central idea. One more example is needed.	The topic is introduced. The central idea is somewhat clear. More examples are needed.	
Organization	All examples and details are organized logically. A variety of transitions links ideas from one sentence to the next.	Most of the examples and details are organized logically. A variety of transitions links ideas from one sentence to the next.	Some of the examples seem to be out of order. More or better transitions are needed.	
Voice	The personal tone connects with the reader. The writer shares feelings and ideas.	The writer connects with the reader most of the time. A more personal tone would help.	The writer connects with the reader some of the time. The tone is personal some of the time.	
Word Choice	Comparisons and well-chosen adjectives convey the meaning precisely.	Most comparisons and adjectives convey the meaning precisely.	Some comparisons are vague or confusing. More adjectives would help convey meaning.	
Sentence Fluency	Varied sentence beginnings help the writing flow. The review is enjoyable to read.	In one or two places, sentence beginnings are not varied. The review is enjoyable to read.	Writing is easy to read, but a few sentences start the same way.	
Conventions	Different types of adjectives are used correctly. The writing is easy to read.	Minor errors in the use of adjectives do not distract the reader.	There are a few errors in the use of adjectives, but they do not interfere with meaning.	

⊕Presentation   The review is legible and neat. The title and the writer's name are at the top of the page.

CCSS Common Core State Standards
Poetry Review

Writing descriptive texts can engage the Common Core State Standards for both Narrative and Informative/Explanatory writing. The rubrics for the poetry review, however, are all drawn from informative/explanatory standards. The Ideas rubric reflects standards **W.4.2,** with its focus on clearly introducing a topic, and **W.4.2,** which emphasizes using examples to support the topic. With its focus on using

3	2	1	
The topic is not introduced clearly. The central idea is not clear. Too few examples are provided.	The topic is not introduced. A central idea is not present. Examples may be unrelated.	The topic is not introduced. Examples are not provided.	**Ideas**
The organization of examples and details is hard to follow. Transitions, if they are used, mislead or confuse the reader.	The examples are not organized. Transitions are confusing or missing.	There is no organization to the writing. It is very difficult to follow.	**Organization**
The writer has only a weak connection with the reader. The writing sounds too formal.	The writer does not connect personally with the reader. The voice is inconsistent.	The voice is inappropriate and/or absent. The writing is flat.	**Voice**
Comparisons do not convey the writer's meaning clearly. More adjectives are needed.	Comparisons may be confusing. Adjectives may be repeated or overused.	Comparisons and adjectives are confusing or not used.	**Word Choice**
Sentence beginnings are repetitive. Writing is dull.	Many sentences begin the same way. The writing is choppy.	The sentences begin the same way. Some sentences are incomplete or incorrect.	**Sentence Fluency**
Some errors in the use of adjectives make the writing harder to understand.	Several errors in the use of adjectives make reading and understanding difficult.	The writing contains many errors in the use of adjectives. It is very difficult to read.	**Conventions**

See Appendix B for 4-, 5-, and 6-point descriptive rubrics.

transitions to link ideas, the Organization rubric reflects standard **W.4.2**. The Word Choice rubric is drawn principally from standard **W.4.2,** which underlines the importance of using precise language. The Conventions rubric addresses standards **L.4.1** and **L.4.2,** which involves command of the conventions of grammar, usage, capitalization, spelling, and punctuation.

Find Evidence in the Model

Small-Group Collaboration
Assign a small group of students and tell them to evaluate the model using the rubric. Assign one person in each group to record the group's findings and one person to report the findings to the class. Instruct students to score the model for each trait based on evidence in the text. Remind students to read closely to identify examples to support their high or low scores. Note: Although the models were written to score high in each trait, students should not assume each trait would receive a 6, the top score.

Teacher-Led Discussion
Bring the class back together and have the reporters present their findings and scores. Prompt groups to provide evidence and examples for their scores from the model as needed.

Additional Rubrics

Appendix B includes 4-, 5-, and 6-point rubrics that can be used with any piece of descriptive writing. The rubrics are also available as blackline masters in the back of this Teacher Edition.

CCSS Common Core State Standards (pp. Z20–Z30)
Writing: W.4.6
Language: L.4.3c
Speaking and Listening: SL.4.1a, SL.4.1b, SL.4.1c, SL.4.1d, SL.4.2, SL.4.3, SL.4.6

Analyze
Close Reading for the Traits

Week 1 • Day 4

Student Objectives

- Read a model poetry review. (p. 401)
- Use the poetry review rubric. (pp. 402–403)
- Use the model poetry review to study **Ideas, Organization,** and **Voice**. (pp. 404–405)

Find Evidence in the Model

Evaluate the Model Have volunteers read each section on pages 404–405. Determine whether students agree with Marta's assessment. Use the questions below to initiate the discussion. Be sure students back up their answers with specific examples from the model.

Discuss Audience, Task, Purpose Ask students one or more of the following questions as they analyze the model:

- **Audience** Who is the audience? (Possible response: all readers)

- **Task** How does the writer share his feelings about the poem? (Possible responses: He uses examples from the poem to show his feelings.)

- **Purpose** What is the writer's purpose for writing this report? How do you know? (Possible responses: To inform the readers; the report includes details from the poem being reviewed.)

Using the Poetry Review Rubric to Analyze the Model

Did you notice that the model on page 401 points out some key elements of a poetry review? As he wrote "My Playful Friend, 'The Wind,'" Marcus West used these elements to help him review a poem. He also used the 6-point rubric on pages 402–403 to plan, draft, revise, and edit the writing. A rubric is a great tool to evaluate writing during the writing process.

Now let's use the same rubric to score the model. To do this, we'll focus on each trait separately, starting with Ideas. We'll use the top descriptor for each trait (column 6), along with examples from the model, to help us understand how the traits work together. How would you score Marcus on each trait?

- **The topic is introduced clearly.**
- **The review has a central idea, and several examples offer support.**

I knew from the very first sentence that this essay is about a poem called "The Wind" by Robert Louis Stevenson. Marcus makes it clear that his purpose is to explain the way the poem describes a child's experience with the wind. He gives several examples.

In the first and second verses of the poem, the child explains how he knows the wind is there. He says that he saw the wind "toss the kites on high."

English Language Learners

BEGINNING

Identifying a Poem's Subject Write the following poem on the board: *O Wind!/Are you a gale or a breeze?/Do you rustle the leaves gently/or blow them off the trees?* Ask students what the poem is about. **(Wind)** Repeat for other short and simple poems.

INTERMEDIATE

Identifying a Poem's Subject Have students write a four-line poem about something from nature, for example, grass, rain, the sun, winter, or a bird. As you read each poem to the group, have students tell the central idea of the poem. Then ask them to identify the supporting details.

Organization
- All examples and details are organized logically.
- A variety of transitions links ideas from one sentence to the next.

Marcus organizes his thoughts around a central idea. Each paragraph talks about a particular feeling or image that the poem brings to mind. In this example, he explains how Stevenson made the wind seem real.

Stevenson makes both the child speaker of the poem and the wind real characters. He makes the wind seem lively and real. He treats it like a person. The child always speaks to the wind directly. He says, "O wind," "O you," and "O blower." Maybe he is teasing the wind a little. In fact, the reader almost expects the wind to answer the child back.

Voice
- The personal tone connects with the reader.
- The writer shares feelings and ideas.

I really like the way Marcus uses a personal tone to describe the poem. Here's a good example. He says that the poet helps the reader feel what it is like to play in the wind. He supports that idea by imagining how readers might respond to "The Wind."

A child who reads the poem might think, "Yes, I know that feeling." An older person reading the poem might feel like a child again.

Poetry Review   **405**

Discuss the Traits Ask students one or more of the following questions to discuss the traits in the model:

Ideas Where is the topic introduced in the review? Why is it introduced there? **(right at the beginning; because the reader needs to know the topic before encountering the examples)**

Ideas Which paragraph contains examples of how the wind sounds, looks, and feels to the child? **(the third paragraph)**

Organization How is the review organized? **(Possible response: The writer introduces the title and author first. Then he describes the poem before telling what he thinks about the poem.)**

Voice What feeling does Marcus want to convey about the poem? **(Possible response: The poem is carefree and playful like a young child.)**

ADVANCED/ADVANCED HIGH
Elements of a Poetry Review Ask students about a book they have read recently. What did they like about it? Did they enjoy the style of writing? What are some examples from the book that they particularly liked? Tell students that in a poetry review, they will identify the same sorts of things.

CCSS **Common Core State Standards** (pp. Z20–Z30)
Language: L.4.3c
Speaking and Listening: SL.4.1a, SL.4.1b, SL.4.1c, SL.4.1d, SL.4.3, SL.4.6

Analyze
Close Reading for the Traits

Week 1 • Day 5

Student Objectives

- Read a model poetry review. (p. 401)
- Use the poetry review rubric. (pp. 402–403)
- Use the model poetry review to study Word Choice, Sentence Fluency, and Conventions. (pp. 406–407)

Discuss the Traits Ask students one or more of the following questions to discuss the traits in the model:

Word Choice What adjective does Marcus use that conveys the meaning precisely? Explain your choice. (Possible response: *lively*; It gives the feeling that the wind is a live being.)

Sentence Fluency What sentences with different beginnings does Marcus use? Why are these sentences enjoyable to read? (Possible response: *The child knows the wind is there... Yet everything the lively wind does... Because of this, the child claims...* The variety makes the sentences interesting.)

Conventions Does Marcus use different types of adjectives correctly? (Yes, Marcus uses different types of adjectives correctly.)

Strategies for Writers Online
Go to **www.sfw.z-b.com** for additional online resources for students, teachers, and parents.

Using the Rubric to Analyze the Model
Poetry Review

Word Choice
- Comparisons and well-chosen adjectives convey the meaning precisely.

Sometimes the writer uses comparisons to make his descriptions clear. He compares something he is describing to something else that is familiar to the reader. In this example, he is describing the rhythm and rhyme of the poem. The adjective *playful* is a good choice. Then, when he compares rhythm and rhyme to skipping and singing, he makes his meaning clearer to me.

> The rhythm in this poem makes it seem playful. It is easy to imagine a little boy or girl outside, pretending the wind is a friend. The rhythm goes *tah-DUM, tah-DUM,* like a child skipping. Each two lines end with words that rhyme, like a child's song.

Sentence Fluency
- Varied sentence beginnings help the writing flow.
- The review is enjoyable to read.

The writer does a good job of varying the beginnings of his sentences. Almost every sentence begins differently from the one before it. This makes his writing easy to read and understand. It also makes it more interesting.

> In the first and second verses of the poem, the child explains how he knows the wind is there. He says that he saw the wind "toss the kites on high." He also heard it make sounds like the swish of "ladies' skirts across the grass." The child also shows how strong the wind is when he says, "I felt you push."

Tech Tips
Online Reviews

Find Online Book Reviews Reviews influence how readers make choices about the texts they read. The Internet has flooded us with opinion, ranging from reviews in *The New York Times Book Review* to a blog post made by a first grader in response to his favorite bedtime story. Use Goodreads or another "digital bookshelf" to locate reviews of poetry collections for elementary students, and ask students to "review the reviews." What makes a review effective or persuasive? To whom are book reviews written? Do different modes or media have an effect? How would images or audio help or hurt?

See **www.sfw.z-b.com** for further information about and links to these websites and tools.

Conventions
- Different types of adjectives are used correctly. The writing is easy to read.

I read through the whole review, and the writer uses adjectives correctly to describe and compare. In this example, the writer uses the adjectives *lively* and *easier* to describe and compare the wind.

The child knows the wind is there and has seen the things it does. Yet everything the lively wind does is easier to see than the wind itself.

✚Presentation The review is legible and neat. The title and the writer's name are at the top of the page.

My Turn! Now it's my turn to write a poetry review! I'll use the rubric and good writing strategies to help me. Follow along to see how I do it.

✚Presentation Remind students of the importance of how a piece of writing looks. Create and show an example of messy, poorly presented writing. Ask students how a reader would react when trying to get through the example. **(Possible response: with annoyance and frustration)** Explain that if a reader cannot make out the words due to poor handwriting, he or she has no hope of understanding what the writer wants to say. Also mention the importance of including the title and writer's name at the top of the page.

Using a computer is an excellent way to create neat, legible text. Encourage students to use a word-processing program if at all possible.

Think About the Traits

Once students have thoroughly discussed the model, ask them which traits they think are most important in a poetry review and have them explain why. **(Possible response: Ideas are most important because the object of the review is to explain the central idea with examples.)**

Differentiating Instruction

ENRICHMENT
Expand on Comparisons Challenge students to use comparisons to convey meaning and images precisely. Have them choose something in nature, such as snow or water, and write a paragraph or poem using as many comparisons as possible to describe it. Encourage students to use their imagination to come up with unusual comparisons.

REINFORCEMENT
Choose a Poem Reassure students who have not read poetry that you will help them choose and understand a poem. Present a limited selection of level-appropriate poems for students to choose from. Allow students time to read the poems several times before they decide. You may wish to allow students to work in pairs to choose a poem and write a review.

CCSS **Common Core State Standards** (pp. Z20–Z30)
Writing: W.4.2d
Language: L.4.3a, L.4.3c, L.4.6
Speaking and Listening: SL.4.1a, SL.4.1b, SL.4.1c, SL.4.1d, SL.4.3, SL.4.6

Write
Poetry Review

Week 2 • Day 1

Student Objectives

• Read and understand a prewriting strategy. *(p. 408)*

Prewrite

Focus on Ideas

Gather Information Read aloud how Marta selected, read, and made notes about a poem. Ask:

• What questions will her notes answer? (What is the poem about? How does it make me feel? What did it help me see?)

Have students browse through books and magazines to choose a poem they like. The poem Marta chose is from *Renascence and Other Poems* (1917):

> I will be the gladdest thing
>   Under the sun!
> I will touch a hundred flowers
>   And not pick one.
> I will look at cliffs and clouds
>   With quiet eyes,
> Watch the wind bow down the grass,
>   And the grass rise.
> And when lights begin to show
>   Up from the town,
> I will mark which must be mine
>   And then start down!

Online Writing Center

 Provides **interactive graphic organizers** as well as a variety of graphic organizers in PDF format.

Prewrite
Focus on Ideas

The Rubric Says	The topic is introduced clearly. The review has a central idea, and several examples offer support.
Writing Strategy	Jot down some ideas about a poem you find interesting.

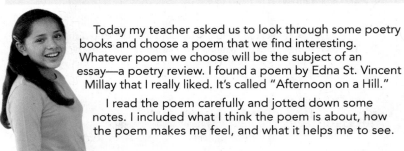

Today my teacher asked us to look through some poetry books and choose a poem that we find interesting. Whatever poem we choose will be the subject of an essay—a poetry review. I found a poem by Edna St. Vincent Millay that I really liked. It's called "Afternoon on a Hill."

I read the poem carefully and jotted down some notes. I included what I think the poem is about, how the poem makes me feel, and what it helps me to see.

My Notes

• painted pictures in my mind
• describes a happy day on a hill
• Verse 1: happy in the sun
• happy like a child
• a hundred flowers
• "gladdest"—a funny, happy word

• Verse 2: time passing
• cliffs and clouds
• the grass bowing and rising
• looking "with quiet eyes"
• Verse 3: going home
• getting dark
• lights from town

Write

Choose a poem that you find interesting. Read it. Then jot down your thoughts and feelings about it.

English Language Learners

BEGINNING/INTERMEDIATE

Sentence Frames Read a brief poem or story to students. Ask, *What is the poem/story about?* If students answer with one word, model a complete sentence and have them repeat it. For example, if a student says, *Wind,* then model the following sentence: *The poem is about wind.* Using the same strategy, model other sentence frames, such as *I liked the poem because _____. The poem made me laugh/cry/wonder about wind.*

ADVANCED/ADVANCED HIGH

Sentence Frames Introduce the following sentence frames. Have students repeat them. Suggest they use some of the frames in their poetry reviews.

The poem made me want to _____.
When the poet said, _____, it made me think about _____.
After reading the poem, I felt _____.
I learned about _____ from reading this poem.

Prewrite

The Rubric Says All examples and details are organized logically. A variety of transitions links ideas from one sentence to the next.

Writing Strategy Make a Network Tree to organize examples and details.

I know that I need to organize my ideas before I write. I'll use a Network Tree. The central idea goes at the top. The verses go in the second level. The details are grouped by verse and go in the third level. Each set of details will become a paragraph.

Writer's Term

Network Tree
A **Network Tree** organizes information according to the level of ideas. At the top is the central idea. Key details that support the central idea go on the next level. Details that support these go on the bottom level.

Network Tree

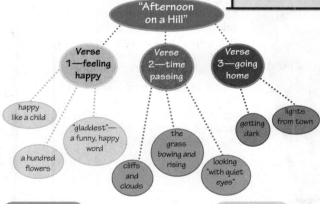

Analyze
Look at Marta's notes and her Network Tree. How will they help her write a good review?

Write
Look at the notes that you made about your poem. Use a Network Tree to organize your ideas.

Poetry Review **409**

Collaborative Conferencing

PEER TO PEER Have students show their Network Tree to a partner and give a short summary of what it includes. The partner asks one or two questions to clarify information he or she did not understand.

PEER GROUPS Have groups of three or four students pass their Network Trees around the group. Tell students to point out a detail they like and one detail they do not understand in each organizer.

TEACHER-LED Work with pairs of students. Have each student show his or her Network Tree and give a short verbal summary. Coach the students in reacting with questions and constructive suggestions.

Write
Poetry Review

Week 2 • Day 2

Student Objectives

• Make a Network Tree to organize details and examples. (*p. 409*)

Prewrite

Focus on  Organization

Organize Details and Examples
Read page 409 aloud while students follow along in their books. Ask how Marta used her Network Tree to organize her notes. (She organized them according to verses from the poem.) (Go to **www.sfw.z-b.com** for the downloadable graphic organizer.) Discuss how a Network Tree can help students plan their reviews.

Writer's Term

Network Tree A Network Tree can translate directly into the paragraphs of a piece of writing. The topic sentence of each paragraph can be written from the information in the middle level of circles. The details to support each topic sentence can be found in the circles of the third level.

CCSS **Common Core State Standards** (pp. Z20–Z30)
Writing: W.4.2a, W.4.2b, W.4.4, W.4.5, W.4.6, W.4.8, W.4.9a, W.4.10
Language: L.4.3c, L.4.6
Speaking and Listening: SL.4.1a, SL.4.1b, SL.4.1c, SL.4.1d, SL.4.3, SL.4.6

Write
Poetry Review

Week 2 • Day 3

Student Objectives

- Begin writing, using first-person point of view. *(pp. 410–411)*

Draft

Focus on  Voice

Develop Tone and Voice Have students read Marta's thoughts as she prepares to write her draft. Ask:

- What is the meaning of *tone*? (Tone is the writer's attitude toward the subject of his or her writing.)

- What tone does Marta want to set for her writing? (personal)

- How will using first person set a personal tone? (Possible response: It will sound like Marta is speaking directly to the reader in a friendly way.)

Point out the second paragraph and remind students that the draft is a first, or "rough," copy. They will have plenty of opportunities to make changes to the content as well as to check for mistakes in spelling, grammar, and punctuation.

Online Writing Center

Provides an **interactive writing pad** for drafting, revising, editing, and publishing.

T410 More Writing Practice

Write a Poetry Review

Draft

Focus on **Voice**

The Rubric Says The personal tone connects with the reader. The writer shares feelings and ideas.

Writing Strategy Use first person (*I, me, my*) to share your thoughts about the poem.

Now it's time to write my draft. The rubric tells me that I need to use a personal tone to connect with the reader. To do that, I should use first-person point of view when I tell readers about the poem. That means I should use the words *I, me,* and *my* to talk about my reactions. To help readers understand the poem, I will describe it and offer specific examples. I will also include my personal feelings and opinions.

As I write my draft, I know that the most important thing is to express my ideas. If I make any mistakes, I will fix them later on when I edit my writing.

410 More Writing Practice

Differentiating Instruction

ENRICHMENT

Compare Poems Have students write a poetry review comparing two poems that have similar themes or are by the same poet. Explain that their Network Trees can focus on similarities and differences between the poems.

REINFORCEMENT

Support Voice Give students additional reinforcement for the concept of tone. Explain that a writer's tone can be formal, informal, friendly, angry, playful, or any number of descriptions. Choose short passages from a humorous short story, a set of assembly instructions, and a newspaper article. Discuss the tone of each piece and why it's appropriate for the purpose and audience. Point out words and phrases that the writers of the pieces use to establish the tone.

Proofreading Marks

⌐ Indent	ℓ Take out something
≡ Make uppercase	⊙ Add a period
/ Make lowercase	¶ New paragraph
∧ Add something	ⓢ℗ Spelling error

[DRAFT]

"Afternoon on a Hill"
a poem by Edna St. Vincent Millay

personal tone

The words of Edna St. Vincent Millay's poem "Afternoon on a Hill" seem to paint pictures in my mind. The words she chose help me see and feel the things that she imagined. This poem is about being happy wherever you are.

Millay tells a story in this poem. She goes out in the country during the day. She sits in the sunshine on top of a hill. She looks at flowers and clouds. At the end of the day, when it gets dark, she goes back home.

Analyze

What personal feelings about the poem does Marta share in her review? What words shows that Marta is writing from the first-person point of view?

Write

Use your notes and Network Tree to write your own draft. Remember to write in the first person and create a personal tone by sharing your feelings about the poem.

Poetry Review 411

Collaborative Conferencing

PEER TO PEER Have students exchange drafts with a partner. Have them underline in their partner's draft one detail they don't understand and ask for clarification.

PEER GROUPS Have students work in small groups and pass their drafts around the group. Group members circle their favorite detail in pencil and explain why they liked it.

TEACHER-LED Meet with individuals and discuss the tone of the drafts. With students, look for ways to use first person and set a personal tone.

Write
Poetry Review

Week 2 • Day 4

Student Objectives
• Complete a draft.

Continue Drafting a Poetry Review Read the model draft aloud as students follow along in their books, or ask student volunteers to read the draft aloud. Explain that this is not Marta's complete draft—just the first two paragraphs. Point out the highlighted sentence and discuss how it sets a personal tone.

Ask students to look back at Marta's Network Tree on page 409. Explain that each item on the second level of the Network Tree represents the topic of a paragraph in the body of the review.

Finally instruct students to begin their own drafts.

CCSS **C**ommon **C**ore **S**tate **S**tandards (pp. Z20–Z30)
Writing: W.4.2a, W.4.2b, W.4.4, W.4.5, W.4.6, W.4.9a, W.4.10
Language: L.4.3c
Speaking and Listening: SL.4.1a, SL.4.1b, SL.4.1c, SL.4.1d, SL.4.3, SL.4.6

Write
Poetry Review

Week 2 • Day 5

Student Objectives

- Revise to include examples. (*p. 412*)

Revise

Focus on Ideas

Use Examples On page 412, read Marta's thoughts about adding details and examples to her review. Ask students to study the draft and identify what was added to the sentences. Discuss why adding examples helps the reader. What would it be like to read the review if the writer did *not* include examples from the poem? (Possible responses: It would be confusing, because the reader would not know exactly what the writer is talking about. The reader would not get a good sense of the poem.)

Tell students that sometimes it's easier to spot places that need examples in someone else's writing. Have students exchange drafts with a partner and point out places that seem like they could be illustrated with an example from the poem.

Strategies for Writers Online

Go to **www.sfw.z-b.com** for additional online resources for students, teachers, and parents.

Revise

Focus on **Ideas**

The Rubric Says   The review has a central idea, and several examples offer support.

Writing Strategy   Use examples from the poem.

I've finished my draft. Now I'll check to make sure I've used the best examples from the poem to support my central idea, an afternoon on a hill.

example from the poem

She says, "I will be the gladdest thing."
"Gladdest" is a funny word but a good choice. Millay's choice of words is important. Some words sounds
like a little child who is really happy and excited. The poet
    She says that even though she will see "a hundred flowers," she will "not pick one."
shows that she wants to protect nature, too. ∧

[DRAFT]

example from the poem

Write

Read your draft. Make revisions to add the details and examples that best support your central idea.

412   More Writing Practice

English Language Learners

BEGINNING/INTERMEDIATE

Comparative Adjectives Write *sun* and *moon* on the board. Ask, *Is the sun bright or dark?* Repeat for *moon*. Ask, *Which is brighter?* Model the sentence, *The sun is brighter than the moon.* Demonstrate how to create a comparative adjective by adding the *-er* ending and how to construct a sentence using the comparative adjective. Have students create their own examples.

ADVANCED/ADVANCED HIGH

Varied Sentence Beginnings Write the following sentence on the board: *The wind whispers in my ear like it wants to tell me a secret.* Challenge partners to work together to determine how the sentence can be changed so the beginning is different but the point of the sentence remains the same. If needed, prompt students with new sentence starters, such as *In my ear* or *Whispering*.

Revise

The Rubric Says Comparisons and well-chosen adjectives convey the meaning precisely.

Writing Strategy Use *like* to compare one thing to another.

The rubric tells me that using comparisons will help make my writing clearer. I read my draft again. My thoughts about the second verse are not very clear. I put in some comparisons that will help the reader understand just what I mean. I'll use good adjectives like *bending* and *floating* in the comparison, too.

[DRAFT]

In the second verse, Millay compares the clouds and bending

grass with time. She describes how she watches "with quiet

added comparison
It feels slow, like time passing.

eyes" as clouds move across the sky. When the wind makes the

added comparison

The bending grass and floating clouds are like clocks in nature.

grass bow down and rise, she has time to watch it rise.

used helpful adjectives

Analyze

Look at Marta's revisions. What word does she use to show that she is making a comparison? How do her comparisons make the descriptions clearer?

Write

Read your draft again. Look for descriptions that aren't clear. Revise to add comparisons that will make them clearer.

Poetry Review **413**

Collaborative Conferencing

PEER TO PEER Have partners read their drafts aloud to each other. Tell them to discuss the comparisons they used and how well they work.

PEER GROUPS Have students work in groups of three or four and pass their drafts around the group. Each student underlines in pencil one statement he or she feels could be supported with an example from the poem.

TEACHER-LED Meet with pairs of students. Choose one passage from each draft that could be revised by adding a comparison and help students develop a comparison together.

Write
Poetry Review

Week 3 • Day 1

Student Objectives

• Revise to include comparisons. *(p. 413)*

Revise

Focus on

Include Comparisons Have student volunteers read the draft excerpt aloud, once without the revisions and once with the revisions. Help students compare the versions. How do the comparisons Marta added help the reader understand the poem? **(Possible response: They make the comparison in the poem clearer and more understandable.)**

Direct students' attention to the adjectives *bending* and *floating*. Ask:

• What if Marta had used the adjective *moving* to describe the grass and clouds? What kind of picture would that paint for the reader? **(Possible response: It would be vague and dull.)**

Explain that carefully chosen words allow writers to express themselves more precisely.

CCSS Common Core State Standards (pp. Z20–Z30)
Writing: W.4.2b, W.4.2c, W.4.2d, W.4.4, W.4.5, W.4.9a, W.4.10
Language: L.4.1f, L.4.2d, L.4.3a, L.4.3c, L.4.6
Speaking and Listening: SL.4.1a, SL.4.1b, SL.4.1c, SL.4.1d, SL.4.3, SL.4.6

Write
Poetry Review

Week 3 • Day 2

Student Objectives

- Revise for varied sentence beginnings. *(p. 414)*

Revise

Focus on

Vary Sentence Beginnings Read Marta's thoughts about revising her work on page 414. Then direct students to study the draft excerpt and identify the changes Marta made. Ask:

- What word had she used too often? *(she)*

Next write these words on the board: *The, It, This,* and *I.* Explain that these are among the words most often used to begin a sentence. Stress that there is nothing wrong with using these words to begin sentences. However, students should avoid using them too often.

Revise

Focus on **Sentence Fluency**

The Rubric Says	Varied sentence beginnings help the writing flow.
Writing Strategy	Start sentences in different ways.

It's time for me to revise my writing. According to the rubric, it's important to use different types of sentence beginnings. If I start every sentence the same way, my writing won't flow and will be hard to understand.

I looked over my essay and found a place where too many sentences began the same way. Three sentences in a row began with *She!* Do you think my changes improve this part of my review?

varied sentence beginnings

[DRAFT]

Millay tells a story in this poem. She goes out in the country during the day. ~~She sits~~ **Sitting** in the sunshine on top of a hill, ~~She~~ **she** looks at flowers and clouds. At the end of the day, when it gets dark, she goes back home.

Write

Read through your draft. Make revisions so that your sentences begin in different ways.

414 More Writing Practice

Optional Revising Lessons

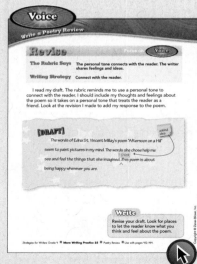

More Writing Practice 35

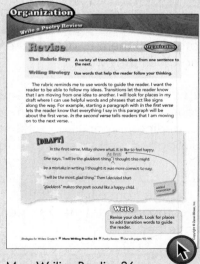

More Writing Practice 36

Go to ⟹ **Strategies for Writers** at **www.sfw.z-b.com.**

Edit

The Rubric Says   Different types of adjectives are used correctly.

Writing Strategy   Make sure adjectives are used correctly.

Now I'll proofread my review for spelling, punctuation, and capitalization. The rubric says to make sure I've used adjectives correctly. I'll look for places where I've described and compared people, places, or things.

Writer's Term_____

Comparative Adjectives
Comparative adjectives describe the differences between two things. If an adjective has one syllable, the comparative is formed by adding **-er**. Adjectives with two syllables or more form the comparative by adding the word **more**. When a two-syllable adjective ends in **-ly**, the **-y** is changed to **-ier**.

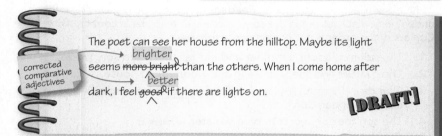

The poet can see her house from the hilltop. Maybe its light
                                    brighter
seems ~~more bright~~ than the others. When I come home after
                         better
dark, I feel ~~good~~ if there are lights on.

corrected comparative adjectives

[DRAFT]

Analyze

First look at how Marta revised her sentences. How do her revisions help the writing flow better? Then look at the edits. Do you think the adjectives are used correctly and effectively? Explain your answer.

Write

Conventions

Edit your draft. Make sure you have used adjectives correctly to describe and compare.

For more practice using adjectives, use the exercises on the next two pages.

Poetry Review   415

Related Grammar Practice _____

Student Edition page 465

Go to ➡ Appendix A: Grammar Practice

Write
Poetry Review

Student Objectives

• Edit for correct use of adjectives. *(p. 415)*

Edit

Focus on **Conventions**

Check Comparative Adjectives

Have students read the information about comparative adjectives in the Writer's Term box. Discuss the changes Marta made in her draft.

Direct students to begin checking all types of adjectives in their drafts. Remind them to edit their drafts for spelling, punctuation, and capitalization as well. Make sure they use the proofreading marks that are found on page 411.

If some of your students are having trouble identifying and correctly using adjectives or comparative adjectives, you may wish to teach the mini-lessons on pages T416 and T417.

Writer's Term _____

Comparative Adjectives Some comparative adjectives do not follow the *-er* formation rule. Two of the most commonly used adjective/comparative adjective pairs with an irregular formation are *good/better* and *bad/worse*.

CCSS **C**ommon **C**ore **S**tate **S**tandards (pp. Z20–Z30)
Writing: W.4.4, W.4.5, W.4.6, W.4.9a, W.4.10
Language: L.4.1f, L.4.2a, L.4.2d, L.4.6

Poetry Review   T415

Mini-Lesson

Student Objectives

• Use adjectives correctly. *(p. 416)*

Adjectives

Ask students to explain what an adjective does. **(An adjective tells us more about a noun.)** Then write the word *dog* and ask students to suggest adjectives that would tell more about a dog.

Next write the following sentences on the board: *That's a brown big dog. That's a big brown dog.* Say the sentences aloud and ask students which one sounds more correct to them. **(That's a big brown dog.)** Ask students what is wrong with the first sentence. **(The adjectives are out of order.)** Explain that when a noun is described by more than one adjective, the adjectives go in a certain order. Write *Size* → *Age* → *Color* → *Material* on the board and explain that this is the correct order for adjectives. Write *That's a big brown dog* on the board beneath the headings on the board with *big* under *Size* and *brown* under *Color*. Give one or two more example sentences with the adjectives written beneath the appropriate headings. Have student volunteers come up to the board and add more sentences.

Online Writing Center

Provides **interactive grammar games** and **practice activities** in student eBook.

Adjectives

Know the Rule

An **adjective** describes a noun. It tells what the noun is like. When two or more adjectives describe a noun, they are listed in a particular order. Look at the chart to see the order of certain kinds of adjectives.

Size	Age	Color	Material
big	young	red	wooden
little	old	blue	silk
teeny	teenaged	yellow	golden
tall	elderly	purple	woolen
short	antique	green	cotton

Practice the Rule

Number a sheet of paper 1–8. Read the sentences below. Decide if the underlined adjectives are in the correct order. If the order is correct, write **Correct.** If the order is not correct, write **Incorrect.**

1. The poem is about a mother and her <u>tall teenaged</u> son. Correct
2. The mother and the son live in a(n) <u>wooden old</u> house. Incorrect
3. One day, the mother plays her <u>little golden</u> harp, and a large pile of clothes appear. Correct
4. The son tries on a <u>cotton blue</u> sweater. Incorrect
5. The mother chooses a <u>yellow silk</u> blouse. Correct
6. One neighbor picks out a <u>purple woolen</u> coat. Correct
7. The neighbors carry home some clothing in a <u>red big</u> basket. Incorrect
8. At the end, the mother says that tomorrow she will play her <u>golden antique</u> flute! Incorrect

Related Grammar Practice

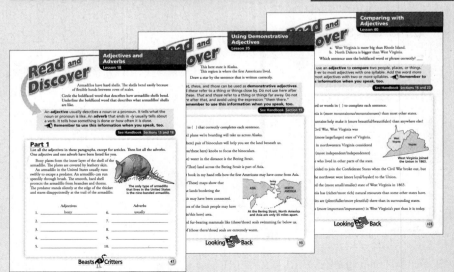

Pages 47, 93, 103

Go to ⟹ **G.U.M. Student Practice Book**

Comparative Adjectives

Know the Rule

Comparative adjectives are used to describe the differences between two nouns or pronouns.

When an adjective has only one syllable, the comparative is often formed by adding -er.
> **Example: bright/brighter**

When an adjective has two syllables or more, the comparative is often formed by using the word **more** before the adjective.
> **Example: important/more important**

When a two-syllable adjective ends in -ly, drop the -y and add -ier.
> **Example: early/earlier**

Practice the Rule

Number a sheet of paper 1–8. Read each sentence. Write the correct form of the adjective in parentheses.

1. I used to think that poetry would be (difficult/more difficult) to understand than prose.

2. I discovered that reading poems is (interesting/more interesting) than I expected.

3. Understanding poetry is a lot (easy/easier) than I thought it would be.

4. There is one form of poetry that I think is (good/better) than other forms.

5. It is called haiku, and, in my opinion, it is (beautiful/more beautiful) than other kinds of poetry.

6. With only three lines, haiku is (short/shorter) than most other poems.

7. The way haiku uses language is much (exciting/more exciting) than other forms of poetry.

8. The poet must paint a mental picture in (few/fewer) words than most poetry forms allow.

Poetry Review **417**

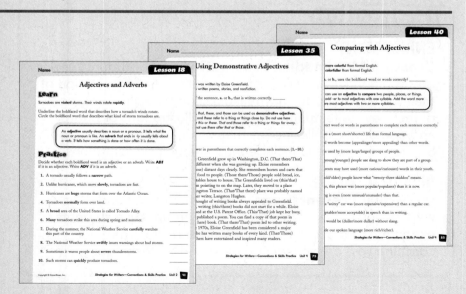

Pages 41, 75, 85

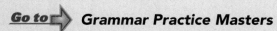
Go to ➡ *Grammar Practice Masters*

Conventions

Mini-Lesson

Student Objectives

- Use comparative adjectives correctly. *(p. 417)*

Comparative Adjectives

Explain that when we talk about two things, we can compare them—we can see if they are the same or different. One way to describe the differences is by using comparative adjectives. Emphasize that comparative adjectives are used when talking about two things. Review the rules for forming comparative adjectives. Write several examples on the board (e.g., *tall/taller, green/greener, weary/wearier, exciting/more exciting, annoying/more annoying*). Ask volunteers for additional examples.

Point out two objects in the room and ask students to suggest ways of comparing them using comparative adjectives. As each student suggests a comparison, ask other students if the adjective has been used correctly and how the adjective should be spelled. Write responses on the board, and then help students determine if the spelling is correct.

CCSS **C**ommon **C**ore **S**tate **S**tandards (pp. Z20–Z30)
Writing: W.4.6
Language: L.4.1d, L.4.2d, L.4.4a, L.4.6

Poetry Review **T417**

Write
Poetry Review

Week 3 • Day 4

Student Objectives

- Discuss preparation for publishing and presentation. *(p. 418)*
- Use a final editing checklist to publish their work. *(p. 418)*

Publish ⁺Presentation

Publishing Strategy Read aloud and discuss Marta's choice for publishing her poetry review. Ask students to suggest ways she could enhance her presentation. **(Possible responses: add music or illustrations)** Discuss techniques for preparing and giving an oral presentation, such as practicing the material beforehand, making eye contact during the presentation, and modulating one's voice to create interest and hold listeners' attention.

Review Marta's final checklist. Have students make checklists of their own and then use them to publish their work. Encourage students to practice before presenting their work by reading their poems and reviews aloud several times. Suggest that they read the material to a parent or another adult as well.

 Strategies for Writers Online
Go to **www.sfw.z-b.com** for additional online resources for students, teachers, and parents.

Publish ⁺Presentation

Publishing Strategy	Read your response aloud to the class.
Presentation Strategy	Use neat handwriting or word processing. Put your name and the page number on each page.

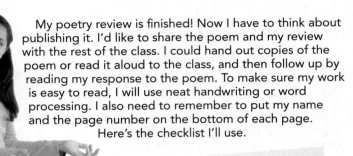

My poetry review is finished! Now I have to think about publishing it. I'd like to share the poem and my review with the rest of the class. I could hand out copies of the poem or read it aloud to the class, and then follow up by reading my response to the poem. To make sure my work is easy to read, I will use neat handwriting or word processing. I also need to remember to put my name and the page number on the bottom of each page. Here's the checklist I'll use.

My Final Checklist

Did I—

✔ use adjectives correctly to describe and compare?

✔ indent every paragraph?

✔ use neat handwriting or word processing?

✔ put my name and the page number on each page?

Write

Make a checklist for your own poetry review. Then make a final draft. Practice reading the poem and your essay before reading them aloud to your class.

418   **More Writing Practice**

Differentiating Instruction

ENRICHMENT

Create a Multimedia Presentation Have students use presentation software to create a multimedia presentation of their review. Students may make a slide for each paragraph of their review featuring appropriate illustrations or photos and one or two bullet points that summarize the paragraph. Students should also include music in their presentations.

REINFORCEMENT

Individual Presentations Allow students to read their work to you individually or to a small group. Give students extra time to practice reading aloud and allot time for a coaching session with you on presentation techniques.

"Afternoon on a Hill"
a poem by Edna St. Vincent Millay
a review by Marta

The words of Edna St. Vincent Millay's poem "Afternoon on a Hill" paint pictures in my mind. The words she chose help me see and feel the things that she imagined. I think this poem is about being happy wherever you are.

Millay tells a story in this poem. She goes out in the country during the day. Sitting in the sunshine on top of a hill, she looks at flowers and clouds. At the end of the day, when it gets dark, she goes back home.

In the first verse, Millay shows what it is like to feel happy. She says, "I will be the gladdest thing." At first I thought this might be a mistake in writing. I thought it was more correct to say, "I will be the most glad thing." Then I decided that "gladdest" makes

Online Posting Sites

Find Places to Post Reviews Reviews only matter when they can be read. As a class, spend time looking for potential venues for posting/sharing students' reviews. Weigh the attributes of different environments: Does the site allow readers to "rate" the effectiveness of a review or provide feedback? Can the writer post a video or other multimodal text? Post student reviews, allowing them choice in audience, mode, process and responsibility for publication. Revisit the reviews after posting, and examine the feedback given regarding the usefulness/helpfulness of students' writing.

See **www.sfw.z-b.com** for further information about and links to these websites and tools.

Write
Poetry Review

Week 3 • Day 5

Student Objectives

- Use a poetry review rubric. (pp. 402–403)
- Share a published poetry review. (p. 419)

Presentation Strategy Explain to students that even though they are reading their poetry reviews to the class, they still need to make sure their text is neatly written and has their name and the page number on each page. This ensures that all of the pages stay in order and do not get lost. If students are using a computer, help them use the header-footer function.

Ask students to use the rubric to evaluate Marta's poetry review. Have groups of students score the writing on each of the six traits, and then present their scores to the class. Encourage students to support their opinions with examples.

CCSS Common Core State Standards (pp. Z20–Z30)
Writing: W.4.4, W.4.5, W.4.6, W.4.9a, W.4.10
Speaking and Listening: SL.4.4, SL.4.5

Reflecting on a Poetry Review

Ask students to reflect on the experience of writing a poetry review. Ask:

- What was the most difficult thing about writing a poetry review? What did you enjoy most?
- How was writing a poetry review different from other types of writing you have done?
- What did you learn about writing from this experience?
- What will you do differently the next time you have a similar writing assignment?

Have students discuss their answers to these questions in class or write about them in their journals.

the poet sound like a happy child. I think Millay is trying to show how a child feels. These words make me feel very happy, too. Poets often use words in surprising ways to express their feelings.

In the second verse, Millay compares the clouds and bending grass with time. She describes how she watches "with quiet eyes" as clouds move across the sky. It feels slow, like time is passing. When the wind makes the grass bow down and rise, she has time to watch it rise. The bending grass and floating clouds are like clocks in nature. They also make me think about how things change as time goes by. I think the second verse is a tiny bit sadder than the first verse.

In the third verse, Millay shows that a lot of time has gone by. The sky must be darker than it was earlier in the day. People in the town are starting to turn lights on in their houses. The poet can see

Marta, page 2

Strategies for Writers Online

Go to **www.sfw.z-b.com** for additional online resources for students, teachers, and parents.

her house from the hilltop. Maybe its light seems brighter than the others. When I come home after dark, I feel better if there are lights on. Lighted windows make a house feel welcoming. I think Millay feels good about going home.

Millay's choice of words shows that she enjoys nature. She says that she will watch "the wind bow down the grass" and "the grass rise." The poet's words also show that she wants to protect nature. She says that even though she will see "a hundred flowers," she will "not pick one."

The poet likes being alone on the hill, looking at the flowers and clouds as she sits in the sun. She also likes going back to her family. One place is not better than the other. They are both important, and you can be happy wherever you are.

Marta, page 3

Analyze
Use the rubric to evaluate Marta's poetry review. Are all the traits of a good poetry review there? Then use the rubric to check your own poetry review.

CCSS **Common Core State Standards** (pp. Z20–Z30)
Writing: W.4.4, W.4.9a, W.4.10
Language: L.4.3c, L.4.5a
Speaking and Listening: SL.4.1a, SL.4.1b, SL4.1c, SL.4.1d, SL.4.3, SL.4.6

Poem Planner

WEEK 1

Day 1
Introduce
Poem

Student Objectives
- Review the elements of a poem.
- Consider purpose and audience.
- Learn the traits of descriptive writing.

Student Activities
- Read and discuss **What's in a Poem?** (p. 422)
- Read and discuss **Why Write a Poem?** (p. 423)
- Read **Linking Descriptive Writing Traits to a Poem.** (p. 424)

Day 2
Analyze
Close Reading of the Model

Student Objectives
- Read a model poem.

Student Activities
- Read **"Do-si-do."** (p. 425)

Day 3
Analyze
Introduce the Rubric

Student Objectives
- Learn to read a rubric.

Student Activities
- Review **"Do-si-do."** (p. 425)
- Read and discuss the **Poem Rubric.** (pp. 426–427)

WEEK 2

Day 1
Write
Prewrite: Ideas

Student Objectives
- Read and understand a prewriting strategy.

Student Activities
- Read and discuss **Prewrite: Focus on Ideas.** (p. 432)
- Apply the prewriting strategy.

Day 2
Write
Prewrite: Organization

Student Objectives
- Make a Three-Column Chart to organize details and examples.

Student Activities
- Read and discuss **Prewrite: Focus on Organization.** (p. 433)
- Reflect on the model Three-Column Chart.
- Apply the prewriting strategy.
- Participate in a peer conference.

Day 3
Write
Draft: Word Choice

Student Objectives
- Begin writing, using figurative language.

Student Activities
- Read and discuss **Draft: Focus on Word Choice.** (p. 434)
- Apply the drafting strategy.

WEEK 3

Day 1
Write
Revise: Organization

Student Objectives
- Revise the poem to fit a shape.

Student Activities
- Read and discuss **Revise: Focus on Organization.** (p. 437)
- Reflect on the model draft.
- Apply the revising strategy.
- Participate in a peer conference.

Day 2
Write
Revise: Sentence Fluency

Student Objectives
- Revise lines for a natural, smooth flow.

Student Activities
- Read and discuss **Revise: Focus on Sentence Fluency.** (p. 438)
- Reflect on the model draft.
- Apply the revising strategy.

Note: Optional Revising Lessons are located at **www.sfw.z-b.com**

Day 3
Write
Edit: Conventions

Student Objectives
- Edit for correct use of prepositional phrases.

Student Activities
- Read and discuss **Edit: Focus on Conventions.** (p. 439)
- Apply the revising strategy.

Note: Teach the Conventions mini-lessons (pp. 440–441) if needed.

Analyze
Close Reading for the Traits

Student Objectives
- Read a model poem.
- Use the poem rubric.
- Use the model poem to study Ideas, Organization, and Voice.

Student Activities
- Review **"Do-si-do."** (p. 424)
- Read and discuss **Using the Rubric to Analyze the Model.** (pp. 428–429)

Analyze
Close Reading for the Traits

Student Objectives
- Read a model poem.
- Use the poem rubric.
- Use the model poem to study Word Choice, Sentence Fluency, and Conventions.

Student Activities
- Review **"Do-si-do."** (p. 424)
- Read and discuss **Using the Rubric to Analyze the Model.** (pp. 430–431)

Write
Draft

Student Objectives
- Complete a draft.

Student Activities
- Finish the draft.
- Reflect on the model draft. (p. 435)
- Participate in a peer conference.

Write
Revise: Ideas

Student Objectives
- Revise to include descriptive details.

Student Activities
- Read and discuss **Revise: Focus on Ideas.** (p. 436)
- Reflect on the model draft.
- Apply the revising strategy.

Write
Publish: +Presentation

Student Objectives
- Discuss preparation for publishing and presentation.
- Use a final editing checklist to publish their work.

Student Activities
- Read and discuss **Publish: +Presentation.** (p. 442)
- Apply the publishing strategy.

Write
Publish: +Presentation

Student Objectives
- Use a poem rubric.
- Share a published poem.

Student Activities
- Share their work.
- Use the rubric to reflect upon and evaluate the model and their own writing. (pp. 426–427, 443)

To complete the chapter in fewer days, combine the learning objectives and activities in a way that supports students as they write.

Resources at-a-Glance

Grammar, Usage & Mechanics

Differentiating Instruction

For additional Differentiating Instruction activities, see Strategies for Writers *Differentiated Instruction Activities at* **www.sfw.z-b.com.**

English Language Learners

Collaborative Conferencing

Tech Tips

 Strategies for Writers Online

Go to **www.sfw.z-b.com** for additional online resources for students, teachers, and parents.

Online Writing Center

Provides IWB resources, assessments, interactive games and practice activities, videos, eBooks, and a virtual file cabinet.

Introduce
Poem

Student Objectives

- Review the elements of a poem. (*p. 422*)
- Consider purpose and audience. (*p. 423*)
- Learn the traits of descriptive writing. (*p. 424*)

What's a Poem?

Select one or two short poems to show and read to the students. Ask students what differences they see and hear between the poems and prose (non-poetry) pieces they have read. (**Possible responses: Poetry is set in lines; it may not be in complete sentences; it has a rhythm; it might rhyme.**)

What's in a Poem?

Read and discuss the elements of a poem with students. Tell them to think about the elements in relation to the poems you read aloud. Show the poems again to illustrate the concept of lines in poetry. Have students help you find examples of figurative language in the poems. If the poems feature alliteration, read them aloud again so that students can hear the effect. Say another example such as the following: *Sighing, soothing, the whispers of the wind sound in my ears.*

Strategies for Writers Online
Go to **www.sfw.z-b.com** for additional online resources for students, teachers, and parents.

What's a Poem?
It's a special form of writing that expresses feelings and impressions. Precise words and descriptive language create vivid imagery.

What's in a Poem?

Lines
A poem is written in lines. Lines may be written as whole or partial sentences. In a shape poem, the lines are arranged to look like the subject of the poem.

Figurative Language
Figurative language is used to create interesting comparisons. *Metaphor* and *simile* are two types of comparisons. A *simile* compares two unlike things using the word *like* or *as*. A *metaphor* compares without using the word *like* or *as*. Can you tell which comparison is used in this example? *The tiny red car looked like a giant ladybug.*

Alliteration
Alliteration is the repetition of beginning consonant sounds. Can you tell which consonant sound repeats in this example? *Two twigs on a tree tapped a merry tune for me.*

Descriptive Text Exemplars (Poem)

Grimes, Nikki. *My Man Blue*. Puffin, 2002. The relationship between a young boy named Damon and his mother's friend Blue unfolds through a set of 14 poems. From Damon's initial suspicion of Blue to his admitted admiration for him, Grimes skillfully describes the challenges and rewards of friendship.

Blake, William. "The Echoing Green." *Songs of Innocence*. Dover, 1971. **CCSS** In his poem, Blake describes children at play in springtime. With rhythm and imagery, he captures the day's activities "on the echoing green" in a way that readers will appreciate and enjoy.

Why write a Poem?

Writing poems is a great way to express yourself! Here are a few reasons to write poems on a variety of subjects.

To Express Yourself

Writing a poem is a good way to express your feelings. You might write a poem to express your feelings about the beauty you see in nature. You might also write to express your feelings on a topic that you feel strongly about, such as saving the rainforests. Poetry is a great way to express personal thoughts and emotions.

To Describe

Many poems describe a person, a place, or a thing. A poem could also describe something humorous or sad, or anything in between. Descriptive poems include vivid words and comparisons that create a clear picture of the subject.

To Understand

Many poets write about a subject in order to learn more about it. You might write a poem about a math term, such as decimals or fractions, and learn more about it in the process. Writing to explore a subject is a great way to expand your understanding of it.

Why Write a Poem?

Read and discuss with students the reasons for writing a poem. Point out that all writing, including poetry, has a purpose. Writers write for many reasons and for a variety of audiences, and these authentic purposes help to shape the writing. When writing for self-expression, a poet might focus on how he or she feels about the topic of the poem. A descriptive poem would include ample sensory details about the topic to make the readers feel they can actually "see" what the poet sees. When writing for understanding, the poet might explore different aspects of one topic. Whatever the purpose of the poem, however, the poet should feel free to use language in a creative and even experimental way.

Sandburg, Carl. "Fog." *Chicago Poems*. Henry Holt, 1916. CCSS This pithy yet complex poem is one of many celebrated works written by Sandburg. With the use of figurative language, he gives life to the hovering fog and paints a picture in the reader's mind.

Frost, Robert. "Dust of Snow." *The Poetry of Robert Frost: The Collected Poems, Complete and Unabridged*. Henry Holt, 1969. CCSS "Dust of Snow" describes the way one simple happening can transform a remorseful day into a blissful one. True to form, Frost allures readers with his effective use of rhythm and rhyme in this brief yet insightful poem.

CCSS **C**ommon **C**ore **S**tate **S**tandards (pp. Z20–Z30)
Language: L.4.3c, L.4.5a
Speaking and Listening: SL.4.1a, SL.4.1b, SL.4.1c, SL.4.1d, SL.4.3, SL.4.6

Introduce
Poem

Linking Descriptive Writing Traits to a Poem

Have students read page 424. Emphasize that they will follow Marta as she models using the writing process and the descriptive writing traits together.

Discuss with students how each trait applies to a poem. Ask students to imagine how readers would react to reading a poem that was lacking in one of the traits—for example, if the words the poet chose were vague and not especially descriptive.

Linking Descriptive Writing Traits to a Poem

In this chapter, you will write a poem to describe something you have learned in math class. Marta will guide you through the stages of the writing process: Prewrite, Draft, Revise, Edit, and Publish. In each stage, Marta will show you important writing strategies that are linked to the Descriptive Writing Traits below.

Descriptive Writing Traits

 Ideas
- a clear and complete topic
- sensory details and examples that help the reader "see" what is being described

 Organization
- well-organized paragraphs that each tell about one main idea
- transitions that guide the reader through the text

 Voice
- a voice and tone that are appropriate for the purpose and connect with the audience

 **Word Choice**
- precise, descriptive language that creates a picture for the reader

 Sentence Fluency
- different kinds of sentences that make the writing flow

 **Conventions**
- no or few errors in grammar, usage, mechanics, and spelling

Before you write, read Owen O'Reilly's poem on the next page. Then use the poem rubric on pages 426–427 to decide how well he did. (You might want to look back at What's in a Poem? on page 422, too!)

Descriptive Writing Traits in a Poem

 Ideas The poem should focus on one clearly defined topic. Abundant sensory details will paint a picture for the reader and allow the poet to convey rich images in few words.

 **Organization** A poem does not have paragraphs—and may not even have stanzas—but ideas should still be grouped and organized in a way that will be clear to the reader.

 **Voice** An appropriate voice and tone will help the writer connect with the reader and help the reader understand the poet's feelings about the topic.

Do-si-do

by Owen O'Reilly

Round
and round, like a
dot or a dime, spinning
through space, O, shape of mine, *alliteration*
curving, closing, completing circumference, *simile*
widening, like a ripple on a pond, rocking, rolling,
rounding, no beginning or ending, like a playground
hoop or a Ferris wheel, a carousel or a steering wheel,
intersecting line through the center, forming diameter, *metaphor*
dividing into two, equal halves, twin faces on a coin or
on the moon, then dance the line from center, do-si-do
along the rim, and form a radius, like the big hand
on a clock turns 360, pointing to perimeter, the
first spoke on a wheel, O, shape of mine,
spinning through space, like a *simile*
dot or a dime, round
and round.

Poem 425

Word Choice Precise, descriptive words and phrases will help the reader understand exactly the images and feelings the poet wants to convey.

Sentence Fluency In a poem, sentence fluency means paying attention to the length, flow, and rhythm of the lines. Lines may be longer or shorter to create the shape of the poem or express the poet's emotions.

Conventions Poems do not always follow all the conventions of grammar and punctuation. Even so, too many errors in grammar, usage, mechanics, and spelling will make a poem confusing.

Analyze
Close Reading of the Model

Week 1 • Day 2

Student Objectives
• Read a model poem. *(p. 425)*

Read the Model

Explain that poetry is meant to be read both silently and aloud, and that listening to a poem will help students appreciate all its elements. Have students read "Do-si-do" silently and then discuss what makes the poem visually interesting. **(It is circular in shape, reflecting the poem's topic.)** Explain that this type of poem is called a shape poem. Ask students why the middle line is in boldface. **(It reflects the content of the line, which defines a diameter.)** Explain that shape poems often use typographic devices. Next have students close their eyes as you read the poem aloud twice. Discuss the ways in which listening to the poem allowed students to notice different things about it.

Elements of a Poem

Use the notes on the model to discuss the elements of a poem. Refer students to What's in a Poem? on page 422 to review the elements. Discuss how each element helps the poet get the images and feelings across.

CCSS **Common Core State Standards** (pp. Z20–Z30)
Writing: W.4.6
Language: L.4.3c
Speaking and Listening: SL.4.1a, SL.4.1b, SL4.1c, SL.4.1d, SL.4.2, SL.4.3, SL.4.6

Analyze
Introduce the Rubric

Week 1 • Day 3

Student Objectives

- Learn to read a rubric. (pp. 426–427)

Introduce the Rubric

Explain the Rubric Explain that a rubric is a tool for planning, improving, and assessing a piece of writing. Tell students that a rubric helps a writer focus on key elements, or traits, in writing (**Ideas, Organization, Voice, Word Choice, Sentence Fluency, Conventions,** and **Presentation**). Point out that column 6 describes a very good poem, one that has received the highest score in all categories. This is what students should strive for in their own writing.

Discuss the Rubric Guide students in a discussion of the rubric. Read the descriptors that go with each trait and take a moment to point out the ways the traits support each other (e.g., **Word Choice** supports **Ideas**). Remind students to keep the rubric in mind when they write their own poem and again when they revise it.

Poem Rubric

Use this rubric to analyze the model. Then use it to plan and score your own poem.

	6	5	4	
Ideas	Descriptive details create a clear picture of the subject.	Most of the details are descriptive and create a clear picture.	Several details are not descriptive enough to create a clear picture.	
Organization	The poem's form or shape fits the subject.	The poem's form or shape fits the subject fairly well.	The form or shape somewhat fits the subject.	
Voice	The writer's personality comes through and connects with the audience.	The writer's personality comes through and connects most of the time.	The writer's personality comes through in a few places.	
Word Choice	Descriptive words and figurative language bring meaning to the writer's message.	Most words are descriptive. Figurative language adds meaning.	Some words are descriptive. Figurative language adds some meaning.	
Sentence Fluency	The words and lines flow naturally and smoothly.	Most of the words and lines flow smoothly.	Some of the words and lines flow smoothly.	
Conventions	The writing contains no errors. Prepositional phrases are formed correctly.	A few errors are present but do not confuse the reader. Prepositions are formed correctly.	Several errors confuse the reader. Some prepositions may be confused, such as *to* and *by*.	

+ Presentation The poem is legible and placed neatly on the page.

426 More Writing Practice

CCSS Common Core State Standards

Poem

Writing a poem engages students in all aspects of the writing process, drawing on skills emphasized in various narrative and informative/explanatory standards, as well as skills related to the production and distribution of writing (standards **W.4.4, W.4.5,** and **W.4.6**) and the range of writing (**W.4.10**).

Online Writing Center

Provides a variety of **interactive rubrics,** including 4-, 5-, and 6-point models.

	3	2	1	
	Some details stray from the subject. Some do not create a picture.	Vague details do not create a clear picture.	Details are not descriptive or related to the subject.	**Ideas**
	The form or shape does not fit the subject.	The form or shape is not appropriate.	The writing is not in poem form.	**Organization**
	The writer's personality fades away by the final line(s).	The writer's personality does not match the topic or audience.	The writer's personality is hidden or absent.	**Voice**
	Few descriptive words are used. Comparisons are weak.	Words are ordinary or vague. Comparisons are not used.	Words are not descriptive. Many are used incorrectly.	**Word Choice**
	Many lines do not flow smoothly.	Lines do not flow well.	The writing is not arranged in lines.	**Sentence Fluency**
	Many errors confuse the reader. Prepositional phrases are not formed correctly.	Serious errors stop the reader. Prepositional phrases are not formed correctly.	The writing has not been edited.	**Conventions**

See Appendix B for 4-, 5-, and 6-point descriptive rubrics.

Poem **427**

Specifically, the Ideas rubric for this poem calls on standards **W.4.2** and **W.4.3,** which emphasize the use of description, while the Word Choice rubric reflects standards **W.4.2** and **W.4.3,** which focus on choosing precise words for effect.

Find Evidence in the Model

Small-Group Collaboration
Assign a small group of students and tell them to evaluate the model using the rubric. Assign one person in each group to record the group's findings and one person to report the findings to the class. Instruct students to score the model for each trait based on evidence in the text. Remind students to read closely to identify examples to support their high or low scores. Note: Although the models were written to score high in each trait, students should not assume each trait would receive a 6, the top score.

Teacher-Led Discussion Bring the class back together and have the reporters present their findings and scores. Prompt groups to provide evidence and examples for their scores from the model as needed.

Additional Rubrics

Appendix B includes 4-, 5-, and 6-point rubrics that can be used with any piece of descriptive writing. The rubrics are also available as blackline masters in the back of this Teacher Edition.

CCSS **Common Core State Standards** (pp. Z20–Z30)
Writing: W.4.6
Language: L.4.3c
Speaking and Listening: SL.4.1a, SL.4.1b, SL.4.1c, SL.4.1d, SL.4.2, SL.4.3, SL.4.6

Analyze
Close Reading for the Traits

Week 1 • Day 4

Student Objectives

- Read a model poem. *(p. 425)*
- Use the poem rubric. *(pp. 426–427)*
- Use the model poem to study **Ideas, Organization,** and **Voice.** *(pp. 428–429)*

Find Evidence in the Model

Evaluate the Model Read each section on pages 428–429 with students. Determine whether students agree with Marta's assessment. Use the questions below to initiate the discussion. Be sure students can back up their answers with specific examples from the model.

Discuss Audience, Task, Purpose Ask students one or more of the following questions as they analyze the model:

- **Audience** Who is the audience? (Possible response: all readers)

- **Task** How does the writer show that he understood the topic? (Possible response: The shape he chose to use.)

- **Purpose** What is the writer's purpose for writing this report? How do you know? (Possible responses: To entertain the readers; the shape and figurative language are fun.)

Using the Poem Rubric to Analyze the Model

Did you notice that the model on page 425 points out some key elements of a poem? As he wrote "Do-si-do," Owen O'Reilly used these elements to help him describe a math concept, the circle. He also used the 6-point rubric on pages 426–427 to plan, draft, revise, and edit the writing. A rubric is a great tool to evaluate writing during the writing process.

Now let's use the same rubric to score the model. To do this, we'll focus on each trait separately, starting with Ideas. We'll use the top descriptor for each trait (column 6), along with examples from the model, to help us understand how the traits work together. How would you score Owen on each trait?

 **Ideas** • Descriptive details create a clear picture of the subject.

The writer uses interesting details to describe the properties of a circle, such as circumference, diameter, and radius. His descriptions and the page design help the audience "see" his subject.

> O, shape of mine, curving, closing, completing
> circumference, widening, like a ripple on a pond,

English Language Learners

BEGINNING

Alliteration Ask students to tell a name that begins with the letter *M.* Then ask for other words beginning with *M* including a verb, a noun, and an adjective that describes the noun. Then put the words together in a sentence. For example, *Manny makes merry music.* Underline each letter *M* to illustrate the idea of alliteration. Have students create other examples with different letters.

INTERMEDIATE

Elements of a Poem Write this simple four-line poem on the board: *Roses are red/Tulips are too/Fifi's flowers are flourishing/And they all are for you!* Clarify any vocabulary students may not know, such as *roses, tulips,* and *flourishing.* Then identify the following elements of the poem: lines, alliteration, rhythm, and rhyme.

 • The poem's form or shape fits the subject.

Owen's poem looks like a circle on the page. I noticed that each line grows longer to the middle of the poem. Then, the lines become shorter to fit the shape. I like the way he divides the shape poem in half by placing details about diameter in the middle of the poem. The middle line is the longest line in the poem.

intersecting line through the center, forming diameter,

 • The writer's personality comes through and connects with the audience.

Owen's enthusiasm for his subject comes through loud and clear. It's also clear that he knows the properties of circles. I wonder if he wants to be a math teacher when he grows up. I'm sure his students would have fun writing shape poems of their own!

on the moon, then dance the line from center, do-si-do
along the rim, and form a radius, like the big hand
on a clock turns 360, pointing to perimeter, the
first spoke on a wheel, O, shape of mine,

Poem 429

Discuss the Traits Ask students one or more of the following questions to discuss the traits in the model:

Ideas Choose another detail that helps you picture the poem's subject. How does that detail help you "see" a circle? (Possible response: *like a playground hoop or a Ferris wheel;* These objects are round, so they help me imagine a circle.)

Organization Why do you think the poet made the poem fit a circle shape? (Possible responses: To better help the reader visualize the subject; It makes the poem fun to read.)

Voice How does Owen feel about the poem's subject? (Possible responses: He enjoys circles a great deal; He thinks circles are fun.)

ADVANCED/ADVANCED HIGH
Descriptive Details Have students use a Web graphic organizer to write down ideas about their selected math concepts. Each "branch" of the web should contain an aspect of the math concept that they want to explore. For each aspect, have students list words they can use to accurately and creatively describe it. Then have them include examples for each.

CCSS Common Core State Standards (pp. Z20–Z30)
Language: L.4.3c, L.4.6
Speaking and Listening: SL.4.1a, SL.4.1b, SL.4.1c, SL.4.1d, SL.4.3, SL.4.6

Analyze
Close Reading for the Traits

Week 1 • Day 5

Student Objectives

- Read a model poem. *(p. 425)*
- Use the poem rubric. *(pp. 426–427)*
- Use the model poem to study **Word Choice, Sentence Fluency,** and **Conventions**. *(pp. 430–431)*

Discuss the Traits Ask students one or more of the following questions to discuss the traits in the model:

 What figurative language does Owen use in his poem? How does it help you understand his ideas?
(Possible response: *like the big hand on a clock turns 360;* The big hand on a clock looks like the radius of a circle, which is what Owen wants to describe.)

Sentence Fluency Why do you think Owen wrote the poem as one long sentence?
(Possible response: It means the poem goes on without any breaks, just like the outline of a circle.)

Conventions Does Owen use prepositional phrases correctly in the poem? **(Possible response:** *Yes, Owen uses prepositional phrases correctly.)*

> **Strategies for Writers Online**
> Go to **www.sfw.z-b.com** for additional online resources for students, teachers, and parents.

T430 More Writing Practice

Using the Poem Rubric to Analyze the Model

Word Choice

- Descriptive words and figurative language bring meaning to the writer's message.

Owen uses a lot of descriptive words and figurative language to describe a circle, especially alliteration and similes. Alliteration—the repetition of beginning consonant sounds—is an effective way to use words that make an impression on the audience. Can you find where Owen used alliteration and simile in these lines?

> widening, like a ripple on a pond, rocking, rolling, rounding, no beginning or ending, like a playground hoop or a Ferris wheel, a carousel or a steering wheel,

Sentence Fluency

- The words and lines flow naturally and smoothly.

Owen's poem is actually one very long sentence. Did you notice that the first and last set of lines repeat? Even though they don't rhyme, they do help create the poem's rhythm and flow. I think the poem would be fun to read aloud in rounds, like one big circle!

> first spoke on a wheel, O, shape of mine,
> spinning through space, like a
> dot or a dime, round
> and round.

430 More Writing Practice

Tech Tips
Online Writing Tools

Use Online Writing Tools Writing doesn't have to be solitary. Use this opportunity to nudge students toward writing collaboratively and, if possible, to do so with someone outside of the classroom. Use the connective resources discussed in earlier tips to find partner classes with whom students can work. Then use an online writing tool with real-time updates (like Google Docs) to have students compose their poems together. You'll want to establish some means of keeping track of versions of their work for unpacking later, another benefit of most online tools. Again, the goal is to create a cohesive poem—together.

See **www.sfw.z-b.com** for further information about and links to these websites and tools.

Conventions
- The writing contains no errors.
- Prepositional phrases are formed correctly.

I read the poem again carefully. Every word is spelled correctly and the commas help the reader pause at the right places. Owen also uses prepositional phrases that add details. Many of them can be found in the comparisons. Here's my favorite: *like a ripple on a pond.* How many can you find in these lines?

> equal halves, twin faces on a coin or
> on the moon, then dance the line from center, do-si-do
> along the rim, and form a radius,

+Presentation The poem is legible and placed neatly on the page.

My Turn!
Now it's my turn to write a shape poem! I'll use the rubric and good writing strategies to help me. Follow along to see how I do it.

Differentiating Instruction

ENRICHMENT
Write a Long Sentence Remind students that the poem is one long sentence. Challenge students to write the longest sentence they can. Then have them read the sentence aloud and revise it to try to add rhythm and flow.

REINFORCEMENT
Reinforce Rhythm Help students understand the concept of rhythm in a poem. Read aloud a poem or part of a poem that has a strong rhythm (e.g, "The Midnight Ride of Paul Revere" by Henry Wadsworth Longfellow or "At the Seaside" by Robert Louis Stevenson) and clap to the beat. Then read the poem aloud again and have students clap along. Read the model aloud and have students clap to the beat.

+Presentation Remind students of the importance of the way a piece of writing looks. Explain that a poem normally does not take up all the space on a page, as prose does. Therefore, when the poem is neatly placed in the center of the page, it is more attractive and appealing to the reader. Legible writing is essential, allowing the reader to enjoy the poet's words without having to struggle to make them out.

Encourage students to use a computer to type their poems. They can use the word processor's functions to produce clear, legible type and center the poem appealingly on the page.

Think About the Traits

Once students have thoroughly discussed the model, ask them which traits they think are most important in a poem and have them explain why. **(Possible response: Sentence Fluency is a more important trait because rhythm and flow are important in a poem.)**

CCSS **C**ommon **C**ore **S**tate **S**tandards (pp. Z20–Z30)
Writing: W.4.6
Language: L.4.1f, L.3.3c
Speaking and Listening: SL.4.1a, SL.4.1b, SL.4.1c, SL.4.1d, SL.4.3, SL.4.6

Write
Poem

Week 2 • Day 1

Student Objectives

• Read and understand a prewriting strategy. (p. 432)

Prewrite

Focus on Ideas

Gather Information Read and discuss how Marta selected her subject and found information to use in her poem. Have students read Marta's notes and ask why she listed everyday examples of right triangles. **(She wants to use them for images in the poem.)**

Help students brainstorm math concepts that could make good shape poems. Encourage students to think beyond just shapes. Can they imagine making a shape poem about lines, rays, or plus signs?

Take Notes on Source Information

Have students consult their math books and make notes about their chosen subjects.

Prewrite

Focus on **Ideas**

The Rubric Says	Descriptive details create a clear picture of the subject.
Writing Strategy	Choose a topic. Make a list of details.

My teacher has asked us to show what we have learned in math class by writing a poem. The assignment is to describe a concept from math class. To do this, I must choose a topic. The model poem is a shape poem about a circle. I think I'll write a shape poem about a triangle.

I want my reader to be able to "see" what I'm describing. First I'll look through my math book and make a list of the properties of triangles. Then I'll list some everyday examples of objects that look like triangles.

My Notes

Triangles	Everyday Examples
• 3 sides	• road sign
• 3 vertices (corners)	• slice of pizza
• 3 angles	• musical triangle
Kinds of Triangles	• scout badge
• right triangle	• half a diamond
• isosceles triangle	• 3-cornered scarf
• equilateral triangle	• jack-o'-lantern eyes
Right Triangle	• guitar pick
• one long side	
• two shorter sides	
• right angle	

Write

Choose a geometric shape. Jot down some math terms that tell more about the shape. Then list examples of the shape.

English Language Learners

BEGINNING/INTERMEDIATE

Math Words As a class, brainstorm a list of math words. Define any words students do not know. Have students categorize their words into operations, symbols, names of mathematicians, and types of math. Have students tell what math topic they would like to write a poem about.

ADVANCED/ADVANCED HIGH

Three-Column Chart Using the ideas they brainstormed earlier, have students organize the details and examples into a Three-Column Chart. Which aspect of the math concept should be described at the beginning of the poem? In the middle? At the end? Ask students to describe to a partner why they organized their ideas the way they did. Partners should give feedback. Discuss as a group.

Prewrite

Focus on **Organization**

The Rubric Says   The poem's form or shape fits the subject.

Writing Strategy   Use a Three-Column Chart to plan the poem.

I'm going to write a shape poem about a triangle. When I'm finished, I want my poem to look like a triangle on the page.

First, I need to decide which details about triangles I will write about at the beginning of my poem. Then I will decide which details to put in the middle, and, last, how to end it.

> **Writer's Term**
>
> **Sequence**
> The **Sequence** is the order topics are arranged in writing.

Three-Column Chart

Beginning	Middle	End
• introduce my subject, a triangle	• describe a right triangle	• restate properties of a right triangle
• name the properties of a triangle	• name the properties of a right triangle	
• compare to everyday examples	• compare to everyday examples	

Analyze
Look at Marta's organizer. How will it help her write her shape poem? Do you agree with the way she has organized her ideas? Why or why not?

Write
Use a Three-Column Chart to plan your poem. Choose details to put in the beginning, middle, and end.

Poem 433

Collaborative Conferencing

PEER TO PEER Have students show their chart to a partner. Students should either affirm that their partner's chart looks complete or point out one type of detail they feel could be added.

PEER GROUPS Have groups of three or four students share their charts. Tell students to discuss the categories and whether any details should be moved from one category to another.

TEACHER-LED Meet with individual students to discuss their charts. Ask students questions about the details and categories to encourage them to think critically about their choices.

Write
Poem

Student Objectives

• Make a Three-Column Chart to organize details and examples. (p. 433)

Prewrite

Focus on

Organize Details and Examples
Read page 433 aloud while students follow along in their books. Ask how Marta used her Three-Column Chart to organize her notes. (**She organized them according to where in the poem she wants them to appear.**) (Go to **www.sfw.z-b.com** for the downloadable graphic organizer.) Point out that Marta did not list every detail in her chart; instead she listed the types of details she will include in the beginning, middle, and end of her poem. Give students time to create their own Three-Column Charts.

Writer's Term _____

Sequence The sequence of events in a poem is just as important as the sequence in a story. Certain events can appear in the beginning, the middle, or the end of a poem.

CCSS **Common Core State Standards** (pp. Z20–Z30)
Writing: W.4.2a, W.4.2b, W.4.2d, W.4.4, W.4.5, W.4.6, W.4.8, W.4.10,
Language: L.4.3a, L.4.3c, L.4.6
Speaking and Listening: SL.4.1a, SL.4.1b, SL.4.1c, SL.4.1d, SL.4.3, SL.4.6

Write
Poem

Week 2 • Day 3

Student Objectives

• Begin writing, using figurative language. (*pp. 434–435*)

Draft

Focus on **Word Choice**

Draft a Poem Have students read Marta's thoughts as she prepares to write her draft. Make sure students understand that this draft is a first, "rough" copy and that they will have time to revise as well as edit their work. Explain that they might not get the shape of their poem exactly right the first time. Once they get something down on paper, they will be able to see more clearly how their words can fit into a shape and then make changes accordingly.

Write examples of similes and metaphors on the board. Ask volunteers to supply additional examples.

✎ Writer's Term _____

Simile and Metaphor Both of these figures of speech feature prominently in poetry because a comparison is an efficient way to create a striking image for the reader. By comparing a new idea or concept to something familiar, the poet makes it easier for the reader to visualize that idea.

➤ Online Writing Center

Provides an **interactive writing pad** for drafting, revising, editing, and publishing.

Draft
Focus on Word Choice

The Rubric Says Descriptive words and figurative language bring meaning to the writer's message.

Writing Strategy Use figurative language.

Now it's time for me to write my shape poem. Words are always important, but I know they are especially important in poetry because there are fewer words in poems. Each word I use has a big job to do.

I know that figurative language can help the reader understand or "see" the topic. I want to include similes or metaphors in my poem.

As I write my draft, I will also look out for mistakes in grammar and spelling, but I know I can fix my mistakes later. Here's my draft.

✎ Writer's Term _____

Simile and Metaphor
A **simile** compares two unlike things using the word *like* or *as*. A **metaphor** compares without using the word *like* or *as*.

Differentiating Instruction

ENRICHMENT
Complex Shapes Challenge students to write their poems in more complex shapes, such as a star or crescent, or to write a poem about more than one shape, using a different shape for each stanza.

REINFORCEMENT
Focus on Simile and Metaphor Work with students to give them additional practice with similes and metaphors before they begin drafting. Write several examples of both and have students identify which are similes and which are metaphors. Work with students individually to craft one simile or metaphor to include in their poems.

[DRAFT]

The Right Triangle

A

triangle

has three

vertices and

three sides, — *simile*

just like a

tasty slice of pizza

or a plastic pick. To tell

if a triangle is truly a right

triangle, look at the right angle,

one that has a square corner. The sides — *alliteration*

join together to make a perpindiculer place.

Yes, it sure is the right triangle in this triangle poem,

one right angle, two other vertices, and three sides.

Analyze

What is the subject of Marta's poem? Did she write a shape poem? How can you tell?

Write

Use your notes and chart to write your poem. Remember to describe the subject with figurative language. Try to write the poem in the shape of its subject.

Poem **435**

Collaborative Conferencing

PEER TO PEER Have students exchange drafts with a partner. Each student tells what he or she likes best about the partner's poem and explains why.

PEER GROUPS Have students pass their poems around the group. Each student writes a question about each poem on a sticky note attached to the poem.

TEACHER-LED Meet with pairs to discuss students' poems. Have students show and read their poems to you and each other. Facilitate a discussion about the similes and metaphors the students used and how they might be improved.

Write
Poem

Week 2 • Day 4

Student Objectives

• Complete a draft.

Continue Drafting a Poem Read the model draft aloud as students follow along in their books. Point out the underlined phrases. Discuss whether the comparison to pizza and a guitar pick is a good choice for the simile. Ask:

• How does the simile help the poet make her point? (Both the pizza slice and the guitar pick are good examples of triangles.)

Discuss why Marta put just the letter *A* on the top line of her poem. (Because it forms a sharp point for the top of the triangle-shaped poem.)

Have students draft their shape poems. Tell students to think about where they want to use similes and metaphors as they write.

CCSS **Common Core State Standards** (pp. Z20–Z30)

Writing: W.4.2b, W.4.2d, W.4.4, W.4.5, W.4.6, W.4.10

Language: L.4.3a, L.4.3c, L.4.5a, L.4.6

Speaking and Listening: SL.4.1a, SL.4.1b, SL.4.1c, SL.4.1d, SL.4.3, SL.4.6

Poem **T435**

Write
Poem

Student Objectives

• Revise to include descriptive details. *(p. 436)*

Revise

Focus on Ideas

Include More Descriptive Details
Read aloud Marta's thoughts about adding more figurative language to her poem. Have students look at the draft on page 435. Ask:

• Do you agree that the poem could use more descriptive language?

Then read Marta's revision on page 436. Discuss the simile Marta added. Ask:

• Why are these comparisons an effective way to convey the idea of a right angle to a reader? **(Because everyone knows what a piece of paper and a door look like, it's easy to picture the corners on those items.)**

Tell students that sometimes it's easier to tell what might be missing from a poem if they hear it out loud. Suggest to students that they read their poems aloud before revising them.

 Strategies for Writers Online
Go to **www.sfw.z-b.com** for additional online resources for students, teachers, and parents.

Revise

Focus on (Ideas)

The Rubric Says — Descriptive details create a clear picture of the subject.

Writing Strategy — Use details that help the reader "see" the subject.

After I wrote my draft, I decided that my poem could use more figurative language. I found lines near the end of my poem that were not very descriptive. I added comparisons that will create a clear picture of my subject. Do they help you "see" what I'm describing?

[DRAFT]

one that has a square corner. The sides
, like the corner on a piece of paper, even a classroom door
join together to make a perpindiculer place.

 added figurative language

Write

Remember to use figurative language that helps your reader "see" your subject. Revise your poem to replace any dull lines with creative ones.

English Language Learners

BEGINNING/INTERMEDIATE
Prepositions Draw a house on the board. Draw a butterfly on the house and ask, *Where is the butterfly?* Students should answer, *The butterfly is on the house.* Write the sentence, circle *on,* and underline *the house.* Repeat for other prepositions, such as *beside, over, on top of,* and *inside.* Tell students the circled words are prepositions. Say each word and have students repeat it.

ADVANCED/ADVANCED HIGH
Figurative Language Describe personification, simile, and metaphor to students. Write the following sentences on the board: *A circle is a smiling face. A circle is like a shining sun. The circle wrapped her arms around me and gave me a hug.* Have students tell what type of figurative language is used in each sentence. Then have students revise one portion of their math poems to include figurative language.

Revise

The Rubric Says   The poem's form or shape fits the subject.

Writing Strategy   Make sure to follow the shape of the poem.

The rubric says the poem's shape should fit the subject. Here's what I did to shape the beginning lines of my poem:

- The word *triangle* can be divided to make shorter lines. I used a hyphen to connect the syllables.
- Even though *tasty* is descriptive, I am describing a triangle, not a pizza.
- The word *truly* makes the line too long. I'll remove it.

[DRAFT]

Before revising:

A
triangle
has three
vertices and
three sides,
just like a
tasty slice of pizza
or a plastic pick. To tell
if a triangle is truly a right

After revising:

A
tri-
angle
has three
vertices and
three sides, like
a slice of pizza or a
plastic pick. To tell if a
triangle is a right triangle,

Analyze

How did Marta revise her writing to improve the shape of her poem?

Write

Revise your poem to make sure the lines match the shape of your subject.

Poem 437

Collaborative Conferencing

PEER TO PEER Have partners exchange drafts. Tell students to use pencil to circle one place where they think the shape of their partner's poem could be improved and to make a suggestion for a revision.

PEER GROUPS Have students work in groups of three or four and pass their drafts around the group. Each student points out a place where he or she may be having difficulties improving the poem's shape or adding details. The rest of the group makes suggestions.

TEACHER-LED Meet with pairs of students. Have the students exchange poems. Coach them in making helpful suggestions for making revisions to improve the poems' shapes.

Write
Poem

Week 3 • Day 1

Student Objectives

- Revise the poem to fit a shape. *(p. 437)*

Revise

Focus on  Organization

Study the Shape Read Marta's description aloud as students follow along in their books. Then have students silently read and study the draft excerpt with Marta's revisions. Tell students to reread each bullet in Marta's description and then look at the revised poem to see what Marta has done. Ask:

- How have Marta's revisions improved the shape of the poem? **(The line of the triangle is much smoother and straighter.)**

The types of changes being made at this stage may be easier to make if students are using a computer. Encourage students to type their poems so that they can more easily try out revisions and see how the changes affect the shapes.

CCSS Common Core State Standards (pp. Z20–Z30)
Writing: W.4.2a, W.4.2b, W.4.2d, W.4.4, W.4.5, W.4.10
Language: L.4.1e, L.4.3a, L.4.3c, L.4.5a, L.4.6
Speaking and Listening: SL.4.1a, SL.4.1b, SL.4.1c, SL.4.1d, SL.4.3, SL.4.6

Write
Poem

Week 3 • Day 2

Student Objectives

• Revise lines for a natural, smooth flow. *(p. 438)*

Revise

Focus on  Sentence Fluency

Improve the Flow Read Marta's words with students. Have student volunteers read the draft excerpt once without the revisions and once with the revisions. Discuss why the revised version has a smoother flow. **(Possible response: Repeating the word *triangle* interrupted the flow. *Yes, it sure is* contains several short words in a row, which sounds choppy.)**

Explain that the best way to tell whether lines are flowing smoothly is to read the poem aloud, preferably more than once. Suggest that students read the poem aloud once or twice to themselves and then read it aloud to a classmate who can make additional suggestions for improving the flow of the language.

 Online Writing Center

Provides **interactive proofreading activities** for each genre.

Revise   Focus on **Sentence Fluency**

The Rubric Says   The words and lines flow naturally and smoothly.

Writing Strategy   Adjust the length of lines for a smooth flow.

To help me hear how my lines flow, I read my poem aloud. I found that several lines were uneven and interrupted the flow. Here are the changes I made. Do you think I've improved the lines?

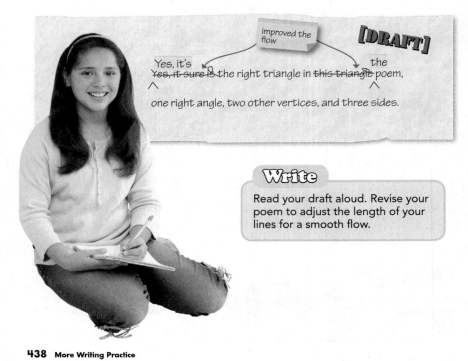

improved the flow

[DRAFT]

Yes, it's
~~Yes, it sure is~~ the right triangle in ~~this triangle~~ poem,
                                              the

one right angle, two other vertices, and three sides.

Write

Read your draft aloud. Revise your poem to adjust the length of your lines for a smooth flow.

Optional Revising Lessons

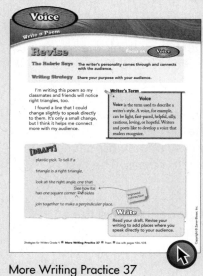

More Writing Practice 37

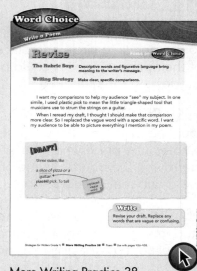

More Writing Practice 38

 Go to ⟹ **Strategies for Writers** at **www.sfw.z-b.com.**

Edit

The Rubric Says   The writing contains no errors. Prepositional phrases are formed correctly.

Writing Strategy   Check prepositions and prepositional phrases.

Next I'll check my spelling, capitalization, and punctuation. Also, the rubric reminds me to make sure that I've used prepositions correctly.

✎ Writer's Term____

Prepositional Phrases

A **preposition** is a word that shows the relationship between its object (a noun or a pronoun) and another word in the sentence. The preposition and the words that follow it form a **prepositional phrase**.

Example: The tiny red car flew **down the road**.

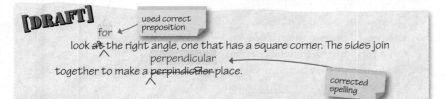

[DRAFT]

used correct preposition

for

look at the right angle, one that has a square corner. The sides join

perpendicular

together to make a ~~perpindicular~~ place.

corrected spelling

Analyze

Look at Marta's sentence revisions and corrections. How do they make the poem easier to understand?

Write   **Conventions**

Edit your draft for spelling, capitalization, and punctuation. Make sure all your prepositions are correct.

For more practice with prepositions, use the exercises on the next two pages.

Poem 439

Related Grammar Practice ____

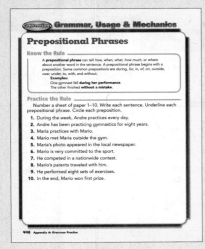

Student Edition page 448

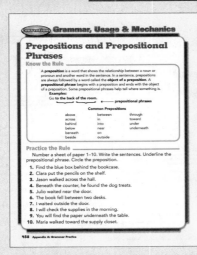

Student Edition page 458

Go to ➡ Appendix A: Grammar Practice

Write
Poem

Week 3 • Day 3

Student Objectives

- Edit for correct use of prepositional phrases. (*p. 439*)

Edit

Focus on **Conventions**

Check Prepositional Phrases

Explain that the object of the preposition is the noun or pronoun that follows a preposition and completes its meaning.

Point out the changes Marta made in her draft. Ask students to identify the prepositional phrase in the draft. (*for the right angle*)

Have students check the prepositional phrases in their drafts as they edit for spelling, punctuation, and capitalization.

If some of your students are having trouble identifying and correctly using adjectives or comparative adjectives, you may wish to teach the mini-lessons on pages T440 and T441.

✎ Writer's Term ____

Prepositional Phrases can be used to add variety to writing. They can help vary the subject-verb-object pattern of sentences and break up choppy passages by creating longer sentences. See the list of prepositions on page T488.

CCSS **Common Core State Standards** (pp. Z20–Z30)
Writing: W.4.4, W.4.5, W.4.6, W.4.10
Language: L.4.1e, L.4.1f, L.4.2a, L.4.2d, L.4.6

Mini-Lesson

Student Objectives

• Identify prepositional phrases. (p. 440)

Prepositional Phrases

Write the following on the board: *how, when, what, how much, where.* Explain that prepositional phrases answer these questions within a sentence. Write the following sentences on the board. Then have students identify the prepositional phrases and tell whether each one tells how, when, what, how much, or where:

I have to take a test on Thursday.

We've been learning all about shapes in math class.

I'll learn my math facts by practicing them every night.

I'll go to my friend Nina's house to study.

I think only half of the twenty students in my class will be ready for the test.

Have students think of additional sentences with prepositional phrases and identify which questions the phrases answer. See the list of prepositions on page T488.

Conventions Grammar, Usage & Mechanics

Prepositional Phrases

Know the Rule

A **prepositional phrase** can tell *how, when, what, how much,* or *where.* A prepositional phrase begins with a preposition and ends with a noun or a pronoun. Some common prepositions are *for, in, of, on, to, under,* and *with.*

Example: The cat sleeps **under** the bed **in** my guitar case.

Practice the Rule

Number a sheet of paper 1–10. Write the prepositional phrase in each sentence.

1. The poem has the shape of a right triangle.
2. It describes the properties of a right triangle.
3. Find a right angle in the lower left corner.
4. Three sides are joined together in a triangle.
5. Do you know about musical triangles?
6. Last year I played the triangle in a concert.
7. On a road trip, we saw a triangle-shaped sign.
8. Did you ever play a guitar with a triangle pick?
9. I borrowed one from my brother.
10. Look for triangles everywhere you go!

Related Grammar Practice

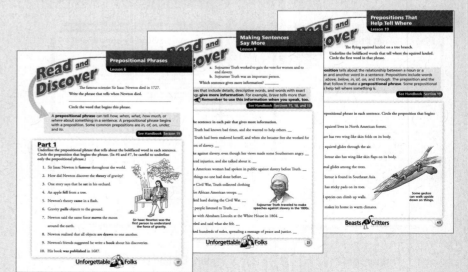

Pages 17, 21, 49

Go to G.U.M. Student Practice Book

More Prepositional Phrases

Know the Rule

A **preposition** tells about the relationship between a noun or a pronoun and another word in a sentence. Prepositions include words that help tell where, such as *above, at, below, in, of, on,* and *through*. The preposition and the words that follow it make a **prepositional phrase**. Some prepositional phrases help tell *where* something is.

Practice the Rule

Number a sheet of paper 1–10. Write each sentence with the correct preposition. Underline the prepositional phrase.

1. I see right triangles (on/with) that welcome mat.
2. We decorated a large flowerpot (by/with) colorful triangle shapes.
3. The pot sits (above/between) a rosebush and a maple tree.
4. Some leaves fell (into/through) the pot.
5. A creek flows (through/over) the rose garden.
6. A narrow footpath follows the creek (in/on) one side.
7. The path continues (over/with) a small bridge and then ends.
8. Metal rods (beneath/by) the bridge form triangles.
9. A yellow sign (on/through) the bridge says "Yield."
10. We hung copper triangles (at/in) trees as wind chimes.

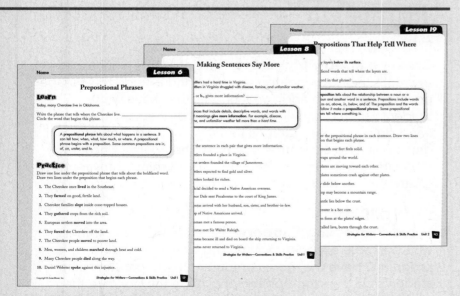

Pages 17, 21, 43

Go to *Grammar Practice Masters*

Mini-Lesson

Student Objectives

- Use prepositional phrases correctly. *(p. 441)*

More Prepositional Phrases

Explain that prepositional phrases always begin with a preposition and end with either a noun or a pronoun. The ending noun or pronoun is called the object of the preposition. Being able to identify the object of the preposition is important.

On the board, write *I am going to school.* Underline *to school* and then circle *school.* Explain that *to school* is the prepositional phrase and *school* is the object of the preposition. The entire phrase tells *where* the subject is going.

Write more sentences such as the following on the board:

Marta read her poem to the class.

She worked hard on the poem.

Yesterday she asked the teacher for extra help.

She'll talk some more about her poem after class.

Have volunteers underline the prepositional phrases and circle the objects of the prepositions. Then have them tell what information each prepositional phrase provides.

CCSS Common Core State Standards (pp. Z20–Z30)
Writing: W.4.6
Language: L.4.1e, L.4.6

Write
Poem

Student Objectives

- Discuss preparation for publishing and presentation. *(p. 442)*
- Use a final editing checklist to publish their work. *(p. 442)*

Publish +Presentation

Publishing Strategy Read aloud and discuss Marta's choice for publishing her poem. Help students list the steps Marta will have to take to submit her poem: find out the requirements for submitting poems to the magazine, create a neat copy of the poem, write a cover letter, and then submit the poem by mail or e-mail. Ask students to suggest other ways she might publish her poem, such as placing it on the school's website, showing it to family and friends, binding it with other poems into a class book, and so on.

Review Marta's final checklist. Have students make checklists of their own, and then use them to publish their work.

⬤ Strategies for Writers Online
Go to **www.sfw.z-b.com** for additional online resources for students, teachers, and parents.

Write a Poem

Publish +Presentation

Publishing Strategy	Submit poem to a magazine or online publisher of children's poetry.
Presentation Strategy	Make the poem look great on the page.

My poem is finished! My next step is to publish it. I have decided to submit my poem to a student magazine that we read in my English class. My teacher will help me write a cover letter to the editor.

I'll type my poem on the computer, using a font that is the right size for the shape of my poem. I'll remember to save my work often! When my poem is ready to go, it will be easy to submit it electronically. To make sure my poem looks great on the page, I'll use this checklist.

My Final Checklist

Did I—
- ✔ check the prepositions and prepositional phrases?
- ✔ look over the words and sentences for correct spelling, grammar, and punctuation?
- ✔ give my poem a title and put my name on the page?
- ✔ make sure the poem is neat and easy to read?

Write

Make a checklist to prepare your final copy. Write a cover letter, and send your poem to a magazine that publishes poetry written by students. You may even want to enter a poetry-writing contest!

Differentiating Instruction

ENRICHMENT

Create a Poetry Magazine Have students work together to create their own poetry magazine and include their shape poems, along with additional poems they have written. Students should add illustrations to the poems, either hand-drawn or photographs found on the Internet. Students may also add introductions to the poems. Encourage students to use word processing or publishing software to create their magazine.

REINFORCEMENT

Word-Processing Support Pair students with partners who are more experienced in using word-processing programs. Have the more computer-literate partners help students choose appropriate fonts, type the poem in the appropriate shape, and center the poem on the page.

The Right Triangle
by Marta

A

tri-

angle

has three

vertices and

three sides, like

a slice of pizza or a

guitar pick. To tell if a

triangle is a right triangle,

look for its right angle, one that

has a square corner. See how its sides

join together to make a perpendicular

place, like the corner on a piece of paper,

even a classroom door. Yes, it's the right triangle

with one right angle, two other vertices, and three sides.

Analyze

Use the rubric to evaluate Marta's poem. Then use the rubric to score your own poem.

Tech Tips

Writing Websites

Use Writing Websites Publishing work for a global audience requires that writers carefully consider how their thoughts fit the modes of expression they are using. Ask students to move their written poem into a collaborative and multimodal writing space like Glogster or Popplet. Working in pairs (either with a face-to-face or electronic writing partner), create a presentation of the poem that uses at least three different modes (e.g., audio, image, motion). Then ask students to provide a rationale for their choices. How does each mode communicate? How did the partners come together to make those decisions?

See **www.sfw.z-b.com** for further information about and links to these websites and tools.

Write
Poem

Week 3 • Day 5

Student Objectives
- Use a poem rubric. *(pp. 426–427)*
- Share a published poem. *(p. 443)*

Presentation Strategy Explain to students that a neatly and attractively presented poem will make a good first impression. If they submit their poem to a publisher, they will be competing for the publisher's attention with all the poems submitted by other students. A sloppy or poorly presented poem will be passed over for one that is easy to read and displayed in an appealing way.

Ask students to use the rubric to evaluate Marta's poem. Have groups of students decide how to score the writing on each of the six traits, and then ask the groups to present their scores to the class. Students should support their opinions with examples.

CCSS **C**ommon **C**ore **S**tate **S**tandards (pp. Z20–Z30)
Writing: W.4.4, W.4.6, W.4.10
Language: L.4.1e
Speaking and Listening: SL.4.1a, SL.4.1b, SL.4.1c, SL.4.1d, SL.4.4, SL.4.5

Grammar Practice The mini-lessons in this section are designed to reinforce targeted grammar, usage, and mechanics skills that students can transfer to their writing. These pages are referenced throughout the Teacher Edition in the Related Grammar section. Or you may wish to use the Table of Contents on this page to choose specific lessons that will benefit your students. To provide valuable additional practice, follow up each mini-lesson with an exercise from **More Practice,** which begins on page 476.

Appendix A
Grammar Practice

Kinds of Sentences

Know the Rule

A **declarative** sentence tells something. A declarative sentence ends with a period. An **imperative** sentence gives an order. An imperative sentence ends with a period. An **interrogative** sentence asks something. An interrogative sentence ends with a question mark. An **exclamatory** sentence shows strong feeling. An exclamatory sentence ends with an exclamation point. Choose the punctuation for the effect you want.

Examples:
I would like to visit Hawaii**.** *(declarative)*
Get the map of Hawaii**.** *(imperative)*
Have you been to Hawaii**?** *(interrogative)*
I can't wait to go to Hawaii**!** *(exclamatory)*

Practice the Rule

Number a sheet of paper 1–10. Next to each number, write the kind of sentence.

1. Hawaii became a state in 1959. declarative
2. Where is Hawaii located? interrogative
3. What is Hawaii's tallest mountain? interrogative
4. Name the eight main Hawaiian islands. imperative
5. Hawaii has two national parks. declarative
6. Where is Pearl Harbor? interrogative
7. Find the Hawaiian islands on a map. imperative
8. Hawaii is in the Pacific Ocean. declarative
9. What a beautiful place Maui is! exclamatory
10. Find the cost of airfare to Hawaii. imperative

Appendix A: Grammar Practice **445**

Conventions

Mini-Lesson

Student Objectives

- Identify the four kinds of sentences. *(p. 445)*

Kinds of Sentences

There are four kinds of sentences. A declarative sentence tells something. An imperative sentence gives an order. An interrogative sentence asks something. An exclamatory sentence expresses strong feeling. Each kind of sentence ends with a particular mark of punctuation.

Display these sentences on the board. Have students identify the kind of sentence and tell how they know.

- *The snowstorm dumped a foot of snow!* (exclamatory: expresses strong emotion, exclamation point)

- *Would you like to go sledding in the park?* (interrogative: asks something, question mark)

- *Go get your sleds from the garage.* (imperative: gives an order, period)

- *The roads are safe to drive on.* (declarative: tells something, period)

Explain that using different kinds of sentences adds variety and interest to speaking and writing. For more practice with this skill, see page 476.

CCSS **Common Core State Standards** (pp. Z20–Z30)
Language: L.4.1f, L.4.3b

Conventions

Mini-Lesson

Student Objectives

- Correct run-on sentences and comma splices. (p. 446)

Avoiding Run-ons and Comma Splices

Correct run-on sentences by adding a comma and conjunction after the first independent clause or by making two complete sentences. Correct comma splices by adding a conjunction after the comma or by making two complete sentences.

Display these sentences on the board. Discuss with students the error in each and ways to correct it.

- *I like basketball, I don't like football.* (comma splice: add the conjunction *but* after the comma; make two complete sentences)

- *My friend Ella won a race at recess today she won a race yesterday, too.* (run-on: add a comma and the conjunction *and* after *today*; make two complete sentences)

Have students name other conjunctions they could use to correct run-ons and comma splices. (but, or) For more practice with this skill, see page 476.

CCSS **Common Core State Standards** (pp. Z20–Z30)
Language: L.4.1f, L.4.2a, L.4.2c

 Conventions **Grammar, Usage & Mechanics**

Avoiding Run-ons and Comma Splices

Know the Rule

A **run-on sentence** is two complete sentences that run together without either a comma or a conjunction such as *and*. A **comma splice** occurs when two complete sentences are separated by only a comma. A conjunction after the comma is missing. To fix these types of sentence errors, add what is missing or make two separate sentences.

Examples:

I went to Paris I loved the city. *(incorrect)*
I went to Paris, **and** I loved the city. *(correct)*

I went to Paris, I loved the city. *(incorrect)*
I went to Paris. I loved the city. *(correct)*

Practice the Rule

Number a sheet of paper 1–10. Write **RO** after each run-on sentence. Write **CS** after each comma splice.

1. Paris is the capital of France it is located on the Seine River. **RO**
2. The Louvre is in Paris, it is one of the world's largest museums. **CS**
3. The Luxembourg Gardens is a large public park in Paris it was built in the seventeenth century. **RO**
4. The Eiffel Tower is a famous landmark my tour group from school decided to see it. **RO**
5. The Eiffel Tower has three levels we took the elevator ride to the top. **RO**
6. I loved Paris I especially liked walking around the city. **RO**
7. The food was delicious the people were very nice. **RO**
8. Our group was in Paris for two weeks, I never felt homesick. **CS**
9. The plane flight home was long I fell asleep. **RO**
10. My family met me at the airport, I was happy to be home. **CS**

Participles and Participial Phrases

Know the Rule

A **participle** is a verb form that acts like an adjective. In other words, a participle tells more about a noun or pronoun. A **participial phrase** is a phrase made up of a participle and the other words needed to complete the meaning.

Examples:
The young Jim Lovell's **failed** experiment taught him a lot. *(participle)*
The **exploding** rocket fell to the ground. *(participle)*
Exploding in the air, the rocket fell to the ground. *(participial phrase)*

Practice the Rule

Number a sheet of paper 1–10. Next to each number, write the sentence. Underline the participles and circle the participial phrases.

1. <u>Excited</u>, Lovell wanted to see if his rocket would fly.
2. The rocket, (soaring upward) finally exploded and crashed.
3. <u>Disappointed</u>, Lovell was determined to figure out what went wrong.
4. (Selected by NASA in 1962) Lovell was their youngest test pilot.
5. (Heading for the moon) the crew realized they were on a grand adventure.
6. (Amazed with space,) the crew enjoyed a smooth flight.
7. Then, suddenly, <u>exploding</u> sounds filled the spacecraft.
8. <u>Flashing</u> lights lit up the control panel.
9. (Understanding the situation) the crew sprang into action.
10. <u>Trained</u> pilots know how to quickly deal with problems.

Conventions

Mini-Lesson

Student Objectives

- Understand participles and participial phrases in sentences. (p. 447)

Participles and Participial Phrases

Participles are verb forms that act like adjectives. A participial phrase is a participle and any other words that complete the phrase. Both participles and participial phrases describe nouns or pronouns. Display these sentences. Point out each underlined participle or participial phrase. Have students identify the word that each describes.

- *Running toward me*, my dog looked like a large floppy doll. (dog)

- *Amazed*, I watched him leap over a fence. (I)

Participles and participial phrases do not always appear at the beginning of a sentence. Discuss with students how they could revise the first sentence so that the participial phrase does not appear at the beginning. (My dog, running toward me, looked like a large floppy doll.)

Explain that using participles helps writers add colorful details to their writing. For more practice with this skill, see page 476.

CCSS **C**ommon **C**ore **S**tate **S**tandards (pp. Z20–Z30)
Language: L.4.2a

Conventions

Mini-Lesson

Student Objectives

- Identify prepositional phrases and the words they modify. (p. 448)

Prepositional Phrases

Prepositional phrases begin with a preposition and end with a noun or pronoun. They can tell about a noun, pronoun, verb, adjective, or adverb in a sentence. Display these sentences on the board. Have students identify the prepositional phrase in each and the word that the phrase describes.

- *The team ran onto the field.* (onto the field, ran)

- *The player at first base is my favorite.* (at first base, player)

- *He is the best in the league.* (in the league, best)

Have students list some other prepositions they use. (Possible responses: across, out, from, toward, under, with)

Prepositional phrases enable writers to tell *how, how much, what, when,* or *where* about another word in a sentence. They make writing more descriptive. Refer students to page 488 for a list of prepositions to use in their writing. For more practice with this skill, see page 477.

CCSS **Common Core State Standards** (pp. Z20–Z30)
Language: L.4.1e

Prepositional Phrases

Know the Rule

A **prepositional phrase** can tell *how, when, what, how much,* or *where* about another word in the sentence. A prepositional phrase begins with a preposition. Some common prepositions are *during, for, in, of, on, outside, over, under, to, with,* and *without.*

Examples:
One gymnast fell **during her performance**.
The other finished **without a mistake**.

Practice the Rule

Number a sheet of paper 1–10. Write each sentence. Underline each prepositional phrase. Circle each preposition.

1. (During) the week, Andre practices every day.
2. Andre has been practicing gymnastics (for) eight years.
3. Maria practices (with) Mario.
4. Mario met Maria (outside) the gym.
5. Maria's photo appeared (in) the local newspaper.
6. Mario is very committed (to) the sport.
7. He competed (in) a nationwide contest.
8. Mario's parents traveled (with) him.
9. He performed eight sets (of) exercises.
10. (In) the end, Mario won first prize.

Appositives and Appositive Phrases

Know the Rule

An **appositive** is a word or phrase that identifies, explains, or means the same thing as a noun. Appositives follow the nouns they identify and are usually separated from the rest of the sentence by commas.

Examples:

Wilheim Roentgen, **a German scientist,** discovered the X-ray.

Roentgen, **an only child,** was educated by his parents.

Practice the Rule

Number a sheet of paper 1–10. Beside the number write the appositive phrase.

1. Roentgen's invention, the X-ray, revolutionized medicine.
2. Doctors use the machine to find out if a fracture, a break in a bone, has occurred.
3. Jake Gladstone, the clumsiest boy in our class, fell off his bike.
4. His bike, a brand new model, slid on gravel.
5. Brian, my quick-thinking brother, decided to get Jake to the hospital.
6. The hospital, the tallest building in town, was built in 1950.
7. The doctor, an expert in bone injuries, ordered an X-ray for Jake.
8. Jake, a very impatient person, hated waiting around the emergency room.
9. While he waited, he learned that one machine, the PET scan, can tell doctors what's happening in a person's brain.
10. Another machine, the PillCam, takes pictures of a person's digestive system.

Conventions

Mini-Lesson

Student Objectives

- Identify appositives and appositive phrases. *(p. 449)*

Appositives and Appositive Phrases

An appositive is a word or phrase that describes a noun or pronoun. Appositives come after the word they describe and are usually set apart by commas. Display these sentences on the board. Have students identify the appositive phrase in each sentence.

- *Paul Robeson, a famous African American, was an actor and a singer.* (a famous African American)

- *Shawn, the first to present his report, talked about African American astronauts.* (the first to present his report)

Explain that if an appositive is one word or is used to identify the noun it follows, it might not be set off by commas. Display this sentence and have students identify the appositive.

- *My friend Sue talked about rap music.* (Sue)

Explain that appositives enable writers to give information about people and things in sentences. For more practice with this skill, see page 477.

CCSS **C**ommon **C**ore **S**tate **S**tandards (pp. Z20–Z30)
Language: L.4.3b

Conventions

Mini-Lesson

Student Objectives

• Write plural nouns. *(p. 450)*

Plural Nouns

A plural noun names more than one person, place, or thing. Form plural nouns by adding *–s* or *–es* to the singular form. Sometimes minor spelling changes must be made (knife, knives; cherry, cherries).

Display these sentences on the board. Have students identify the plural nouns and explain how each was formed.

- *My friends and I played in the neighborhood park.* (friends, added -s to friend)

- *We watched the fallen leaves blow across the grass.* (leaves, changed the f of leaf to v and added -es)

- *The small yellow birds we saw are called finches.* (birds, added -s to bird; finches, added -es to finch)

Explain to students that using singular and plural nouns will make their writing more precise. For more practice with this skill, see page 477.

CCSS **Common Core State Standards** (pp. Z20–Z30)
Language: L.4.6

Conventions Grammar, Usage & Mechanics

Plural Nouns

Know the Rule

A **singular noun** names one person, place, or thing (*grape*). A **plural noun** names more than one (*grapes*).

- To make most nouns plural, add *-s* to the singular noun (*apple, apples*).
- If the noun ends in *s, ch, sh, x,* or *z*, add *-es* (*peach, peaches*).
- For most nouns that end in a consonant and *y*, change the *y* to *i* and add *-es*. (*berry, berries*).
- For most nouns that end in a vowel plus *y*, just add *-s* (*toy, toys*).
- For most nouns that end in *f* or *fe*, change the *f* to *v* and add *-es* (*calf, calves*).
- For some nouns that end in *f*, just add *-s* (*staffs*).

Practice the Rule

Number a sheet of paper 1–10. Beside each number write the plural form of the noun to complete the sentence.

1. Many people look for _____ to save energy. (way) **ways**
2. Taking _____ instead of driving cars can save gasoline. (bus) **buses (also accept busses)**
3. Getting to work by boat is available in some _____. (city) **cities**
4. Another thing people do is to check that their _____ are working properly. (chimney) **chimneys**
5. To save water, do not run _____ unless they are full. (dishwasher) **dishwashers**
6. _____ can help by using their air conditioners less. (company) **Companies**
7. You could also try turning up room _____. (temperature) **temperatures**
8. Riding in _____ is another way to save energy. (carpool) **carpools**
9. _____ should check that their windows keep out cold air. (family) **Families**
10. Many people believe that saving energy will improve our _____. (life) **lives**

Personal Pronouns and Compound Personal Pronouns

Know the Rule

A **pronoun** is a word that takes the place of one or more nouns or pronouns. Use the following **personal pronouns** and **compound personal pronouns** to talk about yourself or about yourself and someone else:
- personal pronouns: *I, me, we, us*
- compound personal pronouns: *myself, ourselves*

Use the following **personal pronouns** and **compound pronouns** to refer to other people and things:
- personal pronouns: *she, her, it, he, him, you, they, them*
- compound personal pronouns: *herself, himself, itself, yourself, yourselves, themselves*

Example:
I made **myself** a sandwich.

Practice the Rule

Number a sheet of paper 1–10. Write each sentence. Underline each personal pronoun. Circle each compound personal pronoun.

1. Adrianna cooked the whole meal herself.
2. He decided to buy himself an ice cream cone.
3. Many people like to cook for themselves.
4. The meal she cooked for herself tasted awful.
5. The new oven cleans itself.
6. Did she teach herself to cook?
7. Frank made himself an iced coffee.
8. Robert splashed her with spaghetti sauce.
9. Latoya grew the tomatoes herself.
10. Rather than eat out, they decided to cook for themselves.

Conventions

Mini-Lesson

Student Objectives

- Recognize personal pronouns and compound personal pronouns. *(p. 451)*

Personal Pronouns and Compound Personal Pronouns

Use personal pronouns and compound personal pronouns to talk about yourself, yourself and another person, or other people and things. Display these sentences on the board. Have students identify the pronouns in each.

- *The librarian taught us how to find books in the library.* **(us)**
- *I told myself to listen carefully to her.* **(I, myself, her)**
- *Now we can find books and articles for ourselves.* **(we, ourselves)**

Tell students that they should not use compound personal pronouns as the subjects of sentences. Have students correct the faulty pronoun usage in this sentence: Cheryl and myself went to the library. **(Cheryl and I went to the library.)**

Explain to students that if they use pronouns, they don't have to repeat the same nouns over and over. For more practice with this skill, see page 478.

CCSS Common Core State Standards (pp. Z20–Z30)
Language: L.4.6

Student Objectives

- Form the past tense of verbs. (p. 452)

Past-Tense Verbs

Use past-tense verbs to show action that happened in the past. Usually, but not always, the past tense is formed by adding *-ed* to the present-tense form. Display these verbs on the board. Have students form the past tense of each and use the verb in a sentence. Possible answers are shown.

- *jump* (jumped; I jumped over a puddle.)
- *hurry* (hurried; We hurried to class.)
- *run* (ran; I ran all the way home.)
- *ask* (asked; I asked my teacher a question.)
- *write* (wrote; I wrote a letter to my aunt.)

Remind students that they should memorize the past tense of verbs, such as *run* and *hide,* that change spelling.

Explain that using past-tense verbs in writing tells readers that certain actions happened in the past. For more practice with this skill, see page 478.

CCSS **Common Core State Standards** (pp. Z20–Z30)
Language: L.4.2d, L.4.6

 Grammar, Usage & Mechanics

Past-Tense Verbs

Know the Rule

The **tense** of a verb lets you know whether something happens in the past, present, or future. **Past-tense verbs** show action that happened in the past. Many verbs in the past tense, though not all of them, end with *-ed.*

Examples:
A huge flaming object **dropped** on farmland in New Jersey.
The year **was** 1938.

Practice the Rule

Number a sheet of paper 1–10. For each sentence, write the past-tense verb.

1. A radio broadcast about an alien invasion once frightened a lot of people.
2. The broadcast aired on October 30, 1938.
3. The program lasted for sixty minutes.
4. The program sounded like a real news bulletin.
5. It fooled many people.
6. People hid in cellars.
7. Some even wrapped their heads in towels.
8. They worried about poison gas.
9. The broadcast was a fake.
10. Later people protested the fake broadcast.

Present-Tense Verbs

Know the Rule

The **tense** of a verb lets you know whether something happens in the present, past, or future. **Present-tense verbs** show action that is happening now.

Examples:

Grizzly bears often **travel** alone.

The grizzly bear **is** North America's largest meat-eating animal.

Practice the Rule

Number a sheet of paper 1–10. Beside each number write the present-tense verb or verbs in each sentence.

1. The grizzly bear lives in the northern United States and in Canada.
2. The hind legs of grizzly bears are extremely powerful.
3. Sometimes grizzly bears walk on their hind legs.
4. Grizzly bears eat both plants and animals.
5. In preparation for winter, grizzly bears gain about 400 pounds.
6. Grizzlies dig dens for winter hibernation.
7. Normally grizzly bears avoid contact with humans.
8. Experts agree that the grizzly is an aggressive bear.
9. Despite their size and weight, grizzlies run very quickly.
10. Today only about 1,000 grizzlies live in the continental United States.

Appendix A: Grammar Practice 453

Mini-Lesson

Student Objectives

- Identify and use present-tense verbs. *(p. 453)*

Present-Tense Verbs

Use present-tense verbs when you want to tell about action that is happening now. Display these sentences on the board. Have a different volunteer read each sentence. Have the rest of the class identify the present-tense verb in each sentence.

- *Marie likes social studies class.* (likes)
- *Toni and Jason prefer math.* (prefer)
- *Learning about history requires a lot of reading.* (requires)
- *Music is my favorite class.* (is)

Remind students that the spelling of present-tense verbs can be different for different subjects. Have them revise the second sentence using only *Jason* as the subject. (prefers)

Explain to students that being able to use different tenses, such as the present tense and past tense, enables them to write about things that happen at different times. For more practice with this skill, see page 478.

CCSS **C**ommon **C**ore **S**tate **S**tandards (pp. Z20–Z30)
Language: L.4.6

Conventions
Mini-Lesson

Student Objectives

• Identify and use future tense verbs. (p. 454)

Future-Tense Verbs

Use future-tense verbs to tell about actions that will happen in the future. Future-tense verbs are formed by adding the helping verb *will*. Display these sentences on the board. Have students identify the future-tense verb in each.

- *I will walk to Li's apartment after school.* (will walk)

- *He and I will play one of his computer games.* (will play)

Display these sentences on the board. Have students revise each using the future tense of the verb.

- *Kara asks Lilly for lunch on Saturday.* (will ask)

- *Lilly's mom drives her to Kara's home.* (will drive)

Explain to students that future-tense verbs, like present- and past-tense verbs, enable them to write about actions that occur at different times. For more practice with this skill, see page 479.

Note: Some helping verbs, such as *will* are called **modal auxiliary verbs.** They are used with a main verb to indicate time and mood.

CCSS **C**ommon **C**ore **S**tate **S**tandards (pp. Z20–Z30)
Language: L.4.6

Future-Tense Verbs

Know the Rule

The **tense** of a verb lets you know whether something happens in the present, past, or future. **Future-tense verbs** show action that will happen. Verbs in the future tense use the helping verb *will*.

Examples:
Janine **will look** for books on her topic tomorrow.
She hopes the librarian **will help** her.

Practice the Rule

Number a sheet of paper 1–10. Beside each number write the future-tense verb in each sentence. Be sure to include both the helping verb and the main verb.

1. Manuel will need help picking a topic.
2. He will ask his older sister for help.
3. She will help him in the evening.
4. Peter will choose an interesting topic.
5. Monique will finish her paper on time.
6. I will write about Marco Polo.
7. I will read all about my topic.
8. I will check my paper for spelling mistakes.
9. Also, I will make a neat copy of my paper.
10. My classmates will enjoy my paper.

Helping Verbs

Know the Rule

Helping verbs come before the main verb in a sentence. Helping verbs work with the main verb to show time and mood. Helping verbs also start many questions. Some helping verbs such as *can,*, *may*, *must*, and *will* are called **modal auxiliaries**.

Common Helping Verbs

am	was	has	can
is	were	have	may
are	will	had	must

Example:
Service dogs **are helping** people all across the country.

Practice the Rule

Number a sheet of paper 1–10. Write each sentence. Underline the helping verb once and the main verb twice.

1. Bessie, a golden retriever, is watching Jake very carefully.
2. Bessie has become Jake's key to freedom.
3. Jake must use a wheelchair to get around.
4. Bessie will help Jake with tasks.
5. Bessie's specialty is helping children with special needs.
6. Every day Bessie and her ten-year-old owner will learn more about each other.
7. Bessie was trained for many months at a special service dog center.
8. Was Jake's scent used for training Bessie?
9. Bessie is trained to follow Jake's scent.
10. Bessie can learn new things every day.

Mini-Lesson

Student Objectives

• Identify and use helping verbs. (p. 455)

Helping Verbs

Helping verbs (*was, were, had, may, will,* and others) come before the main verb in a sentence. Helping verbs also start many questions.

Display these sentences on the board. Have students identify the helping verb and the main verb in each sentence.

• *I have learned a lot about newspapers today.* (have, learned)

• *Working at a newspaper must be exciting.* (must, be)

• *Can you name your town's main newspaper?* (Can, name)

Have volunteers give their own examples of questions that begin with a helping verb. (Possible answers: Did you finish your homework? Are we going to the museum today?)

Remind students that they use the helping verb *will* to form future-tense verbs. Explain that helping verbs help show when the action of the main verb happens. For more practice with this skill, see page 479.

Note: Some helping verbs, such as *can, could, may, might, must, should, will* and *would* are called **modal auxiliary verbs.** They are used with a main verb to indicate time and mood.

CCSS **Common Core State Standards** (pp. Z20–Z30)
Language: L.4.1c, L.4.6

Appendix A: Grammar Practice **T455**

Conventions

Mini-Lesson

Student Objectives

- Form and use present perfect-tense verbs. (p. 456)

Present Perfect-Tense Verbs

Present perfect-tense verbs show that action that happened in the past may still be happening in the present. To form the present perfect tense, add *has* or *have* to the past participle of the verb. Display these incomplete sentences. Have students add *has* or *have* to form the present perfect tense.

- *We _____ worked on our report for two weeks.* (have)

- *Jane _____ written only half of her report.* (has)

- *Jamal and Keith _____ researched photographs for their report.* (have)

Point out the main verb *written* in the second sentence. Explain to students that the past participle of a verb does not always end with *-ed*. Give them examples, such as *eaten, given,* and *done*. Have students use the verbs in sentences of their own. For more practice with this skill, see page 479.

CCSS Common Core State Standards (pp. Z20–Z30)
Language: L.4.6

T456 Appendix A: Grammar Practice

Conventions Grammar, Usage & Mechanics

Present Perfect-Tense Verbs

Know the Rule

The **tense** of a verb lets you know whether something happens in the present, past, or future. **Present perfect-tense** verbs show that an action that happened in the past may still be taking place now, in the present. To form the present perfect tense, add the helping verb *has* or *have* to the past participle of a verb. The sentence *Joe has known Shana for three years* is in the present perfect tense. In other words, Joe met Shana three years ago, and he still knows her today.

Examples:
Brian **has practiced** every day this week.
The rest of us **have** not **practiced** every day.

Practice the Rule

Number a sheet of paper 1–10. Beside each number write the present perfect-tense verb. Be sure to include both the helping verb and the main verb.

1. Martha has attended every practice.
2. We have waited an hour for the beginning of practice.
3. We have rehearsed the play many times.
4. James has worked hard learning his lines.
5. People have performed in school plays for years.
6. Most times I have worked behind the scenes.
7. Jack has had a leading role only once.
8. There have been many successful school plays.
9. All her life Tina has thought of being in a professional play.
10. For years I have dreamed about getting a great role.

Adverbs

Know the Rule

An **adverb** is a word that describes a verb. It tells *how, when,* or *where* about a verb. Many adverbs end with *-ly.*

Examples:

The sauce cooked **slowly** on the stove.

Maria **often** makes spaghetti sauce.

Practice the Rule

Number a sheet of paper 1–10. Beside each number write the adverb and the verb it describes.

1. Yesterday Carmen bought some groceries. **Yesterday; bought**
2. First she cut the peppers. **First; cut**
3. Later she sliced the mushrooms. **Later; sliced**
4. She skillfully added spices. **skillfully; added**
5. Carmen used the hot pepper sparingly. **sparingly; used**
6. Manuel cheerfully set the table. **cheerfully; set**
7. Soon the guests arrived. **Soon; arrived**
8. Manuel greeted guests warmly. **warmly; greeted**
9. Everything was properly prepared. **properly; was prepared**
10. Everyone completely enjoyed the meal. **completely; enjoyed**

Appendix A: Grammar Practice 457

Conventions

Mini-Lesson

Student Objectives

- Identify adverbs and the verbs they modify. *(p. 457)*

Adverbs

Adverbs tell *how, when,* or *where* about verbs. Adverbs often, but not always, end in *-ly.* Display these sentences on the board. Have students identify the adverb in each and the verb that it describes. Discuss with students what the adverbs tell about the verbs.

- *My sister and I walked slowly home from school.* (slowly, walked, how)
- *We looked everywhere for our pet cat.* (everywhere, looked, where)
- *My mother finally found it under my bed.* (finally, found, when)
- *The cat purred loudly as I petted it.* (loudly, purred, how)

Explain to students that being able to use adverbs enables them to add important details about verbs to their writing. For more practice with this skill, see page 480.

CCSS Common Core State Standards (pp. Z20–Z30)
Language: L.4.6

Conventions
Mini-Lesson

Student Objectives

- Identify prepositional phrases. *(p. 458)*

Prepositions and Prepositional Phrases

A prepositional phrase begins with a preposition and ends with a noun or pronoun. The noun or pronoun is called the object of the preposition.

Display these sentences on the board. Have students identify the prepositional phrase in each, as well as the preposition that begins the phrase and the object of the preposition.

- *Yesterday we rode our bikes in the park.* **(in the park, in, park)**
- *At noon we stopped and ate lunch.* **(At noon, At, noon)**

A sentence may have more than one prepositional phrase. Have students identify the prepositional phrases in this sentence.

- *Liam laid his bike on the ground beside the picnic table.* **(on the ground, beside the picnic table)**

Explain that prepositional phrases make writing clearer and more vivid. For more practice with this skill, see page 480.

CCSS Common Core State Standards (pp. Z20–Z30)
Language: L.4.1e

Prepositions and Prepositional Phrases

Know the Rule

A **preposition** is a word that shows the relationship between a noun or pronoun and another word in the sentence. In a sentence, prepositions are always followed by a word called the **object of a preposition**. A **prepositional phrase** begins with a preposition and ends with the object of a preposition. Some prepositional phrases help tell where something is.

Examples:

Go **to the back of the room.** ← prepositional phrases

Common Prepositions

above	between	through
across	in	toward
behind	into	under
below	near	underneath
beneath	on	
beside	outside	

Practice the Rule

Number a sheet of paper 1–10. Write the sentences. Underline the prepositional phrase. Circle the preposition.

1. Find the blue box (behind) the bookcase.
2. Clara put the pencils (on) the shelf.
3. Jason walked (across) the hall.
4. (Beneath) the counter, he found the dog treats.
5. Julio waited (near) the door.
6. The book fell (between) two desks.
7. I waited (outside) the door.
8. I will check the supplies (in) the morning.
9. You will find the paper (underneath) the table.
10. Maria walked (toward) the supply closet.

Coordinating Conjunctions

Know the Rule

A **coordinating conjunction** connects words in a sentence. Common coordinating conjunctions are *and, but,* and *or.* Put a comma before a coordinating conjunction when it is used to form a compound sentence.

Examples:
Carla **and** Diane are taking art lessons.
Carla likes using watercolors, **but** she does not like using colored pencils.

Practice the Rule

Number a sheet of paper 1–10. Write each sentence. Circle the coordinating conjuction and underline the words or sentences it connects.

1. Kim (and) Barbara completed their assignment on Tuesday.
2. Ariella's watercolor painting is original (and) exciting.
3. I want to work in oils (or) pastels.
4. Our art teacher loves painting, (but) she does not like drawing.
5. I studied art for two years, (but) then I switched to photography.
6. I like to paint the sea (and) flowers.
7. Jackson (or) Cole will take you to the art fair.
8. The paper (and) paints are on the table.
9. I am taking art lessons (and) swimming lessons.
10. I want to work as an artist (or) an architect.

Mini-Lesson

Student Objectives

- Identify and use coordinating conjunctions. *(p. 459)*

Coordinating Conjunctions

Coordinating conjunctions, such as *and, but,* and *or,* connect words in a sentence. Display these sentences on the board. Have students identify the coordinating conjunctions and the words they join.

- *Tina ordered spaghetti and salad for lunch.* (and, spaghetti, salad)
- *Would you like to drink water or juice?* (or, water, juice)

A comma followed by a coordinating conjunction can be used to form compound sentences. Display these sentences. Discuss with students how they could use a comma and a conjunction to form a compound sentence.

- *I wanted to order a pizza _____ Mom insisted that we cook dinner.* (, but)
- *Vincent likes Italian food _____ he also likes Mexican food.* (, and ; but)

Explain that using conjunctions can help prevent repetition in writing. For more practice with this skill, see page 480.

CCSS **Common Core State Standards** (pp. Z20–Z30)
Language: L.4.2c

Appendix A: Grammar Practice **T459**

Conventions
Mini-Lesson

Student Objectives

• Recognize and use interjections. *(p. 460)*

Interjections

An interjection can stand alone followed by an exclamation point. It can also begin a sentence. An interjection that begins a sentence is followed by a comma. Display these sentences on the board. Have students identify the interjection and the punctuation that follows it.

• *Hey, would you like to watch a movie?*

• *Wow! That sounds like a great idea.*

Discuss with students why *would* is not capitalized. (It's not the first word of the sentence.) and why *That* is capitalized. (*That* begins the sentence.)

Have students use *oops* and *ouch* in sentences of their own. (Possible answers: Oops, I broke my pencil. Ouch! This splinter in my finger hurts.)

Explain to students that interjections can help them express emotion and add colorful details to their writing. For more practice with this skill, see page 481.

CCSS Common Core State Standards (pp. Z20–Z30)
Language: L.4.3b

Interjections

Know the Rule

An **interjection** is a word that expresses strong emotion. It can stand alone, followed by an exclamation point. It can also begin a sentence. When an interjection begins a sentence, it is followed by a comma.

Examples:
Wow! Did you hear that wind?
Okay, let's get inside.

Common Interjections

ah	hurrah	ouch
bam	my goodness	phew
bravo	oh	rats
eek	oh dear	ugh
good grief	oh my	whoops
gosh	okay	wow
hey	oops	yikes

Practice the Rule

Number a sheet of paper 1–10. Beside each number write the interjection as it appears in the sentence and the punctuation that follows it.

1. (Eek!) The baseball just shattered the window.
2. (Hey,) we've got to get inside.
3. (Good grief!) The wind is ripping trees apart.
4. (Rats!) My tree house is ruined.
5. (Ouch,) a branch just hit my arm.
6. The storm is nearly over. (Hurrah!)
7. (My goodness,) we have a big mess to clean up.
8. You did a great job cleaning up. (Bravo!)
9. (Oh dear,) the wind is picking up again.
10. (Oh my,) here we go again!

Progressive Verbs

Know the Rule

Progressive verbs show that an action is happening, was happening, or will be happening. The action happens for a length of time. Progressive verbs are made from the *-ing* form of a verb along with a form of the verb *to be*.

Present Progressive	I *am walking*.	I am walking right now. I have not finished my walk.
Past Progressive	I *was walking* when it started to rain.	In the middle of walking, the rain began. My walk had not ended yet.
Future Progressive	I *will be walking* to school next year instead of taking the bus.	Over a period of time, I will walk to school many times.

Practice the Rule

Number a sheet of paper 1–10. Write the progressive form of the verb in parentheses that makes sense in each sentence.

1. Next year, Kevin _____ how to play the saxophone. (learn) **will be learning**
2. Last year, he _____ the violin. (study) **was studying**
3. Nisha cannot read while she _____ to music. (listen) **is listening**
4. While Jayden _____ his guitar, a string broke. (tune) **was tuning**
5. I could see Amy's eyes move while she _____ her music. (read) **was reading**
6. Jayden and Amy _____ to try out for the band this afternoon. (plan) **are planning**
7. If they make it, they _____ together in the band! (play) **will be playing**
8. Mr. Mohr _____ music again next year. (teach) **will be teaching**
9. Mr. Mohr _____ forward to teaching Jayden, Amy, and Kevin. (look) **is looking**
10. The band members _____ that they will win the district band contest. (hope) **are hoping**

Mini-Lesson

Student Objectives

• Form progressive tenses of verbs. *(p. 461)*

Progressive Verbs

Progressive verbs show that an action is still happening (present progressive), was happening (past progressive), or will be happening in the future (future progressive). The progressive forms end with *–ing* and are preceded by a helping verb. Discuss with students the helping verbs that are used with the present progressive (*am, are, is*), the past progressive (*was, were*), and future progressive (*will be*). Then have students identify the progressive verbs, including the helping verbs, in these sentences.

• *My class is studying the history of Mexico.* **(is studying)**

• *We were reading about Mexico City when the bell rang.* **(were reading)**

• *Next week we will be writing reports on different countries.* **(will be writing)**

Explain to students that progressive verbs help them tell exactly when an action is happening. For more practice with this skill, see page 481.

CCSS **Common Core State Standards** (pp. Z20–Z30)
Language: L.4.1b, L.4.2d

Conventions

Mini-Lesson

Student Objectives

- Correctly use homophones. (p. 462)

Homophones

Homophones are words that sound the same but are spelled differently and have different meanings. *Too* and *two* are homophones. So are *see* and *sea*.

Help students correctly use these pairs of homophones in sentences of their own. **(Possible answers are shown.)**

- *knew, new* **(I knew the answer. Is that a new book?)**

- *hour, our* **(I finished the test in an hour. Our playground is great.)**

- *rode, road* **(I rode the rollercoaster at the park. The road has a lot of traffic.)**

Have students list other pairs of homophones they know. **(Possible answers: right/write, principal/principle, four/for)**

Explain to students that using the correct homophone in their writing helps make the meaning of a sentence clear. For more practice with this skill, see page 481.

Homophones

Know the Rule

Homophones are words that sound the same but have different spellings and meanings.

Examples:
He **knows** the kind of flowers I like best.
The flowers tickle my **nose.**

Common Homophones	Meaning
eye	the organ of sight
I	personal pronoun referring to oneself
hear	to perceive sound
here	at or in this place
its	belonging to it
it's	it is
sea	a large body of salt water
see	to perceive with the eye
read	to have grasped the meaning of printed or written words
red	a color

Practice the Rule

Number a sheet of paper 1–5. Write the word that best completes each sentence correctly.

1. Last week I _____ everything I could about bees. (red/read)
2. Finally _____ decided to raise bees myself. (I/eye)
3. _____ in my yard, I have two beehives. (Here/Hear)
4. I have a protective suit I _____ when working with my bees. (where/wear)
5. _____ of my favorite things is to watch my bees. (Won/One)

CCSS **Common Core State Standards** (pp. Z20–Z30)
Language: L.4.1g, L.4.2d, L.4.4a

Using the Right Word

Know the Rule

Some words and phrases are often misused in writing. Using the correct word will make your writing less confusing for your readers.

Examples:

accept, except	**Accept** is a verb that means to receive: *I **accept** your apology.*
	Except is usually a preposition that means excluding: *I liked all of the books **except** this one.*
than, then	**Than** is a conjunction used in comparisons: *I like chicken better **than** fish.*
	Then is an adverb that indicates time: *First we'll cook, and **then** we'll eat.*
your, you're	**Your** is a possessive pronoun: *Where is **your** hat?*
	You're is a contraction of the words *you are*: ***You're** going to be late.*
could have, could of	Do not use **could** (*would, should*) **of** when what you mean is **could have**: *I **could have** won the contest.*

Practice the Rule

Number a sheet of paper 1–10. Write each sentence, correcting any words or phrases used incorrectly.

1. *Your*
   You're report is excellent.
2. I swim better *then* my brother.
3. Jen is busy every day *except* Tuesday.
4. Bret could *have* of done a better job.
5. *You're* Your a great baseball player.
6. Get yourself a snack and *then* begin your homework.
7. Please *accept* except my apologies for being late.
8. Marcus would *have* of called, but he was at soccer practice.
9. Ali is taller *than* then Mia.
10. Everyone handed in their homework *except* accept Duncan.

Mini-Lesson

Student Objectives

- Correctly use frequently confused words and phrases. (p. 463)

Using the Right Word

Some words and phrases are often misused in writing and in speaking. Usually these words and phrases have similar sounds. They sometimes sound even more alike when they are pronounced by people in different parts of the country. Discuss with students which word or phrase in parentheses correctly completes each sentence.

- *I _____ helped you last night. (could of, could have)* **(could have)**

- *Your book has better pictures _____ the one I'm reading. (than, then)* **(than)**

- *_____ supposed to list any books you used for your report. (Your, You're)* **(You're)**

Encourage students to keep a list of words or phrases that they often misuse and to check the list when they write.

Explain to students that using the correct word or phrase makes writing less confusing for readers. For more practice with this skill, see page 482.

CCSS Common Core State Standards (pp. Z20–Z30)
Language: L.4.1g, L.4.2d, L.4.4a

Conventions

Mini-Lesson

Student Objectives

- Identify pronouns and their antecedents. *(p. 464)*

Pronoun Antecedents

A pronoun antecedent is the noun that a pronoun refers to, or replaces. A pronoun should agree with its antecedent in number (singular or plural) and gender (male or female).

Display these sentences on the board. Discuss with students the pronoun in each and its number and gender. Then have students identify the antecedent.

- *My friend Carla decided that she would learn about Dr. Martin Luther King, Jr.* (she, singular, female, Carla)

- *Dr. King gave his life for the cause of freedom.* (his, singular, male, Dr. King)

Point out that plural pronouns can refer to both males and females in a sentence. Discuss this example.

- *Crystal and David gave their report on the African American astronaut Mae Jemison.* (their, plural, Crystal, David)

Explain to students that using pronouns correctly makes writing clearer for readers. For more practice with this skill, see page 482.

CCSS **Common Core State Standards** (pp. Z20–Z30)
Language: L.4.4a, L.4.6

Conventions Grammar, Usage & Mechanics

Pronoun Antecedents

Know the Rule

A pronoun takes the place of a noun. The noun that a pronoun replaces is called its **antecedent**. When you write a pronoun such as *he, she, him, her, they, them,* or *it,* be sure that the antecedent—or word that the pronoun replaces—**is clear**. Also be sure that the pronoun agrees in number (singular or plural) and in gender (male or female) with the noun that it replaces.

Examples:

Melissa read an article about Alice Ramsey and **her** adventures.

Melissa was in the library when **she** read the article.

Practice the Rule

Number a sheet of paper 1–10. Write each sentence, using the correct pronoun. Underline its antecedent.

1. Melissa wrote in _____ journal about Alice Ramsey. (her/his)
2. Alice Ramsey lived a long time ago, but _____ adventures are still interesting to read about. (her/their)
3. Melissa decided to write _____ paper on Alice Ramsey. (her/their)
4. Melissa's two friends, Eileen and Kevin, wrote _____ papers on Eleanor Roosevelt. (his/their)
5. Melissa used the Internet for most of _____ research. (her/their)
6. Eileen and Kevin used the library for _____ research. (his/their)
7. Melissa learned a lot about Alice Ramsey and _____ life. (her/his)
8. Melissa's friends worked hard on _____ papers, too. (her/their)
9. Melissa presented _____ paper on Tuesday. (her/his)
10. Eileen and Kevin presented _____ papers on Wednesday. (his/their)

Comparative and Superlative Adjectives

Know the Rule

The **comparative form** of an **adjective** compares two people, places, or things. The **superlative form** compares three or more people, places, or things. For most short adjectives, add *-er* to compare two people, places, or things and *-est* to compare three or more. For most longer adjectives, use *more* to compare two persons, places, or things and *most* to compare three or more. Remember, the superlative form usually is preceded by the article *the*.

Comparing With Adjectives

- Adjectives ending with *e*:   wide
  Drop the *e* and add *-er* or *-est*.   wider
                                                  widest

- Adjectives ending with a consonant and *y*:   silly
  Change the *y* to *i* and add *-er* or *-est*. sillier
                                                  silliest

- Some adjectives with two syllables and all   impressive
  adjectives with more than two syllables: more impressive
  Use *more* or *most* instead of *-er* or *-est*. most impressive

Practice the Rule

Number a sheet of paper 1–8. Write each sentence, choosing the correct form of the adjective.

1. The cheetah is the world's (faster/**fastest**) land mammal.
2. The (speedier/**speediest**) insect is the hawk moth.
3. The (swifter/**swiftest**) mammal in the water is the killer whale.
4. Dinosaurs were big, but today's blue whales are even (most gigantic/**more gigantic**).
5. The (slower/**slowest**) animal on Earth is the three-toed sloth.
6. The (smaller/**smallest**) mammal on Earth is the bumblebee bat.
7. The pygmy shrew is just a little bit (**bigger**/biggest) than the bumblebee bat.
8. Which is (**more beautiful**/most beautiful), a cardinal or a robin?

Mini-Lesson

Student Objectives

- Recognize comparative and superlative adjectives. *(p. 465)*

Comparative and Superlative Adjectives

Comparative adjectives compare two people, places, or things. Superlative adjectives compare three or more. Add *-er* or use *more* to form most comparative adjectives. Add *-est* or use *most* to form most superlative adjectives. Display these sentences on the board. Have students identify the comparative or superlative adjective in each sentence.

- *The Mississippi River is wider than the Ohio River.* (wider, comparative)

- *The longest river in the world may be the Nile River in Egypt.* (longest, superlative)

- *Yolanda is the student in our class who is most interested in rivers.* (most interested, superlative)

Discuss with students how each adjective was formed. (added *-er* to *wide*; added *-est* to *long*; used *most* before *interested*)

For more practice with this skill, see page 482.

CCSS **Common Core State Standards** (pp. Z20–Z30)
Language: L.4.2d, L.4.4a, L.4.6

Conventions

Mini-Lesson

Student Objectives

- Identify adverbs that compare two actions. *(p. 466)*

Comparing With Adverbs

Add *-er* to short adverbs to compare two actions (faster). For most adverbs ending with *-ly*, use the word *more* before the adverb (more slowly). Display these sentences and discuss the adverbs that compare actions. Have students tell how the adverb is formed.

- *Paula worked harder than her partner on their poster.* **(harder, add -er to hard)**

- *Jaime printed the words on the poster more carefully than I did.* **(more carefully, use more with carefully)**

Tell students that the word *than* usually follows an adverb that compares two actions. Have students point out the word *than* in each sentence.

Explain to students that using adverbs to compare actions allows them to give readers accurate information about what is happening in a piece of writing. For more practice with this skill, see page 483.

CCSS **Common Core State Standards** (pp. Z20–Z30)
Language: L.4.2d, L.4.6

Conventions **Grammar, Usage & Mechanics**

Comparing With Adverbs

Know the Rule

You can use **adverbs** to compare two actions. Add *-er* to short adverbs to compare two actions. For most adverbs that end in *-ly*, use *more* to compare two actions.

Examples:

Comparing With Adverbs

One Action	Joe runs **fast**.
	Alexa swims **gracefully**.
Two Actions	Joe runs **faster** than Lee.
	Alexa swims **more gracefully** than Laetifa.

Practice the Rule

Number a sheet of paper 1–10. Beside each number write the comparative form of the adverb.

1. The new coach spoke _____ than last year's coach. (calmly) more calmly
2. Of the two competitors, Clarisse performed _____. (skillfully) more skillfully
3. Wanda swam _____ than Dan. (rapidly) more rapidly
4. Matt answered _____ than Peter. (politely) more politely
5. Austin will complete his training _____ than Katie. (soon) sooner
6. The winner completed his routine _____ than I did. (expertly) more expertly
7. The broad jump began _____ than the high jump. (late) later
8. Austin speaks _____ than Matt. (softly) more softly
9. Katie's relay team ran _____ than our team. (swiftly) more swiftly
10. Mike cheered _____ than Matt. (loudly) more loudly

Comparing With Superlative Adverbs

Know the Rule

You can use the **superlative form** of adverbs to compare three or more actions. Add -*est* to short adverbs to compare three or more actions. For most adverbs that end in -*ly*, use *most* to compare three or more actions. Sometimes you will need to change the spelling of a word in order to add an ending. For example, you might need to change the *y* to *i* before adding -*est*.

Examples:
Of the five of us, Noah arrived **earliest**.
Of all the students in our class, Arun writes **most powerfully**.

Practice the Rule

Number a sheet of paper 1–10. Beside each number write the superlative form of the adverb.

1. Of the five girls, Angela spoke _____. (politely) **most politely**
2. Of all the competitors, Ethan performed _____. (skillfully) **most skillfully**
3. The teacher in our school who speaks _____ is Mr. Henderson. (calmly) **most calmly**
4. The person in our class who sings _____ is Rachel. (sweetly) **most sweetly**
5. Of the ten members in our debating club, Andrew answers questions _____. (confidently) **most confidently**
6. Chloe and I arrived early, but Jayden arrived _____. (early) **earliest**
7. Who jumped _____ in your class? (high) **highest**
8. Recently five students were absent with the flu, but _____ only two students were absent. (recently) **most recently**
9. Everyone works hard at math, but Emma works _____ of all. (hard) **hardest**
10. Jason can run _____ of anyone in the class. (fast) **fastest**

Mini-Lesson

Student Objectives

- Identify adverbs and the verbs they modify. (*p. 467*)

Comparing With Superlative Adverbs

Add –*est* to short adverbs to compare three or more actions (latest). For most adverbs that end in -*ly*, use *most* before the adverb to form the superlative (most calmly). Display these sentences on the board. Have students identify the superlative adverbs that compare three or more actions.

- *Of all the choir members, Elliot sang loudest.* (**loudest**)

- *Of all the violinists, Linda played most confidently.* (**most confidently**)

Display this sentence on the board. Discuss the mistake of forming the superlative by adding both *most* and -*est*. Have students tell the correct way to form the superlative in the sentence.

- *Of the trumpet players, Sarah plays most skillfulliest.* (**most skillfully**)

Explain that superlative adverbs enable writers to describe clearly how three or more actions are related. For more practice with this skill, see page 483.

CCSS **Common Core State Standards** (pp. Z20–Z30)
Language: L.4.6

Conventions

Mini-Lesson

Student Objectives

- Recognize and form abbreviations. *(p. 468)*

Abbreviations

An abbreviation is a shortened form of a word. The abbreviation *St.* stands for the word *Street*. Point out that most abbreviations begin with an uppercase letter and end with a period. Have students list abbreviations they know. **(Possible responses: Mr., Mrs., Ave.)**

Display these abbreviations on the board. Have students explain what each means.

- *Jr.* **(Junior),** *Sept.* **(September),** *Mon.* **(Monday),** *Dr.* **(Doctor)**

Then write these words and have volunteers write the abbreviation of each.

- *February* **(Feb.),** *Wednesday* **(Wed.),** *Post Office* **(P.O.)**

Explain that abbreviations are appropriate for addresses in letters, on envelopes, and in emails. Point out that in writing, however, students should use words rather than their abbreviations.

Tell students that learning abbreviations will enable them to easily figure out the meaning of abbreviations when they see them. For more practice with this skill, see page 483.

CCSS **Common Core State Standards** (pp. Z20–Z30)
Language: L.4.2d, L.4.4a, L.4.6

Conventions Grammar, Usage & Mechanics

Abbreviations

Know the Rule

An **abbreviation** is a shortened form of a word. Most abbreviations begin with an uppercase letter and end with a period. An **initial** is an uppercase letter with a period after it. An initial takes the place of a person's name.

Common Abbreviations

Titles	Mr., Mister	Dr., Doctor	Sen., Senator
Addresses	St., Street	Rd., Road	P.O., Post Office
Initials	M. L. King Jr., Martin Luther King Junior	J. F. Kennedy, John Fitzgerald Kennedy	R. L. Stine, Robert Lawrence Stine
Months	Jan., January	Mar., March	Aug., August
Days	Mon., Monday	Thurs., Thursday	Sat., Saturday

Practice the Rule

Number a sheet of paper 1–10. Beside each number write the correct abbreviation for each underlined word.

1. <u>Doctor</u> Rodriguez Dr.
2. <u>Friday</u> Fri.
3. <u>Mister</u> Tully Mr.
4. <u>Nathaniel Anthony</u> D'Amore N. A.
5. Thomas Jones <u>Junior</u> Jr.
6. 53 Winter <u>Road</u> Rd.
7. <u>August</u> 14, 2012 Aug.
8. 33 Temple <u>Street</u> St.
9. <u>Post Office</u> P.O.
10. <u>Saturday</u> Sat.

Capitalization

Know the Rule

Capitalize the first letter in proper nouns and proper adjectives.
Examples:
We are learning about **Mexico**.
Have you ever eaten at a **Mexican** restaurant?

Proper Nouns and Adjectives

Geographical Names	Holidays	Dates	Historic Documents, Periods, and Events	Organizations
Pacific Ocean	Fourth of July	April	Bill of Rights	American Red Cross
Mount Grey	Thanksgiving	Sunday	Colonial Era	Republican Party
Nile River	Father's Day	January	Great Depression	Warren Community Chorus
Canada	Labor Day	Wednesday	Revolutionary War	European Union

Practice the Rule

Number a sheet of paper 1–10. Beside each number write the sentence with capitalization errors corrected.

1. My friend from germany is coming to visit.
2. We learned about the great depression last month.
3. My project is due on monday.
4. The european union was created more than 50 years ago.
5. This painting shows the english countryside.
6. My favorite holiday is thanksgiving.
7. Our test will be on the revolutionary war.
8. My mother belongs to the warren community chorus.
9. Let's get together on friday.
10. We will have a big party on the fourth of july.

Mini-Lesson

Student Objectives

- Capitalize proper nouns and proper adjectives. *(p. 469)*

Capitalization

Begin proper nouns (Mother's Day, Río Bravo) and proper adjectives (Chinese, Mexican) with an uppercase letter. Proper nouns name geographical places, holidays, dates, organizations, and historical documents. The word *the* that comes before some proper nouns is usually not capitalized.

Display these sentences. Have students capitalize the proper nouns and proper adjectives.

- *Last thursday we studied the american civil war.* **(Thursday, American Civil War)**

- *One important document of that era is called the gettysburg address.* **(Gettysburg Address)**

Point out that plural adjectives, like plural nouns, may be more than one word. Have students capitalize the proper adjective and proper noun in this sentence.

- *The first african american member of the supreme court was Thurgood Marshall.* **(African American, Supreme Court)**

Explain that capitalization helps readers recognize proper nouns and proper adjectives. For more practice with this skill, see page 484.

CCSS **Common Core State Standards** (pp. Z20–Z30)
Language: L.4.2a

Conventions

Mini-Lesson

Student Objectives

• Write titles correctly. *(p. 470)*

Titles

Capitalize the first, last, and all important words in a title. Underline the title of books, magazines, newspapers, movies, and works of art, or italicize if using a computer. Put quotation marks around the titles of stories, poems, and songs.

Display these items on the board. Discuss with students how they would capitalize and punctuate each title if writing with a pencil or on a computer.

• *a poem titled my dog fred* (**"My Dog Fred"**)

• *a book titled lizard goes to mars* (**Lizard Goes to Mars** or *Lizard Goes to Mars*)

• *the movie pirates of the caribbean* (**Pirates of the Caribbean** or *Pirates of the Caribbean*)

• *a story titled my new best friend* (**"My New Best Friend"**)

Explain to students that writing titles correctly helps avoid confusion in writing. For more practice with this skill, see page 484.

Titles

Know the Rule

Capitalize the first word, the last word, and all the important words in a title. Verbs, such as *is* and *are*, are important words. Capitalize *the* only if it is the first word in a title. **Underline** the titles of books, magazines, newspapers, movies, works of art, and long musical compositions. If you are writing on a computer, put these titles in **italics**. Put **quotation marks** around the titles of shorter works, such as songs, stories, and poems.

> **Examples:**
> *Charlotte's Web* (book title)
> *Aladdin and the Wonderful Lamp* (book title)
> *Sports Illustrated for Kids* (magazine title)
> "America the Beautiful" (song title)
> "The Desert Scare" (story title)

Practice the Rule

Number a sheet of paper 1–10. Beside each number, write the sentence correctly.

1. Sarah, Plain and Tall is one of my favorite books. <u>Sarah, Plain and Tall</u>
2. Take the sky was the poem I chose to recite. "Take the Sky"
3. My mother reads the Chicago Tribune every morning. <u>Chicago Tribune</u>
4. I watched the movie National Velvet last night. <u>National Velvet</u>
5. I wrote about the painting Cape Cod Afternoon. <u>Cape Cod Afternoon</u>
6. A Wrinkle in time is a novel written by Madeline L'Engle. <u>A Wrinkle in Time</u>
7. The singing of The Star-Spangled Banner closed the program. "The Star-Spangled Banner"
8. The last piece of light is my favorite short story. "The Last Piece of Light"
9. Cobblestone is a great history magazine. <u>Cobblestone</u>
10. Tomorrow I will start reading the book Summer of The Swans. <u>Summer of the Swans</u>

CCSS **Common Core State Standards** (pp. Z20–Z30)
Language: L.4.2a

Commas in a Series

Know the Rule

A **series** is a list of three or more items in a sentence. A series can consist of single words, phrases, clauses, or sentences. Commas are used to separate items in a series. The last comma in the series goes before the word *and* or the word *or*.

> **Examples:**
> Three of the smartest dogs are **the border collie, the poodle, and the golden retriever**. *(phrases in a series)*
> Every day **I take my dog to dog school, I give him plenty of exercise, and I play with him**. *(clauses in a series)*

Practice the Rule

Number a sheet of paper 1–10. Write the sentences. Add commas where they are needed.

1. Of the litter of puppies, Skidboot was the biggest, most colorful, and most energetic.
2. Skidboot chased chickens, tore up trash, and ran after pets.
3. Mr. Hartwig taught Skidboot to fetch, to jump, and to obey commands.
4. Skidboot learned to fetch the phone, to lead horses, and to chase balls.
5. He also learned to sit, to lie down, and to wait.
6. Skidboot performed for local schools, rodeos, and state fairs.
7. He was a loyal, obedient, and smart dog.
8. Skidboot was a friend with a cold nose, wagging tail, and loyal spirit.
9. Skidboot won contests, competitions, and people's hearts.
10. Skidboot brought joy, amazement, and pleasure to people's lives.

Mini-Lesson

Student Objectives

- Recognize when to use commas in a series. *(p. 471)*

Commas in a Series

A series is three or more words, phrases, or clauses in a sentence. Separate the items in a series with commas. The last comma appears before the word *and* or *or*. Display these sentences on the board. Have students identify the items in a series in each sentence and explain where to use commas.

- *My dog is smart funny and lazy.* **(smart, funny, and lazy)**
- *My friend Kiran my cousin Janelle and my neighbors like pit bulls.* **(My friend Kiran, my cousin Janelle, and my neighbors)**

Explain that no commas are necessary if the items in a series are separated by *and* or *or*. Display this sentence.

- *Do you have a beagle or a poodle or a pit bull?*

Explain to students that using commas in a series helps prevent confusion for the reader. For more practice with this skill, see page 484.

CCSS **Common Core State Standards** (pp. Z20–Z30)
Language: L.4.6

Conventions

Mini-Lesson

Student Objectives

- Use commas correctly after introductory phrases or clauses. (p. 472)

Commas After Introductory Phrases or Clauses

Put a comma after an introductory phrase or introductory clause in a sentence. Display these sentences on the board. Discuss if and where a comma is needed in each sentence. (Hint: No comma is needed in the second sentence because the introductory clause is already followed by a comma.)

- *Before the play people talked and laughed with their friends.* (comma after *play*)

- *As the lights in the theater grew dim, the audience became quiet.* (correct)

- *During intermission juice and cookies were available.* (comma after *intermission*)

Remind students that a comma acts as a pause in sentences. Have volunteers read aloud the example sentences, pausing where commas appear.

For more practice with this skill, see page 485.

CCSS **Common Core State Standards** (pp. Z20–Z30)
Language: L.4.6

Commas After Introductory Phrases or Clauses

Know the Rule

Use a **comma** to show a pause in a sentence. When a sentence begins with an **introductory phrase** (a group of words without a subject and a predicate) or a **clause** (a group of words with a subject and a predicate), put a comma between it and the rest of the sentence.
Examples:
During the first week of June, we are going on a family picnic.
When we get to North Carolina, we will have to find a place to stay.

Practice the Rule

Number a sheet of paper 1–10. Write each sentence, adding commas where needed. If a sentence needs no comma, write **Correct**.

1. When we arrived at my aunt's house, the picnic table was already set.
2. In the beginning, we were having a really good time. Correct
3. When we sat down to eat, there was food everywhere.
4. As I took a sip of my orange juice, I spotted an ant.
5. Within minutes, ants swarmed over all our food.
6. My aunt jumped up and screamed. Correct
7. After a moment, she calmed down.
8. Acting quickly, my aunt grabbed our plates and put them inside.
9. Everything happened so quickly that I could hardly think. Correct
10. Luckily for us, the ants never returned.

Parentheses

Know the Rule

Use **parentheses** to set off an explanation, example, or other information in a sentence. Parentheses enclose information that is helpful but not necessary to the meaning of the sentence.

Examples:

The San Francisco earthquake **(1906)** killed more than 3,000 people.
An earthquake **(also known as a quake)** is caused by two blocks of earth deep under the ground suddenly slipping past each other.

Practice the Rule

Number a sheet of paper 1–10. Write each sentence, adding parentheses where needed.

1. The epicenter(the point of Earth directly above the earthquake's origin)is where the most damage occurs.

2. An earthquake's aftershocks(the smaller earthquakes that occur later) often cause additional damage.

3. Seismographs(instruments that record earthquakes)tell scientists how strong an earthquake is.

4. Tsunamis(very large ocean waves caused by underwater earthquakes) can destroy coastal regions.

5. More people died in the earthquake and tsunami in Japan in 2011 than died in the Kobe earthquake(1995).

6. The largest recorded earthquake was in Chile in 1960(May).

7. The 1960 earthquake caused damaging tsunamis in Hilo(Hawaii).

8. It's a good idea to have an emergency kit(flashlight, batteries, water, bandages)ready just in case.

9. The magnitude(the amount of energy released)of an earthquake is measured by the Richter scale.

10. The Richter scale(named for Charles Richter)was invented in 1934.

Appendix A: Grammar Practice **473**

Mini-Lesson

Student Objectives

• Use parentheses correctly in sentences. *(p. 473)*

Parentheses

Use parentheses to set off, or enclose, information that is not necessary to the meaning of the sentence. Such information may include explanations or examples.

Display these sentences on the board. Discuss with students where and why parentheses should be added.

• *The Super Bowl first played in 1967 is one of the most popular sports events in the United States.* (first played in 1967)

• *Roman numerals I, V, XV, and so on are used to identify each Super Bowl.* (I, V, XV, and so on)

• *Super Bowl XLV or Super Bowl forty-five saw the Green Bay Packers defeat the Pittsburgh Steelers.* (or Super Bowl forty-five)

Explain to students that parentheses enable them to add interesting or informative details to sentences. For more practice with this skill, see page 485.

CCSS **Common Core State Standards** (pp. Z20–Z30)
Language: L.4.6

Mini-Lesson

Student Objectives

- Use semicolons correctly in sentences. (*p. 474*)

Semicolons

Use a semicolon to combine two closely related independent clauses. Also use a semicolon to correct run-on sentences. In both cases, the semicolon goes after the first independent clause. Display this sentence pair and run-on sentence. Have students use a semicolon to combine the sentence pair and to correct the run-on. Check that students understand not to capitalize the second independent clause.

- *Hawaii is the newest of the fifty states in our country. It became a state in 1959.* (**...country; it...**)

- *Hawaii consists entirely of islands they were formed by volcanoes on the ocean floor.* (**...islands; they...**)

Explain to students that using a semicolon to combine related sentences can help them add sentence variety to their writing, which makes writing more interesting. For more practice with this skill, see page 485.

CCSS Common Core State Standards (pp. Z20–Z30)
Language: L.4.1f

Semicolons

Know the Rule

A **semicolon** can be used instead of a comma and a conjunction to join two related independent clauses. You can use a semicolon to fix a run-on sentence.

Example:
The plane took off; we were on our way to Venezuela.

Practice the Rule

Number a sheet of paper 1–10. Use a semicolon to combine each pair of sentences or to fix a run-on sentence. Remember, the first word of the second clause should not be capitalized unless it is a proper noun.

1. Venezuela is the sixth largest country in South America; Brazil is the largest country.
2. Venezuela lies on the northern coast of South America; Its geography is unique. *its*
3. Venezuela is close to the equator; As a result, the country has only two seasons. *as*
4. The dry season lasts from December to April; The wet season lasts from May to November. *the*
5. In ancient times, Indian tribes lived in Venezuela; They farmed, hunted, and fished for their food. *they*
6. Christopher Columbus was the first European to visit Venezuela;he arrived in 1498.
7. Caracas is Venezuela's capital; It sits next to a long valley that stretches from the east to the west. *it*
8. On one side of the valley are the slopes of Avila National Park; On the other side are the hills of the southern suburbs. *on*
9. Caracas grew during the years of the oil boom;gleaming skyscrapers now line the city.
10. Caracas has great weather; The temperature is almost always like spring. *the*

Colons

Know the Rule

Use a **colon**
- in a sentence before a list.
- between the hour and minutes in expressions of time.
  Examples:
  Jess grows three kinds of vegetables: tomatoes, peppers, and corn.
  Please meet me at 2:10 P.M.

Practice the Rule

Number a sheet of paper 1–10. Write each sentence, adding colons where needed.

1. The bus will leave at 9:00 A.M.
2. Bring the following items: sunglasses, good walking shoes, and lunch.
3. There were three sandwich choices for lunch: tuna, cheese, and ham.
4. My travel bag held everything: shirts, pants, a jacket, and shoes.
5. We saw some amazing things: a waterfall, rare birds, and an antelope.
6. At 2:30 P.M. we took a break.
7. By 3:00 P.M. we were ready to continue our hike.
8. I realized I forgot some items: bug spray, sunscreen, and extra water.
9. To get home, we traveled three ways: a bus, a train, and a taxi.
10. We got home at 6:00 P.M.

Appendix A: Grammar Practice **475**

Mini-Lesson

Student Objectives

- Use colons correctly in sentences. *(p. 475)*

Colons

Use a colon before a list of items in a sentence. Also use a colon between the hour and minutes in expressions of time (7:45 A.M.)

Display these sentences. Discuss where colons should appear and why.

- *We carried the following instruments trumpets, drums, and flutes.* (instruments:, before a list of items)

- *At 615 P.M., the band met in the gym.* (6:15, to separate the hour and minutes)

Point out to students that the same key on a computer keyboard is used for a colon and a semicolon. They first need to press the Shift key before keying a colon.

Explain to students that a colon before a list of items makes a sentence easier to read. Using a colon in expressions of time makes the expression immediately clear to readers. For more practice with this skill, see page 486.

CCSS **C**ommon **C**ore **S**tate **S**tandards (pp. Z20–Z30)
Language: L.4.6

More Practice

Kinds of Sentences

Label each sentence **declarative**, **imperative**, **interrogative**, or **exclamatory**.

1. Bring the poster over here. imperative

2. Have you finished your project? interrogative

3. Cal wrote about border collies. declarative

4. His paper was so well done! exclamatory

5. When is the next report due? interrogative

Avoiding Run-ons and Comma Splices

Write **RO** after each run-on sentence. Write **CS** after each comma splice.

1. Tornadoes form from powerful thunderstorms, they look like rotating funnel-shaped clouds. CS

2. Severe weather conditions can be scary tornadoes are one of nature's most violent storms. RO

3. A tornado warning means that a tornado has been seen, it also means that people should find shelter immediately. CS

4. My brothers and I saw a tornado once we were really scared. RO

5. Storm chasers go close to tornadoes, it's very dangerous. CS

Participles and Participial Phrases

Write the sentences. Underline the participial phrase and circle the participle.

1. (Walking) confidently, Marcus stepped up to the plate.

2. (Excited,) Marcus couldn't wait to show the fans his swing.

3. (Understanding) the situation, Marcus focused his attention on hitting the ball.

4. (Cheering) wildly, the fans jumped to their feet when Marcus hit a home run.

5. Marcus, (trotting) around the bases, waved at the fans.

CCSS **Common Core State Standards** (pp. Z20–Z30)
Language: L.4.1f, L.4.2c, L.4.3b

More Practice

Prepositional Phrases

Write the prepositional phrase or phrases in each sentence.

1. Our trip began <u>in Colorado</u>.
2. We skated <u>over the lake</u> and hiked <u>up the mountain</u>.
3. Some <u>of our friends</u> stayed <u>in the cabin</u>.
4. <u>After our hike</u> we cooked a great supper.
5. We cooked fresh fish <u>in a skillet</u>.

Appositives and Appositive Phrases

Write the appositive phrase in each sentence.

1. Robert Fulton, <u>an American engineer and inventor</u>, developed the first commercially successful steamboat.
2. Fulton, <u>a well-known portrait painter</u>, had always been interested in mechanical inventions.
3. Fulton painted a portrait of Benjamin Franklin, <u>one of the most famous Americans of his time</u>.
4. Fulton designed his first working submarine, <u>the *Nautilus*</u>, between 1793 and 1797.
5. Fulton and Robert R. Livingston, <u>the U.S. Ambassador to France</u>, built a steamboat together.

Plural Nouns

Write the plural form of each noun.

1. letter letters
2. noise noises
3. wolf wolves
4. puppy puppies
5. turkey turkeys
6. porch porches
7. berry berries
8. roof roofs

CCSS **Common Core State Standards** (pp. Z20–Z30)
Language: L.4.1e, L.4.6

More Practice

Personal Pronouns and Compound Personal Pronouns

Write the pronouns in each sentence. Underline each personal pronoun. Circle each compound personal pronoun.

1. Felipe did the entire project (himself.)
2. <u>He</u> worked on <u>it</u> for four weeks.
3. Nadia did not do the project by (herself.)
4. <u>She</u> completed <u>it</u> with a partner.
5. Nadia and James were proud of (themselves) for working together well.

Past-Tense Verbs

Write the past tense of the verb in parentheses.

1. Andrew _____ his dog Buster yesterday morning. (walk) **walked**
2. Buster _____ the ball with Andrew for an hour. (chase) **chased**
3. Buster _____ high in the air to catch the ball. (jump) **jumped**
4. Last week Andrew _____ Buster a bath. (give) **gave**
5. Yesterday Buster _____ in the dirt again! (roll) **rolled**

Present-Tense Verbs

Write the present-tense verb or verbs in each sentence.

1. Dolphins <u>spend</u> most of their time beneath the surface of the water.
2. Because they <u>have</u> streamlined bodies, they <u>swim</u> very quickly.
3. Dolphins <u>live</u> in pods of up to a dozen dolphins.
4. They <u>communicate</u> with clicks, whistles, and other sounds.
5. Some dolphins <u>perform</u> tricks at aquariums.

CCSS **Common Core State Standards** (pp. Z20–Z30)
Language: L.4.2d, L.4.6

More Practice

Future-Tense Verbs
Write the future tense of the verb in parentheses.
1. Carlos _____ his skateboarding this afternoon. (practice) **will practice**
2. He _____ the skateboarding contest next month. (enter) **will enter**
3. He hopes he _____. (win) **will win**
4. If he wins, he _____ a cash prize. (get) **will get**
5. Carlos _____ very happy if he wins. (be) **will be**

Helping Verbs
Write the helping and main verb in each sentence. Underline the helping verb once and the main verb twice.
1. The whole class is going to the Grand Canyon.
2. We will earn the money for the trip.
3. Our teacher is helping us.
4. We will have a great time.
5. Everyone should visit the Grand Canyon if possible.

Present Perfect-Tense Verbs
Write the present perfect-tense verb in each sentence.
1. Olivia has practiced horse jumping for five years.
2. She has worked hard with her horse Nina.
3. Nina has been a wonderful partner.
4. For years Olivia has dreamed of winning a horse-jumping contest.
5. Olivia has enjoyed working with Nina.

CCSS **Common Core State Standards** (pp. Z20–Z30)
Language: L.4.1c, L.4.6

More Practice

Adverbs

Write the adverb or adverbs in each sentence. After each adverb, write the word that it describes.

1. Cesar carefully prepared his presentation. carefully; prepared
2. First, he thoroughly researched his topic. First, thoroughly; researched
3. Then, he rehearsed his presentation. Then; rehearsed
4. He delivered his presentation skillfully and smoothly. skillfully, smoothly; delivered
5. The class clapped loudly for Cesar. loudly; clapped

Prepositions and Prepositional Phrases

Write the sentences. Underline each prepositional phrase. Circle each preposition.

1. We went (to) the game (on) Saturday.
2. (In) the morning, we packed our lunches.
3. (During) the second quarter, our team played much better.
4. (At) the end (of) the game, we cheered until we were hoarse.
5. Cold water felt good (on) our dry throats.

Coordinating Conjunctions

Write each sentence. Circle the coordinating conjuction and underline the words or sentences it connects.

1. Kara (and) Emilio love studying insects.
2. They learned that insects can live on the bodies of plants (and) animals.
3. Insects are everywhere, (but) most of the time we don't see them.
4. I love learning about insects (and) plants.
5. What should I study next, reptiles (or) birds?

CCSS **Common Core State Standards** (pp. Z20–Z30)
Language: L.4.1e, L.4.2c, L.4.6

More Practice

Interjections

Write the interjection and the punctuation that follows it.

1. (Good grief!) I really messed up that test.
2. (Hey,) how did you do on the test?
3. (Oh dear,) I should have studied harder.
4. (Bravo!) You got a perfect score.
5. (Yikes!) You almost ran into the table.

Progressive Verbs

Write the correct form of the verb in parentheses to show continuing action.

1. I _____ my garden next weekend. (plant) **will be planting**
2. While I _____ about my garden, I should order the seeds. (think) **am thinking**
3. A rabbit hopped by while I _____ my flowers. (water) **was watering**
4. When the flowers _____, they are beautiful. (bloom) **are blooming**
5. This summer, I _____ my garden very much. (enjoy) **am enjoying**

Homophones

Write the word that correctly completes each sentence.

1. I can _____ someone coming down the hallway. (here/hear)
2. _____ think it might be my friend Dana. (I/Eye)
3. I can _____ her coming down the hall. (sea/see)
4. _____ Dana! (Its/It's)
5. _____, Dana, how are you? (Hay/Hey)

CCSS **Common Core State Standards** (pp. Z20–Z30)
Language: L.4.1b, L.4.1g, L.4.2d, L.4.3b, L.4.4a

More Practice

Using the Right Word

Write each sentence, correcting any words or phrases used incorrectly.

1. You're
   Your right; I should have studied harder.
2. have
   You could of pestered me more to study.
3. than
   You did better on the test then I did.
4. except
   I like everything about school accept tests.
5. your
   You did a good job on you're test, though.

Pronoun Antecedents

Write each sentence. Write the pronoun in parentheses that correctly completes each sentence. Underline the pronoun's antecedent.

1. <u>Alysa</u> wrote _____ paper on Amelia Earhart. (his/**her**)
2. She learned that <u>Earhart</u> took _____ first flying lessons in California. (**her**/their)
3. In 1931 <u>Earhart</u> married <u>George Putnam</u>, and together _____ formed a successful partnership. (she/**they**)
4. <u>Brian</u> and <u>Rafael</u> wrote _____ papers on Roberto Clemente. (his/**their**)
5. <u>Clemente</u> played all of _____ professional baseball games with the Pittsburgh Pirates. (**his**/their)

Comparative and Superlative Adjectives

Write the form of the adjective in parentheses that best completes each sentence.

1. Miguel is _____ than Alma. (tall) **taller**
2. Sarah is the _____ person in our class. (friendly) **friendliest**
3. Li is a _____ runner than Alonzo. (fast) **faster**
4. The _____ speaker in our class is Natasha. (confident) **most confident**
5. Vikram has a _____ voice than Ali. (soft) **softer**

CCSS **Common Core State Standards** (pp. Z20–Z30)
Language: L.4.1g, L.4.2d, L.4.4a, L.4.6

More Practice

Comparing With Adverbs
Write the form of the adverb in parentheses that best completes each sentence.

1. My dog runs _____ than yours. (quickly) more quickly
2. The competition began _____ than we thought it would. (late) later
3. The winning dog performed _____ than the runner-up. (skillfully) more skillfully
4. My dog barks _____ than yours. (often) more often
5. Your dog eats _____ than my dog. (noisily) more noisily

Comparing With Superlative Adverbs
Write the form of the adverb in parentheses that best completes each sentence.

1. Who jumped _____ in the race? (quick) quickest
2. Of all the hikers, Ramon climbed _____. (fast) fastest
3. We started at 6 A.M., which is the _____ we have ever started earliest hiking. (early)
4. Of all of us, Liza screamed _____ when she saw the snake. (loud) loudest
5. The _____ we can get home is 4 P.M. (soon) soonest

Abbreviations
Write the correct abbreviation for each underlined word below.

1. Friday Fri.
2. Mister Owens Mr.
3. 227 Commercial Street St.
4. 18 Meadow Road Rd.
5. Doctor Chen Dr.
6. Eileen Marie McCoy E.M.
7. December Dec.
8. Monday Mon.

CCSS **C**ommon **C**ore **S**tate **S**tandards (pp. Z20–Z30)
Language: L.4.2d, L.4.6

More Practice

Capitalization
Write the paragraph, correcting all errors in capitalization.

My favorite holiday is the fourth of july. This year, my family is traveling to new mexico to celebrate the day. We will leave on sunday and return on saturday. We plan to visit the museum of indian arts and culture.

Titles If students work on a computer, underlined titles should be italics.
Write each sentence, correcting errors in the use of titles.

1. Last month we read the book the cricket in times square. The Cricket in Times Square

2. Showery Times is my favorite poem. "Showery Times"

3. Next month we will study the painting Golden Sun Flowers. Golden Sun Flowers

4. Baseball Youth is a magazine with great stories and articles about young baseball players. Baseball Youth

5. How many times have you seen the movie stuart little? Stuart Little

Commas in a Series
Write the sentences. Add commas where they are needed.

1. Adrianna, Leon, and I went hiking together.

2. Leon carried the camera, Inez carried the food, and I lugged the water.

3. Leon's camera is small, light, and durable.

4. Leon took pictures of mountains, lakes, and birds.

5. We saw crows, hawks, and blue jays.

CCSS **Common Core State Standards** (pp. Z20–Z30)
Language: L.4.2a, L.4.6

More Practice

Commas After Introductory Phrases or Clauses

Write the sentences. Add commas where they are needed.

1. After the race ended, we went out to eat.
2. By the time the food arrived, we were starving.
3. In the beginning, we hardly talked at all.
4. After we had eaten, we were much more talkative.
5. On the way home, we stopped to see Nana.

Parentheses

Write the sentences. Add parentheses where they are needed.

1. Eleanor Roosevelt (1884–1962) became First Lady of the United States in 1933.
2. Before she became First Lady, Mrs. Roosevelt worked with the Women's Trade Union League (WTUL) to improve working conditions for women and children.
3. Her mother (Anna Hall Roosevelt) died when Eleanor was only eight.
4. Her husband (Franklin D. Roosevelt) got polio in 1921.
5. In 1939, Mrs. Roosevelt defended Marian Anderson (1897–1993) when the singer was not allowed to perform at Constitution Hall.

Semicolons

Write the sentences. Add semicolons where they are needed.

1. I researched my paper for three hours; now I can begin writing.
2. The first page will introduce my topic; the second page will explain it.
3. I presented my paper; everyone in the class thought it was good.
4. I will keep my paper in a safe place; I may want to refer to it someday.
5. Mom and Dad were proud of my report; they hung it on the refrigerator.

CCSS **C**ommon **C**ore **S**tate **S**tandards (pp. Z20–Z30)
Language: L.4.1f, L.4.6

More Practice

Colons

Write the sentences. Add colons where they are needed.

1. Bring the following to class tomorrow:paper, pencils, and colored markers.

2. The sale will begin at 10:00 A.M.

3. Mia's class will sell the following items:books, toys, and games.

4. All school sales will end at 2:00 P.M.

5. Here is how to study your spelling words:read the words, say the words, and write the words.

CCSS Common Core State Standards (pp. Z20–Z30)
Language: L.4.6

T486 Appendix A: Grammar Practice

Transitions

Transition words and phrases can help make the meaning of your writing clearer by connecting sentences and paragraphs. Below are words that you can use to make it easier for readers to understand what you are trying to say.

Words and Phrases That Can Show Time Order; Temporal Words

about	after	as soon as	at	before
during	finally	first	second	third
later	meanwhile	next	soon	then
until	today	tomorrow	yesterday	

Words and Phrases That Can Show Likenesses and Differences

Likenesses:	also	both	in the same way	
	likewise	similarly		
Differences:	although	however	in contrast	instead
	on the other hand		unlike	yet

Words and Phrases That Can Show Cause and Effect

because	as a result	however	since	thus
therefore				

Words and Phrases That Can Show Location

above	across	around	behind	below
beneath	beside	between	down	in back of
in front of	inside	near	next to	on top of
outside	over	under		

Words and Phrases That Can Conclude or Summarize

finally	in conclusion	lastly	therefore

CCSS **Common Core State Standards** (pp. Z20–Z30)
Language: L.4.1c, L.4.2, L.4.3c

Prepositions

Prepositions link nouns, pronouns, and phrases to other words in a sentence. There are many prepositions in the English language. These are some of the most common ones:

at	after	against
around	among	below
before	between	beside
beyond	from	inside
into	onto	over
past	through	underneath
upon	within	

CCSS **Common Core State Standards** (pp. Z20–Z30)
Language: L.4.1e

Appendix B

Rubrics

Text Type-Specific Rubrics This section contains 4-, 5-, and 6-point rubrics that can be used with any piece of Narrative, Informative/Explanatory, or Opinion/Argument writing or when writing descriptive elements in any of the text types. Rubrics based on the six traits of writing can help students identify their writing goals and better understand the expectations of each writing assignment. Rubrics also provide valuable self-assessment for students during the revising process.

Narrative Writing Rubric

	4	3	2	1
Ideas	The topic is just the right size—not too big or too small. Descriptive details introduce and develop the setting, narrator, characters, and plot. Carefully selected ideas completely satisfy the needs of the reader.	The topic is the right size. Details introduce and develop the setting, narrator, characters, and plot. The ideas selected by the author frequently meet the needs of the reader.	The topic is too big or too small. Some details develop the setting, narrator, characters, and plot. The ideas selected by the author sometimes meet the needs of the reader.	The writing is not a narrative. Details are unrelated or not included.
Organization	The narrative unfolds logically and naturally. Transition words and phrases help sequence the events. A strong beginning leads to a satisfying conclusion.	Some events are not connected or are out of order. Transition words and phrases are needed to help sequence the events. The beginning and the conclusion work, but may not be strong.	The narrative does not unfold logically and naturally. Events are out of order. Transition words and phrases are confusing or missing. The beginning or the conclusion is weak.	The writing is disorganized and very difficult to follow. Transition words and phrases are not used. No beginning or conclusion is evident.
Voice	The voice, mood, and tone are just right for the purpose. Dialogue, if used, reveals each character's voice clearly.	The voice, mood, and tone are just right in places, but inconsistent. Dialogue, if used, somewhat reveals the characters' voices.	The voice sounds disinterested. Mood and tone are weak. Dialogue, if used, does not uniquely distinguish the characters' voices.	Voice is flat. Mood and tone are absent. Dialogue, if used, does not sound right for some of the characters.
Word Choice	Words and phrases consistently help the reader "see" the characters and "experience" the events. Nouns and verbs are clear and precise. Modifiers are carefully selected.	Some words and phrases help the reader picture characters and events, but some are too general. Certain nouns and verbs are weak, requiring too much help from modifiers. Modifiers are satisfactory.	Many words and phrases are too general. They keep the reader from picturing the characters and events clearly. Nouns and verbs lack clarity or precision. Too many or too few modifiers are used, and many of them are weak.	Many words are not used correctly. They distract the reader.
Sentence Fluency	Varied sentence beginnings, lengths, and patterns make the writing flow smoothly. Several particularly well-crafted sentences add style and interest. The paper is effortlessly read aloud with inflection or feeling.	There is some variation in sentence beginnings, lengths, and patterns. The sentences are correct, and one or two sentences add style. The paper can be read aloud with inflection or feeling.	Many sentences have the same beginnings, lengths, and patterns. This interrupts the flow of the writing. The sentences are mostly correct but ordinary. It is difficult to read the paper with inflection.	Sentences are poorly written or incorrect. The writing does not flow.
Conventions	Spelling, grammar, punctuation, and capitalization are correct. The narrative contains no errors.	There are a few grammatical errors that may cause the reader to pause momentarily, but meaning is clear.	Many errors are present, and some confuse the reader.	The writing has not been edited. Serious errors make the narrative hard to understand.

Informative/Explanatory Writing Rubric

	4	3	2	1
Ideas	The topic is introduced clearly. Information and examples develop the main idea(s). Carefully selected ideas completely answer the reader's main questions.	A topic is introduced. Most of the information and examples develop the main idea(s). The ideas chosen by the author frequently answer the reader's main questions.	A topic is introduced, but little of the information or examples develops the main idea(s). Some of the reader's questions are answered.	A topic is not introduced. Information and examples are incomplete or unrelated to the topic.
Organization	Information is organized into a strong and thoughtful introduction, a body, and a satisfying conclusion. Varied and appropriate transitions connect the ideas.	Information is organized into an introduction, a body, and a conclusion. More or better transitions are needed.	Information is not well organized. The introduction, body, and conclusion may be poorly developed. Transitions are confusing or not helpful.	The writing is not organized. Introduction and conclusion may both be missing. Transitions are not used.
Voice	The voice sounds interested and informative. It fully connects with the audience and conveys the writer's purpose well.	The voice sounds informative and mostly connects with the audience. It conveys the purpose some of the time.	The voice sounds informative in places. It conveys the purpose, but often fades out.	Voice is weak or absent. It does not connect with the audience or convey the writer's purpose.
Word Choice	Precise language and domain-specific vocabulary are used. Definitions are complete and helpful. Nouns and verbs are clear and precise, supported by a few carefully selected modifiers.	Some precise language, domain-specific vocabulary, and definitions are used. Some nouns and verbs are weak, requiring help from modifiers. Modifiers are satisfactory.	Little precise language and domain-specific vocabulary is used. Definitions are missing or incorrect. Nouns and verbs lack clarity or precision. Too many or too few modifiers are used, and many of them are weak.	Precise language and domain-specific vocabulary are not used.
Sentence Fluency	Clear, concise sentences make the text flow smoothly. Sentence beginnings, lengths, and patterns are varied for effect. The paper is effortlessly read aloud with inflection.	One or two sections of the writing do not flow smoothly. In these sections, several sentences may have the same beginnings, lengths, or patterns. The paper can be read with inflection.	In many places, the writing does not flow smoothly due to repetitive sentence beginnings, lengths, and patterns. It is difficult to read the paper with inflection.	Sentences are incomplete or incorrect.
Conventions	The text contains no errors. Spelling, grammar, punctuation, and capitalization are correct.	The text contains some errors in spelling, grammar, punctuation, and capitalization. One or two errors may cause the reader to pause momentarily, but meaning remains clear.	Many errors are present. Some errors are basic or repeated. The errors interfere with meaning in places.	The writing has not been edited. Serious errors make the writing hard to understand.

Opinion Writing Rubric

	4	3	2	1
Ideas	The writer states a clear opinion. The perfect details and facts are chosen to support the writer's reasons.	The writer states an opinion. Some details and facts are well chosen to support the writer's reasons.	The writer states an opinion, but few details are well chosen to support the writer's reasons.	The writer does not state an opinion. Reasons are not provided.
Organization	The text is organized logically and creatively. Helpful, appropriate, even unique transitions link the writer's opinion and reasons. A compelling conclusion clearly supports the opinion statement.	The text is organized logically. More or better transitions are needed to link the opinion and reasons. The beginning and the conclusion are functional. The conclusion relates to the opinion statement.	The text is not organized logically. Transitions may not show how the writer's ideas are related. Either the beginning or the conclusion is weak. The conclusion may not relate to the opinion statement.	The text is not organized as an opinion. Transitions are not used. Ideas are hard to follow. No beginning or conclusion is evident.
Voice	The voice is clearly convincing and totally fits the writer's purpose. The mood and tone are appropriate and engage the audience.	The voice is convincing and fits the writer's purpose. The mood and tone are engaging some of the time.	The voice is convincing in some places. The mood and tone are incorrect or inconsistent. They lose the audience.	The voice is weak or absent. The tone is not appropriate.
Word Choice	Precise words and fair language convey the writer's opinion. No biased words or phrases are used. Nouns and verbs are clear and precise, supported by a few carefully selected modifiers.	Some words are too general. One biased word or phrase may be used. Some nouns and verbs are weak, requiring help from modifiers. Modifiers are satisfactory.	Most words are weak. A few biased words or phrases may be used. Nouns and verbs lack clarity or precision. Too many or too few modifiers are used, and many of them are weak.	Words are weak, biased, or used incorrectly.
Sentence Fluency	A variety of sentence patterns adds interest and style. Great variation in sentence beginnings and lengths makes the writing flow very smoothly. The paper is effortlessly read aloud with inflection.	Some sentence patterns are varied and add interest. Some variation in sentence lengths and beginnings is evident. The writing flows smoothly in some places, but not in others. The paper can be read with inflection.	Too many sentences share the same pattern. The writing does not flow smoothly due to a lack of variation in sentence lengths and/or beginnings. It is difficult to read the paper with inflection.	Sentences are poorly written or incomplete. The writing is hard to follow.
Conventions	The text contains no errors. Spelling, grammar, punctuation, and capitalization are correct.	There are some errors in spelling, grammar, punctuation, and capitalization. One or two of these errors may cause the reader to pause momentarily, but meaning remains clear.	Many errors are present. Some errors are basic or repeated. The errors interfere with meaning in places.	The writing has not been edited. Serious errors make the writing hard to understand.

Descriptive Elements in the Text Types Rubric

	4	3	2	1
Ideas	The topic is clear, focused, and complete. Sensory details and examples are related to and develop the main ideas. The description helps the reader experience what is being described very clearly.	The topic is clear but may not be focused or complete. Sensory details and examples develop most of the main ideas. The description sometimes helps the reader experience what is being described.	The topic is not clear or focused. Details and examples develop some of the main ideas. The reader cannot always experience what is being described.	The topic is not clear. Details and examples are unrelated or missing. The reader cannot experience what is being described.
Organization	The description is well organized into a strong introduction, body, and conclusion. Details support the topic. Appropriate transitions connect the ideas and guide the reader.	Most of the description is organized. The introduction, body, and conclusion are functional. Most of the details support the topic. More or better transitions are needed to connect the ideas and guide the reader.	Some of the description is organized. The introduction, body, or conclusion may be weak. Few of the details support the topic. More and better transitions are needed to connect the ideas and guide the reader.	The description is not organized and does not have an introduction or conclusion. Details are missing. Transitions are not used.
Voice	The writer's voice connects strongly with the audience. The mood and tone match the purpose perfectly.	The writer's voice connects with the audience in places. The mood and tone match the purpose, but are inconsistent.	The writer's voice does not fit the purpose or the audience well. The mood and tone are inappropriate or inconsistent.	The writer's voice is weak or absent. It does not connect with the audience.
Word Choice	Precise, descriptive language and creative comparisons create a clear picture of the subject. Nouns and verbs carry the descriptive load with help from a few carefully chosen modifiers.	Some of the language is precise, but some is vague. Some of the comparisons create a clear picture of the subject. Many nouns and verbs depend upon modifiers for specificity. Modifiers are satisfactory.	Most of the language is not descriptive. Comparisons are ineffective. Nouns and verbs lack clarity or precision. Too many or too few modifiers are used, and many of them are weak.	The language is very basic and limited. Comparisons are not used.
Sentence Fluency	A variety of sentence beginnings, lengths, and patterns keeps the description interesting. It is effortless to read aloud with inflection or feeling. The writing flows very smoothly.	Some sentences share the same beginnings, lengths, or patterns. Some of the writing flows smoothly. The paper can be read aloud with inflection or feeling.	Several sentences in a row have the same beginnings, lengths, or patterns. The flow of the writing may slow or stall in parts. The paper is difficult to read aloud with inflection or feeling.	Sentences are not varied or interesting. The writing does not flow. The description is very difficult to read.
Conventions	The description contains no errors. Spelling, grammar, punctuation, and capitalization are correct.	The description contains some errors in spelling, grammar, punctuation, and capitalization. One or two of these errors may cause the reader to pause momentarily, but meaning remains clear.	Many errors are present. Some errors are basic or repeated. The errors interfere with meaning in places.	The writing has not been edited. Serious errors make the writing hard to understand.

Narrative Writing Rubric

	5	4	3	2	1
Ideas	The topic is just the right size—not too big or too small. Descriptive details introduce and develop the setting, narrator, characters, and plot. Carefully selected ideas completely satisfy the needs of the reader.	The topic is the right size. Most details introduce and develop the setting, narrator, characters, and plot. Carefully selected ideas satisfy most of the reader's needs.	The topic is the right size. Some details introduce and develop the setting, narrator, characters, and plot. The ideas selected by the author frequently meet the needs of the reader.	The topic is too big or too small. Some details develop the setting, narrator, characters, and plot. The ideas selected by the author sometimes meet the needs of the reader.	The writing is not a narrative. Details are unrelated or not included.
Organization	The narrative unfolds logically and naturally. Transition words and phrases help sequence the events. A strong beginning leads to a satisfying conclusion.	The narrative unfolds logically and naturally. Transition words and phrases help sequence most of the events. The beginning or the conclusion is strong.	Some events are not connected or are out of order. Transition words and phrases are needed to help sequence the events. The beginning and the conclusion work, but may not be strong.	The narrative does not unfold logically and naturally. Events are out of order. Transition words and phrases are confusing or missing. The beginning or conclusion is weak.	The writing is disorganized and very difficult to follow. Transition words and phrases are not used. No beginning or conclusion is evident.
Voice	The voice, mood, and tone are just right for the purpose. Dialogue, if used, reveals each character's voice clearly.	The voice, mood, and tone are just right most of the time. Dialogue, if used, reveals the characters' voices.	The voice, mood, and tone are just right in places, but inconsistent. Dialogue, if used, somewhat reveals the characters' voices.	The voice, mood, and tone do not sound right for some of the characters. Dialogue, if used, does not uniquely distinguish the characters' voices.	Voice is flat. Mood and tone are absent. Dialogue, if used, does not sound right for some of the characters.
Word Choice	Words and phrases consistently help the reader "see" the characters and "experience" the events. Nouns and verbs are clear and precise, supported by a few carefully selected modifiers.	Words and phrases frequently help the reader "see" most of the characters and "experience" most of the events. Nouns and verbs are mostly clear and precise. Most modifiers are carefully selected.	Some words and phrases help the reader picture characters and events, but some are too general. Certain nouns and verbs are weak, requiring too much help from modifiers. Modifiers are satisfactory.	Many words and phrases are too general. They keep the reader from picturing the characters and events clearly. Nouns and verbs lack clarity or precision. Too many or too few modifiers are used, and many of them are weak.	Many words are not used correctly. They distract the reader.
Sentence Fluency	Varied sentence beginnings, lengths, and patterns make the writing flow smoothly. Several particularly well-crafted sentences add style and interest. The paper is effortlessly read aloud with inflection or feeling.	Most sentence beginnings, lengths, and patterns are varied. One or two sentences add style. The paper is easily read aloud with inflection or feeling.	There is some variation in sentence beginnings, lengths, and patterns. The sentences are correct but ordinary. The paper can be read aloud with inflection or feeling.	Many sentences have the same beginnings, lengths, and patterns. This interrupts the flow of the writing. The sentences are mostly correct but ordinary. It is difficult to read the paper with inflection.	Sentences are poorly written or incorrect. The writing does not flow.
Conventions	Spelling, grammar, punctuation, and capitalization are correct. The narrative contains no errors.	There are a few minor errors, but they do not make the narrative difficult to read.	There are a few grammatical errors that may cause the reader to pause momentarily, but meaning is clear.	Many errors are present, and some confuse the reader.	The writing has not been edited. Serious errors make the narrative hard to understand.

Strategies for Writers.

Informative/Explanatory Writing Rubric

	5	4	3	2	1
Ideas	The topic is introduced clearly. Information and examples develop the main idea(s). Carefully selected ideas completely answer the reader's main questions.	The topic is introduced clearly. Most of the information and examples develop the main idea(s). Almost all of the reader's main questions are answered.	A topic is introduced. Some of the information and examples develop the main idea(s). The ideas chosen by the author frequently answer the reader's main questions.	A topic is introduced, but little of the information or examples develops the main idea(s). Some of the reader's questions are answered.	A topic is not introduced. Information and examples are incomplete or unrelated to the topic.
Organization	Information is organized into a strong and thoughtful introduction, a body, and a satisfying conclusion. Varied and appropriate transitions connect the ideas.	Information is organized into an introduction, a body, and a conclusion. Most transitions are varied and appropriate.	Information is organized into an introduction, a body, and a conclusion. More or better transitions are needed.	Information is not well organized. The introduction, body, and conclusion may be poorly developed. Transitions are confusing or not helpful.	The writing is not organized. Introduction and conclusion may both be missing. Transitions are not used.
Voice	The voice sounds interested and informative. It fully connects with the audience and conveys the writer's purpose well.	The voice sounds informative and mostly connects with the audience. It conveys the purpose fairly well.	The voice sounds informative and connects with the audience somewhat. It conveys the purpose some of the time.	The voice sounds informative in places. It conveys the purpose, but often fades out.	Voice is weak or absent. It does not connect with the audience or convey the writer's purpose.
Word Choice	Precise language and domain-specific vocabulary are used. Definitions are complete and helpful. Nouns and verbs are clear and precise, supported by a few carefully selected modifiers.	Precise language and domain-specific vocabulary are used. Most definitions are complete and helpful. Nouns and verbs are mostly clear and precise. Most modifiers are carefully selected.	Some precise language, domain-specific vocabulary, and definitions are used. Some nouns and verbs are weak, requiring help from modifiers. Modifiers are satisfactory.	Little precise language and domain-specific vocabulary is used. Definitions are missing or incorrect. Nouns and verbs lack clarity or precision. Too many or too few modifiers are used, and many of them are weak.	Precise language and domain-specific vocabulary are not used.
Sentence Fluency	Clear, concise sentences make the text flow smoothly. The sentence beginnings, lengths, and patterns are varied for effect. The paper is effortlessly read aloud with inflection.	Most of the sentences flow smoothly. The sentence beginnings, lengths, and patterns are varied. The paper is easily read aloud with inflection.	One or two sections of the writing do not flow smoothly. In these sections, several sentences may have the same beginnings, lengths, or patterns. The paper can be read with inflection.	In many places, the writing does not flow smoothly due to repetitive sentence beginnings, lengths, and patterns. It is difficult to read the paper with inflection.	Sentences are incomplete or incorrect.
Conventions	The text contains no errors. Spelling, grammar, punctuation, and capitalization are correct.	The text contains very few errors in spelling, grammar, punctuation, or capitalization. The meaning remains clear.	The text contains some errors in spelling, grammar, punctuation, and capitalization. One or two errors may cause the reader to pause momentarily, but meaning remains clear.	Many errors are present. Some errors are basic or repeated. The errors interfere with meaning in places.	The writing has not been edited. Serious errors make the writing hard to understand.

Opinion Writing Rubric

	5	4	3	2	1
Ideas	The writer states a clear opinion. The perfect details and facts are chosen to support the writer's reasons.	The writer states a clear opinion. Most details and facts are well chosen to support the writer's reasons.	The writer states an opinion. Some details and facts are well chosen to support the writer's reasons.	The writer states an opinion, but few details are well chosen to support the writer's reasons.	The writer does not state an opinion. Reasons are not provided.
Organization	The text is organized logically and creatively. Helpful, appropriate, even unique transitions link the opinion and reasons. A compelling conclusion clearly supports the opinion statement.	The text is organized logically. Most details and transitions are needed to link the opinion and reasons. The beginning is strong, and the conclusion supports the opinion statement.	The text is organized logically. More or better transitions are needed to link ideas and reasons. The beginning and the conclusion are functional. The conclusion relates to the opinion statement.	The text is not organized logically. Transitions may not show how the writer's ideas are related. Either the beginning or the conclusion is weak. The conclusion may not relate to the opinion statement.	The text is not organized as an opinion. Transitions are not used. Ideas are hard to follow. No beginning or conclusion is evident.
Voice	The voice is clearly convincing and totally fits the writer's purpose. The mood and tone are appropriate and engage the audience.	The voice is convincing and fits the writer's purpose. The mood and tone are appropriate and engaging most of the time.	The voice is somewhat convincing and fits the writer's purpose. The mood and tone are engaging some of the time.	The voice is convincing in some places. The mood and tone are inconsistent. They lose the audience.	The voice is weak or absent. The tone is not appropriate.
Word Choice	Precise words and fair language convey the writer's opinion. No biased words or phrases are used. Nouns and verbs are clear and precise, supported by a few carefully selected modifiers.	Most words are precise and fair. No biased words or phrases are used. Nouns and verbs are mostly clear and precise. Most modifiers are carefully selected.	Some words are too general. One biased word or phrase may be used. Some nouns and verbs are weak, requiring help from modifiers. Modifiers are satisfactory.	Most words are weak. A few biased words or phrases may be used. Nouns and verbs lack clarity or precision. Too many or too few modifiers are used, and many of them are weak.	Words are weak, biased, or used incorrectly.
Sentence Fluency	A variety of sentence patterns adds interest and style. Great variation in sentence beginnings and lengths makes the writing flow very smoothly. The paper is effortlessly read aloud with inflection.	Most sentence patterns are varied and add interest. Variation in sentence beginnings and lengths makes the writing flow smoothly. The paper is easily read aloud with inflection.	Some sentence patterns are varied and add interest. Some variation in sentence lengths and beginnings is evident. The writing flows smoothly in some places, but not in others. The paper can be read with inflection.	Too many sentences share the same pattern. The writing does not flow smoothly due to a lack of variation in sentence lengths and/or beginnings. It is difficult to read the paper with inflection.	Sentences are poorly written or incomplete. The writing is hard to follow.
Conventions	The text contains no errors. Spelling, grammar, punctuation, and capitalization are correct.	The text contains very few errors in spelling, grammar, punctuation, or capitalization. The meaning remains clear.	There are some errors in spelling, grammar, punctuation, and capitalization. One or two of these errors may cause the reader to pause momentarily, but meaning remains clear.	Many errors are present. Some errors are basic or repeated. The errors interfere with meaning in places.	The writing has not been edited. Serious errors make the writing hard to understand.

Descriptive Elements in the Text Types Rubric

	5	4	3	2	1
Ideas	The topic is clear, focused, and complete. Sensory details and examples are related to and develop the main ideas. The description helps the reader experience what is being described very clearly.	The topic is clear and focused. Most sensory details and examples are related to and develop the main ideas. The description helps the reader experience what is being described most of the time.	The topic is clear but may not be focused or complete. Sensory details and examples develop most of the main ideas. The description sometimes helps the reader experience what is being described.	The topic is not clear or focused. Details and examples develop some of the main ideas. The reader cannot always experience what is being described.	The topic is not clear. Details and examples are unrelated or missing. The reader cannot experience what is being described.
Organization	The description is well organized into a strong introduction, body, and conclusion. Details support the topic. Appropriate transitions connect the ideas and guide the reader.	Most of the description is organized, featuring an introduction, body, and conclusion. Most details support the topic. One or two more transitions are needed to connect the ideas and guide the reader.	Most of the description is organized. The introduction, body, and conclusion are functional. Some of the details support the topic. More or better transitions are needed to connect the ideas and guide the reader.	Some of the description is organized. The introduction, body, or conclusion may be weak. Few of the details support the topic. More and better transitions are needed to connect the ideas and guide the reader.	The description is not organized and does not have an introduction or conclusion. Details are missing. Transitions are not used.
Voice	The writer's voice connects strongly with the audience. The mood and tone match the purpose perfectly.	The writer's voice connects with the audience most of the time. The mood and tone match the purpose.	The writer's voice connects with the audience in places. The mood and tone match the purpose, but are inconsistent.	The writer's voice does not fit the purpose or the audience well. The mood and tone are inappropriate or inconsistent.	The writer's voice is weak or absent. It does not connect with the audience.
Word Choice	Precise, descriptive language and creative comparisons create a clear picture of the subject. Nouns and verbs carry the descriptive load with help from a few carefully chosen modifiers.	Most of the language is precise. Most comparisons create a clear picture of the subject. Nouns, verbs, and modifiers are mostly strong.	Some of the language is precise, but some is vague. Some of the comparisons create a clear picture of the subject. Many nouns and verbs depend upon modifiers for specificity. Modifiers are satisfactory.	Most of the language is not descriptive. Comparisons are ineffective. Nouns and verbs lack clarity or precision. Too many or too few modifiers are used, and many of them are weak.	The language is very basic and limited. Comparisons are not used.
Sentence Fluency	A variety of sentence beginnings, lengths, and patterns keeps the description interesting. It is effortless to read aloud with inflection or feeling. The writing flows very smoothly.	Most of the sentences feature varied beginnings, lengths, and patterns, making the writing interesting. Most of the writing flows smoothly. The paper is easy to read aloud with inflection or feeling.	Some sentences share the same beginnings, lengths, or patterns. Some of the writing flows smoothly. The paper can be read aloud with inflection or feeling.	Several sentences in a row have the same beginnings, lengths, or patterns. The flow of the writing may slow or stall in parts. The paper is difficult to read aloud with inflection or feeling.	Sentences are not varied or interesting. The writing does not flow. The description is very difficult to read.
Conventions	The description contains no errors. Spelling, grammar, punctuation, and capitalization are correct.	The description contains very few errors in spelling, punctuation, or capitalization. Grammar is correct, and meaning is clear.	The description contains some errors in spelling, grammar, punctuation, and capitalization. One or two of these errors may cause the reader to pause momentarily, but meaning remains clear.	Many errors are present. Some errors are basic or repeated. The errors interfere with meaning in places.	The writing has not been edited. Serious errors make the writing hard to understand.

Narrative Writing Rubric

	6	5	4	3	2	1
Ideas	The topic is just the right size—not too big or too small. Descriptive details introduce and develop the setting, narrator, characters, and plot. Carefully selected ideas completely satisfy the needs of the reader.	The topic is the right size. Most details introduce and develop the setting, narrator, characters, and plot. Carefully selected ideas satisfy most of the reader's needs.	The topic is the right size. Some details introduce and develop the setting, narrator, characters, and plot. The ideas selected by the author frequently meet the needs of the reader.	The topic is too big or too small. Some details develop the narrative. Some details are unrelated. The author did not consider the needs of the reader.	The topic is undeveloped. Too few details develop the narrative. Some details are not included.	The writing is not a narrative. Details are not included.
Organization	The narrative unfolds logically and naturally. Transition words and phrases help sequence the events. A strong beginning leads to a satisfying conclusion.	One or two events in the middle are not connected or are out of order. Transition words and phrases help sequence most of the events. The beginning or the conclusion is strong.	Some events are not connected or are out of order. Transition words and phrases are needed to help sequence the events. The beginning and the conclusion work, but may not be strong.	The narrative does not unfold logically and naturally. Events are out of order. Transition words and phrases are confusing or missing. The beginning or the conclusion is weak.	The narrative does not unfold logically. Events are out of order. Transition words and phrases are not used. The beginning or the conclusion is missing or problematic.	The writing is disorganized and very difficult to follow. No beginning or conclusion is evident.
Voice	The voice, mood, and tone reveals each character's voice clearly.	The voice, mood, and tone are just right for the purpose. Dialogue, if used, reveals the characters' voices.	The voice, mood, and tone are just right most of the time. Dialogue, if used, reveals the characters' voices.	The voice, mood, and tone are inconsistent. Dialogue, if used, somewhat reveals the characters' voices.	The voice sounds disinterested. Mood and tone are weak. Dialogue, if used, does not uniquely distinguish the characters' voices.	Voice is flat. Mood and tone are not used. Dialogue is not used.
Word Choice	Words and phrases consistently help the reader "see" the characters and "experience" the events. Nouns and verbs are clear and precise, supported by a few carefully selected modifiers.	Words and phrases frequently help the reader "see" most of the characters and "experience" most of the events. Nouns and verbs are mostly clear and precise. Most modifiers are carefully selected.	Words and phrases help the reader picture characters and events, but some are too general. Certain nouns and verbs are weak, requiring too much help from modifiers. Modifiers are satisfactory.	Some words and phrases help the reader picture the characters and events, but some are too general. Nouns and verbs lack clarity or precision. Too many or too few modifiers are used, and many of them are weak.	Many words and phrases are too general. They keep the reader from picturing the characters and events clearly. Nouns and verbs are vague, unclear, or confusing. Modifiers may be missing entirely.	Many words are not used correctly. They distract the reader.
Sentence Fluency	Varied sentence beginnings, lengths, and patterns make the writing flow smoothly. Several particularly well-crafted sentences add style and interest. The paper is effortlessly read aloud with inflection or feeling.	Most sentence beginnings, lengths, and patterns are varied. One or two sentences add style. The paper is easily read aloud with inflection or feeling.	There is some variation in sentence beginnings, lengths, and patterns. The sentences are correct but ordinary. The paper can be read aloud with inflection or feeling.	Many sentences have the same beginnings, lengths, and patterns. This interrupts the flow of the writing. The sentences are mostly correct but ordinary. It is difficult to read the paper with inflection.	All or almost all the sentences follow the same pattern. Lengths and beginnings do not vary, making the writing robotic or rambling.	Sentences are poorly written or incorrect. The writing does not flow.
Conventions	Spelling, grammar, punctuation, and capitalization are correct. The narrative contains no errors.	There are a few minor errors, but they do not make the narrative difficult to read.	There are a few grammatical errors that may cause the reader to pause momentarily, but meaning is clear.	Many errors are present, and some confuse the reader.	Several serious errors make the narrative hard to understand.	The writing has not been edited.

Informative/Explanatory Writing Rubric

	6	5	4	3	2	1
Ideas	The topic is introduced clearly. Information and examples develop the main idea(s). Carefully selected ideas completely answer the reader's main questions.	The topic is introduced clearly. Most of the information and examples develop the main idea(s). Almost all of the reader's main questions are answered.	A topic is introduced. Some of the information and examples develop the main idea(s). The ideas chosen by the author frequently answer the reader's main questions.	A topic is introduced, but little of the information or examples develops the main idea(s). Some of the reader's questions are answered.	A topic is introduced, but information and examples do not develop the main idea(s). The author did not think about what questions the reader might have.	A topic is not introduced. Information and examples are incomplete or unrelated to the topic.
Organization	Information is organized into a strong and thoughtful introduction, a body, and a satisfying conclusion. Varied and appropriate transitions connect the ideas.	Information is organized into an introduction, a body, and a conclusion. Most transitions are varied and appropriate.	Information is organized into an introduction, a body, and a conclusion. More or better transitions are needed.	Information is not well organized. The introduction, body, and conclusion may be poorly developed. Transitions are confusing or not helpful.	Information is only partly organized. The introduction or the conclusion is missing. Transitions are not used.	The writing is not organized. Introduction and conclusion may both be missing. Transitions are not used.
Voice	The voice sounds interested and informative. It fully connects with the audience and conveys the writer's purpose well.	The voice sounds informative and mostly connects with the audience. It conveys the purpose fairly well.	The voice sounds informative and connects with the audience somewhat. It conveys the purpose some of the time.	The voice sounds informative in places. It conveys the purpose, but often fades out.	The voice consistently sounds flat. It may sound uninformed or uninterested. It does not convey the purpose.	Voice is weak or absent. It does not connect with the audience or convey the writer's purpose.
Word Choice	Precise language and domain-specific vocabulary are used. Definitions are complete and helpful. Nouns and verbs are clear and precise, supported by a few carefully selected modifiers.	Precise language and domain-specific vocabulary are used. Most definitions are complete and helpful. Nouns and verbs are mostly clear and precise. Most modifiers are carefully selected.	Some precise language, domain-specific vocabulary, and definitions are used. Some nouns and verbs are weak, requiring help from modifiers. Modifiers are satisfactory.	Little precise language and domain-specific vocabulary is used. Definitions are missing or incorrect. Nouns and verbs lack clarity or precision. Too many or too few modifiers are used, and many of them are weak.	Some domain-specific vocabulary is used incorrectly. Clarification and definition are not provided for the reader. Nouns and verbs are vague, unclear, or confusing. Modifiers may be missing.	Precise language and domain-specific vocabulary are not used.
Sentence Fluency	Clear, concise sentences make the text flow smoothly. Sentence beginnings, lengths, and patterns are varied for effect. The paper is effortlessly read aloud with inflection.	Most of the sentences flow smoothly. The sentence beginnings, lengths, and patterns are varied. The paper is easily read aloud with inflection.	One or two sections of the writing do not flow smoothly. In these sections, several sentences may have the same beginnings, lengths, or patterns. The paper can be read with inflection.	In many places, the writing does not flow smoothly due to repetitive sentence beginnings, lengths, and patterns. It is difficult to read the paper with inflection.	All or almost all the sentences have similar beginnings, lengths, or patterns. The writing sounds robotic or rambling.	Sentences are incomplete or incorrect.
Conventions	The text contains no errors. Spelling, grammar, punctuation, and capitalization are correct.	The text contains very few errors in spelling, grammar, punctuation, or capitalization. The meaning remains clear.	The text contains some errors in spelling, grammar, punctuation, and capitalization. One or two errors may cause the reader to pause momentarily, but meaning remains clear.	Many errors are present. Some errors are basic or repeated. The errors interfere with meaning in places.	Serious errors stop the reader frequently and make the writing hard to understand.	The writing has not been edited.

Opinion Writing Rubric

	6	5	4	3	2	1
Ideas	The writer states a clear opinion. The perfect details and facts are chosen to support the writer's reasons.	The writer states a clear opinion. Most details and facts are well chosen to support the writer's reasons.	The writer states an opinion. Some details and facts are well chosen to support the writer's reasons.	The writer states an opinion, but few details are well chosen to support the writer's reasons.	The writer's opinion is not clear. Facts are inaccurate or unrelated to the writer's reasons.	The writer does not state an opinion. Reasons are not provided.
Organization	The text is organized logically and creatively. Helpful, appropriate, even unique transitions link the writer's opinion and reasons. A compelling conclusion clearly supports the opinion statement.	The text is organized logically. One or two more transitions are needed to link the opinion and reasons. The beginning is strong, and the conclusion supports the opinion statement.	The text is organized logically. More or better transitions are needed to link the opinion and reasons. The beginning and the conclusion are functional. The conclusion relates to the opinion statement.	The text is not organized logically. Transitions may not show how the writer's ideas are related. Either the beginning or the conclusion is weak. The conclusion may not relate to the opinion statement.	The text is not organized logically. No transitions are used. Ideas are hard to follow. The beginning or the conclusion is missing.	The text is not organized as an opinion. No beginning or conclusion is evident.
Voice	The voice is clearly convincing and totally fits the writer's purpose. The mood and tone are appropriate and engage the audience.	The voice is convincing and fits the writer's purpose. The mood and tone are appropriate and engaging most of the time.	The voice is somewhat convincing and fits the writer's purpose. The mood and tone are engaging some of the time.	The voice is convincing in some places. The mood and tone are incorrect or inconsistent. They lose the audience.	The voice is flat and does not fit the writer's purpose. The mood and tone do not engage the audience.	The voice is weak or absent. The tone is not appropriate.
Word Choice	Precise words and fair language convey the writer's opinion. No biased words or phrases are used. Nouns and verbs are clear and precise, supported by a few carefully selected modifiers.	Most words are precise and fair. No biased words or phrases are used. Nouns and verbs are mostly clear and precise. Most modifiers are carefully selected.	Some words are too general. One biased word or phrase may be used. Nouns and verbs are weak, requiring help from modifiers. Modifiers are satisfactory.	Most words are weak. A few biased words or phrases may be used. Nouns and verbs lack clarity or precision. Too many or too few modifiers are used, and many of them are weak.	Many words are overused and ineffective. Several biased words and phrases are used. Nouns and verbs are vague, unclear, or confusing. Modifiers may be missing.	Words are weak, biased, or used incorrectly.
Sentence Fluency	A variety of sentence patterns adds interest and style. Great variation in sentence beginnings and lengths makes the writing flow very smoothly. The paper is effortlessly read aloud with inflection.	Most sentence patterns are varied and add interest. Variation in sentence beginnings and lengths makes the writing flow smoothly. The paper is easily read aloud with inflection.	Some sentence patterns are varied and add interest. Some variation in sentence lengths and beginnings is evident. The writing flows smoothly in some places, but not in others. The paper can be read with inflection.	Too many sentences share the same pattern. The writing does not flow smoothly due to a lack of variation in sentence lengths and/or beginnings. It is difficult to read the paper with inflection.	Almost all sentences are alike. The writing is boring and does not flow smoothly.	Sentences are poorly written or incomplete. The writing is hard to follow.
Conventions	The text contains no errors. Spelling, grammar, punctuation, and capitalization are correct.	The text contains very few errors in spelling, grammar, punctuation, or capitalization. The meaning remains clear.	The text contains some errors in spelling, grammar, punctuation, or capitalization. One or two of these errors may cause the reader to pause momentarily, but meaning remains clear.	There are some errors in spelling, grammar, punctuation, and capitalization. The errors interfere with meaning in places.	Many errors are present. Some errors are basic or repeated. The errors make the writing hard to understand.	Serious errors stop the reader frequently and make the writing hard to understand. The writing has not been edited.

Descriptive Elements in the Text Types Rubric

	6	5	4	3	2	1
Ideas	The topic is clear, focused, and complete. Sensory details and examples are related to and develop the main ideas. The description helps the reader experience what is being described very clearly.	The topic is clear and focused. Most sensory details and examples are related to and develop the main ideas. The description helps the reader experience what is being described most of the time.	The topic is clear but may not be focused or complete. Sensory details and examples develop most of the main ideas. The description sometimes helps the reader experience what is being described.	The topic is not clear or focused. Details and examples develop some of the main ideas. The reader cannot always experience what is being described.	The topic and main ideas are not clear. Few sensory details and examples are included. The reader has to work to experience what is being described.	The topic is not clear. Details and examples are unrelated or missing. The reader cannot experience what is being described.
Organization	The description is well organized into a strong introduction, body, and conclusion. Details support the topic. Appropriate transitions connect the ideas and guide the reader.	Most of the description is organized, featuring an introduction, body, and conclusion. Most details support the topic. One or two more transitions are needed to connect the ideas and guide the reader.	Most of the description is organized. The introduction, body, and conclusion are functional. Some of the details support the topic. More or better transitions are needed to connect the ideas and guide the reader.	Some of the description is organized. The introduction, body, or conclusion may be weak. Few of the details support the topic. More and better transitions are needed to connect the ideas and guide the reader.	The description is not well organized. The introduction or conclusion is missing or problematic. Details are missing. Transitions are misused or missing.	The description is not organized and does not have an introduction or conclusion. Details are missing. Transitions are not used.
Voice	The writer's voice connects strongly with the audience. The mood and tone match the purpose perfectly.	The writer's voice connects with the audience most of the time. The mood and tone match the purpose.	The writer's voice connects with the audience in places. The mood and tone match the purpose, but are inconsistent.	The writer's voice does not fit the purpose or the audience well. The mood and tone are inappropriate or inconsistent.	The writer's voice does not fit the purpose or the audience. The mood and tone are inappropriate.	The writer's voice is weak or absent. It does not connect with the audience.
Word Choice	Precise, descriptive language and creative comparisons create a clear picture of the subject. Nouns and verbs carry the descriptive load with help from a few carefully chosen modifiers.	Most of the language is precise. Most comparisons create a clear picture of the subject. Nouns, verbs, and modifiers are mostly strong.	Some of the language is precise, but some is vague. Some of the comparisons create a clear picture of the subject. Many nouns and verbs depend upon modifiers for specificity. Modifiers are satisfactory.	Most of the language is not descriptive. Comparisons are ineffective. Nouns and verbs lack clarity or precision. Too many or too few modifiers are used, and many of them are weak.	The language is not descriptive. Comparisons are confusing. Nouns and verbs are vague, unclear, or confusing. Modifiers may be missing.	The language is very basic and limited. Comparisons are not used.
Sentence Fluency	A variety of sentence beginnings, lengths, and patterns keeps the description interesting. It is effortless to read aloud with inflection or feeling. The writing flows very smoothly.	Most of the sentences feature varied beginnings, lengths, and patterns, making the writing interesting. Most of the writing flows smoothly. The paper is easy to read aloud with inflection or feeling.	Some sentences share the same beginnings, lengths, or patterns. Some of the writing flows smoothly. The paper can be read aloud with inflection or feeling.	Several sentences in a row have the same beginnings, lengths, or patterns. The flow of the writing may slow or stall in parts. The paper is difficult to read aloud with inflection or feeling.	Many sentences have the same beginnings, lengths, or patterns. The writing does not flow smoothly.	Sentences are not varied or interesting. The writing does not flow. The description is very difficult to read.
Conventions	The description contains no errors. Spelling, grammar, punctuation, and capitalization are correct.	The description contains very few errors in spelling, punctuation, or capitalization. Grammar is correct, and meaning is clear.	The description contains some errors in spelling, grammar, punctuation, and capitalization. One or two of these errors may cause the reader to pause momentarily, but meaning remains clear.	Many errors are present. Some errors are basic or repeated. The errors interfere with meaning in places.	Serious errors stop the reader frequently and make the writing hard to understand.	The writing has not been edited.

Scope and Sequence

	K	1	2	3	4	5	6	7	8
Collaborative Conferencing									
	●	●	●	●	●	●	●	●	●
Differentiated Instruction									
	●	●	●	●	●	●	●	●	●
English Language Learner Support									
	●	●	●	●	●	●	●	●	●
Grammar, Usage, and Mechanics									
abbreviations/acronyms			●	●	●	●	●	●	●
abstract nouns				●		●	●		●
action verbs			●	●	●	●	●	●	●
active and passive voice							●	●	●
adjective and adverb clauses						●		●	●
adjectives	●	●	●	●	●	●	●	●	●
adjectives, order of					●				
adverbs			●	●	●	●	●	●	●
apostrophes			●	●	●	●	●	●	●
appositives					●	●	●	●	●
articles		●	●	●	●	●	●	●	●
capitalization	●	●	●	●	●	●	●	●	●
clauses						●	●	●	●
collective nouns			●					●	●
colons				●	●	●	●	●	●
comma splices					●	●	●	●	●
commas	●	●	●	●	●	●	●	●	●
commas, direct address					●	●	●	●	●
commas, introductory elements, *yes* and *no*			●	●	●	●	●	●	●
common nouns		●	●	●	●	●	●	●	●

Grammar, Usage, and Mechanics (cont.)

	K	1	2	3	4	5	6	7	8
comparative adjectives		●	●	●	●	●	●	●	●
comparative adverbs			●	●	●	●	●	●	●
complete sentences	●	●	●	●	●	●	●	●	●
complex sentences				●		●	●	●	●
compound personal pronouns (reflexive and intensive pronouns)			●	●	●	●	●	●	●
compound sentences	●	●	●	●	●	●	●	●	●
compound subjects and predicates						●	●	●	●
compound-complex sentences								●	●
conjunctions	●	●	●	●	●	●	●	●	●
contractions		●	●	●	●	●	●	●	●
coordinate adjectives								●	●
coordinating conjunctions			●	●	●	●	●	●	●
correlative conjunctions						●		●	●
dangling and misplaced modifiers							●	●	●
dashes							●	●	●
declarative sentences	●	●	●	●	●	●	●	●	●
demonstrative pronouns and adjectives		●	●	●	●	●	●	●	●
dependent and independent clauses				●		●	●	●	●
dialogue, punctuation with			●	●	●	●	●	●	●
direct and indirect objects					●	●	●	●	●
direct quotations			●	●	●	●	●	●	●
direct speech, punctuation with			●	●	●	●	●	●	●
double negatives				●	●	●	●	●	●
ellipses									●
end punctuation	●	●	●	●	●	●	●	●	●

Grammar, Usage, and Mechanics (cont.)

	K	1	2	3	4	5	6	7	8
exclamation points	●	●	●	●	●	●	●	●	●
exclamatory sentences	●	●	●	●	●	●	●	●	●
forms of *be*			●	●	●	●	●	●	●
frequently confused words			●	●	●	●	●	●	●
good and *well*				●	●		●		●
helping/auxiliary verbs			●	●	●	●	●	●	●
homophones			●	●	●	●	●	●	●
imperative sentences		●	●	●	●	●	●	●	●
indefinite pronouns		●					●	●	●
infinitive phrases							●	●	●
initials				●	●	●	●	●	●
interjections				●	●	●	●	●	●
interrogative sentences	●	●	●	●	●	●	●	●	●
irregular verbs			●	●	●	●	●	●	●
items in a series, punctuation with			●	●	●	●	●	●	●
kinds of sentences			●	●	●	●	●	●	●
letters, parts of and punctuation	●	●	●	●	●	●	●	●	●
linking verbs			●	●	●	●	●	●	●
modal auxiliaries					●			●	●
negatives				●	●	●	●	●	●
nonrestrictive/parenthetical elements, punctuation with							●	●	●
nouns	●	●	●	●	●	●	●	●	●
parallel structure									●
parentheses					●	●	●	●	●
participial phrases					●			●	●
past tense		●	●	●	●	●	●	●	●
perfect tenses					●	●	●	●	●
periods	●	●	●	●	●	●	●	●	●

Grammar, Usage, and Mechanics (cont.)	K	1	2	3	4	5	6	7	8
personal pronouns			●	●	●	●	●	●	●
phrases				●	●	●	●	●	●
plural nouns, regular and irregular	●	●	●	●	●	●	●	●	●
possessive nouns		●	●	●	●	●	●	●	●
possessive pronouns		●	●	●	●	●	●	●	●
predicate nouns and adjectives						●	●	●	●
prepositional phrases			●	●	●	●	●	●	●
prepositions	●	●	●	●	●	●	●	●	●
progressive verbs					●		●	●	●
pronoun-antecedent agreement				●	●	●	●	●	●
pronouns	●	●	●	●	●	●	●	●	●
pronouns, shifts in number and person							●		●
pronouns, vague (unclear or ambiguous antecedents)				●			●	●	●
proper nouns	●	●	●	●	●	●	●	●	●
question marks	●	●	●	●	●	●	●	●	●
quotation marks	●	●	●	●	●	●	●	●	●
quotations from a text, punctuation with					●	●	●	●	●
relative pronouns and adverbs					●		●	●	●
run-on sentences				●	●	●	●	●	●
semicolons					●	●	●	●	●
sentence fragments			●	●	●	●	●	●	●
sentence types			●	●	●	●	●	●	●
sentences, expanding and rearranging			●	●	●	●	●	●	●
simple sentences		●	●	●	●	●	●	●	●
singular nouns			●	●	●	●	●	●	●
subject and object pronouns			●	●	●	●	●	●	●

	K	1	2	3	4	5	6	7	8
Grammar, Usage, and Mechanics (cont.)									
subject and predicate	●	●	●	●	●	●	●	●	●
subject-verb agreement			●	●	●	●	●	●	●
subordinating conjunctions				●		●	●	●	●
superlative adjectives		●	●	●	●	●	●	●	●
superlative adverbs			●	●	●	●	●	●	●
titles			●	●	●	●	●	●	●
transitive and intransitive verbs							●	●	●
using the right word			●	●	●	●	●	●	●
variations from standard English						●	●	●	●
verb moods								●	●
verb tense, shifts in						●		●	●
verbals and verb phrases					●		●	●	●
verbs/verb tenses	●	●	●	●	●	●	●	●	●
Graphic Organizers									
5 W's Chart	●	●		●			●	●	
Argument Map							●	●	●
Attribute Chart			●		●	●			
Biography Map		●					●		
Business Letter Organizer				●					
Cause-and-Effect Chain						●	●	●	●
Character Chart	●							●	
Concept Map						●			
Five-Column Chart	●				●				
Five Senses Chart	●	●	●				●		
Flow Chart									●
Four-Paragraph Organizer					●				
Main Idea Table		●		●	●			●	●
Network Tree	●	●	●	●	●	●	●		
Observation Chart				●				●	

	K	1	2	3	4	5	6	7	8
Graphic Organizers (cont.)									
Opinion Chart			●						
Order Chain			●						
Order-of-Importance Organizer			●		●		●		
Outline					●	●	●	●	●
Paragraph Organizer					●		●		
Pro-and-Con Chart						●	●		
Problem-Solution Chart/Frame				●				●	●
Sequence Chain		●	●	●	●	●	●		●
Spider Map		●		●	●	●	●		
Story Map/Frame	●	●	●	●	●	●	●	●	●
Storyboard	●	●	●			●	●		
Support Pattern						●			
Three-Column Chart	●	●							
Timeline		●			●				●
Two-Column Chart	●	●							●
Venn Diagram	●	●	●				●		
Web	●	●	●	●	●	●	●	●	●
Handwriting									
Corrective Strategies	●	●							
Pencil Grip	●								
Listening and Speaking									
	●	●	●	●	●	●	●	●	●
Oral Language Development									
	●	●							
Rubrics and Checklists									
	●	●	●	●	●	●	●	●	●
Tech Tips									
	●	●	●	●	●	●	●	●	●

Scope and Sequence

	K	1	2	3	4	5	6	7	8
Text Exemplars/Mentor Texts	●	●	●	●	●	●	●	●	●
Traits for Writing	●	●	●	●	●	●	●	●	●
Writing in the Content Areas	●	●	●	●	●	●	●	●	●
Writing Genres and Text Types									
Adventure Story					●				
All About Book	●	●							
Argument Essay							●		●
Argument/Opinion Writing	●	●	●	●	●	●	●	●	●
Biographic Sketch/Biography					●	●	●	●	●
Book of Facts	●	●							
Brochure				●					
Business Letter				●		●	●	●	●
Cause-and-Effect Report							●	●	
Character Sketch					●				
Compare-and-Contrast Book/Paper/Essay	●	●	●		●	●			
Descriptive Elements in Writing	●	●	●	●	●	●	●		●
Descriptive Paragraph					●				
Directions/Map	●	●							
Editorial					●			●	●
E-mail							●		
Explanatory Essay						●	●		●
Eyewitness Account							●		
Fable			●	●		●			
Fairy Tale	●								
Folktale		●		●					
Formal Proposal									●

Writing Genres and Text Types (cont.)

	K	1	2	3	4	5	6	7	8
Friendly Letter	●	●	●	●	●				
Geographic Description								●	
Hero Biography		●							
Historical Episode							●	●	●
How-To Directions/Guide/Essay/Paper	●		●	●	●	●			●
I Like…Because… Book	●	●							
Informative/Explanatory Writing	●	●	●	●	●	●	●	●	●
Interview Questions	●								
Map/Directions	●	●							
Memoir									●
Movie Review		●							
My Favorite…	●								
My Favorite Book	●	●							
My Favorite Person	●								
My Favorite Poem	●								
My Friend's Favorite…	●								
Mystery						●			
Narrative Writing	●	●	●	●	●	●	●	●	●
News Article	●								
Next Generation Writing Assessment			●	●	●	●	●	●	●
Observation/Observation Report	●					●	●	●	●
Opinion Paper/Paragraph/Essay			●	●		●			
Opinion Speech			●			●			
Opinion/Argument Writing	●	●	●	●	●	●	●	●	●
Personal Narrative	●	●	●	●	●	●		●	
Photo Essay	●	●							
Picture Book	●								
Picture Description	●	●							
Place Description	●	●							

Scope and Sequence

	K	1	2	3	4	5	6	7	8
Writing Genres and Text Types (cont.)									
Play					●	●		●	
Poem	●	●	●	●	●	●	●	●	●
Poetry Review					●				
Poster	●	●							
Problem-Solution Essay				●				●	
Recipe	●	●							
Research Report			●	●	●	●	●	●	●
Response to Literature			●	●	●	●	●	●	●
Rhyme	●	●							
Rules		●							
Scientific Observation									●
Short Story							●		●
Song Lyrics	●	●							
Speech	●	●					●		●
Story	●								
Story About a Friend			●						
Story About an Event	●								
Story About Me	●	●							
Story About My Friend	●								
Story Retelling	●	●							
Summary	●	●			●		●	●	
The Best...	●								
The Best... (Advertisement)		●							
Travel Brochure	●	●							
Website Review								●	
Writing Process									
Prewrite	●	●	●	●	●	●	●	●	●
Draft	●	●	●	●	●	●	●	●	●

	K	1	2	3	4	5	6	7	8
Writing Process (cont.)									
Revise	●	●	●	●	●	●	●	●	●
Edit	●	●	●	●	●	●	●	●	●
Publish	●	●	●	●	●	●	●	●	●
Writing Readiness									
Left-to-Right Concept	●								
Letter Formation	●								
Making Sentences	●								
Making Words	●								
Spacing	●								
Top-to-Bottom Concept	●								

Index

word picture, T370
words (of a character), T390
writer's terms
    adverbs, T257
    appositives, T159
    attribute chart, T133
    beginning, T89
    body, T276
    categorize, T203
    cliché, T391
    commas, T91
    comparative adjectives, T415
    conclusion, T276
    details, T16
    detail sentences, T366
    dialogue, T61, T88
    direct quotations, T65
    fact, T296
    first-person point of view, T19
    formal tone, T158
    homophones, T139
    interview, T36
    introduction, T276
    lead, T136
    loaded words, T256
    main idea, T275, T365
    metaphor, T434
    negatives, T209
    network tree, T297, T409
    opinion, T248, T318
    order-of-importance organizer, T249
    outline, T177
    paragraph, T156
    past-tense verbs, T281
    play format, T87
    plural nouns, T371
    prepositional phrases, T439
    pronouns, T183, T325
    punctuating a friendly letter, T303
    reasons, T250, T274
    run-on sentences, T393
    sentence types, T90
    sequence, T433
    sequence chain, T15
    simile, T434
    source, T155

    spider map, T387
    stage directions, T88
    story map, T59, T85
    subject-verb agreement, T43
    supporting details, T206, T365
    supporting evidence, T319
    third-person point of view, T40
    timeline, T37
    tone, T158, T278
    topic sentence, T366
    transition words, T38, T323
    transitions, T368
    web, T155
    word choice, T320
    word picture, T370
writer's workshop, Z18
writing in the content area.
    See content area writing
writing process
    draft, T16–T17, T38–T39, T60–T61, T86–T87, T112–T113, T134–T135, T156–T157, T178–T179, T204–T205, T228–T229, T250–T253, T276–T277, T298–T299, T320–T321, T344–T345, T366–T367, T388–T389, T410–T411, T434–T435
    edit, T21, T43, T65, T91, T117, T139, T161, T183, T209, T233, T257, T281, T303, T325, T349, T371, T393, T415, T439
    prewrite, T14–T15, T36–T37, T58–T59, T84–T85, T110–T111, T132–T133, T154–T155, T176–T177, T200–T205, T226–T227, T248–T249, T274–T275, T296–T297, T318–T319, T342–T343, T364–T365, T386–T387, T408–T409, T432–T433
    publish, T24, T46, T68, T94, T118, T142, T164, T186, T212, T234, T260, T284, T306, T328, T350, T374, T396, T418, T442

    revise, T18–T20, T40–T42, T62–T64, T88–T90, T114–T116, T136–T138, T158–T160, T180–T182, T206–T208, T230–T232, T254–T256, T278–T280, T300–T302, T322–T324, T346–T348, T368–T370, T390–T392, T412–T414, T436–T438
writing to multiple sources, Z14–Z15, T106–T107, T222–T223, T338–T339
writing traits.
    See traits of writing